SURVEY OF LONDON
VOLUME XLI

PREVIOUS VOLUMES

OF THE SURVEY OF LONDON

* *Original edition out of print. Photographic facsimile available from* Survey of London *section (DG/AE/SL), Greater London Council, or from AMS Press Inc., 56 East 13th Street, New York, and the agents of AMS Press.*

† *Out of Print.*

The Oratory Church. A view drawn by its architect Herbert Gribble in 1878, before building began

SURVEY OF LONDON

GENERAL EDITOR: F. H. W. SHEPPARD

VOLUME XLI

Southern Kensington: Brompton

THE ATHLONE PRESS
Published for the Greater London Council
1983

Published 1983 *by*
THE ATHLONE PRESS
at **44** *Bedford Row, London* WC1

© GREATER LONDON COUNCIL 1983
PUBLICATION NUMBER 7168/1297/5

British Library Cataloguing in Publication Data
Survey of London
    Vol. 41: Southern Kensington: Brompton
    1. Architecture — England — London
    2. London (England) — Buildings
    I. Greater London Council
    720′.9421   NA970
    ISBN 0 - 485 - 48241 - X✓

Printed in Great Britain by Hazell Watson and Viney Limited
for the Greater London Council Supplies Department

Preface

This is the third volume of the *Survey of London* to be concerned with Kensington. The first was published in 1973 under the title *Northern Kensington,* and the second in 1975 as *The Museums Area of South Kensington and Westminster.* Work on the remainder of Kensington was then suspended for several years, during which two volumes on the Grosvenor Estate in Mayfair were prepared and published. The present volume marks the resumption of work on Kensington, which will be completed in a year or two by the publication of a fourth volume describing the Kensington High Street and Earl's Court areas. It is intended that the final volume should also contain a general review of the whole of South Kensington.

The present volume covers a triangular portion of the ancient parish of Kensington extending westward from Knightsbridge Green as far as the railway line which forms the boundary between Kensington and Hammersmith. At its narrower eastern end it includes both sides of Brompton Road, while further west it is bounded on its north side by Old Brompton Road and on its south side by Fulham Road. Building began around Knightsbridge in the 1760's and spread sporadically westward down these three main roads, along which there sprang up numerous villa residences, many of them set in well-planted groves and surrounded by the nurseries and market gardens for which Brompton was famous in the early nineteenth century.

But this idyllic scene did not last long, and by the 1840's it and the small remnants of earlier development at Little Chelsea in the Fulham Road were being submerged by the advancing tide of streets and squares. This process was accelerated by the opening of the Metropolitan Railway in 1868, until by the end of the century the whole area had been covered with bricks and mortar. Most of this present volume is therefore concerned with nineteenth-century residential development on the Alexander, Smith's Charity, Gunter and other estates which make up this area, but it also includes studies of several churches and of such varied subjects as Brompton Oratory, Brompton Cemetery, Harrods, and Brompton Hospital.

On behalf of the Council I should like to thank the many people who have given help in the preparation of this volume. Many of their names are recorded in the List of Acknowledgments, and without their generous assistance much of the research for this study could not have been done. I am particularly grateful to my colleagues, the Advisory Members of the Historic Buildings Panel — Sir John Betjeman, Sir Hugh Casson, Dr. Henry Cleere, Sir Osbert Lancaster and Mr. Ian L. Phillips — who, despite the many demands made upon them, have given their valuable time and knowledge at numerous meetings of the Panel. I also wish to thank two former Advisory Members — Lord Reilly and Sir John Summerson, both of whom have retired since the publication of the last volume. The Council is very fortunate to have had the help of two such distinguished Members for so long. Sir John has, indeed, advised the Council and its predecessor, the London County Council, in all matters relating to historic buildings since the establishment by the L.C.C. of a special sub-committee for their management in 1953; and his connexion with the *Survey of London* has been even longer. Everyone who cares for the well-being of the historic fabric of London owes him a deep debt of gratitude.

No preface to this volume would be complete without reference to the immense contribution made by Dr. Francis Sheppard, the General Editor of the *Survey of London,* who retired at the end of 1982 whilst the book was being printed.

Dr. Sheppard was appointed General Editor by the former London County Council in 1954 and has been associated with every volume since then. Under his guidance, inspiration and leadership the *Survey of London* has grown in stature and is recognised by leading authorities throughout the world. Dr. Sheppard has maintained the highest possible standard of accuracy but his devotion to excellence has in no way diminished his most interesting style which has kept the human reality behind London bricks and mortar. Dr. Sheppard has made a notable and significant contribution to London's history and fortunately for Londoners it remains available for future generations.

Associated with Dr. Sheppard in the work on this volume were Mr. P. A. Bezodis, Deputy Editor, and Mr. J. Greenacombe and Mr. V. R. Belcher, Assistant Editors (all of the Director General's Department), who with Dr. Sheppard wrote most of the text and edited all the material. The architectural content was provided by the staff of the Historic Buildings Division of the Department of Architecture and Civic Design under the aegis of the Surveyor of Historic Buildings, Mr. Ashley Barker. The drawings were made by the Division's draughtsmen, Mr. John Sambrook, Mr. Alan Fagan, Mr. Roy Bowles and Mr. R. Weston, under the general guidance of Mr. Sambrook. Several chapters of the text were written by Mr. Andrew Saint, the Architectural Editor, who also organised the drawing and photographic programmes: Dr. J. M. Robinson also contributed to these aspects of the work, particularly in its earlier stages. Many of the photographs were specially taken for the volume by members of the Council's Photographic Unit, under the supervision of Mr. Roy Ferriman. Printing arrangements were made by the Central Reprographic Service of the Supplies Department, particularly by Mr. Leslie Needs and Mr. Arnold Riley, with their respective support teams of Mr. Reg. Corke, Mr. Ivor Croad, Mr. Peter Durrell and Mr. Brian Rees.

NORMAN HOWARD

Chairman, Historic Buildings Panel
Greater London Council
County Hall
January 1983

Acknowledgments

The Council has received help from many quarters in the preparation of this volume, and the names of persons and institutions to whom it tenders its grateful thanks are listed below. Of individuals it is proper to mention especially Mr. Ian Anstruther and Mrs. Anstruther (Susan Walker) for their courtesy in giving access to the archives of the Alexander (Thurloe) estate and for their advice and information about its history; and Miss Dorothy Stroud, whose studies of that estate and of the Smith's Charity estate, augmented by her personal advice and comments, have been of the greatest help in the preparation of the work.

Among institutions and other bodies the Congregation of the London Oratory must be first named, for their patience in giving access to their archives and their building and in answering requests for information over a protracted term of years. The Servite Friars have also most kindly allowed access to their buildings and records. The description of Brompton Hospital was greatly facilitated by the help given to the Council's officers by Mr. J. R. Plant, Secretary to the Board of Governors, and other members of the staff of the Hospital, especially Brigadier H. R. W. Vernon, and Miss Varley. The history of Evelyn Gardens was much assisted by the kindness of Major A. E. Daw and Mr. C. J. P. Lindon, Chairman and Secretary of C. A. Daw and Son, Limited, in allowing the use of the firm's archives. Especial thanks should also be given to the Local Studies Department of Kensington Central Public Library and Mr. B. R. Curle and Mr. T. M. Egan for their great help to the work in continuation of that given in previous years.

It is a pleasure to acknowledge the assistance given by the following, in addition to those already mentioned: Mr. A. S. Alcock; Mr. F. D. Allen; Fr. Philip Allen, O.S.M.; Mr. Hugh Anderson; Mrs. Alison Anstead; Mrs. Inette Austin-Smith; Major D. H. Back; Rev. C. John G. Barton; Mr. David Beasley; Mr. P. J. Bishop; Prof. Sanborn C. Brown; Mr. Alban Caroe; Mr. Martin Caroe; the Right Rev. Patrick Casey; Sir Hugh Casson; Miss Louisa Chafee; Mr. Toby Cholmeley; Fr. Gerard M. Corr, O.S.M.; Mr. J. Cotter; Lord Craigmyle; Mr. F. Cranmer; Mr. Alan Crawford; Mr. Stephen Croad; Mr. S. E. Cronk; Rev. M. C. Crowdy; Mr. Christopher Da Costa; Commander John David; Rev. Gary Davies; Mr. Simon Day; Mr. James Dearden; the Very Rev. Charles Dilke; Mr. G. P. Dyer; Mr. G. Eke; Mr. Denis Evinson; Mrs. P. A. Fox; Mr. Andor Gomme; Miss M. Gooding; Mr. David Green; the Hon. C. J. G. Guest; Mr. N. C. Hall; Mr. H. M. Hambly; Mr. Roy Heron; Mr. E. R. C. Holland; Mr. Stratton Holland; Miss Diana Howard; Mr. Sidney Hutchison; Dr. A. H. Jenniskens; Mr. Paul Joyce; Rev. Manus P. Keane, S.J.; Mr. I. N. Kendal; Miss Jean M. Kennedy; Mr. J. M. Keyworth; Mr. Daniel Lamb; Mrs. Isabella Leland; Lady Logan; Mr. J. H. Love; Mr. A. C. McDougall; Mr. Edward MacParland; Mr. D. R. G. Marler; Mr. John Mason; Mr. Anthony Mauduit; Mr. J. W. Milliken; the Very Rev. M. S. Napier; Mrs. Rachel Nelson; Mr. M. K. Nield; His Grace the Duke of Norfolk; Mrs. Belinda Norman-Butler; Mr. A. G. Peake; Miss Fiona Pearson; Mr. A. R. Perry; Mr. C. Pettiward; Mr. P. C. Phillips; Mr. Harold Poupart; Mr. J. W. Prevett; Rev. Richard Price; the Lord Reilly; Mr. and Mrs. Julian Ridsdale; Mr. T. J. Rix; Miss Jane Roscoe; Lady Rose; the late Mr. Michael Ross-Wills; Mr. Frank Seton; Mr. L. A. Sheppard; Mr. P. L. Slight; Peter and Alison Smithson; Mr. I. H. Stewart; Mlle. N. Tassoul; Sir Peter Thorne; Madame Claude Trialle; Mr. J. R. Turner; Miss Alison Turton; Rev. R. Turvey; Mrs. C. Vivian; Mr. David M. Walker; Mr. Peter Watson; Mrs. Deborah Weiner; Miss Carol Wheeler; Mr. A. M. Wherry; Mr. James S. Wilson; Miss G. M. Wyatt; Miss I. Wynniatt-Husey.

The Armouries, H.M. Tower of London; Bank of England Museum and Historical Research Section; Bibliothèque Nationale, Paris; Bibliothèque Publique, Liège; Bibliothèque Royale Albert 1er, Brussels; Bodleian Library; W. and F. C. Bonham and Sons Limited; British Library; British Telecom, Solicitor's Office; Broughton and Company; Carden, Godfrey, Macfadyen and Sturgis; Dartmouth College Library, New Hampshire; Ealing Borough Central Services and Records; Ealing Central Library; Eleusis Club; Farley and Company; Gemeentelijke Archiefdienst Maastricht; Goldsmiths' Company; Guildhall Library; Harrods Limited; Hedges and Butler Limited; Hereford

Record Office; House of Fraser Limited; House of Lords Record Office; London Transport Plan Room; Margate Public Libraries; Museum of London; National Monuments Record; National Register of Archives; Norfolk Record Office; Post Office, London Postal Region, Building and Mechanisation Division; Post Office, Solicitor's Office; Public Record Office; Richmond Central Library, Surrey; Royal Institute of British Architects; Royal Marsden Hospital; Royal Mint; Frederick Sage Limited; Shepherd's Bush Library (Archives Section); Society of Australian Genealogists; South Australian Genealogy and Heraldry Society; South Carolina Historical Society; State Library of South Australia; Suffolk Record Office; Surrey Record Office; Unigate; Unigate Properties Limited; Westminster Public Libraries; Wightscot Photographers Limited; Winkworth and Company.

The Council also acknowledges with thanks the help received from other owners and occupiers who have allowed access to their buildings for inspection and measurement, and also the co-operation of those firms that have permitted the use of their scaffolding for the study of buildings under renovation.

Owners of photographs and other illustrations reproduced in this volume are acknowledged in the List of Plates.

Contents

Plates *at end*

End Pocket
Map of the Area

List of Plates

List of Figures

Note: Many of the drawings in this volume show buildings conjecturally restored to their original state, and should in no case be construed as a record of their exact appearance at the time of publication

CHAPTER I

Brompton Road: Introduction

As an official name, 'Brompton Road' did not exist until 1863.* It now denotes the portion of the old highway from London to Fulham stretching south-westwards from Knightsbridge as far as Pelham Street, beyond which it becomes Fulham Road. But until 1935 Brompton Road extended only as far as the junction with Thurloe Place (opposite the Brompton Oratory); after this, Fulham Road began.[1]

Today the broad arterial Cromwell Road seems a more logical westward continuation of Brompton Road than the relatively tranquil offshoot between the Oratory and Pelham Street. But before 1855 there was no Cromwell Road,[2] while not till after 1939 did West Cromwell Road connect with Hammersmith via Talgarth Road and so provide a major thoroughfare between London and the west. Cromwell Road's construction, coinciding with the main period of building development in South Kensington and Earl's Court, made Brompton Road into one of the busiest highways of the capital and contributed to the bustling commercial identity that it enjoys today.

Nevertheless there was always much traffic on the old turnpike road, which linked London not only with Little Chelsea and Fulham but also (via Putney Bridge) with parts of Surrey as well, and which from 1726 to 1826 was maintained by the Kensington Turnpike Trustees. Anciently, the eastern end of this highway was known indiscriminately as the road to Fulham or the road to Brompton. The name 'Brompton', now used loosely, then applied most precisely to the settlement which lay westwards of what is now South Kensington Station, just off the turnpike road along the lane to Earl's Court. This lane, generally called Brompton Lane or Bell and Horns Lane, diverged from the main road at the Bell and Horns, an inn sited opposite the Oratory where Empire House now stands. After the frontages of Brompton Road nearer London had been built up, the original nucleus of

Brompton became known as Old Brompton and Brompton Lane as Old Brompton Road — which name survives today except in the short stretch east of South Kensington Station, where its line is represented by Thurloe Place.

Before 1863 therefore, 'Brompton Road' was in general an unofficial term, usually to be construed as meaning the part of the Fulham turnpike road connecting Knightsbridge with Brompton Lane and thus with Old Brompton.† As with other main roads out of London, the different developments along its length had separate names and numbers, which were not abolished until 1863.

Brompton Road before Development

The ancient parish boundaries of Kensington enclosed a thin corridor encompassing the whole of Brompton Road up to Knightsbridge Green on the north, and up to the lane later to become Sloane Street on the south. On neither side of the road was the hinterland within the parish of much depth behind the frontages. Northwards, extending to Knightsbridge and its continuation to the old village of Kensington, was an outlying portion of the parish of St. Margaret's, Westminster; on the south side lay the parish of Chelsea.‡ But these administrative divisions did not coincide especially well with property boundaries at the time of first development. On the south side one major freeholder, the trustees of Smith's Charity, held lands both in Kensington and in Chelsea, while on the north side the boundary between Kensington and St. Margaret's, Westminster, divided another freehold of some antiquity, that of the Tathams and later of the Moreaus.

Until 1760 no special development had occurred on either side of the turnpike road. The character of the land was generally speaking horticultural. Since Brompton like much of Kensington was excellent nursery ground, it was intensively cultivated. Nurserymen, some very prosperous, feature often in early property transactions in the district,

---

*In this introductory chapter, sources are not given for statements authenticated in succeeding chapters.

†Use of the term 'Brompton Road' in the twenty years or so preceding 1863 is confusing. In the *Post Office Directory* it is restricted as an address to the eleven houses later to become Nos. 38-58 (even) Brompton Road, at the east end of the north side. However the parish authorities spoke of these houses as in Brompton Place, and used 'Brompton Road' to refer not only to the turnpike road from Knightsbridge as far as the Bell and Horns, but also to its continuation towards Old Brompton along the line of the present Thurloe Place, then also known as Bell and Horns Lane or Brompton Lane. During this period, some of the detached houses along the north side of this lane, in the vicinity of the present Victoria and Albert Museum, were numbered by the parish as in Brompton Road.

‡The boundaries were altered when the London boroughs superseded the parish vestries in 1900. On the north side, the City of Westminster took over from Kensington all its properties east of Montpelier Street, including Nos. 2-130 (even) Brompton Road, and a small quadrilateral north of Cheval Place including the east and south sides of Rutland Street, the south end of Montpelier Walk and both sides of Fairholt Street. South of Brompton Road, a strip of land along the north-west sides of Basil Street, Walton Place and Walton Street was ceded by Chelsea to Kensington. These changes are shown on fig. 1. Unless otherwise stated, this chapter follows ancient parish rather than modern borough boundaries.

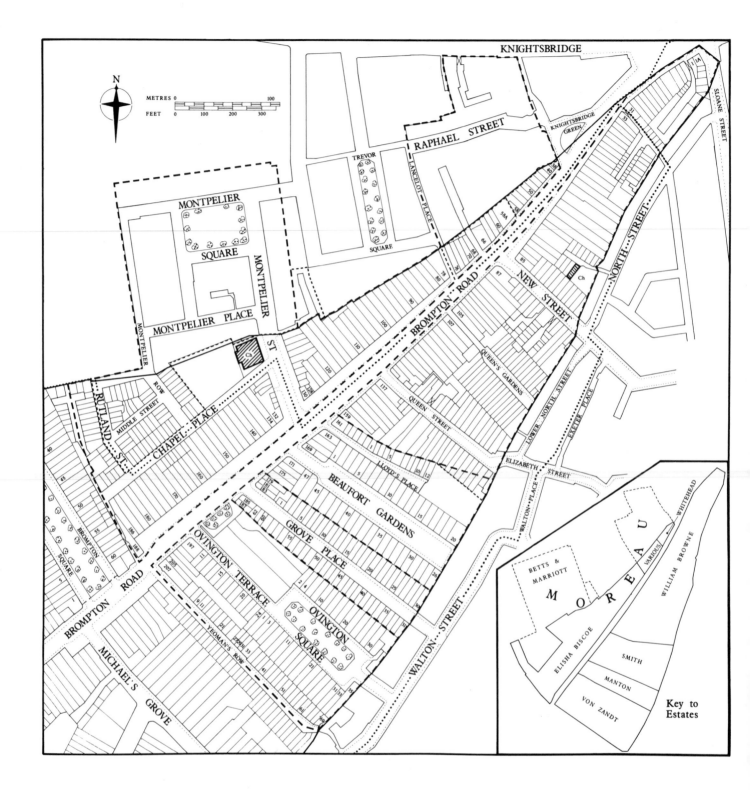

Fig. 1. Principal estates along Brompton Road discussed in Chapters I-III. Based on the Ordnance Survey of 1862-72. The solid line represents the boundary of the ancient parish of Kensington, the broken line shows estate divisions, and the dotted line shows boundaries of the London boroughs between 1900 and 1964. The street names given are those of the 1860's, while the house numbers are those generally in use since that period.

the most celebrated being Henry Wise of Brompton Park Nursery.[3] A surviving inventory of 1760 lists the effects of David Anderson, nurseryman, who tended lands in the region of the modern Beaufort Gardens, Beauchamp Place and Ovington Square; it evokes an air of quaint, rustic cottage life at Brompton which was then soon to be broken.[4] Another deed of 1763 concerning the garden of Sir Thomas Dyer (where Ovington Square now stands) requires the lessee, John Hooper, gardener, to reserve annually for Sir Thomas and his wife a peck of apples, a peck of pears and a quantity of cherries and plums, 'the best and choicest fruit and produce of two hundred standard trees growing or to grow on the said demised premises'.[5]

Interspersed between these walled nursery gardens were occasional cottages and, more particularly, frequent hostelries of the type that dotted the main thoroughfares around London. These grew commoner as the road approached Knightsbridge, a district well known in the early eighteenth century, not to say notorious, for its inns. Several of these clustered around the major junction next to Knightsbridge Green where the roads from Fulham and from Kensington met: the Swan, sited roughly on the present corner of Brompton Road and Sloane Street; the World's End (later the Fulham Bridge), set back from the north side of the road between Knightsbridge Green and what is now Lancelot Place; and the Rose or Rose and Crown, an important coaching inn facing Knightsbridge proper and therefore not in Kensington. By 1760 several further houses had been built around this junction, most of them in St. Margaret's parish, while Knightsbridge eastwards between here and Hyde Park Corner was beginning to attract ribbon development. Further west along Brompton Road, the main inn was the Bell and Horns at the corner of Brompton Road and Brompton Lane.

Early Development

With striking simultaneity, development commenced in about 1763-4 at several points along both sides of the eastern part of Brompton Road, as far as Yeoman's Row on the south and Brompton Square on the north. The coincidence tallies precisely with a well-attested building boom in London, but it is the worthier of remark because it took place on three separate freeholds and on one large tract of copyhold land.

The landholdings along Brompton Road were at the time quite fragmented (fig. 1). On the south side, proceeding westwards from what is now Sloane Street, the first holding was that of William Browne: his eleven acres of copyhold land are now represented along the frontage by Nos. 1-159 (odd) Brompton Road, with a depth to the parish boundary a little to the north of the present Basil Street and Walton Place. There followed three small freeholds, now covered respectively by the sites of Beaufort Gardens, Beauchamp Place and Ovington Square, before the extensive properties of the trustees of Smith's Charity began west of Yeoman's Row. On the north side of Brompton Road, the whole frontage westwards from Knightsbridge Green as far as what is now Cheval Place, with a sizeable holding behind in both Kensington and St. Margaret's, Westminster, was until 1759 in a single freehold ownership, latterly that of the Moreau family. West of this large property, where Brompton Square, Holy Trinity Church and the Oratory now stand, was a twelve-acre site which until 1749 was held as a single copyhold. Beyond the Bell and Horns began what was to become the Alexander estate, whose frontage to Brompton Road extended as far as what is now the south end of Alexander Square; after this came further lands of Smith's Charity. These last estates are discussed in detail in subsequent chapters.

The development of the 1760's was preceded by a small flurry of property transactions on these lands. Of these, the most important was the sale at auction in 1759 and ensuing break-up of the large estate of the Moreaus along the north side of the road. The largest purchaser, Elisha Biscoe, was a lawyer practised in speculation and connected by family with the Brownes and Braces who owned much property hereabouts (see fig. 2 on page 11). In conjunction with Thomas Rawstorne, ironmonger, Biscoe from 1764 undertook ribbon development all along the frontage between the present Lancelot Place and Cheval Place. Some of the original houses of Biscoe's Buildings (later Brompton Row) survive, albeit in much altered condition. A proprietary chapel behind the houses in Rawstorne (now Montpelier) Street provided Brompton with its first place of worship, which was not to be supplemented until Holy Trinity Church was built in 1826-9.

On the south side of the road, the frontage of William Browne's copyhold estate was developed from 1764 under the auspices of two main builders, Joseph Clark(e) and William Meymott. Besides the several terraces built along the main road here (known most generally as Queen's Buildings) were some side streets and courts, among them Queen's Gardens (later obliterated by Harrods) and Queen Street (now Hans Road). The whole of the frontage up to the present No. 159 Brompton Road was by no means completed when the building boom faded in about 1770, so that development dribbled on here until the early 1790's. West of Browne's land was a small three-and-a-half-acre freehold (where Beaufort Gardens now stands); this was bought in 1763 by Thomas Smith, musical instrument maker, and promptly developed with a short terrace facing the main road called Brompton Grove. The last and perhaps most interesting of these early developments came a little further west, on the site of Ovington Gardens and Square and the east side of Yeoman's Row, all then the freehold of Sir Thomas Dyer. Here from 1765 a terrace arose along Yeoman's Row, but facing Brompton Road three sizeable detached houses were built by William Southall, carpenter.

Excepting Southall's Buildings, these early developments of the 1760's were almost all orthodox houses in long or short terraces. Those facing the turnpike road tended to have long front gardens to shield them from dust and noise; these were reduced almost to nothing later on by road-widenings and the growth of single-storey shops in front of old houses. But at first few of these houses functioned as shops. They were good-class homes taking advantage of Brompton's reputation for good air and salubrity. The smaller dwellings and workshops were concentrated on William Browne's land in the back courts and streets, which in the nineteenth century were to degenerate.

For half a century from 1770, much of the new building along Brompton Road consisted of modest infilling and completion. On the north, a handful of new houses were built in about 1777-80 and 1794-6 east of Lancelot Place, on ground close to the Fulham Bridge tavern. Opposite, Henry Holland between about 1781 and 1791 helped finish development on William Browne's estate, laying out New Street (now the northern end of Hans Crescent) and completing Queen Street (Hans Road) so as to allow good communication between Brompton Road and his personal undertaking of Hans Town at the northern tip of Chelsea (Plate 3). The effect of Hans Town and its later outliers within the large Cadogan estate in northern Chelsea upon the district of Brompton Road was in the long term great. Some of those who worked in Brompton when building on a large scale recommenced in the 1820's were based in Chelsea or had connexions with Holland and his circle. Further, the strategic position of Knightsbridge and Brompton Road in relation to fashionable addresses like Cadogan Place and Hans Place was to make them a magnet for shopping and aid in the growth of stores like Harrods.

One important development did occur along the south side of Brompton Road at the end of the eighteenth century. this was the construction between about 1785 and 1800 of Michael's Place, Michael's Grove and Brompton Crescent on Smith's Charity land west of Yeoman's Row. The brainchild of the theatre architect Michael Novosielski, it was probably more ambitious in terms of design than anything previously built in the locality. But little is known of its appearance, and the crescent was completed after Novosielski's death in 1795. It was certainly no success financially. Yet it may have been this development which first attracted theatrical and musical personalities to Brompton, their suburb *par excellence* for much of the ensuing century.

The Growth of 'New Brompton'

A survey made by Joseph Salway in 1811 to show drainage along the turnpike road to Fulham well records the appearance of 'New Brompton' (as the district was sometimes now called to distinguish it from Old Brompton further west) just before a new wave of building occurred (Plates 4, 5). The houses along the north side of Brompton Road are all shown in elevation; most have good gardens, some with

trees, and few as yet are shops. Shortly after this, in the boom of the 1820's, the buildings became denser and the character of ribbon development began to be lost. On the south side, Grove (now Beauchamp) Place filled up the gap between Brompton Grove and Southall's Buildings, though it progressed slowly at first. On the north side there was more activity, anticipated by nine houses built between 1818 and 1824 close to Knightsbridge Green (later Nos. 42-58 Brompton Road). West of this, the back lands behind Brompton Row were developed at the same time as Trevor Square and Montpelier Square were going up in St. Margaret's parish, while in Kensington proper Brompton Square was started in 1821. Beyond the Bell and Horns, Alexander Square and the surrounding streets were laid out from 1826, and on Smith's Charity land, Onslow Terrace was the precursor of larger developments to follow in the 1830's. The principals in these several undertakings were closely linked. The central figure was James Bonnin, a builder involved at Trevor Square, Brompton Square, Alexander Square, Onslow Terrace and Grove Place; his career is given in some detail on pages 61 and 101.

In 1826-9 'New Brompton' acquired its own church in the shape of Holy Trinity, just west of Brompton Square. The suburb by now boasted some coherence, individuality and prosperity. A directory of 1827-8 lists altogether a hundred 'nobility, gentry and clergy' inhabiting Queen's Buildings, Brompton Grove, Brompton Square (as yet unfinished) and Brompton Row; of these, forty-three lived in Brompton Row.[6] Tradesmen and craftsmen were concentrated particularly in Queen's Buildings. Several 'professors' and teachers, two attorneys and a scattering of journalists and minor writers made their homes in Brompton at this period. But the most distinctive inhabitants were musicians and actors, especially comedians, whose genial presence enlivened the district well into the late Victorian era (see Appendix).

In the 1830's and '40's the Brompton Road district, though engulfed now in the broader development of London, remained prosperous and residentially desirable. Canvassing for a new parish school in 1841, the vicar of Holy Trinity wrote: 'Brompton will never, I am persuaded, require poor schools for more than 300 children. The neighbourhood increases in *respectability*, as well as numbers: and two squares are projected which will take away a large number of our present back streets.'[7] Though this last remark betrays concern for improvement, the new developments of Ovington Square and Thurloe Square did not touch the area most in need of reform, around New Street. Ovington Square and Terrace (1844-52) however, in superseding Southall's Buildings, set the pattern for later building, namely reconstruction with shops facing the main road and houses behind.

In 1844 a local antiquarian, T. Crofton Croker, perambulated the whole turnpike road and published an amiable, illustrated account of what he saw in *Fraser's Magazine*.[8] Afterwards collected as *A Walk from London to*

Fulham (1860), his essays afford a clear picture of the Brompton and Fulham Roads shortly before commerce took a dominating hold of the main frontages. Another celebrant of the locality's charms at this period, W. Carew Hazlitt (grandson of the essayist), regretted from the vantage-point of the 1890's the vanished Brompton of his youth, and particularly Old Brompton, 'the ancient mansions which abounded there, the historical sites or records, the fine residences in grounds, the market gardens, and, best of all, the old Vale',* all of which had given place to 'a dismal moraine of bricks and mortar'. 'I judge it to have been one of the truest pleasures of my life, if not one of its greatest privileges, to contemplate with my own eyes the beautiful hamlet of Old Brompton, as it appeared prior to the Exhibition of 1851, which virtually destroyed it,' added Hazlitt.[9]

Communications became an issue in Brompton from the 1830's. In 1836 a scheme was devised in connexion with the Birmingham, Bristol and Thames Junction Railway (architect, William Hosking) for bringing in a line to a terminus at Knightsbridge Green, with a large triangular market and arcade at the angle between Brompton Road and Knightsbridge (Plate 10c). The object of this enterprise, stated the promoters of the Knightsbridge Market Company, was to establish a point 'to which the produce of the north and west of England, of Wales, and Ireland, as well as that of the market gardens about Hammersmith and its vicinity, can be brought with the greatest rapidity and at the smallest possible cost'; and they prophesied for the venture 'a great pre-eminence over every other metropolitan market yet established.'[10] Alarmed, the Bromptonians united in opposition. For this and many other reasons, the line and market were never built. Yet at later dates up to 1846 proposals continued to be canvassed for bringing in a railway to a terminus at Knightsbridge Green, and the prolonged uncertainty may have affected property values along the north side of Brompton Road between Brompton Square and Knightsbridge Green close to the projected course of the line.[11]

Brompton Road itself started slowly to improve in surface though not yet in width, after its management passed in 1826 from the Kensington Turnpike Trust to the Commissioners of Metropolis Turnpikes. The very heavy wear on this and other local 'lines' was ascribed in the 1840's particularly to the traffic of 'Omnibus and Market Garden Carriages' bearing 'produce from market gardens and heavy return loads of manure'.[12] Along some portions of the road, the difference of levels between the worn-down highway and the made-up ground supporting ribbon development on either side was quite dramatic; opposite Brompton Row, the roadway ran narrowly through 'a sort of gorge' between the still-ample front gardens of the flanking houses.[13]

Two things focussed increasing public attention upon the state of Brompton's roads in the 1850's and '60's. One was the growth of official 'South Kensington' round Exhibition Road, deriving from the Great Exhibition of 1851 and confirmed by the establishment of the South Kensington Museum in 1856-7. Henceforward, Brompton Road became the main thoroughfare leading to London's new cultural quarter, and any deficiency in the district was loudly and publicly complained of. The columns of *The Builder* (whose editor, George Godwin the younger, was a lifelong inhabitant of Brompton) were particularly prolific in suggestions for street improvements.[14]

The other change came about through the formation of Cromwell Road, started in 1855 to serve the rapid growth of residential South Kensington, that 'city of palaces' which arose in these years, in the words of William Pepperell, 'under the magic touch of capitalists and builders like Mr. Freake and others'.[15] This wide new road (not carried to its full length for over twenty years) connected with the eastern end of Brompton Road via Thurloe Place, highlighting a growing difference between the sections west and east of the old Bell and Horns. From now on the upper part of the old highway began to take on a candidly commercial character, whereas the section between the Bell and Horns and Pelham Street was quieter and still predominantly residential.

This distinction was confirmed by the first significant widening of Brompton Road, which was started in 1862 to improve access to the International Exhibition of that year. As this exhibition was situated just off the new Cromwell Road (where the Natural History Museum now stands), it affected Brompton Road more directly than its predecessor. The improvements carried out between 1862 and 1873 were between Knightsbridge Green and Thurloe Place only. On the section so widened, various small strips of ground in front of Brompton Row and Queen's Buildings disappeared and the private gardens were drastically curtailed.[16] The main frontage thus ceased to be residentially desirable, although the property behind remained eligible. In 1860, for instance, Brompton Grove was pulled down and replaced by a row of dour shops facing the road but with a 'square', Beaufort Gardens, behind. Again, in 1866-8 further frankly commercial buildings arose at Nos. 187A-195 (odd) Brompton Road in place of the remnant of the old Southall's Buildings, but a row of large private houses was built along the east side of Ovington Gardens behind.

In confirmation of these changes, the name of Brompton Road became official in 1863 and the old terrace names and numbers disappeared. Henceforward commercial activity gathered pace. Tattersalls, the great horse auctioneers, removed in 1864 from Hyde Park Corner to a large site in St. Margaret's parish right behind Nos. 38-58 (even) Brompton Road, so perpetuating the association with horseflesh peculiar to these environs since the days of the coaching inns and affecting several local shops and pubs. Opposite, C. D. Harrod was between 1860 and 1889 in the process of transforming a small grocer's shop into a

*Brompton Vale was a small agglomeration of picturesque cottages which stood in the vicinity of the present Queensberry Place.

great department store. The instance of Harrods was not an isolated one; in Knightsbridge further east, Woollands and Harvey Nichols went through similar stages in the same years. Knightsbridge and Brompton Road, or at least their southern sides, were thus becoming fashionable for shopping. By 1884 Harrods' custom could be described as 'world-wide'.[17] Yet its premises then consisted of motley additions to the original houses built on William Browne's estate a hundred years before.

Brompton Road since 1890

Between 1893 and 1908 there occurred, not before time, a great rebuilding of the whole south side of Brompton Road between Sloane Street and Brompton Place, including Harrods. In 1859, thinking of this district, George Godwin the younger (who had been brought up in New Street) had contrasted in *The Builder* the generally good amenities of Brompton with 'rows of houses just behind all the gay, airy surface, which are absolute hot-beds of disease. Each room is occupied by a family, at a high rent, and the doctor is a constant visitor.'[18] At this time William Browne's old estate was in the hands of Lord Kensington's creditors and was so heavily encumbered by debt that little could be done with it. The problems of its ownership were finally resolved in 1888, when the freehold effectively passed to the Goddard family, who undertook rebuilding as soon as the leases expired.

The dominant achievement of this reconstruction was the new Harrods, which for exuberance and scale (if not for architectural finesse) rivals anything in London. The designer of Harrods, C. W. Stephens, was also active on neighbouring sites at Nos. 79-85 and 137-159 (odd) Brompton Road, making his much the most powerful hand in this part of the street. But the reconstruction of the estate, excepting two houses by Voysey and one by Mackmurdo at Nos. 12-16 (even) Hans Road, was adjudged by contemporaries to lack architectural quality. Writing in 1905, A. E. Street lamented that, despite a general improvement in street architecture, 'Brompton Road is perhaps peculiarly unfortunate: a thoroughfare of unusual breadth, with ample room for good-sized trees on one side, it was not without possibilities of being made a stately approach to the region of big churches and palaces beyond. Commercialism, however, has decreed otherwise, and nowhere is the particular stamp of architecture which one connects with the big, braggart, unregenerate shop more noticeable than here.'[19]

This rebuilding and the several pieces of infilling that occurred on the north side of Brompton Road in the same period by no means drummed the lowlier tradesman out of the area. Some small shops and public houses were indeed still built (for instance between Nos. 33 and 61 in 1898-1900), while most of the older shops remained modest; Beauchamp Place, for example, remained plain and unaffected in character until well after 1945. But along the main frontage they were increasingly overshadowed by grander concerns, drapers like Tudor Brothers, Gooch, Owles and Beaumont, and of course the overwhelming emporium of Harrods. There were also daintier small shops like Spikings the bakers with its tea room (No. 108) and, close to Knightsbridge, a rash of arcades: Park Mansions Arcade on the north side of the street (1897-1900), Brompton Arcade (1903-4) and the Knightsbridge Station Arcade (1903-4) opposite. This last was built in connexion with the Piccadilly tube railway, which opened in 1906. As this line originally offered two stations close together, 'Knightsbridge' at Nos. 29-31 and 'Brompton Road' at No. 206, it swelled still further the road's commercial significance. Hitherto Brompton Road had been served only by horse omnibus, but from now on the shopping district was quick to reach. All photographs of this part of Brompton Road taken since 1900 during the working week show crowded pavements and busy traffic. This boom seems to have been unanticipated when rebuilding took place on the Goddard estate, where shopkeepers appear to have been confined to two floors of retailing at most, with flats above. At Harrods, for instance, the directors were already anxious in 1912 to displace some of the flats they had so recently built on upper floors along Brompton Road and Basil Street — a process which took many years to carry out in its entirety.

Meanwhile further west, the old houses of Michael's Place were demolished in the late 1880's and succeeded between Nos. 209 and 251 (odd) by Brompton Road's first taste of the Queen Anne style. Here the conflict of commercial and residential pressures was resolved by having shops along the frontage but making the houses above accessible from a separate street behind. Further back were two further rows of houses sharing a cramped communal garden. By contrast the grand Mortimer House, built in its own grounds with a high brick wall on two sides, together with the gardens of Alexander Square opposite helped to perpetuate the old-style, suburban character of this part of the street. The difference between Brompton Road's western half and the commercial section to its east was now more than ever marked, a dramatic point of demarcation being from 1880 the bulk and from 1892-3 the alien *seicento* façade of Herbert Gribble's Brompton Oratory, entirely eclipsing the impoverished appearance of the established church's secluded Holy Trinity behind. On the opposite corner, the Bell and Horns and the old buildings behind it survived until 1909-15, when most of the present Empire House, Hotel Rembrandt and flats were built.

The history of Brompton Road since 1918 broadly confirms previous trends. Big blocks of flats arose at Nos. 78-94 (1934-5) and 197-205 (1929-30), but there were no new department stores to rival Harrods, merely a scattering of smaller smart shops, the harbingers of today's boutiques. In the squares and residential areas behind, there was some infilling and much conversion of small houses in streets like Rutland Street, Fairholt Street and Montpelier Walk into 'bijou' dwellings.

Since 1945, rebuilding has taken place on a much enlarged scale, with office blocks predominating now over flats. Few of these, particularly on the north side, have blended well with earlier development. A very large comprehensive scheme of rebuilding carried out in 1955-60 on the Tattersalls site and adjoining land between Knightsbridge Green and Lancelot Place seems especially wanton in its disregard of the street frontage. Yet this development would have been dwarfed in scale had the 'Knightsbridge Intersection Scheme' gone ahead. This project, fathered in the late 1950's by Capital and Counties Property Company Limited (which by then owned the frontage of Brompton Road between Sloane Street and Hans Crescent), would have imposed upon the complicated junction where Brompton Road meets Knightsbridge a huge traffic circulation system. Vast swathes of property on all sides of this junction would have come down in favour of office blocks, and a large 'island' development in the centre was to crown the whole. Plans for carrying out this scheme were well advanced in 1964 when the advent of a Labour Government committed against further office building in central London caused its withdrawal.[20]

Further west, the surviving houses of the old Brompton Row have suffered from the intermittent insertion of office buildings between Montpelier Street and Cheval Place. By contrast, an attempt was made at Nos. 190-212 (even) Brompton Road, following further road-widening, to return the south end of Brompton Square to something loosely resembling its original character.

Changes on the south side of Brompton Road, though considerable, have been less drastic. The numerous boutiques, notably between Sloane Street and Hans Crescent and in Beauchamp Place, make a fascinating study in the ephemeral fashions of window-display and shop-front. Between them, the unchanging bulk of Harrods offers a reassuring token of permanence and prosperity.

Brompton Road, Existing Buildings

Since the frontage of Brompton Road is divided into separate estates treated in several different chapters, the following list is appended of existing buildings along its whole length, together with their dates of original erection and their architects and builders, where known. Sources are given only if more detailed information is not supplied elsewhere.

South Side (odd numbers)

Nos. 1-9 (with Nos. 1, 2 and 2A Sloane Street). W. Duvall Goodwin, architect, 1903-4; alterations by W. Curtis Green and Partners, architects, 1932-4.[21]

Nos. 13-27 (with Nos. 2-8 Basil Street and Brompton Arcade). Shops and arcade by G. D. Martin, architect, and Perry and Company, builders, 1903-4; superstructure by G. D. Martin and W. F. Harber, architects, 1909-10.

Nos. 29-31 (with Basil Street Hotel). Ground floor (converted) originally Knightsbridge Station, by Leslie W. Green, architect, 1903-5; superstructure by Delissa Joseph, architect, 1910-11.

No. 33. Riley and Glanfield, architects, 1957-8.[22]

No. 35. James D'Oyley, architect, Lilly and Lilly, builders, 1893.[23]

No. 37. W. Reason, builder, 1898.[24]

Nos. 39-41. T. H. Adamson and Sons, builders, 1898.[25]

Nos. 43-45. Martin Wells and Company, builders, 1898-9.[26]

Nos. 47-49. James Smith and Sons, builders, 1899.[27]

No. 51. G. R. Tasker and Sons, ?architects, 1899.[28]

No. 53. Eedle and Meyers, architects, 1898.[29]

No. 55. Architect and builder unknown, c. 1898-9.

No. 57. James Smith and Sons, builders, 1899-1900.[30]

No. 59. William Downs, builder, 1899-1900.[31]

No. 61. Percy Henry Adams, architect, William Downs, builder, 1899-1900.[32]

Nos. 63-77. Martin, Wells and Company and James Carmichael, builders, 1903-4.

Nos. 79-85 (with Nos. 46-54 Hans Crescent). C. W. Stephens, architect, James Carmichael, builder, 1903-4.

Nos. 87-135 (Harrods). C. W. Stephens, architect, John Allen and Sons, builders, 1901-5.

Nos. 137-159 (with Nos. 2-10 Hans Road). C. W. Stephens, architect, Holloway Brothers, builders, 1903-6.

No. 161. G. A. Burn, architect, Thomas Stimpson, builder, 1860-1.[33]

Nos. 163-169 (Collier House). Industrial Investment Services Limited with Gilbert Ash Limited, builders, 1961-2.[34]

Nos. 171-175 (with Nos. 48-50 Beaufort Gardens). Igal Yawetz and Associates, architects, 1974-6.[35]

No. 177. G. A. Burn, architect, Richard Batterbury, builder, 1860-1.[36]

Nos. 179-181. Built in 1825 and leased to William Farlar, ironmonger, in 1831.

No. 183. Ernest R. Barrow, architect, Lawrence and Sons, builders, 1927.[37]

Nos. 185-187. Leased to George Benjamin Sams, statuary and mason, 1825.

Nos. 187A-191. Clifford Derwent and Partners, architects, 1964.[38]

Nos. 193-195 (Hereford House, with No. 11 Ovington Gardens). Denis Clarke Hall and Partners, architects, 1963-4.[39]

Nos. 197-205 (Ovington Court, with Nos. 1A-7 Yeoman's Row). Murrell and Pigott, architects, 1929-30.[40]

No. 207 (The Bunch of Grapes). Leased to James Walters, victualler, 1845.[41]

No. 209. Leased to Charles Patrick Smith, upholsterer, 1887.

No. 211. R. J. Worley, architect, G. and G. Green, builders, 1886-7.

Nos. 213-215. Samuel Chafen, builder, 1886-7.

Nos. 217-225. Mark Manley, builder, 1886-7.

Nos. 227-235. Alexander Thorn, builder, 1886-7.

Nos. 237-249. S. and R. Cawley, builders, 1888.

No. 251. Matthews Brothers, builders, 1889.

The Hour Glass. Sidney Castle, architect, 1936.

No. 285. *c.* 1830, largely rebuilt in 1981.

No. 287. *c.* 1808, probably rebuilt or altered *c.* 1830.

Nos. 289-293. *c.* 1830.

Nos. 295-301. Architect unknown, 1934-5.

Nos. 303-307. Temple and Foster, builders, 1871.

Nos. 309-313. Probably rebuilt *c.* 1835; refronted 1871.

No. 315. *c.* 1808, altered.

North Side (even numbers)

Nos. 2-22 (Park Mansions, with Nos. 127-151 Knightsbridge). G. D. Martin, architect, A. Kellett, builder, 1897-1900.[42]

Nos. 24-26 (formerly All Saints' Schools). Leased in 1839, much rebuilt *c.* 1885.[43]

Nos. 44-58 (Caltex House, with No. 1 Knightsbridge Green). Stone, Toms and Partners, architects, 1955-7.

Nos. 58A-64 (Silver City House). Frank Scarlett, architect, 1955-7.

Nos. 66-76 (Lionel House). Gunton and Gunton, architects, 1960.

Nos. 78-94 (Princes Court). G. Val. Myer and F. J. Watson-Hart, architects, 1934-5.

Nos. 96-104 (Trevor House). William H. Robbins, architect, 1959-60.[44]

Nos. 106-110. Sheppard Robson and Partners, architects, Costain Construction Limited, builders, 1981-2.[45]

No. 116. Rebuilt by Kenneth Gibson, architect, 1955-6.[46]

Nos. 118-122. Largely rebuilt by Elgood and Hastie, architects, 1932-3.[47]

Nos. 124-126. Hubbard Ford Partnership, architects, Crouch Construction Limited, builders, 1982-3.[48]

No. 128. Leased to William Rose, carpenter, 1767; altered.

No. 130. Rebuilt *c.* 1850, builder unknown.

No. 132 (The Crown and Sceptre). Leased to Thomas Rawstorne, ironmonger, 1766; altered.

Nos. 134 and 136. Leased to George Longstaff, bricklayer, 1766 (No. 134 much rebuilt).

No. 138. Leased to Thomas Longstaff, mason, 1766; front rebuilt.

Nos. 140-148. Duke, Simpson and MacDonald, architects, Harry Neal, builders, 1980-2.[49]

Nos. 150 and 152. Leased to George Gibbons, carpenter, 1766.

No. 154. Battley Sons and Holmes, builders, 1905.[50]

No. 156. Leased to George Gibbons, carpenter, 1766.

Nos. 158-166. C. H. Elsom and Partners, architects, 1959-60.[51]

No. 168. Leased to Joseph Clark, carpenter, 1768; much rebuilt *c.* 1835.

Nos. 170-174. Leased to Joseph Clark, carpenter, 1767-8.

Nos. 176-178. Wills and Kaula, architects, 1954-5.[52]

Nos. 180-186. A. J. Fowles and Partner, architects, 1963.[53]

No. 188. Leased to Joseph Clark, carpenter, 1768.

Nos. 220-244 (Empire House, with Nos. 1-7 Thurloe Place). Paul Hoffmann, architect, 1910-16.

Nos. 250-262 (St. George's Court and Garage). Robert Angell and Curtis, architects, Sir Lindsay Parkinson and Company, builders, 1934-5.

Nos. 264-268. John Mechelen Rogers, architect, Henry R. Wagner, builder, 1879-80.

Nos. 270-280 (Crompton Court, with Nos. 91-93 Pelham Street). C. Stanley Peach, architect, W. Moss and Sons, builders, 1933-5.

CHAPTER II

Brompton Road, South Side

Nos. 1-159 (odd) Brompton Road, Hans Crescent and Hans Road

All these properties, stretching from the corner of Sloane Street to the present No. 159 Brompton Road and to the parish boundary with Chelsea behind (see fig. 1 on page 2), were first developed between about 1764 and 1793 on the site of Long Close or Long Field. Until 1842 this ground was copyhold land held of the manor of Earl's Court. In the early seventeenth century Long Close had been part of the very extensive local landholdings of Sir William Blake. After Blake's death in 1630 it was among lands which descended to his son, grandson and subsequently to his great-great-granddaughter Anna Maria Harris (fig. 2). On her death in 1760, the bulk of her property descended to Harris Thurloe Brace, her only son by her second marriage; this became the Alexander or Thurloe estate. But Long Close was inherited instead by William Browne of Cursitor Street, the grandson of Anna Maria's first marriage to John Browne of the City, leather-seller. It was under William Browne's auspices that development of this estate began shortly after 1760.[1]

The Development of William Browne's Estate

The one important structure on Long Close before 1760 was the Swan or New Swan inn, which occupied a group of buildings facing the lane later enlarged into Sloane Street, with a tap house (later the Clock House inn) facing Brompton Road (Plate 7b). The inn dated back at least to 1699, but had been largely rebuilt in 1755-6 when a new lease was granted by Anna Maria Brace and William Browne to Joseph Barnham, innkeeper.[2] There was a yard with stables and coach-houses stretching to the west roughly up to the present Hooper's Court, beyond which the rest of Long Close was probably used as garden land in connexion with the inn.

The rebuilding caused a dispute between the vestry of Kensington and that of St. Margaret's, Westminster, in whose parish a small portion of the inn lay. According to Kensington sources, the 'officers' of St. Margaret's cunningly cut down the tree that was the 'ancient land mark' between the parishes, 'with a view to depriving the parish of the benefit of the tree and by that means to take in the New Inn Coach Houses Stables and outhouses lately built by Mr Joseph Barnham and to deprive this parish of any benifit'.[3]

Development started in the immediate environs of the inn. Here twelve houses known initially as Gloucester Row were erected under building leases of 1764 from Joseph Barnham to Joseph Clark(e), carpenter, and William Meymott, carpenter. Clark's contributions to the district are discussed below; he built the four houses next to the Swan, all leased in 1764.[4] Meymott, a substantial builder based in Southwark and Bermondsey, built the following eight, leased in 1764-7.[5] Like most of the houses along the frontage of Brompton Road, these were small and orthodox Georgian terrace houses.

In 1766 William Browne was formally 'admitted' to the copyhold tenure of the property and began immediately to develop those portions of his estate not covered by the lease of 1755 to Barnham, that is to say the whole frontage west of Hooper's Court.[1] He now signed articles of agreement with Joseph Clark to develop the remainder of Long Close as far as its westward boundary next to the Red Lion inn, which stood at the entrance to the present Brompton Place.[6] By this agreement Clark was to receive seventy-one-year leases from midsummer 1766 of any houses he erected, with the possibility of a later twenty-one-year extension. Here described as 'of Brompton Road, builder', Clark was the most prolific developer in the boom years of 1764-8 hereabouts. A deed of 1772 refers to him as Joseph Clark 'the elder' and therefore presumably distinguishes him from Joseph Clark 'the younger' of St. Margaret's, Westminster, builder, who erected houses at Prospect Place, Old Brompton, in association with Jacob Leroux in 1764.[7] Besides the houses he built under lease from Browne, the elder Clark also developed part of the east side of Yeoman's Row (known initially as Clark's Buildings) and in 1766-8 constructed fourteen houses in Brompton Row (Nos. 158-188 on the north side of Brompton Road, some of which survive). Little activity is known on his part after 1770.

Clark at first called his whole development here Queen's Buildings, in honour of Queen Charlotte. His original idea appears to have been to fill the frontage along Brompton Road as far as the Red Lion without substantial breaks for streets, since in 1766 no development on Lord Cadogan's lands to the south was envisaged. What is now Hans Crescent, therefore, was not conceived at this time. However one or two courts were required for access to the back lands; here the early development was undertaken particularly by William Meymott and by John Hooper of Knightsbridge, gardener. Near the eastern end Hooper's Court was laid out by Hooper and Meymott in about

1767-8 with small houses and stables, originally in a T-shape.[8] Behind this they built a tiny terrace called Garden Row, which briefly enjoyed pleasant views south wards, before North (now Basil) Street was laid out on Lord Cadogan's land immediately adjoining. Further west, Queen's Gardens was developed in about 1768-70, debouching into the Brompton Road roughly in the centre of the present site of Harrods. Here Meymott built some thirty small houses, with a public house (the Buttercup) and two other houses facing the main road at the north end.[9]

Clark himself built both at the east end of Queen's Buildings, where some sixteen houses (on the site of Nos. 29-61 Brompton Road) were leased to him or his nominees in 1766-7,[10] and at the west end next to the Red Lion where some eight or nine houses arose in 1768-9 (where are now Nos. 137-159 Brompton Road).[11] East of these a street was planned, originally Queen Street (now Hans Road), but Clark made little progress with this.[12]

The development was therefore completed by other undertakers in sporadic bursts of activity up to about 1793. In 1775-8 ten further houses were added along the frontage. Continuing Clark's eastern terrace westwards were five quite substantial houses (Plate 7a), three of which were leased to Laurence Laforest, victualler, and one each to Crispus Claggett, builder, and Henry Gandy, esquire;[13]* further west and stretching westwards from Meymott's buildings at the corner of Queen's Gardens a further five were built, three under agreement with Thomas Callcott of Kensington, bricklayer, and one each under lease to James Humphrey, gentleman, and John Moore, carpenter.[15]

The remainder of the frontage was completed between 1781 and 1791 under the auspices of Henry Holland, the celebrated architect. His intervention in Long Close stemmed from his much larger commitments in developing Hans Town on Lord Cadogan's land to the south. Though planned by an agreement of 1771, the major works at Hans Town (including the laying-out of Sloane Street and Hans Place) were not started until towards the end of that decade.[16] Holland was doubtless keen to arrange good communications between Hans Town and Brompton Road to its north, and this seems to have been the main object of his activities on William Browne's land. Firstly however he developed a small plot of land along Brompton Road east of Queen's Gardens (now on the site of Harrods) with six houses. These were leased in 1781-3, chiefly to Holland's nominees (William Vale, bricklayer; Reuben Jackson, plumber; Richard Paine, carpenter).[17] The one house leased to Holland himself may have been of interest; a photograph of c. 1900 shows it as stuccoed, with the remnants of a pediment over the second floor (Plate 26a). Of the others little can now be said.

Then in August 1789, with Hans Town well on the way to maturity, Holland accepted two further 'takes' from William Browne. One involved Queen Street, where William

Birks, a local tallow chandler, had recently undertaken some development on the west side.[18] Holland now took the whole east side from Brompton Road as far south as the boundary with the Cadogan estate. This, with the remaining frontage along the main road between Queen's Gardens and Queen Street, was quickly developed under sub-leases by Birks under Holland.[19] Probably Holland's main purpose here was to ensure a good width for Queen Street as far as his own Elizabeth Street, which extended southward into Hans Place. Further east, he took another tract for similar reasons, but here he had to construct a street not previously planned to join his Exeter Street on Lord Cadogan's land. This tract consisted of the remaining frontage along Brompton Road between his own buildings of 1781-3 and Crispus Claggett's house of 1775, with the whole depth to the estate and parish boundary. New Street was laid out down the centre to connect with Exeter Street (both together now form Hans Crescent). The west side of New Street was let out to tradesmen in small plots, but two small courts (Richmond Buildings and New Court) were also formed here. The east side was leased directly by Browne to Richard Holland, Henry's builder brother, who kept a large plot at the back for a timber-yard (accessible from North Street) and sub-let most of the rest. Eight houses were built along Brompton Road east of New Street and two to its west, all in 1790-1. Their lessees were the Reverend John Trotter; Robert Ashton, statuary and mason; Arthur Wilson, bricklayer; John Herman, glazier; Thomas Zieltzke, pastrycook; and William Warwick, builder.[20]

Finally, a small piece of infilling occurred in about 1809-10 on the site of the Hollands' timber-yard, which by then was the property of Henry Holland's nephew, Henry Rowles the builder. Under an agreement of 1809 with Rowles, the young James Bonnin took the yard, which was renamed Sloane Place, and built a series of six small houses on its eastern side, accessible from North Street.[21] Bonnin was to be an important figure in Brompton developments of the 1820's; his career is discussed on page 61. Facing these houses, a small Wesleyan place of worship was built, known as the Sloane Place Chapel. Little is known of this chapel, which held only a hundred people. William Pepperell, visiting it in about 1871, pronounced it dwarfed, dingy and situated in about the lowest part of 'a very low neighbourhood'.[22]

By the time that Sloane Place was built Holland's conception of Hans Town was virtually realized, so that the development of Long Close was no longer isolated but merged with the streets of northern Chelsea immediately behind. Horwood's map of 1794 (Plate 3), for instance, shows building well advanced along both sides of North Street (now Basil Street), while not long afterwards houses sprang up all along Exeter Street and Elizabeth Street, respectively the continuations of New Street and Queen Street.

---

*'Matthew Brittingham' is rated for one of these houses in 1778,[14] shortly after construction; possibly the architect Matthew Brettingham is meant. Crispus Claggett was later the proprietor of the Apollo Gardens, Lambeth, and in 1792-5 rebuilt the Pantheon in Oxford Street.

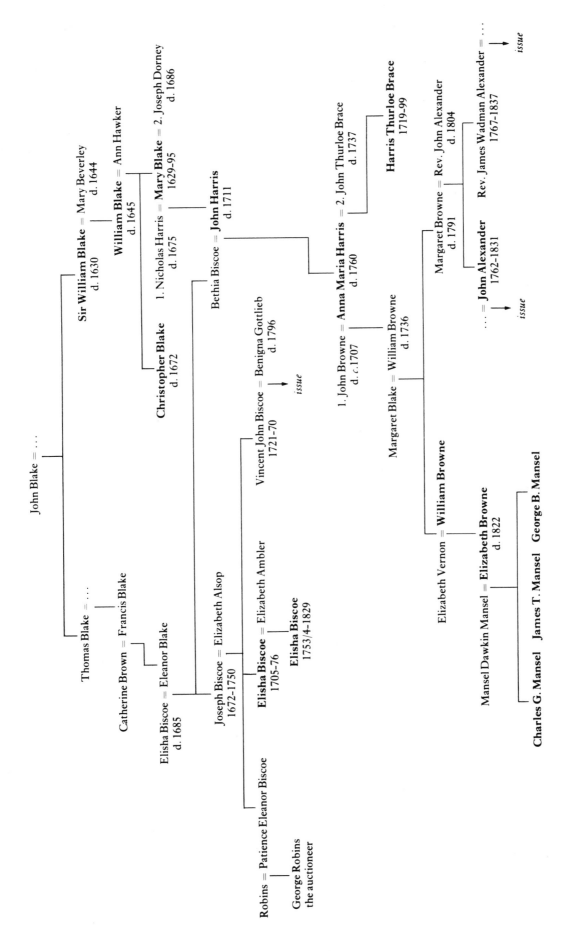

Fig. 2. Abridged pedigree of the Browne, Blake and Biscoe families: significant landowners in Brompton shown in bold

The original name of the whole frontage along Brompton Road from Gloucester Row to the Red Lion was
Queen's Buildings, but this quickly became confusing as
different terraces arose at different dates. New names
therefore soon appeared, but these rather added to the
confusion than detracted from it. On Horwood's map of
1794 the houses between Gloucester Row (or Buildings)
and New Street are shown as Queen's Row; those between
New Street and Queen's Gardens as Queen's Buildings;
those between Queen's Gardens and Queen Street as The
Terrace or Brompton Terrace; and those between Queen
Street and the Red Lion as Boston Row. But these relatively simple distinctions were soon abandoned. From
about 1800 Gloucester Row became most frequently
known as Queen's Buildings, Knightsbridge; Queen's
Row as Queen's Buildings, Brompton; the stretch between
New Street and Queen Street as Middle Queen's Buildings (with four houses next to the corner with Queen
Street numbered separately as in Brompton Terrace); and
Boston Row became Upper Queen's Buildings.[23] The
situation was mercifully rectified in 1864, when the whole
road was renumbered and the motley assortment of terraces became Nos. 1-159 (odd) Brompton Road.

Queen's Buildings and its shallow hinterland composed
the nucleus of late-Georgian Brompton and in early years
had something of the cohesion and independence of a
'London village'. None of the houses built here was large,
but most were at first decently inhabited. T. C. Croker,
writing in 1845, mentions five artists or engravers, one
writer and one doctor of note as having lived in Queen's
Buildings, while in one of the houses lived the incumbent of
the Brompton Chapel, the Reverend Richard Harrison.[24]
Most of the houses along Brompton Road, especially west
of New Street, enjoyed substantial front gardens to shield
them from the traffic. After about 1830, however, the
district began to deteriorate. Shops began to take over the
frontage and single-storey erections to cover the front
gardens, while the back courts and streets slipped into
multi-occupation. As fashionable development moved
westwards the area gained some notoriety, and George
Godwin, whose boyhood had been passed in a house on the
west side of New Street, inveighed in *The Builder* against the
district's insalubriousness.[25]

The Ownership of the Estate, 1799-1898

In 1799 William Browne settled the whole of Long Close
upon his only child, Elizabeth Browne, who was then about
to marry M. D. Mansel, esquire. After her death in 1822
the estate passed to her three sons, and in 1842 they, as
the copyhold tenants, sold it for £26,000 to the second
Lord Kensington, who was the lord of the manor of Earl's
Court and therefore, in 'feudal' terms, their overlord. The
copyhold tenure was thereby extinguished, and the property became freehold.[26]

From 1842 until 1888 the Brompton estate, as Long
Close was now always called, formed part of the second
Lord Kensington's estate, the history of which will be
described in *Survey of London* volume XLII, and which for
these years need only be summarised here.

In the early 1840's Lord Kensington was 'in a state of
hopeless and irretrievable insolvency'.[27] His principal
purpose in buying the Brompton estate was perhaps to
create a fresh asset, unencumbered by any previous family
settlements, which his innumerable creditors could use as
an additional security for their money. He may also have
hoped for a rise in value of this land when and if the West
London Railway (in which he was himself heavily interested) built a branch through to a terminus at Knightsbridge
Green, a project in serious contemplation between 1836
and about 1844 (see page 5).

To pay the purchase money Lord Kensington immediately mortgaged the estate for £27,000 to the London
Assurance Loan Company, a second mortgagee advanced
another £12,000,[28] and scores of creditors having
registered judgments for debt against him quickly fastened
upon this new property.[29] When he died in 1852 Lord
Kensington had certainly never himself received a single
penny from his Brompton estate. In 1892, when it and
Lord Kensington's remaining unsettled estates in Wales
were still in the hands of receivers acting on behalf of the
mortgagees and other creditors, the mortgages stood at
some £64,000.[30] The judgment debts amounted to over
£56,000, annuities totalling £2,231 per annum were still
outstanding, and there were arrears of interest of over
£117,000.[31]

But by this time the value of the Brompton estate was
beginning to rise. In the early 1840's many of the original
leases granted in the 1760's had been renewed by the
mortgagees for terms of forty-four years, and by around
1890 these had expired;[32] and many other leases had
been renewed in or about 1858.[29] One sagacious creditor,
John Goddard, formerly an actuary for an assurance company, had evidently foreseen all this, and in the 1870's and
'80's he had been buying up many of the annuities and
judgment debts, his long-term aim being clearly to obtain
possession of the estate.[31] In 1888 William Watkins, a
friend of Goddard's apparently acting on his behalf,
brought a successful action for foreclosure against the
second Lord Kensington's surviving trustee, and was
granted the equity of redemption of all the remaining
unsettled estates (including that at Brompton), subject to
the claims of the mortgagees and other creditors.[33]

In 1892 John Goddard died, leaving his estate, valued
at some £64,000, to his son, John Goddard II, a merchant
in the City.[34] Since 1876 John Goddard had received any
surplus rents from either the Brompton or the unsold
Welsh estates that might remain after payment of the
mortgagees' interest,[35] and now these were paid to his
son.[36] The Goddards were not yet, however, involved in
the management of the Brompton estate, lease-renewals
for which were between 1888 and 1898 granted by Wat-

kins as equitable owner in fee and/or by the mortgagees' solicitor.[37]

The Goddards' long campaign to acquire possession of the Brompton estate finally triumphed in May 1898 when Watkins transferred his equity of redemption in this and the unsold Welsh lands of the second Lord Kensington to John Goddard II.[38] Goddard's title was, however, still subject to the old mortgages for £64,000 and to the payment of the annuities and judgment debts, many of which he already owned.[39]

The Rebuilding of the Estate

The reconstruction of the Brompton estate was doubtless contemplated immediately after William Watkins and John Goddard I effectively acquired the freehold in 1888. All attendant circumstances indicated rebuilding. At that stage the existing fabric between Sloane Street and Lloyd's (now Brompton) Place was mostly over a hundred years old. Nearly all the buildings along the frontage to Brompton Road had been converted to retailing and had undergone heavy wear, while many of the properties in the side streets and back courts were in candid truth slums. Brompton Road itself, thanks chiefly to the presence of the ever-expanding Harrods, was beginning to prove a magnet for fashionable shopping, so that handsome ground rents could be expected.

At the same time, the tone of the Hans Place district southwards was improving markedly, as rebuilding there and on other northerly parts of the Cadogan estate gathered pace in the 1880's. In 1889 Earl Cadogan, temporarily in financial straits, parted with the freehold of a sizeable segment of land north of Hans Place which included both sides of North Street and bordered on the estate of Watkins and Goddard; leases here expired in the early 1890's.[40] In 1892 this property came into the hands of Ralph Vivian of Hans Place, who in conjunction with the estate agents Sidney Marler and Herbert Bennett of Sloane Street formed a company called the Belgravia Estate Limited. This syndicate promoted a rebuilding from 1894 onwards with the assistance of C. W. Stephens, an architect who had been prominent in the redevelopment of Hans Place over the previous decade.[41]

On the Brompton estate the first intimation of rebuilding occurred in 1888-9, when Kensington Vestry bought from Watkins a strip of land in front of Nos. 35-45 (odd) Brompton Road for street widening.[42] There followed in 1894-5 an agreement for a new building line all along Brompton Road from Hooper's Court westwards to Brompton Place.[43] Reconstruction of the whole estate proceeded in stages between about 1892 and 1908, according to the expiry of outstanding leases. Throughout, the freeholders (that is to say Watkins before 1898 and John Goddard II thereafter) depended upon the professional advice of the mortgagees' solicitor, T. E. Jennings, and their surveyors, at first Arthur Garrard and then after his death his son A. Norman Garrard, both of V. Buckland

and Garrard, a very experienced firm in all matters of estate development. Their policies were naturally more dictated by questions of value than of appearance, but an important effort was made to promote coherence with the Belgravia Estate Limited's rebuildings to the south and to resolve the problems created by parish and estate boundaries here. To this end, a strip of land all along the north-west of North (now Basil) Street east of New Street (now Hans Crescent) was acquired from the syndicate in 1898 so that the respective freeholders could develop their lands to mutual advantage.[44] In addition, Watkins and Goddard co-operated with the complicated rebuilding plans of Harrods, whose premises crossed the boundaries of the two estates. C. W. Stephens, already architect to the Belgravia Estate Limited and to Harrods, was also entrusted by Goddard with the rebuilding of much of the Brompton Road frontage, an appointment which doubtless helped to simplify affairs.

Apart from this arrangement, no especial desire to promote architectural coherence can be detected. The policy of the freeholders was in essence to erect shops along Brompton Road, some singly and some in blocks, with flats or offices above. Of the side streets New Street (from 1904 part of Hans Crescent) took its character chiefly from Harrods, but Hans Road was at first reserved for houses. Where special buildings arose, as at Harrods or Nos. 12-16 Hans Road, this was due to developers or lessees, not to the freeholders.

Along Brompton Road east of Hans Crescent, rebuilding began in small blocks of loosely Queen Anne character, starting with the 'Daisy' and adjacent premises at Nos. 33 and 35, next to Hooper's Court (Plate 20a).[45] Westwards from here, Nos. 37-61 (odd) were variously rebuilt by an assortment of architects, builders and clients between about 1898 and 1900 (Plate 20b, c). Brief details of the surviving buildings here may be found on page 7. The feature worthiest of remark was at No. 59, where Kodak Limited took the lower floors in 1900 and fitted them out with some decorative *art nouveau* interiors contributed by their architect, George Walton (Plate 22a, c); these have all gone.[46]

East of Hooper's Court, reconstruction up to the corner with Sloane Street started later, in 1903-4. Here development was marked by a penchant for fashionable shops in arcades, but complicated by the intrusion of the Great Northern, Piccadilly and Brompton Railway (now the Piccadilly Line). This line, first proposed in 1897 and mostly built in 1902-5, passed hereabouts under the southern frontage of the street. Its first Knightsbridge Station was built in 1903-5 at Nos. 29-31 Brompton Road. Designed by Leslie W. Green in the railway company's beloved ox-blood-red faience and decked out with an unusual amount of ornament, it boasted a small shopping arcade but at first had no superstructure (Plate 14d).[47] Next to this, a major development of shops and flats (Imperial Court) with another arcade (Brompton Arcade) was planned at Nos. 13-27 on behalf of the successful Oxford Street draper D. H. Evans. The architect here was G. D. Martin, who had just in 1897-1900 erected the large block opposite at Nos. 2-22 (even) Brompton Road, including the 'Park Mansions Arcade'. But because of disputes with the railway, only the shops and the arcade were built in 1903-4. The upper storeys followed on later, in 1909-10, and then to a prettier and less lofty design by Martin's assistant and successor, W. F. Harber, incorporating not flats but showrooms for Tudor Brothers the drapers, who occupied many of the shops below (Plate 19b).[48] At the same date the superstructure of Nos. 29-31 was added to the design of Delissa Joseph, as part of the Basil Street Hotel behind.[49] Later, the ground floor of the old station building was reconstructed, and in 1933 new entrances to Knightsbridge Station were made at the corners of Sloane Street and Hans Crescent.[50]

From No. 63 Brompton Road westwards as far as No. 159, the rebuilding again took place in larger units. Architecturally this part of the frontage, together with both sides of New Street (Hans Crescent) as far as Basil Street, appears to have been under the control of one man, C. W. Stephens, whose career is outlined in the account of Harrods below. Besides the dominating bulk of Harrods itself, stretching all the way from Hans Crescent to Hans Road and south-east to the estate boundary, Stephens certainly designed the large flanking blocks fronting Brompton Road at Nos. 79-85 and 137-159 (odd) on either side of Harrods, as well as Nos. 32-44 Hans Crescent.

The first of these, Nos. 79-85 Brompton Road with a return at Nos. 46-54 Hans Crescent (1903-4), was a speculation of shops and flats (Hans Crescent Mansions) on behalf of Stuttaford and Company, wholesale merchants in capes.[51] Here Stephens seems to have taken the general lines of the new Brompton Road front of Harrods (built in 1901-5) as a guide, so that the building has shop windows up to the first floor and a turret at the corner, while the entrance to the flats in Hans Crescent directly faces a similar entrance to flats originally constructed over Harrods opposite (Plate 21c). Here however the facings are of red brick and stone and lack the terracotta brio of Harrods. South of this building, Nos. 32-44 Hans Crescent (mainly of 1908), with a warehouse at the rear (Plate 21b), was Harrods' manufacturing building, details of which are given on page 22. It was replaced in 1972-4 by a development sponsored by Capital and Counties Property Company Limited, for whom Dallas A. Mailer was project architect.[52] Further west beyond Harrods, the large site at Nos. 137-159 Brompton Road and Nos. 2-10 Hans Road up to the estate boundary was undertaken by Holloway Brothers the builders in 1903-6.[53] Development took place in stages and comprised two blocks with flats (Hans Court) over and shops facing the main road. Stephens' elevations here, of red brick with giant attached columns and blank rusticated arches in stone, differ radically from those of Harrods (Plate 26d).

The one building along this part of the frontage for which the architect appears unrecorded is Nos. 63-77 Brompton Road, but again it is likely that the responsibility was Stephens'. Here Gooch the outfitters, in their time a rival to Harrods, rebuilt in 1903-4 to a unified, neatly gabled and bayed Tudor design with their shops below and 'Knightsbridge Mansions' above. Later, a good new shop front along the whole length was installed during major alterations of 1928, to a design by G. Alan Fortescue.[54] Gooch's later ceased trading and the shop front disappeared, to be replaced by individual fascias.

Between Hans Crescent and Hans Road, the complete quadrilateral from Brompton Road to Basil Street was reconstructed between 1894 and 1911 by Harrods, which dominated the entire district. The gradual rebuilding of this vast emporium is considered below. Here however it must be said that when redevelopment was first planned in the early 1890's, nobody ever envisaged that Harrods would occupy the whole of its present site—or indeed much property west of the old Queen's Gardens. Matters here were complicated by the alienation of a sizeable freehold site on the west side of Queen's Gardens to the London School Board in 1874. But the Queen's Gardens School, built to designs by E. R. Robson in 1874, did not prove popular. Harrods opened negotiations to buy the site in 1896, but did not obtain possession until 1902.[55]

Hans Road

The unforeseen growth of Harrods profoundly influenced the fate of Hans Road, the only part of John Goddard's estate to be rebuilt with private houses. Reconstruction began here in 1892 with the expectation that this would provide a smart residential address. There was indeed some talk of renaming the street Hans Gardens; one architect involved here, Basil Slade, in advocating this suggested planting 'a few lime trees on the sidewalk' to 'lend tone to the name', and subsequently reported that the name was unanimously supported by his syndicate, who 'are nearly all residents on the Cadogan Estate and know the proper tune to play in the neighbourhood'.[56] These hopes were not to be fulfilled.

The east side of Hans Road, where the houses erected survived less than twenty years, may be briefly dealt with. Here perhaps fourteen houses were built: Nos. 9 and 11 (built by A. Bush and Sons, 1894), Nos. 13-19 (built by J. J. Messor, 1895), Nos. 21 and 23 (built by A. Bush and Sons and designed by Basil Slade, 1893-4), and Nos. 25-35 (built by C. A. Daw and Son, 1893-4).[57] These were good houses; long leases of five of Daw's houses fetched an average of £3,550 and the sixth, the larger No. 25, was sold for £5,425.[58] At the corner of North (Basil) Street next to the entrance to the Queen's Gardens School, the Friend at Hand public house was rebuilt in a cheerful stripey style by Dear and Winder, architects, in 1894.[59] All these buildings disappeared in 1908-12, as Harrods bought up the leases and expanded on to the sites.

Possibly the external walls of some of the houses were re-used and merely reclothed in terracotta, but if so their plans were altered out of all recognition.

On the west side of Hans Road the houses survive. They merit full discussion, since two were designed by C. F. A. Voysey and one by A. H. Mackmurdo, while surviving records of the firm mainly responsible for development here, C. A. Daw and Son, shed some light on proceedings.

A building agreement for both sides of Hans Road (as Queen Street became in 1886) between the corner blocks at either end was secured in 1891 by Thomas Newcomen Archibald Grove. This gentleman already had some experience in local property dealings but was also interested in progressive causes, being founder and editor of the *New Review*. From 1892 he sat intermittently as a Liberal M.P. Grove promptly in 1891 underlet most of the west side here to Daws, covering the sites of Nos. 18-34 (even), and kept the remainder for himself, intending to occupy one of three houses (Nos. 12-16) to be constructed there.[60] At this stage the plan was that Grove's original architect, William C. Marshall of Marshall and Vickers, should design the whole street elevation. But by November 1891, dissatisfied with Marshall's elevation, Grove had dispensed with his services and hired in his place the as yet little-known C. F. A. Voysey.[61] By the spring of 1892 Voysey had matured his plans for Nos. 12-16 but Daws had already begun building at Nos. 18-26, probably following Marshall's outline designs, so that a sad discrepancy in storey heights and character occurred. Daws did not continue with Marshall either but with Frederick G. Knight, an architect responsible for much good-quality Queen Anne work on the Cadogan estate. Knight designed the interior features and perhaps some external details of Nos. 18-26, probably most of No. 28, and evidently the whole exterior of the handsomer and richer Nos. 30-34 (Plate 21a).[62] Of these buildings Nos. 18-26 were built in 1892-3, Nos. 28-34 apparently in 1894-5.[63] Except for No. 34, a small group of flats, they were all private houses; Nos. 18-26 sold for prices varying from £4,350 to £4,750.[64]

Meanwhile Archibald Grove's own houses at Nos. 12-16 were running into difficulties. These were perhaps as much due to Voysey's inexperience of speculative architecture as to Grove's fickleness. Under the contract agreed between them, Voysey was to have 5 per cent on the cost of No. 12 and only 2½ per cent on the other two. But in 1892 Grove decided temporarily to postpone No. 12, the slightly larger house which he had earmarked for himself. When therefore Nos. 14 and 16 were finished, Voysey insisted on charging 5 per cent on one of them. Grove refused this, and Voysey instituted proceedings. So when in the summer of 1893 Grove became ready to go forward with No. 12, he turned instead to another Arts and Crafts firm of architects, Mackmurdo, Hornblower and Walters. Voysey was thus supplanted for the third of his houses by a colleague whom he had known and pre-viously admired, A. H. Mackmurdo. In compensation he was awarded £127 at law, a proportion of his claim.[65]

This dispute (doubtless as much the result as the cause of soured relations between architect and client) sorely reduced the quality of this still-exceptional group of houses. Voysey's original scheme ingeniously adapted his customarily horizontal tidied-up Tudor idiom of architecture to the needs of London terrace housing. Its casual discipline, clever placing of bay windows and slight asymmetries show study of Norman Shaw's houses on Chelsea Embankment and Queen's Gate. In an early elevation the upper storeys were to be roughcast and the eaves of the green-slated roof were to overhang (Plate 23a),[66] but on revising the project in May 1892 Voysey toned down this rustic element, accepted red brick and Ketton stone dressings for the fronts, and above the third-floor windows designed a parapet that sloped neatly up to the party walls (fig. 3). A similar parapet occurs at the back, which though plainer is hardly less effective (Plate 23b). When the chance of No. 12 was lost, some of the delicacy of this scheme disappeared. As executed, Nos. 14 and 16 were perfectly symmetrical, though because one window has been lowered and another added to the mezzanine at No. 14 this is no longer the case.

In planning the houses (fig. 3), Voysey justified his reputation as an original but practical and economical architect. The levels of the reception rooms at Nos. 14 and 16 were split, a low-ceiled mezzanine room being inserted at the front of the houses between the hall and the smaller drawing-room, while the dining-room and the main drawing-room at the back were higher. Yet all the rooms were well lit and there seems to have been no extravagant recourse to iron in the sections. The houses were built by Thomas Gregory and Company at the modest costs of £3,418 and £3,618.[67] Internally, the finishings were simple, with oak-boarded floors, sunk and painted panelling to frieze height and plain fireplaces, above which were spaces for 'Mr. F. Hollyer's photographs of the works of Burne-Jones'.[68] The staircases were characteristic of Voysey, with sturdy tapering newel posts and stout square balusters (Plate 23d). At first-floor level might be found, at least at No. 16, a quaint metal stair-guard with four bucolic figures in silhouette. The only other special decorative features were two relief panels by Conrad Dressler, perhaps those at first intended for the hoods over the front doors; these are now placed within the porches (Plate 23c). The houses were soon tenanted and the first occupant of No. 16, the novelist Julian Sturgis, was to commission a small country house from Voysey at Puttenham, Surrey, in 1896.[69]

At No. 12, A. H. Mackmurdo faced the unenviable task of replacing Voysey's projected third house without plagiarizing his design. His solution, though skilful, was perhaps not quite skilful enough. Like much of Mackmurdo's architecture it has an awkward originality.[70] The motifs of the front (Plate 22b, d), which is formal and symmetrical, derive closely from the Queen Anne houses

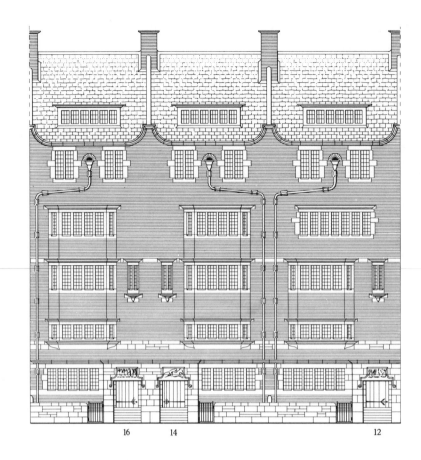

16   14   12

FEET   10   0   10   20   30
METRES 1   0   1   2   3   4   5   6   7   8   9   10   11

Scale for elevation

FEET   10   0   10   20   30   40
METRES   0   5   10   15

Scale for plans

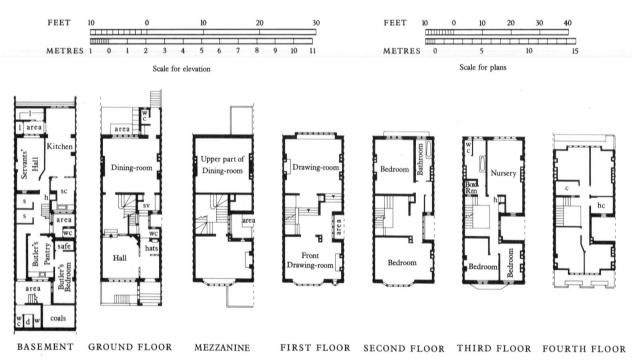

BASEMENT   GROUND FLOOR   MEZZANINE   FIRST FLOOR   SECOND FLOOR   THIRD FLOOR   FOURTH FLOOR

Fig. 3. Nos. 12-16 (even) Hans Road. Plans of No. 16 and preliminary elevation of group (1892). C. F. A. Voysey, architect

c	cistern room	hc	housemaid's closet	sc	scullery
d	dustbins	l	larder	sv	servery
h	hoist	s	stores	w	wood store

of Cheyne Walk, so that the pedimented porch, keystones and strong plaster cornice seem obtrusively classical besides Voysey's elevation. Yet Mackmurdo adhered to Voysey's storey levels, and the prominent oriel over the porch evidently derives from the smaller versions next door. Internally, the plan and finishings also faithfully follow upon Voysey's lead, though the introduction of a modicum of classical detailing everywhere betrays Mackmurdo's more eclectic decorative sympathies. (If anything, there is less of English *art nouveau* in Mackmurdo's house than in Voysey's pair.) This house was again built by Thomas Gregory and Company; it was erected in 1893-4 and first occupied in 1895, though not by Archibald Grove, who after brief residence in a house on the other side of Hans Road moved away from the district.[71]

The Estate in the Twentieth Century

John Goddard II died in 1906 with 'effects' valued at £986,000. This great wealth stemmed originally from the fact that Lord Kensington had had an absolute title to the Brompton estate upon which he had been able to pile huge debts; and with this disastrous example no doubt in his mind, John Goddard II had tied up his estates as strictly as any far-sighted landowning aristocrat. A trust with the much-favoured term of five hundred years was established, from which ample provision was made for his family, and subject to this his only son, John Goddard III, was to have a life interest only in all his real property, with the remainder to the latter's eldest son.[72]

By 1909 John Goddard III had increased his father's mortgage on the Brompton estate from £30,000 to over £117,000.[73] In 1921, however, Harrods Limited (who had hitherto held the greater part of their island site only upon leasehold tenure) bought the freehold of their premises from the trustees of the will of John Goddard II. The purchase price was £263,850, of which some £64,000 was paid to the heirs of Lord Kensington's mortgagees, some £119,000 to John Goddard III's mortgagees, and the balance of some £80,000 to John Goddard II's will trustees. Thus all the mortgages were redeemed; but the annuities and judgment debts were still being paid in 1921.[74]

When John Goddard III died in 1953 his settled land was valued at the enormous sum of £754,000, a figure which doubtless owed much to the continuing commercial prestige of the Goddard Knightsbridge Estate, as the estate was now most usually called.[75] His son John Lemuel Goddard became tenant in tail in possession, but in 1956 sold almost all the remainder of the estate for approximately two million pounds to Capital and Counties Property Company.[76] The chairman of this company at that date was Leslie S. Marler, grandson of Sidney Marler, one of the directors of the Belgravia Estate Limited which had since 1894 owned much of the adjacent land to the south. Most of this land had passed into the hands of Capital and Counties, and a principal object of the purchase of 1956 was to amass property in the district in preparation for a large redevelopment project known as the Knightsbridge Intersection Scheme, of which brief details are given on page 7. This scheme, which would have involved the demolition of all the buildings along the frontage of Brompton Road from Sloane Street to Hans Crescent, fell through in 1965.[77] In 1977 Capital and Counties sold most of their properties hereabouts, excluding the west side of Hans Road and Nos. 137-159 (odd) Brompton Road, to the B.P. Pension Fund for forty-five million pounds.

Harrods

Harrods is untypical of the great London department stores in having risen not from a drapery or general goods business but from a grocer's shop. In 1853 Charles Henry Harrod, previously a wholesale grocer and tea-dealer of Cable Street, Stepney and of Eastcheap, took over from Philip Henry Burden a small house and grocery facing the Brompton Road and then known as No. 8 Middle Queen's Buildings.[78]* Then and for many years afterwards the district was not conspicuously salubrious. Queen's Gardens, a narrow lane two doors away from the shop, contained a few little cottages and a large woodyard where in 1886 rats abounded, while at the same date North Street behind was said to be 'a mass of filth from one end to the other'.[80] Along this sector of Brompton Road the shops were single-storey erections tacked on to the fronts of the original houses of 1781-3 (Plate 26a).

From about 1860 C. H. Harrod's energetic son Charles Digby Harrod began to take over the running of the business. In 1864 (when the premises became known as No. 105 Brompton Road) the son married a fellow-grocer's daughter, and a few years later the father retired to York Cottages, Thurloe Place nearby.[81] The firm was now making its first advances, especially in tea, upon which according to C. D. Harrod's brother they built up 'a very nice counter trade which you know was when I left it [*c.* 1866] about 200 to 250 per week and very profitable'.[82] These profits allowed Harrod to add his first new departments, build a new shop front, move his family away to Esher, and in 1873 to add a two-storey extension at the back.[83] The key to this expansion was his adoption of the 'co-operative' or 'civil service' method of retailing, whereby the shopkeeper was able to charge low prices by taking cash only and refusing credit, thus saving considerable sums. Most such early establishments were limited companies run by costly boards of directors, but Harrod saved here too by keeping the business in personal ownership. He also attracted custom by delivering all goods free of charge.[84]

---

*The usual date given for the foundation of Harrods is 1849,[79] which appears to be when the premises at No. 38 Eastcheap were opened. But C. H. Harrod had been at Cable Street since 1835, while ratebooks and directories show no evidence for a shop in Brompton before 1853.

Fig. 4. Harrods, site plan *c.* 1885

In 1879 Harrod took over Nos. 101 and 103 Brompton Road adjacent to the east.[69] Considerable rebuilding followed and further departments were added. In the early 1880's the number of employees rose from a hundred to nearly two hundred, and in 1883 the separate departments included 'groceries, provisions, confectionery, wines and spirits, brushes and turnery, ironmongery, glass, china, earthenware, stationery, fancy goods, perfumery, drugs, etc. The provision department was the leading feature of the Stores.' According to *The Chelsea Herald*, Harrod's business 'which at one time was a purely local one, is now world-wide, and his clients — or customers — rank from the "Peer to the peasant" '.[85]

During the course of additions at the back in December 1883 a devastating fire virtually burnt out the shop, causing some £30,000 to £50,000-worth of damage.[86] Harrod was equal to the crisis, hired temporary premises and reputedly fulfilled all his Christmas orders.[87] In 1884 the old site was hastily reconstructed to the design of Alfred Williams, assistant district surveyor for Kensington, who had been Harrod's architect since at least 1881.[88] The rebuilt store was little more handsome than its predecessor and perpetuated the single-storey extension towards the street (Plate 26a), but it stretched back to embrace many of the old cottage sites on the east side of Queen's Gardens and was of course built on a 'thoroughly fire-proof principle'. General provisions, meat, flowers and fruit were sold at ground level. In the 'warehouse' above were silver goods, lamps, china, saddlery, turnery, ironmongery and brushes. On the second floor along with games were the departments 'sure to find favor with the gentler sex', namely

perfumery and patent medicines, while in the attic were beds and bedding. At an intermediate level was a large furniture department.[89]

The next landmark was 1889, when Harrods became a limited company under the chairmanship of Alfred James Newton, a reputable City merchant, with a capital of £141,400. Soon afterwards C. D. Harrod retired. His place as general manager was taken by Richard Burbidge, who had previously been with Whiteleys and other stores.[90] Almost immediately a more forward-looking phase of expansion began. Further new departments opened, adjoining properties were secured, and a depository was acquired at Barnes. Following a further surge in trade the board determined in 1894 on erecting premises 'of very substantial character'.[91]

This decision proceeded from the knowledge that rebuilding was then being contemplated on the whole of the quadrilateral now occupied by Harrods (fig. 4). As is explained in greater detail on page 13, the main site of Harrods lay on the freehold estate of John Goddard I and William Watkins, whose long-delayed rebuilding plans for the whole of their Brompton Road frontage were afoot by 1892. Behind this, the equally decrepit south end of Queen's Gardens and the whole of North Street came in 1892 into the hands of the Belgravia Estate Limited, which co-operated with Goddard and Watkins on a mutual plan of reconstruction. One of the directors of this syndicate, Herbert Bennett of Marler and Bennett, estate agents in Sloane Street, was also a director of Harrods.[92] This connexion enabled Harrods to negotiate an arrangement whereby the Belgravia Estate Limited rebuilt this portion of North Street (subsequently Basil Street) on a line further south and Harrods took most of the new street's northern frontage, thus extending its premises southwards into Chelsea and stopping up the old south end of Queen's Gardens.[93]

As yet however the company does not seem to have thought generally of expanding west of Queen's Gardens, where they held no leases. The presence here of a small but quite recent London board school, erected in 1874 to the design of E. R. Robson, constituted one difficulty.[94] This school never proved popular, perhaps because of a plethora of local voluntary schools; but despite rumours of its demolition as early as 1892, Harrods did not secure the promise of a sale until 1897 and entered into possession only in 1902, when the school was finally amalgamated with another in Marlborough Street, Chelsea.[95] A graver problem was that from 1893, under the rebuilding plans of Watkins and Goddard, good new houses were being erected all along the east side of Hans Road (see page 14).

The architect chosen for the reconstruction of Harrods, C. W. Stephens, confirms the link with the Belgravia Estate Limited's activities to the south. At this point in his curiously obscure career, Stephens' reputation was wholly local. He had been to the fore in the 1880's, partly on behalf of Sir Herbert Stewart and other local residents but

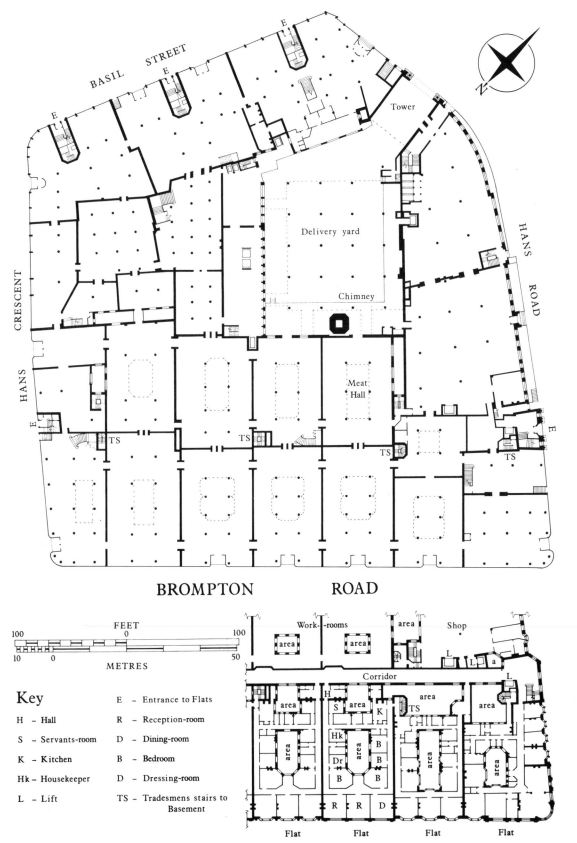

19

BASIL STREET

CRESCENT

HANS

Tower

Delivery yard

Chimney

Meat Hall

HANS ROAD

TS   TS   TS   TS

E   E

BROMPTON   ROAD

FEET
100   0   100
METRES
10   0   50

Key

H – Hall   E – Entrance to Flats

S – Servants-room   R – Reception-room

K – Kitchen   D – Dining-room

Hk – Housekeeper   B – Bedroom

L – Lift   D – Dressing-room

TS – Tradesmens stairs to Basement

Work-rooms   area   Shop

area   area   L L a

Corridor   L

area   H   area   K   TS   area

S   S

Hk   B

area   Dr   area   B   area   area

B   B

R   R   D

Flat   Flat   Flat   Flat

Fig. 5. Harrods, ground-floor plan of store and excerpt from plan of typical floor of flats, *c.* 1912

partly too on his own account, in the redevelopment of Hans Place close by on the Cadogan estate, and he had his office in the short southern section of Hans Road beyond North Street.[96] His buildings here and elsewhere in the district were of a banal Queen Anne character, but presumably he was a competent businessman and an effective planner. Stephens was the architect employed by the Belgravia Estate Limited to lay out the new Basil Street.[97] In 1892 he designed a new chimney shaft for Harrods, having also worked recently for the store's nearby rival, Harvey Nichols of Lowndes Terrace, Knightsbridge.[98] But 1894 was the *annus mirabilis* for Stephens, bringing him not only the prospect of reconstructing Harrods but also the huge and fashionable commission of Claridge's in Mayfair (1894-8). Later there came other sizeable projects, including the two buildings flanking Harrods along the Brompton Road at Nos. 79-85 and 137-159 (see page 14). From 1913 until his death in 1917 Stephens was in partnership with E. J. Munt, previously his assistant.[99] All his commercial buildings belong to the ornate, eclectic school of late Queen Anne architecture which continued to flourish well after the first proponents of that style had moved on to chaster effects. But Harrods, bulging expansively out of its rich casing of Doulton's terracotta, is unique among them.

The transformation of Harrods into the vast department store known today was a piecemeal business, since sites were acquired only gradually, business had to be kept going, and building regulations required that such large undertakings had to be divided into several structurally separate entities. Generally speaking, the rebuilding proceeded anti-clockwise from 1894 until 1912, from Basil Street and Hans Crescent round into the Brompton Road and so finally into Hans Road. Throughout, it was Stephens' arduous task to combine the requirements of each individual sector with a semblance of unity.

The first site at Harrods known to have been rebuilt by Stephens was in the middle of Hans Crescent, where in 1894 the properties then called Nos. 8 and 9 New Street were redeveloped to give a new side entrance to the existing shop.[100] Part of this elevation survives, incorporating a pediment. It is of the pink Doulton's terracotta characteristic of the whole reconstruction, but is less ornamental than some later portions. Shortly afterwards in 1895-6 John Allen and Sons of Kilburn, contractors for most of the rebuilding, began the first large work along the north side of Basil Street and at the corner with Hans Crescent;[101] and in 1897-8 the gap in Hans Crescent between this block and the side entrance of 1894 was filled. The elevations here have all disappeared but followed the style established in 1894, with pavilions at the corner and centres and a turret at the end of Basil Street. Significantly, the shop was confined to the ground floor, with five storeys of income-generating flats above.[102]

The rebuilding of the Brompton Road frontage came next (Plate 26). Here Harrods had gradually expanded in the early 1890's until by 1895 they occupied all but one of the old shops between Hans Crescent (then New Street) and Queen's Gardens (the final shop, at the corner with Queen's Gardens, was not secured until 1901). But beyond this, leases on the further stretch westwards from Queen's Gardens to Hans Road (Nos. 111-135 Brompton Road) were also due to expire, and a new building line including the whole frontage from Hans Crescent to Hans Road had been established in 1894-5. In 1897 therefore Harrods acquired promises from the Goddards' representatives of leases for the whole of this extended frontage, and from the London School Board of the sale of the school site on the west side of Queen's Gardens.[103] These agreements paved the way for a rebuilding of almost all the modern site, less only the east side of Hans Road.

Stephens must now have produced a design for rebuilding along the Brompton Road according to a more ornamental elevation and with superior flats above the store, which was here to occupy not only the ground but the first floor as well. In 1901 the general lines of this design were agreed with the London County Council and the first instalment, at the corner of Hans Crescent and Brompton Road, was built by John Allen and Sons.[104] The idea, perhaps not followed precisely, was to undertake a block 200 feet by 120 feet in area every summer until the new front was complete.[105] Meanwhile in 1902-3 Allens also erected on the school site in the centre of the quadrilateral the well-known meat hall and, behind this, a covered delivery yard with four storeys of warehouses and offices above, accessible from Hans Road. The Brompton Road front was completed to the corner of Hans Road in 1903-5, technically in five blocks of building.[106] This campaign included construction of the prominent terracotta dome and richly sculptured pediment over the centre of the front. In the case of at least one block the two storeys of shop were erected first, temporarily roofed in and opened for business, leaving the superstructure of flats to be added a little later (Plate 26b, c).

The last stages of the rebuilding were in Hans Road, where difficulties in acquiring some of the new-built houses occasioned delay and a specially incoherent elevational design, which may prompt suspicion that some of the houses may not have been wholly reconstructed (Plate 27b). The site of Nos. 13-23 nearest the corner with Brompton Road seems to have been rebuilt first, by James Carmichael in 1908-9.[107] The remainder, from No. 25 Hans Road southwards to Basil Street, arose in two stages in 1910-12 again through Carmichaels. Here several problems occurred. A projected 'Coronation Tower' over the entrance to the delivery yard had to be curtailed because residents and lessees opposite objected (Plate 27a); a pub, the Friend at Hand, had temporarily to be rehoused on the new premises; but a restaurant and a short-lived roof garden (the 'Rock Tea Gardens') here were eventually allowed.[108]

By 1912 therefore Harrods had been to all intents entirely reconstructed and occupied the whole of its present site (Plate 27b, fig. 5). Already claimed by Richard

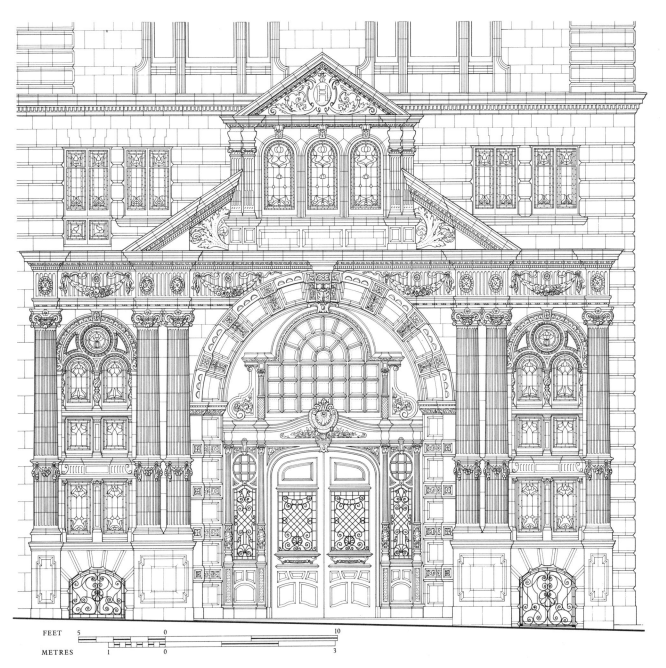

Fig. 6. Harrods, elevation of original entrance to flats from Hans Road. C. W. Stephens, architect

Burbidge in 1905 as the largest building of its kind in London under one roof,[109] it still continued to exceed all its rivals seven years later. Only one small portion of the old Harrods remained, on the north side of the delivery yard. Nevertheless there was little internal unity to the building. An American observer, Joseph Appel (a manager with the great Philadelphia store of Wanamaker's), commented in 1906: 'Harrods is totally unlike American stores in construction being simply a series of separate stores side by side connected by archways. Goods are sold only on two floors as building laws do not permit going any higher'.[110]

Though this was not quite accurate, legislation did materially influence the store's internal planning. Under the London building acts of this period, all buildings over 250,000 cubic feet in capacity had to be subdivided with party walls and fire-resisting doors. Exemptions were granted only with reluctance, particularly to buildings over sixty feet in height, like Harrods. The London County Council (General Powers) Act, 1908, amended the position slightly but still invested the Council with discretionary authority over 'additional cubical extent', for which Harrods was frequently obliged to apply.[111] The London County Council was also the ultimate arbiter of what were for the time very stringent escape provisions at Harrods under the Factory and Workshop Act, 1901. These regulations led to a number of costly disputes. When for instance Harrods wished in 1911 to arrange a kitchen high up on the Hans Road front, they were for a time baulked by the London Fire Brigade's long-standing opposition to the 'general tendency to increase the height of buildings in all large stores and emporiums'.[112]

Because of these laws large London buildings of this period were slow to adopt the type of steel-framed construction and open interior increasingly common elsewhere. In contrast to, for instance, L. C. Boileau's Bon Marché building in Paris (1872-87), Messel's Wertheim Store in Berlin (1896), or Sullivan's Schlesinger and Mayer Store in Chicago (1899-1902), where the shop extended well upwards in the building and the interiors were relatively unrestricted, London department stores of the period were planned with retailing on the lower floors alone. Above them might be wholesale departments, accommodation for the workforce or separate flats, depending on the locality and the policy of the management. The important thing was that access to these upper floors had to be wholly separate, so as to evade the limitations on 'cubical extent'.

At Harrods the company decided to build flats, which Stephens arranged with particular attention to providing natural light for the store below. The most elegant flats faced the Brompton Road, had at least fifteen rooms and a superficial footage of over 5,000 square feet each, and rented at £400-500 per annum.[113] They enjoyed ample space for circulation and were arranged around large light-wells, which descended to illumine skylights over the first-floor showrooms (fig. 5). Beneath these skylights were well-holes allowing light to the ground floor (Plate 29a). (Naturally this source had in many parts of the store to be supplemented by arc lamps.) For the gentry, access to the flats (which were named Hans Mansions) was from lifts or staircases within entrances in Hans Road (fig. 6) and Hans Crescent, but by a makeshift device the service staircases rose from a dingy sub-basement through the store itself, from which they were entirely enclosed.

The original finishing of the shop interiors was very lavish, too greatly so for Joseph Appel, who in 1906 caught himself 'admiring the fixtures and really not seeing the goods . . . Mr. Burbidge says they get the land so cheap — ground rent — that they can afford to spend money on luxurious fittings. But really it is because they are among such elaborate surroundings in London, beautiful public buildings, elaborate castles and private homes, and so on, that they have to decorate more luxuriously than we do.'[113] Appel emphasises particularly the copious use of glass, intended no doubt to make essentially small spaces look larger and lighter, and the ubiquity of carpets. Old photographs show very ornate plasterwork to the ceilings and to

the capitals of the many interior piers and columns (Plates 28, 29). A booklet produced by Harrods in 1909 also mentions rich marble and woodwork, the latter 'mainly composed of natural Ancona Walnut, Mahogany, inlaid Satinwood and Oak', and adds: 'the ceilings and frescoes are worthy of special note, being painted and modelled by French Artists in the Renaissance style'.[105] These Frenchmen were employed by the shopfitters Frederick Sage Limited, the firm chiefly responsible for the interiors. 'For five full years, from 1900 to 1905', says this firm's history, 'the House of Sage devoted almost the whole of its resources to Harrods and thereby consolidated its own reputation as the first name among shopfitters'.[114] Among Sage's works almost certainly were the *art nouveau* shop fronts on the ground and first floors, for which glass was supplied by Pilkington and Company.[113]

The old interiors and their equipment (which included a very early 'escalator' in the form of a moving belt installed in 1898) have nearly all disappeared. The one notable exception is the meat hall, described by Appel as 'probably the most magnificent in the store and handsomely painted with large designs and figures'.[113] Doultons, the suppliers of terracotta for the façades, were commissioned to line this part of the building with their tiles and entrusted the designs to W. J. Neatby.[115] His scheme of 'ceramic murals', carried out early in 1903, leaves the piers and arches relatively plain and concentrates decoration on the upper walls surrounding the light-well, which display bold and colourful roundels of animal life beneath trees conceived in a luxuriant *art nouveau* taste (Plate 30b, c). There are also some small almond-shaped scenes on the main walls and a series of bulbous marble counters (not in their original positions).

During the rebuilding of Harrods, trade was continually expanding. The cost of the works doubtless exceeded a million pounds (three quarters of which sum had been spent by 1905), but this was amply justified by returns. Between 1890 and 1910 yearly profits rose steadily from £13,500 to just over £210,000, and turnover in 1906 was put at £2,100,000. So many new departments were opened that before reconstruction was complete there was already pressure for further expansion.[116]

The company already had small manufacturing premises and a warehouse on the east side of Hans Crescent at Nos. 34-36 and behind; in 1908 Stephens rebuilt this with the rest of the block down to the corner with Basil Street, so that the whole of Nos. 32-44 Hans Crescent were available for these facilities. This coarse, bayed building (Plate 21b) was demolished in 1972.[117] Close by, on a site in Chelsea bounded by Pavilion Road, Rysbrack Street and Stackhouse Street, Stephens erected a further building in 1912, while across Brompton Road large premises for storage went up in 1912-13 on the south side of Trevor Square. These buildings were variously interconnected with each other and with the main store by subway.[118]

Despite these attempts to keep manufacturing, warehousing and wholesaleing out of the main building and thus preserve the flats, the pressure to expand upwards there proved inexorable. In 1908 occurred the first of an increasing stream of major alterations to Stephens' as yet unfinished building. In 1912, just as the quadrilateral was complete, the first of the flats on the Brompton Road frontage were abolished. Others gradually followed, until in 1927 a policy was formally adopted to bring the whole building into commercial use.[119]

So frequent were the alterations at Harrods that from 1913 at the latest the firm employed a 'house architect', M. Mostyn Brown, who at first worked in conjunction with Stephens.[120] His successor from 1920, Louis D. Blanc (later architect for the new D. H. Evans store in Oxford Street), made many important internal changes. His most extensively visible scheme for Harrods was carried out in 1929-30, when as part of the campaign to abolish the flats the whole of Stephens' elevation to Basil Street was reconstructed.[121] The result was a handsome classical front somewhat in the manner of the new Selfridges, with giant pilasters of a primitive order running through the upper storeys (Plate 27c). The materials are brown Doulton's terracotta or faience (then unfashionable, but chosen to cohere with Stephens' elevations) above a ground floor of granite enclosing fine bronze shop windows supplied by Frederick Sage Limited.[122] Later, in 1934, Blanc reconstructed a large block in the heart of the store including the banking hall, which was rebuilt to a chaste, classical taste but has since been removed (Plate 30a). Soon afterwards he was replaced by John L. Harvey, who in 1939 extended Blanc's Basil Street elevation round into Hans Crescent and built a large escalator hall behind the façade here.[123] The complete reconstruction of this front along Hans Crescent then intended has, however, never materialised.

Until 1921, most of the main island block on which Harrods is situated was still held on leasehold from the Goddard family and their trustees, but in that year the company secured the whole of this site freehold at a cost of £263,850.[124] Much later, in 1959, Harrods together with the several other stores then forming part of the Harrods group came into the ownership of the House of Fraser. Of the various structural alterations made to the interior since that date, the most important has been the installation of a bank of escalators on the west side of the stores in 1981.[125] By contrast, the external appearance of the building has changed little since 1945.

Nos. 161-177 (odd) Brompton Road, Brompton Place and Beaufort Gardens

In the earlier eighteenth century the site now covered by these properties was a small freehold parcel of land, some three and a half acres in extent, called Skitts or Scottish Close (see fig. 1 on page 2). This close was one of several scattered properties in Kensington owned by Henry Hassard (or Hazard), who died in 1706. All of these eventually passed in 1730 to Sir Thomas Reynell, baronet. Skitts Close included two 'messuages' in the north-east corner

near the entrance to the present Brompton Place, but most of it was leased and cultivated as garden ground by a succession of nurserymen, latterly David Anderson, who took a twenty-one-year term from Reynell in 1741.[126] Soon afterwards Reynell disposed of his Kensington properties, which came in 1744-6 into the hands of Isaac Preston of Beeston St. Lawrence, Norfolk, and Thomas Preston of Friday Street, City of London, merchant.[127] The Prestons gradually sold off the various holdings; Skitts Close was bought in 1760 by Barbara Oram, a local widow, who in turn sold it in 1763 to Thomas Smith of Piccadilly.[128] Smith, a musical instrument maker, was perhaps a figure of some substance; he is described in his one known publication (of 1766) as 'Musical Instrument Maker to His Majesty'.[129]

Brompton Grove and Brompton Place

The lease to Anderson having now expired, Smith prepared to develop the land. In 1764 he granted ninety-nine-year leases (from 1761) of most of the ground to Charles Ross, a well-known carpenter of St. James's, Piccadilly.[130] By then Ross was clearly well advanced with a row of seven terrace houses along the frontage to Brompton Road, set back behind a drive and common garden (Plate 3). All were occupied by 1766, two by members of the Gideon family, the widow and daughter of the wealthy stockbroker Sampson Gideon—a sufficient indication of a good class of house.[14] The land at the rear was left vacant, doubtless affording long gardens and an unimpeded prospect. The houses became known as Brompton Grove, a name later extended also to buildings further west. Nothing is known of their appearance, though at the time of their demolition in 1860 they were described as 'a block of dull, heavy houses with palings.'[131] To their east, the old houses in the north-east corner of the land were excluded from the ground let on long lease to Ross; instead they were wholly or in part transformed in about 1765 into the Red Lion inn, henceforward an important public house in this area of Brompton.[14]

In 1801 the freehold of this small estate was sold by Thomas Smith's widow Cecilia and his grandson Thomas Cafe, 'Staffordshire warehouseman', to a neighbour of theirs, Martin Lloyd of Gloucester Place, St. Marylebone.[132] Sixteen years later Lloyd (by now of Sudbury, Middlesex) granted a new lease of parts of the Red Lion standing on the east side of a passageway which from about this time became known as Lloyd's Place (now Brompton Place).[133] This appears to have allowed land at the back of the inn to be released for building, for in 1825 Nos. 1-6 Brompton Place, the first of twelve small surviving cottages, were built on the same side of this passageway, followed in 1830-2 by Nos. 7-12. All these were leased by Lloyd to William Paul of Sloane Street, plumber and glazier, for terms expiring in 1885.[134] They are uniform brick two-storey cottages, noteworthy only for their survival (Plate 8c).

Beaufort Gardens

Eventually the title of the estate passed from Martin Lloyd to his cousin Richard Lloyd, a builder, who in 1843 renewed the leases of the Red Lion and adjacent properties so as to fall out along with the original leases to Ross in 1860. But he died in 1859, just one year before this occurred. His trustees, Charles Cartwright Quentery (a nephew) and Thomas Howard (builder), and his executor William Cartwright Quentery (another nephew) now prepared to redevelop the estate.[135] A plan was submitted in March 1860 by George Adam Burn, an architect who had been chief assistant to Thomas Hopper and latterly had had some experience in designing iron churches.[136] By this plan, the narrow passageway into Lloyd's Place was to be realigned and widened, the Red Lion (hitherto occupying premises on both sides of this passageway) rebuilt on the eastern corner site, Brompton Grove demolished, and eight new houses with shops built along the frontage to Brompton Road (Plate 18a). The shops were to be in two groups of four, with a new forty-foot gated roadway between them leading to an elongated square behind, which was intended to be called Brompton Grove and to contain forty-seven houses.[137]

Work began immediately. In 1860-1 the Red Lion was duly rebuilt to Burn's designs by the local builder Thomas Stimpson on behalf of Robert Lathbury, victualler.[138] It still survives as No. 161 Brompton Road, with the upper floors rendered on top of the original stock brickwork (Plate 18b). Behind it and at the end of Lloyd's Place (where an exchange of ground was made with Lord Kensington's estate to the north-east so as to regularize the boundaries), stables were built or rebuilt by John Baker, livery-stable keeper.[139] Along Brompton Road, Burn's eight shops were built at a cost of some £11,000 by Richard Batterbury and leased in 1861 to Robert Lathbury and Charles Stedman, both victuallers.[140] They were briefly called Nos. 1-8 Grove Terrace East, but in 1864 became Nos. 163-169 and Nos. 171-177 (odd) Brompton Road. Of these No. 177 alone survives, considerably changed in elevation.

The new square (which, *The Builder* sardonically observed, 'will present two permanent sanitary adjuncts, a livery stable and dung-yard at one corner, and a busy slaughter-house at another'[141]) was not much slower to be developed. Four houses on the western side, Nos. 44-47, were leased to Burn in October 1861 and a further one, No. 43, in February 1863.[142] In the latter month the Quenterys, having changed its name from Brompton Grove to Beaufort Gardens, sold the undeveloped remainder of the freehold to Jeremiah Little, a substantial builder with a proven record of success in North Kensington.[143] Jeremiah's son Henry Little promptly undertook the development under his father, and both sides were complete by 1870. Some of the Littles' houses were let on long leases for prices in the region of £2,300 each, but others were sold freehold.[144] At Jeremiah Little's death in 1873,

he owned only fourteen from a total of forty-two built on his land.[145] Directories show that early inhabitants were of high standing, with two Members of Parliament, one dowager countess and several officers from the services residing in Beaufort Gardens in 1870. At the time of the 1871 census, 311 persons were in residence in the forty-two inhabited houses of Beaufort Gardens (Nos. 21-26 being as yet untenanted). These ranged from No. 20, where the eighth Viscount Midleton's household consisted of nine members of his family and twelve servants, to several households with small families and only two or three servants.[146]

The houses of Beaufort Gardens are of an orthodox high-class Kensington type, with four main storeys and a full attic above ground, light-brick walling, porticoes and plentiful Italianate 'compo' dressings (Plate 18d). G. A. Burn's five houses (Nos. 43-47) present a slightly simpler appearance than those of the Littles, but the general similarity makes it probable that he designed all the houses in Beaufort Gardens as well as the shops and the Red Lion along the Brompton Road.

Burn's commercial buildings along the frontage of Brompton Road have all gone, with the forlorn exceptions of No. 161 and No. 177. For many years Nos. 163-169, having acquired a coating of stucco over the original stock brickwork (Plate 18c), was the seat of Owles and Beaumont, a large local drapery store, but the shop closed in 1960 and the block was then demolished; Nos. 171-175 followed on a few years later. The buildings which replaced them are listed on page 7. Beaufort Gardens, by contrast, survives virtually intact though now almost entirely occupied as flats.

The freeholds of the properties in Lloyd's Place were sold by the Quenterys in 1871.[147] The livery stables at the south end are now garages for Harrods, but Paul's cottages of 1825-32 remain in residential occupation. The name of Brompton Place was substituted for Lloyd's Place in 1938.

Nos. 179-187 (odd) Brompton Road and Beauchamp Place

One-time inhabitants of Beauchamp Place might marvel were they to know the esteem in which their street is currently held. 'Once it was just another turning off Knightsbridge,' enthused the *Evening Standard* in 1974 with scant topographical precision. 'Now it's become a soft but steady pulse-beat of London fashion.'[148] 'A delightful narrow street chock full of antique shops', it was termed in another journalist's panegyric of similar date;[149] and in 1972 Beauchamp Place won the London Tourist Board's Cleary Trophy for the best shopping street in the metropolis.[150]

This destiny has been arrived at from modest but not uneventful beginnings. The thin two-acre site of the street (see fig. 1 on page 2), fronting Brompton Road and stretching south-east to the parish boundary, is blank on the maps of Horwood (1794) and Starling (1822), when at least along the main road all around had been thoroughly built up (Plates 2a, 3). Its eighteenth-century history is obscure. In 1763, when development was just starting on Brompton Grove and Southall's Buildings immediately to the east and west, the nephew and heir of William Oram, deceased nurseryman of Brompton, sold the freehold of what was probably this site to one Joseph Kaye.[151] But effective control of it soon passed to the Aitkens family of Mayfair, carpenters. In 1768 Alexander Aitkens, as administrator of the effects of David Anderson (another nurseryman who had cultivated much of the ground hereabouts), assigned to John Aitkens, of Market Street, Mayfair, the remainder of a ninety-nine-year term on the land dating from 1724.[152] Then in 1794 John Aitkens, by now apparently the freeholder, died, leaving a life-interest in the as-yet undeveloped land to his daughter Mary Ann Manton.[153] She was the wife of Joseph Manton (1766-1835), gunmaker, of Davies Street, Berkeley Square.

'Joe' Manton was celebrated as the most ingenious and elegant sporting gunsmith of his day; his career has been meticulously chronicled by W. Keith Neal and D. H. L. Back.[154] In 1819, when at the height of his fame, Manton moved his shop from Davies Street to larger premises in Hanover Square. But because of a fall in demand for his guns and high legal fees arising from lawsuits over patents, he from about this time met with increasing financial pressures which at first he seems to have been unwilling to heed. As a result his business began to fail, he was briefly imprisoned for debt in November 1825 and in January 1826 he was declared bankrupt. Following further bouts in detention as a debtor in the King's Bench Prison in 1828-9 and 1830-1, Manton with his family's aid resumed work for a time. He died intestate with effects of only £100 in June 1835 and was buried at Kensal Green Cemetery.[155]

Manton's financial crisis coincided with and greatly disrupted the first development of his wife's land, following expiry of the lease of 1724 in 1823. Perhaps to raise money on mortgage by improving the property, the Mantons fast set about development. Under agreements of November 1824 a new street called Grove Place (after Brompton Grove nearby) was to be laid out and houses built under the authority of a local attorney, John Henry Goodinge of Brompton Grove, who was to receive ninety-nine-year leases. The beneficial interests of Manton's many children were safeguarded, but Manton himself was to receive £420 in rent per annum. The building agreement stipulated that the houses facing Brompton Road were to be of at least the third rate and were to be stuccoed

on the ground storey, while those in Grove Place behind were to be of at least the fourth rate. The whole development was to be complete by Christmas 1828. The plan and elevations were provided for Goodinge by Robert Darley of Jermyn Street, the obscure architect probably also responsible at just this time for the design of Brompton Square opposite (see page 40). Manton's professional representative was Samuel Lahee, an auctioneer, surveyor and house agent of New Bond Street.[156]

None of these parties was able to mitigate the forthcoming disaster, and none perhaps was specially skilled in the delicate business of speculative house-building. In May 1825 Goodinge mortgaged his agreements in this and another site nearby in Montpelier Street to Joseph Delevante of Kimbolton Place, Fulham Road, for £1,600.[157] Meanwhile sixteen of the houses, five called Nos. 1-5 Grove Terrace (now Nos. 179-187 Brompton Road) and eleven in Grove Place (now Nos. 1-9, 50 and 51 Beauchamp Place) were in course of building. All except No. 183 Brompton Road survive; they are plain and orthodox, of three storeys above ground in Beauchamp Place and four in Brompton Road. The original ground storeys, now mostly replaced by shop fronts, were all stuccoed (Plate 15).

Immediately before Manton failed, at a time when the gunmaker was raising money wherever he could, eleven of these houses were leased on 10 November 1825 to the building tradesmen responsible for them, presumably in an attempt to avoid lawsuits and claims under the agreement of November 1824.[158]* Six days later Manton was committed to the King's Bench, leaving five houses built but unleased.

Following Manton's failure, development in Grove Place ground to a halt for fifteen years. But the five unleased houses (Nos. 179, 181 and 183 Brompton Road and Nos. 50 and 51 Beauchamp Place) proved a great source of trouble. William Farlar, the freeholder and developer of Brompton Square opposite, had been responsible for the three facing Brompton Road. Though he made repeated attempts to obtain his leases from Manton and Goodinge, he met with no success, for in November 1826 Manton had been obliged to make over his life interest in the estate to Sir Richard Sutton, a prominent sportsman who had advanced him a large sum to help him out of his difficulties. In addition Goodinge, having for some time failed to pay the full ground rent due from him as developer to Manton's creditors and assignees, was himself declared an insolvent debtor in February 1828. Faced with this situation, Manton with his creditors obtained an action for ejectment against all those occupying parts of the estate as yet unleased. Ever sanguine, Manton himself seems to have supposed that he might thus regain

*The original lessees in Beauchamp Place were: No. 1, Samuel Symons; Nos. 2 and 3, Joseph Clarke, builder; Nos. 4 and 5, James Bonnin, builder; Nos. 6 and 7, William Barrat, builder; Nos. 8 and 9, William Wellbeloved, gentleman. Nos. 185 and 187 Brompton Road were leased to George Benjamin Sams, statuary and mason.[159]

title even to the houses built by Farlar and by Thomas Harrison (the undertaker of Nos. 50 and 51 Beauchamp Place). He was sharply reprimanded by Sir Richard Sutton's lawyer in these terms: 'If by the ejectment you expect to recover possession of the Houses which Farlar and Harris[on] have built in the honest Confidence that as soon as finished they would have their Leases, you will I am persuaded find yourself wrong. Yet supposing you were right in strictness of law surely you do not seriously contemplate such a piece of wickedness and injustice as to attempt to wrest the possession of the Houses from the individuals who, under your Eye, have laid out thousands in building them, and you have not expended one farthing.'[160] The action for ejectment proved the last straw for Farlar, who promptly undertook a Chancery suit to obtain the long-sought leases; these were finally awarded to him and to Harrison in 1831.[161]

Also in 1831, matters righted themselves sufficiently for John Baker of Chatham, gentleman, and George Godwin of Alexander Square, surveyor, to take over the estate in trust for the Manton family.[162] But the arrangement did not quicken the pace of development. No further building took place until 1841, six years after Manton's death, when leases for eight further small houses, Nos. 52-59 Beauchamp Place, were granted by his daughter Caroline Manton to John Bellworthy.[163] At much the same time Nos. 60-62, three two-storey houses, were put up on land attached to No. 185 Brompton Road.

Soon after this, the street was practically completed down to the parish boundary under further leases granted by Caroline Manton. The main undertaker was Thomas Holmes of Belgrave Street South, a builder prolific at this time elsewhere in Kensington, particularly at Hereford Square. Holmes over-extended himself and came to grief in 1847, but by then his activities in Beauchamp Place appear completed. All the leases (of Nos. 10-30 on the north-east side and Nos. 33-49 on the south-west side) were granted between June 1844 and March 1846, mainly to Pimlico builders and tradesmen associated with Holmes. He himself took few leases directly but in several cases assigned houses to John Brannan Quick, paper-hanger, and took sub-leases back under him. Some other builders were involved, for instance William Emmins, who erected Nos. 28-30.[164] Two further houses at the south end, Nos. 31 and 32, were added by John Gooch, builder, in 1850.[165]*

The later houses built in Beauchamp Place were again ordinary, with stucco ground floors and surrounds to the windows. Those at the south-east end of Beauchamp Place (Nos. 26-30 on the north-east side and 31-36 on the south-west side) have extra storeys, all seemingly original. A smattering of houses appears to have included shops from the start, but these were in a minority. Most were modest middle-class homes, though the Kensington Vestry did receive a complaint in 1864 to the effect that two houses in the street 'are kept as common brothels'. The Grove Tavern, now prominent at Nos. 43-44, seems to have made its appearance in about 1867.[167] The census of 1871 shows that at that time more than half the dwellings were occupied by more than one household; there were lodging-houses in abundance, and one house, No. 33, was inhabited by no less than nineteen people.[168]

By the 1870's the freehold interest in the estate was in the hands of Thomas Randall, a solicitor, and various representatives of the Manton family, who were mostly living near Melbourne following the emigration of Joseph's son Frederick Manton to Australia. The Mantons' share appears to have been bought out in 1875-6 by agents of the Lygon family.[169] In honour of the chief title held by this dynasty, Grove Place was renamed Beauchamp Place in 1885. Photographs taken at the turn of the century show many but by no means all of the houses functioning as shops (see Plate 15a). The transformation into a street almost exclusively of shops and restaurants is a post-war phenomenon and its fashionable status more recent still.

Along Brompton Road, the few old houses of Grove Terrace (from 1864 Nos. 179-187 Brompton Road) rather surprisingly survive, with the exception of No. 183, which was rebuilt to designs by Ernest R. Barrow in 1927.[170]

Nos. 187A-207 (odd) Brompton Road, Ovington Square, Ovington Gardens, and the east side of Yeoman's Row

These sites today centre upon Ovington Square. In itself a typical enough small early-Victorian development of 1844-54, it possesses a rare interest because the reminiscences of its main entrepreneur, William Willmer Pocock, survive, shedding light on facets of nineteenth-century house-building that are commonly obscure. First however, something must be said of the somewhat individual mixed development that preceded Ovington Square and the other buildings around it.

Southall's Buildings, Yeoman's Row and Other Early Developments

The freehold interest in this whole site of just over five acres between Yeoman's Row (an ancient lane leading to the Quail Field in the parish of Chelsea) and the boundary

---

*First lessees were as follows: William Barrat(t), builder, No. 22; Nathaniel Date, gentleman, No. 49; Charles Delay, plasterer, No. 10; Benjamin Eatly, bricklayer, Nos. 11 and 47; Edward Falkner, linen-draper, No. 23; William Gaul, gentleman, No. 26; Henry Hart, paper-hanger, Nos. 31, 32 and 46; Thomas Holmes, builder, No. 37; Thomas Johnson, corn merchant, No. 27; James Keene, cheesemonger, Nos. 16 and 17; William Kimber, plumber, No. 15; George Lyng, No. 14; John Brannan Quick, paper-hanger, Nos. 18-21, 33-36 and 38-45; George Roberts, carpenter, Nos. 12 and 48; John William Smith, baker, No. 28; John Thorne, builder, No. 30; Thomas Wallis, plasterer, No. 25; John Winchester, plumber and glazier, No. 13; Issachar Woods, upholder, Nos. 24 and 29.[166]

of the field on which Beauchamp Place was built (see fig. 1 on page 2), was vested in the early eighteenth century in Edward Starke of Brompton. From him it descended to his daughters Eleanor and Elizabeth, and after the latter's death to her daughter Elizabeth Jones (d.1777), who in 1735 married Sir Thomas Dyer, fifth baronet (1695-1780).[171] Like other lands in this vicinity, much of it was cultivated before his death in 1760 by the local nurseryman David Anderson and used chiefly for fruit trees. It may possibly at one time have been a nursery garden for Brompton Hall, a large house at Old Brompton further west at one time owned by the Dyer family.[172] After Anderson died, his house in the north-western corner of the site passed to a City broker, William Shergold.[173]

In 1763 Sir Thomas and Lady Dyer granted the whole of this 'garden ground' on an eighty-one-year lease to John Hooper of Knightsbridge, gardener, who was also active in developing Long Close further east. Hooper promptly made an agreement whereby William Southall of Newman Street, St. Marylebone, carpenter, would take most of the land for the remainder of the term but lease back to Hooper a strip at the west end next to Yeoman's Row.[174]

Instead of the terrace houses which arose elsewhere along the main road, Southall proceeded to erect three substantial houses. These were at first called Southall's Buildings but later Brompton Lower Grove, Lower Brompton Grove or merely Lower Grove, and numbered in succession to the houses in Brompton Grove to the east. The westernmost and largest house, with a frontage of a hundred feet to the road, was leased in March 1765 to Bartholomew Gallatin of Park Street, Mayfair, Colonel of the 2nd Troop of Horse Grenadiers.[175] Known as Grove House, Brompton,* or No. 11 Brompton Grove, it was a handsome detached house of five windows' width and three full storeys. An unusual appendage was the 'complete riding house ninety foot by thirty' on the west side next to the stables; it was deemed suitable for 'age or youth that are learning to ride, or wish to take exercise on horse back in bad weather'.[176] Grove House was always well inhabited. Following Gallatin's death in about 1782 his widow sub-let the house to Sir George Savile the politician, who died there in 1784.[177] In 1793 it was bought by Sir John Macpherson, who had briefly and somewhat dubiously governed India in succession to Warren Hastings.[178] Known locally as the 'Gentle Giant', Macpherson occupied Grove House (which he used as part security for a mortgage of £10,000 from the East India Company in 1805[179]) until his death in 1821; during his tenure a single-storey drawing-room was added on the east side, allegedly for entertaining the Prince Regent.[180] Subsequently the house was briefly tenanted by William Wilberforce (1823-5) and then by the literary editor William Jerdan.[181] It was pulled down in about 1844, and

its site is now occupied by the present roadway of Ovington Gardens together with some of the houses on its west side.

Southall seems to have been less successful with his other two houses here and was soon encumbered by mortgages, finally ceding control of all these properties in 1771.[182] In 1769 however he had leased the house to the east of Gallatin's, later No. 10 Brompton Grove, to Sir John Astley, baronet;[183] between about 1826 and 1828 this was the home of the composer and pianist Muzio Clementi.[14] Next door, No. 9 Brompton Grove was completed at about the same time and first occupied by Thomas Jemmett; from about 1782-3 until his death in 1797 it was the residence of James Petit Andrews, lawyer, antiquarian and reformer, and later of John Sidney Hawkins, antiquary (d. 1842).[184] Little is known about these houses, but they were ample in size and compared favourably with other dwellings hereabouts. They survived until about 1866.

Though these three houses had good gardens, none stretched as far as the parish boundary. The ground behind in part remained unbuilt on (Plate 3). But a narrow lane or 'driftway' on the west side of Grove House led out of Brompton Road down to The Hermitage, a secluded house in its own grounds just south of the original terrace of houses in Yeoman's Row. This house's history is obscure. It was on the portion of ground leased to Southall, but no very substantial house seems to have been built here by him. Horwood's map of 1794 shows a small square building, but on Starling's map of 1822 it has been much extended. This enlargement may have been due to the celebrated *diva* Angelica Catalani and her husband and manager Paul de Valabrègue ('uomo avido e senza scrupoli'), whose brief tenure in 1811-14 coincided with the height of her British popularity and with a rise in The Hermitage's rateable value.[185] Subsequently the house was used as an asylum for the insane, and it was pulled down when Ovington Square was constructed in 1846.[186] A lithograph of about 1840 suggests an extensive, rather rambling, two-storey house, possibly stuccoed, with three modest 'Venetian windows' on the garden front (Plate 11a).[187]

The strip of land between Yeoman's Row and the 'driftway' leading to The Hermitage which had been retained by John Hooper in 1763 was soon developed, chiefly by the prolific Joseph Clark, carpenter, in about 1765-6. Facing Brompton Road were two plots extending to a depth of about 130 feet. On the eastern one, adjacent to the driftway, he built a public house set back from the road with extensive stabling behind; appositely called the Carpenter's Arms, it soon ceased being a pub and became No. 13 Brompton Grove.[188] The house later had literary occupants (John Banim, editor, 1822-4; Gerald Griffin, Irish novelist and dramatist, 1824[189]) and was demolished in about 1844. Next to it at the corner with Yeo-

*Not to be confused with Grove House, Old Brompton Road, or Grove House, Kensington Gore, for which see *Survey of London*, vol. XXXVIII, 1975, pp. 11, 12.

man's Row stood the house tenanted by the Shergold family. This, having perhaps been reconstructed by Clark, was sub-let by him to Henry Cooley.* By 1770 there was a pub here known as the Bunch of Grapes, which name was retained when it was rebuilt in 1844.[191]

Behind these properties a row of fourteen small cottages sprang up on the east side of Yeoman's Row. These were at first called Clark's Buildings, but in 1768 the name of Yeoman's Row first appears for them in the ratebooks. Joseph Clark built the ten northernmost houses, which were leased to him or his nominees by Hooper in 1766-7;[192] the remainder were apparently all leased to John Stuttard of Kensington, carpenter, in about 1771.[193] Nine of Clark's cottages survived until about 1960 as Nos. 9-25 (odd) Yeoman's Row (Plate 9a, b). They were of two full storeys with an attic and a basement. By a pleasing arrangement, the houses alternated between wider front-ages of three windows' width with pedimented door-hoods, and narrower ones of two windows' width with straight-headed hoods. South of these, Nos. 27-33 (odd) are the only survivors now of the original mid-Georgian development along the south side of Brompton Road (Plate 9d). They are simple houses of three storeys with basements which still incorporate the core of Stuttard's original work; at least one (No. 29) still has a tolerably original interior, with plain panelling throughout the main rooms. The present facing and stucco doorcases of these houses perhaps date from 1879, when they are known to have been altered.[194]

Ovington Square and Later Development

By the 1830's the freehold of all the properties described above had passed to Sir Thomas Richard Swinnerton Dyer, seventh baronet. On his death in 1838 they were inherited by his widow Elizabeth, daughter of John Stan-derwicke of Ovington House, Hampshire. She promptly married Frederick, Baron Von Zandt, a Bavarian noble-man, but remained childless when he too died in 1842.[195] As Baroness Von Zandt, she presided between 1844 and 1852 over the redevelopment of most of this small estate, including Ovington Square, Ovington Terrace (now the west side of Ovington Gardens), the sites of Nos. 197-207 (odd) Brompton Road and Grove Cottages on the east side of Yeoman's Row at its southern end. After her death in 1864 the freehold passed to her first hus-band's cousin, Sir Thomas Richard Swinnerton Dyer, ninth baronet.[196] He it was who with his second son Henry Clement Swinnerton Dyer oversaw the completion of what was to become Ovington Gardens and Nos. 187A-195 (odd) Brompton Road.

The main developer of Ovington Square and Terrace, William Willmer Pocock (1813-99), was an architect, the son of William Fuller Pocock of Trevor Square, Knightsbridge, also an architect. A staunch Wesleyan, the elder Pocock had been long connected with Knightsbridge and Brompton and promoted family alliances with other dissenters prominent in the local building world. In 1840 W. W. Pocock married Sophia, daughter of Samuel Archbutt, a prosperous builder who operated extensively in Belgravia and Chelsea, while in 1844 his brother Tho-mas married a daughter of the yet more successful builder Seth Smith. After working for a time with his father William Willmer Pocock began striking out on his own, usually in conjunction with the Archbutt family. In 1839 he built houses with Samuel Archbutt junior, a lawyer, in St. Luke's Street, Chelsea, and in about 1842 he took on from his father-in-law a plot in Lowndes Street, on which he had cleared £1,500 by midsummer of 1844.[197]

At this point Pocock was looking for further ventures. The leases of Lower Grove, as Southall's Buildings had come to be called, were falling in and Baroness Von Zandt was looking for bids for redevelopment, but she did not or was not in a position to offer all the land together. Pocock therefore at first considered Grove House and its large garden on their own, but concluded that 'the land for building purposes was not worth as much as the house would let for'. But hearing afterwards that Baroness Von Zandt was willing also to lease the adjacent site of The Hermitage and its large garden, 'I at once put on my boots, and leaving the house with my informant, but keeping my own counsel, I then and there went to the Agent and made an offer that was accepted for the whole of the land.' Promptly he involved Thomas Archbutt, the builder son of Samuel; 'I let him nearly half my land at Brompton, at a small advance of rent beyond what I was to pay, and between us, we had got 20 houses fairly on the way before the year was out, tho' I had only taken land from the Michaelmas.' They acted so quickly because the Metro-politan Building Act of 1844 was due to come into force in the parish at the end of the year, Kensington having been exempt from previous London building regulations. So strong was the building boom in 1844 on this account, records Pocock, that he and his father took brick fields in Battersea to ensure supplies. Few of these bricks, however, were used here.[197]

The site divided itself into four parts, most of which became Pocock's preserve. In the rebuilding that took place along Brompton Road north-east of Yeoman's Row he was not the sole operator. Here the Bunch of Grapes public house on the corner (now No. 207 Brompton Road) was rebuilt by other parties together with the adja-cent property (now the site of Nos. 203 and 205) in a plain stock-brick style, with livery stables behind (Plate 16c, d). All these were leased in 1845.[198]

East of No. 203 was the site of Grove House, part of Pocock's take and regarded by his father as 'the cream of the whole'. Here in 1844-5 he constructed three houses with shops on the old forecourt, 'forming the openings to fit the doors, windows etc., from the old house I had

---

*A cistern dated 1770 with the initials HC was noted hereabouts by the topographical illustrator Appleton in 1888.[190]

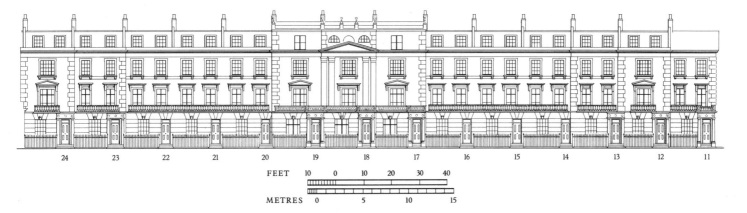

Fig. 7. Nos. 11-24 Ovington Gardens. W. W. Pocock, architect, 1845

marked for the purpose, they being of a superior character'. These shops, Nos. 197-201 (odd) Brompton Road (now demolished), were stuccoed and had vigorously rusticated Gibbs surrounds to the upper windows (Plate 16a).[199]

A second but minor area of operations was the east side of Yeoman's Row. Here Baroness Von Zandt relet the old cottages immediately south of the Bunch of Grapes to a local builder, George Brown. Beyond these, Pocock in 1846-8 built a row of eighteen cottages on the site of The Hermitage and its garden. Most of these were leased to local small builders who worked with Pocock and Archbutt, principally Henry Thomas Adams, bricklayer, and William Chapman, carpenter. They were called Grove Cottages and have now all been demolished, their sites being occupied by Nos. 35-57 (odd) Yeoman's Row.[200]

The heart of Pocock's project lay on the ground behind the frontages. Here he laid out an access road from Brompton Road with houses at first on its south-west side only, originally Nos. 1-14 Ovington Terrace (later Nos. 11-24 Ovington Gardens), all leased in 1845.[201] This led to Ovington Square, a thinnish rectangle inserted behind the remaining houses in Brompton Lower Grove, which for the time being survived. All but two of the original thirty-five houses in the square occupied the long sides (Nos. 1-33 on the south-west, Nos. 2-32 on the north-east).[202]

Architectural formality was attempted here but hardly achieved, for despite the pace of first building Pocock did not complete the square (begun in 1844) until 1852. The greatest coherence appears along the south-west side of Ovington Gardens, where a pilastered, mildly Grecian elevation centres upon the present No. 18 (Plate 17c, fig. 7). During the building of these and the first houses in the square, Pocock and Thomas Archbutt occupied The Hermitage, whence Pocock and his family moved briefly into No. 3 Ovington Square in about 1846. Thereafter Archbutt fades from the picture, having secured leases only of Nos. 8-11 Ovington Terrace (now Nos. 18-21 Ovington Gardens) and — under Pocock — of Nos. 2-14 (even) on the north-east side of the square. In the event

Pocock had to finish some of Archbutt's houses. He comments: 'had he been content with this one "speculation"', he would have done very well'; presumably therefore his partner overreached himself elsewhere.[203]

Pocock alone proceeded to demolish The Hermitage and finish the square, which was completed with two individual houses, Nos. 34 and 35, flanking a short exit road (known until 1881 as Vincent Street) leading out over Smith's Charity land to Walton Street. This land (in the parish of Chelsea) he took 'almost on my own terms, as I could give an equivalent in means of access to the whole. With very little trouble and outlay, I cleared perhaps, £5,000 out of this in a few months.' This refers to the houses in Vincent Street, now known as Nos. 36-42 (even) and 37-43 (odd) Ovington Square; they were built by Pocock in conjunction with Samuel Archbutt junior in about 1849-51, following on from other development by him along the north side of Walton Street, also on the Smith's Charity estate in Chelsea, around this time.[204]

Ovington Square proved a success for Pocock. His houses were occupied promptly and fetched good prices; in 1852 he was paid £1,250 for a seventy-two-year term on No. 30 Ovington Square, one of the last houses to be completed and one of the few to be provided with stabling.[205] Pocock himself seems not to have had to part with many head leases or to incur an especial number of mortgages. Capital for the initial development came from profits on earlier undertakings along with a small loan from Thomas Knight of Thistle Grove; later on there were advances from W. F. Pocock, Knight and others as trustees of the Chelsea Building Society.[206] The best testimony to Pocock's success is his own: 'I happened to mention to Mr. Thos. Cubitt how much per acre I had given for the Land, and he seemed to think it too much. I mentioned it to Mr. Seth Smith, and he said I should make £10,000 out of it in seven years. It was virtually completed in less than 5 years, and my gains greatly exceeded his estimate.'[197]

All the houses thus erected apart from Nos. 34 and 35 at the end of the square have orthodox plans, with two rooms on each floor, Italianate stucco fronts and four full storeys above ground, and all are about eighteen feet in width (Plate

17a, b). Some have two windows on the upper floors, others display a species of single Venetian window. At the ends and in the middle of the two ranges in the square are pillared porticoes, but the balconies and other details are not consistent, nor do the ranges match precisely. Some of these infelicities were doubtless due to changes during development. Internal details naturally vary also, but all conform to the Italian or late Grecian styles popular in the 1840's.

The thirty-five houses in the terrace and square inhabited in time for the census of 1851 contained on average five persons each, mainly minor gentry or professional people with two or three servants per household. The one aristocrat, Lord Arthur Lennox at No. 21, enjoyed the largest complement, with five servants and five members of his family; next door at No. 22 were the landscape painters William and Emma Sophia Oliver, at No. 18 the Sicilian-born artist Guglielmo Faija, and at No. 4 could be found a fading actress, Mrs. Nisbett (Lady Louisa Boothby), under the care of her mother.[207] The first occupant of No. 33 was another painter, James Go(o)dsell Middleton, who in 1852, shortly after his arrival, exhibited portraits of W. W. Pocock and his wife at the Royal Academy. He was succeeded by a better-known artist, Edwin Long, who lived at No. 33 from about 1860 to 1875.[208]

The central garden was leased to Pocock in 1854.[209] No further development occurred from then until Elizabeth Von Zandt died ten years later. Her heir, Sir Thomas Richard Swinnerton Dyer, ninth baronet, and his son Henry Clement Swinnerton Dyer now promoted the development of the remnants of Brompton Lower Grove in agreement with Charles Aldin, the well-known Kensington builder. Here, immediately across the roadway from Ovington Terrace, Pocock had 'reserved and planted a small strip of land to mask an ugly wall belonging to my Freeholder and prevent a nuisance'; he now received from Aldin 'nearly £1,000 for giving this up, to enable houses of a superior class to be erected on the land behind it'. Under his plan of about 1866, Aldin built ten houses (Nos. 1-10 Ovington Gardens) facing Ovington Terrace. Behind these he laid out a mews, while on the site of the houses facing the main road arose six shops with accommodation above (Nos. 187A-195 Brompton Road). All these buildings were leased to Aldin or his nominees in 1867 or 1868 and occupied expeditiously.[210] They were built in a downright orthodox stock-brick style with stone dressings and had four storeys above ground (Plate 17d). In 1869 the street became formally known as Ovington Gardens; seven years later the older houses were renumbered to allow for the newcomers, Nos. 1-14 Ovington Terrace becoming Nos. 11-24 Ovington Gardens.

Later reconstruction along Brompton Road has led to the demolition of both Pocock's and Aldin's shops and to the disappearance of Nos. 11 and 12 Ovington Gardens from the original composition of Ovington Terrace. The present Nos. 187A-195 (odd) Brompton Road date from 1963-4 (Plate 24a);[211] brief details of these buildings will be found on page 7. West of these is Ovington Court

(Nos. 197-205 Brompton Road and Nos. 1A-7 Yeoman's Row), a large block of flats designed by Murrell and Pigott in 1929-30.[212] In the square, little has changed. The narrow mews between Nos. 32 and 34 in the south-east corner allowed the modest No. 32A, designed for W. I. Turner by Clough Williams-Ellis, to be inserted in 1924.[213] Nearby, Nos. 22-26 (even) were replaced in 1957 after war damage by steel-framed, brick-faced flats designed by Walter and Eva Segal for Apex Properties (Plate 17b).[214] This building respects the scale of the surrounding houses, though not their style.

It remains to say something of the history and character of Yeoman's Row since 1850. By that time some thirty-four cottages had been built on the west side on the Smith's Charity estate (see pages 92 and 97), and the street had become a refuge for a large and almost exclusively working-class population. The census of 1851 shows that within the sixty-eight little houses in Yeoman's Row there lived 1,020 inhabitants—a figure substantially larger than that of all the residents (including servants) in the great houses of Grosvenor Square in Mayfair. The average number of inhabitants in each house was 15, but in one case there were 28 people, forming 6 separate households. Only two houses were in undivided occupation, one of the householders here being 'a proprietor of houses'. Male householders included building tradesmen (48), coachmen or grooms (21), labourers (18), coachworkers and shoemakers (11 each), tailors (9), and gardeners and furniture workers (5 each). Female householders included laundresses (12), charwomen (5) dressmakers (4) and nurses (3).[215]

By 1881 the total population had fallen to 888 and the average number of inhabitants in each house to 13. The number of householders in the building trades had declined to 30, while labourers had increased to 27; and five policemen now lived in Yeoman's Row. Otherwise there was little change.[216]

Nos. 27-33 (odd) are of particular interest as they are now the only survivors of the houses enumerated in the census of 1881. At that date Nos. 29 and 33, with 25 inhabitants in each, had the highest number of residents of all the houses in the street. At the former there were seven separate households and at the latter four. Despite having been 'altered' (and presumably improved) in 1879, a condition for the renewal of the sub-lease of all four houses in 1890-1 was that they should be 'put in thorough repair and kept so'.[217] In 1905-6 each of the four floors of No. 27 was in separate occupation, the weekly rents ranging from 5s. 6d. to 7s.[218] As late as 1938 the Kensington Borough Council was considering declaring all four houses 'to be a clearance area'.[219]

The long process whereby this overcrowded sump assumed its exclusive modern *chic* began in the 1890's with the appearance of middle-class studios on the Smith's Charity estate on the west side. The tension which evidently existed between the residents on either side of the street came to a head in 1931-2 when the London

County Council was induced to act against various sheds and pigeon-houses on the forecourts of the old Grove Cottages, which were decidedly raffish. A studio-dweller opposite, however, wrote in defence of one of the L.C.C.'s victims in these terms: 'the majority of the people down here are a very ignorant and dirty crowd and this man is a distinctly different class and quite an acquisition to the street . . . the pidgeons with their cooings are quiet compared with the usual quarrelsome dogs and cats to say nothing of the usual sample of owner!'[220]

All this heralded impending gentrification. Neo-Georgian brick houses in smart pairs duly arose on the sites of Nos. 35-57 to designs by E. Walcot Bather, Nos. 35-49 being built in 1937-8 and Nos. 51-57 following on in 1953-4.[221] Further north, the old Georgian Nos. 9-25 survived a threat of 1938 but finally succumbed in 1960, when they were replaced with a neat row of houses in similar style by J. J. de Segrais, architect (Plate 9c).[222] With these disappeared what John Betjeman at the time called 'the last glimpse of the village of Brompton, when it stood in the market gardens of Knightsbridge'.[223]

Nos. 209-251 (odd) Brompton Road

The land between Yeoman's Row and the entrance to Crescent Place, extending as far as the former parish boundary on the south, belongs to the Smith's Charity estate, and the history of the present and former buildings on the site is described in Chapter VI.

Nos. 275-315 (odd) Brompton Road

The group of buildings between Crescent Place and Draycott Avenue consists of a small neo-Georgian public house (the Hour Glass) and a range of shops of various dates, each with two or three storeys of residential accommodation above. Except where later rebuilding has taken place the upper storeys are generally rendered and have a variety of window dressings. The history of the buildings is as obscure as their appearance is undistinguished.

The strip of land on which they stand has a long frontage to the main road, but is shallow and of uneven depth. At the end of the eighteenth century it appears to have been either waste land or copyhold of the manor of Earl's Court.[224] At that time only two buildings stood here — a small structure, perhaps a shop, which had been erected in about 1798[14] approximately where No. 285 now stands, and a larger but probably hardly more substantial building of earlier date on the site of the present No. 315, at the corner of Blacklands (or, on some maps, Whitelands) Lane, later Marlborough Road and now Draycott Avenue. On the other side of the lane stood the Admiral Keppel tavern (in the parish of Chelsea) and the building at No. 315, which had a low rateable value, may have been no more than a shop or other adjunct of the tea garden which was one of the attractions of the inn.[225]

The greater part of the land was probably enfranchised at some time between 1783 and 1831, a period for which the court rolls of the manor are no longer extant, but the site of this building remained copyhold until 1866.[226]

No building activity of note took place until 1806 when a sixty-year lease of most of the land was granted to one James Duddell,[227] and a fair-sized detached house, double-fronted but of little depth, was built in the middle of the plot and shortly afterwards assigned, together with the leasehold interest, to a John Gray. At about the same time the southernmost house at No. 315 was rebuilt and let to a greengrocer, and, in the absence of any evidence of further rebuilding, may still form the core of the present building there. Other premises, which were occupied by a milkman, were erected on the site of, and may likewise form the core of, the present No. 287. Lastly, in this initial phase of building activity, four small houses were built in 1809 to the north of, and adjoining, the southern corner house. Perhaps little more than small shops which are barely visible on Starling's map of 1822, this range was originally known as Keppel Place.[228]

In 1817 the freehold or copyhold of the whole plot (including the copyhold of the site of No. 315) was acquired by George Willmer, who occupied the detached house for the next seven years before moving to King's Parade, King's Road, Chelsea.[229] Shortly after his departure the house was demolished and between 1826 and 1832 eight houses were erected in its place, of which only Nos. 289-293 survive in any recognisable form. The rebuilding was organised by Thomas Gray of Marylebone Street near Golden Square and later of Piccadilly, a stationer, who had succeeded to the lease of 1806, and in about 1830 the name Gray's Place was adopted for his range of buildings instead of Keppel Place.[230]

In 1831 Willmer granted a lease to George Godwin the elder of the narrow strip at the northern end of the ground (occupied at the present time by the Hour Glass and No. 285), which had not been included in the land leased in 1806.[231] Godwin seems to have rebuilt No. 285 (which, however, was largely rebuilt again in 1981[232]) and also erected other small houses and lock-up shops, now demolished, on the site.[14] Finally, this second phase of building was brought to an end in 1835 when the four houses near the southern end of the frontage, which had been built in 1809, were rebuilt or substantially enlarged.[14] The three southernmost of these may form the basis of the building fabric of Nos. 309-313 despite later alterations.

By the mid 1830's the whole frontage was occupied by some nineteen buildings, mostly of a nondescript character, and all apparently with shops on the ground floor.[233] The buildings at the northern end, which were leased to Godwin, were numbered from north to south as 1-5 (consec.) Crescent Place, Fulham Road (not to be confused with the houses of the same number which were erected later in Crescent Place itself on the Smith's Charity estate), and the remainder were numbered from south to north as 1-14 (consec.) Gray's Place. In 1862 they were all renumbered as 35-75 (odd) Fulham Road, from north to south, and in 1935 renumbered again as 275-315 (odd) Brompton Road when this part of Fulham Road was incorporated into Brompton Road. The enlarged Hour Glass now occupies the sites of Nos. 275-283.

In his will, which was proved in 1832, Willmer left all his freehold and copyhold property to the children of his daughter, Sarah, who had married James Wilkin. The prolific Sarah Wilkin had several children and the administration of the will proved a complex affair for Willmer's trustees.[234] The problem was partly resolved in 1867 when the Metropolitan District Railway Company bought the southern half of the ground in order to construct its railway line, which had been authorised by Act of Parliament in 1864.[235] Only three houses had to be demolished, however, and these were replaced in 1871 by the present Nos. 303-307 (odd), which were built by Temple and Foster of Paddington in a florid Franco-Italian manner with elaborate architraves to the windows and a high, mansarded attic storey.[236] In the same year Nos. 309-313 (odd) were apparently refronted with coarse stone or cement ornamentation;[237] No. 313 has since been further altered.

In 1934-5 Nos. 295-301 (odd) were rebuilt as a pair of shops with three storeys of flats above in brown brick with projecting stone bays,[238] and in 1936 the Hour Glass public house, which had begun life as a beer shop in the 1830's, was rebuilt on an enlarged site in a simple neo-Georgian red-brick manner to the designs of Sidney Castle.[239]

CHAPTER III

Brompton Road, North Side

On the north side of Brompton Road, the modern borough of Kensington now stretches no further east than Montpelier Street, the frontage beyond up to Knightsbridge Green having been ceded to the City of Westminster in 1900 (see fig. 1 on page 2). Anciently a thin strip of Kensington extended as far east as Knightsbridge Green, but in terms of land ownership the parish boundary with St. Margaret's, Westminster, hereabouts was never of great significance. From the earlier seventeenth century until 1759 a very substantial tract of land in both parishes here was in a single freehold block. This holding (some twenty-five acres in extent) was bounded by Brompton Road on the south, where it stretched west from Knightsbridge Green to the point where Cheval Place now debouches into the road east of Brompton Square; the only exception on this side was a narrow strip of the Brompton Road frontage reaching westwards from Knightsbridge Green about half way to the present Lancelot Place, which seems until 1705 to have been in other hands. On its north side the boundaries were not so regular, but some portions extended up to the western continuation of Knightsbridge and another detached piece occupied the site of the present Ennismore Gardens. The holding comprised portions of the fields or closes known as Wellfield, Greenfield and West or Wett Meads.[1]

Like much of eastern Kensington, this property belonged in the early seventeenth century to Sir William Blake, being part of the hundred acres of meadow and pasture land in St. Margaret's Westminster, Chelsea, Knightsbridge and Kensington which that gentleman owned at his death in 1630.[2] Subsequently it passed to the Tatham family, which by 1675 also held thirty-three acres of copyhold land in Kensington, including the thirteen acres adjoining westwards to this freehold, where Brompton Square, Holy Trinity Church, and the Oratory now stand.[3] By 1690 the freehold property belonged to Thomas Powell of Hackney, citizen and cutler of London, and his wife Elizabeth, daughter of Henry Tatham of Clapham.[4] They disposed of it in 1717 to Peter Laroche, and he duly resold it the following year to Philip Moreau (1656-1733), who since 1705 seems to have been the owner of the thin strip of land previously referred to immediately south-west of Knightsbridge Green, later the site of Nos. 38-58A Brompton Road.[5]

The property remained in the hands of the Moreau family until 1759. They were prosperous Huguenot merchants who maintained strong European connexions.[6] But Philip Moreau, who died worth 'near £50,000',[7] and his son James Philip Moreau (c. 1681-1748) both lived on their Knightsbridge estate. Their large house (Plate 4a) lay just in St. Margaret's parish, fronting the west side of Knightsbridge Green (where Caltex House is now entered). It had been occupied at some point in the late seventeenth century by the celebrated Catherine, Viscountess Ranelagh, but was 'new built' again by James Philip Moreau.[8] Later it was to become a boarding house, known confusingly enough as Grosvenor House, Knightsbridge;[9] it was finally demolished in about 1864.

Of the several other buildings on the estate before 1759, much the most important was the large and ancient Rose or Rose and Crown inn, on Knightsbridge itself close to Knightsbridge Green, with various adjacent stables and dwellings, all in Westminster. There was another inn, the World's End or Fulham Bridge, just in Kensington (where No. 66 Brompton Road later stood), and a scatter of smaller houses, of which two sheltered behind a walled garden along the strip of Kensington between the Fulham Bridge and the house of the Moreaus, on the property which had been separately held until 1705.[10] Most of the estate however was still garden or meadow land in horticultural use and much of it was tenanted by local innkeepers.

After James Philip Moreau's widow, Esther, died in 1753, the estate passed to their grandson, Charles Frederick Moreau (1735-84). He appears not to have lived at Knightsbridge, which was slowly being encumbered with suburban development. On coming of age, he raised mortgages of over £5,000 on the property in 1757-8 and put up the whole for auction in 1759.[11] By this time he had taken holy orders, accepted a living in Dorset and married, but his subsequent behaviour belied these promises of a settled existence. By 1773 he had arrived on his own in South Carolina, where in 1778 he became the second rector of St. Michael's, Charleston.[12]* Meanwhile his wife Ann was left in London unprovided for, and reduced to petitioning for relief from small debts.[14] Moreau died at Charleston in 1784, leaving a very modest estate;[15] where and how the proceeds of the sale of 1759 were dissipated remains a mystery.

The auction of 1759 divided the Moreau property into nine lots. The estate was therefore dismembered and the parts then in Kensington fell into three separate freeholds. These consisted of the short frontage along Brompton

---

*"On one occasion, Mr Moreau ascended the pulpit and announced as his text, John xvi 16: "A little while and ye shall not see me". At this unlucky moment his foot slipped from the step on which he was elevated, and he disappeared from the sight of the congregation.'[13]

Road from Knightsbridge Green as far as what became No. 58A Brompton Road; an equally small section from here up to the corner of what is now Lancelot Place; and a much larger property stretching westwards from Lancelot Place as far as No. 188 Brompton Road, together with Montpelier Street, Cheval Place and lands behind in both parishes. For reasons of size and convenience the first two freeholds are taken together below.

Nos. 38-76 (even) Brompton Road

The purchaser in 1759-60 of the modest freehold immediately south-west of Knightsbridge Green with its two small houses was Joseph Pickles, a brushmaker of the City of London, acting here on behalf of two paper-stainers in partnership, Benjamin Crompton and William Spinnage. (At the same time they also bought the important staging inn on Knightsbridge itself, the Rose and Crown, which probably interested them more.)[16] In time the ownership was consolidated in the hands of Spinnage's son and daughter-in-law, who lived in the more easterly house next to Knightsbridge Green. Some low and insignificant cottages, at first known as Gibbon's Rents after their lessee of 1797, Eleazar Gibbon, and depicted on Salway's survey of 1811, were built on part of the Spinnages' garden (Plate 4a). To the west of the various houses here a portion of garden ground, later the site of the Brompton National School, for the time being survived.[17]

Excepting this last-mentioned ground, the different interests were all bought up by a lawyer, Nathaniel Gostling, between 1803 and 1808. In 1817 he disposed of them for £1,999 to William and John Whitehead of Little Cadogan Place, Chelsea, builders.[18] The Whiteheads were considerable developers, chiefly in Chelsea, where their name is commemorated in Whitehead's Grove; they probably had enjoyed close links with Henry Holland and were involved in building some of the outer areas after the original nucleus of Hans Town had been completed.[19] Here the Whiteheads elected to build a terrace of nine plain four-storey brick houses with shops (later Nos. 42-58 even Brompton Road) immediately west of the corner house facing Knightsbridge Green (Plate 7d). One deed indirectly connects the surveyor-architect George Godwin the elder (who certainly worked with the Whiteheads in Chelsea) with these houses, though whether he designed them does not transpire.[20] Responsibility for building them was divided between four separate undertakers (Edward Dolman, Charles Jewell, William Harding and William Jones), who received leases of varying length from William Whitehead.[21] Construction proceeded slowly between 1818 and 1824, at which date the Whiteheads sold the freehold of the whole for £3,500 to William Beach of Sloane Street, with whose family the property long remained. Rather later, in 1841-2, the corner house facing Knightsbridge Green came 'in hand' and its site was

rebuilt with two further houses on Beach's behalf by George Todd of Marlborough Road, Chelsea, builder, to the designs and meticulous specifications of one Charles Downes, architect.[22] These later additions (Nos. 38 and 40 Brompton Road) matched well with the houses adjacent to the west.

The houses of the Whiteheads and of Beech were initially called Nos. 1-11 Brompton Road, at a time when the street had no such official name; they became Nos. 38-58 (even) Brompton Road in 1864. They were doubtless much affected when the new Tattersalls horse mart was built immediately behind them (in St. Margaret's parish) in 1864, but survived until about 1955.

West of the properties bought by Crompton and Spinnage, the land as far as Lancelot Place (then a small 'driftway' leading to the Rose and Crown) was purchased in 1759-60 by William Wildman Barrington, Viscount Barrington.[23] The large World's End or Fulham Bridge tavern was the one building here, with stabling behind it in St. Margaret's parish. Barrington promptly disposed of it in 1762 to its licensee, the victualler John Butcher, who in turn assigned it in 1776 to Edward Snape, farrier.[24] In about 1777-80 the Fulham Bridge itself appears to have been rebuilt and three small brick houses (Nos. 60-64 even Brompton Road) were added immediately to its east (Plate 7c). At the back of part of these premises appeared 'a certain Ride for Exercising and Shewing of Horses' and a forty-three-stall stable, harbingers perhaps of the time when Tattersalls was to move its auction rooms from Hyde Park Corner to this district in 1864, and evidence that dealing in horses was then already an established tradition in the locality.[25] From the early nineteenth century the entrance to Fulham Bridge Yard was known as Tullet or Tullett Place after a licensee of the time, Richard Tullet. By 1794 a house also existed at the corner with Lancelot Place (No. 76 Brompton Road), and in about 1795-6 four higher houses (Nos. 68-74 even) were built between this and the Fulham Bridge Yard under the aegis of Obadiah Reeve of Limehouse, timber merchant, thus completing a short terrace known until 1864 as Brompton Place (Plate 4a).[26] A few years later, in about 1810, Lancelot Place obtained its name and dignity as a means of access to the new Trevor Square in St. Margaret's parish behind.

The one remaining piece of vacant ground here, between Nos. 58 and 60 Brompton Road, lay vacant until 1841-2, at which date the Brompton National School was (in Crofton Croker's words) 'wedged in there'.[27] Early incumbents of Holy Trinity, Brompton had had some difficulty in securing a permanent school site, but in 1841 purchased this confined plot, formerly known as the 'Melon Ground', from George Watson Wood.[28] A picturesque but symmetrical small edifice in Tudor style (Plate 10b), the school was designed by George Godwin the younger and built by James Bonnin junior for £1,100; it accommodated just over two hundred girls and two hundred boys.[29] It survived until about 1889-90, when the school moved to the old Brompton Chapel in Montpelier

Street. It was then acquired and demolished by an art dealer, William Benjamin Creigh, who promptly replaced it with No. 58A Brompton Road, an over-scaled tall, red-brick building in Queen Anne taste (Plate 14c). Ambitiously styled 'The Art Workshops', it evidently included craft studios. But in 1893 the business was wound up, and henceforward No. 58A was used as a depository.[30] Among later alterations were a shop front and ornamental doorway designed in about 1921 by E. Vincent Harris when the ground floor was converted for the use of Macfisheries Limited.[31]

Further changes occurred along this short stretch of Brompton Road between 1885 and 1910. The Fulham Bridge (No. 66) underwent alterations in 1888 when its lease was renewed (Plate 7c), and in 1894 changed hands for £20,000.[32] Next to it at Nos. 60-64 (even), the existing small houses were knocked down and ornate showrooms and flats fronted in red brick with dressings of Doulton's terracotta were erected in 1905-6 for Humber Limited, motor and bicycle manufacturers, to designs by R. A. Briggs (Plate 14c); John Allen and Sons of Kilburn

were the builders.[33] Further west, the fronts of Nos. 68 and 76 (even) Brompton Road had been stuccoed and altered by 1900, while in between, Nos. 70-74 (even), a virile building of brick and stone with oriel windows and in a forthright mixture of styles, went up in 1896 for Cooper and Company, grocers and tea-dealers (Plate 14a). The builders here were Stimpson and Company and the architect F. E. Williams.[34]

Severe bomb damage having been incurred between Nos. 58 and 66 Brompton Road, the whole section of Brompton Road from Knightsbridge Green to Lancelot Place with Tattersalls behind was scheduled for comprehensive redevelopment after the war of 1939-45. All the existing premises were demolished from 1955 onwards and the present office buildings were erected thereafter. They include the very substantial Caltex House (No. 1 Knightsbridge Green and Nos. 44-58 Brompton Road), designed by Stone, Toms and Partners and built in 1955-7 for Edger Investments Limited;[35] Silver City House of 1955-7 (Nos. 58A-64 Brompton Road) by Frank Scarlett for Beaufort Estates;[36] and Lionel House (Nos. 66-76

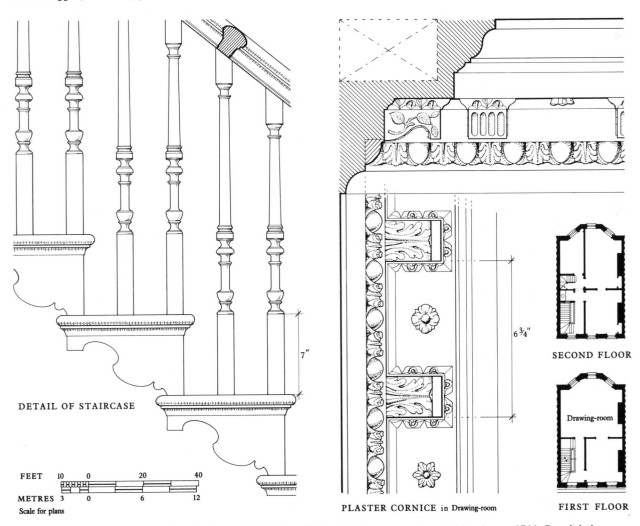

DETAIL OF STAIRCASE

FEET 10 0 20 40
METRES 3 0 6 12
Scale for plans

PLASTER CORNICE in Drawing-room

SECOND FLOOR

Drawing-room

FIRST FLOOR

Fig. 8. No. 142 Brompton Road, plans and details in 1979. John Serjeant, carpenter, building lessee, 1766. *Demolished*

Brompton Road) by Gunton and Gunton for the City of London Real Property Company Limited (1960).[37] None calls for much notice, though Caltex House (Plate 24c) boasts a large external sculpture of sea horses, designed by F. Belsky and executed in reinforced concrete covered with a coating of plastic metal.[38]

Nos. 78-188 (even) Brompton Road (formerly Brompton Row)

West of what is now Lancelot Place the estate of the Moreaus consisted of five 'closes', described in the auction particulars of 1759 as 'rich Meadow Land, and well situated for Garden Ground, or for building'.[39] This substantial tract (see fig. 1 on page 2), at that time partly used by tenants of the Rose and Crown inn, was bought by Elisha Biscoe of Bedford Row, the Inner Temple and Heston, Middlesex.[40] Biscoe (1705-76), a prosperous attorney well versed in property speculation, was connected through his grandmother with those Alexanders, Braces and Brownes who owned much of the local land (see fig. 2 on page 11).[41] He had witnessed both mortgages of the Moreau estate in 1757-8 and therefore knew it previously.[42]

Plainly Biscoe wished to develop the land as soon as was practicable. In 1764 he signed articles of agreement with Thomas Rawstorne of St. Martin in the Fields, ironmonger (and later of Islington, where Rawstorne Street, Finsbury, perpetuates his name).[43] By this agreement Rawstorne was to organize the building of houses, fifty-six in all, along the frontage of Brompton Road. A new street, originally Rawstorne Street but from about 1825 called Montpelier Street, was to debouch into Brompton Road approximately halfway along. East of this street the shallowness of Biscoe's property made a mews behind impracticable. But west of Rawstorne Street a mews lane (originally Chapel Row) was projected behind the houses, terminating at the 'driftway' which marked the western boundary of the development. In due course (probably in the 1820's when Brompton Square was built) the short section of this driftway between Brompton Road and the mews became known as Cheval Place, a name in 1910 extended also to Chapel Row (or Place). All the land to be built on initially lay in Kensington, leaving about seven and a half acres in Biscoe's possession as yet undeveloped, most of it in St. Margaret's parish but some of it then still in Kensington.

The development was at first named Biscoe's Buildings, but by 1790 had become known as Brompton Row. Most of the houses along the main frontage were put up by building tradesmen and leased to them quickly and efficiently between 1766 and 1768.* The terms varied, but were mostly a little shorter than the 105-year period

suggested in the original articles of agreement. Many of the houses were mortgaged back immediately to Elisha Biscoe's brother Vincent John Biscoe (1721-70), a West India merchant.[45] Characteristically, the first building to be leased was a public house, the Crown and Sceptre at No. 132 Brompton Road, on the western corner with Montpelier Street.[46] The largest undertakers were Joseph Clark(e), carpenter and builder, who erected all sixteen of the westernmost houses (Nos. 158-188 Brompton Road)[47] and William Rose, carpenter, who was involved with fourteen of the sites in the eastern sector of the development (Nos. 104-130 Brompton Road).[48] In Rose's case however all may not have gone well. After mortgaging many of his properties to a timber merchant, he became bankrupt and was dead by 1771.[49] Like several other of the craftsmen involved here, Rose had been previously based in St. Marylebone.

Biscoe's Buildings were the most substantial of the terrace houses built in Brompton during the boom of the 1760's. Salway's plan of 1811 (Plates 4c, 5b) shows all except two as of three windows' width, while most enjoyed four storeys above ground, some having dormers and some full attics. The houses were protected from the dust and noise of Brompton Road by good front gardens, trees or shrubs, and in some cases shared carriage drives. The more westerly houses were also raised well above the level of the roadway, a feature perpetuated today in the stepped pavement along this portion of Brompton Road. The last house at the extreme western end (No. 188) differed from the rest in extending westwards over Cheval Place by means of an archway (Plate 6b) and in breaking forward from the main building line.

Of these houses (Plates 4c, 5b, 6, 8a, b, d, fig. 8), fifteen at the time of writing retain discernible traces of their original size and form (Nos. 120, 122, 128, 132-138, 150, 152, 156, 168-174 and 188 even Brompton Road). All these have been grievously altered and most have been stuccoed, but several retain sufficient of their interiors to show that they varied in plan (some had three-sided bays at the back) and were quite handsomely finished. Of the survivors one, No. 168, commands particular interest as the experimental residence between about 1798 and 1802 of Benjamin Thompson, Count Rumford. This house was sufficiently unusual and well-documented for its history to be discussed in detail below. No other house was of comparable interest, but much of Brompton Row was originally well inhabited by people of some prosperity.

After Elisha Biscoe's death in 1776 the freehold interest in the Brompton Row properties was divided. Most of the houses west of Montpelier (Rawstorne) Street descended through his daughter Catherine Frances to the Rolfes of Heacham Hall, Norfolk. The freeholds of these properties

---

*First lessees for Brompton Row were as follows: Nos. 78, 80 and 82, John Butcher, brewer; Nos. 84, 86 and 88, Francis Kendill, carpenter; Nos. 90, 92 and 94, Richard Martin, carpenter; Nos. 96 and 98, John and Richard Stokes, bricklayers; Nos. 100 and 102, John Stokes, bricklayer; Nos. 104-118 and 122-130, William Rose, carpenter; No. 120, Richard Warwick, plumber; Nos. 134 and 136, George Longstaff, bricklayer; Nos. 138 and 140, Thomas Longstaff, mason; No. 142, John Serjeant, carpenter; No. 144, John Cowcher, plasterer; Nos. 146-156, George Gibbons, carpenter and builder; Nos. 158-188, Joseph Clark, carpenter.[44]

were bought by Charles Goodwin of King's Lynn in 1837 and began to be sold off just before the original leases expired. The eastern houses and the remaining undeveloped land behind the frontage passed to Elisha Biscoe junior (1753/4-1829).[50]

Along Brompton Road itself, alterations naturally occurred over the years; many of the houses were stuccoed and the front gardens of all were severely curtailed by road widenings. The only house that seems to have been entirely rebuilt before the leases fell out round about 1870 was No. 130 at the east corner with Montpelier Street. In 1868-9, Nos. 142-146 were acquired by the novelist and playwright Charles Reade with a view to building a theatre here, but the scheme came to naught.[51] Not until the Edwardian period did other of the old houses start to disappear. In the

eastern sector three adjacent houses (Nos. 108-112) were rebuilt and a fourth (No. 114) was refronted, all in red brick and stone, at this time. Of these Nos. 108 and 110 (1902-3) were designed by the architects Louis A. Blangy and Frans van Baars (Plate 8a). No. 108 was the model premises of a fashionable local baker, Spiking and Company, and included a small refreshment gallery where shoppers could take sustenance after an arduous afternoon at Harrods (fig. 9). It retained some fashionable Art Nouveau touches until its demolition in 1982.[52] Further west, No. 154 was rebuilt in 1905.[53]

A first substantial change in scale came in 1934-5 when the houses between Nos. 78 and 94 Brompton Road were replaced by Princes Court (initially Knight's Court), a large block of steel-framed flats designed on behalf of

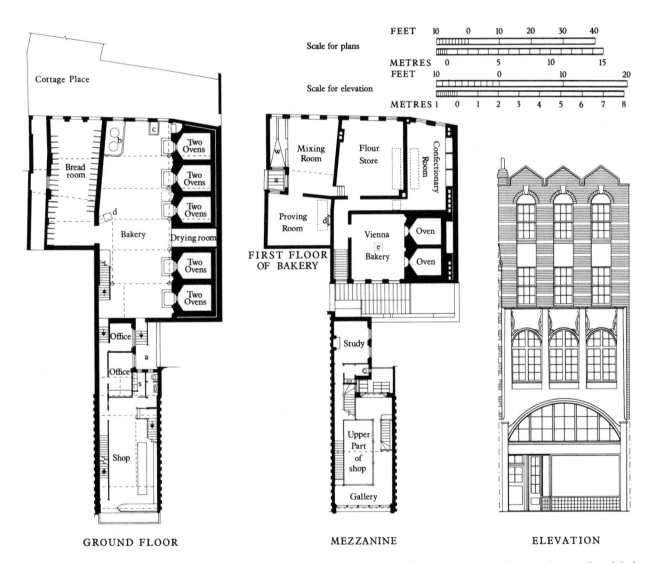

GROUND FLOOR   MEZZANINE   ELEVATION

Fig. 9. No. 108 Brompton Road, plans as built in 1903 and elevation in 1981. Louis A. Blangy and Frans van Baars, architects. *Demolished*

a area   c coal shoot   s scullery
b boilers   d dough shoot   w washing space

F. L. Griggs by G. Val. Myer and F. J. Watson-Hart (Plate 24b).[54] Among the shops on the ground floor was one at No. 78 designed by Wells Coates for Cresta Silks. A few years previously, in 1929, Coates had installed on the ground floor of the old No. 78 the first of a celebrated series of shops for this firm, but the rebuilding necessitated a new design.[55] Cresta Silks continued to occupy the shop until 1979-80, but latterly none of Coates's work remained.

Since 1945 the surviving portions of the first development have been inexorably whittled away, with blocks of offices and shops arising along Brompton Road at Nos. 96-104 (1959-60), 106-110 (1981-2), 124-126 (1982-3), 140-148 (1980-2), 158-166 (1959-60), 176-178 (1954-5) and 180-186 (1963). Brief details of these buildings are given on page 8.

Brompton Chapel

In conjunction with the houses of Brompton Row, Elisha Biscoe and Thomas Rawstorne also erected a proprietary chapel at the north corner of Rawstorne (Montpelier) Street and Chapel Row (Cheval Place). It was built under an agreement of April 1768 between Rawstorne, the Reverend Richard Harrison of Tottenham Court Road and the Reverend Seth Thompson of Kensington, and leased to the three of them in the following year.[56] The agreement stated that a chapel was 'thought necessary and of great utillity' to the development and stipulated that the partners were to contract with proper persons for building and furnishing the chapel. Shares in the enterprise were divided into six parts. Harrison, who held two of the sixth shares, was appointed the first 'Morning Minister' at £80 per annum and Thompson, with one sixth share, the first 'Afternoon Minister' at £40; Rawstorne retained the other shares, and the pew rents were divided between the parties after deducting the expenses. Harrison, a preacher of some note, continued here until his death in 1793.[57]

A modest, square brick building entered from Rawstorne Street, the Brompton Chapel was dignified with a pediment and a small bellcote (Plate 10a). Within were galleries on three sides resting on columns, and a minimal projection for a sanctuary at the west end.[58] After Holy Trinity, Brompton, was opened in 1829 the chapel (sometimes now known as St. John's Chapel) probably became less frequented. In 1832 the freehold was sold for £440 to the Reverend George Allan of Brompton.[59] When William Pepperell made his survey of places of worship in Kensington in about 1871, he found the chapel 'strictly Georgian in its character, Georgian indeed to the backbone . . . It is simply ugly outside, and very little more may be said of it inside . . . It has successfully resisted all modern innovations; no alterations of any kind have taken place, excepting that a coating of stucco has been bestowed upon the front. The same is true of the character of the public service.'[60]

The chapel was for sale again in 1878, and in 1888 it became a church school when the Brompton National School building at No. 58A Brompton Road was closed. The architect for this conversion was C. H. M. Mileham and the builders were Dove Brothers, who also made later alterations.[61] The school finally closed in 1939, at which date the building's elevations were still essentially unchanged. But drastic alterations were made subsequently for W. and F. C. Bonham and Sons Limited, auctioneers, particularly by J. Newton-Smith of Haynes and Carpenter, architects, in about 1953-4.[62] The building still survives in carcase as Bonham's Montpelier Galleries, but has been raised by a storey, re-stuccoed in a rather Germanic manner, and bereft of all its Georgian features, internal and external.

No. 168 Brompton Road

Benjamin Thompson, Count Rumford (1753-1814), scientist, philanthropist and domestic reformer, bought No. 45 Brompton Row (as that house was then called) in the summer of 1798.[63] At this point in his quixotic career he was severing his connexions with the Court of Munich, where he had spent most of the previous fifteen years, and intending to settle permanently in Britain. Soon after moving to London he inaugurated the Royal Institution, which he conducted more or less as a personal enterprise before falling out with the managers and withdrawing in 1801. At this period he lived at least partly in the Institution's rooms in Albemarle Street and also travelled widely, and therefore he may have been little at Brompton. Indeed he appears to have resided there permanently for only a year or so, in 1801-2.[64] Yet at about the time that he was losing control of the Royal Institution, Rumford embarked on a series of internal alterations at Brompton Row to make his house a model of modern domestic convenience. These works were complete by June 1801, when the Swiss scientist M. A. Pictet stayed with Rumford at Brompton and wrote a long account of the house. They were undertaken by Rumford himself with some help from Thomas Webster, the architect whom he had employed at the Royal Institution.[65]

As described by Pictet,[66] the house remained orthodox in plan, with two rooms on each floor. On ground level were parlour and dining-room, on the first storey drawing-room and bedroom, on the second bedrooms, and on the third a bedroom and surprisingly, Rumford's study, which enjoyed a view to open country northwards out of a bowed window. The outbuildings towards Chapel Row (now No. 41 Cheval Place) included besides the usual stabling and 'offices' a chemical laboratory, probably that described in 1802 as 'the Octagon room in New Building';[67] they were connected with the house by a covered way warmed by heating pipes.* The most visible eccentricity of

---

*Rumford steam-heated the lecture room at the Royal Institution, but there is no evidence that this was done at Brompton Row.

the house was the double-glazing of the front windows, effected by means of three-sided projecting glass cases in which plants could be placed.

Inside, Rumford arranged the main rooms so as to conceal the services as far as was practicable. Thus the chimney-breasts, which contained 'close stoves' of brick and earthenware rather than the standard fireplaces or cast-iron stoves, did not protrude, having cupboards and hinged flaps for tables on either side. In summer the stoves were hidden by frames of cloth painted to look like panelling. In the bedrooms, the beds could be converted to form sofas during the day; in the dining-room, a folding screen enabled the space to be made larger or smaller and meals to be served in greater privacy; while in the kitchen, described by Rumford in one of his essays,[68] the roaster, boiler and other devices could be concealed behind panels of sheet-iron so that 'on entering it, nobody would suspect it to be a kitchen'.

Pictet also adverts opaquely to Rumford's colour scheme for the house. 'Even in the choice of colours it can be seen that the owner's taste has been aided by the physical principles of the mixture of colours; these, as he has discovered, are always harmonious to the eye when they are respectively the complement of the colours that the whole prismatic spectrum can offer. You see how the discoveries of Newton can be applied to the choice of a ribbon as to the system of the world.'

Rumford never stayed long enough at Brompton to make full use of his improvements. In May 1802 he went to Paris, to all intents on a short visit, but he returned, if at all, only for brief periods.[69] The house was let at first on short tenancies under the supervision of his housekeeper Bessey Williams and was rated to Rumford until 1807, when the Reverend William Beloe, translator of Herodotus, took it on.[70] The head lease remained with Rumford's daughter until at least 1831, when much of his furniture and effects was sold.[71] At about this time a thorough reconstruction of the house appears to have occurred. Nothing now seems left of his schemes, though the south-facing front of the stable block retains an essentially mid-Georgian appearance.

Cheval Place and Montpelier Street Area

In 1824 Elisha Biscoe junior sold the freehold of some seven and a half acres of the remaining undeveloped land immediately north of Brompton Row; this passed through the hands of the auctioneers John and Joseph Robins to John Betts of Brompton Row, esquire, and Thomas Weatherley Marriott of Knightsbridge, ironmonger.[72] Most of this ground, which crossed the parish border, was empty and lay in the parish of St. Margaret's, Westminster; here Betts and Marriott set about the development of Montpelier Square, beginning with its south side.[73] But the part of it immediately north of Chapel Row (Cheval

Place) then belonged in Kensington parish (though in 1900 it was transferred to the City of Westminster). Here a number of small streets sprang up, mainly apparently under the aegis of Marriott, Betts having sold his interests.[74] Many of the first houses, which were leased between 1825 and 1830, survive on the north side of Cheval Place (west of Montpelier Walk), both sides of Fairholt (until 1936 Middle) Street, the southern portions of Montpelier Walk (originally Montpelier Row) and the east and south sides of Rutland Street (the east-west section of which was until 1874 known as Rutland Terrace).[75] They are mostly small houses of two windows' width and two original storeys above ground, stuccoed at least up to first-floor level (Plate 13c).

Under whose supervision these streets were laid out and by whom, if by any individual, the houses were designed does not seem to be known. Edward Evans Marriott, a brickmaker and the brother of T. W. Marriott, was much involved in the development and is described at least once as 'surveyor';[76] while Ernest Oswald Coe, an architect otherwise known only for a few topographical drawings, witnessed leases of two houses on the east side of Montpelier Walk in 1829.[77] The lessees were generally small tradesmen of no especial note. The small section of this estate west of Rutland Street was developed by William Farlar of Brompton Square and sold to him in 1830 (see page 44).[78]

Since the war of 1914-18, these houses have been much 'gentrified' and some have been wholly rebuilt. Perhaps the most interesting examples are on the north side of Fairholt Street, where Nos. 3, 4 and 5 were rebuilt for Ethel Snagge in 1925-8 by the architects Baillie Scott and Beresford, with early-Georgian sashes but retaining the old rough brick facings (Plate 13d).[79]

East of Montpelier Walk, the north side of Chapel Row immediately west of the Brompton Chapel had been let by Elisha Biscoe to Thomas Rawstorne in 1770 and formed no part of the sale of 1824.[80] The few houses built here were probably demolished after the original lease ran out, and the present Nos. 2-10 (even) Cheval Place with Relton Mews behind were erected in a simple polychromatic brick style in 1873-5.[81] One of the houses, No. 2 Cheval Place with Nos. 12 and 13 in Relton Mews, was extended and converted for use as the Knightsbridge station of the Metropolitan Fire Brigade in 1879 at a cost of £1,192, but reverted to other use when the station in Basil Street came into operation in 1907.[82] At the corner of Montpelier Walk, Nos. 16-22 Cheval Place have recently been rebuilt.

In Montpelier (Rawstorne) Street itself the undeveloped portions of Biscoe's land were gradually built up after 1800. In about 1808-9, chiefly under the auspices of William Jones, plumber, small brick houses were built along its eastern side as far as what is now Montpelier Mews; these included the surviving Nos. 2-8 (even) Montpelier Street.[83] The more northerly of these houses were later demolished and replaced by a nurses' home for

St. George's Hospital at No. 14 Montpelier Street, erected by Higgs and Hill to designs in a Queen Anne style by Stephen Salter in 1895-6.[84] Opposite, the land on the west side of the street behind the Crown and Sceptre was partly sub-let for building in 1776 to John Hooper, gardener,[85] but the surviving houses (Nos. 1-11 odd Montpelier Street) appear to date from between 1867 and 1871.

Brompton Square Area

This area now consists principally of Brompton Square, an elongated rectangle with a crescent at the north end, laid out and built up with terrace houses under the auspices of William Farlar, ironmonger, between 1821 and 1835. With it are associated some smaller properties in the surrounding back streets and more recent buildings along Brompton Road, erected following successive road-widenings here (fig. 10).

This district, together with the adjacent lands westwards where Holy Trinity Church and the Brompton Oratory stand, amounts to approximately twelve acres. In the early eighteenth century all this land was called Oldfield and was copyhold of the manor of Earl's Court. By 1700 the 'customary tenant' or copyholder was Henry Tatham of Clapham, of the Tatham family which had also owned the freehold of the lands immediately eastwards (see page 33). After his death his holdings here passed in 1747 to 'the young gentlewoman whom he had brought up from infancy, called Mary Tatham', by this time the wife of John Erskine of the Middle Temple.[86] Soon afterwards Erskine was ordained, and after residence at Foxearth and Gosfield in Essex subsequently became Dean of Cork.

In 1749 and 1768 the Erskines disposed of their interests in the future sites of Holy Trinity Church and the Brompton Oratory respectively, leaving only the easternmost five acres in their hands. These were inherited after their deaths in the 1790's by a minor, Mary Tatham Browne, perhaps their grand-daughter and certainly the daughter of Arthur Browne (d. 1805), a prominent academic at Trinity College, Dublin, and the last Prime Serjeant of Ireland; she also owned other holdings further west in Old Brompton (in the vicinity of the present Gledhow and Wetherby Gardens) which had descended to her by a similar path.[87] In 1812 the five acres at 'New Brompton' were enfranchised and therefore became the freehold of Mary Tatham Browne.[88]

From 1762 this land had been tenanted as garden ground by John Butcher of the Fulham Bridge tavern and a succession of occupiers on short leases.[89] Development overtook the five acres from 1820 onwards, a decade of widespread building activity in London generally and Brompton in particular. It seems impossible now to determine who first decided to build a square here or when, but among those involved at an early date were James Bonnin, the prolific local builder whose career is described on page 61; William Farlar, who is discussed in some detail below; and John Henry Goodinge, a local attorney and developer.[90] The square was probably planned and the houses were in some sense designed by a surveyor-architect of considerable obscurity, Robert Darley of Jermyn Street. Darley, who left property in Dublin when he died in 1833, was probably a member of the family of architect-builders of that name which built widely in Ireland in the eighteenth and early nineteenth centuries and which had particular connexions with Trinity College, Dublin;[91] at Brompton Square, he was regularly Farlar's representative between 1822 and 1828, but the Irish connexion prompts the possibility that he acted originally on behalf of Mary Tatham Browne. Darley, Farlar, Goodinge and Bonnin, it is worth adding, all had a hand in developing Beauchamp Place opposite, which was started in 1824, soon after Brompton Square (see page 25).

The first evidence for activity dates from March 1821, when work on a house on the east side of 'Brompton Square' had been started by Bonnin, who at this point was also building in Trevor Square, Knightsbridge.[92] Bonnin began building here on the promise of a ninety-nine-year lease of the frontage along Brompton Road between Cheval Place and Cottage Place to a depth of some 165-190 feet, in other words as far north as the present No. 9 on the west side and No. 54 on the east side of the square, together with further ground to the west of the square. Then in September 1821, with the earliest houses well advanced, a new principal came to the fore. This was William Farlar (1786-1867), who came originally from Isleworth in Middlesex. Farlar had a substantial furnishing ironmongery business in the West End, based initially in Wardour Street and later in Piccadilly. At this time he was just finishing a small speculation in Ebury Square, Pimlico, which he seems to have taken over from the builder Alexander Robertson in 1819; he therefore had some experience of speculative development, having probably started as a supplier to Robertson.[93]

Under the new arrangement, Bonnin was to build houses on the land he had agreed for, as before, but he was now to receive his leases from Farlar. The eastern portion of his 'take' was to form the south end only of the projected square, of which evidently Farlar was expecting soon to become the freeholder and main promoter.[94] This came about early in 1823 when, with the scheme well under way, Farlar purchased the whole freehold from Mary Tatham Browne and granted many ninety-seven-year leases for completed houses.[95]

The plan under which Farlar and Bonnin proceeded envisaged the square in accordance with its present form, except at the north end. In addition two groups of buildings were projected on Bonnin's 'take' in the south-west corner of the property: Brunswick Place, a group of six houses and shops facing Brompton Road immediately west of the square; and Cottage Place, six further dwellings in three pairs on the east side of the lane that separated the estate from the adjacent property to the west (Plate 13b).

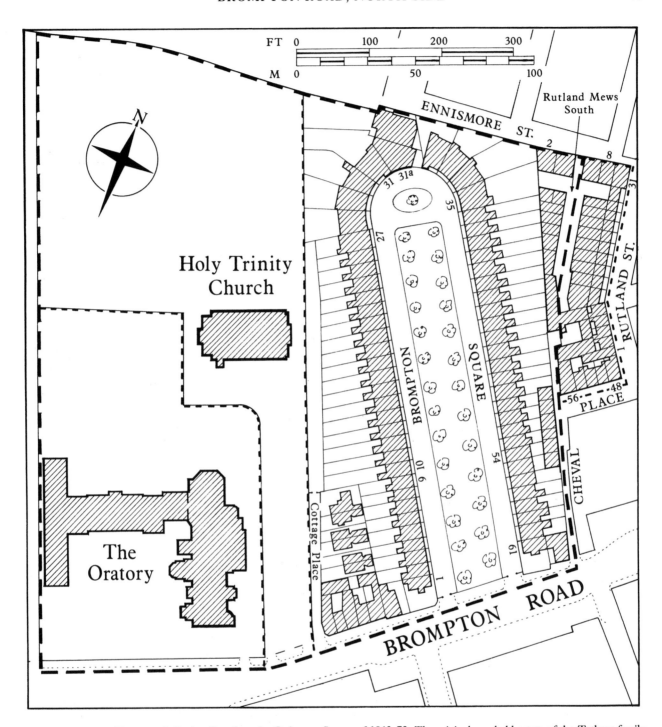

Fig. 10. Brompton Square and district. Based on the Ordnance Survey of 1862-72. The original copyhold estate of the Tatham family is shown, with its subdivisions into the sites of the Oratory, Holy Trinity Church and Brompton Square. The strip next to Rutland Street was added to the Brompton Square Estate in 1830. The house numbers shown are modern

For the time two areas were left unplanned: a large plot at the north end of the square abutting northwards on the Earl of Listowel's lands in St. Margaret's parish, and a thinner remnant behind the east side (where Rutland Mews South was later built).

Construction on what was termed the Brompton Square Estate proceeded apace between about 1821 and 1826, by which time all the houses of Brunswick Place and Cottage Place and thirty-one in the square had been let on long terms to a variety of building tradesmen and indi-

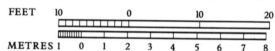

Fig. 11. Nos. 28-35 Brompton Square, elevations as built, from viewpoints shown on site plan

viduals.[96]* Bonnin probably controlled development on the land he had originally agreed for, comprising Cottage Place, Brunswick Place and the south end of the square (Nos. 1-9 and 54-61). His agreement with Farlar stated his intention of living at No. 1, which he did for a short period in 1823-4 before moving on to other developments; the house was probably occupied in conjunction with an office and yard next door in Brunswick Place. Two other houses in the square (Nos. 58 and 59) were leased to him, but with the houses north of his 'take' he had nothing to do.[97]

Farlar himself perhaps undertook many of the houses, having given up his ironmongery business when he purchased Brompton Square and become in some sense a builder as well as a developer. But several other building tradesmen were involved; after Bonnin, William Barrat of North Street, Brompton, builder, was connected with the leasing of the largest single number, six in all.[98] Most interesting of the head lessees was the well-known comedian William

Farren (1786-1861), who successively took leases of three houses in Brompton Square (No. 23 in 1825, No. 25 in 1826 and No. 30 at the north end in 1837).[99] He was the first of a long line of early-Victorian actors whose residence enlivens the sober chronicle of the square (see page 253).[100] Farlar himself lived on the east side of the square, firstly at No. 48 (c. 1823-35) and latterly at No. 36 (c. 1835-51).[101]

Robert Darley's contribution to the development of Brompton Square emerges only through his applications to the Westminster Commissioners of Sewers to build drains

*Building tradesmen named as original head lessees or as parties to first leases for the main sides of Brompton Square up to 1826 were as follows: William Barrat, builder, Nos. 5, 6, 12, 13, 54 and 55; James Bonnin, builder, Nos. 1, 2, and 55-61; William Cock, plumber, No. 4; James Dean, timber merchant, No. 3; Thomas Jenkins, carpenter, No. 21; Joseph Hale Miller, painter and glazier, Nos. 19 and 20; William Paul, plumber, Nos. 15 and 61; Richard Russell, carpenter, Nos. 10 and 11; John Souter, stonemason, Nos. 7, 8 and 9; Lancelot Edward Wood, stonemason, No. 60. Thomas Milton, stonemason, received leases of No. 16 in 1828 and of No. 17 in 1831.

32   33   34   35

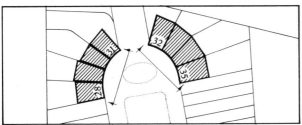

on Farlar's behalf.[102] The draining of Brompton Square
proved problematic, because the main sewer ran into an old
and inadequate sewer in Yeoman's Row which was unequal
to the extra task. So Farlar and the early inhabitants of the
square got up a petition in November 1825 to the Commissioners, urging them to rebuild the Yeoman's Row
sewer. In it they claimed that 'the Brompton Square sewage
is wholly inoperative and is serviceable only as a Cess-pool
to the adjoining Houses containing a continual Depth of
Water and Filth to the extent of three feet above the
bottom of the Sewer by which the Houses of your
Petitioners are rendered damp and unwholesome and the
foundations injured in various respects . . . Your Petitioners cannot but look forward to the approaching Winter

with the utmost uneasiness . . .'[103]

The houses built in the square were of a plain, unvar-
nished urban character, having the orthodox stuccoed
ground storey and three levels above (Plate 12a, b). Their
frontages of between sixteen and eighteen feet allowed
only two windows for each house. In plan too they were
conventional, having only small single-storey back projections. Bonnin's houses at the south end of the square,
following the model already set by him in Trevor Square,
had dormer windows above the second floor, whereas
those further north enjoyed full attics; but there is no
especial difference in the detail of the elevations between
Bonnin's 'take' and the portions which Farlar developed
himself. There were no porches or other pretentious
features, but Farlar did provide handsome entrance gates,
lamps and piers at the entrances from Brompton Road
(Plate 11d). For the management of the square itself with
its 'pleasure garden' Farlar secured a private Act of Parliament in 1824.[104]

By 1826, when a national slump in house building
slowed down the pace of many developments, the greater
part of Brompton Square had already been completed.
The whole of the west side (Nos. 1-27) was finished and
all the houses there were occupied, while on the east side

nearly all the houses up to No. 45 were tenanted; north-wards of No. 45 a few new houses stood empty. The completion of the east side (up to No. 36) proceeded more slowly, but all the houses here were built and most were occupied by 1830, apart from Nos. 36-38. Along this eastern range, it seems that more of the later houses were disposed of on short terms or yearly tenancies.[105]

Behind the east side of Brompton Square, Farlar's original freehold was restricted, allowing very little room for stabling, of which only Nos. 62-72 (even) Cheval Place had been built by 1825. He therefore arranged with Thomas Weatherley Marriott, since 1824 the owner and developer of the neighbouring Montpelier estate, to take the west side of Marriott's projected Rutland Street and the short section of the north side of Chapel Row (now Cheval Place) to its west. Having built a set of stables and other buildings here, he purchased the freehold from Marriott in 1830 to add to his own. Most of these buildings survive in altered guise, the ten tiny cottages at Nos. 11-29 (odd) Rutland Street having a quaint charm owing to latticework (not an original feature) in their windows (Plate 13a). South of these was a group, now Nos. 1-9 (odd) Rutland Street and 48-60 (even) Cheval Place, which in 1839 included stables and coach-houses, 'police and engine stations', a National School (at Nos. 56 and 58 Cheval Place) and Farlar's own works in the mews at what is now No. 60 Cheval Place. Here he had a smith's shop, workshop, warehouse and an engine intended for pumping water to his estate and the vicinity. To its north was a tract which for the time being remained vacant.[106]

Farlar's buildings in Rutland Street were probably in the main erected by William Aslat, bricklayer and builder, a shadowy figure closely associated with Farlar in this second phase of the Brompton Square estate. Aslat was described between about 1829 and 1832 as of Rutland Street, but in 1834 he briefly had an address at No. 20 Vale Place, Hammersmith, where Anthony and Edward Aslat were also builders.[107] In Brompton Square, William Aslat received leases of the last houses built on the east side, Nos. 36-38, in 1832 (by which time Nos. 36 and 38 had already been tenanted for two years). At the same time Farlar leased to him the north end of the square, as yet entirely undeveloped.[108] For this large plot, Farlar had most probably at first intended a single substantial villa set in its own grounds, perhaps for himself. But by the time that building finally took place here, development on the Manners estate (Rutland Gate) to the north-east was getting under way, while on the Earl of Listowel's lands immediately to the north of Brompton Square it was probably being talked of. The idea of providing access from the Brompton Square estate to the prospective streets northwards and thence to Hyde Park beyond seems therefore to have weighed with Farlar and Aslat (if after 1832 the latter continued to be involved).

The plan therefore followed was to construct two small quadrants of four houses each on the rather cramped site (fig. 11); between them space was left for a future road which would debouch on to the lands northward when building there proceeded. The two stuccoed groups (Nos. 28-31 on the west and Nos. 32-35 on the east) were built in about 1834-5.[109] It seems likely that they were started by Aslat but not finished by him, for at just this time his name disappears from the records and that of a young local architect, John Blore (1812-82), enters the story. Blore, who lived close by in Michael's Place, later listed among his works 'the Completion of a Crescent of Houses opposite my own residence'; the phrase can bear more than one interpretation, but unquestionably connects Blore with these particular buildings.[110] Most probably, Blore was responsible for their Greek external detailing. Each house has a porch with Doric columns, and there are giant Ionic pilasters at the end against the upper storeys with ornamental cartouches above in the attics (Plate 12c). Several have now been disfigured with extra storeys, and the symmetry of the composition has been lately damaged by the extension of No. 31A in the style of the original elevations.

Besides being larger than earlier houses in the square, those in the crescent possessed unusual structural interest. An auction notice of 1842 speaks of 'bar iron plates and bonds to the extent of 40 tons in weight placed within the walls of these abodes' and pronounces their quality 'a refreshing contrast to modern buildings'.[111] The rationale for such a contrivance is not clear, but it may be borne in mind that Farlar had been in the iron trade and that his brother John remained in the business after William's retirement. An ultimately abortive branch of the Birmingham, Bristol and Thames Junction Railway which was from 1836 planned a little to the north of the crescent probably came too late to influence the construction of the houses. But it may have made them harder to sell, since several were not leased for some years.[112]

For whatever reasons, Farlar's financial position deteriorated steadily from the time of his association with Aslat in the early 1830's. In 1832 Aslat and he had together mortgaged the site of the north end of the square together with Aslat's Nos. 36-38 on the east side. Over the next few years Farlar drew increasingly on these securities.[113] In 1835, when he claimed to be deriving 'upwards of £2,200' annually from the estate, his application to an insurance company for a loan of £28,000 was refused.[114] Then in 1838-9 matters came to a head. In quick succession the estate was re-mortgaged and the greater part (including the main sides of the square but excepting Nos. 36-38) then sold outright to a solicitor, William Batty.[115] In 1840 Farlar, doubtless expecting bankruptcy, assigned his remaining interests in Nos. 36-38 to his daughter Mary.[116] In 1842 the crescent and the properties in Rutland Street were auctioned and mostly bought by John Squire of Pall Mall East, who proceeded to sell off many freeholds individually.[117] By one means or another Farlar delayed entire failure and went on living at No. 36 until 1848, when he was declared bankrupt and imprisoned for eight months.[118]

Farlar was discharged from bankruptcy in 1849, returned for two years to No. 36 Brompton Square, perhaps lived briefly also at No. 61 at the south end of the square, but then moved away in about 1852 to Hammersmith.[119] He never recovered from his reverses, and the rest of the Farlar family tale is a sorry one. In 1851 Mary Farlar died in Whitechapel; her father fruitlessly contested her will, but in the end it turned out that she left little except debts. John Farlar, William's brother, died in 1857, also worth virtually nothing, and in 1867 William Farlar himself died at No. 3 Ashley Terrace, Hammersmith, with effects under £50. The affairs of all three Farlars remained unsettled for several years after their deaths.[120]

Meanwhile at Brompton Square, William Batty and a colleague in 1849 bought the outstanding interests in the crucial gap between the houses in the crescent,[121] doubtless intending to open the road out of the square northwards, where development was now proceeding.* But John Elger, the principal promoter there, wishing to defend the exclusiveness of what is now Ennismore Gardens, firmly refused to countenance the opening. There followed intermittent acrimony in the columns of *The Builder*, where George Godwin championed the 'Bromptonians', 'Thurlovians, Oratorians and Montpellierians' in their desire to promote a through road northwards (Exhibition Road did not then exist) and re-establish lost links with 'the aroma of the Serpentine and other verdant influences of the Hyde'. A Bill was even promoted in Parliament in 1854, but it failed.[123]

All this time Elger remained adamant against the suggested road, and in 1854 he was able to secure from Batty for his own use the controversial empty segment in the crescent along with the remaining vacant land between Rutland Street and the east side of the square.[124] On the former he built a motley set of north-facing structures (Nos. 36-38 Ennismore Gardens, with a narrow back elevation called No. 31A Brompton Square) which earned further execration from *The Builder* and to this day disfigure the north end of Brompton Square. On the latter site he laid out Rutland Mews South 'not leaving a foot of garden — no, not for half a yard of cabbage', editorialized Godwin.[125] Access from Brompton Square and Cheval Place to these developments was firmly shut off. Regarded as disastrous at the time, this mischance proved modern Brompton Square's salvation, since no through traffic clogs the square.

A brief résumé of the census of 1841 adequately conveys the character that Brompton Square maintained for much of the rest of the century. At the time of that census sixty of the sixty-one houses in the square were inhabited, mostly by families of 'independent' means with about two or three servants each. Besides the actors previously mentioned, there were two lodging-houses and three educational establishments with living-in pupils;

those at Nos. 55 and 61 were small 'seminaries' with four and three pupils each respectively, at No. 14 lived a governess with two assistants and four charges, but at No. 28, one of the houses in the crescent, was a fully fledged girls' school with two schoolmistresses, five assistants, twenty-six pupils, a housekeeper and four servants, making no less than thirty-eight inhabitants altogether.[126]

One early resident of note in Brompton Square was the social reformer Francis Place, who took No. 21 'on a lease of 7-14-21 years' at £60 a year in 1833. He commented: 'The house had been let at 80£ a year but it was sadly out of condition and the putting it into condition — the expense of removing fitting up the library carpets etc. cost me 360£.' Place chose Brompton Square because his second wife, the actress Louisa Simeon Chatterley, had lived at No. 15 from about 1825 until their marriage in 1830. This house Place pronounced 'neat in good condition and rather elegantly fitted up and furnished. The square was occupied by genteel quiet people, and was nicely kept. The House was well situated the front in the Square, the back looking over a small garden had an uninterrupted view as far as Chiswick, and was so circumstanced in respect to situation that it was not at all likely it would be built on.' Despite this idyllic picture, Place's own residence in Brompton Square was not happy. He was plagued by financial problems, separated from his wife in 1851, and moved to Earl's Court in 1853 shortly before his death.[127]

The later history of the Brompton Square estate has not been specially eventful. A Blue Plaque at No. 6 draws attention to the fact that the young French poet Stéphane Mallarmé resided quite briefly at a lodging-house here in 1863, just before and after his marriage to Marie Gerhard, a German governess.[128] Though many houses in the body of the square have been heightened, extended at the back and in particular have received new front windows on the ground floor, only one has been visibly rebuilt: No. 26, refronted in a subdued Queen Anne manner in 1889-90 by Frederick Horton, architect, on behalf of the builder John Garlick, and now whitewashed.[129] Next door to this, No. 27 is noteworthy for an altered rear elevation exhibiting Gothic details of powerful ferocity, probably dating from around 1860. At the south end facing Brompton Road the changes have been more extensive. At a quite early date (between 1843 and 1852), the south-facing elevations of both the end houses, Nos. 1 and 61, were tidied up, raised by a storey and dignified with porches. On the west side, Nos. 1 and 2 together with portions of the old Brunswick Place were demolished in 1881 and replaced by a branch of the London and Westminster Bank, a late Italianate building in Portland stone designed by F. W. Porter and built by J. T. Chappell (No. 200 Brompton Road and Nos. 1 and 2 Brompton Square).[130] West of this, four further houses in Brunswick Place and the two

---

*A road between the houses is plainly to be seen on Thomas Allom's perspective of about 1844 showing the intended layout of John Elger's development in Ennismore Gardens and Princes Gate.[122]

southernmost ones in Cottage Place disappeared when the Brompton Road Station of the Great Northern, Piccadilly and Brompton Railway was built, in the characteristic full-blooded faience of the early tubes, in 1906.[131] Not much later the two remaining pairs of semi-detached houses in Cottage Place were demolished, leaving only the much-altered Gladstone public house at the corner (latterly No. 212 Brompton Road) to testify to the original development here.

Opposite, on the east side of the square, No. 61 Brompton Square and an associated shop at No. 190 Brompton Road were pulled down in 1893-4 as part of a road-widening scheme. The reduced site remained empty for some years; building operations on some flats started in 1900 but came to naught. The properties were auctioned in 1902 and in 1907-8 Nos. 190-196 Brompton Road (Saville Court), a small block of shops and flats, were put up by J. J. Wheeler, builder, to designs by R. J. Worley's firm (Worleys and Armstrong).[132]

More recent alterations at the south end of Brompton Square have stemmed from further road-widening in Brompton Road by the Greater London Council. Following a decision of 1968, all the buildings along the frontage between Cheval Place and Cottage Place, comprising Nos. 190-212 (even) Brompton Road, were demolished. A new neo-Georgian southern flank wall was provided for No. 60 Brompton Square, while at the corner with Cottage Place a small building was erected in similar style for the Territorial Army, which by this time occupied the disused Brompton Road Station. The designs for these were provided by the G.L.C. Architect's Department, Historic Buildings Division, the job architects being Norman Harrison and William Garner. This left an empty site where the bank had stood at the south-west corner of the square. This was disposed of by the G.L.C. and filled in 1979-81 by a new house, No. 2 Brompton Square, designed by Heber-Percy Parker Perry Associates. Though steel-framed, this house imitates the old elevation of neighbouring houses towards the square, while towards Brompton Road it follows with variations the flank elevation provided by the G.L.C.'s architects at No. 60 Brompton Square.[133]

At the north end, the appearance of the crescent was further confused in 1981-2, when the narrow No. 31A Brompton Square was refronted and extended eastwards into the 'gap', as part of a rebuilding of Nos. 36-38 Ennismore Gardens for the Government of Malaysia by King and Pache, architects.[134] The new south-facing elevation respects the style of the old houses but makes it hard to discern their original arrangement and extent, and only partly fills the gap between them.

Of other alterations outside Brompton Square only one calls for comment. This is the conversion of the stables at the north end of Rutland Mews South into four small but handsome Tudor town houses, now Nos. 2-8 (even) Ennismore Street. This was effected with much skill in 1921-2 by A. M. Cawthorne, architect.[135]

Holy Trinity Church, Brompton

This church was built in 1826-9 to designs by T. L. Donaldson and has been variously extended since, principally by Arthur Blomfield in 1879-82. It occupies a site which, including the 'avenue' approach from Brompton Road to the south and the open burial ground to the north, comprises some three and a half acres in all.

In the early eighteenth century this land, together with the ground on either side where Brompton Square and the Brompton Oratory now stand, was copyhold of the manor of Earl's Court, the 'customary tenants' being from 1747 the Reverend John Erskine of Foxearth, Essex (later Dean of Cork) and his wife Mary (née Tatham) (see page 40). But in 1749 the Erskines sold their interest in the future site and surroundings of Holy Trinity, then a piece of 'garden ground' with a narrow means of access from Brompton Road, for £460 to the Governors of St. George's Hospital for use as a 'Common Burial Place for the use and benefit of such poor sick and lame persons and objects of Compassion as then were or thereafter might come to said Hospital'.[136] For the sixteen previous years since its foundation at Hyde Park Corner, the hospital had used burial facilities within the parish of St. George's, Hanover Square, but had been asked in 1747 by that parish's authorities to find an alternative site. The new ground was promptly paled in and given new gates, and a chaplain was appointed at £20 per annum to bury the dead. But the previous occupants of the ground, James and Mary Hoare, were retained to help with the burials and maintenance. They also grew vegetables on the portion of the ground not required for burials, and for years 'greens' from the site were regularly served up to patients at Hyde Park Corner.[137]

In 1822 the Kensington Vestry set up a committee to augment church accommodation in the parish with the aid of money from the Commissioners for Building New Churches. Some altercation ensued as to which end of the parish should be thus favoured, but after 'tumultuary discussion' it was resolved in 1823 to build a church on an unspecified site 'between Old and New Brompton' and plans were publicly solicited.[138] Subsequently an increase in funds voted by Parliament to the Commissioners made it possible also to erect a 'chapel' (later St. Barnabas, Addison Road) in the western district of the parish, but the church at Brompton generally enjoyed some priority of funds and attention. Under an arrangement of February 1825, the Commissioners agreed to grant £10,000 if both churches were built and this sum were matched by the parish. In the event the total expense to the parish for both churches came to nearly £16,000. (The cost of building Holy Trinity, Brompton, was computed in 1833 at nearly £10,734, of which the Commissioners contributed some £7,407. The site cost £4,000, of which £3,000 was for the copyhold interest and £1,000 for enfranchising the freehold.)[139]

By 1825 the burial-ground site at Brompton had been agreed for with St. George's Hospital and the lord of the manor, Lord Kensington.[140] In April 1826 the land was duly conveyed to the Church Building Commissioners, and two months later plans for the church were submitted by the young architect Thomas Leverton Donaldson, whose scheme had been selected from several sent in. Work proceeded between 1826 and 1829 without notable event. There was however some trouble towards the end of the work with the contractor, Archibald Ritchie, whose 'very peculiar character' and dilatoriness obliged Donaldson in 1828 to reinstate a foreman over his head.[141] The church, which had 1,505 sittings (606 free and 899 rented), was consecrated on 6 June 1829, when the Reverend Percival Frye (a nephew of Kensington's vicar, Archdeacon Pott) was instituted as incumbent.[142] In the following October a large district was assigned to it, stretching west as far as the Kensington Canal and north to the Kensington Turnpike.[141]

Donaldson's design (Plate 31a) exemplified 'Commissioners' Gothic' at its baldest. It consisted of a five-bay clerestoried nave with two aisles, a small projecting sanctuary flanked by vestries and a west tower with lobbies on either side containing stairs to the galleries. There was a porch in the centre of the southern aisle and an entrance to the vaults at the same point on the northern side. The windows were uniformly lancets without tracery or significant moulding, a group of three serving to dignify the east end. The materials were stock bricks with Suffolk facings and Bath stone dressings, while the roofs, of Bangor slates, were everywhere hidden behind what one critic termed a 'paltry coping'.[143]

The interior, of which no view survives, appears not to have been quite so coarse. The most individual feature was the open-timber nave roof. According to the same commentator this was 'panelled by ribs, which rest on corbels representing busts of both sexes in every variety of costume, and the intermediate spaces are plastered, and pierced with quatrefoil apertures at intervals, as ventilators; the whole design, as well as the application of the corbels in such a situation, is perfectly new, and peculiar to the modern taste'.[144] This does not survive, but the aisle roofs do; these rest on similar corbels, are tied and cross-braced and have cusped tracery of early Tudor character between the struts. Also remaining from Donaldson's interior are the three galleries (with altered fronts), the arches to the tower, chancel and nave arcade, and the piers to the arcade (Plate 32a, b). To judge from the details of these features, Donaldson had undertaken basic but not extensive study of Early English forms. The west gallery originally included seats for the choir and an organ in the tower arch beneath an ogee canopy. The font, a 'hemispherical basin', stood in the middle of the nave closely boxed in by seats, while the pulpit and desks were at the front of the nave. The altar table had no reredos, the customary inscription being on the east wall. The seating was all of deal.

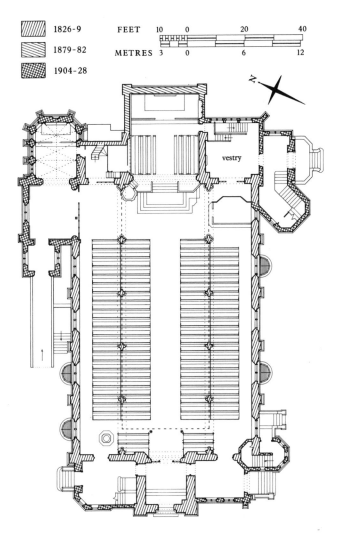

▨	1826-9
▨	1879-82
▨	1904-28

FEET 10 0 20 40
METRES 3 0 6 12

vestry

Fig. 12. Holy Trinity Church, Brompton, plan

From the start nobody seems to have been happy with the appearance of Holy Trinity, Brompton. In the year of the consecration the churchwardens may be found pleading with the Church Building Commissioners for the 'addition of some architectural ornament'; and in 1830 E. J. Carlos, the critic before referred to, savaged Donaldson's design in *The Gentleman's Magazine*, dubbing it a 'complete specimen' of what used to be called Carpenters' Gothic and comparing it adversely with J. H. Taylor's 'excessively faulty' church of St. John's, Walham Green.[145] The planting of a handsome avenue leading from Brompton Road in about 1831 helped to beautify the church's environs, but did nothing for the building itself.[146] After some few years of endurance a youthful new vicar, the Reverend William J. Irons, promoted improvements to the value of about £800 in which one of the churchwardens, Stroud Lincoln (an important figure in the financing of development in Alexander Square and Pelham Crescent), played a prominent part. The local architect John Blore was called in and from 1843 installed tracery in the aisle windows (Plate 31b, d), substituted a completely new window in place of Donaldson's obtrusive main southern entrance and porch, and refurbished the little chancel with a wide reredos, sedilia, stalls and stained glass by William Warrington. The results were found satisfactory but, commented *The Builder*, the church 'will require a large expenditure . . . to give anything approaching to an ecclesiastical appearance to its most unsightly exterior'.[147]

The only significant addition known in the next thirty years occurred in 1863, when to designs by E. C. Hakewill the present font was installed (Plate 32d) and at the east end of the south aisle a circular window was put in as a memorial to Stroud Lincoln, with glass again by Warrington. This is the only one of the earlier stained windows fixed in the church to survive. By 1872 also the old high pews had given way to lower ones in oak. In that year George and Henry Godwin prepared plans for a vicarage to be built near the church's south porch, but the proposal came to nothing.[148]

The inevitable major enlargement and alterations were delayed until 1879-82. They were promoted by a new vicar, William Covington, who in February 1879 asked (Sir) Arthur Blomfield to report on the capabilities of Holy Trinity, Brompton. At first Covington wished to delay works till the new Brompton Oratory building was finished lest 'a strong appearance of competition and rivalry' be given,[149] but it soon transpired that this would prolong affairs too much. A building committee was therefore formed, subscriptions were solicited, and in August with a tender of £1,990 Dove Brothers won the contract for the first phase of the work, an extended chancel with a parish room beneath. These were effectively finished by Christmas 1879.[150] Structurally, Blomfield merely pushed out from the old building by a few feet and built up over the north vestry, but internally the whole was transformed. The new chancel, in correct Early English style, was raised well above the nave, faced internally in two colours of brick with stone dressings, and given a handsome five-light east window of stepped lancets (Plate 32c, fig. 12). The floor was at first of plain Minton tiles and there were few costly fittings.

Gradually further improvements were made. In 1880 Brindley and Foster supplied a new organ, and in 1881 an open stone pulpit was procured from Thomas Earp, a lectern given, and stained glass by Heaton, Butler and Bayne placed in the chancel windows as part of a general scheme of decoration. This year also saw a gateway in Dumfries stone erected to a design supplied by H. D. Shepard, an independent architect who assisted Blomfield in these works in some capacity. The gateway was originally sited at the south end of the avenue facing Brompton Road but was later moved (in 1908) to the north boundary of the churchyard. In 1882 Blomfield and Dove Brothers set about improving the nave for an estimated

£1,530. This involved a clever new tripartite wooden vault under a roof of higher pitch, improved gallery fronts and seats, and alterations under the tower. As part of this work the clerestory windows were simplified, slightly enlarged, and reglazed with clear glass.[151]

The broad reredos in gold mosaic, with many figures, was designed by J. R. Clayton of Clayton and Bell, made in Italy (probably by Salviati) and installed early in 1885 (Plate 32c). In the following year Arthur Blomfield designed a new west window, which was promptly stained by Heaton, Butler and Bayne. The same firm proposed a scheme of glass for the aisle windows in 1891, but few seem to have been inserted before 1900.[152]

In 1899 a new vicar, the authoritative A. W. Gough, arrived. He remained until his death in 1931, and during his prosperous cure much extension and embellishment were undertaken. In 1901 a proposal for a new south-east porch was first mooted and plans procured from Arthur Blomfield junior of Sir Arthur Blomfield and Sons; this, in revised form so as to include a vestry, staircase and other rooms, was eventually erected in 1906 by the builders J. Dorey and Company for £1,259.[153] It has crenellated parapets and is the first of several extensions to the church to adopt a later style of Gothic. Internally, two large paintings by G. W. Ostrehan were installed in the chancel in 1903.[154] Shortly after this, the architect Harry Wilson advised on altering one of these and supervised some minor changes. The only feature in the church definitely known to be Wilson's is the figurative bas-relief over the sedilia, executed to his designs in plaster by E. Lanteri in 1906. The Byzantinizing marble chancel steps and screen wall were inserted in 1914, but the handsome matching pulpit is, surprisingly, of 1927, designed by J. B. Mendham with help from Francis Eeles.[155] Later fittings in the chancel, including desks, stalls and panelling, are mainly of 1953.

The current south-western and north-western porches were first proposed in 1910, when the obscure R. W. Knightley Goddard presented plans for rebuilding the vestibules here with two 'small towers' for the stairs to the galleries. W. Downs the builder undertook the southern porch for £1,123 in 1913, but its northern counterpart was delayed by the war.[156] Subsequently, Gough's priority was for a memorial chapel, for which Goddard first produced an unsolicited design in 1917. But it seems most likely that this, the adjacent northern transept and indeed the north-western porch also were all ultimately designed by Arthur Blomfield junior. The small vaulted memorial chapel was built in 1920, the north-western porch probably in 1924, and the north transept with its own small porch in 1926-8.[157]

The church's interior has been several times redecorated since 1945, and much of the structural woodwork is now painted a light colour. An altar and other appurtenances were erected at the east end of the south aisle in 1959, and the organ from St. Mark's, North Audley Street, was introduced with new cases in 1978-9, at a cost of some £60,000.[158]

In the north-west corner of the churchyard a 'church house', erected to designs by Laurence King, was dedicated in 1965. It replaced a small infants' school built in 1871 at the expense of C. J. Freake the builder to supplement the main parish school, then in Brompton Road.[159] The churchyard itself, said to have been the last provided adjacent to a church in central London, was closed as early as 1854; a century later most of the gravestones were removed and the dead reinterred at Brookwood Cemetery.[160]

The London Oratory of St. Philip Neri and the Church of the Immaculate Heart of Mary

At the opening of the great church in 1884 *The Tablet* commented that it would 'bring home vividly to many that thought can find expression in other forms than words',[1] and it is easy to feel that the building does indeed assert the ultramontane trend of thought in Victorian Roman Catholicism — especially, perhaps, that of Catholics not born into the Church. In its demonstration of the Romanizing tendency of converts the late-Victorian Congregation of the London Oratory conformed to its origins, when in 1848 the community established by Newman at Maryvale near Birmingham was joined by another society of recent converts under Frederick Faber. The following year Faber led a Congregation of Oratorians to London, where they established a house and church in King William Street, Strand. A year later, with the Catholic Hierarchy newly restored in Britain, the Oratorians aspired to 'a good, large and stately church', of Italianate style, in a better position. A committee of rich Catholic laymen under Lord Arundel (later the fourteenth Duke of Norfolk) looked for a site. By 1852 the aim had declined from St. James's to Pimlico or Argyll House east of Regent Street.[2] Then in the late summer the Fathers of the Oratory suddenly settled on a site at Brompton, although its comparative remoteness rather went against the tradition of urban evangelism of the Congregations of St. Philip Neri.[3] Newman, who had advocated a grand and central metropolitan position, was not impressed by Faber's apologia for Brompton as 'the Madeira of London', and thought the site 'essentially in a *suburb* . . . a neighbourhood of second-rate gentry and second-rate shops'.[4] One of the Fathers wrote jestingly (to his mother) that they would be 'far enough from Chelsea chapel [St. Mary's, then on the site of the present No. 105 Cadogan Gardens] to seem not to interfere with it, and just near enough to draw away the rich part of its congregation', but the avoidance of proximity to other Catholic chapels was in fact a motive for going to the suburbs.[5]

The site of three and a half acres had, as copyhold of the manor of Earl's Court, been sold in 1768 by the Reverend John Erskine and his wife Mary (see page 40). The purchaser was David Barclay, an insurance broker, on whose death two years later the land passed to a nephew, Alexander Barclay, wax-chandler. It accommodated a house and wax-bleacher's establishment when the Barclays sold it in 1819 for £4,000 to Robert Pollard, who set up a boys' boarding school there, known as Blemell House.[6] He promptly extended the buildings greatly,[7] as can be discerned on Plate 11c. Enfranchised in 1830,[6] the site was sold by Pollard to the Congregation of the Oratory in November 1852 for £16,000.* This was through the agency of George Godwin, architect and editor of *The Builder*, who later said the price was calculated to give the same return in interest as the site's anticipated yield as building land, and thought it a notable instance of Brompton's rising land values at that time. The recipients in trust for the Congregation were Mrs. Bowden, a widow and benefactress, and the architect J. J. Scoles, a Catholic by birth.[9]

The southernmost part of the site was soon being sold for £2,000 to the Commissioners for the Exhibition of 1851. (The sale was concluded in January 1854.) They had great plans for their own land immediately to the west, and threw the ground into Brompton Lane (now Thurloe Place) to widen the approach to the projected Cromwell Road.[10]

An attempt early in 1853 by the Vicar of Holy Trinity, Brompton, to prevent the establishment of a Catholic community so close to his church was unsuccessful,[11] and during that year an Oratory House with its own chapel and library was built for the Congregation, together with a temporary public church that nevertheless survived in use until 1880 (Plate 33a, b).[12]

Possibly influenced by the hostility felt from Holy Trinity, Brompton, on the east, the first intention was to place the public church on the west side of the Oratory House, with the private chapel of the Congregation on the east. Then, by April 1853, it was decided to transfer the latter to the west wing of the house and make it serve also as a public church, pending the erection of a larger place of worship on the eastern part of the site.[13] By July or August, however, this idea was in turn modified to allow the building of a temporary public church on the eastern part, within the future site of the nave of the great church.[14]

The designer of the Oratory House, as of the temporary church, was J. J. Scoles. Like the Oratorians' residence at Birmingham and the London Congregation's country villa at Sydenham, the Oratory House is in a very restrained Italianate (a 'giant haystack petrified', according to one contemporary versifier[15]). The pedimented south face of the western range was meant to be finished with statues of

---

*A well-carved mid-Georgian Rococo wooden chimneypiece in one of the reception rooms in the Oratory House is said to have come from the previous buildings on the site,[8] and might suit a house of the 1770's.

saints that were never added, and neither were the papal arms in the tympanum, where the stone still awaits carving.[16] Preparations for ashlaring the east front are also apparent. This range (paid for by the fourteenth Duke of Norfolk[17]) contains the Congregation's chapel, known as the Little Oratory, and above it the library — both of them (especially the chapel) elaborated subsequently. Within the residential part of the house the well-proportioned refectory is notable, and so are the long high corridors, which were, as a periodical said, 'well adapted for exercise in wet weather'.[18]*

The contractor was William Jackson of Pimlico, a native of Ireland and a Catholic. He had speculative interests nearby as a house-builder, and was said in the *Illustrated London News* to have himself provided half the purchase-money given to the Fathers for the land to widen Brompton Lane and afford improved access to the new developments by him and others westward.[19] One of the Fathers wrote (to Lady Arundel) that the house was 'not to be run up by contract [evidently meaning, rather, competitive tendering] in the usual way of houses that are to stand only 99 years while the lease lasts' but at Jackson's 'fair estimate of what it will cost to build it really well and substantially'.[20] Nevertheless the contract seems to have been let by Jackson to another builder, Charles Delay, and the plastering, for example, further subcontracted.[21] And however well the work was done, it was not completed without alarms at Jackson's own finances. These fluctuated during a chequered career, so that early in 1854 they brought him, 'highly excited and very much out of temper', near to bankruptcy.[22] (Jackson's trouble was probably caused by the delay of the Commissioners for the Exhibition of 1851 in concluding their purchase of his leasehold interest in Lord Harrington's estate west of the Oratorians' land.[23]) The contract for the house had, it seems, been made at about £18,020.[24] Eventually the total cost, including furnishings and fittings, was £29,316.[25]

The Oratory House would in any event have absorbed most of the money available for building, agreeable to Newman's advice that it would subsequently be easier to collect money for a church than a residence.[26] Jackson's contract for the church was evidently made at only £3,500,[27] the final cost, with furnishings and fittings, being £5,549.[28] Long, low, and narrow, of the plainest brick externally, the church was given an acceptable interior by Scoles, with a thirty-foot-deep sanctuary and an open wooden roof of dull red or chocolate and dark blue. It held 1,200 worshippers.[29]

In 1858 the roof had to be lifted off and replaced on heightened walls to accommodate a large Bishop organ presented by the Dowager Duchess of Argyll: at the same time Scoles introduced a flat, many-panelled ceiling over

clerestory windows, additional chapels were made, and the sanctuary deepened to some forty-seven feet (Plate 33c, d). Much of the cost of this was met by the Duchess, who also gave the stalls and sanctuary pavement of variegated woods put in place by Messrs. Holland in 1863-4 and later adapted by the same firm for use in the present church.[30] Still very plain externally, the church had internally, *The Building News* thought, 'the proportion and somewhat the appearance of an ancient Roman Basilica.' The chapels, decorated by an Oxford Street tradesman, Charles Nosotti, deserved study by students of polychromy.[31] By the 1860's the added chapels made the original church almost unrecognizable on plan (fig. 10).[32]† A later comment, that the effect of the interior was made by the simulated marbling of the walls and pilasters, suggests that the Fathers already aimed in paint at something of the all-over colouring achieved in the present church by a wonderful variety of stones.[33]

Within the Oratory House Scoles added an organ gallery in the Little Oratory in *c.* 1858.[34] In 1871-2 the organ was transferred to a new case and gallery at the north end as part of the elaborate scheme which includes the new altar, apsidal sanctuary, longitudinal stalls, and ceiling decoration (Plate 34a). The designer was J. Hungerford Pollen, then connected with the Science and Art Department next door at the South Kensington Museum.[35] The south or entrance end of the chapel retains Scoles's organ gallery on its arcaded screen and now communicates with the southward extension of this range made about the same time by the building in 1872-3 of St. Wilfrid's and St. Joseph's Halls. Who the responsible architect was here is not known, but the plans were approved by J. A. Hansom as 'consulting architect'.[36] St. Wilfrid's Hall, on the first floor, is a dignified room, generally in the sober style of the Oratory House but with decoration on the doorcase (and formerly also on the now-lightened wall-pilasters) rather of the Italian-Renaissance type favoured at that time in the Science and Art Department.

In May 1874 the Congregation, conscious that the exterior of the temporary church was 'almost contemptible', issued an appeal for funds for a permanent church, to which the fifteenth Duke of Norfolk subscribed £20,000.[37] (Newman's advice was being justified by munificent donations which recurrently augmented the building funds; but it may be remarked that various works of construction and adornment have also been paid for by individual Fathers.)

In May 1875 the Fathers accepted 'as the ground work of a plan for the new Church' a 'Fergusson-Moody' design.[38] This signifies that they had again turned to figures in the art-world associated with the Science and

---

*Scoles's designs for the south front of the west wing, now largely concealed by a later extension, are possessed by the Congregation.

†Their dedications are shown on a plan in the *Oratory Parish Magazine* for January 1926. Photographs of side-altars *c.* 1870 are in an album in the Library of the Congregation. The exterior after 1858 is illustrated, very crudely, in a print in Kensington Central Library, 282 ORA/C/1332.

Art Department next door, where a style deriving from the Italian Renaissance was being cultivated in a convinced if idiosyncratic manner. The names referred to are those of an instructor in decorative art there, F. W. Moody, in conjunction with James Fergusson, architect as well as theorist and historian of architecture. Fergusson had recently been a Professional Examiner in Art to the Department,[39] and had made illustrated suggestions for a non-Gothic domical cathedral in the 1873 edition of his *History of the Modern Styles of Architecture*.[40] In October a larger plan by Moody was under consideration.[41] Already a dome is referred to, and a chapel and sacristy of similar lengths flanking the sanctuary, as in the church that was built.[42] But it was later recalled that many of the Fathers now developed 'a fever for architecture', so that 'there were almost as many plans as Fathers', and the 'Fergusson-Moody' scheme was finally rejected in December 1875.[43] Moody was paid £155 for his designs, of which he exhibited an interior view, admired by the *British Architect*, at the Royal Academy in 1877.[44]*

The future architect of the church had, however, appeared in public by March 1876. In that month *The Building News* published a design for the church 'about to be erected', in the Renaissance style 'for which the congregation have a strong predilection', and basically similar to what was ultimately built (Plate 35a). A week later it printed a disclaimer from the architect, that the design was 'merely a suggestion of what he thought suitable'.[45] The author of the design in question was Herbert Gribble (1847-94), a twenty-nine-year-old Devonian living nearby in Chelsea. He had himself been a pupil at the National Art Training School of the Science and Art Department in the neighbouring Museum, and then from about 1867 a pupil of J. A. Hansom. Despite this last hint of a Catholic background he is said to have been a recent convert of the Fathers.[46] He had certainly been in touch with them in a matter of design so early as April 1874, when he had been sketching a 'banner' in the room of Father Keogh (the Father Superior at the time the church was begun).[47] One of the Fathers later said Gribble had prepared the design published in *The Building News* 'at the private instigation of one or more of the Fathers' but had made it public without authority.[48] Gribble's connexion with the Fathers may well have owed something to his work for Hansom on the church of St. Philip Neri at Arundel in about 1868-73. This is likely already to have brought him in contact with the Oratorian-educated fifteenth Duke of Norfolk and to have predisposed the Fathers to an architect associated with their great friend and patron.

Late in 1877, however, it was decided to hold a competition for the design, announced in January 1878.[49] It was not limited to Catholics, and offered prizes of £200 and £75. The chief requirements were two. The style was to be 'that of the Italian Renaissance', and the sanctuary, at least sixty feet deep, was to be 'the most important part of the Church. . . . Especially the altar and tabernacle should stand out as visibly the great object of the whole Church.'[50] The nave was to be of a minimum width (50 feet) and maximum length (175 feet). The subsidiary chapels were to be 'distinct chambers', not mere side-altars. Choice of material was unrestricted and although estimates of cost were required no limit in that respect was stated—an omission criticized by architectural journalists and disgruntled competitors, whose designs called for expenditure ranging from £35,000 to £200,000.

Apart from Gribble himself, the thirty pseudonymous competitors included Henry Clutton, H. B. Garling, E. W. Godwin, George Goldie, Temple Moore (aged twenty-two), G. G. Scott junior, and J. D. Sedding.†

In May 1878 it was decided to employ Alfred Waterhouse at a fee of £105 to report on the designs but not to determine the Fathers' choice.[51] The following month Waterhouse submitted his report.[52] One general comment of his was that many entries were so much in the prescribed style as to be under-fenestrated for a northerly latitude. Of the thirty, he identified twelve as worth particular consideration: the designs of Garling, Godwin (Plate 35c), Temple Moore and Sedding were among those excluded. The chosen twelve were by A. J. Adams, Adams and Kelly, Edward Clarke, H. Clutton, G. Goldie, Gordon and Flockhart, G. E. Grayson, H. Gribble, G. G. Scott junior, Bernard Smith, Tasker and Bonella, and Vicars and O'Neill. From these Waterhouse himself calculated the cost of executing four 'as being most likely to repay the trouble'. They were by Adams and Kelly (£97,702 by Waterhouse's reckoning), Gordon and Flockhart (£169,865), Gribble (£91,775) and G. G. Scott junior (£64,660). For an unknown reason and perhaps simply in error Waterhouse took Gribble's own estimate to have been close to his, at £91,000, whereas Gribble had in fact claimed his design would cost only £35-40,000 unashlared or £65-70,000 ashlared. The impression conveyed by Waterhouse's comments on the individual designs is of greatest liking for those of Gordon and Flockhart (' . . . the work of a Master [*sic*]. The interior seems to me to be very nearly perfect . . . ') and G. G. Scott junior (a design 'of no ordinary merit. . . . I feel that it is impossible to speak too highly of its beauty, its quiet dignity, its absence of all vulgarity and its concentration of effect around the high altar . . . '). Adams and Kelly had produced 'a pleasing and refined design' with acoustical hazards. Gribble's design showed notable merits and defects. Chiefly it was his planning — very close to his 1876 scheme — that

---

*Unsigned and undated drawings on paper watermarked 1874 in the possesion of the Congregation may relate to these designs.
†Of the designs of these seven entrants only those of Clutton and Godwin were published in architectural periodicals. Godwin's, Temple Moore's and some preliminary drawings by Scott are at the R.I.B.A. The competitors are listed in the *Oratory Parish Magazine* for March 1927, pp. 43-4.

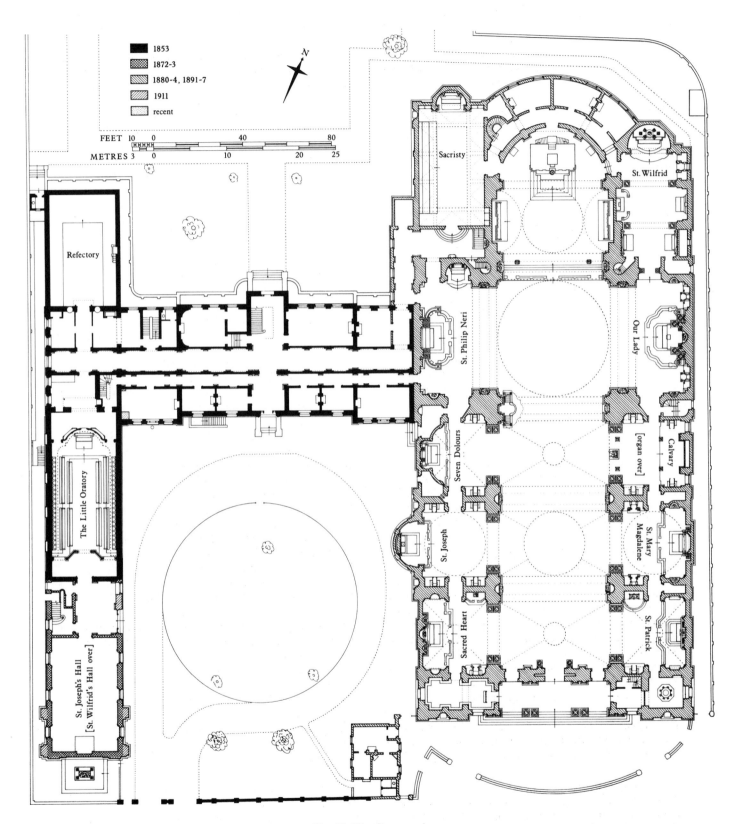

Fig. 13. The Oratory, plan

Waterhouse admired. 'The design appears to me a very sensible one, well thought out and well proportioned. Indeed in all its arrangements it shews exceptional excellence, as e.g. the position of the Confessionals; the openings into and the accessibility of the side chapels; the admirably contrived passage round the church for processions and for gaining access to the different parts of the Church when the Nave might be crowded . . . .' Judging from Waterhouse's general comments on the designs he was also doubtless pleased by Gribble's avoidance of harsh lighting and of the placing of windows behind the altars.[53] The pulpit was under the dome—'a position I should be rather afraid of '—and there were one or two remediable 'weaknesses of construction'. It was Gribble's elevations, however, that displeased Waterhouse. 'They lack dignity and breadth and are embellished with so much extraneous ornamentation as to be almost vulgar and commonplace.'

Nevertheless it was Gribble's design that was chosen by the Fathers for their first prize and for execution.[54] Their second prize they gave to a competitor not among Waterhouse's select four, Henry Clutton (Plate 35b). This latter choice was not altogether unreasonable, however, in the light of Waterhouse's own comments on this 'good design', which found nothing badly amiss and merit in the 'somewhat severe' exterior.[52] It seems, from the rejection of Scott's design, that the likely cost of execution as estimated by Waterhouse was not the factor telling for Gribble: but perhaps the Fathers put their faith in Gribble's own lowest estimate for completion without ashlaring. Gribble was a skilful draughtsman and his interior perspectives may also have helped him, although Waterhouse had said their colouring was 'to me most unpleasing'.[52]

The Fathers' decision drew criticism in the architectural press.[55] The similarity of Gribble's design to his earlier offering suggested the competition had been an expensive nullity, and there was disquiet among architects when it became known that the Fathers had not followed Waterhouse's preferences. There seems no foundation for the suspicion that the Fathers had departed from any undertaking in that respect. Some of the objections were certainly groundless. Nevertheless a statement from Waterhouse's office designed to make clear his limited role coupled this with a plea that future public competitions should be definitively judged by a professional referee. Furthermore, Clutton, as second prizeman, soon announced he had 'since had reason to decline that honour'.[56] Evidently, therefore, unhappiness at the outcome was felt in respected quarters.

The two designs that were liked by all three of *The Builder*, *The Building News* and the *British Architect* were by Gordon and Flockhart and G. E. Grayson—the latter a competitor who had, as it happens, been only mildly

praised by Waterhouse ('a sensible design').[57]* Generally the periodicals regretted a lack of originality, so that 'souvenirs of tit-bits have been transported from nearly all the famous Italian churches'.[58] The absence of centralizing plans, theoretically permitted by the specified dimensions, was noticed, but the longitudinal space available almost enforced the usual oblong plan.

The Fathers decided that in carrying out his design Gribble should be associated with another architect, and after considering C. A. Buckler (evidently a non-competitor, unless he was the sole unidentified entrant), Clutton, Goldie and the obscure J. T. Walford decided on the last, whose design was one of the five that had gone unnoticed even in *The Builder*'s lengthy review of the competition. (Temple Moore's was another.)[59]

Adjustments were made to Gribble's design in 1878-9, when many quite small changes were submitted for the Fathers' approval. A little ornamentation was removed from the exterior. The intended realization of the church in brick was changed to Portland-stone ashlaring.[60] An important change was to the dome. The competition design would have provided for a single, shallow concrete shell, but this was replaced by a design for a higher dome of double, inner and outer, construction, that would nevertheless still have been of low silhouette compared with that of the dome actually built after Gribble's death (Plate 36a, c).[61]

Gribble's original competition design was not published, but his modified design was published, as being his 'selected design', in May 1879.[62]

Although the interior and general effect of the church very fully met the Fathers' Italianate requirements (Frontispiece), it may be observed that Gribble gave the lower part of the exterior and particularly of the façade a smooth, neat, rectangularized treatment that seems to show Wrennish and French influences rather than Italian.

In September 1879, after competitive tendering, a contract was concluded with the builder George Shaw of Westminster for the carcase less the outer dome and façade.[63] (The architect's clerk of works was Joseph Seed and the builder's foreman Tinckam.[64]) At the same time a temporary iron church, to be built in front of the Oratory House to Gribble's design, was contracted for with Messrs. Croggan: at 113 by 76 feet it was thought one of the largest of iron churches.[65] The total cost arising from its construction was £2,679.[66]† In March 1880 the foundations of the permanent church were begun.[68] Gribble decided not to carry them down thirty feet to the gravel, but to build on dry, compacted sand.[69] The foundation stone was laid in June—the ceremony being, according to *The Builder*, 'a perfect muddle'.[70] The church, still lacking its outer dome and façade, was consecrated and opened in April 1884.[71]

---

*For comments on the entries see these three periodicals for 21, 28 or 29 June 1878. Designs by Clutton, Grayson, J. Kelly, G. Nattress and Vicars and O'Neill were illustrated in *The Building News* in August and on 15 November 1878 and *The Builder* on 4 July 1885.

†It was sold in June 1884 and re-erected as a Sailors' and Soldiers' Institute at Alexandria, where it survived until the late 1940's: its site, close to the present Seamen's Institute, is now occupied by a mosque.[67]

A notable constructional feature was Gribble's use of concrete vaulting, by the example, he says, of the 'temple' of Minerva Medica at Rome. In the nave it was seven to fourteen inches thick and in the inner dome it was (or was intended to be[72]) one to two feet thick. An account of the building of the church published by Gribble in 1885 reveals with candour the element of personal experimentation and tentative, anxious pragmatism in a Victorian architect's approach to his constructional problems. Of the wrought-iron trusses in the roof, for example, he wrote, 'whether this scheme will turn out satisfactory or not, time will show. . . . 'The cost was sleepless nights for Gribble, and, at first, tie-rods across the nave itself.[73] Gribble used Devonshire 'marbles' extensively inside, from near his native Plymouth.[74] These were supplied, ready for fixing, by J. and E. Goad of that city, where Gribble designed their premises.[75]* The building stone was specified as best brown Portland, the roof-slates North Wales Duchess, the timber Baltic, and the wrought iron best Swedish or its equivalent.[76] It was announced that the caps and ornamental parts of the interior would be in carton pierre and fibrous plaster.[77] The Oratorians' neighbour, the Science and Art Department, evidently regarded Gribble as an expert on building materials, and employed him in 1886 to improve its 'construction collection'.[78]

The cost of the work rose eventually, by the end of 1885, to vindicate Waterhouse's judgment at a total of some £93,302. This was made up of £69,682 to the contractor, £10,352 to the marble merchant, £4,777 to the architects, £1,098 to their clerk of works and £7,393 for fittings and sundries.[65] The Builder had, however, prophesied that it would be a 'costly' design,[79] and Gribble was pleased to have held the expense to less than 7d. a cubic foot.[80]

By the end of 1881 his association with Walford had become disharmonious, and in February 1882 the Fathers had shown their confidence in him by his appointment as sole architect: Walford was evidently aggrieved.[81] In 1885 the Fathers gave Gribble an honorarium of £100.[82] In the same year, however, an alternative scheme for the sanctuary by J. H. Pollen was evidently being considered,[83] and in 1888 its decoration was given to J. Cosgreave, who removed pediments from Gribble's doors and designed the present wall-treatment (for foreign, not Devonshire, marbles).[84]

In 1890 it was decided to add the façade at the south end. Of thirteen Fathers five voted against Gribble's employment as architect, and his design was only adopted after a split vote.[85] It was an amended version of his competition design, a little closer in its pedimented finish to the Oratorians' Chiesa Nuova at Rome, and crowned by a statue of the Virgin, not, as in the competition design, St. John the Baptist.[53] A tender was accepted from D. Charteris in 1891-2, but some breach, probably caused by a misunderstanding about the estimates, opened between

Gribble and the Fathers.[86] This was patched up: in 1893, however, when Gribble was probably already afflicted with a fatal sickness, his services were dispensed with and the upper part of the façade, less the superstructure of the flanking towers, was completed to his design under the supervision of the clerk of works, Peter Shaw (Plate 37b).[87] Who carried out the excellent ornamental stone-carving on the exterior is not known: one sculptor employed by Gribble at the Oratory in 1891 on unidentified work connected with 'tablets' was Alfred Toft of Trafalgar Studios, Manresa Road, Chelsea.[88] In the years 1890-5 some £14,302 was spent on the building.[89] Shaw in 1896 designed the pleasant, cylindrically chimneyed lodge, built in the following year, and also the paving in front of the portico, curtailed for road-widening in 1971-2.[90] (In 1897 he called himself 'architect' and lived at Bedford Park.[91])

Gribble, who died in 1894 aged forty-seven, had greatly regretted the failure to construct his outer dome.[92] The want was, in a manner, supplied when 'a Client of Saint Philip' (Mrs. Daglish-Bellasis[93]) offered to pay for it on the saint's tercentenary in 1895. The design was to be provided by the architect George Sherrin, who in 1894 had suggested an alternative domical finish to the flanking towers,[94] but the lantern was designed by his young assistant, E. A. Rickards (Plate 37a).[95] The steel-framed dome was built in 1895-6 to the silhouette, higher and steeper than Gribble had proposed, which shows so effectively from some of the quiet streets north of the Brompton Road.[93] The influence of Pietro da Cortona is evident. (Stanley Adshead thought Sherrin had impaired Rickards's design by elevating the lantern in relation to the dome—'let us push it up a foot or so'.[95])

At the same time Cardinal Newman's memorial was erected by a committee under the fifteenth Duke of Norfolk in front of St. Joseph's Hall (Plate 41e). It was designed by Bodley and Garner and made by Farmer and Brindley, whose artist, L. J. Chavalliaud, modelled Newman's statue.[96]

The last external work of consequence was the facing of St. Wilfrid's and St. Joseph's Halls with stone to a design by Leonard Stokes in 1911 intended to rise one storey higher.[97]

Within the Oratory House the delightful library (Plate 34b) has been fitted up and decorated, particularly above gallery level, at various dates since 1859 (for example, in 1910[98]). The beautiful private chapel of the Little Oratory still chiefly shows Pollen's work of 1871-2, augmented in 1954 by grisaille and trompe l'oeil paintings by Edgar Ritchard to the architectural design of Adrian Brookholding-Jones (Plate 34a).[99]

In planning his great church Gribble's generally Italian effect had been perfectly deliberate, 'so that' (he said) 'those who had no opportunity of going to Italy to see an Italian church had only to come here to see the model of

*For the dome construction (Plate 36b) and the 'marbles' see The Building News 2, 16, Dec. 1881, pp. 724, 790, 16 Feb. 1883, p. 182, and Herbert Gribble, 'How I built the Oratory' in Merry England, vol. v, 1885, pp. 260-72.

one.'[100] His original coloured interior perspective of the competition design for the nave[101] shows a perhaps rather light-weight decorative scheme employing arabesque motifs and *grotteschi*. By 1885 his proposals for the sanctuary, at least, were strongly coloured in red marbles.[101] With internal walls in Keene's cement, however, the church in its early days lacked its full intended richness,[100] although at the opening the Lady Chapel and St. Wilfrid's Chapel already displayed their fine old altars from northern Italy and Flanders (see below and Plates 40b, c, 41a). In 1895 the twelve marble apostles carved by Giuseppe Mazzuoli *c.* 1679-95 for Siena Cathedral and ejected thence by Gothic zeal in 1880 were acquired to adorn the nave (Plate 41c, d).[102] In many of the subsidiary chapels as well as in the sanctuary much of the early decoration and painting was by J. Cosgreave and the Spanish artist V. Codina-Langlin respectively.[103]

The present interior (Plates 38, 39) takes much of its character from decoration in 1927-32 by Commendatore C. T. G. Formilli, an Italian architect long resident in Kensington, who was on occasions employed by the Italian and British governments.[104] He was here both the designer and contractor, at an estimated price of no less than £31,000, which was, furthermore, to be considerably exceeded. His versatility extended to designing the suspended scaffolding for his workmen. He provided the high-relief figures in the spandrels and over the keystones of the arches in the nave, the Stations of the Cross between the pilasters in the nave, and other panels in relief (all in stucco, and some or all of it executed in Milan); the yellow Siena marbling between the pilasters in the nave and at the crossing (which was adopted when Formilli failed to find a marble of the bright green colour he would have preferred); the Venetian-made mosaics under the dome, flanking the windows, and in the ceiling; much of the gilding throughout; some painting in the ceiling; the coloured motifs in the windows; and (extra to the main contract) the great mahogany pulpit (Plate 40a). Formilli's declared aim was by his colouring to make the interior 'still more in keeping with the traditions of the Catholic Church', and it seems that his proposed designs were pleasing to Pope Pius XI.[105] The effect is more billowy and abounding than in Gribble's proposals. The Father Superior of the time said, 'We ought I suppose to have advertised a competition, employed British architects and British labour, and had a thoroughly British scheme of decoration. But we did none of these things, and I for one do not regret it. I can imagine the sort of thing we should have got . . . .' Formilli was not, however, allowed to substitute polychrome marble for the old wood-block floor bedded in concrete. (The Fathers had preferred this to a boarded floor, which Gribble had originally recommended as 'most essential for comfort, when sitting, or during the devotion of the "Way of the Cross".'[106])

Some features of the church, viewed clockwise and excluding copies of works elsewhere, are the following:[107]

Fig. 14. The Oratory, confessional box from former church

Chapel of the Sacred Heart. Decorated by Geoffrey Webb *c.* 1935:[108] altar and reredos by Gribble.

Chapel of St. Joseph. Decorated by Andrew Carden of Carden, Godfrey and Macfadyen 1964: altar by Scoles (1861) from the old church:[109] statue of St. Joseph, Belgian, erected 1884:[110] marble doorcases survive from scheme by George Aitchison, *c.* 1897-8.[111]

Chapel of the Seven Dolours. Altar and reredos by Gribble given by Flora, Duchess of Norfolk: altarpiece painted at Rome for Fr. Faber in 1859 or earlier by Ferenc Szoldatits (1820-1916), a Hungarian follower of the Nazarenes domiciled there: the Fathers thought of him as a German.[112]

Chapel of St. Philip. Altar and baldacchino by Gribble, made by Farmer and Brindley, given by 15th Duke of Norfolk (Plate 41b):[113] alto-relievo in Italian cement in tympanum of baldacchino by Girolamo Moneta of Milan, (estimated price £90):[114] wall-reliefs on either side of baldacchino by Laurence Bradshaw, *c.* 1927:[115] apse of Blessed Sebastian Valfré by Thomas Garner, 1901-3:[116] paintings on either side of baldacchino attributed to Guercino.[117]

Sacristy. Altar and reredos from the Chapel of the Sacred Heart in the old church.[118]

Sanctuary. Altar rails and wooden stalls and floor from old church: wall treatment designed by J. Cosgreave, 1888-90:[119] altarpiece and paintings at sides by B. Pozzi, 1924-7:[120] seven-branch candle-holders designed by William Burges, presented by third Marquess of Bute, 1879.[121]

Chapel of St. Wilfrid. The altar and baldacchino of the saint (Plate 40b, c), installed before the opening in 1884, originally formed the High Altar of the monastic church of St. Remy at Rochefort in Belgium, but had been bought, through the dealer Cools and the firm of Duveen, from the church of St. Servaas at Maastricht in Holland, which had itself bought the altar in 1811, after the suppression of St. Remy. It lacks two angels that knelt on brackets at each side of the baldacchino, and the door of the tabernacle has been changed within its oval opening. (De Feller visited St. Remy in 1771 and said the High Altar, 'un vrai chef d'oeuvre', was the work of the architect Étienne Fayn (1712-90), which, if true, gives a later date for it than the style suggests.)[122] Statue of saint by V. Codina-Langlin:[123] apse decorated by J. Cosgreave:[124] altars of St. Teresa of Lisieux and of the English Martyrs by David Stokes, 1936-8:[125] bas-relief on former by Arthur Pollen: triptych over latter by Rex Whistler.

Lady Chapel. The altar, with its reredos (Plate 41a), is from the Chapel of the Rosary in the church of San Domenico at Brescia. It was made in 1693 by the Florentine Francesco Corbarelli and his sons Domenico and Antonio and, as would appear from the term 'Arch.' in the contemporary inscription, was also designed by them. It was bought for £1,550, received in instalments from February to May 1881, and restored over a period of two years.[126] The central recess was altered to receive the figure of Our Lady from the old Oratory church and originally in King William Street.[127] The statues of St. Rose of Lima and St. Pius V to left and right of the altar are by Orazio Marinali, *c.* 1690-2 (the latter signed with his initials).[128] The rest of the figure sculpture, including the St. Dominic and St. Catherine of Siena now moved from the altar to niches in the side walls of the chapel, is by the Tyrolean, Thomas Ruer (d. 1696).[129] Two other statues, of angels, have been removed from either side of the altar to the organ gallery, where they overlook the Chapel of St. Mary Magdalene: of these, the one on the right as seen from that chapel is by Santo Calegari (1662-1719) and signed by him and was formerly on the Gospel side of the Lady Altar.[130]*

Organ gallery. The organ by J. W. Walker and Sons, 1954, to specifications by Ralph Downes: two angels, see *Lady Chapel* above.

Chapel of St. Mary Magdalene. Decorated by J. Cosgreave: altar and reredos by Gribble: mosaic panels on either side of altar by A. Capello of Chelsea, 1883-4.[132]

Chapel of St. Patrick. Altar from Naples: reredos by Gribble: altarpiece and lateral paintings by Pietro Pezzati: paintings on wooden panels at each side of altar perhaps by Frans Floris:[133] war memorial, 1918-21, designed by L. Berra, executed by Daniells and Fricker of Kilburn, with Pietà of Italian carving.[134]

The plain confessionals in four of the chapels are from the old church (fig. 14).[135]†

---

*In the period 1884-93 it was reported that other parts of the chapel in which this altar had stood at Brescia had been installed in a now-demolished house of Cyril Flower, later Lord Battersea, at what was latterly numbered 7 Marble Arch.[131]

†The altar of St. Philip from the old church is now in the Lady Chapel of St. Patrick's Church, Wapping.[136] For the location of other features from the old church in 1934 see H. M. Gillett, *The Story of the London Oratory Church*, 1934, pp. 49-50.

CHAPTER V

The Alexander Estate

During the first half of the nineteenth century the Alexander estate in South Kensington consisted of six separate plots of land having a total area of some fifty-four acres.[1] Only one of these plots is within the area described in this volume — a triangular block of some fourteen acres bounded on the north-west by Thurloe Place, on the east by Brompton Road, and on the south (approximately) by the underground railway and South Kensington Station (see fig. 15). Three more of the six plots were described in *Survey of London* volume XXXVIII, where a general account of the estate is to be found on pages 8-11. The other two plots, consisting of a tiny piece of land now part of the site of Barker's store in Kensington High Street, and of some twenty acres on the west side of Gloucester Road, will be described in volume XLII.

The whole estate is here called after its nineteenth-century owners, the Alexanders, under whose auspices it was developed, but it has often been known as the Thurloe estate, after the Puritan statesman John Thurloe (1616-1668). His association with the estate is supposed to derive from a present of some land which he is said to have received from Oliver Cromwell himself.[2] However, no documentary proof that either Cromwell or Thurloe ever owned land in this area has been found: on the contrary, the surviving evidence suggests that Thurloe could never have been the owner of this estate. The tradition of his ownership no doubt developed because in the eighteenth century one of his descendants acquired an interest in the property through marriage (see below).[3]

The Ownership of the Estate

In the early seventeenth century most of the lands which were later to make up the Alexander estate belonged to a vintner, Sir William Blake, who at the time of his death in 1630 owned some 370 acres in Kensington, Knightsbridge and Chelsea.[4] Soon afterwards this large holding was broken up, and several pieces of land, including most of what was to become the Alexander estate, descended to his son and grandson. By the early eighteenth century these had passed into the ownership of Sir William's great-great-grand-daughter, Anna Maria Harris, whose first husband was John Browne (see fig. 1 on page 11). But after his death she in 1712 took as her second husband John Thurloe's grandson, John Thurloe Brace, and it is from this marriage that the estate's peripheral connexion with John Thurloe stems.

Anna Maria Brace died in 1760 leaving the bulk of her property in Brompton and South Kensington to Harris Thurloe Brace, her only son by her second husband.[5] Excluded from this inheritance, however, were some eleven acres of copyhold land of the manor of Earl's Court which had already passed to William Browne, Anna Maria's grandson by her first marriage, and a small piece in the vicinity of Trevor Square. The eleven copyhold acres, though usually described as being in Knightsbridge, were in fact on the south side of Brompton Road with a frontage to that highway extending (in modern terms) from Sloane Street almost to Brompton Place. They remained the property of the Browne family and their heirs until purchased by the second Lord Kensington in 1842 and have never been owned by the Alexanders. Their development and later history are described in Chapter II.

When Harris Thurloe Brace died unmarried in 1799 he left his estates to his mother's two great-grandsons by her first marriage, the brothers John and James Wadman Alexander.[6] James received land and property in the town and county of Bedford, while John, a lawyer then aged about thirty-seven, inherited the Brompton and South Kensington estate. After his death in 1831 this passed to his son Henry Browne Alexander, and in 1885 to his grandson William Henry Alexander; and on the latter's death in 1905 to Lady George Campbell, a grand-daughter of James Wadman Alexander, who in 1879 had married the fourth son of the eighth Duke of Argyll.[7] Lady George Campbell died in 1947 leaving the estate to her daughter Joan. On Joan Campbell's death in 1960 the property passed by her will in trust (under terms varied in 1974) for Ian Anstruther, a grandson of Lady George, and his family.

Harrison's Nursery

In 1799, when John Alexander inherited the estate, the greater part of the area under consideration here was being cultivated as a nursery garden.[8] The proprietor was then John Harrison, but the nursery had been founded some fifty years earlier by Henry Hewitt (d. 1771) and his brother Samuel (d. 1793).[9]* After Henry's death the business was carried on by Samuel in partnership with his nephew, Henry Hewitt junior, and William Smith. By 1789 Samuel had retired and Henry junior was in partnership with his nephew, John Harrison, and John

---

*A lease to the Hewitts from Anna Maria Brace in 1757 of a messuage used as a seed shop or counting-house, and some three and a half acres of ground used as a nursery and flower garden, states that these properties 'are and have been for some years' in the tenure of the Hewitts.[10]

Fig. 15. The Alexander Estate. Based on the Ordnance Survey. The two areas within the dotted lines were sold at the time of the construction of the underground railway (pp. 79, 81). The inset map shows the area behind the Bell and Horns prior to its redevelopment in 1909–27

Cook. Cook soon dropped out, and in 1790 Hewitt assigned his share to Harrison, who thereby became the sole proprietor. The nursery was then held under a thirty-three-year lease from Harris Thurloe Brace expiring in 1821, at £60 per annum. It stocked fruit trees and also specialised in herbaceous and greenhouse plants, and in vegetable and flower seeds. The seed-shop and counting-house were on the western part of the site next to the road, where the Thurloe Street entrance to South Kensington Station is situated (see Plate 2a).[11]

John Harrison was succeeded by his brother Samuel, who in 1815 increased the size of the nursery by leasing a further eight and a half acres from the trustees of the adjoining Smith's Charity estate.[12] (This is the area where Pelham Crescent, Place and Street were subsequently built.) In 1819 Harrison entered into partnership with William Bristow,[13] and in 1821 they obtained a new lease from John Alexander extending their tenure of the nursery on his estate up to 1842, subject to Alexander's right to repossess a small part of it if he should require it for building.[14] But the firm continued in business only until November 1832, when both Harrison and Bristow were declared bankrupt.[15] Two years before the crash Harrison had become the first occupant of one of the new houses in Alexander Square,[16] built, as described below, on land which up to 1826 had formed a part of his nursery.

The Bell and Horns

Adjoining the nursery were two old-established public houses. To the west, in the vicinity of its present-day successor, stood the Hoop and Toy, and to the east, at the junction of what are now Thurloe Place and Brompton Road, was the Bell and Horns. The site of the Bell and Horns was a small detached portion of the manor of Earl's Court and had formed no part of John Alexander's inherited estate.[17] But when the property came on to the market in 1808 Alexander bought the freehold for £1,260.[18] There had been a public house on the site since at least the 1720's. It was then called the Bell, and this is the name under which it was licensed until the late 1780's.[19] The name Bell and Horns suggests a merger of two taverns, and in fact there had been a public house called the Horns in Brompton, 'over against the Pond', in the early eighteenth century. Latterly known as the Ship and Horns, this survived until the early 1780's. On the other hand the Bell is referred to as the Bell and Horns in the abuttals of a lease in 1773.[20] Salway's view of 1811 (Plate 11b) shows it after a refronting of 1808-9.[21]*

In 1824-5 the old Bell and Horns was replaced by a new brick-built public house erected for Thomas Goding of Knightsbridge, brewer and wine and spirit merchant, to whom Alexander granted a thirty-five-year lease of the property.[22] Goding's architect was Francis Edwards

(1784-1857), who later designed the Lion Brewhouse on the South Bank for Messrs. Goding and Company (1836) and was frequently employed by the firm for public houses and other works.[23] Although never again completely rebuilt, the Bell and Horns was altered, enlarged and partially reconstructed for the Lion Brewery in 1855-6, when it was given the Italianate stucco façades which survived until the building was demolished in 1915 (Plate 42a, b). At the same time a yard next to the Fulham (now Brompton) Road was covered with single-storey buildings, including a shop and a coffee-room. Francis Edwards was again the architect, in association with his son, also Francis, and the contractor was William Chutter of Upper Stamford Street. In 1879 further improvements and alterations costing not less than £500 were made for the Lion Brewery, this time by a J. Edwards, architect.[24] The site of the Bell and Horns is now occupied by the eastern corner of Empire House.

The Hoop and Toy

This inn, which unlike the Bell and Horns had descended to John Alexander with the rest of the estate, was apparently a building of some antiquity, if an article in *The Builder* of 1874 is to be trusted. The writer there — perhaps the editor, George Godwin — recalls it as 'a brick and timber building of the latter part of the fifteenth or the commencement of the sixteenth century'.[25] The main front was not to the roadway but faced southwards over a garden. At the west end, immediately next to the road, was a small two-storey weather-boarded cottage which was latterly occupied by a gardener called Dunn.[26] How long the building had been in use as a public house is difficult to determine, but it had certainly been licensed since 1760, when it was called the Hoop and Grapes. Its name was changed to the Hoop and Toy in *c*. 1775.[27]

The old house was pulled down in 1844 and replaced by a differently oriented two-storey stucco-faced building fronting directly on the roadway. This was erected by John Carnelly, the licensee, under an agreement with H. B. Alexander of July 1844, and with financial assistance from Whitbread and Company, the brewers. Carnelly was to spend at least £1,000 on the new building, whose elevations, plans and specifications had been approved by Alexander's surveyor. In the following December Alexander granted a sixty-year-lease of the premises to Carnelly at £60 per annum.[28] This building survived until the Hoop and Toy was reconstructed in its present form in 1927 (see page 86).

The Development of Alexander Square

In 1826 John Alexander exercised his right (reserved in the lease of 1821) to repossess for development part of

---

*The watercolour of the Bell and Horns by T. Hosmer Shepherd in Kensington Central Library, which shows the site at the junction of two roads more clearly than Salway, was painted in the 1850's, after Brompton Lane (Thurloe Place) had been widened, and some thirty years after the building which it depicts had been demolished, and is probably based on Salway's view.

the ground in the occupation of Harrison and Bristow; and in June he entered into an agreement to let this plot to the builder James Bonnin.[29] The area in question was a piece of about four acres on the eastern side of the estate which included the whole of Alexander's frontage to the Fulham (now Brompton) Road southwards of the Bell and Horns. Here the development was to comprise what are now Alexander Square, North Terrace, the eastern halves of Alexander Place and South Terrace, and some building in Thurloe Place and Brompton Road.

The James Bonnin with whom Alexander concluded the agreement was the builder who more effectively than any other left his stamp on present-day Brompton. Born in about 1782,[30] he is first encountered hereabouts in 1806, when he was living in a house in Exeter Street, Hans Town, Chelsea.[31] He was soon involved in a number of developments in the Hans Town area, some of them under lease from the contractor Henry Rowles.[32] By 1810 he had moved to North Street, where his premises were described as formerly part of Richard Holland's timber yard.[33] Bonnin was then calling himself a carpenter, but in a directory for 1816-17 he is listed as a timber merchant with an address in Sloane Place.[34] In c. 1819-20 he was involved in building on Viscount Dungannon's estate at Knightsbridge (including Trevor Square),[35] and in 1821 he undertook the initial development of Brompton Square, where he was briefly the first occupant of No. 1.[16] In 1822 he entered into an agreement to erect a row of houses, called Onslow Terrace, on the Fulham Road frontage of the Smith's Charity estate, immediately to the south of Alexander's property. At the rear of this he built a cottage, with a workshop and timber yard, for his own occupation, where he lived from 1826 until 1838.[36] His career ended in bankruptcy in 1846 (see page 101), but by then he was able to claim that he had built no fewer than three hundred houses in Kensington, the majority of them on the Alexander and Smith's Charity estates, and inhabited, moreover, 'by parties whose respectability is of great advantage to the Parish'.[37]

From about 1830 onwards Bonnin was assisted in his business by his second son, James Bonnin junior (b. 1808), variously described as pewterer, carpenter or builder, who in the 1840's was perhaps the dominant figure. In 1848 he too was declared bankrupt.[38]

Under the terms of his agreement with Alexander the elder Bonnin was required to lay out streets and build houses in accordance with a plan approved by Alexander's surveyor. Who this was is not certain, although two years earlier it had been a Mr. Leonard — perhaps the T. Leonard of King Street, Covent Garden, who was a land surveyor.[39] The plan annexed to the agreement provided for the layout of the new streets to be in the form of a reversed capital E, the upright being represented by the roadway in front of the two east-facing terraces of Alexander Square, and the lateral strokes by the three westward-leading streets now called North Terrace, Alexander Place and South Terrace.* Alexander Square, which is unnamed on the plan of June 1826 but so called by May 1827,[40] bears rather a pretentious designation for what is little more than a pair of terraces set back from the Fulham (now Brompton) Road behind ornamental plantations. On the plan the streets leading out of the 'square' terminate abruptly at the eastern boundary of Harrison's nursery, but their westward continuation at a future date is clearly implied, and in the case of Alexander Place and South Terrace this was done some fourteen years later. In the meantime they were closed by iron railings on dwarf walls. This was no doubt a concession to Bonnin by Alexander who had originally required a high brick wall to be built down the western side of the site in compliance with his own undertaking to Harrison (in the lease of 1821) to wall off the nursery from the ground Alexander took back for building.[41] Harrison, whose acquiescence in this change must be presumed, was still able to train his trees and plants against the blank return fronts and garden walls of the westernmost houses in these streets.[42]

The layout provided for seventy-two houses — four more than were eventually built. In the east-facing ranges of Alexander Square the houses were to be four storeys high over basements. Here the two corner houses and two centre houses in each range were to be 22 feet wide and 30 feet deep, and the intermediate houses 18 feet wide and 28 feet deep. On the short north and south frontages of the square and along the streets leading out of it the houses were to be three storeys high over basements and not less than 17 feet wide and 27 feet deep.[43]

By provisions usual in such agreements it was laid down that as soon as the houses were built and covered in they were to be leased by Alexander to Bonnin or his nominees for a term of eighty years from Midsummer 1826 at ground rents ranging between £2 and £10 per house. During the first two years the total of these ground rents was to be £50, and thereafter it was to rise by stages to £400 in the seventh year. At least two houses were to remain unleased until the whole building programme was completed.

The building agreement does not mention any architect's name, nor is there any reference to the houses having to conform to an approved elevation. But Bonnin undertook to work to a precise and comprehensive set of specifications which even extend to the details of the interior finishing.

Externally the houses were to be faced with good malm stocks, not inferior in quality to those used in Brompton Square, and stuccoed on the ground storey. The round-headed front doors were to have 'large handsome fanlights' and the first-floor front windows 'handsome wrought iron balconies', whilst the areas were to be protected by stout iron railings. All the houses were to have two rooms on a floor (fig. 16), finished at each level in a

*This plan is reproduced in Dorothy Stroud, *The Thurloe Estate*, 1965.

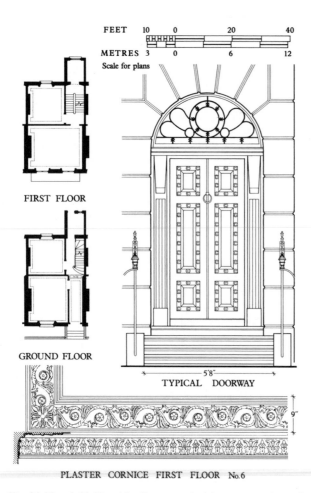

FEET 10   0   20   40
METRES 3   0   6   12
Scale for plans

FIRST FLOOR

GROUND FLOOR

TYPICAL DOORWAY

PLASTER CORNICE FIRST FLOOR No. 6

Fig. 16. Nos. 6-11 Alexander Square, typical doorway, cornice and
plans. James Bonnin, builder, 1830-2

manner appropriate to their use — kitchens in the
basement, parlours on the ground floor, drawing-rooms on
the first floor, bedrooms on the second, and in the taller
houses, attic rooms above. The two drawing-rooms were
to communicate by folding doors. The parlours could
either connect in the same way, or could be treated as
separate rooms, in which case the intervening wall was to
contain (probably on one side only) a 'handsome'
segmentally arched recess for a sideboard. Drawing-rooms
and parlours were to have 'large handsome cornices' (fig.
16), papered walls with gilt mouldings, and marble
chimneypieces; and the joinery was to include a 'deep
handsome moulded skirting', four-panel doors moulded
on both sides, and double-faced architraves or pilasters
around the doors and windows. The houses had only one
staircase, which was to be of wood with a 'handsome'
mahogany handrail. The bedrooms and attics were to have
Portland stone chimneypieces, papered walls, and 'neat'
cornices. In the kitchens there were to be two Portland
stone chimneypieces, a deep skirting of wood or compo,
deal floors, proper cupboards and large dressers and
shelves with three drawers.

Apart from the houses just described Bonnin also
undertook to erect ten small semi-detached cottages along
the road frontage (now called Thurloe Place) immediately
to the west of the Bell and Horns, and a little row of shops
along the short frontage of the Fulham Road between the
Bell and Horns and North Terrace. They were to be
'equally respectable', built of good materials, and finished
to the satisfaction of Alexander's surveyor. Erected over
basements, the cottages were to have two storeys, and the
shops three.

A builder of Bonnin's experience would hardly have
needed a professional architect to translate the
specifications into plans and elevations, so precisely do
they describe the characteristic terrace house of the
1820's. However, it has been argued that the greater
sophistication of the main ranges of Alexander Square as
compared with Bonnin's houses in Brompton Square
points to the hand of an architect, and the name usually
mentioned in this connexion is that of George Godwin the
elder (1789-1863), a surveyor now remembered, if at all,
as the father of George Godwin, junior (1813-88), the
architect, social reformer and, for many years, the editor of
The Builder.[44] Godwin senior was certainly involved in the
development (where he was also an early resident), though
in circumstances which suggest he was acting as Bonnin's
rather than Alexander's surveyor. In May 1828 he applied
to the Westminster Commissioners of Sewers for leave to
build two sewers, one in front of Onslow Terrace, Fulham
Road (one of Bonnin's developments on the Smith's
Charity estate), and another in Alexander Square. When
originally submitted by Bonnin himself in December
1827 this latter application had been refused, and it may
be surmised that Bonnin then decided to employ the
services of a surveyor in his dealings with the sewers
commissioners.[45]

Alexander had allowed Bonnin seven years in which to
complete the development, a realistic schedule which
should have produced about ten new houses a year. In fact
the rate of progress was very uneven and the greatest
number of leases — for half the intended number of
houses — was granted in 1827. The properties leased in
that year comprised the ten cottages to the west of the Bell
and Horns and the five shops to the south, the sites on the
north side of North Terrace and on the south side of
South Terrace, and the north and south ranges of
Alexander Square (Nos. 1-4 and 21-24).

Not all these houses were built by Bonnin himself, and
the very first lease to be granted by John Alexander under
the agreement of 1826 was in fact to Charles Henry
Blore, builder. Dated 11 January 1827, this was for No. 7
York Cottages,[46] as the ten small houses to the west of the
Bell and Horns were originally called (probably in
commemoration of the Duke of York, who had died only a
few days earlier): later the cottages were renumbered Nos.
2-11 (consec.) Thurloe Place. Blore himself occupied
No. 7 from 1828.[16]

Another builder here was William Barrat(t) of North
Street near Sloane Street, Chelsea. He erected Nos. 9 and

10 York Cottages and subsequently lived at No. 10, where he had built a large 'shed' adjoining the west side of the house, no doubt to be used in connexion with his business. In 1863 the then occupant of No. 10, William Henry Marler, estate agent, was given permission to convert the 'shed' into an estate agent's office.[47] Bonnin himself was not directly the lessee of any of York Cottages, though he probably built Nos. 3-6 and 8, and perhaps also Nos. 1 and 2, the latter pair being leased to the licensee of the adjoining Bell and Horns.[48] All ten houses here were demolished in 1909 and the site is now covered by Empire House, Dalmeny House and the Rembrandt Hotel.

At Alexander Place (Plate 42a), as the Fulham Road frontage between the Bell and Horns and Alexander Square was originally called, the builders appear to have been Bonnin himself and Lancelot Edward Wood of King's Road, Chelsea, statuary, who had previously been associated in the building of Trevor Square. One of the first inhabitants of Alexander Place was Bonnin's nineteen-year-old builder-son, James Bonnin junior, who occupied No. 2 from 1827 until c. 1838.[16] In 1841 the five shops here were in the hands of an ironmonger, a plumber (Wright Maydwell), a stationer, a statuary (George Sams) and the proprietor of a ham and beef shop.[49]

The north side of North Terrace and the south side of South Terrace were both leased in December 1827 to John Bailey, esquire, the proprietor of Bailey's Hotel in Berkeley Square.[50] (These two streets were then called North Street and South Street.) Bailey, who had dabbled in speculative building in Berkeley Square,[51] was not, of course, himself the builder of any of the houses here, but he was evidently financing the building and the leases to him were a device, frequently encountered on the Alexander estate, of securing the lessee's investment. In these circumstances the lessee would often sub-let the properties to the actual builders at an enhanced ground rent.*

In North Terrace the builder of part, if not the whole, of the northern range (Plate 43b) was probably the statuary Lancelot Edward Wood, who was Bailey's lessee at No. 5, and a party to the lease at Nos. 6 and 7.[52] Only four of the seven houses here had been built when the lease of the whole range was granted to Bailey in 1827 but the others were added soon afterwards. No. 7, which had a bigger frontage than the others and also its own private back entrance from Thurloe Place, was sold in 1830 for £1,327 10s.[53] All the houses on the north side of North Terrace were demolished in c. 1909.

In South Terrace, where the houses leased to Bailey are now numbered 1-11 (odd), only No. 3 was subsequently sub-let to a building tradesman. This was John Skinner of Cumberland Street, Chelsea, bricklayer.[54] Nos. 1-9 were first occupied in 1828-9, but No. 11, a slightly wider house than the others, had been leased to Bailey as a vacant site and was not built until about 1830, being first occupied in 1831.[16] Both Nos. 1 and 7 have been raised a storey, the former in 1982.

The short northern and southern arms of Alexander Square, numbered respectively 1-4 and 21-24 (consec.) — the former now completely demolished — were really little more than extensions of the two ranges on the north side of North Terrace and the south side of South Terrace, and except for the two double-fronted corner houses (Nos. 1 and 24 Alexander Square) there was nothing in their appearance to distinguish them from their neighbours numbered in those two streets (Plate 43b). None of these eight houses was leased to Bonnin and there is no evidence that he was involved with the building of any of them. On the north side, where all four houses were occupied by the end of 1828,[16] the lessees were William Paul of Sloane Street, Chelsea, plumber and glazier (No. 1), Robert Badcock of Michael's Place, Brompton, livery-stable keeper (No. 2), Elizabeth Purkis of South Audley Street, widow (No. 3), and John Latchford of Warwick Row, Pimlico, esquire, the last of whom took up residence at No. 4 in 1828.[55]

On the south side the occupancy of the houses was not completed until 1829,[16] although they included in No. 24 the first house in the square to be taken. Here the occupant, from before December 1827, was Bonnin's own surveyor, George Godwin the elder. He was also the lessee of the house from John Alexander, in September 1827, at which time he gave his address as Brompton Square: previously it had been New Street (now Hans Crescent), Brompton.[56] In 1836 he moved from Alexander Square to No. 11 Pelham Crescent and for several years No. 24 was let to tenants, though Godwin continued to pay rates for what the collector described as 'offices' in Alexander Square.

From 1845 until 1863 (the year of the elder Godwin's death) No. 24 was the business address of the firm of George Godwin and Son, architects,[57] although it was not until 1847 that the younger George Godwin made his home here,[16] removing to Cromwell Place in 1872. A life-long bachelor, George junior shared the house for many years with one of his younger brothers, the architect Henry Godwin, also a bachelor, who remained here after George had moved to Cromwell Place.[58] Yet another brother (and architect), Sidney Godwin, was also living here in 1851.[59]

Like the former No. 1, No. 24 Alexander Square presents only a single-bay return front to the square, its main three-bay façade with central front door being on the east side facing Brompton Road, from which it is separated by a private garden, now somewhat curtailed. There is no back garden. An extension on the south side is contemporary with the main structure and probably served as the office for which Godwin paid rates. Originally only one storey high, with stuccoed walls and three large

---

*For an example of how this worked see the leasing history of No. 8 Pelham Crescent, described on page 94.

east-facing windows, it was heightened in brick in 1972.[60]

The lessees of the other three houses on the south side of the square, none of them residents, were Joseph Bennett of Yeoman's Row, builder (No. 21), Wright Barringer of Onslow Terrace, Brompton, gentleman (No. 22) and Margaret Murray of Sloane Street, Chelsea, spinster (No. 23).[61] (Neither the bay window at No. 23, nor the attic storey at No. 21, is original.)

All the lessees in Alexander Square were granted the privilege of 'walking' in the two plantations. In September 1827 these were described as 'lately laid out', though the enclosing brick walls and iron railings were not completed until October.[62]

The year 1827 also saw the start of work on the southern of the two east-facing ranges of Alexander Square (Nos. 13-20, Plate 44a), and it is this date, rather than the date of completion, which appears in the little pediment above the centre of the range. The eight houses here were leased by Alexander in 1828 (Nos. 16-20) and 1829 (Nos. 13-15) and first occupied between 1829 and 1831.[63] Apart from Bonnin, the lessees were William Whitehead of Little Cadogan Place, Chelsea, builder and bricklayer (No. 13), James Whitehead of Sloane Street, Chelsea, plumber (No. 20), and two booksellers, for whom this was evidently a speculation, David Murray of Chelsea (No. 18) and John Murray the younger of Coventry Street, St. James's (No. 19). In 1832 John Murray sold his lease to the then occupant of No. 19 for £875; but David Murray let his house to tenants for short periods at a rack rent (of £60 per annum), and this continued until 1854 when his executors sold the lease for £705.[64] Particulars of the house prepared for that sale show how closely No. 18 conformed to the specifications of 1826. By 1854, however, the two former parlours on the ground floor had been made into one 'spacious' dining-room. The walls of the bedrooms were, as before, hung with paper, but the dining-room and the two 'elegant' first-floor drawing-rooms (the latter still communicating by folding doors) were 'painted, grained, and decorated'. In the hall the paintwork was grained and the walls were papered with 'marble paper varnished'. The window lighting the staircase contained stained glass. Whatever the provision of water closets may have been in 1826, by this time there were three, one on the second floor, one on the ground floor 'conveniently placed' in a lobby at the back of the hall, and one in the basement for the servants.[65]

The two main ranges of Alexander Square are separated by Alexander Place, which also falls chronologically between them. Slightly wider than the two parallel streets to north and south, as befitting its central position, Alexander Place was in 1828 intended to be called Eton Street.[66] But that designation quickly gave way to York Place, the name used in the earliest leases, and by the time the first occupants of the houses were in residence in 1831 it had been renamed, for no very obvious reason, Alfred Place. Also known as Alfred Place East (in differentiation

from Alfred Place West, now Thurloe Street), it was given the name Alexander Place only in 1920, the original Alexander Place next to the Bell and Horns having by then been demolished. Eight houses (two fewer than originally intended) were built here in 1829 in two short facing terraces (now numbered 4-10 even, and 1-7 odd), and they were all leased in December of that year to John Gibson, esquire, of Reading.[67] Like John Bailey in North and South Terraces, Gibson had evidently invested in the

FEET   10   0   10

METRES 1   0   1   2   3   4   5

Fig. 17. No. 3 Alexander Place, elevation and plan of front. James Bonnin, builder, 1829-30

development by lending money to the builder, or builders, and the houses were first leased to him in order to provide adequate security. Bonnin was undoubtedly the principal builder here but only Nos. 1, 3, 4 and 10 were subsequently leased back to him by Gibson in 1830.[68] Gibson's other lessees were James Bonnin, junior, in his first appearance on the estate in that role (No. 6), William Jarman of Knightsbridge, paper-stainer (No. 8), and two 'gentlemen' investors (Nos. 5 and 7).[69] All eight houses have attractive bow windows on the ground floor — a feature expressly prohibited by the building agreement unless sanctioned by both Alexander and Bonnin; and although each range is only four houses long they form self-contained architectural units in which the two end houses are slightly projected (Plate 43c, fig. 17). The houses are finished with a moulded cornice instead of the simple brick parapet and three-inch-thick coping stone which was all that was required by the specifications. Nos. 1 and 4 each have a pretty Gothick window let into the east flank wall at first-floor level. At the other end of the ranges the west-facing flank walls of Nos. 7 and 10 overlooking Harrison's nursery were reserved for the nurseryman to train his plants against and probably had no windows.

The gardens at the rear of the houses on the north side were somewhat shorter than originally intended because Bonnin had already appropriated the piece of back land now occupied by No. 2 Alexander Place for the newly founded Western Grammar School (see page 67). The entrance to the school was by the passageway alongside No. 4 now used to give access to No. 2.[70]

In 1830, the only year between 1827 and 1833 in which no building leases were granted, work started on the northern of the two east-facing ranges of Alexander Square (Nos. 5-12, Plate 44c). This was built by Bonnin himself and with only one exception he was the lessee of all the houses there. While work on this range was still in progress John Alexander died (in January 1831) and his estate devolved on his elder son, Henry Browne Alexander, who continued the development without interruption. The leases for Nos. 5-12 Alexander Square were granted by him at various dates between June 1831 and October 1832 and the houses filled up with inhabitants between 1832 and 1834.[71] At No. 7 the lessee was one of Bonnin's mortgagees, Robert Bradley, a silk merchant of Shoreditch then resident at Michael's Place, who lived here from 1836 in succession to William Bradley, the first occupant.[72]

In appearance the northern range is very similar to the southern, but some of the details are different, and one in particular suggests that Bonnin was having to make some modification in the design of the houses in order to conform to the requirements of the estate's new surveyor. He, unlike his probable predecessor, Mr. Leonard, was a distinguished architect, George Basevi (1794-1845). According to the Architectural Publication Society's *Dictionary* (of 1852) Basevi became surveyor in 1829; but the *Dictionary* also says he was appointed surveyor to the adjoining Smith's Charity estate in the same year, whereas in fact he had held that post since September 1828.[73] Whether or not the *Dictionary*'s date is entirely reliable it is clear that Basevi did not become the Alexander estate surveyor (a post he retained for the rest of his life) until after the development was well under way — too late to make any significant changes, but not too late to introduce small alterations in the design of the houses still to be built.

The particular feature which points to Basevi's influence here is the form of the front doors in the northern range of Alexander Square. In the earlier southern range, in Alexander Place, and in South Terrace the houses have conventional six-panel front doors, the largest panels being at the top and the smallest in the centre. But in the northern range the panels of the front doors are differently proportioned, with iron-studded frames (Plate 44b, fig. 16). In her history of the Alexander estate Miss Dorothy Stroud drew attention to Basevi's use of these iron-studded doors in other, later, houses known to have been designed by him on both the Alexander and Smith's Charity estates,* and she traced the source of the design to a seventeenth-century illustration of the great bronze doors of the Pantheon in Rome. Basevi probably picked up the idea from his master, (Sir) John Soane, who had used this type of door at his own house in Lincoln's Inn Fields, and at the Bank of England.[74] On Bonnin's development these doors occur at Nos. 5-12 Alexander Square, at Nos. 8-11 North Terrace, and at No. 4 South Terrace, all houses erected in or after 1830.

Basevi presumably sanctioned the bow window on the southern return flank of this range, at No. 12 Alexander Square, but it seems unlikely that he was answerable for Bonnin's use here of the very conventional anthemion-patterned ironwork for the balcony windows. Like the southern range, the northern range of Alexander Square has a small pediment embossed with the date when work started, in this case 1830.

The last houses to be erected under the agreement of 1826 were Nos. 2-8 (even) South Terrace and Nos. 8-11 (consec.) North Terrace. The four in South Terrace were probably built together in 1832, Nos. 6 and 8 being leased in October of that year to James Lowther of Osnaburgh Street, Regent's Park, gentleman, who shortly afterwards moved into No. 8.[75] But the leases for Nos. 2 and 4 were held back by Alexander (as provided for in the building agreement) until the whole of the development had been completed, and are dated 9 September 1833.[76] Here the lessee was James Bonnin, junior. Nos. 2, 4 and 6 were all occupied in 1834, the residents of Nos. 2 and 4 having bought their houses from Bonnin (and his mortgagee) for £630 and £600 respectively.[77] The ironwork of the balconies at the four houses is, uniquely on this development, the same as in Pelham Crescent.

Of the four houses on the south side of North Terrace, No. 11 is conspicuously unlike any other house on the estate. Leased in March 1833, it has a wholly stuccoed front, with a bow rising through all three storeys, while the windowless flank wall on the east side, which is also stuccoed, has been dressed with Doric pilasters and is finished with a pediment. The lessee here was Lewis Kennedy, esquire, a lawyer and one of Bonnin's mortgagees.[78] He was then living in Hans Place, Chelsea, but soon afterwards removed into the recently completed

*For example in Pelham Crescent (in the 1830's) and in Thurloe Square (in the 1840's). The number of panels in these studded doors varied: in Pelham Crescent there are four, in Thurloe Square only two (see fig. 19).

No. 5 Alexander Square, the back windows of which directly overlook the flank wall of No. 11 North Terrace.[79] From these circumstances it may be conjectured that Kennedy, with the intention of occupying the house in Alexander Square already in mind, had agreed with Bonnin to buy No. 11 while it was yet unbuilt, and in order to enhance the view from his own back windows had the house erected to a more 'interesting' design, presumably with the permission of Alexander's surveyor. It is not known whether Bonnin was employed as the builder. Kennedy himself paid the rates for No. 11 (from 1834) but the house was evidently let to tenants.[80]

Westwards of No. 11, Nos. 8-10 North Terrace were leased in July 1833 to John Latchford, esquire, lessee and first occupant of No. 4 Alexander Square, who was evidently financing their building; and in 1834-5 his widow granted sub-leases to Bonnin (of No. 10) and to two other building tradesmen, Wright Maydwell of Alexander Place, Fulham Road, plumber and glazier (No. 9) and John Legeytt Colchester of North Terrace, builder (No. 8).[81] No. 8 was first occupied in 1835 and Nos. 9 and 10 in the following year.[16] The design of the houses is basically as prescribed in the agreement, though Nos. 9 and 10 have bowed ground-floor windows,* and at the latter house the two upper floors project as a canted bay ill-related to the ground-floor front. In the early 1860's, when No. 8 was in the hands of the proprietors of the Turkish baths recently opened on the site of No. 2 Alexander Place (see page 85), it was extended over its back garden to make an entrance from North Terrace to the 'private baths'.[82]

Occupants

Most of the houses built under Bonnin's agreement were occupied within a year of their being leased by the ground landlord, and by 1836 every house on the estate had been taken.[16] From 1833 some of the residents had been deemed worthy of inclusion in *Boyle's Court Guide*, and the respectability of the development as a whole is confirmed by the returns of the census of 1841, where 65 per cent of the householders in the four principal streets (including the square) described themselves as of independent means.[83] Among those who did deign to give their occupations the professions were represented by an accountant, a barrister, a surgeon and a student at law (William Hazlitt, son of the essayist, at what is now No. 4 Alexander Place[84]); the armed services were represented by a naval man, and 'trade' by a wine merchant, a bookseller, a mine agent, and a navy agent. There were also several 'clerks', and one artist (Thomas Harper) at No. 23 Alexander Square. Most families had one or two servants (generally female) living in, and in the four-storey houses in Alexander Square the number was usually either two or three.

Among the nineteenth-century inhabitants of this part of the estate were few interesting or well-known names, although one or two architects occur. There is a Blue Plaque in Alexander Square to the younger George Godwin, whose family's long association with No. 24 has already been described. In 1841 the young Edward Charles Hakewill, architect son of Henry Hakewill, was living at No. 17 Alexander Square, where his widowed mother had taken up residence in 1839 (later he had a house of his own at No. 8 Thurloe Square);[85] and in the early 1880's Herbert Gribble occupied No. 10 Alexander Square, no doubt on account of its proximity to the Oratory, which was then building.[86]

Not many of Brompton's large theatrical community chose to live on the Alexander estate and some of the few who did are mentioned in the Appendix at the end of the volume. One intriguing figure, whose presence as a lodger at No. 23 Alexander Square is revealed only in the census of 1851, is a thirty-year-old Irishman calling himself Dion Page. Married, with an eighteen-year-old Spanish-born wife, 'Jessey', Page gave his designation as 'gentleman and dramatic author', and this description, taken together with Page's date of birth and unusual Christian name, suggests that he may have been the Irish dramatist Dion Boucicault living incognito.[87]

At No. 3 South Terrace the first occupant, from 1829 until 1832, was William Glascock, a naval captain and author of several now-forgotten works of fiction, 'whose pen', in the opinion of T. Crofton Croker, 'has enriched the nautical novel literature of England with the same racy humour which has distinguished his professional career.' In 1832 Glascock moved to No. 21 Alexander Square where he resided until 1834.[88]

Other residents have included the nurseryman Samuel Harrison at No. 12 Alexander Square from 1830 until his bankruptcy in 1832,[16] and the journalist G. A. H. Sala, who was briefly the occupant of No. 1 Alexander Square in *c.* 1870-1.[57]

The Estate in the 1830's

The failure and bankruptcy of Harrison's nursery in 1832 presented Alexander with an unexpectedly early opportunity to press ahead with the development of the area to the west of Alexander Square, Harrison's lease having been not due to expire until the end of 1842.[89] But although the nursery ground was repossessed there was no immediate development, unlike on the adjoining Smith's Charity estate where some of the land formerly in Harrison's occupation was being laid out for building in 1833 (see page 92). In both cases the advice as to whether to proceed or not would have been Basevi's, as surveyor to the two

---

*The bay window at No. 8 is perhaps not the original.

estates, and it may be that at a slack period for the building industry in London generally, he was trying to limit the amount of land being made available to builders in order to reduce the risk of overbuilding. If he seemed to be favouring the Smith's Charity estate it was probably because no significant development had taken place there for some thirty years. Whatever the reason for holding back on Alexander's property, seven years elapsed between the granting of the last leases under the 1826 agreement (in September 1833), and the first moves to develop the area to the west early in 1840.

The Western Grammar School

In 1835, however, a small piece of Harrison's former nursery at the west end of North Terrace was used to provide a new site for the Western Grammar School, which had hitherto been occupying premises erected by Bonnin on a plot of land at the back of Alexander Square, where the present No. 2 Alexander Place now stands.[90]

Founded in 1828, the Western Grammar School was one of the new independent proprietary schools. The first of these was probably the Liverpool Institute, which had opened only in 1825, and was quickly followed by many others, both in London and the provinces. The new schools were financed by the sale of shares rather like a joint-stock company. Control of the school and of its curriculum was thus placed in the hands of the share-holders or proprietors, who were, of course, frequently the parents. In 1831 The Quarterly Journal concluded that the reason why so many such schools had been established was that for parents it was easier 'to found a school, and make it good, than run the doubtful chance of placing their sons where they may learn nothing to any purpose.'[91]

At the Western Grammar School, where the shares cost £15 apiece, the proprietors were each permitted to hold up to three of the one hundred shares originally available, and had the right to nominate one pupil to the school in respect of each share. They had also to pay nine guineas annually towards the running expenses. The school was managed by an elected committee of proprietors and honorary officers, many of them local residents, under the presidency of Sir Theophilus Lee of Crescent House, Brompton, one of Bonnin's mortgagees.* Other members of the committee included the journalist William Jerdan, the master builder Seth Smith (both of them proprietors), and William Fuller Pocock, the school's honorary architect, who designed the premises in Alexander Place.[93]

The school originally offered an 'efficient system of Education' using the 'Madras system ... practised at Charterhouse'. This was the method, also known as the monitorial system or the system of mutual instruction, by which the masters taught only the monitors who in turn passed on the instruction they had received to their school-fellows. But it soon proved to be 'inefficient in its application to the course of studies of this institution' by 'comparison with the more ancient and established methods of tuition', and after only four years was abandoned. The school's curriculum included Latin, Greek, French, English language and literature, composition, elocution, mathematics and drawing, with occasional lectures in science and art.[94] Interest in the performing arts was not, however, encouraged, as the actor and local resident John B. Buckstone discovered in 1838. Wishing to place his son at the school, Buckstone applied to become a proprietor and was turned down 'on the ground that I am an actor, and that such a person in a public school would incite in the boys a desire to see plays, which would unsettle their minds'.[95]

At first the teaching was free of any religious or denominational bias, thereby reflecting the interdenominational character of the early committee, which included several prominent Nonconformists (Smith and Pocock) as well as ordained ministers of the Church of England. In 1836, however, the proprietors applied to be taken into union with King's College, London, and in order to be accepted the school had to adopt an Established Church stance. Thereafter the headmaster and permanent staff had to be practising members of the Church of England, and pupils received instruction in 'the doctrines and duties of Christianity as taught by the Established Church'.[96]

According to a report in The Morning Post the proprietors' decision to erect new premises in North Terrace was occasioned by the imminent expiry of the lease of their building in Alexander Place.[92] This explanation, however, does not quite fit the known facts, for no lease had been granted, but the report may perhaps refer to some difficulty over the tenure of the old building, which in the absence of the school's records cannot now be determined. Nor is there evidence to show why Alexander and his surveyor were willing to see North Terrace turned into a permanent cul-de-sac, unless, of course, they found compensation in the prospect of a handsome building to close the vista down the street.

As honorary architect Pocock was responsible both for designing the new school, to which he gave an impressive façade in his favourite Greek Doric style, and for supervising its construction. The foundation stone was laid in June 1835, the ceremony being attended by both the architect and the (unnamed) builder, and under the stone was placed a plaque bearing Pocock's name and the inscription 'Bromptoniae et Musarum Gratiâ Idibus Junii — A.D. 1835'.[92] The cost of the new premises, or at any rate some part of it, was defrayed out of a building fund created by levying a charge of £1 per annum on the proprietors.[97]

*A later statement that the school was founded under the patronage of Earl Cadogan appears to be incorrect.[92] Apart from the fact that there is no patron named in an early list of honorary officers, the second Earl, who held the title from 1807 until his death in 1832, was a certified lunatic. His successor, the third Earl, did, however, become patron of the school.

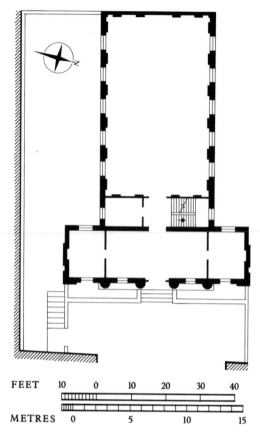

FEET   10   0   10   20   30   40

METRES   0   5   10   15

Fig. 18. Western Grammar School, North Terrace, plan as built.
W. F. Pocock, architect, 1835-9

That the builder was not Bonnin is clearly demonstrated by an incident relating to the wall which under the terms of the 1826 agreement he had previously erected across the west end of North Terrace where it abutted on Harrison's nursery. In order to obtain access to the school site from North Terrace the wall had to be taken down, and on 25 May 1835 this was duly effected. But its removal was evidently done without Bonnin's consent for on the same day he and his workmen erected a temporary wooden fence in its place, and a fortnight later the temporary fence was replaced by a permanent new dwarf wall with iron railings. This new wall was allowed to remain until the school building was completed in March 1836, when Alexander had it removed. Once again Bonnin responded with another temporary wooden fence, soon followed by the building of a solid brick wall completely shutting off the new school from North Terrace. In the summer of 1836 Alexander sued Bonnin in the Court of Common Pleas, but the final verdict of the Court, given in 1838, was for the latter. The dispute seems to have been settled privately later and the wall was eventually removed for good.[98]

In August 1839 Alexander granted an eighty-year lease of the site jointly to Pocock and Joseph Fuller of Stewart's

Grove, Chelsea, esquire, presumably on behalf of the proprietors.[99] Whether the new building had by then been brought into use is not clear, for it was not until 1843 that the school began to pay rates on its new premises and stopped paying them on the old ones. On the other hand the old building in Alexander Place, which was subsequently converted into a Nonconformist chapel, was hired out to a congregation of Baptists from 1838, though perhaps only on Sundays. At the time of the 1841 census the building in North Terrace was in the care of a 'janitor'.[100]

Only the front part of the school still survives. This is the pedimented stucco-faced building at the head of North Terrace, which is now occupied as a private house. It is five bays wide and two storeys high over a basement, but little more than one room deep (Plate 43a, b). This part of the building may perhaps have served as the headmaster's house.* Behind was a large hall or schoolroom (see fig. 18), which may originally have been open to the roof. (Such an arrangement was better suited to the Madras system of teaching, which did not require the provision of separate classrooms, than to the 'established methods of tuition' to which the school had recently returned.) By the 1920's the back building contained at least two storeys[102] and had probably undergone extensive alteration.

The Western Grammar School closed in 1912, but its last headmaster, the Reverend Elias James Huelin, who had held the post for more than fifty years, continued to live there until his death in 1917 at the age of eighty-eight. The building was subsequently used as a furniture repository.[103] The conversion of the site into two private residences in 1927-9 is described on pages 84-5.

The Development of the Thurloe Square Area

The dispute over the wall in North Terrace did not lead to any lasting breach between Bonnin and H. B. Alexander, and within a few years both Bonnin and his son James were playing leading roles in the early development of Thurloe Square.

The first intimation that the ten acres or so of ground repossessed by Alexander after Harrison's bankruptcy in 1832 was to be laid out for building came in April 1840 when Bonnin applied to the Westminster Commissioners of Sewers to build a sewer along the south side of 'a new square proposed to be laid between Pelham Road [now Street] and Old Brompton Road . . . intended to be called Thurloe Square'. This sewer was to continue eastwards 'along a new road about to be formed' — the western half of South Terrace — and to connect at its west end with the sewer in Pelham Place.[104] Bonnin's application was accompanied by a printed, though

*The census of 1861 shows the school premises occupied by the headmaster and his family, two teachers and two house servants.[101]

undated, plan showing the proposed layout of the development drawn up by H. B. Alexander's estate surveyor, George Basevi.[105] This layout, which is virtually that built, calls for little comment except to note that at this early stage Basevi envisaged more, and therefore smaller, houses in the square itself — sixty-two as compared with fifty-six when first completed; while in the 'new road' entering the west side of the square (now Thurloe Street), where forty houses were later built, the plan calls for only fifteen 'cottages', ranged in two terraces with very substantial gardens.

Basevi himself is known to have provided the designs for the houses in Thurloe Square, and there is a strong probability that he did the same for a row of 'villas' in Thurloe Place of which four (now Nos. 18-21) still survive. But there is no evidence that he was the architect of any of the other houses erected on the estate during the period of his surveyorship. Similarly on the Smith's Charity estate Basevi is only known to have designed the more important groups of houses, for example Pelham Crescent and Egerton Crescent.

Here on the Alexander estate the development continued on conventional lines, under building leases granted by H. B. Alexander for terms of between eighty and eighty-five years. But instead of placing the responsibility for the whole in the hands of a single builder, as his father had done with Bonnin senior in 1826, Alexander, no doubt on Basevi's advice, appears to have entered into separate agreements with several builders.[106]

In the course of this development, which was spread over a decade though concentrated in the period between 1840 and 1846, 149 new houses and two mews were erected on the estate. Together they yielded ground rents totalling nearly £1,200 a year, a sum equivalent to about £120 an acre. This was perhaps rather more than Alexander would have received if he had entrusted the work to a single builder. (On the Smith's Charity estate in the early 1840's the developer C. J. Freake successfully offered a ground rent equivalent to just over £50 an acre for the large plot of land where Onslow Square was subsequently built.)

Although Bonnin and his son James Bonnin, junior, were still prominent during the early stages of this new phase of development, three other builders were also very much to the fore, and after about 1843 they had almost all the work in their hands. These were Thomas Holmes, John Gooch, junior, and Henry William Atkinson.

Between them these three were responsible for the west side of Thurloe Square, the whole of Thurloe Street, and Thurloe Place between York Cottages and the Hoop and Toy public house. Holmes and Gooch make their début on the estate in 1842 as the builders of Nos. 12-16 (consec.) Thurloe Place, a short terrace of five houses immediately to the east of Thurloe Square.[107] They were both young, Holmes being only twenty-one, and Gooch twenty-four; both their fathers were in the building trade,

and they may even have been related by marriage. (Holmes's father, Lauret, was a builder and stonemason of John (now Crawford) Street, Edgware Road, who in the late 1830's and early '40's was involved in the development of part of the Bishop of London's estate in Paddington.[108])

In 1842 Thomas Holmes was the building lessee of a house in Norland Square in northern Kensington, and in 1845, while still heavily engaged on the Alexander estate, he agreed to develop the whole of Hereford Square on the Day estate in Gloucester Road.[109] During these years his address was in Belgrave Street South (now Lower Belgrave Street), where he is variously described as mason, statuary and builder. On both the Alexander and Day estates much of the finance for his building operations was supplied by a local resident, George Pinckney Whitfield (successively the occupant of No. 9 Alexander Square, 1841-7, No. 27 Thurloe Square, 1847-54, and No. 27 Hereford Square, 1854-6), who had also lent money to Holmes's father. A Yorkshireman in his late fifties, Whitfield is described as an 'independent' in the census of 1841, and ten years later as a 'proprietor of houses'.[110] On the Alexander estate nearly all the houses built by Holmes were leased in the first instance to Whitfield and subsequently re-leased by him to Holmes or the latter's nominees.

Whitfield's financial support did not prevent Holmes in 1847 from following Bonnin senior into the bankruptcy court, a fate which also overtook John Gooch in the same year.[111] Later, however, both he and Holmes recovered, and in 1851 Gooch (already a widower at the age of thirty-three) was describing himself as a builder employing four men. He was then living with his father in Montpelier Street, where a few months later he died.[112]

Unlike Gooch and Holmes, who were both Londoners by birth, Henry William Atkinson came from the provinces. Born in Salisbury, he was aged about thirty-four in 1842. He managed to avoid bankruptcy in 1847, and in 1851, when he described himself as a builder employing four men, he was engaged in erecting some of the very big houses round the east crescent of The Boltons.[113] From 1845 to 1851 he lived at No. 35 Cheyne Walk, Chelsea.[57] Another builder, John Atkinson, of Queen Street, Chelsea, who was doubtless a relation, witnessed several of the leases granted to H. W. Atkinson, and in one case (that of No. 6 Thurloe Street) was himself the recipient of the building lease.

South Terrace and Alexander Place

The first houses to be built on this part of the Alexander estate were in South Terrace and Alexander (then Alfred) Place, both newly extended westwards to connect with Thurloe Square. Now numbered 10-22 (even) and 13-33 (odd) South Terrace and 9-19 (odd) and 12-22 (even) Alexander Place, these houses contrast sharply with the earlier ranges in these streets by reason of their greater height and somewhat austere aspect. Rising to four full storeys (over basements), they have stuccoed ground floors, jointed to imitate stone, above which are three storeys of the plainest brickwork surmounted by a stuccoed cornice. The front entrances are flanked by Doric pilasters. Each house is two bays wide and conventionally planned. The ranges are contiguous with the earlier houses but set back further from the roadway. At three of the four junctions of the older and newer ranges this set-back is partly concealed by a portico or porch. It is difficult to believe that Basevi had anything to do with the design, apart from giving his approval, and none of the houses have studded front doors.

In South Terrace, where building began in 1840, all but two of the houses were leased in the first instance to Stephen Phillips, a timber merchant who lived in Clerkenwell and had a business address at No. 76 New Broad Street, City. He was a big investor in suburban building developments in Islington, Paddington and Kensington, and an important source of finance for the Bonnins on both the Alexander and Smith's Charity estates.[114]

On the south side of South Terrace James Bonnin, junior, was evidently the principal builder, being the lessee either directly from Alexander, or indirectly from Phillips, of Nos. 13-25 (odd) and No. 33 in 1840-1.[115] Another builder here was Henry Thomas Adams of Rutland Terrace, Brompton, to whom Phillips sub-leased No. 27 in 1841.[116] Some of the houses were first occupied in 1841, and apart from No. 25 the rest had filled up by the end of 1844.[16]

On the north side five houses (now Nos. 12-20 even) were erected by John Chapman of Marlborough Road, Chelsea, builder.[117] Of these Nos. 12 and 14 were sub-leased by Phillips to Chapman in 1842-3, and, after the latter's death in August 1843, sub-leases of Nos. 18 and 20 were granted to his brother-in-law and acting executor, the builder Thomas Holmes.[118] The two other houses on the north side, flanking Chapman's five and now numbered 10 and 22, were sub-let respectively to James Buckley of Onslow Place, Brompton, plumber, in 1841, and John Thorne of Caroline Street, Pimlico, builder, in 1844.[119] Nos. 10-22 were first occupied between 1842 and 1845, John Chapman being briefly the first resident of No. 12, from 1842 until his death.[16]

In Alexander Place, where James Bonnin, junior, was the main builder,[120] the northern range (Nos. 12-22 even) was erected in 1840-1 and the southern range (Nos. 9-19 odd) in 1840-2. Bonnin himself was the lessee, in December 1840, of Nos. 9 and 11, and, in 1841, of Nos. 12, 14 and 18; and he was the sub-lessee at Nos. 15, 16, 17 and 20.[121] At these last four houses the head lease had been granted, in 1841-2, to Stroud Lincoln, esquire, of Alexander Square, who in addition to the four houses which he is known to have let to Bonnin, also had the head lease of No. 22.[122] Like Stephen Phillips, Stroud

Lincoln was one of the Bonnins' more important financial backers, both on the Alexander estate and more particularly on the Smith's Charity estate. In the 1830's he had provided Bonnin senior with standard mortgages on the security of houses in Alexander Square, where he himself was successively the first occupant of No. 23 (1827-33) and No. 8 (1834-50).[16]

The other lessees in Alexander Place, apart from Bonnin and Lincoln, were James Quance of Marlborough Road, Chelsea, oil and colourman (at No. 13) and Henry Hart of Knightsbridge, house decorator (at No. 19), both leases being dated 1842.[123]

Nos. 9-19 Alexander Place were first occupied between 1841 and 1845, and Nos. 12-22 between 1842 and 1844.[16] From 1848 to 1852 James Bonnin, junior, lived at No. 15. This was the period when he was trying to rebuild his career after his bankruptcy (in 1848), and by 1851 he had regained his position sufficiently to have two women servants living in, while in his business he was employing five men and a clerk in the timber yard.[124]

Behind Nos. 12-22 Alexander Place the ground now occupied by Thurloe Close was laid out in 1842 as a small mews of ten stables. Known as Thurloe Mews, it was built by the younger James Bonnin and Edward Saul of Brompton, carpenter, though at Bonnin's request the lessee, in November 1842, was G. P. Whitfield.[125] This was the first time a mews had been built on the Alexander estate. None had been provided for the houses in Alexander Square, and Basevi had not thought it necessary to include any in his layout plan. Whether or not Thurloe Mews was built with any particular residents in mind, nine of its ten stables were first taken by occupants of houses in Thurloe Square (including Whitfield himself).[16]

The entrance to the mews was by a narrow roadway adjacent to No. 22 Alexander Place, which survives as the approach to Thurloe Close, but which originally continued northwards into Thurloe Place,[126] where the northern end also survives as the private cul-de-sac giving access to Nos. 17 and 17A Thurloe Place. On Basevi's layout it is shown a little to the east of where it was actually constructed, with sites for 'cottages' along its eastern frontage. The connexion between the two ends was severed in 1848 when the middle section of the roadway and some adjoining land behind the Western Grammar School (now part of the site of No. 17A Thurloe Place) were taken to provide extended back gardens at Nos. 26-28 Thurloe Square.[127]

Thurloe Mews was swept away when Thurloe Close was laid out here in 1927 (see page 84).

Thurloe Square

The square was laid out for building in 1840 and the houses erected over a period of some six years. The south side (Nos. 1-12 consec.) was the first to be built, in

Fig. 19. Thurloe Square, elevations, plans and details. George Basevi, architect, 1840-6

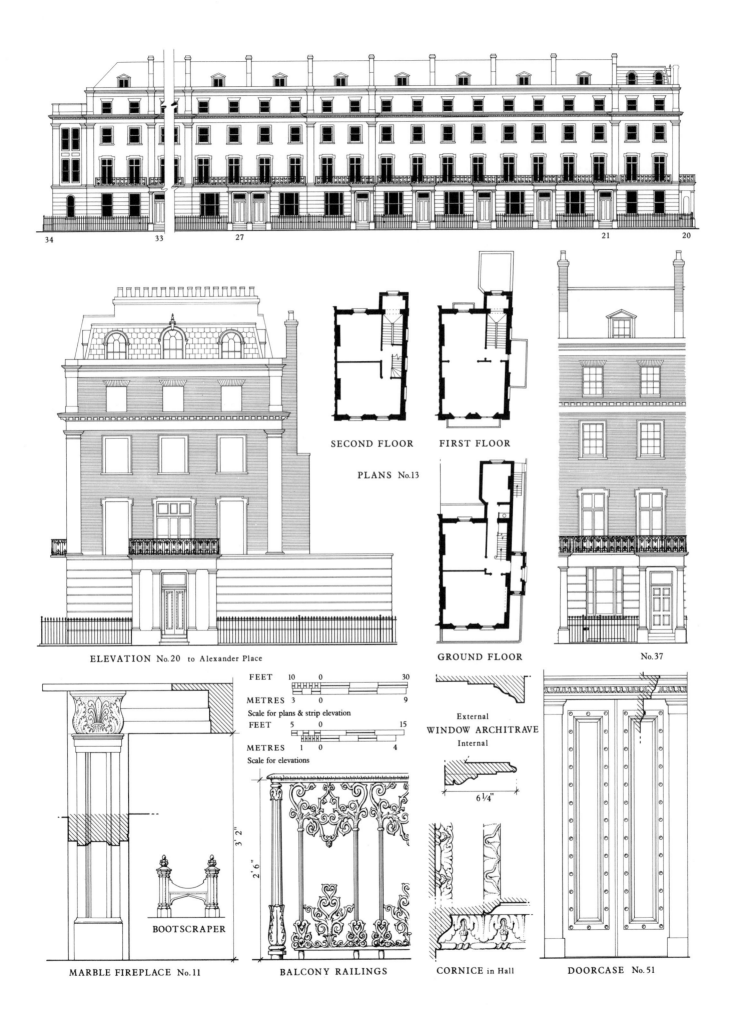

34   33   27   21   20

SECOND FLOOR   FIRST FLOOR

PLANS No.13

ELEVATION No. 20 to Alexander Place

GROUND FLOOR   No. 37

FEET   10   0   30
METRES   3   0   9
Scale for plans & strip elevation

FEET   5   0   15
METRES   1   0   4
Scale for elevations

External
WINDOW ARCHITRAVE
Internal

6¼"

3' 2"

2' 6"

MARBLE FIREPLACE No. 11   BOOTSCRAPER   BALCONY RAILINGS   CORNICE in Hall   DOORCASE No. 51

1840-2. This was followed by the north-east range (Nos. 20-33), which was begun late in 1842 and completed in 1844. All the other ranges were started during 1843. On the west side the southern range (Nos. 45-56) was completed in 1845, the northern range (Nos. 34-44) in 1846; and on the east side the southern range (Nos. 13-19) was also completed in 1846. No. 33 was the first house in the square to be occupied, in 1843, and No. 15 the last, in 1849.[16]

Thurloe Square is the only development on the Alexander estate for which Basevi is definitely known to have been the architect, his authorship being acknowleged in contemporary sources.[128] Although none of his drawings for the square has survived, an undated lithograph (Plate 45a) of the south-east range (Nos. 13-19) evidently represents a stage earlier than the final design, since what it shows differs in several respects from what was built. The whole block is there given a fully stuccoed or (less probably) ashlared front; it has no dormer windows, no balconies overlooking the square, open instead of enclosed porches at Nos. 13 and 19, and six-panel front doors like those used in Alexander Square.

Already at the time the lithographic view was made a sequence of projecting pillared porticoes was intended to be ranged along the front — an early instance of what was about to become the hall-mark of respectable residential London. The earlier design nevertheless has a more traditionally late-Georgian air about it than was to be possessed by Thurloe Square as built, where a different effect was produced by the substitution of grey gaults plentifully dressed with stucco for the uniform facing shown in the lithograph. This emphasized the rectangularity of the design and gave advance warning of some of the more forbidding aspects of later South Kensington. It contrasts with the luxuriance of the neo-rococo ironwork of the balconies (see fig. 19).

The five ranges of houses are not (and never have been) absolutely identical in appearance. The most noticeable variation occurs on the south side, where, instead of pilasters, long and short quoins were used to define the terminal pavilions which here, on the evidence of the sole survivor (at Nos. 11-12), had the width of two houses, not one as elsewhere. This range also differs from most of the square (and conforms to the lithograph) in lacking dormer windows. In the long north-east range the façade is articulated by the projection forward of two of the houses near the centre, each being defined by pilasters (Plate 45c, fig. 19). A unique and certainly original feature is the three-storey stuccoed porch facing the Victoria and Albert Museum on the return face of the north-east corner house (No. 33), which forms a conspicuous object in Thurloe Place (Plate 45b). In the south-west range the ground-floor windows are segmentally arched, not straight-headed, and this range has in the dressing of all the first-floor windows the added frieze and architrave which in the north-west range are used to accentuate the centre and ends.

Apart from the corner houses, which have their entrances on the return fronts (see plan on fig. 19), the houses in Thurloe Square have internal plans that follow the conventional arrangement for two-bay houses with entrance halls at one side. Despite their greater size than the earlier houses on the estate they still have only one staircase (fig. 20). Basevi's characteristic studded doors, here having only two panels (see fig. 19), survive at more than half the houses.

The south side of the square was largely built by James Bonnin, senior; but all twelve houses here were first leased, in 1841-2, to one of his financial backers, the timber merchant Stephen Phillips.[129] In 1841-3 Bonnin took sub-leases from Phillips of Nos. 1, 3-5, 7-10 and 12,[130] which he then promptly mortgaged, many of them either to Robert John Ashton of Pelham Crescent, solicitor, or to Alexander Frederick Ashton of Brompton, gentleman.[131] Phillips sub-let the other three houses in this range to Henry Hart, house decorator (No. 2), James Buckley, plumber (No. 6) and Henry Thomas Adams, builder (No. 11).[132]

Perhaps because the south side was finished well in advance of the rest of the square, these houses remained unoccupied until the latter part of 1845, No. 8 being the last to be taken, in 1846.[16]

In c. 1867 five houses here (Nos. 1-5) were demolished for the construction of the underground railway, and part of this site was subsequently redeveloped as studios, now No. 5 Thurloe Square (see page 81).

The entire east side of the square (with the possible exception of Nos. 13 and 18) was evidently built by James Bonnin, junior, and he himself was in May 1843 the lessee of No. 33, this lease being witnessed by John R. Murfey and Thomas Cary, 'carpenters in the employ of the said James Bonnin jnr'.[133] All the other houses on this side were first leased to G. P. Whitfield, from whom Bonnin took sub-leases of at least twelve.[134] For the north-east range (Plate 45c, fig. 19), where the houses were occupied between 1843 and 1848,[16] the leases to Whitfield are dated 1843 (Nos. 25-32) and 1844 (Nos. 20-24).[135] In the south-east range, the shortest in the square, but the longest in building, the houses were leased over a period of some three and a half years, the first in December 1843 (Nos. 18 and 19) and the last (No. 13) in May 1846.[136] They were first occupied between 1845 and 1849.[16]

After completing their work on the east and south sides of the square neither of the Bonnins played any further part in the development of the Alexander estate. This was presumably by their own volition, as they had in 1843 entered into fresh commitments on the Smith's Charity estate (see page 97), which doubtless absorbed the greater part of their attention thenceforward.

The development was briefly noticed for the first time in *The Builder* in November 1843, when one builder was singled out for mention by name among those then engaged on the work. This was not, as might have been expected, either of the Bonnins but Thomas Holmes.[137]

In Thurloe Square Holmes built nine houses (Nos. 34-42) in the north-west range where work started in 1843.[138] He himself was the lessee of No. 42, and he was the first occupant, in 1845-7, of No. 36, this latter house having been first leased, in 1844, to G. P. Whitfield, as were Nos. 34-35, 37-38 and, in 1845, Nos. 39-41.[139]

At the southern end of this range No. 44 was evidently built by H. W. Atkinson, who was the lessee of the house from H. B. Alexander in September 1845.[140] But at the adjoining No. 43 the identity of the builder is uncertain. According to the district surveyor in 1845 it was Evan Jones of Marlborough Road, Chelsea, a builder not otherwise known to have been involved in the development.[141] But when the house was leased, in January 1846, to a widow living in Knightsbridge, one of the witnesses was the builder John Gooch, junior, who had also witnessed Atkinson's lease of No. 44 and may perhaps have been involved in the building of both these houses.[142]

In the south-west range, which was leased between 1843 and 1845, Gooch was the builder of Nos. 45-48, 50 and 51 (though the lessee of No. 48, in 1844, was the house decorator Henry Hart), and Atkinson, who had applied to lay the drains at all the houses, the builder of Nos. 49 and 52-56.[143] Gooch's nephew, William Gooch, a builder, of Albert Terrace, Knightsbridge, witnessed some of the leases, as did the builder John Atkinson, and both men were probably involved in assisting their respective namesakes.

In the south-west range the houses were occupied between 1844 and 1846, and in the north-west range between 1845 and 1848.[16] Five houses at the southern end of the west side (Nos. 52-56) were demolished for the underground railway in c. 1867.

With the possible exception of the south-west range, all the houses on the east and west sides, including those at the corners, originally had a single pedimented dormer window overlooking the square (see Plate 45b and fig. 19), and a few, for example Nos. 16, 26, 33, 37 and 41, still retain this feature. At some of the corner houses, however, these original dormers were soon displaced by prominent round-headed windows set in steeply pitched mansard roofs (see for example No. 20 in Plate 45c). When this was done is not generally recorded, but at No. 34 it took place between 1856 and 1861.[144] A rather distant view of the south and east sides of the square in c. 1872 shows only Nos. 19 and 20 (and perhaps also No. 13) with mansard roofs and round-headed windows, all the other houses on the east side still having their original dormers.[145]

The communal garden of nearly two acres in the centre of the square was laid out informally with shrubs and small trees, though not quite along the lines suggested by Basevi in his original plan, which had envisaged two enclosures separated by a road linking Alexander Place and Thurloe Street. All the lessees in the square were granted the privilege, 'under due regulations', of walking in the

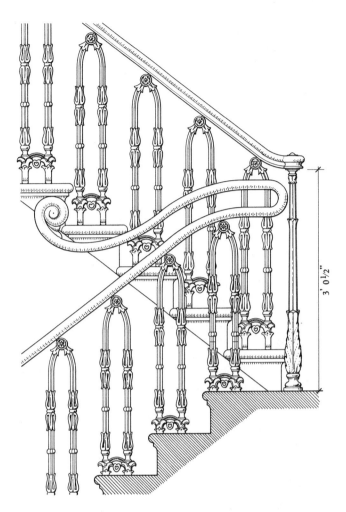

Fig. 20. No. 37 Thurloe Square, detail of staircase

communal garden, which was to be maintained out of an annual charge levied on the lessees of £3 10s. This money was also to cover the cost of maintaining the roadway and lighting the square. The original iron railings around the enclosure were removed during the war of 1939-45 and their replacements, which were erected in 1977 by Mr. Ian Anstruther, are of a slightly different pattern.

The nature of the occupation of the houses in the square when they were still recently built is shown by the census of 1851.[146] On the night of the census only four of the fifty-six houses were either uninhabited or in the care of servants, and many were still in the occupation of the first residents. On average each house contained six or seven occupants, of whom two or three were servants.

Over half of the householders were pursuing (or had retired from) careers in the professions or in trade and business. In the former category the law was well represented with four practising barristers (among them William Digby Seymour, who lived at No. 29), an attorney, and a barrister not in practice who described himself as 'retired judge Slave Trade department'. This was the forty-six-year-old resident at No. 56, Michael S. Melville. Banking, medicine, insurance and accounting all had at least one representative. At No. 49 the householder was the Inspector-General of Inland Revenue, William Garnett, author of a *Guide to Property and Income Tax*, and next door to him at No. 50 lived the Principal Committee Clerk of the House of Commons, Robert Chalmers.

About a dozen householders could be said to be in trade or business. These included a bookseller (David Murray, at No. 4, who was also a brewer and employed four men), a cheesemonger, a tobacco manufacturer and 'hop merchant master', a distiller, a retired brewer, a coal merchant and an engraver.

The armed services were represented by a naval captain (later Admiral Sir Edward Belcher, the first occupant of No. 22[16]), and by two army officers, one of them retired. A third retired army man was absent from his house on the night of the census. This was Lieutenant-Colonel H. B. Smith, formerly of the Madras cavalry. He was the first occupant of No. 34, which he had bought from Holmes (the builder) and G. P. Whitfield (the lessee) for £1,660 in October 1845, Holmes receiving £1,500 and Whitfield £160.[147] In the conveyance the house is said to have been 'very much added to and improved by Thomas Holmes'. In 1846 Smith incurred the displeasure of the ground landlord, H. B. Alexander, by erecting an observatory on top of his house without permission — perhaps the box-like structure just visible above the cornice in Plate 45b. 'I will not, as it is done, object to it', said Alexander in a testy letter to Mrs. Smith, ' — tho' it ought not to have been done without previous assent from me and approval by my Surveyor. I hope this will not be forgotten in the future.'[148]

Two of the householders in 1851 were clergymen: Guillaume Daugars, minister at the French Protestant Church in St. Martin's-le-Grand, whose establishment at No. 13 consisted of himself, his wife, five daughters and a sister-in-law, but no living-in servants; and Richard Boyne of the established church, who 'not having the care of Souls' lived in retirement with his wife and son at No. 18 in the care of one male and four female servants.

Another ten householders (seven of them women) described themselves as fundholders or annuitants, while seven (including two who also described themselves as fundholders) derived their income from land or houses, or both, among them G. P. Whitfield, who lived at No. 27. One of the 'fundholders' was the entomologist and conchologist, Thomas Vernon Wollaston, the occupant of No. 25 from 1849 until 1855.[149]

Other householders included a lodging-house keeper (at No. 42, where two lodgers were in residence); two gentlemen describing themselves only as Master of Arts (one from each of the two ancient universities); an actor, Thomas P. Cooke (at No. 35); and the professor of Italian language and literature at University College, London. This last was Antonio Carlo Napoleone Gallenga who

occupied No. 21 from 1847 until 1851.[16] Born in Parma, Gallenga had been forced into exile after taking part in political activity in Italy in 1830, and in 1846 he had become a British subject. As well as holding various academic posts, both here and abroad, he was successively a newspaper correspondent, leader writer for *The Times*, author, and a deputy in both the Piedmontese Parliament and the Italian Chamber.[150]

Other residents of Thurloe Square have included the architect and district surveyor, Edward Charles Hakewill, who lived at No. 8 from 1854 to 1867,[151] and Sir Henry Cole, the first director of the South Kensington (now Victoria and Albert) Museum. Cole moved into No. 33, for which he had offered a rent of £250 a year, on 22 December 1873, having resigned from the museum in the previous May. In the following June he was making unspecified alterations at the house. He left it in 1877.[152]

Thurloe Place

The development described here comprises all the houses built in the 1840's along the south frontage of what was then called Old Brompton Road, between York Cottages on the east and the Hoop and Toy public house on the west. These buildings did not form one continous range, Thurloe Square making a sizeable break in the middle, and the two parts were originally distinguished as Thurloe Place and Thurloe Place West, each with its separate sequence of house numbers.

Basevi had not intended to have any north-facing houses along the eastern section of Thurloe Place. On his layout the frontage here is marked by a wall enclosing the garden of the northernmost of a row of seven 'cottages' facing a narrow roadway which linked Thurloe Place with Alexander (then Alfred) Place. This roadway, which extended behind the back gardens of the houses in the north-east range of Thurloe Square, was laid out in about 1842,[126] and (as previously mentioned) its northern end still survives as the cul-de-sac leading southwards out of Thurloe Place next to No. 16. But the seven cottages were never built, and instead of a garden wall next to Old Brompton Road there arose a terrace of five houses, originally Nos. 1-5 (consec.) and now Nos. 12-16 (consec.) Thurloe Place.

Begun in 1842, they were built by John Gooch, junior, and Thomas Holmes, and first occupied by the end of 1843.[16] Nos. 13 and 14 were leased directly to Gooch in November 1842, while at the same time two (Nos. 12 and 16) of Holmes's three houses were leased to his financial backer, G. P. Whitfield. Holmes's third house (No. 15) was leased in the following year to its first occupant, Edward Paul Bocquet of Robert Street, Adelphi, esquire.[153] In 1843 Gooch sold his two leases to a furnishing undertaker, Abel Birch, of Middle Row, Knightsbridge, who in 1851 was living at No. 13.[154]

This short range is broadly similar in style to the brick and stucco manner of Basevi's Thurloe Square and the

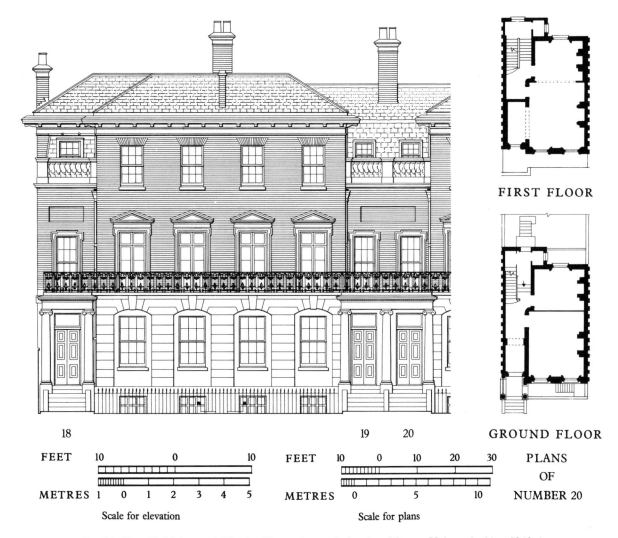

FIRST FLOOR

GROUND FLOOR

18

19   20

FEET   10   0   10   FEET   10   0   10   20   30   PLANS
                                                                                        OF
METRES 1   0   1   2   3   4   5   METRES   0   5   10   NUMBER 20

Scale for elevation   Scale for plans

Fig. 21. Nos. 18-20 (consec.) Thurloe Place, plans and elevation. Thomas Holmes, builder, 1843-4

studded two-panel front doors are identical. There are, however, no columned porches, and for its date the ironwork is decidedly old-fashioned. Originally all five houses contained only three full storeys over basements with a dormer window in the roof,[155] but subsequently (probably in the 1870's) the two end houses, Nos. 12 and 16, which project forward from the central three and have channelled stucco quoins, were each given an extra full storey (in a matching style) and steep mansard roofs with two dormers.

Holmes was doubtless also the builder of a pair of very small semi-detached cottages fronting on to the narrow roadway leading south out of Thurloe Place. These were leased to Whitfield in 1843, and first occupied later that year.[156] Originally called Thurloe Cottages, they survive only in a completely recast form as the present No. 17 Thurloe Place (see page 83).

In 1878-9 the Kensington Vestry planted plane trees along the eastern section of Thurloe Place between the north-east corner of Thurloe Square and No. 6 York Cottages. The cost (and that of similar planting elsewhere in the parish) was defrayed out of Kensington's share (£100) in a private gift for this purpose made available in 1878 to ten metropolitan parishes.[157]

The western part of Thurloe Place, from the north-west corner of Thurloe Square to the Hoop and Toy public house, was developed between 1843 and 1847. It originally comprised five pairs of linked semi-detached 'villas' (instead of the five pairs of semi-detached but unlinked 'cottages' proposed on Basevi's plan), a short terrace of four two-storey houses (Nos. 28-31 Thurloe Place), and two very plain three-storey houses (Nos. 32 and 33).

Of the ten 'villas' only four still survive (now Nos. 18-21 Thurloe Place), and these are perhaps the most distinguished of any of the original houses on the Alexander estate (Plate 46b, fig. 21) although, facing north, they are not much noticed. Their design cannot with certainty be ascribed to Basevi. But in November

1843 *The Builder* told its readers that 'Beautiful villas', as well as 'a splendid square', were being built on Alexander's estate 'under the direction of Mr. Basevi, the architect.'[137] The 'villas' are doubtless those under construction in Thurloe Place West, since this description is inapplicable to any other houses on the estate. That Basevi's 'direction' here amounted to architectural authorship is suggested partly by the quality of the design and partly by the fact that he is known to have been the architect of the 'splendid square' (Thurloe Square) with which the villas are coupled in *The Builder*'s comment.

The builders of these ten houses, originally numbered 1-10 (consec.) Thurloe Place West and later Nos. 18-27 (consec.) Thurloe Place, were Thomas Holmes (Nos. 18-23) and John Gooch, junior (Nos. 24-27). All Holmes's houses were, as usual, leased to G. P. Whitfield, the leases being dated in July, October and November 1843, while those leased to Gooch were granted in December of the same year.[158] Some of the houses were occupied in 1844 and the rest in 1845.[16] Nos. 22-26 were demolished for the extension of Exhibition Road in *c*. 1867, and No. 27 in *c*. 1895.

After the completion of No. 27 there was no more building in Thurloe Place West until 1846, when John Gooch, junior, assisted by H. W. Atkinson, started work on six houses. These included a short terrace later renumbered 28-31 (consec.) Thurloe Place, for which the leases were granted to the builders in February and June 1847.[159] Originally composed of four two-bay houses (No. 28 was demolished in *c*. 1895), this terrace is only two storeys high over a basement, with a stuccoed ground storey, and a deep bracketed cornice which was probably once crowned by a balustrade. Nos. 29 and 31 have had single-storey shops built out in front, and only No. 30 still retains its original Doric porch and attractive area-iron-work. Among the first occupants of this range was the history painter James Clarke Hook, who took up residence at No. 30 (then No. 13 Thurloe Place West) in 1848.[160]

The architect of Nos. 28-31 was John Blore (1812-82), a local man living in Michael's Place, whom Alexander had appointed as estate surveyor after Basevi's accidental death in October 1845.[161] The son of an 'experienced Builder of many years' standing in this neighbourhood' — perhaps the builder C. H. Blore of York Cottages mentioned on page 62 — John Blore had received what he himself described as 'the basis of my practical education' in his father's workshops and on his father's buildings, before being articled for five years to the architect Robert Wallace in 1827. During that time he worked on some of Wallace's best buildings, including the Athenaeum, Post Office and Royal Hotel in Derby. Blore's own buildings in Kensington comprise, among others, Hereford Square, Drayton Terrace and Drayton Grove (all on the Day estate), and in Chelsea, on the Colvill

estate, Anderson, Coulson and Lincoln Streets and a prominent range in the King's Road built as part of the same development.[162]

Blore himself claimed responsibility for a 'range of residences called Thurloe Place West' in the curriculum vitae which he submitted with his unsuccessful application for the post of Superintending Architect to the Metropolitan Board of Works in 1855. This certainly included Nos. 28-31 Thurloe Place, but may not have extended to Nos. 32 and 33, two plain three-storey houses erected in 1846-7 by Gooch and Atkinson. These were first occupied by a baker (at No. 33 in 1847) and a grocer (at No. 32 in 1848); but the shops which now mask the ground storey of both houses were added much later.[163] Westwards of No. 33 the Hoop and Toy public house was completely rebuilt in 1844 (see page 60).

Thurloe Street

Until it was renamed in 1939 Thurloe Street was known as Alfred Place West, perhaps on account of Basevi's original intention to link it directly with Alfred (now Alexander) Place by means of a road cutting Thurloe Square garden in two. Building began here in the autumn of 1844[164] and by the end of 1846 most of the houses had been leased, though (for reasons explained below) there was a delay in completing some of the houses on the north side, where No. 25 was not leased until January 1851.

On the south side, the first to be completed, there were originally two terraces, each comprising nine houses. The three central houses in each range (Nos. 8-12 and 26-30 even) were three storeys high over basements, and the flanking houses generally two storeys high.* The central houses are conventionally planned with side hallways and dog-leg staircases at the rear. But the surviving two-storey houses have a less commonly encountered plan in which there are two back rooms occupying the whole width of the house, and the staircase, starting at the rear of the hallway, rises steeply towards the front of the house. In elevation the two-storey houses have many similar characteristics to Nos. 27-37 (odd) Egerton Terrace on the Smith's Charity estate (see Plates 43d and 51c), which were erected at precisely the same time and also have unconventional plans (see page 100). Different builders appear to have been involved, although H. W. Atkinson, one of the principal operators in Thurloe Street, was also building elsewhere in Egerton Terrace. A common denominator was Basevi's surveyorship of both estates, though the houses would not have been finished at the time of his death.

The eastern range, Nos. 2-18 (even) Thurloe Street, was begun in July 1845 and substantially completed by the following January. In the records of the district surveyor H. W. Atkinson (wrongly called J. W. Atkinson) appears as the

---

*A symmetrical arrangement was clearly the intention, though in the eastern (and only surviving) range the three easternmost houses have extra storeys, those at Nos. 2 and 6 being evidently early additions,[165] while that at No. 4 is modern (1981).

builder of all nine houses, but other builders were also involved, including John Atkinson and John Gooch, junior. H. W. Atkinson himself was the lessee from H. B. Alexander of Nos. 2 and 4 (in November 1845) and Nos. 14 and 16 (in May 1846). No. 6 was leased to John Atkinson (in June 1847), Nos. 8-12 to Wright Maydwell, of Alexander Place, Fulham Road, plumber (in November 1845), and No. 18 to John Gooch, junior (in November 1846).[166] The houses were all occupied in 1846-7, two of the first inhabitants being the painter Robert Hannah, at No. 2 (1847-65), and R. W. Skeffington Lutwidge, uncle of Lewis Carroll (Charles Lutwidge Dodgson), at No. 4 (1846-64). Carroll himself often stayed here with his uncle, who was a barrister and a Commissioner in Lunacy, and had a fondness for acquiring new gadgets. After a visit in 1852 Carroll wrote: 'He has as usual got a great number of new oddities, including a lathe, telescope stand, crest stamp, a beautiful little pocket instrument for measuring distances on maps, refrigerator, &c. &c.'* No. 6 was the town house of the actress Marie Litton (Mrs. Wybrow Robertson) who died there in 1884.[167]

The western range (Nos. 20-36 even) was built in 1845-6 by John Gooch, junior, probably with assistance from his nephew William Gooch, also a builder, and H. W. Atkinson, both of whom witnessed some of the leases. All nine houses were leased by Alexander in February and May 1846, eight of them directly to Gooch, and they quickly filled up with occupants.[168] The whole range was demolished for South Kensington Station in c. 1867, but the western end of it can be seen in a photograph of the 1860's showing the construction of the underground railway in Harrington Road (Plate 47a). Just visible is the two-storey bow which graced the west end of No. 36. This, the westernmost house in the range, occupied a triangular site tapering towards the junction with Pelham Street, and was double-fronted. (For the present Nos. 20-34 even Thurloe Street see page 80.)

Between Nos. 18 and 20 was the entrance to Alfred Place Mews, which extended behind both ranges on the south side of the street. Laid out in 1846-7, it contained eighteen stables, the majority being originally leased to the builder, John Gooch, junior.[169] Several of the residents of Thurloe Square were among the first to take stables here.[16] The entire mews was demolished in the late 1860's for South Kensington Station and the underground railway.

On the north side of Thurloe Street there are two ranges of houses, originally contiguous but now separated by Exhibition Road, which was extended southwards into Alfred Place West in c. 1867. To the east Nos. 1-13 (odd) were begun, though not completed, during the lifetime of George Basevi (whether to his designs is not known), while to the west of Exhibition Road Nos. 25-43 (odd) were built after Basevi's death to the designs of his successor, John Blore.

In the eastern range, which originally comprised eleven houses (Nos. 1-21 odd), the buildings are three storeys high over basements and two bays wide, with fully stuccoed if plainish fronts, Ionic porches and a bracketed cornice surmounted by a balustrade — this last feature now surviving in part only at No. 13. There is a continuous balcony at first-floor level, with an iron railing of the same lacy pattern as that used in Thurloe Square. Like the houses opposite on the south side, Nos. 1-13 are set back from the street behind small front gardens. The builders of this range were John Gooch, junior, (with assistance from William Gooch) and Thomas Holmes. Nos. 1-11 (odd), begun late in 1844, were all leased to Gooch in the following January (Nos. 1-5) and May (Nos. 7-11), and were first occupied between 1845 and 1847,[170] Gooch himself being the first ratepayer, from 1845-7, at No. 5, which may have served him for an office as well as a house.† At No. 9 an early occupant (from 1850 until his death in 1887) was the dramatist and novelist, John Palgrave Simpson.[171]

Thomas Holmes began work on the adjoining Nos. 13-21 in 1845, and the houses here were all leased in March and May 1846, the lessees being Holmes's financial backer, G. P. Whitfield (Nos. 15-21) and Henry Hart of Knightsbridge, house decorator (No. 13). Nos. 13-21 filled up with inhabitants in 1847-8.[172]

The contrast in styles between the two ranges on the north side of Thurloe Street has been somewhat diminished by the cutting-through of Exhibition Road in c. 1867, but must have been quite striking when the houses were new and the ranges contiguous. For, as in Thurloe Place West, Blore scorned to continue the style of the houses already erected and produced instead his own more up-to-date designs. His houses are taller — four full storeys over basements, rather than three — and being built mainly of grey Cowley bricks they are unmistakeably Victorian (Plate 47c), whereas Nos. 1-13, though Victorian in date, belong in appearance to the Georgian tradition. Blore did not, however, altogether ignore the earlier houses, giving his range the same channelled-stucco ground storey and Ionic porches; but the ironwork of the balconies is different and there are no front gardens. Blore's terrace, now slightly curtailed by the removal of one house (No. 23) at the east end, was evidently at first symmetrical in its basic composition. It has a central projection three houses in width with the central house (No. 33) projected further forward, and, to judge from the westernmost house at No. 43, which also projects, the now demolished No. 23 (the site of which was thrown into Exhibition Road) formed a balancing pavilion at the eastern end. In the middle house, No. 33, (and also at No.

---

*In 1864 Lutwidge moved from here to No. 101 Onslow Square.[57]
†In 1847-8 he was the ratepayer at No. 28.

43) the three upper storeys have centrally positioned tripartite windows, that on the first floor topped by a small pediment, but as usual Blore was unwilling to sacrifice a conventional ground-floor plan for the sake of his elevation and the symmetrical effect is spoilt by the off-centre porch.* (How Blore composed the ground floor at No. 43 is not known, but here he was able to avoid the problem by placing the entrance on the return front.)

The whole of the western range (Nos. 23-43 odd) was built by Thomas Holmes, who started work at the west end in May 1846, and by August the carcases of four houses (Nos. 37-43) were ready to be leased.[173] The lessee of these, as of all the other houses in the range, was Holmes's financial backer G. P. Whitfield, who sub-leased some of them back to the builder. The leases for Nos. 31-35 followed in December 1846.[174] The extent to which the houses were unfinished at the time of leasing is shown by an agreement which Holmes made in December 1846 to sell No. 41 for £700. Much work was then still outstanding, including the whole of the plastering and the glazing and hanging of the sash windows, all of which Holmes undertook to complete.[175]

The remaining four houses in Blore's terrace (Nos. 23-29) were begun in September or October 1846. But after work had gone on for some six weeks disaster struck, and on 12 November three of the houses, Nos. 23-27, collapsed, killing one of the labourers. (By another account all four fell down.) At the inquest, held nearby in the Hoop and Toy, Thomas Hanniland, a carpenter employed by Holmes, said he thought the cause of the fall was that the houses had been run up too quickly in damp weather. 'They had been only five weeks in erecting, when they ought to have been two months.' Against this, however, the district surveyor, T. L. Donaldson, said that 'a house might as well be run up in six weeks as in six months', and he could not complain of haste. Hanniland said the weather had been very wet and he thought the lower parts were not sufficiently set to bear the weight of the upper parts.[176]

Several witnesses said that since the use of bonding timber in party walls had been prohibited by the recent Building Acts party walls were not so sound as they had previously been. Criticism was also levelled at the iron hoops which Blore had required to be used in the party walls. Hanniland, who (being a carpenter) not surprisingly considered iron an unsatisfactory substitute for timber, thought that the wall would not have buckled if bond timber had been used in it.

Blore, on the other hand, thought that iron, though not as good as timber, was a satisfactory substitute. He blamed the accident on 'the reckless system of running up a heavy weight of materials to the height of twenty feet or more, without any support, and to a number of men running up a scaffold with a wall in such a state'. He also thought the materials were not of the best.

During the investigation Holmes revealed that he was employing Messrs. Emmins to supply the lime and labour while he himself supplied the bricks. On the question of the quality of the materials the foreman of the bricklayers, who had worked for the prominent public-works contractor, Thomas Grissell, said he had used worse mortar on Government buildings, and he could not account for the fall.

Faced with conflicting 'expert' evidence, the 'very intelligent' jury came to the unexceptionable conclusion that the houses fell down because they were not 'securely built'. This the jurymen blamed on the speed of building, the dampness of the weather, the height of the houses and the lack of timber in the party walls. They also believed that 'an effectual supervision of the work in all its divisions was not exercised by the persons having authority over it at the time.'

The whole incident was reported in some detail in *The Builder*, where the editor, George Godwin, delivered himself of some trenchant comments on the working of the Building Acts. He offered no criticism of the builder, Thomas Holmes, however, 'a very respectable man, [who] has executed some dozens of houses under our own eyes'. But it can have been of little comfort to Blore that to avoid 'the chance of being misinterpreted' Godwin decided to 'withhold comment' on Blore's 'share in the transaction', and furthermore identified him as 'the same gentleman who recently thought fit to advertise an impudent piece of special pleading, to contradict a fact stated in our columns.' Godwin added, 'Were we actuated by motives such as he was silly enough to ascribe to us on that occasion, the present occurrence would offer opportunity far too tempting to be passed over'.

As a result of the accident, further compounded no doubt by Holmes's bankruptcy in June 1847, the completion of Nos. 23-29 was delayed by a year or more, and the leases for Nos. 23, 27 and 29 were not granted until December 1847, while that for No. 25 was held back until January 1851, by which time the house was already occupied.[177] Holmes considered the accident to be one of the principal causes of his misfortunes in that immediately afterwards his creditors began to press for payment, thereby forcing him into bankruptcy.[178] It seems also to have cast something of a damper over the other houses in this range, with the result that they all remained unoccupied for several years.[16]

The first inhabitants of these houses included a farmer (with ninety-seven acres), two solicitors, a landed proprietor, a mine owner, a Church of England clergyman ('not having the care of souls'), the proprietor of a boarding school and two widows with private incomes.[179] The boarding school was at No. 39, where on the night of the census in 1851 nine pupils were in residence. Among later occupants were (Sir) J. C. Robinson, superintendent of the art collections at the South Kensington Museum, who

*For another example of this same fault see the centre house of Blore's terrace on the west side of Drayton Gardens, Plate 67a.

lived at No. 33 from 1858 until 1861, and Joseph Aloysius Hansom, the architect and inventor, who first occupied No. 25 in 1867-9 and then moved next door to No. 27 where he remained until *c.* 1872. Hansom's architect son, Joseph Stanislaus Hansom, continued at No. 27 until 1913, though for most if not all of that time this was only his office. In 1888 J. S. Hansom wrote to his patron, the Duke of Norfolk, 'I have spent several hundreds on 27 Alfred Place West.... Now I have got my office back there and have let the upper part, having had to do it all up at a cost of over £100.... My desire to keep house and office together [probably at Palace Gardens Terrace] has been a failure which I shall not repeat.'[180]

South Kensington Station and the Extension of Exhibition Road

In the late 1860's two events occurred which significantly altered the appearance and to some extent the character of the western end of the estate. These were the construction of South Kensington underground station and its approaches, largely on Alexander's property, though also on part of the adjoining Smith's Charity estate, and the related extension of Exhibition Road southwards from Cromwell Road into Alfred Place West (Thurloe Street). In 1864 the Metropolitan Railway Company had obtained Parliamentary authority to extend its line from Notting Hill Gate to a new station at South Kensington; and in another Act, passed at the same time, a new company, the Metropolitan District Railway Company, was authorised to build a line extending eastwards from South Kensington to Tower Hill, and westwards, via Gloucester Road, to join the West London Railway at West Brompton. Both Acts authorised the building of a station at South Kensington and the extension of Exhibition Road.[181]

As the owner of an already developed urban estate H. B. Alexander was naturally concerned to minimise any disturbance to his property, and he had a clause inserted in the Acts requiring the railways to run in covered cuttings where they crossed his land, a rather futile provision as it turned out, for the only two places where the railway was to traverse the estate were at Gloucester Road and South Kensington stations. The former was erected on un-developed land, but at South Kensington the proposed site, at the junction of Alfred Place West and Pelham Street, was already built up. In evidence to a Select Committee of the House of Lords the railway companies' engineer, (Sir) John Fowler, stated that this site had been chosen after consultation with other interested parties, including the Commissioners for the Exhibition of 1851, and the builder C. J. Freake, who had just finished developing part of Alexander's property on the south side of Cromwell Road and in Cromwell Place. But in countering the suggestion that Freake's opposition to the siting of a station next his houses had been a decisive factor he was less than convincing: 'Mr Freake represents a great

number of influential persons in that neighbourhood — The Duke of Rutland and some of his tenants and lessees live in that district, he represents them, and I therefore was very glad to be possessed of Mr Freake's views on the subject.' The attitude of the 1851 Commissioners was known to be uncompromising. They wanted a station in the vicinity because their own recently acquired estate was poorly served by public transport, but they would not have it on their property. When asked if he regarded the Commissioners as rivals Alexander replied 'They are neighbouring but not very neighbourly land owners'.[182]

Alexander himself was really no more neighbourly than the Commissioners, sharing their view that other people's property would make a better site for the station than his own built-up land. A nearby alternative which he favoured was Brompton Hall, an old house in extensive grounds at the corner of Old Brompton Road and Cromwell Lane (Harrington Road).[183] But he was unable to persuade Parliament, or the railway companies, to reconsider their preferred site.

The 1851 Commissioners, not content merely to keep the station off their own land, had clauses inserted in the Acts requiring that it should be used only by passengers, and that the building itself should be of 'an ornamental character'. In 1864 Fowler had told the Select Committee that the railway companies were proposing that the north side should have 'a handsome elevation . . . so that people going down the [extended] Exhibition Road would see a good looking building'; and in 1867, when there was evidently still a possibility that the station would have a frontage to Alfred Place West, or be visible from Exhibition Road, the Commissioners produced a plan for an entrance here looking up Exhibition Road.[184] Had this latter suggestion been carried into effect emerging passengers would at least have been pointed firmly in the direction of museumland. As it is the present two-way exit from the station at what was always a confusing road-junction leaves many passengers bewilderingly disoriented.

To provide the railway companies with the land they required for the new station Alexander had to convey to them all of his houses on the south side of Alfred Place West, the whole of Alfred Place Mews, and twenty-three houses in Thurloe Square, twelve on the west side (Nos. 45-56) and eleven on the south (Nos. 1-11).[185] The loss of part of Thurloe Square was, of course, the greatest blow; but to preserve as far as possible the amenities and character of the square the companies were forbidden to put an entrance to the station there; and where houses in the square were demolished 'an ornamental Wall or Structure' was to be erected 'in lieu thereof'.[186] For the sale of Nos. 1-11 Thurloe Square Alexander received £3,000 from the Metropolitan District Railway.[187]

Occupants of houses required for demolition were individually compensated, many of them in the opinion of *The Building News* claiming 'ridiculously high prices' but receiving 'very little more than one half of the amount claimed'. For No. 52 Thurloe Square £5,250 was sought on the grounds that 'rents had enormously increased of late years, and the Museum at Kensington had added to the value of the houses in the neighbourhood'. Here the displaced householder, a seventy-two-year-old bronchitic, was 'much annoyed' at having to leave his house as he could, so he claimed, 'only breathe freely in the locality'. He had, therefore, been obliged to acquire another house in the square, at No. 24 — on the best side, retorted the railway company. The jury awarded him £3,100, a sum which although considerably less than the claim, nevertheless indicates that the rental value was considered to have doubled in the twenty years since the house was built.[188] In Alfred Place West (Thurloe Street) £1,980 was sought for a house which in 1850 had been bought for just £850. In this case the jury awarded £1,350, less than the railway company had originally offered in compensation.[189]

The station itself was at first to be called Brompton Exchange, but soon acquired the name of South Kensington. Like Gloucester Road Station to its west, it was to be shared between the Metropolitan and the Metropolitan District Railways and laid out jointly for the two companies by Fowler as the common engineer. His original plan seems to have envisaged two sets of double tracks, the northern ones to be used by the Metropolitan and the southern ones by the District Railway. They were to be roofed by a pair of simple curved iron arches, of the type used at other stations along the line, with one span covering either set of tracks and meeting the other upon columns on the central platform.[190]

In 1867-8 the northern tracks only were constructed according to this plan, together with the station building, a simple but pretty essay in the white-brick Italianate style favoured by the two companies (Plate 48a). Metropolitan trains ran west to Notting Hill Gate and District trains east to Westminster Bridge from Christmas Eve, 1868.[191] From 1 August 1870 District trains continued westwards to Gloucester Road, still using the northern tracks at South Kensington but crossing immediately over to the southern tracks as they left the station.[192] Partly to ease the congestion caused by this arrangement, and partly 'to increase the accommodation of visitors to the ensuing International Exhibition', the southern platforms and tracks were added in 1871.[193] By this time separate sidings were deemed necessary for the two companies, between whom relations had cooled. This meant a change in Fowler's original plans, with one siding being provided for the Metropolitan Railway next to their tracks and another for the District Railway to the south of theirs. As a result, the southern arch had to be broader and more elliptical than its northern counterpart. It came to rest on the south side on further columns, with a lean-to roof covering the District Railway's siding.[190]

The original exterior of the booking hall was soon masked from view by shops along Pelham Street (1879-80)

and Alfred Place West (1881).[194] It survived until 1905-6, when the arrangement of the station was affected by the construction of the deep-level Great Northern, Piccadilly and Brompton Railway (Piccadilly Line). The consortium which laid out this line controlled the District Railway and so was able to build its own South Kensington Station adjacent to the District's platforms, with a separate entrance in Pelham Street (Plate 48b). This station, designed by Leslie W. Green, was opened in 1907 (see page 117).[195] The Metropolitan Railway Company took the opportunity to reconstruct the Metropolitan and District Railway station building and concourse and to re-roof the platforms. This was undertaken by the architect George Sherrin, who had been working at High Street, Kensington. Sherrin took down the old station building and arranged a glazed arcade between Thurloe and Pelham Streets with steps down into a new concourse. Round the corner between the two streets, provision was made for roofing over the open tracks and building single-storey shops, though this seems not to have been carried out for a few years. At platform level, Fowler's iron spans were removed, the tracks were exposed to the elements, and small independent wooden roofs on iron columns were put up on each of the platforms.[196] This essentially is the arrangement which still survives.

Of the forty-two houses which Alexander had conveyed to the railway companies for the station only nineteen were in the event demolished, though others had their back gardens curtailed. But the companies were under no obligation to sell the surviving houses back to Alexander, and the majority were subsequently sold off as independent freeholds.* In one or two places where the houses had been demolished the surplus parts of the site were redeveloped. The largest of these was on the south side of Thurloe Street (Alfred Place West) between the station and the narrow passage, just west of No. 18, which is all that survives of the way into Alfred Place Mews. In 1879 Arthur Heald, esquire, of Finborough Road, an accountant with an office in the Strand, was proposing to lease this site from the Metropolitan Railway for a range of buildings comprising eight shops with artists' studios and chambers above. But there were objections and Heald eventually withdrew leaving the development to a builder, John Whittlesea, of St. Stephen's Avenue, Shepherd's Bush, who erected the present Nos. 20-34 (even) Thurloe Street here in 1880-1.[198] Designed in all probability by Whittlesea's surveyor, the architect Edwin George Wyatt, this commonplace row of houses with ground-floor shops (but no studios) in a debased Italianate style, occupies the site where Fowler had in 1864 hoped to see a 'good looking building'. The shops were first occupied (in 1882-3) by a bric-a-brac dealer, a glass manufacturer, bakers, a furrier, tailors, a jeweller, florists and a dairy. A later resident of the houses was Alan Cole, younger son of Sir Henry Cole, and a senior official

---

*A few houses have been repurchased by the Estate, for example, Nos. 9-11 Thurloe Square in 1934.[197]

successively in the Science and Art Department and the Board of Education, who lived at No. 20 from 1894 until 1908.[57]

Whittlesea was also the building lessee (from the Metropolitan Railway Company) of the vacant site on the west side of Thurloe Square, where No. 52 was erected in 1888-9. Here, however, Whittlesea himself was not the builder (perhaps because he was then living in Brighton), and the house was erected for him under contract by Messrs. Cooke and Battson of Airlie Gardens, whose tender, at £1,560, was the lowest submitted. The architect of this rather undistinguished example of the late 'Queen Anne' style was the little-known A. Benyon Tinker.[199] The house was first occupied in 1890.[57]

Just across the road from the site of No. 52, on the south side of Thurloe Square where the five houses west of No. 6 had been demolished, there was another vacant site, difficult to use for houses by reason of its acutely triangular shape, which was taken by the builder William Douglas for a block of seven artists' studios (now No. 5 Thurloe Square). Erected by Douglas between 1885 and 1887,[200] the largely unadorned front which this rather gaunt-looking building presents to the square has big plain north-facing windows and broad stretches of dark-red brickwork. From the west and south the striking wedge shape of the building is very apparent. Plans of the studios (amended several times over) were submitted to the Metropolitan Board of Works on Douglas's behalf by a surveyor, C. W. Stephenson, who is known to have designed other buildings and may have been the architect here.[201] Artists of no great distinction took studios in this building from 1888.

For the extension of Exhibition Road, authorised by the Acts of 1864 and carried out by the railway companies in c. 1867, Alexander had to give up seven houses on the north side of Alfred Place West (between and including the present Nos. 13 and 25 Thurloe Street) and a further seven in Thurloe Place (Nos. 22-28 consec.).[202] The reason for the extension was to provide adequate access from the station to Cromwell Road and parts beyond (particularly the estate of the 1851 Commissioners). Old Brompton Road (Thurloe Place) was thought to be too narrow for this purpose, and Cromwell Place, which was parallel to the proposed extension, was then still a private road which could be shut off at any time, as indeed it was during the Exhibition of 1862.[203]

The frontages of the new road between Thurloe Place and Thurloe Street, originally left undeveloped behind new brick walls,[204] were partially filled up with shops in the early 1870's. On the west side of Exhibition Road Nos. 1-5 (odd) are the more or less unaltered survivors of a row of five single-storey shops, described as 'recently erected' in November 1871, which were designed by E. W. Griffith of Westbourne Grove, architect.[205] Now, and for many years, the premises of Messrs. Lamley and Company Limited, the booksellers, who took over Nos. 1 and 3 in 1879, they were originally occupied in 1872 by a firm of

upholsterers.[57] The two other shops in this row, Nos. 7 and 9 (first occupied by a cigar merchant and a confectioner respectively), were rebuilt in c. 1895-6 together with the south-west corner of Exhibition Road and Thurloe Place. In that redevelopment two of the original houses in Thurloe Place (Nos. 27 and 28) which had survived the cutting through of Exhibition Road were pulled down. The corner block, now numbered 11-17 (odd) Exhibition Road and 25-28 (consec.) Thurloe Place, is a four-storey building with ground-floor shops and shaped gables in the artisan mannerist style of the early seventeenth century. The architect was W. H. Collbran.[206] At the southern end of this side the small shop at No. 1A was erected in c. 1897.[57]

On the east side of Exhibition Road the shops have a more complicated history illustrating the chops and changes to which even a very ordinary piece of London's fabric may be subjected. In 1872 three single-storey shops (Nos. 2, 4 and 6) in the same style as Nos. 1-5 were erected in the back garden of No. 13 Alfred Place West (now 13 Thurloe Street). But they were originally set back from the pavement, presumably in order to avoid interference from the Metropolitan Board of Works, which had previously turned down proposals for shops on this site.[207] Nos. 4 and 6 were first occupied by a firm of house agents, and No. 2 by a cow keeper, William Follett, who was also the occupant and freehold owner of No. 13 Alfred Place West.[57] Later extended up to the pavement, they no longer retain their original façades. Neither does the adjoining No. 2A which was built for Follett (though first occupied by a firm of auctioneers) in 1876. Follett's architect here was Henry E. Cooper of Caroline Street, Bedford Square, surveyor, whose florid first designs (not unlike a John Gibson bank) were soon replaced by something much plainer continuing the pattern of pilasters and the balustrade at Nos. 2-6. No. 2A then had a rounded corner and did not extend beyond the front of No. 13 Thurloe Street. But shortly afterwards another architect, George Edwards, was called in to extend the building southwards, and it was probably at this stage (1877-8) that both Nos. 2 and 2A received their present fronts of stripey brickwork (in the case of No. 2A now covered up).[208] No. 2A nevertheless still has its original pierced balustrade of 1876 with its tell-tale curved end and divisions no longer matching those of the shop front below: at No. 2 most of the balustrading and the two urns which stood on it have been removed.[209] Both Nos. 2 and 2A together with Nos. 4 and 6 were later occupied by the Belgravia Dairy Company Limited, successors in 1885 to the cow keeper William Follett.[57]

Northwards of No. 6 the frontage remained undeveloped until William Douglas erected three tall houses here in 1883-4.[210] Built of stock brick with copious red-brick dressings and steeply pitched slate roofs in the French style, they rise to some sixty feet, perhaps in compensation for the shallowness of the site, which tapers to less than ten feet on the return to Thurloe Place. No. 8, a double-fronted house with two tiers of bow windows, was first occupied by Edward Hyde Hewett, C.M.G. (H.M. Consul for the Bights of Benin and Biafra and the Island of Fernando Po), No. 10 by court dressmakers, and No. 12 by Douglas's son John, a builder and estate agent who continued here until 1939.[57] The shop front at No. 8 was added by John Douglas in 1891, probably for Messrs. Reeves, the artists' suppliers, who took over the building in that year.[211]

Twentieth-Century Changes

The first opportunity for any large-scale redevelopment on the estate (the railway station and the extension of Exhibition Road being, of course, outside the Alexander family's control) came in 1906 when all the leases granted under the agreement of 1826 expired together in a block. But in the event only a relatively small though important area behind and including the Bell and Horns was selected for wholesale redevelopment (whether by W. H. Alexander, before his death in April 1905, or by his heir Lady George Campbell is not known). Situated at the junction of two important and increasingly busy thoroughfares, this area (see fig. 15) had been the first to be developed, and the houses here were the smallest and least prepossessing on the estate. Another good reason for redeveloping here was the opportunity it provided for some much-needed road widening, particularly on the Brompton Road side.

By 1906 an arrangement had been made with a development company, Metropolis Estates Limited, though under what terms and conditions is not known, and in that year the company's architect, Howard Chatfeild Clarke, submitted proposals to the London County Council to redevelop the Thurloe Place frontage between the Bell and Horns and No. 12.[212] Since its formation in 1902 under the chairmanship of (Sir) Robert W. Perks, the industrialist, railway lawyer and Liberal M.P., Metropolis Estates had undertaken no other redevelopment; nor did it subsequently have significant interests in any property other than Thurloe Place. Perks and his two co-directors owned just over forty per cent of the shares, but the biggest investors (though not having a controlling interest) were Speyer Brothers, the international banking and finance house with which Perks had had dealings over the setting up (also in 1902) of the Underground Electric Railways Company of London.[213]

The development received something of a setback when Chatfeild Clarke's scheme was rejected by the L.C.C., and nearly three years elapsed before Metropolis Estates were ready to bring forward any fresh proposals.* These were by Delissa Joseph, Chatfeild Clarke's successor as architect to the company. They received the L.C.C.'s approval in 1909, and in the same year all the old houses on the site (the Bell and Horns excepted) were demolished.[212] But in the absence of any detailed information about Delissa Joseph's scheme it is impossible to say to what extent the subsequent piecemeal and rather protracted redevelopment of Thurloe Place represents his original intentions.

The first of the new buildings to go up was the **Rembrandt Hotel** (No. 11 Thurloe Place). Erected in 1910-11, this was designed by Joseph and built by Messrs. Ford and Walters of Kilburn.[215] It has a balconied front towards Thurloe Place, with the centre projecting slightly above a tall entrance and culminating at roof level in a high attic and small dome. It bears marked resemblances to the Brompton Road elevation of the Basil Street Hotel, built to Joseph's designs at exactly the same time.

In 1922 the building was extended across part of the then still undeveloped site to the east. This added a further fourteen feet to the frontage in Thurloe Place (where there is now an entrance to the Rembrandt Rooms), and some sixty feet to the rear frontage in North Terrace. The architects for the extension were R. H. Kerr and Sons, and the contractors were again Ford and Walters.[216] Though designed to match, the extension destroyed the symmetrical composition of the Rembrandt's front to Thurloe Place; but harmony was later restored by the careful treatment given to the front of the adjoining Dalmeny House (see below). In North Terrace this problem did not arise and the architects merely repeated the design of the existing front with no perceptible join between the two. The long façade here is divided up into seven vertical divisions, each three windows wide, alternately faced in stone and red brick. In the stone-faced sections the windows are provided with balconies.†

The eastern part of Thurloe Place is occupied by **Empire House,** a large office block with ground-floor shops extending along both Thurloe Place (Nos. 1-7 consec.) and Brompton Road (Nos. 220-244 even), and having a short return front to North Terrace. Built for the Continental Tyre Company, presumably under a lease from Metropolis Estates, it was begun in the same year as the Rembrandt (1910) but not completed until 1916. The reason for the delay was the continued presence of the Bell

---

*A set of drawings for a proposed development of the whole site, including the Bell and Horns, by R. C. Overton and H. V. Milnes Emerson, architects and surveyors, dated January 1907, and a revised set of drawings, with superior elevations, by Overton and R. Douglas Wells of May 1907, survive in Kensington Library.[214] This scheme is for a range of shops along the ground floor with flats above, and in its unrevised form includes an L-shaped shopping arcade between Brompton Road and Thurloe Place. As far as is known this had no connexion with Metropolis Estates, the client being R. Emerson, esquire, doubtless a relative of H. V. Milnes Emerson.

†Opposite the Rembrandt Hotel, in the centre of the roadway of Thurloe Place, is a cabmen's shelter (fig. 22) which was originally erected a little further to the east in 1897 and moved here in the 1970's. Paid for by the Vicar of St. Jude's Church, Courtfield Gardens, and the residents of Earl's Court, it was evidently a replacement for an earlier shelter. The purpose of these shelters, for which a fund had been established in 1875 under the presidency of Lord Shaftesbury, was to supply cabmen 'when on the ranks, with a place of Shelter where they can obtain good and wholesome refreshments at very moderate prices'. The shelters took various forms, but the best-known type, of which that in Thurloe Place is a good example, was designed by Maximilian Clarke, who was appointed joint honorary architect to the Cabmen's Shelter Fund in 1884.[217]

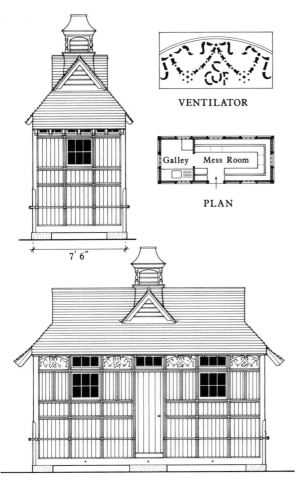

VENTILATOR

PLAN

Galley | Mess Room

7' 6"

Fig. 22. Cabmen's shelter, Thurloe Place, elevations, plan and detail, 1897

and Horns, which was not removed until the autumn of 1915. The odd, if short-lived, effect of this can be seen in Plate 42b, a photograph of *c.* 1912, where the two seemingly separate buildings to right and left of the old Bell and Horns are in fact both parts of Empire House. The Continental Tyre Company's architect was Paul Hoffmann, and the builders were Perry and Company of Bow (for the main part of the structure, 1910-12), and the General Building Company (for the eastern corner, 1915-16).[218]

The three portions of Empire House partake of slightly varying architectural character, though all display wreaths and wings in deft classical allusion to the motor-car tyre (Plate 42b, c). Towards Brompton Road the façade curves gently along the line of the road but the architecture is restrained up to the cornice, above which the ends sprout up into pavilion roofs. In Thurloe Place the building at Nos. 6 and 7, which housed the company's main offices, is altogether more bombastic, with bulbous sculpture over the entrance and a heavy top-knot crowning the roof. The later portion, embracing the prominent corner site, is dominated by a hefty but carefully studied

angle-tower, all in stone, with metal windows in the middle stages. Generally, the building betrays the influence of Vienna and the *Wagnerschule*, interpreted, however, with more enthusiasm than comprehension.

The final stage in the redevelopment of Thurloe Place was the erection in 1926-7 of **Dalmeny House** (Nos. 8-10A Thurloe Place) on the long-vacant site between the Rembrandt Hotel and Empire House (Plate 42a, c). The developers here were the builders, C. P. Roberts and Company Limited of Hackney, and the architect was Horace Gilbert of Finsbury Circus. Gilbert's plans, submitted to the L.C.C. in December 1926, show that the fifth and sixth floors were originally intended to be let to the Rembrandt to provide extra bedrooms, the rest of the building being taken up by flats and, on the ground floor, shops.[219] More liberally fenestrated than its Edwardian neighbours but still stone-fronted, Dalmeny House gives the impression of being a symmetrical composition with a raised centre flanked by two lower wings. The western wing is, however, in reality the front of the 1922 extension of the Rembrandt, the design of which Gilbert repeated in the eastern wing of Dalmeny House in order to obtain an effect of symmetry.

After the completion of the redevelopment of the Thurloe Place site the shareholders of Metropolis Estates voted for the company to go into voluntary liquidation, and in 1928 it was wound up. By then most of the shares (over seventy per cent) belonged to Glyn Mills Bank, though Perks still retained a nominal holding. The company's principal asset was its leasehold property in Thurloe Place, from which it derived an income after all deductions (including the annual ground rent of £975) of just under £1,500 a year. The property there was valued at £58,680 in 1920-4.[220]

By this time the chic *à la mode* domestic architecture of the 1920's was beginning to appear on the estate. The harbinger of this new trend was **No. 17 Thurloe Place** (Thurloe Lodge), which was completely remodelled in 1922-3 for (Sir) Nigel Playfair, the actor manager. For many years a resident in nearby Pelham Crescent, where his lease was soon to expire, Playfair had been enjoying a considerable success with his revival of *The Beggar's Opera* at the Lyric Theatre, Hammersmith (1920-3); and although on his own admission his 'share in the swag was a very small one', he decided to invest it in rebuilding 'two little cottages with a large garden' in the 'little lane opposite Brompton Oratory'.[221]

The 'two cottages' in question were a semi-detached pair originally erected in 1843, which had been converted into a single dwelling in *c.* 1867.[222] Playfair bought up the existing lease and obtained a new long lease of the property from Lady George Campbell 'at a reasonable sum'.[223] He entrusted the job of remodelling the house to Darcy Braddell, a personal friend who had previously designed a cottage for the Playfairs at Sandwich Bay.[224] (Braddell's partner, Humphry Deane, was nevertheless jointly credited with the work in published accounts.[225])

In the recollection of his son Playfair 'took as much interest in the building of his house as he had ever taken in one of his productions at the Lyric. Hardly a day passed without his meeting D'Arcy [sic] Braddell to discuss a new idea or to look over a new plan.'[226] With James Gray Limited of Danvers Street as contractors building work began in May 1922.[227]

The remodelling was extensive — Playfair himself called it a complete rebuilding — and although something of the original cottages may still be vestigially present, what one sees today (particularly within) is mostly by Braddell with some later alterations. The exterior is of plain stock brick under the wide eaves of a shallow-pitched slate roof, with a tripartite window of 'Venetian' form on the west front inserted to light the dining-room. For interior decoration Playfair favoured strong bold colours in unconventional combinations. At No. 26 Pelham Crescent friends had admired his use of black, and his yellow dining-room there with red and black furnishings was deemed 'exceptionally individual'.[228] At Thurloe Place, perhaps under the influence of Braddell, the colour schemes were more muted if no less individual. In the dining-room the waxed silver spruce of the woodwork was offset by emerald green curtains and a green carpet with a magenta border. In the drawing-room the walls were coloured creamy grey with the overdoors and dadoes picked out in soft jade green and a little coral. A striking feature of Playfair's study was the bold chequer-board patterning of the floor.[229]

Playfair and his family took up residence in Thurloe Lodge in the spring of 1923. At first he was pleased with it. But it had cost twice as much as he intended and his finances were no longer buoyant: 'why do we live in this expensive house,' he complained, 'I never liked it'. The last straw was the failure of a new light opera, *Midsummer Madness*, many of whose rehearsals Playfair had directed in the garden, and the family gave up the house either late in 1924 or early in 1925. To his surprise Playfair found that the property sold well and his investment in it proved 'not an unwise one'.[230]

Towards the end of 1926 official approval was being sought for two separate schemes of redevelopment involving the same architect and the same firm of developers. One was a plan to convert the old Western Grammar School building in North Terrace into two private residences, and the other was a proposal for building ten small houses or 'bijou residences' on the site of Thurloe Mews. The architect was Francis Gordon Selby of Westcliffe-on-Sea, who died in 1928 at the age of thirty-eight, and the developers, Simmonds Brothers and Sons Limited, a local firm of builders with an office in the Cromwell Road and works in Kelso Place.[231]

Under their auspices Thurloe Mews was turned from an ordinary, rather run-down collection of stables into a startling enclave of high-class 'Tudor' houses in which timber-framing, roughcast rendering, brick infilling, tile hanging, gables and casement windows were all laid under contribution (Plate 47b). The transformation was signalled by the change of name to **Thurloe Close** (1927).[232] Selby had told the London County Council that he planned to retain as much as possible of the existing buildings, 'including the external and party walls', but it seems doubtful if very much, if anything, of the old stables was in the end retained.[231] Working under an agreement with Lady George Campbell dated 14 March 1927, the developers, Simmonds Brothers, began building in Thurloe Close in the following month and the development was completed by the end of 1930 when all but two of the houses were occupied.[233]

Like the stables which they replaced, the houses in Thurloe Close face inwards onto an open flagged courtyard which also serves as a communal garden. Selby had originally wanted the covered way from Alexander Place to have a rustic flavour (with a roof of oak shingles), and to extend, in Albany-like fashion, down the middle of the courtyard, but the L.C.C. refused its consent for this.[231]

At the Western Grammar School the original intention, shown on an elaborate set of plans which Selby submitted to the L.C.C. in December 1926, had been to keep the whole of the building for conversion into two separate houses.[231] (The site was to include part of the back gardens of Nos. 26-28 Thurloe Square of which the leases were expiring.[234]) But in the end only the eastern portion of the former school was retained. Its conversion into the present **No. 7 North Terrace** (Alexander House) was carried out to Selby's design by Simmonds Brothers in 1927-8.[235] Pocock's original Greek Revival façade (of 1835) was retained (Plate 43a), but behind this the building was virtually gutted and only the staircase compartment and, on the ground floor, the small back room shown on fig. 18 survive from the old building. The staircase itself, which has a mahogany handrail and simple square-section balusters, predates the conversion but is probably not the original. Selby's replanned interior includes, on the ground floor, a pretty octagonal entrance hall flanked, to left and right respectively, by the dining- and drawing-rooms. These are both panelled in imitation of mid-eighteenth-century taste with fluted pilasters, while in the hall the walls are painted to resemble veined marble and the floor paved with black and white marble squares. In the principal bedroom, above the dining-room, the panelling is decorated with rococo-style ornaments. The first occupant of No. 7, late in 1928, was a Mrs. Percy Balfour.[57]

No. 7 North Terrace was Selby's swansong. In September 1927 poor health had obliged him take a long holiday abroad, and he died in Italy in January 1928.[236] Whether or not his death had any influence on events, the proposed conversion of the western portion of the school into what would have been quite a large house did not go forward. Subsequently the unconverted parts of the building were acquired by Sir Harold J. Reckitt, second baronet, who called in Stanley Hall, Easton and Robertson (in one account only the latter two are named) to prepare a new scheme for dealing with the property; and with Dove Brothers as contractors a completely new house, now **No. 17A Thurloe Place** (Amberwood House), was built here in 1928-9.[237]

Occupying approximately the same position as the old schoolroom, the main body of the house is a three-storey building faced in brindled red Sussex bricks with a wide shallow bow on the west side rising through the three storeys. The bowed rooms were the dining-room (ground floor), the drawing-room and the principal bedroom (top floor). These and the other living rooms occupied the south and west sides of the house, the servants' rooms and service areas being on the north and east sides. On each floor the living and service areas were completely separate, each being provided with its own staircase and lift. 'This excellent (and rare) arrangement', to quote *The Architect and Building News* of 1932, 'gives complete seclusion to the owner and his guests.'

The front entrance, at the southern end of the opening out of Thurloe Place, is in a single storey which contains a small hall and a loggia with French windows opening on to the garden. The loggia was given a marble floor and a ceiling of painted wood, and was furnished in limed oak to designs by the architects. A little barrel-vaulted vestibule lit by a Venetian window connects the loggia to the staircase hall in the main body of the house.

Special attention was paid to the garden, which was laid out on several levels, and for which Eric Munday designed a fountain in the form of a sea-horse and a lead cistern bearing Reckitt's initials. A roof garden was made over the entrance hall, loggia and vestibule, and the servants were provided with a separate garden of their own.*

Reckitt called his new house Little Green Lodge after his country house, Little Green, near Petersfield (it was assigned the number 17A Thurloe Place only in 1951), and he occupied it from 1929 until his death, less than eighteen months later, in December 1930.[238]

Another completely new house built at this time is the present **No. 2 Alexander Place**. This was erected as a speculation by Simmonds Brothers in 1929-30 on the site of the Western Grammar School's original premises of 1828.

Since being vacated by the school the old building had been variously adapted to serve as Nonconformist chapel, Turkish baths, and artists' studios. It first served as a chapel in 1838, when the building was hired by a congregation of Baptists, though whether for their exclusive use is uncertain as the school continued to pay

the rates until 1843.[239] Later known as the Thurloe Chapel, its congregations were nominally Baptist until *c.* 1851, and Presbyterian or Free Church of Scotland, *c.* 1851 to 1856. In 1851 the chapel had 340 sittings of which 300 were free, and a morning congregation of 200.[240] In the following year the congregation in association with other Nonconformist groups decided to build themselves a new chapel.[241] A site was secured in Neville Terrace and the new building, known as the Onslow Chapel, was opened in 1856 (see page 143), but the Thurloe Chapel continued in use until *c.* 1861.[57]

In April of that year the building was being fitted up as Turkish baths.[242] 'Establishments are now springing up everywhere', commented *The Builder* knowingly, but 'these baths are an improvement on any we have seen in the metropolis.' The facilities here included a forty-foot-square frigidarium, 'tastefully decorated', with lantern windows extending all round, hot rooms, and a lavatory with 'complete water apparatus'. The proprietors, Edward and Charles Pollard, had also acquired the house at No. 8 North Terrace, which (having been extended behind) provided a completely separate entrance to the private baths.[82]

When the baths closed in 1887 the building was converted into the Alexander Studios, which were first occupied in 1888 by two portrait painters, Henry John Hudson and (Sir) James Jebusa Shannon. Another occupant, from 1911 to 1916, was Gustav Julius Froberg, purveyor of medical massage.[243]

After clearing away the old building Simmonds Brothers began work on No. 2 Alexander Place in April 1929, and by December this was sufficiently advanced for Lady George Campbell to grant a sixty-one-year lease of the house at an annual ground rent of £75. At the request of the builders, who were paid £5,000 by the lessee, it was granted to Lieutenant-Colonel Cecil Du Pré Perton Powney, O.B.E., of Egerton Terrace, who moved into his new home in 1931.[244]

Situated at the end of a narrow private footpath between the back gardens of Alexander Square and the adjoining houses in Alexander Place, No. 2 lies several feet below the general level of the surrounding buildings in the centre of the old school site, part of which has been laid out as a pleasant garden. The house itself is a two-storey building, consisting of two short wings set at right angles to each other with a central entrance placed diagonally in the corner. Reticently neo-Georgian in style, it has rendered walls and a slate roof. The architect is not known.

At **No. 14 Alexander Place** the oak front door, curious

---

*Munday was only one of a small army of sub-contractors employed on the house, among whom the following may be mentioned: Art Pavements and Decorations Ltd. (mosaics, etc.); W. Aumonier and Sons (carving); Baguès Ltd. (ironwork); T. Crowther and Sons, C. Pratt and Sons, Bratt, Colbran and Co. (fireplaces); G. Jackson and Sons Ltd. (fibrous plasterwork); H. T. Jenkins and Son Ltd. (marble work); Vernon Bros. (garden works); J. P. White and Sons Ltd. (garden treillage). Redpath, Brown and Co. Ltd. provided the steel joists needed to support the floors, which were constructed of patent terracotta tubes. A full list of the sub-contractors was given in *The Architect and Building News* for 8 January 1932, which also has plans and photographs of the house.

ground-floor window, wooden shutters and round-headed dormer are the external trappings of a very extensive internal transformation carried in 1929-30 for Mrs. Patrick Morley by R. Douglas Wells. On the ground floor the walls dividing the front room from the hall and the back room were removed to make one large hall-cum-dining-room extending from front to back with a small entrance lobby. The first floor was similarly treated to form a library-cum-sitting-room. This was given a barrel vaulted ceiling (in plaster) and lined with old panelling said to have come from demolished houses in Kensington. In the dining-room the walls were stripped, plastered with Keene's cement and varnished: 'the result', according to Randal Phillips in *Country Life*, 'giving a kind of cloudy marble effect, of delightful surface and warm tone'. For the garden Wells provided elm trellises to screen the party walls and a pergola across the northern end.[245]

The only other noteworthy development of these years was the widening of Thurloe Place, west of Exhibition Road, and the consequent rebuilding in its present form of the **Hoop and Toy** public house. This was carried out in 1926-7 under a long lease from Lady George Campbell to Huggins and Company Limited of the Lion Brewhouse, Broad Street, Golden Square. The architect was Alfred Burr of Gower Street, and the contractors Kirk and Kirk Limited of Upper Richmond Road.[246] In his design Burr had to accommodate an awkward obtuse angle in the frontage of the site where Thurloe Place changes direction. This he did by placing a conspicuous stone-faced tower, capped in copper, at the angle, with, on either side of it, sober stone and brick elevations rising to four storeys.

The widening of Thurloe Place swept away the surviving front gardens, and before long single-storey shops were being added to the houses there (those at Nos. 29 and 31 in 1930-1 and 1928 respectively[247]).

Since the early 1930's little beyond the replacement of war damage has altered the outward aspect of the estate and recent years have been marked by a policy of careful conservation.

The only completely new post-war building is the house at **No. 21 Alexander Place**. Erected in 1954-7, this occupies a previously unbuilt site originally leased in 1844 to the occupant of No. 19 Thurloe Square for a garden.[248] The London County Council had wanted the architects, Robert Bostock and Leonard T. Wilkins, to 'reproduce the existing façades as nearly as possible'. The design nevertheless has a strong flavour of the 1950's about it, the use of glass bricks for the tall staircase window in the west elevation being a particularly telling period detail.[249]

CHAPTER VI

The Smith's Charity Estate

The Smith's Charity estate, which was formed in the seventeenth century, originally consisted of eighty-five and a half acres of land in the parishes of Kensington, Chelsea and St. Margaret's, Westminster. In 1853 a further small plot of former manorial waste on the north side of Fulham Road was purchased, and in 1856 the part of the estate in St. Margaret's parish known as the Carpet Ground, which was detached from the rest, was conveyed to the Commissioners for the Exhibition of 1851 in exchange for a slightly larger parcel of ground in Kensington.[1] Since then, apart from the sale of some plots for ecclesiastical and institutional purposes or for railway construction and road widening, the estate has remained intact. The detailed account of building developments in this volume is confined to Kensington and excludes the fourteen and a half acres in the former parish of Chelsea, but in the calculations of total rental and income the estate is considered as a whole.

Henry Smith, a City merchant and alderman of a highly charitable disposition, was born at Wandsworth in 1548, acquired a considerable amount of property during his lifetime, and from 1620 onwards set up a succession of trusts to dispose of the rents and profits of his lands for charitable uses, making gifts to several towns in Surrey for the relief of the poor.[2] He died in 1628 and by his will decreed that £1,000 should be used to purchase land producing at least £60 per annum, which was to be applied for the relief and ransom of 'the poore Captives being slaves under the Turkish pirates', and that a further £1,000 was to be spent in purchasing more land of equivalent value, the income from which was to be used for the relief of the poorest of his kindred who were unable to work for their living.[3] The dangers to English seamen posed by the Barbary pirates were real enough in the early seventeenth century, but the need for this charity diminished and in 1772, when no claims had been made for many years, the income under this heading was merged with that providing relief to Smith's descendants.[4]

It has always been assumed that the estate in Kensington was acquired under these two dispositions of Henry Smith's will and the charity has been maintained on this basis ever since, although its scope has now been considerably widened to take in much more than payments to Smith's descendants. There is, however, no documentary evidence about the original purchase; no conveyance has come to light. The first reference to an estate in Kensington and adjacent parishes belonging to the charity occurs in a deed establishing new trustees in 1658,* when the estate was described as being in the tenure of Robert Sewell or Seywell,[6] and the first full description is in a lease of 1664.[7] At that time part of the land appears to have been copyhold of the manor of Earl's Court, but by 1675 it was described as entirely freehold.[8]

The lease of 1664 was to Christopher Blake for seventy years at a rent of £130 per annum in consideration of £500 to be laid out by Blake in new buildings and improvements and of the release by Blake of 'his claim to several of the lands'.[7] This second stipulation perhaps indicates that the acquisition of the land by the Smith's Charity trustees had not been a straightforward affair. Blake was the grandson of Sir William Blake, who had amassed a very large estate in Kensington, Knightsbridge and Chelsea during the reign of James I,[9] and who was both a trustee appointed by Henry Smith and one of the executors of his will. The lands which make up the Smith's Charity estate had undoubtedly been part of Blake's holding and were probably conveyed to the trustees by Blake's descendants after his death in 1630.

At the time of the lease to Christopher Blake the estate consisted of a number of fields or closes, one substantial house which had been built by Robert Sewell, and about a dozen smaller houses and cottages. Blake died in 1672 and by his will his leasehold lands passed first to his sister Maria Dorney and then to her son by her first marriage, John Harris.[10] The latter assigned the lease to Richard Calloway of Knightsbridge, innkeeper,[11] and at the time of its expiry in 1734 the leaseholder was Francis Calloway.[12]

Calloway had reached an agreement with the trustees for a new lease at a rent of £250, but this contract was set aside and the trustees agreed to reduce the rent to £200 for a twenty-one-year term. No lease was actually executed even though Calloway remained in possession of the land, and he was soon owing the trustees arrears of rent. Eventually in 1749 he relinquished his interest to William Bucknall, a doctor, in return for an annuity of £30.[12] Bucknall had recently purchased Brompton Hall, a mansion which stood on the north side of Old Brompton Road at its eastern end, opposite the Smith's Charity lands.[13]

In 1750 the trustees granted Bucknall a twenty-one-year lease at an annual rent of £170 for ten years and £200 for

---

*The trustees have generally been recruited from the aristocracy and landed gentry. The Charity Commissioners' latest scheme for the Kensington estate (of 1971) provides that there should be not more than twenty-four or less than fifteen trustees. When necessary, future trustees are to be appointed on the nomination of the Archbishop of Canterbury and the Lord Chancellor.[5]

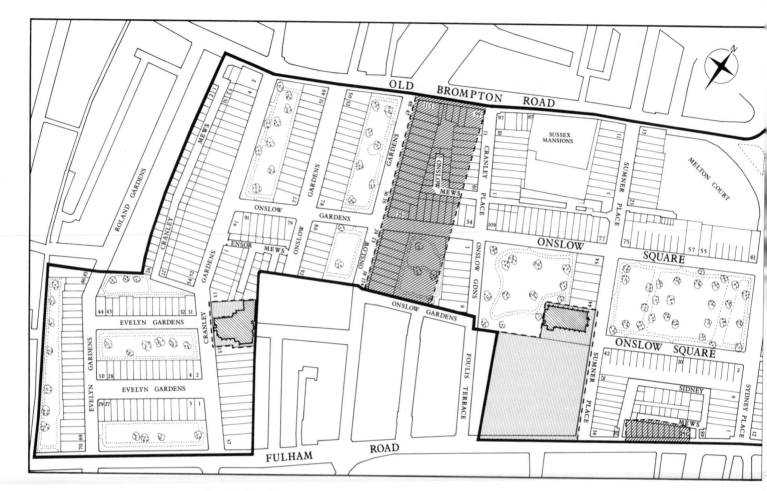

Fig. 23. The Smith's Charity estate in Kensington. Based on the Ordnance Survey

the remainder. He, too, soon fell behind in his rent, however, and by 1759 owed over £800. In return for the payment of most of these arrears, the trustees agreed to grant a new lease for the same length of time as that to Christopher Blake, namely seventy years, at a rent of £151 per annum. Accordingly in 1760 a new seventy-year lease at that rent was made out in the name of Samuel Bucknall, Dr. Bucknall's son.[14]

William Bucknall died in 1763 and Samuel Bucknall in 1770, when the benefit of the lease passed to the latter's two sisters and eventually to their husbands, the Reverend Joseph Griffith, who succeeded the Bucknall family in Brompton Hall, and Morgan Rice of Tooting.[15]

Novosielski and Michael's Place

Of the first building development on the estate, which took place on the south side of Brompton Road in the vicinity of the streets now called Egerton Gardens, Egerton Place and Egerton Terrace, not a house now remains. Here in 1785 Morgan Rice and the Reverend Joseph Griffith let fourteen acres on building leases to Michael Novosielski, architect, for forty-five years plus another sixteen years if they could obtain a renewal of their lease from the Smith's Charity trustees. The ultimate rent, payable in full after five years, was £140 per annum.[16]

Novosielski, who was of Polish descent, was born in Rome in 1750 and came to London as a young man. He is reputed to have assisted James Wyatt at the Pantheon in 1770-2, but was working as a scene-painter when he was invited to remodel the King's Theatre in the Haymarket in 1782. He was later architect for the rebuilding of the theatre in 1790-1 after it had been destroyed by fire, and this was to be his most notable work.[17]

At Kensington he was heavily involved as a speculator from the start, apparently paying for the first houses to be erected and supplying mortgages to builders to whom he granted sub-leases of other houses.[18] To finance this and other smaller-scale speculations, primarily in Piccadilly and St. Marylebone, he had himself to borrow on a large scale, to the extent of £11,000 from the Honourable Mary Bridget Mostyn and at least £16,000 from the bankers Ransom, Morland and Hammersley of Pall Mall.[19]

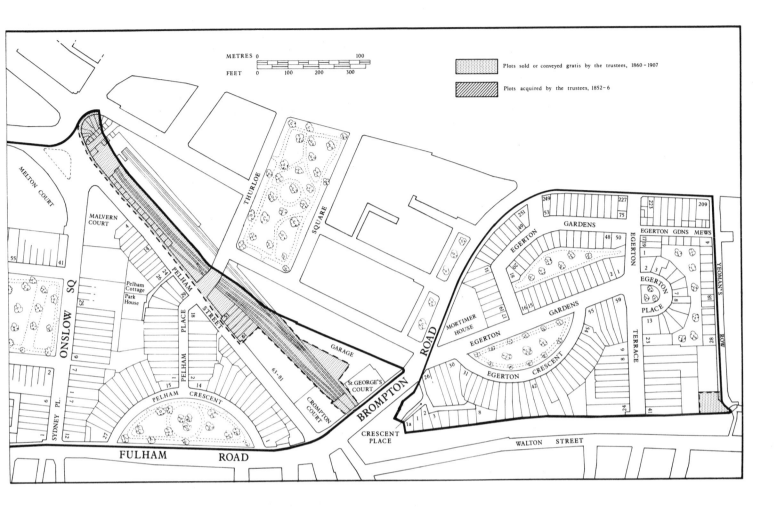

Novosielski's enterprise was essentially a continuation of the kind of ribbon development which had spread along Brompton Road from Knightsbridge since the 1760's, and his major activities were concentrated on the frontage of that road (Plates 2a, 3). Here, immediately to the west of Yeoman's Row, which formed the eastern boundary of the Smith's Charity estate, he proposed to begin by erecting a uniform terrace of fifteen houses set back a little way from the road with a plantation in front.[20] A square was also projected for the hinterland behind the frontage to Brompton Road.[21] Neither the square nor the uniform terrace finally took shape as such, but the house which was intended to form the centre of the terrace was distinguished by a canted bay rising through three storeys.[22]*

Michael's Place, as Novosielski eponymously named the terrace along Brompton Road, eventually consisted of forty-four houses and was completed by about 1795.[23] There is little evidence of its general appearance, but a drawing depicting two of the houses shows that these had

four storeys with relatively plain late-Georgian elevations embellished by simple mouldings with a hint of Greek severity.[24] After the initial range, which appears to have been built under contract, most of the houses were erected under sub-leases granted to Allen Burton of Brompton, bricklayer, and James Clark of Crutched Friars in the City, carpenter.[25] In 1790 Clark was declared bankrupt, the first of several builders on the estate to suffer this misfortune.[26] One of his assignees was James Turner of Whitechapel Road, a timber merchant and surveyor, who was also much involved in Burton's speculations.[27] Other builders who worked on the houses in Michael's Place were Henry Adams of Chelsea, carpenter; Thomas Justice of Brompton, carpenter; Benjamin Leathers of Finsbury, plasterer; and William Smart of St. James's, carpenter.[28]

Most of the houses had narrow frontages and cost about £350 to £450 to buy,[29] but there were two 'double' houses, Nos. 16 and 33, the latter 'a very large handsome and well finished messuage' which was built by Burton and

---

*A later long-term resident of this house, originally No. 8 Michael's Place and later No. 223 Brompton Road, was the architect John Blore, who designed many houses hereabouts. He lived there from at least 1833 until his death in 1882.[23]

briefly occupied by him. In 1792 both were purchased by James Billington and his wife Elizabeth, the celebrated singer. They lived at No. 16 in 1792-3, before selling that house for 900 guineas, and Elizabeth Billington later lived at No. 33 from approximately 1804 to 1807.[30]*

Between Nos. 11 and 12 Michael's Place Novosielski laid out a new road called Michael's Grove (now Egerton Terrace), which originally extended only for some 135 yards south-eastwards from Brompton Road. On the north-east side of the new road a terrace was erected eventually consisting of ten houses although some were not built until after Novosielski's death in 1795.[23] The terrace stood approximately on the site of Egerton Place and the houses were set well back from the road with long front gardens. They also had gardens extending as far as Yeoman's Row at the rear.

At the south end of Yeoman's Row Novosielski built a large house with extensive grounds to the south-west for his own occupation. The house, which was called Bromp-ton Grange, was completed by 1787[23] but there is no record of its appearance.

The final item in Novosielski's enterprise was a shallow crescent of houses opposite to the site now occupied by Egerton Crescent. He planned to call it Novosielski Street, but after his death the name was changed to Bromp-ton Crescent. The crescent was originally intended to consist of twenty-five houses, but the seven easternmost ones were never built, their place being taken by three larger houses erected in 1805-7 and a group of coach-houses and stables. The original houses were thus rather confusingly known as Nos. 8-25 (consec.) Brompton Crescent. They were built under sub-leases granted in 1792 to Thomas Hewson of St. George's, Bloomsbury, surveyor, but it was over ten years before the terrace was completed.[31] The quintessentially South Kensingtonian architect Charles James Richardson lived at No. 22 from 1842 to 1850.[23] At the western end of Brompton Crescent, where it joined Fulham Road, a larger house was built on the site now occupied by Mortimer House. Called Crescent House, it was completed in 1801.[32]

Novosielski died on 8 April 1795 at a time when the building industry in general was encountering severe diffi-culties. At Brompton he left a number of houses which remained unfinished for many years,[22] and at Sidmouth in Devon, where he had another speculation, there was also an uncompleted crescent which still exists today in truncated form as Fortfield Terrace.[33]

In his will, which was made very shortly before his death, Novosielski stated that his estate was subject to mortgages and other incumbrances and that 'on account of the present times it is impossible to ascertain what the amount or surplus of the same may be after paying off such incumbrances'.[34] His debts proved to be very extensive and his widow had to sell Brompton Grange and move to No. 13 Michael's Place.[35] The leases to Novosielski from Rice and Griffith were assigned to Ransom, Morland and Hammersley's bank.[36]

The purchaser of Brompton Grange was John Willett Payne, a captain (later rear-admiral) in the navy and private secretary to the Prince of Wales.[37] Payne lived there until 1801 and two years later sold the house for £3,800.[38] In 1830 it reverted to the Smith's Charity trustees on the expiry of the original lease, and it was occupied from then until 1842 by the famous singer John Braham at a rent of £250 per annum. Braham invested his large fortune in two unsuccessful theatrical ventures at the Colosseum at Regent's Park and the St. James's Theatre. In 1842, when he was heavily in debt, his furniture was seized and the Smith's Charity trustees took possession of the Grange.[39] It was demolished in the following year and the houses in Egerton Crescent, Cres-cent Place and the southern end of Egerton Terrace, together with others now demolished at the south end of Yeoman's Row, were erected in its stead. This develop-ment is described in more detail below.

The Early Nineteenth Century

An important change in the disposition of the Smith's Charity estate took place at the beginning of the nineteenth century when the lease granted to Samuel Bucknall in 1760 was set aside. It had become increasingly clear that the rent of £151 which was payable under that lease represented only a fraction of the real value of the land now that building development had progressed so far westwards, and in 1801 the Attorney General, acting on behalf of the recipients of the charity, instituted a suit in Chancery against the current holders of the lease, the Reverend Joseph Griffith and John Morgan Rice, the grandson of Morgan Rice, and against the charity's trust-ees. The latter were probably friendly parties and offered no defence, merely agreeing to abide by the decision of the court. The Attorney General asked for the lease to be declared void, claiming that under the terms of the trusts set up by Henry Smith the trustees had not had the power in 1760 to grant a lease for such a long term, that the lease had only been executed by seven of the trustees, and that even in 1760 the rent had not been the best that could have been obtained for the land.[40]

The Reverend Joseph Griffith died in 1803, leaving his second wife Harriet as his legatee, and the suit had to be revived.[41] Eventually in 1807 the Lord Chancellor de-livered his verdict and not only set aside the lease but

---

*The most notable occupant of Michael's Place was William Cobbett, who lodged at No. 11 in 1820-1. Inhabitants of these and other houses in Novosielski's development who were connected with the stage (possibly through Novosielski's own associations with the theatre) are listed on pages 253-4. The names of some other residents of houses on the estate are given in Thomas Crofton Croker, *A Walk From London to Fulham*, 1860, and Dorothy Stroud, *The South Kensington Estate of Henry Smith's Charity: Its History and Development*, 1975.

ordered that the rents and profits received by the lessees since the inception of the case in 1801 should be forfeited and invested for the benefit of the recipients of the charity. The sub-leases which had been granted to Novosielski and others were, however, confirmed.[12] The income from them was thenceforth received by the trustees and amounted to £773 per annum in 1807. By 1825 the rental had been increased to £1,023.[42]

At around this time much of the undeveloped part of the estate was occupied by a number of nurseries. There had been nursery grounds at Brompton since the end of the seventeenth century, the most famous being the Brompton Park Nursery, founded in 1681. By 1825 the largest of those located on the Smith's Charity estate belonged to William Malcolm and Company. It consisted of seven and a half acres approximately on the site now occupied by Brompton Hospital and the western part of Onslow Square, and of the fourteen and a half acres of the estate in Chelsea. Malcolm also had another fifteen acres of nursery ground on the sites now ocupied by De Vere Gardens and Queen's Gate Terrace and Elvaston Place.[43]

The site now covered by Pelham Crescent, Pelham Place and Pelham Street formed part of the nursery of Samuel Harrison, which comprised eight and a half acres on the Smith's Charity estate and a further thirteen and a half acres on the Alexander estate immediately to the north. Harrison, who had acquired the ground on the Smith's Charity estate in 1815, was latterly in partnership with William Bristow.[44]

The nursery of Thomas Gibbs occupied five and a half acres immediately to the west of Harrison's ground. Gibbs, who had established his nursery on the estate in 1800,[45] used it both for horticultural purposes and for experiments to produce improved crop seed. He grew specimens of all known kinds of cereal and vegetables used in farming and several kinds of grasses. There were a number of buildings on the premises, including a substantial house which had been erected in 1792, and a small cottage built of pisé, a form of dry-earth construction. Pisé had been popularized by a Frenchman, François Cointereaux, who wrote a number of booklets on the subject and whose ideas enjoyed widespread currency in England. He came to London in 1815 and in the following year built the cottage on Gibbs's nursery at the invitation of the Board of Agriculture. The cottage was still in good condition when Faulkner wrote his *History and Antiquities of Kensington* in 1820.[46] All of the buildings on the nursery were grouped together at the northern end on part of the site now occupied by Melton Court; the last of them was demolished in 1850.

Eighteen and a half acres at the extreme western edge of the estate, known historically as Brompton Heath and at this time still detached from the main part of the estate, were occupied by a Mr. Street, who was also described as a nurseryman, but Starling's map of 1822 appears to show most of his land in use as market gardens. Street was succeeded in 1830 by William Joyce and, although the land was then called Joyce's nursery, it was described as market gardens in the tithe apportionment survey of 1843.[47]

Between Malcolm's and Gibbs's nurseries lay the grounds of Cowper House (Plate 52d). This large house, named after Henry Cowper, its occupant at the beginning of the nineteenth century, stood on the south side of Old Brompton Road on a site now occupied by the western part of Melton Court. It can be identified with the house built by Robert Sewell in the early seventeenth century and said to have been rebuilt by Samuel Bucknall in the eighteenth century.[48] From 1829 until its demolition in 1850 it was used as a private lunatic asylum.[49] A conspicuous feature of the grounds was a long avenue of elms stretching to the Fulham Road, the line of which is preserved in the double row of trees in the eastern part of Onslow Square gardens and the single row in Sydney Close; the present trees are, however, replantings.[50]

Another smaller house stood in an acre of grounds on the site of Sussex Mansions. To its east was a terrace of half a dozen very small houses which had been erected under a building lease granted by Griffith and Rice to Charles Bevan in 1793.[48] The occupants of the houses were invariably poor and the vestry had great difficulty in collecting even the low rates assessed on them.[23] The terrace was demolished in 1852-3.[51]

Bonnin, Basevi, and Pelham and Egerton Crescents

In 1822 James Bonnin, a builder who was then engaged in building Brompton Square and who was to play a major role in the development of both the Smith's Charity and Alexander estates over the next twenty-five years, entered into a building agreement with the Smith's Charity trustees to erect a terrace of eight houses on the north-west side of what was then Fulham Road but is now the western end of Brompton Road. The site is now occupied by St. George's Garage, St. George's Court and Nos. 264-268 (even) Brompton Road. The agreement provided for the granting of sixty-year leases* from 1823 at a total rent of £42 per annum,[52] and the terrace was called Onslow Terrace after the second Earl of Onslow, one of the trustees. No. 1, at the northern end of the terrace, which had extensive grounds at the rear (the site now of St. George's Garage) was leased in 1823 to William Wilberforce the younger, the son of the celebrated emancipationist, but he only lived there for a short while.[53] The most notable later occupant of the terrace was Giuseppe Mazzini, the Italian statesman, who lodged at No. 2 (later renumbered 18 Fulham Road) from 1861 until 1871, when he returned to Italy for the last time.[54]

---

*The trustees had obtained the power to grant building leases for any term not exceeding ninety-nine years in the Act of 1772 which made provision for the disposal of the money originally reserved by Henry Smith's will for ransoming captives of the Turks.[4]

The southernmost house was demolished in about 1866 for the building of the Metropolitan District Railway, and in 1883 shops were built on the forecourts of six of the remaining houses, then numbered 18-28 (even) Fulham Road, by Edward Yates of Walworth Road, a major speculative builder who worked mostly in south London.[55] Yates's shops and Bonnin's houses behind were demolished in 1934.

At the rear of the terrace Bonnin built himself a single-storey cottage with a workshop and timber yard, where he lived and conducted his business from 1826 until 1838.[56]

The surveyor of the trustees' London estate during the building of Onslow Terrace was John Booth. His appointment, probably in 1819, seems to have marked a change of policy by the trustees, the London estate having previously been under the control of the charity's general surveyor, William Clutton, the son of the William Clutton who had been first appointed to that post in 1769.[57] Booth, who was a minor architect,[58] proved somewhat dilatory in carrying out his duties, and his laxness in drawing up the agreement with Bonnin had enabled the builder to erect the workshops and sheds for his own use at the back of Onslow Terrace, much to the chagrin of the trustees.[59] Not surprisingly he was replaced in 1828.

The leases which had been granted to Novosielski in 1785 were due to expire in 1830, and when the trustees wanted a report on the state of the houses erected under these leases and the best method of re-letting them they turned not to Booth but to George Basevi junior. The decision was probably taken at the trustees' meeting on 22 August 1828 as the letter inviting Basevi to undertake the work was written shortly afterwards.[60] This commission appears to have pre-dated Basevi's appointment as surveyor to the neighbouring estate of John Alexander, and may have been given to him because the trustees knew and admired his work in Belgrave Square, by then well advanced.

Like Booth before him, Basevi was only surveyor for the charity's London properties, the country estates remaining under the control of the Clutton family, and his first tasks were humdrum enough but important to the trustees. He was paid £212 for his report on the houses in Michael's Place and nearby streets and further sums for surveys, estimates of dilapidations and statements of the improvements which he considered necessary. These included a new sewer and pavements in Brompton Crescent, which were constructed by James Bonnin at a cost of over £1,350.[61]

Most of the houses erected by Novosielski or his sub-lessees were re-let on twenty-one-year leases at rack rents which produced a considerable improvement in the income of the charity,[62] but some new building also took place, principally in Yeoman's Row. Here the back gardens of the houses in Michael's Grove were shortened and some twenty narrow terrace houses were erected over several years by Edward Aldred of Gray's Place, Kensing-

ton, and Edward William Burgess of Soho, builders, on sixty-three-year leases from 1830.[63] These houses were demolished on the expiry of their leases in 1893. Burgess may also have rebuilt three houses in Michael's Grove, for which he was granted leases for similar terms,[64] but these houses too have been demolished.

Pelham Crescent, Pelham Place and Pelham Street

In 1832 the bankruptcy of Samuel Harrison and William Bristow, the nurserymen,[65] freed some eight and a half acres of land for development, and thereby provided Basevi with the opportunity to make a much more substantial contribution to the appearance of the estate. Here Pelham Crescent and Place and most of Pelham Street (formerly Pelham Road), which were named after Henry Thomas Pelham, third Earl of Chichester, one of the trustees, were laid out under two building agreements with James Bonnin. The first, dated 1 June 1833, covered the eastern half of Pelham Crescent, the eastern side of Pelham Place, both sides of Pelham Street between Pelham Place and Fulham Road, and a short frontage to Fulham Road on each side of Pelham Street. The second agreement, dated 21 October 1838, was for the remainder of Pelham Crescent and Pelham Place and the sites now occupied by Nos. 12-26 (even) Pelham Street. A third agreement, for the building of Nos. 6-10 (even) Pelham Street and a number of houses on the north side of that street which were demolished for the building of South Kensington Station, was made with Bonnin's son, James Bonnin junior, on 25 July 1843. Some of the land covered by the last agreement was taken from the nursery of Thomas Gibbs, whose lease had expired in 1843.

Basevi provided elevations and details for Pelham Crescent (Plate 50a) and nine houses in Fulham Road, six with ground-floor shops to the north of Pelham Street and three without shops between that street and Pelham Crescent. (Only two of the latter were in fact built, and all eight houses, known collectively as Onslow Place, have been demolished.) He also drew the flank elevations of the houses at the junction of Pelham Crescent with Pelham Place and thus determined the lines of the adjoining houses in Pelham Place.[66] Whether he drew out any more elevations is not known (those for the houses without shops in Fulham Road only being prepared at the express suggestion of Reginald Bray, the trustees' clerk and treasurer[67]), but his influence was paramount and it is clear that very little was built during the period of his surveyorship, which lasted until his death in 1845, without his architectural imprimatur.

Under the agreement of June 1833 Bonnin took the ground for eighty years from 1833 at an initial rent of £25 per annum rising annually to £220 in the seventh year, when the development was to be completed. He was to build houses worth at least £800 in Pelham Crescent and £600 in Pelham Place and Fulham Road. Pelham Street was regarded as being of much less importance and Bonnin was allowed to erect stables on its southern side at the backs of the houses in Pelham Crescent, and to erect semi-detached pairs of 'cottages' on the north side to elevations which were to be approved by Basevi but not necessarily provided by him. A plot at the north end of Pelham Place (now occupied by Nos. 16 and 18) was also set aside for cottages. The agreement specified that the leases were to contain covenants that the houses were to be repainted externally every four years including the stucco work, 'each house of an uniform colour with the whole'; that no alterations were to be made to the external appearance of houses without consent; and that, apart from the six shops in Fulham Road and the first two houses in Pelham Street, which were allowed to be used as shops (one was the Pelham Arms public house), all the houses were to be used as private dwellings only.[68]

The trustees covenanted to provide a communal garden in Pelham Crescent for the occupants of the houses in the crescent and Pelham Place. Basevi designed the iron railings enclosing the garden (which were removed during the war of 1939-45) and they were manufactured by May and Merritt at a cost of £333.[69] Thomas Gibbs undertook the planting in the garden.[70]

The agreement of 1838 was also for the granting of eighty-year leases, this time dating from 1838, at an ultimate ground rent of £200 payable in the fifth and succeeding years. Bonnin had to complete the development within six years and, in an extra stipulation not contained in the earlier agreement, he was by then 'to correct all errors that may be made in the elevation' and replace all the materials that were contrary to the specifications. He was permitted to erect three cottages or stables at the back of the houses on the west side of Pelham Place to elevations approved by Basevi.[71]

The third agreement, which was made in 1843 with James Bonnin junior for the western end of Pelham Street, provided for the granting of eighty-three-year leases at a total ground rent of £96 per annum.[72]

James Bonnin senior proceeded with great despatch as soon as he had signed the first agreement in June 1833. In July he disposed of most of the ground on the north side of Pelham Street and the small plot at the end of Pelham Place (the site of Nos. 16 and 18) to James Jolley of St. James's, builder, in a subsidiary agreement.[73] One of the witnesses to the agreement was James Bonnin junior, who was thus clearly assisting his father from the start.*

John Bonnin, a grocer, another of the builder's sons, was paying rates on the first house in Onslow Place by the end of 1833 and all eight houses there were occupied by 1836. No. 1 Pelham Crescent was occupied in 1835, Nos. 2, 4 and 11 in 1836 and the remaining houses in the eastern half of the crescent by 1838. The first six houses in

Pelham Place, originally Nos. 1-6 but renumbered as 2-12 (even) in 1864, were taken by 1839, and the seventh house, now No. 14 followed in 1841.[23]

Only in his arrangements with James Jolley does Bonnin appear to have run into serious difficulties. Building along Pelham Street proceeded slowly and intermittently, and in about 1842 Bonnin and Jolley were on the verge of litigation.[75] One problem was that Jolley had relied on the open Blacklands Sewer which ran parallel to, and a little distance to the north of, Pelham Street, for house drainage. But shortly after building commenced the lower portion of this sewer had been diverted into a new sewer which had been built in Pelham Crescent and Pelham Place, with the result that his houses, lacking proper drainage, 'have been so inundated as to render them uninhabitable, and the Tenants have left them in consequence'.[76] Jolley was eventually declared bankrupt in 1842, and the undeveloped plots on the ground which had been taken by him were transferred to James Firby of Chelsea, gentleman.[77] Firby was also the lessee, in March 1842, of Nos. 16 and 18 (formerly Nos. 8 and 9) Pelham Place, which had been built on a plot included in the agreement with Jolley and which are marked on a plan of 1840 as 'houses built by James Jolley'.[78] Firby was the first occupant of No. 16 in 1842, and No. 18 was let in the following year.[23]

Building under the second agreement proceeded more rapidly. The first houses in the western half of Pelham Crescent were completed by 1840 and the whole crescent was occupied by 1843. The seven houses on the south side of Pelham Street covenanted to be built by this agreement, originally known as Pelham Terrace and later as Nos. 42-48 (consec.) Pelham Street before being renumbered in 1897 as 12-24 (even), were also completed by 1843. (Of these, Nos. 12-18 were rebuilt in 1883-4 in dark brick and stone, probably to the designs of Charles Jones of Ebury Street, architect.[79]) The west side of Pelham Place, originally numbered 10-23 (consec.) from north to south and renumbered in 1864 as 1-29 (odd) from south to north, was completed by 1844.[23]

Bonnin also built two adjoining cottages behind the west side of Pelham Place. The northerly one, called Pelham Cottage, was occupied by Bonnin himself in 1841-2; the other was called Park Cottage (now Park House) after its first occupant, Thomas Park, a tailor.[80] Both are long, narrow, two-storey buildings treated in a pleasantly vernacular manner with informally planned interiors.[81] Approached only by narrow passageways from Pelham Street or Onslow Square, both cottages enjoy almost total seclusion and have been much sought after in recent years. Perhaps inevitably, they have also undergone much alteration. In 1888 a large studio was built (by Killby and Gayford) to the south of Park House and separated from it by a stone-paved courtyard.[82]

*In this deed the younger James Bonnin was described as a builder with an address in Vale Place, Hammersmith, but in 1835-7 he was described as a pewterer with a business in or near the City.[74]

The remaining houses in Pelham Street erected under the agreement of 1843 with James Bonnin junior, of which only Nos. 6-10 (even) survive, were completed by 1848.[23] Six houses were also built in the northward continuation of Pelham Place towards Thurloe Square (Plate 49b). This short stretch of road was originally known as Pelham Place North, but the houses have all been demolished.

Besides James Bonnin senior and junior, a number of other builders assisted with the development. Samuel Archbutt took leases, or was a party to leases, of Nos. 9-21 (odd) Pelham Place, but the applications to connect these houses to the sewer in the road were made by his son, Robert Archbutt.[83] James Buckley of Brompton, plumber and glazier, was the sub-lessee of a house in Onslow Place which he himself occupied and also took leases of No. 18 Pelham Crescent and several houses in Pelham Street now demolished.[84] Robert Cox of Chelsea, builder, was also much involved in building operations in Pelham Street and constructed sewers and pavements there; he was party to a sub-lease of Nos. 55 and 57, which form part of the attractive surviving terrace at Nos. 51-61 (odd) Pelham Street.[85]*

The Bonnins obtained some of the finance needed for the development by the normal method of mortgaging the building leases which were granted to them by the trustees. The intermediary in several of these transactions was Robert John Ashton, an attorney of Queen's Buildings, Brompton, and the mortgagee in a number of instances was his father, Robert Ashton, a retired builder. The Ashtons were later the first occupants of No. 2 Pelham Crescent.[87]

Many of the building leases, however, were not granted to the Bonnins or other builders, or to the occupants of the houses, but to third parties who can usually be presumed to have been providing some of the financial backing for the development. The lessee in such circumstances would normally grant a sub-lease to a builder for virtually the whole term of his head lease at an enhanced ground rent, the money he had evidently made available to the builder being perhaps a capitalisation of the improved ground rent. The builder often then proceeded to mortgage his sub-lease.

To take an example of how this worked, at No. 8 Pelham Crescent the head lease was granted by the Smith's Charity trustees in December 1835 to Ann Wissett of Bruton Street, Mayfair, a widow, for seventy-eight years from 25 March 1835 at a ground rent of £4 per annum. In September 1836 Ann Wissett granted a sub-lease to James Bonnin senior for seventy-seven-and-a-half years, less three days, from 29 September 1835 at a rent of £12 per annum. Bonnin mortgaged the sub-lease in October 1836 for £500 to which £300 was later added, and in January 1840 he assigned the sub-lease for £187, still subject to the mort-

gage of £800 and, of course, to the rent of £12, to the first occupant of the house, George Newman, a wine merchant.[88]

The mortgagee in this instance was Stroud Lincoln, esquire, who lived firstly at No. 23 and then at No. 8 Alexander Square,[23] and who was the most important of Bonnin's early sources of finance. Several of the trustees' leases were granted directly to him and, as indicated by this example, he also provided standard mortgages at five per cent interest.[89] At his death in 1850, when his estate was worth £20,000, he was still the head lessee of seventeen houses on the Smith's Charity estate and nine on the neighbouring Alexander estate.[90]

Another important backer in the 1840's was Stephen Phillips, a timber merchant with an address in New Broad Street in the City.[91] He was the head lessee of nearly all the houses in Pelham Street erected under the agreement with James Bonnin junior,[92] and he was also very much involved in James Bonnin senior's development in Brompton (now Egerton) Crescent (see below). Like Lincoln, Phillips also provided normal mortgages, such as one to James Bonnin junior for £4,000 on the security of four houses in Thurloe Square (on the Alexander estate) and two in Pelham Street.[93]

The price of a new house in Pelham Crescent was about £1,000.[94] No prices are known for houses in Pelham Place when new, but in 1861 five houses there, which were let at rack rents of between £60 and £65 per annum each, were sold at an average price per house of slightly over £700.[95]

The distinguished ensemble of stucco-faced houses in Pelham Crescent and Pelham Place for which Basevi and Bonnin were responsible remains amongst the most attractive in this part of London (Plates 49-50, fig. 24). The two continuous ranges in the crescent, consisting of thirteen houses to the east of Pelham Place and twelve to the west, have three main storeys with basements and attics. At the corners with Pelham Place and in that street itself there are no attic storeys (apart from two later additions). The façades are treated with the kind of austere Graeco-Roman detailing which Basevi handled so well, those in the crescent being slightly more embellished. There the enclosed porches framed by pilasters with highly individual palm-leaf capitals, the horizontal channelling of the stucco on the ground storey, the stringcourse at second-floor sill level and the crowning balustrade were all faithfully executed from Basevi's drawings, as was the unusual provision of casement windows with balconies on both the ground and first floors. The ironwork of the balconies is, however, more ornate and less in keeping than the simple geometrical pattern of interlacing lozenges prescribed by Basevi, but the area railings, with the 'spear' heads matching the palm leafs of the capitals, are as he intended. The six-panelled doors shown in the drawings were

---

*Other building tradesmen who were lessees or sub-lessees of houses in Pelham Crescent, Place and Street were Henry Thomas Adams of Brompton, builder; John Legeytt Colchester of Clareville Street, builder; Henry Hart of Knightsbridge, house decorator; Evan Jones of Chelsea, builder; Benjamin Kendall of Chelsea, plasterer; Thomas Lester of Knightsbridge, plumber; William Long of Little Chelsea, builder; James Quance of Elm Terrace, Fulham Road, plumber; Thomas Smith of Richmond, plumber; William Strickland of Michael's Place, builder; George Symons of Brompton, carpenter; Thomas Taylor of Chelsea, plasterer; John Thomas Wilkins of Brompton, oil and colourman.[86]

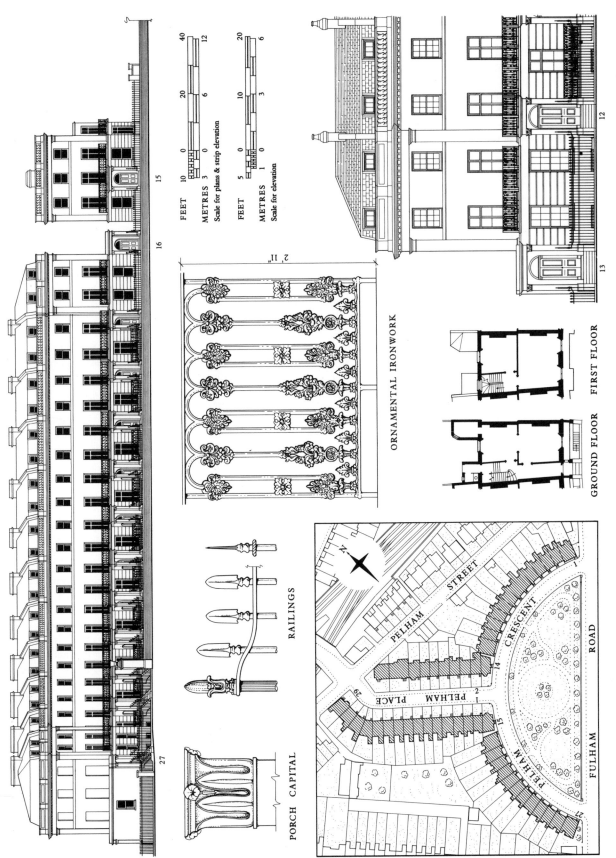

FEET 10 0 20 40

METRES 3 0 6 12

Scale for plans & strip elevation

FEET 5 0 10 20

METRES 1 0 3 6

Scale for elevation

15

16

27

2' 11"

ORNAMENTAL IRONWORK

RAILINGS

PORCH CAPITAL

GROUND FLOOR   FIRST FLOOR

12

13

N

PELHAM STREET

PELHAM PLACE

CRESCENT

PELHAM

FULHAM ROAD

14

29

15

27

1

1

2

Fig. 24. Pelham Crescent, site and house plans, elevations and details. George Basevi, architect, 1833–41

replaced by equally elegant four-panelled ones, some with narrow bands held in place by studs. The latter are similar in design to some of the doors in Alexander Square, where Miss Dorothy Stroud has seen Sir John Soane's influence on Basevi, who was formerly one of his assistants.[96] (The bands are shown on one of the detailed drawings accompanying the second agreement of 1838.) The fanlights were also varied in execution.

In Pelham Place the porches are dispensed with, the first-floor windows have individual balconettes with pattern-book cast-iron railings and the ground-floor windows are fitted with conventional sashes. The end houses of the main blocks on each side are marked by simple square pilasters and canted bays rising through three storeys (including the basement), although not to the height shown on Basevi's drawings. Those at the corner with Pelham Crescent, which are numbered 14 and 15 in the crescent, have porches and ironwork in common with the remainder of the crescent on their south fronts, with the bizarre effect that the balcony ironwork on the principal façade of each house differs from that on the return front. This was not anticipated by Basevi, whose drawings show the same ironwork used in both streets. No. 15 Pelham Place, the centre house on the long west side, is singled out for a different treatment and has a blocked parapet instead of a balustrade, wide architraves to the windows and a continuous balcony at first-floor level with railings which may be of a later date.*

Nos. 16 and 18 Pelham Place are exceptions to the general pattern and consist of an attractive pair of two-storeyed stuccoed houses with wide Doric porticoes (which were added in 1872[98]), overhanging eaves and outside shutters to the windows. In the building agreement Bonnin was to be allowed to build 'a small cottage' on this plot, and in the event he let the ground to James Jolley, as described above.

Pelham Street, too, was to be set aside for semi-detached pairs of 'cottages', and Basevi's responsibility for the houses in this street probably extended only to approving the elevations and materials. Partly no doubt because Bonnin let some of the ground to Jolley, who ran into difficulties, a very heterogeneous collection of houses was in fact erected along its length, most of which has been demolished. The two main groups to survive, Nos. 20-24 (even) and 51-61 (odd), are pleasant small two-storeyed stuccoed houses with basements. Nos. 6-10 (even) were built under the agreement with James Bonnin junior in 1843 and are similar houses, but have been more altered.

Most of the houses in Pelham Crescent and Pelham Place have straightforward plans with side hallways and dog-leg staircases at the rear, two rooms to a floor (although frequently made into one from the beginning by

an arched opening on both ground and first floors) and shallow extensions at the back (fig. 24). In Pelham Crescent a barely perceptible splay to the houses compensates for the curve of the crescent. Here the end houses of each segment have extensions at the side containing the entrances, which were originally single-storeyed but which have now been heightened in two instances, and Nos. 14 and 15, at the corners with Pelham Place, have central entrances.

Shallow cornices and simple chimneypieces provided the main decorative features before the embellishments made by later owners. (Sir) Nigel Playfair, the actor-manager, whose residence at No. 26 Pelham Crescent from about 1910 to 1922 is commemorated by a Blue Plaque, surprised his visitors by his taste in interior decoration which included a dark, bold wallpaper of peacocks, the use of black in the colour scheme of the house, and a yellow ceiling and walls to the dining-room.[99] The architect Philip Tilden decorated No. 3 Pelham Crescent with an elaborate *trompe l'oeil* scheme in the early 1920's when he took up residence there.[100]

At the time of the census of 1841 twenty houses in Pelham Crescent were in substantially normal occupation. Eleven of the householders classified themselves as 'independent' (seven men and four women), and there were also two clergymen, two clerks, a merchant, an architect (George Godwin the elder), a serjeant-at-law, a private tutor and a schoolmistress. There were 122 occupants in the twenty houses (an average of almost exactly six per house), including 42 servants (just over two per house on average), of whom all but three were female. In Pelham Place only seven houses were in normal occupation. Their householders included the judge and journalist Sir John Stoddart and the comedian Frederick Vining, together with two independents (one of each sex), a barrister, a clergyman and a student at law. There were thirty-seven occupants in the seven houses (an average of 5.3 per house). Of these eleven (all female) were servants, divided between five households with two servants each, one with one and one with none.[101]

On the night of the census of 1851 all twenty-seven houses in Pelham Crescent and twenty-one in Pelham Place had their usual complement of inhabitants as far as can be determined. Of the twenty-seven householders in the crescent, thirteen apparently derived their income from such sources as government funds, annuities, house property or land, and of these seven were women including five widows. There were also four merchants, three architects (Godwin, Alexander F. Ashton and William Drew), a senior clerk, an army major, an army superintendent, a barrister, a solicitor, a surgeon and a music publisher. The occupants, excluding visitors, numbered 165 (again an average of almost exactly six per house), of whom 67 (2.5

---

*In a memoir the architect William Willmer Pocock claimed that he had made drawings for five houses in Pelham Place for Samuel Archbutt, who was the lessee of this house, and he may have been responsible for the somewhat coarser treatment here, although the house was apparently completed before Basevi's death.[97]

per house on average) were servants, all but four female. In Pelham Place, of the twenty-one householders ten indicated that they were living on income from investments of one kind or another, and of these six were women, five of them widowed. The occupations represented were those of barrister, solicitor, army agent, army clothier, civil engineer, wine and spirit merchant, confectioner, comedian (Alfred Wigan) and 'bookseller's assistant', while two women kept lodging-houses. Excluding the lodging-houses, the occupants of the other nineteen houses totalled 103 (5.4 per house), of whom 32 (1.7 per house) were servants, all women.[102]

The evidence of the census enumerators' books suggests that Bonnin and the trustees, under Basevi's guidance, catered for a solidly middle-class clientèle, a considerable number of whom could be described as rentiers. Those who had occupations belonged mainly to the professions, with the mercantile element following closely behind.

Other inhabitants of Pelham Crescent during the nineteenth century included the French statesman and historian, François Guizot, who maintained Brompton's tradition as a place of refuge for exiles when he lived at No. 21 in 1848-9 after the revolution of 1848.[103] The actor and actress Robert and Mary Ann Keeley lived at No. 10 from 1856, he until his death in 1869 and she until her death in 1899.[104] Another celebrated theatrical figure, the actor and impresario Charles James Mathews, who pursued an early, brief career as an architect, occupied No. 25 from 1865 to 1870,[105] and Edward John Trelawny, the adventurer and companion of Byron and Shelley, lived at No. 7 from 1861 until 1881.[106]

Sussex Terrace

Another small development which had begun slightly earlier than Bonnin's in Pelham Crescent was the erection of a row of houses known as Sussex Terrace on the south side of Old Brompton Road, on the site of the present block of flats called Sussex Mansions. The builder was Thomas Rice of Brompton, a mason. In an article which was written at a later date in *The Builder*, probably by George Godwin junior, the comment was made that this was looked upon as a 'somewhat hazardous' venture at the time because of the rural nature of the vicinity, and sure enough Rice was declared bankrupt in 1833.[107] The terrace consisted of seven houses to which James Bonnin senior added another for his own residence in 1842-3.[108] This was a substantial bow-fronted end-of-terrace house with its entrance in the middle of the side elevation and a central hallway and staircase across the width of the house. There was also a large yard at the side with a workshop at the rear. Bonnin had given up Onslow Cottage to his builder son James in 1839 and had lived successively at No. 3 Pelham Place, at Pelham Cottage and in South Street before making his home in Sussex Terrace in 1843.[23]

Egerton Crescent, Egerton Terrace and Crescent Place

On the same date, 25 July 1843, that James Bonnin junior had entered into his agreement to complete the building of Pelham Street, James Bonnin senior contracted to undertake a much more substantial development on the site of Brompton Grange. This was made possible by the financial difficulties of the singer John Braham which forced him to give up the mansion and its extensive grounds. In 1843 the trustees decided to demolish the house, and thereby made six acres available for building development. Bonnin agreed to take the land, and the trustees undertook to grant leases to him or his nominees for terms equivalent to eighty-four years from midsummer 1843 at an ultimate total ground rent of £250 per annum, payable in the fifth and succeeding years (the same rent that Braham had been paying for Brompton Grange).[109]

The development produced thirty-four houses in Brompton (now Egerton) Crescent, eighteen in Michael's Grove (now Egerton Terrace) to which two more were added in 1850 at the south end of the east side under an agreement with the builder Benjamin Watts, ten in Yeoman's Row to which two more were also added under Watts's agreement (all now demolished), and thirteen 'cottages' and some stabling in Crescent Place. The houses in Brompton Crescent, made up of twenty-four in the crescent proper and two short return 'wings' of five houses each, were numbered 26-59 (consec.) in continuation of the numbering of the existing late-eighteenth-century houses opposite to the new crescent (see page 90). This numbering was retained both when the latter houses were demolished in 1885 and when the street was renamed Egerton Crescent in 1896 after the Honourable Francis Egerton, one of the Smith's Charity trustees. The houses on the east side of Michael's Grove were numbered 1-10 Grange Villas or The Grange until renumbered as 23-41 (odd) Michael's Grove in 1877. On the west side of the street the northernmost house was called Michael's Grove Lodge, Grange Lodge or simply The Lodge and the houses to the south of it were numbered 1-9 (consec.) Grange Terrace. In 1877 these ten houses were renumbered 6-24 (even) Michael's Grove. The numbers given in 1877 were retained when the street was renamed Egerton Terrace in 1898.

Like Pelham Crescent and its adjoining streets, the development appears to have proceeded rapidly and, judging from the rate of occupancy, successfully. Twelve houses in Egerton Crescent were in occupation by 1845. By 1847 only two houses, Nos. 45 and 47, remained empty and they were taken in 1849 and 1848 respectively. The eighteen houses in Egerton Terrace which were built under the agreement with Bonnin were all occupied by 1848 and those in Crescent Place likewise.[23]

James Bonnin senior's actual involvement in building operations may have been confined to Egerton Crescent and even here he was not the direct lessee from the trustees of any of the houses, though he was sub-lessee of thirteen and a party to two other sub-leases. The principal speculator involved in Egerton Crescent was Stephen Phillips, the timber merchant who was at the same time James Bonnin junior's main backer in Pelham Street. Twenty-eight of the thirty-four houses in the crescent were leased directly to Phillips by the trustees at ground rents, with one exception, of £2 per annum each.[110] Phillips then sub-let the houses, usually to James Bonnin senior or other builders, at improved ground rents, generally £15 per annum.[111] As in Pelham Crescent, these sub-leases were usually mortgaged to obtain additional capital, Bonnin, for instance, borrowing £2,000 from George Newman, the wine merchant of No. 8 Pelham Crescent, on the security of his sub-lease of Nos. 50-53 Egerton Crescent.[112] Stephen Phillips, who was also the lessee of some twenty of Bonnin's houses on the Alexander estate and the owner of extensive property interests in North Kensington, Paddington and Islington, retired to Preston, near Brighton, and when he died in 1862 his effects were valued at nearly £35,000.[113]

Another large-scale undertaker who was active in the vicinity of Egerton Crescent was Benjamin Watts. He was living in Harriet Street, Lowndes Square, when development began, but moved to No. 49 Brompton Crescent in 1845,[114] and in 1851, when he was sixty-eight years old, he described himself as a retired builder.[115] He was the lessee of the terrace of ten houses erected in Yeoman's Row (now demolished) on the actual site of Brompton Grange, as well as of one house in Egerton Crescent, three in Egerton Terrace and ten in Crescent Place. In c. 1850 he also contracted with the trustees to build two more houses at the southern end of Yeoman's Row and Nos. 39 and 41 Egerton Terrace. Two houses in Crescent Place were leased to Benjamin Watts junior, who kept the Admiral Keppel public house in Fulham Road.[116] Benjamin Watts senior, like Phillips, generally granted sub-leases of his houses to other builders at improved ground rents.[117]*

Unlike Pelham Crescent, no drawings survive for Egerton Crescent, but there is no reason to doubt Basevi's responsibility for the design. An obituary which appeared in *The Builder* shortly after his death and which was probably written by the journal's editor, George Godwin the younger, a resident in nearby Alexander Square, stated that 'the new part of Brompton Crescent' was designed by Basevi, and in 1847 the trustees reimbursed Bonnin £22 which 'he had paid Mr. Basevi for drawings', perhaps for Egerton Crescent.[119]

Egerton Crescent does not have a break in the middle, and the continuous stuccoed terrace of twenty-four houses which Basevi designed to fit the curve of the crescent is articulated in a more complex manner than the shorter ranges of Pelham Crescent (Plate 51a, b, fig. 25). Each house is basically a two-bay unit of about twenty-four-foot frontage, but three types can be distinguished. The principal type, which has a basement, three main storeys, and garrets within a conventional mansard roof, is closest to the houses in Pelham Crescent and has similar plain window openings and a continuous stringcourse at third-floor level. The two houses in the centre differ in having a full attic storey with a double-pitch roof behind a tiny linking parapet, but are otherwise identical to the first type.

The terrace is, however, punctuated at regular intervals by a third type of house which is advanced from the general building line. Of four full storeys above ground with a hipped roof, it has quoins at the sides and triple windows at first- and second-floor level, that on the first floor having pilasters with anthemion-and-palmette capitals and a full entablature, and that on the second consisting of a triple sash window in a wide opening. It is in these houses and their relationship to the rest of the terrace that the stylistic changes of the decade since the design of Pelham Crescent are most apparent.

Even within houses of the same type variations are introduced by the placing of the doorways to create a complex rhythm of paired and single porches. Some of the entrance doors still retain the studded bands already noticed in Alexander Square and Pelham Crescent.

The unifying factors are the stuccoed façades, channelled on the ground floor and plain above, the continuous dentilled cornice above the third storey and the balconies, which are joined on all except the projecting houses. The ironwork of the balcony railings, which consists of straight bars relieved by clusters of leaves at top and bottom, is particularly pleasing. The shallow porches too are identical throughout and are formed by square three-quarter columns with conventional Ionic capitals carrying plain entablatures and dentilled cornices. As in Pelham Crescent there are casement windows at both ground- and first-floor level, the former opening on to balconettes with iron railings of the same pattern as those above.

The short, straight wings at the sides of Egerton Crescent, consisting of Nos. 26-30 on the west and Nos. 55-59 on the east, introduce further variety. Formerly each range contained three three-storey houses with basements and garrets flanked by two houses with four full storeys above basements, but the reconstruction of Nos. 26 and 27 after war damage as a single block of flats with an over-fenestrated façade, and other alterations, have marred the symmetry. In both ranges the first-floor windows have straight, bracketed hoods, and there is room for full Ionic porticoes and small front gardens.

---

*Other builders or persons associated with the building trades who were granted sub-leases of houses in Egerton Crescent, Egerton Terrace and Crescent Place were Henry William Atkinson of York Place, Fulham Road, builder; Richard Ball of Queen's Buildings, Brompton, statuary mason; Thomas Braund of Marlborough Road, Chelsea, plumber; James Buckley of Onslow Place, plumber; James Robert Chapman of Pimlico, builder; William Emmins of Montpelier Row, builder; William Fitch of Michael's Grove, builder; John Henderson of Belgravia, builder; William Long of Seymour Walk, Little Chelsea, builder; William Pocock of St. Marylebone, plumber; Thomas Stimpson of Trevor Square, carpenter; William Strickland of Michael's Place, carpenter; Daniel Tidey of Chelsea, builder; Richard Watkins of Pimlico, whitesmith.[118]

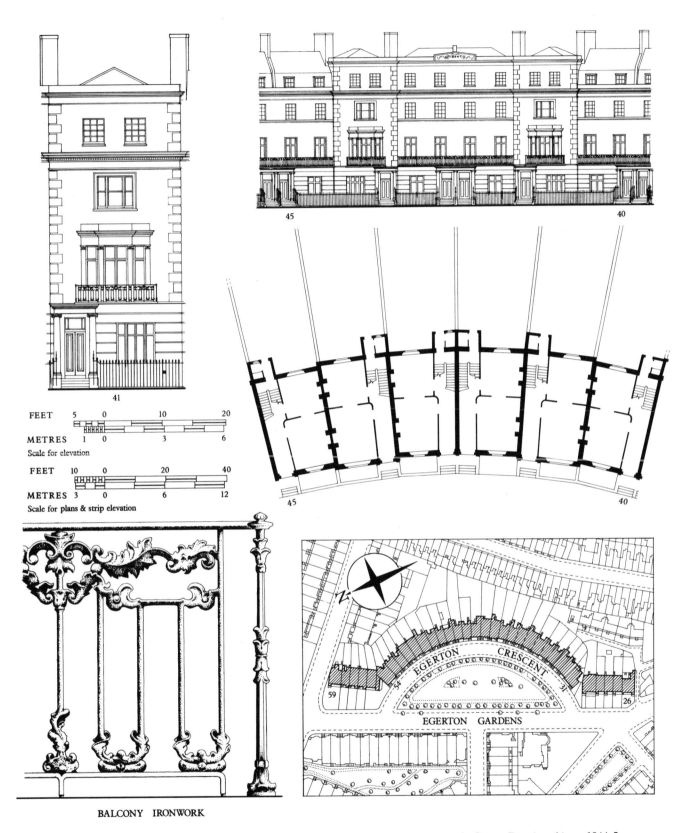

FEET 5 0 10 20
METRES 1 0 3 6
Scale for elevation

FEET 10 0 20 40
METRES 3 0 6 12
Scale for plans & strip elevation

BALCONY IRONWORK

Fig. 25. Egerton Crescent, site and house plans, elevations and detail of balcony ironwork. George Basevi, architect, 1844-5

The interiors are relatively plain and simple. The houses around the crescent are of a conventional side hallway type, and the ground-floor plans drawn on their leases show that they generally had openings between the front and rear rooms and very shallow closet wings at the back of the staircases (fig. 25). Only in the end houses of the short ranges at each side of the crescent was anything more ambitious in plan attempted, the now demolished No. 26, for instance, having had a side entrance and an open-well staircase in the centre of the house. The original decorative features chiefly consist of cast-iron balustrades to the stone staircases and some modest cornices and chimneypieces.

The cul-de-sac of Egerton Terrace contains groups of houses of different design, and Basevi's role here is more uncertain, but characteristically all the houses have stuccoed façades and are pleasing in their variety. They comprise a semi-detached pair of three-storey villas with a bracketed eaves cornice at Nos. 23 and 25, an individual house with a central entrance at No. 6 (where James Robinson Planché, the antiquary and dramatist, was the first occupant), a terrace of two storeys above a semi-basement on the remainder of the east side, and a terrace with three main storeys and garrets, also above a semi-basement, on the west.

The detailing of the terrace on the eastern side is crisper and more inventive and includes sharply incised Greek Corinthian capitals to the prominent porches, straight hoods carried on carved consoles to the ground-floor windows, a deep bracketed cornice and a balustraded parapet (Plate 51c).* The houses in this terrace have wider frontages and greater depth than those opposite, and sometimes they also have an interesting plan variant in the form of an L-shaped hallway in which the staircase makes a quarter turn in its upper flight. Originally they also had flat rear elevations with no closet wings, but most of them have been altered at the back and some also now have added attic storeys.

Charles Gray, who, as an architectural student, helped to found the Architectural Association in 1847, was one of the first occupants of No. 31 Egerton Terrace (formerly No. 5 Grange Villas) from 1846 until at least 1851. He lived there with relatives, including an aunt who derived her income from an annuity and was the rated occupier. Gray was not a prolific architect in later life but produced some highly distinctive buildings including Nos. 56 and 58 Queen's Gate Terrace, Kensington.[120]

The first occupants of the houses built during the 1840's in Egerton Crescent and Terrace differed little in their social composition, in fact, from the inhabitants of Pelham Crescent and Place. At the time of the census of 1851 thirty of the houses in Egerton Crescent appear to have been in normal occupation. These thirty houses were inhabited by 186 people (6.2 persons per house on average), of whom 71 (2.4 per house) were servants, all but two of them women. Nine of the householders described themselves as annuitants or fundholders, including five widows, and four others were landed proprietors, three of them also widows. There were two doctors, two attorneys, two clerks (employed in the War Office and a banking house), an official in the Queen's household, a colonel in the East India Company, a superintendent of mails with the Post Office, a civil engineer, a tax inspector, a music teacher, two merchants, a dealer in fancy goods, a hosier and a retired builder (Benjamin Watts, who, although he did not state it on the census form, received an income from house rents).[121]

The houses surviving from the original development in Crescent Place, Nos. 1A and 1-8, make up a terrace of simple but attractive double-fronted houses, brick-faced except at No. 1A which has been stuccoed, each with two main storeys and a basement and two rooms per floor. Most of them also have small closet wings at the rear. They were originally intended in part to form a buffer between the houses in Egerton Crescent and any undesirable developments which might take place on adjoining land in Chelsea which did not belong to the trustees, 'it being the intention of the said Trustees . . . that the north front of [each house] shall present a neat and clean appearance to the occupiers of houses in Brompton Crescent and be a skreen [sic] from any more unsightly buildings yards or gardens on land not belonging to the said Trustees'.[122] The occupants were not to hang washing or keep pigs and dogs in front of the houses and were not to use them for any trade or business, lunatic asylums and brothels being specifically prohibited.

The small houses in such 'back' streets provided much-needed accommodation for the working population engaged in supplying those numerous services demanded by the nearby well-to-do residents which could best be provided close at hand. In 1851 the twelve occupied houses in Crescent Place were inhabited by no fewer than 105 people. Three households to a single house were common and there were sometimes four. The occupants included married out-servants, several building tradesmen, tailors, dressmakers and milliners, a cowkeeper and dairyman with two living-in milkmen, and that essential Victorian tradesman, the shoemaker, who lived here with his wife and eight children. (The dairyman and shoemaker lived at premises, since demolished, on the west side of the southern arm of the street, where the ban on trades was presumably waived.) Such a pattern of occupancy was probably not to the liking of the trustees, however, for their treasurer and solicitor, Reginald Bray, later said that 'Crescent Place was built against my wish'.[123]

Brompton Hospital

In May 1844 the trustees signed a building agreement with the governors of the Hospital for Consumption and

*The similarity in the general design of these houses to others built at about the same time in Thurloe Street on the Alexander estate, although there are differences in detail, has been noted on page 76.

Diseases of the Chest who soon afterwards built a new hospital on about three acres of the charity's lands. The site was eventually sold to the governors in 1868 and the history of Brompton Hospital (as it became known) is described in Chapter VII.

The Deaths of Basevi and Bonnin

On 16 October 1845 Basevi was killed by a fall while inspecting the western tower of Ely Cathedral. His death deprived the estate of architectural guidance of a high order. The developments undertaken in the seventeen years of his surveyorship produced distinguished, well-mannered terraces which have, for the most part, survived with relatively little alteration, although their façades have been surprisingly disfigured in places by the addition of drainage pipes. Completely stuccoed except in the most minor of houses, the façades vary in style from the unclut-tered late-Regency of Pelham Crescent to the more trans-itional early-Victorian of Egerton Crescent. Philip Tilden remarked of Pelham Crescent, 'How very pleasant it is to live in a crescent',[124] and certainly these gently curved terraces, echoing the grander classical traditions of Bath but with tree-shaded communal gardens in front, retain a serenity which the more ostentatious products of the Ital-ianate style often lack.*

In July 1846 James Bonnin senior was declared bank-rupt.[125] There were no indications in his work on the Smith's Charity estate that he was encountering difficulties, and, judging by the rapid occupancy rate, the houses which he built there seem to have met with the approval of prospective purchasers and tenants. Three years after his bankruptcy he attributed his failure to 'undertaking more than my means would justify, . . . the fluctuations in the funds in 1845 and 1846, and fall in House property with some heavy losses',[126] but his explanation does not accord with what is known about the general economic conditions in these years. Interest rates had begun to rise in 1845-6, but the extreme volatility of the financial markets and the crisis which led to a sharp downturn in building activity did not come until after Bonnin's bankruptcy. Nevertheless he may have been an early victim of the depression which affected builders in South Kensington particularly severely in 1847-8.

His assessment of the reasons for his failure were given in a letter to the Kensington Board of Guardians in which he successfully solicited money to assist him in emigrating to South Australia, some of his children having already emi-grated there. He landed on 26 December 1849 with his wife and four other children but died in Adelaide on 8 January 1850 of 'natural decay'.[127] His builder son James Bonnin junior had also been declared bankrupt in 1848,[128] but he did not emigrate and, after a short spell as Inspector

of Nuisances for the Kensington Board of Guardians in 1848-50,[129] he later resumed his building career in London.

In 1845 the total rental value of the estate amounted to £3,734 per annum.[130] Five years earlier it had been a little over £4,000, but some land had since been let for building and no return on it was yet being received. In fact the substantial increase in the rental value of the estate since 1825 (when it was £1,023) had come, not from the new developments, but from the rack rents obtained from the twenty-one-year leases which had been granted in 1830 of Novosielski's houses in Michael's Place, Michael's Grove and Brompton Crescent.

Charles James Freake and Onslow Square and Gardens

For four decades following the death of Basevi in 1845 the history of the Smith's Charity estate was dominated by one man — (Sir) Charles James Freake (1814-1884), builder, architect, patron of music and the arts, public benefactor and (from 1882) a baronet. On the Smith's Charity estate alone the firm belonging to this titan of the building world was responsible for the erection of some 330 large houses, approximately one hundred separate coach-houses and stables, and two churches. It also undertook the construc-tion of the roads, sewers and other ancillary features of building developments and was responsible for the laying out of half a dozen communal gardens. This estate was the core of Freake's operations but he had already been building in Belgravia before he turned his attention to South Kensington, and he also built extensively in adjacent parts of South Kensington and Westminster, as well as finding the time to erect four large houses in Grosvenor Square, at the same time as he was working on the Smith's Charity estate.[131] In all, in a career extending over nearly fifty years, he built well over five hundred houses as well as innumerable mews buildings, three churches, the National Training School for Music (now the Royal College of Organists), a block of model dwellings in Chelsea, and the former Twickenham Town Hall, the last two now demol-ished.

Freake was the son of Charles Freake, a coal merchant turned victualler, who in the 1820's took a sub-lease from the builder Seth Smith of the Royal Oak public house in Elizabeth Street, Belgravia, on the Grosvenor estate.[132] Freake senior speculated himself in a small way in that vicinity, generally by taking further sub-leases from Smith,[133] and in 1837 he in turn granted a sub-lease of a small mews house in Royal Oak (now Boscobel) Place to his son, Charles James, who was described as a carpenter.[134] In the following year Charles James Freake,

*Besides the houses already referred to, Basevi's work on the Smith's Charity estate also included St. Saviour's Church and Walton Place, both in Chelsea, as well as Sydney Place and perhaps part of Onslow Square in the area to the west of Pelham Crescent which is described in the next section.

now with the designation of builder, was the sub-lessee of Seth Smith for house plots in Elizabeth Street,[135] and over the next five years he built some forty houses on the south side of Eaton Square and in South Eaton Place and Chester Row.

Basevi was involved in the development of Belgravia through his designs for Belgrave Square, but there is no evidence of an association between him and Freake until 1843, when Freake contracted to build the small Gothic church of St. Jude in Turk's Row, Chelsea (now demolished), to Basevi's designs.[136]

Thus when the lease of Thomas Gibbs's nursery expired in 1843 and the Smith's Charity trustees wished to extend development westwards Freake had the ear of Basevi and was able to offer his services to the trustees. They concluded a building agreement with him in April 1844 while he was still completing St. Jude's Church.

This agreement retained some features of a general plan for the development of this part of the estate which had been drawn up by Basevi as early as 1833.[137] In particular a proposed new road connecting Fulham Road with Old Brompton Road took shape as Sydney Place and the eastern side of Onslow Square. Originally Basevi had envisaged that there would be a small square at the southern end of this road opening on to Fulham Road, but by 1844 the proposed square had been moved northwards. It was still to be relatively small with its long axis north-south and with a row of houses on the western side backing on to the avenue of elms which formed the western boundary of Freake's take.[138] In the course of building, however, the square was much enlarged in a westward direction.

The agreement stipulated that seventy-two houses and a pair of cottages were to be erected by 1851 at a graduated cumulative ground rent rising to £390 per annum (about £50 per acre) in the sixth and subsequent years. The houses were to be built to elevational designs and specifications provided by the trustees' architect and surveyor (at that time Basevi) and were all to have stucco fronts with porticoes and the full panoply of dressings and cornices. Freake agreed not to remove any trees without permission, perhaps a provision introduced to protect the famous avenue of elms which led up to Cowper House (see page 91).[139]

Six more building agreements were made with Freake — in 1849, 1850, 1855, 1861, 1862 and 1883 — covering all of the estate to the west of his first take with three exceptions. These were Sussex Terrace on the south side of Old Brompton Road, where houses had been built in the 1830's under leases expiring in 1895; a small plot at the south-western extremity of the estate occupied by a floor-cloth manufactory which was later converted into the factory of Henry Jones, organ-maker; and the site of Brompton Hospital, which was sold in 1868 to the hospital's governors.[140] Freake's last take was still largely undeveloped at his death in 1884 and his executors subsequently made a subsidiary agreement with C. A. Daw and Son under which the houses in Evelyn Gardens were built. During his lifetime, however, Freake's firm under-

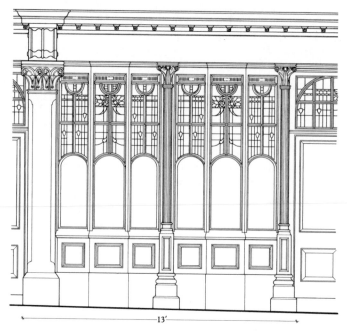

Fig 26. The Cranley Arms, Fulham Road, detail of ground-floor windows

took all the building work, and all but three of the numerous building leases of the houses erected by the firm were granted by the trustees to Freake himself directly. The length of the leases, as specified in the agreements, varied from eighty-six to ninety-nine years. In all slightly more than forty acres were made available to Freake for development, and the total ground rent eventually received by the trustees under the seven agreements amounted to a little over £3,000 per annum, or about £75 per acre.[141]

The Chronology of Development

Freake began building in Sydney Place (which was named after the third Viscount, later Earl, Sydney, one of the trustees) in 1844, and had completed the street by 1846. The first four houses in Onslow Square, Nos. 1-7 (odd), were begun in September 1845[142] and were all occupied by 1847. The whole square, including its western extension, was finished by 1865. Of the streets leading off the square, Sumner Terrace (now Nos. 25-34 Sumner Place and named after George and William Holme Sumner, other trustees) was begun in 1849 and completed by 1851. The northern arm of Sumner Place was begun in the latter year but surprisingly some of the houses do not seem to have been occupied for some ten years. Onslow Crescent (now demolished, on the site of Melton Court) dated from 1851-6.[143]

The three-storey stuccoed terrace with ground-floor shops at Nos. 48-78 (even) Fulham Road was erected in

1853-4 and originally called Cranley Terrace (Viscount Cranley being one of the titles held by the Earl of Onslow). Nos. 54-72 and the Cranley Arms public house (Plate 55d, fig. 26) took the place of a public house called the Old George and a group of houses known as Strong's Place. Most of these had been erected in 1811 by Thomas Strong, victualler, on a piece of former manorial waste, but the public house may well have been established earlier. The site, which encroached on to Fulham Road, had been sold by Lord Kensington, the lord of the manor, to Strong in 1811 and had in turn been purchased by Freake in 1851. He proposed to the Smith's Charity trustees that they should purchase the ground from him and in return grant him leases of the new houses which he planned to build there. The trustees readily agreed, obtaining an Act of Parliament to enable them to pay Freake £5,666-worth of Old South Sea Annuities for the land, in return for which he was to pay them a rent of £170 per annum on a seventy-seven-year lease. The conveyance to the trustees was dated 22 December 1853, by which time Freake had already begun the building of Cranley Terrace.[144]

Behind Cranley Terrace Freake constructed a complex of stables and workshops called Sydney Mews, which was entered through two arched openings between Nos. 48 and 50 Fulham Road on the east and Nos. 74 and 78 on the west. The demand for stabling in the area was still limited in the 1850's and parts of the site were used for Freake's own workshops and a large studio and foundry for Baron Carlo Marochetti, the sculptor, who lived on the south side of Onslow Square, perhaps at first briefly at No. 30 and then at No. 34, from 1849 until his death in 1867.[23] The painter C. E. Hallé recalled working in the studio, 'a large block of buildings at the back of Onslow Square', as a pupil of Marochetti, and it was here that Landseer's lions for the base of Nelson's Column in Trafalgar Square were cast by Marochetti.[145] After the sculptor's death the premises were converted into a number of artists' studios ranged on each side of an arched corridor. The work was in progress by October 1870 and among the artists and sculptors who rented studios in Avenue Studios, as they came to be called after the avenue of elms, were Hallé, (Sir) J. Edgar Boehm, Frank Dicey, John Willis Good, Charles Lutyens, (Sir) Edward J. Poynter, (Sir) Alfred Gilbert, John Singer Sargent, Philip Wilson Steer, George Edward Wade and John Tweed.[146] The studios are ingeniously arranged so that those on the south side of the central corridor are three storeyed with large windows and skylights in the upper storey to admit north light, while those on the other side facing north have only two storeys (Plate 55c). The conversion must have involved a considerable amount of rebuilding and Freake's firm undertook the work.[147]

Besides Strong's Place the trustees were also able to acquire another parcel of land which greatly facilitated the extension of development westwards. This was a three-and-three-quarter-acre plot now occupied by Nos. 99-115 (odd) Old Brompton Road, Nos. 17A-32 and 35-48

Onslow Gardens, most of Onslow Mews and the west side of Cranley Place (see fig. 23). The land had belonged to the Harrington-Villars estate and, after the partition of that estate in 1850-1, it formed part of the portion which was allocated to the Baron and Baroness de Graffenried Villars and sold by them to the Commissioners for the Exhibition of 1851. The plot separated the westernmost part of the Charity's lands, which was known as Brompton Heath but which had long since been used for market gardens and nurseries, from the remainder of the estate, and its acquisition was therefore clearly desirable from the point of view of the trustees. The 1851 Commissioners, in turn, needed the detached part of the Smith's Charity estate in St. Margaret's, Westminster, called the Carpet Ground, to complete their main rectangle bounded by Queen's Gate, Kensington Road, Exhibition Road and Cromwell Road. Although the Carpet Ground was an acre less in extent, the trustees were able to obtain a straight exchange which was agreed in December 1852 and confirmed by the Inclosure Commissioners in 1856. Freake was involved in the negotiations for the exchange and later complained on numerous occasions that he had been the loser by the transaction, even claiming that 'he had given up 2 or 3 millions' by the deal, though with what justification it is difficult to see.[148]

The ground acquired from the 1851 Commissioners became Freake's fifth take in August 1861, when Onslow Square was nearing completion, and he carried his building activities steadily westwards. Cranley Place was begun in 1863 or 1864 and completed by 1867. Building in Onslow Gardens was under way by 1863, the first occupants moved in during 1864, and by 1878 all of the houses in this complex pattern of streets had been completed and occupied.[91] Cranley Gardens was begun in 1875 and by November 1880 notice had been given to the district surveyor for the building of the whole of the west side of the street and the short range to the north of St. Peter's parsonage. A group of houses in the middle of the long western terrace, however, remained uncompleted or unoccupied for a considerable time, and no occupant for No. 38 is listed in the directories until 1900. This was in marked contrast to Onslow Gardens and perhaps indicates that the market for the large Italianate houses in which Freake specialized had finally become satiated. That he himself recognized this is indicated by his decision in 1883 to turn to more compact houses in a red-brick Queen Anne style at Nos. 15-37 (odd) Cranley Gardens to the south of St. Peter's Church.[149]

Office and Staff

Freake either lived on the estate or maintained an office there for most of the years during which the development was proceeding. In the early years he seems to have combined the two. From 1845 to 1847 he had an address at No. 10 Sydney Place, moving thence to No. 19 Onslow Square until 1849. His next address was No. 41 on the north side of the square, where he was living at the time of the census of 1851 with his wife, two infant sons, a nurse, a cook and two house servants.[150] By April 1852 he had moved further along the north side to No. 55, a large house with a forty-foot frontage, where he remained until 1857. He is also listed in the directories from 1856 to 1861 at No. 79 Onslow Square, but this was probably merely an office, and his place of residence seems to have been No. 19 Sumner Place from 1857 to 1860. In the latter year he moved to No. 21 Cromwell Road, which continued to be his London home for the remainder of his life.[143]

It was while living in Cromwell Road that Freake established himself firmly in social circles. The musical and theatrical events, especially the highly fashionable *tableaux vivants*, staged at his home for charity before audiences which included the Prince of Wales and the Duke of Edinburgh, were reported at length in the fashionable press. Freake also moved in Sir Henry Cole's circles, and his erection at his own cost of the National Training School for Music (now the Royal College of Organists) in 1874-5 was the principal factor in securing him a baronetcy in 1882. By the time of his death on 6 October 1884 he was a very wealthy man. Besides his property in Kensington, he owned an estate and a house at Twickenham, another at Kingston-upon-Thames, and left a personal estate worth upwards of £718,000.[151]

Despite moving his residence off the Smith's Charity estate in 1860 Freake generally maintained an office there, usually, in the normal manner of speculative builders, in a house which was awaiting the final fitting out for a tenant or purchaser. A more permanent office was established after his death, at No. 18 Cranley Gardens until 1890, then at No. 42 Cranley Gardens until 1957, and finally at No. 97 Old Brompton Road, where the Freake Estate Office remained until 1963, after which it no longer appears in the directories.[91]

Freake's workforce must have varied from time to time according to the state of his building operations, but in 1867 his employees were said to number nearly four hundred.[152] Some of the names, at least, of his large office staff are known. In 1844 the applications to the Westminster Commissioners of Sewers on his behalf were made by Henry Robert Kingsbury, who also signed the plan presented to the Commissioners in 1847 for the extension of Onslow Square.[153] In a deed of 1846, however, James Waller was described as Freake's clerk, and later many of the building notices given to the district surveyor were in his name; he was the nominal builder of the National Training School for Music and was a trustee of Freake's will.[154]

Charles F. Phelps was another of Freake's 'clerks' in 1856 and is probably identifiable with the Charles Frederick Phelps who was later a builder on the Phillimore and Holland estates to the north of Kensington High Street.[155]

By 1878 applications to the Metropolitan Board of Works on Freake's behalf were being made by Charles Henry Thomas,[156] who played an increasingly important role in the firm during Freake's last years. He also set up an independent architectural practice from about 1880 and was responsible for both the building and design of the surprising group of red brick houses at Nos. 15-37 (odd) Cranley Gardens (Plate 59b) which were the swan song of Freake's firm on the Smith's Charity estate.[157]

Thomas was not alone in the firm in graduating from building practice to architecture. Freake described himself as 'architect and builder' in the census of 1851, and in the directories from 1853 onwards he is invariably described at his office address as 'architect', a designation which was also handed down to James Waller when he was listed at the firm's office address from about 1869. Nevertheless other architects worked for the firm at one time or another. William Tasker was engaged from the early 1850's until at least the mid 1860's,[158] and the young George Edwards was a pupil and assistant in Freake's 'architects office' from 1865 to 1874.[159] W. H. Nash, who later had an independent career as an architect, was employed as a surveyor in the 1860's.[160] In 1871 Henry E. Cooper, architect and surveyor, was living at Brompton Cottage (on the site later occupied by Roland Houses, Old Brompton Road), which was owned by Freake, and he is almost certainly the H. E. Cooper who applied on Freake's behalf in 1872 to the Metropolitan Board of Works to form Reece Mews off Harrington Road.[161]

Finance

Freake's extensive building operations over four decades must have involved a capital expenditure of well over one million pounds, but as no records of his firm have survived information about the financial side of his operations has to be pieced together from fragmentary evidence. Like many builders he evidently had a close relationship with a solicitor, through whom he may have had access to small rentier savings. This was William Pulteney Scott of the firm of Hertslet, Scott and Hertslet, who lived from about 1841 in one of the first houses to be built by Freake, No. 62 Elizabeth Street, Belgravia, before moving in 1846 to No. 8 Onslow Square, where he must have been one of the first residents in the square.[162]*

What set Freake apart from the general run of speculative builders, however, was his early and heavy reliance on institutional lenders, in particular insurance companies. At first the most important of these was the Royal Exchange Assurance, which began to invest in mortgages to house builders in about 1839.[164] Freake was one of their first clients, borrowing from them in that year to complete three houses in Elizabeth Street and ten in Chester Terrace, Belgravia.[165] His father had insured his speculative houses

*Another partner in the same firm, Charles Hertslet, was the first occupant of No. 23 Egerton Terrace, which was built at about the same time as No. 8 Onslow Square on James Bonnin's development in the vicinity of Egerton Crescent.[163]

in Elizabeth Street with the Royal Exchange in 1833,[166] but the Corporation's minutes record that Freake was introduced by Seth Smith.[167] Borrowing on a large scale from insurance companies, though not unknown, was relatively rare at that time (Thomas Cubitt's major loans from the London Assurance Corporation not beginning until 1841[168]), but it was soon to become a common method of raising money for other big 'South Kensington' builders besides Freake.[169]

In February and April 1846 Freake asked to borrow up to £58,000 from the Royal Exchange on the security of houses he was building in Belgravia and in Sydney Place and Onslow Square, but by July he was ready to pay back £22,000 to enable four houses in Eaton Square and one in Onslow Square to be released for sale.[170] This remained the pattern for several years; he would borrow sums either on the security of deposited leases or formal mortgages and pay back sums when he had found purchasers for some of his houses. In 1852, for instance, he asked for No. 30 Onslow Square to be released on payment of £2,000, being 'the entire purchase money',[171] and in 1853 No. 36 was similarly released, William Makepeace Thackeray having contracted to buy it for '£2,100 over three years'.[172] By February 1853 the Corporation's loans to Freake amounted to £96,000,[173] and in August of that year he borrowed a further £30,000 on the security of his freehold estate at Twickenham.[174] This was the high point of Freake's indebtedness to the Corporation, and over the next few years he gradually reduced his commitment until he had repaid all his loans by 1867.[175]

In the late 1850's Freake also turned to another insurance company, the County Fire Office, borrowing chiefly on the security of his burgeoning developments in Exhibition Road. His solicitor by this time was the County Fire Office's own solicitor, Charles Fishlake Cundy, brother of the architect Thomas Cundy II.[176] There is, however, a paucity of evidence about how Freake financed his building operations on the Smith's Charity estate from the mid 1860's, and both this lack of information and the ease with which he was able to reduce his commitment to the Royal Exchange may indicate that from about that date he was able to supply the bulk of his working capital from the proceeds of his earlier houses.

He sold several houses outright at their original ground rent, Thackeray's at No. 36 Onslow Square for example, while some were sold to investors on completion, the assignment of the whole terrace comprising Nos. 9-31 (odd) Onslow Square early in 1847 being a case in point.[177] Other houses were let on short-term leases, some of them, however, being later sold to investors, such as Nos. 42 and 75 Onslow Square and Nos. 1-6, 12 and 25-34 Sumner Place (nineteen houses in all, producing some £1,760 per annum in rack rents) which were sold in 1854 to a Portuguese viscount for £28,700.[178]

The rack-rental values of Nos. 11-29 (odd) Onslow Square, which were comparable in terms of size to most of the houses built in the square up to about 1860, ranged from £110 to £130 per annum for each house.[179] The prices of houses sold individually in Onslow Square varied from £2,000 to £2,600 during the same period; those in Sumner Place fetched £1,500 to £1,700 and in Onslow Crescent £1,400 to £1,500.[180] No. 55 Onslow Square, an exceptionally spacious 'double' house with a forty-foot frontage, was sold for £5,000 in 1861,[181] but even this price should be compared with the much higher ones paid for Freake's houses elsewhere, £6,500 for No. 47 Eaton Square in 1858 for instance,[182] or £9,500 to £11,000 in 1864-70 for Nos. 23-27 (odd) Cromwell Road, subject to improved ground rents.[183] Prices for houses in Onslow Gardens and Cranley Gardens are, unfortunately, not known.

Although Freake's building operations seem generally to have progressed very smoothly, even he was not immune from the fluctuations of the building cycle. In 1848 — a very bad year for builders in South Kensington — he began only six houses (and four of those towards the end of the year) compared with twelve in 1847 (out of an intended eighteen) and twenty-four in 1849.[184] In 1857 — another trough in the cycle — he received a gently chiding letter from Bray and Company, the solicitors to the Smith's Charity trustees, reminding him that he was falling behind in his timetable for building under his agreements, but adding that 'Several circumstances having rendered it difficult for you to fulfil your agreement the Trustees are advised not to require the immediate strict performance of it'.[185] The evidence of the directories suggests that he was having some problem in disposing of houses in Onslow Crescent and Sumner Place at this time, and in the following year he was considering the possibility of allowing shops in Sumner Place.[186] Nevertheless there is no indication that Freake was ever in serious financial difficulties, and by the time of his death he was an immensely rich man.

The value to the charity of his enterprise was also very considerable. By 1884, the year of Freake's death, the total rental of the estate had risen to £11,992, almost exactly three times the income in 1844 when he had entered into his first building agreement. Two years after his death, when additional ground rents from the area covered by his last agreement had been received, the rental stood at £12,072, the highest it was to reach for some twenty-five years or more as the rack rents of Novosielski's houses in the eastern part of the estate were given up in return for the ground rents of the new houses which were erected in their place.

Architecture

In his building operations on the estate Freake was usually very much his own master but initially at least he had to build to the designs of Basevi. The latter's authorship of the houses in Sydney Place was mentioned in his obituary[187] and the short stuccoed terraces there are almost identical to the houses in Egerton Crescent, the only major difference being in the pattern of the balcony railings (fig. 27a).

Sydney Place (type), 1844   No. 5 Onslow Square, 1845   Onslow Square, south side (type), 1845

Fig. 27. Elevations of houses built by C. J. Freake

In the next range of houses to be built, Nos. 1-7 (odd) Onslow Square (Plate 52b, fig. 27b), it is already possible to see a dilution of Basevi's influence, however. This was conceived as a separate group of four houses in the plan of 1844 and was begun in September 1845, shortly before Basevi's death,[188] but the treatment of the façade must have dated from after that unhappy event. Several elements nevertheless closely relate to Basevi's earlier work. The houses are fully stuccoed, with four full storeys, basements and garrets, and parts of the façade project forward with quoins at the angles and characteristic triple windows at second-floor level. The corresponding windows on the first floor, however, are given a fully aedicu-

lated treatment with half-columns instead of pilasters, and at third-floor level there is a continuous Doric frieze with triglyphs and metopes embellished with paterae. This prominent and surprising feature must rank as a solecism in view of the fact that the porticoes have Ionic columns, and it seems likely that Freake embellished Basevi's designs without objection from Henry Clutton, who had been appointed surveyor to the charity's London estates on Basevi's death. A new pattern of crinoline-shaped balcony railings introduced on this group of houses was adopted with minor variations throughout Freake's later developments on the estate wherever iron balcony railings were used.

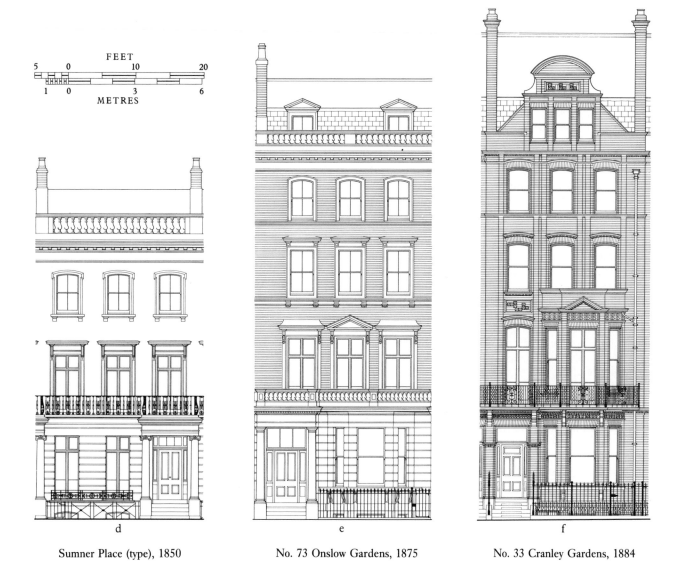

FEET
5   0   10   20
1   0   3   6
METRES

d

Sumner Place (type), 1850

e

No. 73 Onslow Gardens, 1875

f

No. 33 Cranley Gardens, 1884

Thereafter Freake and his staff were clearly in command and Clutton appears to have exercised little or no architectural control, confining his functions to that of surveyor. But there was no sharp break with Basevi's work, and several characteristic motifs were carried over into Freake's houses, such as the break-up of a long terrace by slight projections at the ends and centre, usually defined by quoins and emphasized by the use of triple windows, often sporting the anthemion-and-palmette capitals which Basevi had first used in Egerton Crescent. Apart from Nos. 1-7 Onslow Square, however, the houses in Onslow Square, Onslow Gardens and Cranley Place and the Italianate houses in Cranley Gardens have elevations of grey stock brick with stucco dressings rather than the completely stuccoed façades previously favoured by Basevi elsewhere on the estate and actually specified in the building agreement of 1844. Freake's reasons for this change were probably aesthetic rather than financial and he used stuccoed elevations in some of the shorter terraces — in Onslow Crescent (now demolished) and Sumner Place (Plate 55a, b) and at Nos. 87-97 (odd) Old Brompton Road and Nos. 48-78 (even) Fulham Road.

Until his sudden late conversion to the merits of the Queen Anne style at the southern end of Cranley Gardens in 1883, there was little variation in the basic design of Freake's houses on the Smith's Charity estate. As the development proceeded chronologically and geographically westwards the houses became larger, chiefly through the extension of the ground floor much further back to give greater accommodation at that level, but the basic Italianate formula remained a common denominator. All of the houses in the principal streets have four main storeys, basements and garrets, three-storey houses being restricted to shorter streets such as Sydney Place, Sumner Place and Cranley Place and the shops along the main highways which form the estate boundaries. These smaller houses lack nothing in architectural elaboration, however, the northern arm of Sumner Place in particular with its stuccoed façades and rhythmical window dressings still retaining much of the calm elegance it possessed at the end of the nineteenth century, despite the loss of its crowning balustrade (Plate 55a, fig. 27d).

The long terraces of Onslow Square (Plate 52a, c, fig. 27c) are similar but not precisely identical, the principal unifying features being a deep cornice resting on consoles at third-floor level and rows of Doric porches, those at the ends and centre of each terrace linked together to form colonnades (with the exception now of Nos. 77-109 odd, where reinstatement after war damage has led to extensive modification of the ground floor). On the eastern terrace, originally Nos. 9-31 (odd) but now renumbered 9-25 after the rebuilding of Nos. 25-31 as a single block of flats with a facsimile façade following war damage, pilasters are used at the angles of the projecting parts of the terrace, but elsewhere these give way to quoins. Only on the west side of the square proper, where a group of three quasi-semi-detached houses numbered 44-54 (even) share the frontage with St. Paul's Church, are the houses substantially different. Originally they appear to have had only three main storeys but have since been heightened in a very crude manner.

The first houses to be built in Onslow Gardens, Nos. 1-8 (consec.), which were at first called West Terrace, Onslow Square, introduce cement balustrades to the balconies, canted bays to the end houses of the terrace, and three windows to a floor in each house front, in contrast to two in Onslow Square. Their frontages are wider (twenty-five feet compared with twenty to twenty-four feet generally in the square), but, with the exception of Nos. 26-33 (consec.) Onslow Gardens, all of Freake's subsequent houses on the estate are three windows wide even though the frontages are sometimes as narrow as twenty-two feet. (It was Freake's practice to vary the width of his house fronts even within a continuous terrace.) Frequently the middle window on the ground floor has a pediment, sometimes segmental but usually triangular. At Nos. 17A-48 Freake reverted to iron balcony railings of the familiar pattern, but thereafter used cement balustrades to the balconies of houses in Onslow Gardens. At Nos. 35-48 (Plate 53a) canted bays were also provided on the ground floor of each house, another feature which was to become de rigueur in subsequent houses.

The building of the easternmost terraces in Onslow Gardens was followed by a short lull before the remaining ranges, consisting of Nos. 50-92 (even) and 49-91 (odd) with 1A Cranley Gardens, were begun in 1873-5. During the interval Freake had been building at the southern end of Queen's Gate, and when he resumed in earnest on the Smith's Charity estate his houses differed in one important respect from those which he had previously erected there, namely in the abandonment of the lip-service hitherto paid to the classical ordonnance by the placing of the main cornice at third-floor level with a full attic storey above. Henceforth the Italianate houses in Onslow and Cranley Gardens had a modillion cornice surmounted by a balustraded parapet at roof level and prominent stringcourses dividing the storeys below (Plate 53b, c, fig. 27e). The emphasis which this change gave to the height of the houses was accentuated by placing tall pedimented dormer windows either in line with and interrupting the parapet, as at Nos. 50-92 (even) Onslow Gardens, or set back slightly behind the balustrade, as at Nos. 49-77 (odd).

The treatment of the dormer windows may have derived its inspirations from alterations carried out in 1871-2 at No. 23 Onslow Gardens for the first occupant, Algernon Sidney Bicknell.[189] The work, for which Banks and Barry were the architects, appears to have been extensive and to have included major decorative work in the interior, especially in the staircase compartment and in the first-floor drawing-room, where the elaborate plasterwork of the ceiling includes the monogram 'ASB' as a small motif. On the exterior an elegant surviving iron verandah was added to Banks and Barry's designs, and it seems most probable that the attic storey was raised and pedimented architraves added to the lower dormer windows at the same time (fig. 28). If so, Freake may have admired the effect and decided to adopt a similar design for the dormer windows of the houses he erected subsequently in Onslow Gardens.

The treatment of the façades of the later ranges in Onslow Gardens is extended to those rear elevations which are visible from nearby streets across the long communal gardens (fig. 29). The regularity of these rear elevations is, however, achieved at the expense of convenience, the half-landings of staircases frequently coinciding awkwardly with the lower parts of windows.

In Cranley Gardens, Nos. 2-54 (even) are identical to the later ranges of Onslow Gardens except that on the balconies iron railings once more take the place of cement balustrades. Nos. 1-13 (odd) are slightly different — the Doric porches are paired and the stucco dressings are flatter in profile — but it is only with Nos. 15-37 (odd), to the south of St. Peter's Church, that there is a dramatic change in style. Here Italianate gives way to Queen Anne in the form of four-storey red-brick houses with high gabled attics and cut-and-moulded brickwork (Plate 59b, fig. 27f). Symmetry is eschewed and irregular variations introduced — canted bays in some places, square in others, a segmental gable on one house, a triangular on another. The frontages vary in width, but most of the houses have less depth than those to the north, leaving room at the rear of each plot for a small private garden. As already indicated, the architect of these houses was Charles Henry

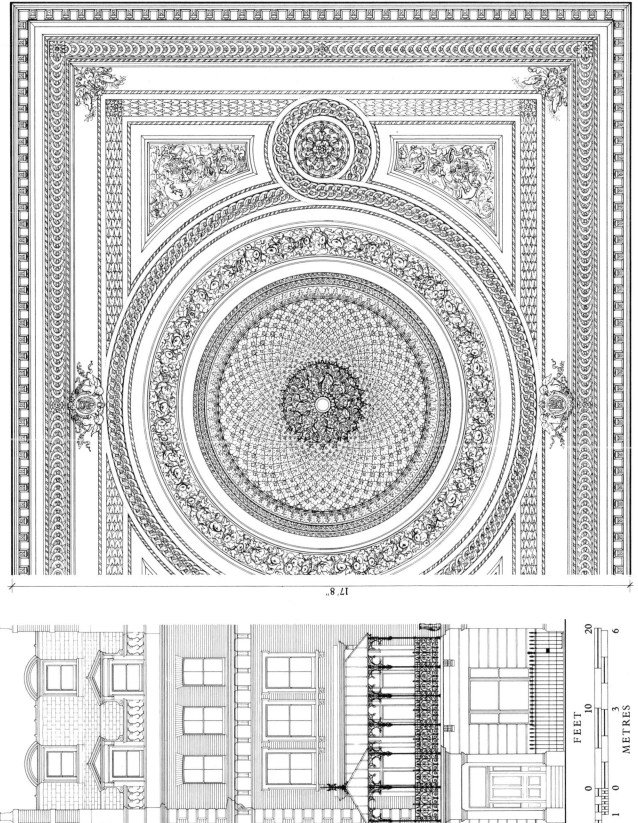

17' 8"

FEET 5   0   10   20

METRES 1   0   3   6

Fig. 28. No. 23 Onslow Gardens, elevation, and detail of first-floor front-room ceiling. C. J. Freake, builder, 1865; alterations and additions by Banks and Barry, architects, 1871-2

Thomas, but he was acting as Freake's employee and the building leases were granted to Freake.[190]

The majority of Freake's houses conformed to the standard London terrace-house plan with a side hallway leading to a dog-leg stair at the rear, in many cases constructed of stone, and two main rooms to a floor in the upper storeys. The basement contained the kitchen and other service quarters, and on the ground floor it became increasingly common from the 1860's as the houses were extended further back on their plots to provide, besides the dining-room and parlour, a third large room which might serve as a library or as the increasingly fashionable billiard-room (fig. 29). In some houses with wider frontages, however, particularly at the ends and centre of terraces, Freake did vary the plan and was able to include substantially more accommodation. In these the staircase was sometimes moved to the centre of the house, or was of the open-well variety, winding around a much-enlarged hall. No. 57 Onslow Square, a particularly spacious house with a forty-foot frontage on the north side of the square, not only had an open-well staircase supported on marble columns, but an additional servants' stair at the side. It had a dining-room, library, morning-room and billiard-room on the ground floor, two 'noble' drawing-rooms on the first floor and thirteen bedrooms and dressing-rooms above. It was also equipped with a four-stall stable and double coach-house at the rear of a large private garden.[191]

Such a house was, of course, large even by the standards of those Freake built towards the end of his development, and was rare in having its own stables attached. It was not, indeed, until the building of Onslow and Cranley Gardens that the number of stables and coach-houses with living quarters above, erected in Onslow Mews, Ensor Mews and particularly the long Cranley Mews, began to keep pace with the number of houses being built and even then fell a little short. Livery stables on a modest scale were also provided at the rear of the houses and shops in Old Brompton Road on a site now occupied by the garage numbered 109 Old Brompton Road.[192]

Occupants

The early residence of Baron Marochetti in Onslow Square, and later the conversion of his foundry into studios, helped to give the square the reputation of an artistic quarter. 'South Kensington' associations were reinforced by the residence of (Sir) Henry Cole at No. 24 in 1856-7 and at No. 17 in 1857-63, and of (Sir) Theodore Martin, the parliamentary agent who wrote a biography of the Prince Consort, at No. 31 from 1852 until his death in 1909. Architects who lived in Freake's houses on the estate included William Railton, whose best-known work is Nelson's Column, at No. 65 Onslow Square from about 1858 until his death in 1877, Anthony Salvin at No. 19 Cranley

Place from 1865 to 1881, Joseph Aloysius Hansom, the founder and first editor of *The Builder* and inventor of the Hansom Cab, at No. 27 Sumner Place from about 1873 to 1877, and Henry Clutton, cousin of the estate surveyor of the same name, at No. 76 Onslow Gardens from 1885 until his death in 1893.[91] (Sir) Edwin Lutyens was born at No. 16 Onslow Square, the London home of his father, the painter Charles Lutyens, on 29 March 1869 and spent much of his early life there.[193] Commemorative plaques mark the residences of Thackeray at No. 36 Onslow Square, Hansom at No. 27 Sumner Place, the historians J. A. Froude and W. E. H. Lecky at Nos. 5 and 38 Onslow Gardens, and the prime minister Andrew Bonar Law at No. 24 Onslow Gardens.*

Thackeray was certainly pleased enough with the situation of his new house at first, describing it in 1853 as 'a pretty little house . . . looking into a very pretty square',[195] but by 1858 he was tiring of it and called it 'a shabby genteel house'.[196] This sort of sentiment was echoed by Margaret Leicester Warren, the daughter of the second Baron de Tabley, whose diaries give a fascinating glimpse of life in the square and its vicinity during the 1870's. She and her sister were forced to leave their Mayfair house at No. 86 Brook Street in 1871 after the second marriage of their father, and lived in reduced circumstances at No. 67 Onslow Square. Her view is, therefore, a somewhat jaundiced one, and she was evidently not impressed when Freake told her 'what a capital situation Onslow Square was and how it used to be called "the vale of Health" '. 'He owns all the houses there,' she added by way of explanation. In May 1872 she commented 'What shall I write of this long Sunday afternoon, sitting in the quiet and sadness of Onslow Square, the trees outside shivering in such a bitter winter wind and the architect's wife next door [Mrs. Railton] playing over and over again "a few more years shall roll, a few more seasons pass," *always* wrong at the same chord!' In September of the same year she wrote, 'The inhabitants of Onslow Square are very neighbourly and send each other small bits of food and old newspapers. They are all very poor.'[197]

Margaret Leicester Warren moved into No. 67 on the day after the census of 1871 was taken, and the facts revealed by the enumerators' books present a different picture.[198] Of the eighty-six houses in Onslow Square, seventy-two had their regular heads of households present on the night of the census and can be presumed to have been in substantially normal occupation. There were 565 inhabitants in these seventy-two houses, of whom 306 were servants, an average of 7.85 persons (including 4.25 servants) per house. The bigger houses in the westward extension of the square at Nos. 85-109 (odd) had the highest complements, averaging exactly ten persons per house, of whom 5.8 were servants. The largest household was fifteen at No. 99, but the highest number of servants

---

*An account of other notable residents is given in Dorothy Stroud's booklet on the estate.[194]

FOURTH FLOOR   THIRD FLOOR   SECOND FLOOR

GROUND FLOOR   FIRST FLOOR

Fig. 29. No. 74 Onslow Gardens, plans and rear elevation. C. J. Freake, builder, 1874

was at No. 9 where a butler, a housekeeper, a cook, a nurse, a nursery maid, two housemaids and a footman waited on a young East India merchant, his wife and three children.

Of the seventy-two householders five were titled (a baronet, a dowager baroness, a baronet's widow and two widows of knights, one of whom was an earl's daughter), nine others lived on income from land or property, and two who described their occupation as 'magistrate' can probably also be placed in the same category. Eight were annuitants, derived their income from dividends or had 'private means'. Of the professions the law was clearly dominant; nine of the householders were barristers (including a Scottish advocate),* two were solicitors and one was a 'law student'. There were eight army and navy officers (including a baronet and a landowner already noted above), some of them retired and others of a venerable age, and two officials of the War Office, one superannuated. Other public employees were an inspector of hospitals, a Poor Law Board inspector, a member of the Queen's household, the Director of the Meteorological Office and a clerk in the Foreign Office. There were seven merchants, two stockbrokers, two clergymen, a physician, a painter (Charles Lutyens), a banker, a sculptor (J. Edgar Boehm at Marochetti's old house, No. 34), a professor of music, the French Commissioner General for the London International Exhibition of 1871 (at No. 52), a retired clerk, and the architect William Railton, who described himself as 'Gentleman retired'. One man and three unmarried women provided no information about their occupations.

Onslow Gardens were still in the early stages of building in 1871 and only twenty houses had what appears to be their normal complement of occupants on the night of the

*Among them was Skeffington Lutwidge, Lewis Carroll's 'Uncle Skeffington' at No. 101, but perhaps the most notable barrister residing in the square was not a householder. He was Albert Venn Dicey, the future Vinerian Professor of English Law at Oxford and author of several major works on law, who was living at his widowed mother's house, No. 50, with his brother, the artist Frank Dicey.

census. There were 175 inhabitants in these twenty houses (an average of 8.75 per house), of whom 106 (5.3 per house) were servants. The largest household was at No. 41, where a thirty-five-year-old stockbroker, his wife and three children were attended by nine servants. At the top of the social scale among the householders were a dowager baroness (Lady Monteagle at No. 17A, whose grandson, the second Baron, was living with her) and two sons of earls, one describing himself as a landowner and the other as a late captain of the First Life Guards. There was one other landowner and three other army officers, including a retired colonel who was a Justice of the Peace for Northamptonshire. Another occupant was late assistant military secretary to the Horse Guards. Two householders held high public office, the Accountant General of the Court of Chancery and an Assistant Secretary to the Treasury, and two had retired from the Indian civil service. Of the remainder, two lived on income from securities or a jointure, one was the stockbroker mentioned above, and one a ship and insurance broker; the others were a barrister, a clergyman (who was also Secretary to the Church Missionary Society), a newspaper proprietor (William Reed) and the historian J. A. Froude, who described himself as 'Man of letters' and lived very comfortably with his wife and two children and seven servants at No. 5.

A comparison can be made between the pattern of occupancy in Onslow Square and Onslow Gardens in 1871 and that of the houses in the vicinity of Queen's Gate, Queen's Gate Gardens and Cromwell Road described in volume XXXVIII of the *Survey of London*. There the average number of inhabitants was 10.9 per house compared with 8.04 in Onslow Square and Gardens combined, and the number of servants waiting on each household was 6.2 compared with 4.5. There was a higher proportion of titled occupants in the larger houses of the Queen's Gate area, and the more purely middle-class character of the Onslow Square area immediately to the south was one of the factors that militated against it in the eyes of Margaret Leicester Warren. One noticeable characteristic of both areas was the small proportion of occupants who could be classified as rentiers when compared with Pelham Crescent, Pelham Place and Egerton Crescent twenty years earlier — perhaps an indication that the houses built by Freake were too big and expensive for most of the people who lived on the modest proceeds of small investments.

Later Changes

Time has been relatively kind to the external appearance of most of Freake's houses. Some additions were made almost immediately, an application to raise No. 75 Onslow Square by a storey in 1862 receiving his endorsement on the grounds that 'there is no objection to adding another storey to any of the houses if it does not interfere with the top of the front wall, and that sooner or later all the lessees

will require it'.[199] The alterations to No. 23 Onslow Gardens have been described above, and No. 1 Sydney Place has also been much altered, probably in 1870, when the premises were first adapted for use as a bank.[91]

Some houses have been demolished, a group of six at the north-eastern corner of Onslow Square, latterly numbered 1-6 Onslow Houses, and No. 2 Pelham Street being replaced by Malvern Court in 1930-1, and Onslow Crescent making way for Melton Court in 1935. The building of the latter also involved the demolition of the Royal Exotic Nursery, one of South Kensington's best-known horticultural establishments, which was at the back of Onslow Crescent and had a frontage to Old Brompton Road. The nursery buildings consisted of a small shop at the side of No. 16 Onslow Crescent and a long conservatory in the form of a Gothic nave and aisles with its gable end towards the street. The conservatory was built (probably by Freake, who was the lessee) in 1872 for John Wills, the florist and nurseryman, who moved to No. 16 Onslow Crescent in that year from another shop further along Old Brompton Road. Wills, who was born in Somerset in 1832, had come to London in 1867 and rapidly established himself as a leading pioneer in the field of floral decoration. In 1882 he entered into partnership with Samuel Moore Segar and the firm still flourishes as Wills and Segar. Wills died in 1895 and No. 16 Onslow Crescent was latterly the residence of the Segar family until its demolition.[200]

These rebuildings presaged a more extensive programme of redevelopment which, but for the intervention of the war of 1939-45, would have transformed Onslow Square and Gardens. In 1939 the Smith's Charity trustees decided to replace Nos. 1-8 Onslow Gardens with a new terrace of houses designed by W. E. Masters sporting Odeon-style entrance doorways, and a building agreement was concluded with Holland, Hannen and Cubitts in July 1939 but was surrendered on the outbreak of war. Plans were also afoot at the same time to redevelop Nos. 103-109 (odd) Onslow Square and the stables behind in Onslow Mews East.[201]

After the war, however, a conservative programme of rehabilitation was considered more appropriate, and, apart from the replacement of the war-destroyed Nos. 25-39 (odd) Onslow Square by two blocks of flats, one, on the site of Nos. 25-31, reproducing the original façade in facsimile, and the other to a modern design by John V. Hamilton of Cluttons, changes have generally been confined to the conversion of houses into flats. In many cases, however, this has involved extensive rebuilding behind existing façades and, at Nos. 77-109 (odd) Onslow Square, considerable alterations to the ground floor. Nos. 1 and 2 Sumner Place were destroyed by bombing and have been replaced by garages.

St. Paul's Church, Onslow Square

The terms of the building agreement of 1850 with (Sir) Charles James Freake under which the ground on the west

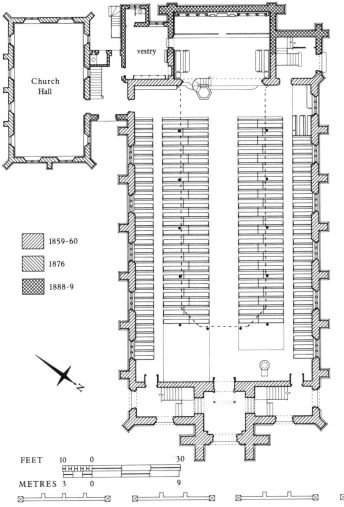

Church Hall

vestry

1859-60

1876

1888-9

N

FEET 10 0 30

METRES 3 0 9

Fig. 30. St. Paul's Church, Onslow Square, plan. Some modern additions omitted

to church records which have since been lost and there is no reason to doubt his attribution to this rather obscure church architect.

The foundation stone was laid in 1859 and the completed church (Plates 56a, 57, fig. 30) was consecrated at Christmas 1860.[206] It seated 1,550 — 1,180 in rented pews and 370 in free seats — and the income was derived entirely from pew rents. The first minister, the Reverend Capel Molyneux, formerly minister of the Lock Chapel in Paddington, was appointed by Freake, who was patron of the living, and a district chapelry was assigned to the church in 1861.[207] The best-known vicar was Hanmer Webb-Peploe, whose incumbency lasted from 1876 to 1909, and who made the church a noted centre of Evangelicalism.[208]

The design of St Paul's, with its entrance at the east end and originally only a very shallow chancel at the west end, is defiantly Low Church. The exterior (Plate 56a) is faced with Kentish rag in a basically Perpendicular style. The nave is divided into seven bays by slender buttresses, and the most prominent features are the tower and spire supported by angle buttresses in the centre of the east front. The junction between tower and spire is unusual, the transitional stage being achieved by chamfering the corners of the tower immediately beneath the spire and placing four crocketed pinnacles on top of the buttresses.

Inside, the 'preaching-box' characteristics of the wide nave (Plate 57) are emphasized by deep galleries around three sides supported by thin octagonal columns with plain capitals, the gallery fronts showing the merest hint of Gothic tracery, and by an open timber roof with prominent tie-beams. Originally a large wooden pulpit and reading desk were placed in the centre and 'quite shut out the west, or communion end'.[209]

The chancel dates largely from 1888-9 when the west (or liturgical east) end of the church was reconstructed and extended by some fifteen feet. The ostensible reason was to provide, by building staircases at the west end, a means of escape from the galleries in case of fire, but the opportunity was taken to embellish the hitherto plain appearance of the interior. A new seven-light window was installed with glass depicting scenes from the life of St. Paul by Clayton and Bell, who also provided the rest of the glass in the chancel. Beneath the large window is a Gothic arcade with ogee-headed arches which originally contained panels of Mexican onyx on which the Commandments, the Lord's Prayer and the Creed were inscribed, but in 1936 these were replaced with pink alabaster. The oak pews and panelling, the pulpit of Caen stone with onyx panels and columns of Devonshire marble approached by winding stone stairs with a brass railing, and the brass lectern in the shape of an eagle all date from the alterations of 1888-9. The roof of the new chancel, like that of the nave, is also wooden, but with hammerbeams instead of tie-beams.

The architect for these alterations was William Wallace; one of the principal donors towards the work was the Countess of Seafield, whose title was Scottish and who

side of Onslow Square was laid out had anticipated the provision of a church or chapel as part of the development, and in March 1859 Freake approached the Smith's Charity trustees, who agreed to present a site here as a free gift.[202] The Ecclesiastical Commissioners readily accepted his proposal to erect a church, to the cost of which he was prepared to contribute at least £5,000.[203]

By June 1859 the designs for the church were sufficiently advanced to be the subject of a comment in *The Building News*, which thought that they did great credit 'to those who have been engaged upon them, under the direction of Mr. Freake'.[204] The *British Almanac for 1861* attributed the design to Freake,[205] but Derek Taylor Thompson, in his booklet entitled *The First Hundred Years* commemorating the centenary of the church in 1960, stated that the architect was James Edmeston (presumably the elder James Edmeston, architect and hymn-writer, who died in 1867, rather than his son, also an architect, who died in 1888[58]). No earlier source naming Edmeston has been found, but Thompson may have had access

may have preferred a Scottish architect. The contractors were Langdale, Hallett and Company, and the cost, apart from the main window, the pulpit, the reredos and the communion rails which were donated by parishioners, was £4,463. Thomas Potter and Sons made the brass eagle lectern and Alfred J. Shirley designed the communion rails, which were paid for by the servants of members of the congregation. The new chancel was consecrated on 23 October 1889.[210]

In 1935-6 renovations and redecoration were undertaken by Trollope and Colls under the architects Gordon and Gordon at a cost of £2,219.[211]

A gabled church hall with ragstone facing was erected on the south side of the church in 1876 to the designs of Edward C. Robins of Southampton Street, Covent Garden, and enlarged by Wallace in 1893.[212] Another smaller hall in ragstone was built in front of the earlier one in 1932 to the designs of William Doddington,[213] but this was demolished in 1969 for new parish rooms, built as part of a scheme which also included a three-storey building incorporating a vicarage and a curate's maisonette. A small courtyard separates the vicarage and maisonette from the church halls. The architect, who chose a modern style in brick in contrast to the earlier church halls, was Eric Brady of Maidment and Brady, and the builders, who carried out the work in 1968-70, were William Blood Limited.[214]

The memorial tablets in the church include ones to Freake, set within a Gothic canopy at the east end, to Webb-Peploe of marble and alabaster in the chancel, and to Anne and John King, an elaborate marble memorial with drapes, a scrolled cartouche and a cherub's head, in the nave. Besides the stained glass by Clayton and Bell, there is a window by Arild Rosenkrantz, made in 1930, on the north side of the nave. The large organ in the eastern gallery was installed in 1885-6 by Lewis and Company and incorporates the stops from the previous organ. The Lewis organ was in turn substantially reconstructed by J. W. Walker and Sons in 1899-1900.[215]

In 1977 St. Paul's was united with Holy Trinity, Brompton. The last service was held in the church on 1 May of that year, and at the time of writing (1982) the future of the building is uncertain.

St. Peter's Church, Cranley Gardens

Now called St. Peter's Armenian Church, this is the second of the two churches which were built by (Sir) Charles James Freake to serve the needs of the occupants of the houses he had built or was about to build on the Smith's Charity estate. St. Peter's (Plates 56b, c, 58, fig. 31) was erected in 1866-7 from designs prepared in Freake's own office, but much of its architectural interest arises from a number of alterations which were made to the interior during the present century under the direction of W. D. Caröe.

The church was built on ground which Freake held from the Smith's Charity trustees by virtue of a building

agreement of 1862. Early in 1865 he approached Dr. A. C. Tait, then Bishop of London and later Archbishop of Canterbury, with a proposal to build a church at his own expense, and sought Tait's aid in obtaining a sufficiently large district for the church.[216] By May 1865 he had obtained a promise from the charity's trustees to convey the site to the Ecclesiastical Commissioners as a free gift, and in June 1866 he made a formal proposal to the Commissioners, through his solicitor Charles Fishlake Cundy, for the erection, endowment and perpetual patronage of a church to seat 1,500 (500 in free seats) which he estimated would cost £7,000 and for which he was prepared to provide an endowment of £1,000.[217] The Commissioners agreed, and the foundation stone was laid by Mrs. Freake on 21 July 1866. After a dispute with the sponsors of the proposed new church of St. Augustine's, Queen's Gate, over the size of the respective districts to be allotted to the two churches, which was resolved by the intervention of Bishop Tait, St. Peter's was consecrated by him on 29 June 1867.[218]

Freake seems to have been at pains to conceal the identity of the actual architect or architects of the building. Some contemporary journals attributed the design to him personally, but *The Builder* was probably more accurate in stating that the church was built by Freake 'from drawings prepared in his own office', with J. Brown as clerk of works and general foreman.[219] A number of fledgling architects are known to have worked under Freake (see page 104), and his principal executant on work of about this date in Grosvenor Square was William Tasker.[220] If experienced outside advice on church-building was needed, however, Thomas Cundy II, who was the brother of Freake's solicitor, Charles Fishlake Cundy, and who was involved in the work in Grosvenor Square as the Grosvenor estate surveyor, would have been well qualified to assist.

The first incumbent to be appointed by Freake, the Honourable and Reverend F. C. E. Byng, was a son of the second Earl of Strafford. Some of the cost of the church appears to have been met by him, perhaps merely the interest charges on a loan which Freake had evidently had to take out, as (Sir) Henry Cole recorded in his diary instances when he was called upon to mediate between the two men on monetary matters.[221] Byng resigned the living in 1890 and nine years later succeeded his brother as fifth Earl of Strafford.[222]

St. Peter's has been described as the High Church equivalent of St. Paul's, Onslow Square, but its services were never particularly 'High'. A later vicar said that 'It has been difficult to define or place from the party, or the theological point of view, except that it has been certainly "Church of England" '. He characterised the congregation as one that 'has always been fortunate in its men. Men who are earning their living in London can hardly live in that part of London unless they are efficient, and on the other hand it is not so expensive as to make it impossible for the returned Colonial Governor, the retired Admiral or

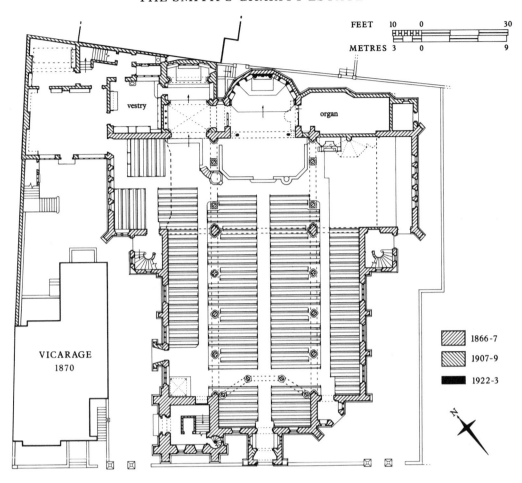

FEET 10 0 30
METRES 3 0 9

1866-7
1907-9
1922-3

N

Fig. 31. St. Peter's Church, Cranley Gardens, plan

General, the retired or senior Civil Servant to live there. We always had a large number of knights in the congregation, which indicates the type of men. Not great men perhaps, not of the first rank, but faithful servants of the State, men who had done something.'[223]

The large and prosperous congregation which the church attracted for much of its history provided the means for extensive embellishments to be carried out. The most important of these were undertaken in two schemes of 1907-9 and 1922-3, in both of which most of the cost was defrayed by Percy C. Morris of Elm Park Gardens, Chelsea, a barrister by profession, and members of his family.[224] Morris appears to have been instrumental in obtaining the services of W. D. Caröe as architect for the work, and the latter's association with the church continued until his death in 1938, when his memorial service was held in St. Peter's.[225] In the work Caröe was assisted by Herbert Passmore, who later became his partner, and whose connexion with the church as an architect and a member of the congregation (in which he served as both churchwarden and sidesman) continued until his death at the age of ninety-eight in 1966.[226] Alban Caroe, W. D. Caröe's son, was architect to the fabric during the final period of the church's history as an Anglican place of worship, having taken over the position in 1958.[225]

The church is basically cruciform on plan with a very broad nave and aisles, wide transepts, a spacious crossing, and a short apsidal chancel. To the north of the chancel is a morning chapel which was added by Caröe in 1907-9, replacing a vestry, and to the south is a large organ chamber which is also principally Caröe's work of the same date.

The exterior (Plate 56b, c), which is in the Decorated style and faced with Kentish ragstone, has been relatively little altered from the time of first building, apart from the addition of a porch on the north side as part of the alterations of 1907-9, and an untidy jumble of accretions at the east end, visible only from Selwood Place. Only the west front can be seen clearly from a distance and here the architectural effect has been concentrated in the form of a tall gabled front with a five-light window and a large tower with a broach spire rising to a height of 160 feet.

In the interior (Plate 58) the walls of the nave and transepts are faced with brick, which was originally cream-coloured with patterns in red and black, but the intended polychromatic effect was largely obliterated by whitewashing in the 1930's.

The west end of the nave is dominated by an elegant stone gallery which is supported on four slim clustered columns and decorated with figure sculpture and other carvings. Originally galleries were only provided in the transepts, but that in the south transept had to be reduced in size when the organ chamber was rebuilt in 1907-9, and to compensate Caröe added the present west gallery. Above the gallery the stained glass in the west window is by Ward and Hughes and dates from the establishment of the church, but it was badly damaged during the war of 1939-45 and is no longer complete.

The nave and aisles are separated by simple stone arcades of wide arches carried on clustered columns. The arcades are continued into the crossing in a more complex and unusual arrangement of triple arches, the outer ones narrow and sharply pointed and the inner wide and high and supported by round columns with crocket capitals. The clerestory windows are alternately pairs of trefoil-headed lights and quatrefoils with glass of 1904-6 by the Arts and Crafts stained-glass artist Mary Lowndes.[227] The remaining glass in the nave and transepts is richly varied and includes work by Ward and Hughes, Clayton and Bell, and Heaton, Butler and Bayne. The roof of the nave is of open timberwork.

The constricted nature of the east end apparently caused problems from the beginning, as the large corbels which once supported the chancel arch were attributed in 1872 to an early alteration in which the lower part of the opening had been widened.[228] The choir projects into the crossing, from which it was originally separated by a dwarf stone screen, but in 1900 this was replaced by marble walls and an ornate wrought-iron screen.[229] The latter was removed when the marble walls were advanced by six feet in 1922-3, but parts of it have been re-erected at the sides of the choir.[230]

The apsidal sanctuary itself was much embellished in 1922-3 to Caröe's design at a cost of over £7,400, partly to remedy its dark and cramped condition and partly to serve as a war memorial. The main structural alteration was the insertion of dormer windows, each consisting of three simple segmental-headed lights filled with stained glass, between the ribs of the roof. A new stone reredos with a sculpture of the Crucifixion was flanked by arcades incorporating a bishop's seat, sedilia and piscina with richly carved Gothic canopies above, all being the work of the sculptor Nathaniel Hitch. (It should, however, be noted that the fine carvings of angels playing musical instruments in the spandrels above the lancet windows, no doubt inspired by the sculptures in the Angel Choir of Lincoln Cathedral, are earlier work which was retained.) A new altar, altar-rail and choir stalls were made by Dart and Francis of Crediton, Devon, a firm much used by Caröe. The glass was by James Powell and Sons, that in the main lights replacing some 'excellent stained glass' by Ward and Hughes, but Powells' glass in these windows has in turn been so badly damaged by bombing that only fragments remain, re-used as decorative borders to clear glass. The general contractors for the alterations were F. Hitch and Company of Ware, Hertfordshire.[231]

If the present appearance of the chancel is largely due to alterations carried out to Caröe's designs, the morning chapel to the north (Plate 58b), which was formed in 1907-9 and originally called the Chapel of the Holy Spirit, is entirely of his creation. Opening off the north transept through a tall stone arch with a low bronze rail and gates, the chapel is faced with Bath stone and has two bays in its upper part and three in the lower including a deep recess beneath the east window which contains the altar and reredos. The chapel is lierne-vaulted in stone and the springers of the main ribs are decorated with statues of angels, apostles, prophets and other Christian figures including, in the mediaeval tradition, Frederick Temple, Archbishop of Canterbury, who had died a short time previously. The main bosses of the vault are carved with the head of Christ and the Holy Dove, while on the subsidiary bosses are angels bearing symbols of the Passion and the insignia of various learned institutions. These include those with which the Morris family were associated, and those of Trinity College, Cambridge, where Caröe studied, and of New College, Oxford, the college of the vicar, the Reverend W. S. Swayne. The lower parts of the walls are arcaded and have sedilia on the north side and a piscina on the south. An opening on the south side of the western bay allows communication with the chancel through an intervening passage.

The stone carving in the chapel, which was carried out by Nathaniel Hitch and his assistant Harold Whitaker, reaches its apogee in the finely detailed reredos which has three niches with lacy canopies above containing figure sculpture, that in the central niche depicting the Crucifixion. The altar beneath is of oak and was made by Dart and Francis to Caröe's design. The marble floor, which was laid Cosmati fashion, is by Arthur Lee and Brothers of Hayes, and the glass of the six-light east window is by James Powell and Sons. Like much else in the chapel, it is of very high quality and rich in detail while restrained in colouring so as to allow a great deal of light to pass through. The general contractors for the construction of the chapel were Collins and Godfrey of Tewkesbury.[232]

The alterations which were made to the organ chamber on the opposite side of the chancel at the same time as the building of the morning chapel constituted but one stage in the history of the organ, which is almost as complex as that of the church itself. The first organ, by Messrs. Hill and Sons, is famous as the instrument on which (Sir) Arthur Sullivan played from 1867 to 1871 as the church's first organist. This was replaced in 1893 by a Willis organ which, in turn, was largely rebuilt in 1908 by J. W. Walker and Sons when the organ chamber was much enlarged and new cases were designed by Caröe. Further alterations were made in 1922-3, and after damage during the war of 1939-45 repairs were carried out. Finally a major restoration was undertaken by Hill, Norman and Beard in 1958.[233]

Of the church's other fixtures and fittings, the present pulpit, which is of wood on a stone base, is the third and dates from 1902; it was designed by John Samuel Alder, architect.[234] An elaborate Gothic wooden canopy at the west end of the north aisle formerly housed the font which is now in the south transept. Another font, which was introduced by the Armenians from a church in Birmingham, is in the morning chapel. A large memorial to Frank Macrae (d. 1915) with an inset painting of St. George, which is in the north aisle, is by Jesse Bayes. At the west end of the nave is a Gothic memorial to Freake similar to that in St. Paul's, Onslow Square, and a memorial to the war of 1914-18 which was designed by Caröe.

The vicarage to the north of the church (Plate 56b) was built in 1870 to the designs of Alfred Williams at an estimated cost of £2,570, for which the endowment of £1,000 given by Freake was used in partial payment.[216] Although built before its Italianate neighbours, it now forms an end-of-terrace house in a contrasting Gothic style in red brick and stone. Its principal feature is a tall recessed arch, asymmetrically placed, at second- and third-floor level containing paired window openings which are divided vertically by decorated stone panels. Above the arch is a gable with an iron finial. The house has been much altered and is now divided into flats.

A two-storey building containing vestries on the ground floor and a church hall with an open-timber roof above was erected to Caröe's designs behind the vicarage as part of the alterations of 1907-9, when the new morning chapel replaced the original vestry.

In January 1973 the last Anglican service was held in the church and its parish was united with that of St. Mary, The Boltons. In June 1975, however, St. Peter's was re-consecrated by the Supreme Catholicos of all Armenians as the cathedral church of the Armenians in London.[235]

The Effect of the Underground Railways

Virtually the only part of the estate to undergo major changes in the period between 1850 and Freake's death in 1884 where he was not involved was in Pelham Street and the adjoining frontage of what was then Fulham Road but is now the western end of Brompton Road. Here the authorisation of the construction of the Metropolitan and Metropolitan District Railways by Acts of Parliament in 1864 led to the sale of some plots of land to the railway companies (see fig. 23) and the subsequent demolition of several houses.

Initially the building of the railways and their joint station at South Kensington affected the neighbouring Alexander estate more than the Smith's Charity estate (see page 79) and in Pelham Street only a few houses at the western end had to be pulled down to make way for the station (Plate 48a). In 1871, however, the remaining houses on the north side of the street to the west of the short stretch of roadway leading to Thurloe Square were demolished so that the station could be enlarged to accommodate separate District platforms. This was in part the result of a quarrel between the two companies which also led to the District acquiring the surviving terrace at Nos. 51-61 (odd) Pelham Street in order to construct its branch line to the station but, in the event, these houses did not have to be demolished.[236]

On the frontage to Fulham Road the last house in Onslow Terrace, with James Bonnin's former cottage and workshops behind, had to be demolished in c. 1866 for the construction of the District railway. They were eventually replaced in 1879-80 by a riding school which was later converted into a garage and two houses and shops now numbered 266 and 268 Brompton Road, the upper storeys of which are faced with red brick and cement dressings in a coarse Italianate style. They were built by Henry R. Wagner of Britannia Street, King's Cross, to the designs of John Mechelen Rogers, architect.[237]

The construction of the deep-level Great Northern, Piccadilly and Brompton Railway (now the Piccadilly Line), which was begun in 1902, produced yet another extension to South Kensington Station on the frontage to Pelham Street. Opened in January 1907, this part of the station was designed by Leslie W. Green and has retained the original façade of ox-blood-red glazed faience (Plate 48b) which he used at several tube stations between 1903 and 1907.[238] A range of two-storey shops, called Station Buildings, was erected shortly afterwards on the frontage to Pelham Street to the east of the station, but was demolished in 1973.[239] At the present No. 49 Pelham Street, on the east corner of the entrance to Thurloe Square, an electricity sub-station was built in 1904 to serve the needs of the railway. Green designed an elaborate Baroque building for the site with four storeys of flats above the sub-station, but in the event only the ground storey was completed. Two more floors, in red brick and stone with bow windows to Pelham Street, were added in the early 1920's to the designs of Stanley A. Heaps, architect to the Underground Electric Railways Company, to provide a dining club for the company.[240]

Evelyn Gardens

When Sir Charles James Freake died in October 1884 a large parcel of ground in the south-western corner of the estate, which he had taken under a building agreement with the Smith's Charity trustees in February 1883, was still largely undeveloped. The trustees appointed under his will were his widow, Dame Eliza Freake, his long-time assistant, James Waller, and Charles Townshend Murdoch, a banker and later M.P. for Reading.[241] Waller soon repudiated his trusteeship,[242] and Lady Freake and Murdoch decided to find another builder to take on the remainder of Freake's obligations under the agreement.

The ground was advertised and in October 1885 an acceptable tender was received from the building firm of C. A. Daw and Son. The approval of the Smith's Charity trustees was obtained, and a building agreement between Freake's trustees and Daws was signed on 24 April 1886.[243] Under this agreement Daws paid £4,000 for Freake's plant and equipment,[244] and undertook to pay an ultimate ground rent of £2,486 18s. (from 1890) to Lady Freake and Murdoch. This represented an improved ground rent of over £1,800 above the ground rent which the executors had to pay to the Charity's trustees under Freake's original building agreement, although his firm had done some preliminary work on the site. Daws eventually bought the improved ground rents at twenty-two-and-a-half years' purchase, a sum amounting to nearly £50,000, or an average of about £700 per house.

Charles Adams Daw, the founder of the firm, was Devonshire-born and had migrated in the early 1860's to London, where he engaged in small-scale speculative building in various parts of Kensington, Paddington and St. Marylebone in partnership with two brothers. In the early 1870's he had branched out on his own and was shortly afterwards joined in business by his son, William Adams Daw, who had been born in 1856.[245] From the mid 1870's their firm had been building houses and flats in De Vere Gardens and Palace Gate, and had encountered some difficulties in disposing of the large houses in De Vere Gardens. In Evelyn Gardens (which was named after William John Evelyn, one of the Smith's Charity trustees), therefore, they sought permission from the charity's trustees to build smaller houses than had been stipulated in Freake's building agreement.[246] After some negotiation the trustees concurred, and, large as they may seem by modern standards, the houses in Evelyn Gardens are modest by comparison with those in De Vere Gardens or with Freake's later Italianate houses in Onslow Gardens and Cranley Gardens. One result was the provision of an abundance of communal garden space, which was even further increased when Daws decided to dispense with the stabling Freake had proposed to build on the north and west of the site, in continuation of Cranley Mews, and lay out those sites as garden ground also. Otherwise the layout which had been devised by Freake was basically adhered to, apart from the extension of the north-south arm of Evelyn Gardens northwards to communicate with Roland Gardens.

The Chronology of Development

Daws began building in 1886 with Nos. 1-7 (odd) and 2-10 (even) Evelyn Gardens.[247] These are in fact larger than subsequent houses in the development, the even-numbered houses on the north side having four main storeys, attics and basements, while those on the south side, although having only three main storeys, have wider, twenty-five-foot, frontages. The firm then concentrated in 1887 on building the northernmost terrace, consisting of

Nos. 31-44 (consec.), originally called Evelyn Terrace, where the houses are narrower, with twenty-one-foot frontages for the most part, and have only three main storeys.[248] The building of the two ranges which had been begun in 1886 was resumed in 1888, but with narrower, or lower, houses.[249] The long north-south range, consisting of Nos. 45-70 (consec.), was begun in 1890. Here the southernmost part of the long communal garden at the back of the houses occupied the site of an organ factory which had been made available to Daws by the Smith's Charity trustees by a separate building agreement of May 1892.[250] By 1895 only Nos. 59, 60 and 64 Evelyn Gardens remained untenanted, and these were all occupied in the following year,[91] thus bringing the whole development of seventy houses to a conclusion in ten years.

Finance

The firm obtained the money to finance its building operations from both institutional and private lenders. Several mortgages were negotiated with the Union Assurance Office, amounting by 1894 to £31,950 at four-and-a-half per cent interest on the security of eighteen houses.[251] A further £24,516 was borrowed from the County Fire Office, principally to buy up improved ground rents from Freake's executors.[252] Individual mortgages were usually arranged through solicitors, the lawyers and their families sometimes supplying money themselves. For instance, in 1887 several mortgages to members of the Torr family were arranged through the solicitors, Torr, Janeways, Gribble and Oddie.[253]

Sometimes the initiative seems to have come from would-be mortgagees, especially in times of easy money conditions. Thomas Peel of Bradford must have made the first approaches, for in December 1887 he was informed by Daws that, 'Just at present we are not desirous of raising any money having recently sold some property but we are almost sure to be able to offer you some securities on our Evelyn Estate within the next 3 or 4 months', and in March 1888 they offered him No. 35 as security for £1,500 but wanted a quick reply 'as just now there is a good deal of money to be had on good terms Mr. Goschen's conversion having disturbed a lot of capital'.[254] Daws were often able to pick and choose, negotiating more favourable interest rates with one potential mortgagee than another. In 1895 they told one particularly irksome individual that he was 'the most nervous and fidgetty mortgagee we have ever had to deal with'.[255]

In the normal manner of Victorian building developments, Daws let some houses in Evelyn Gardens at rack rents, usually on twenty-one-year leases, and sold others outright. No. 1, a spacious end house, was the first to be taken, at a rent of £250 per annum, by John Henry Clutton of the firm of surveyors who managed the Smith's Charity estate.[256] No. 44, also an end house, was let at £290 per annum, but generally rents ranged between

£170 and £210.[257] In the early stages of the development rents were kept deliberately low, however, in order to attract tenants. One house was both let and then sold for low sums for exceptional reasons, as William Adams Daw explained. 'We have sold 2 Evelyn Terrace [No. 32 Evelyn Gardens] cheap', he wrote, 'because Sir F. Burrows [Sir Frederic Abernethy Burrows, baronet and solicitor] is our lawyer and as he acts for Freake's trustees and wished to buy as an investment it suits us to be on the best of terms with him. We pay some £2,000 a year in ground rent to Freake's trustees and are constantly wanting slight alterations in the building agreement and variations of plan etc. which we could not ask for were we on bad terms (or anything but the best of terms) with everybody concerned. And secondly we sold this house for £1,900 . . . because it is let for 21 years at £145 and if this tenant were to leave she would certainly underlet with a premium as similar houses are let for £160 and we now ask £170, so we would derive no further benefit from the house for 21 years.'[258]

The highest price known to have been paid for a house in Evelyn Gardens was £3,400, which Philip Norman, the antiquary, scholar and artist, agreed to give for No. 45, a larger house at the north end of the north-south range with an extension at the rear for a studio. The house was fitted out to Norman's specifications, five fireplaces being selected from the Coalbrookdale Company, for instance.[259] More usual prices ranged from £2,100 to £2,900.[260]

Daws were frequently informing investors or potential purchasers that they had few houses left on their hands, and in 1894 Henry Trollope of George Trollope and Son, on being informed that the cheapest house left would cost £2,600, or £190 per annum, remarked, 'I liked the houses very much and wish I could afford one, but am pleased to see that they have gone off so well'.[261] The firm estimated that it made a profit of about £250 on the sale of each house, but as the estimate was for income tax purposes this figure was probably on the low side.[262]

Architecture

All of the houses in Evelyn Gardens are in the red-brick, Anglo-Dutch, Domestic Revival idiom, but there are variations between groups of houses which generally correspond to their different building dates (Plates 59a, c, fig. 32). There is no evidence, however, about the authorship of the designs. One practice which the firm used elsewhere was to approach an outside architect for either sketch or detailed elevations, to which it would then fit plans. C. F. A. Voysey, to whom Daws went for elevations for houses in Chelsea, rather disparagingly called this a 'shirt-front arrangement';[263] another example of the firm's use of this system occurs in Hans Road (see page 15).

There is some reason to think, however, that in Evelyn Gardens the firm may have dispensed altogether with the services of an outside architect. When its initial plans were submitted to an agent acting for Freake's trustees he com-

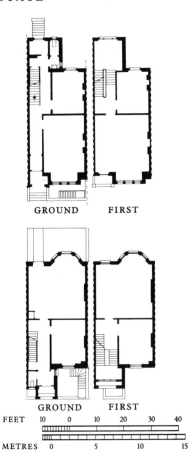

GROUND   FIRST

GROUND   FIRST

FEET   10   0   10   20   30   40

METRES   0   5   10   15

Fig. 32. Evelyn Gardens, typical plans of Nos. 31-44 at top and of Nos. 2-10 (even) at bottom. C. A. Daw and Son, builders, 1886-7

mented about one set of designs that 'The elevation . . . is very ugly as to the upper part. It would be well for you to get out an architect's plan for this . . . I think you may get over the shops in front if you were to design a good elevation.'[264] (A proposal to build shops along part of the frontage to Fulham Road was quickly dropped.) The absence of any reference to an architect in the voluminous correspondence about these houses which survives among the firm's records, and the changes made as building progressed, suggest that all the designs may have been prepared in the firm's own drawing office. Purchasers who wanted alterations made, like Philip Norman who had his own surveyor, negotiated with the firm's foreman, a Mr. Kerswell.[265] According to W. A. Daw, the houses 'were all built together under the same foreman and by the same gangs of workmen who were shifted from one house to another as occasion required'.[266]

Of the first houses to be erected, Nos. 2-10 (even) have 'back to front' features of a kind sometimes found elsewhere in conjunction with communal gardens (Plate 59c). They are four-storey houses with basements and garrets and have projections at the front rising through three main storeys. These projections, which are more usually placed at the rear of houses to accommodate the staircase or to provide additional rooms off its half-landings, contain four storeys at different levels from those of the main house and are capped with free-standing pediments. At their bases, entrance porches project further forward (except at No. 2 where the entrance is at the side), and above the porches are loggias set within arched recesses and entered from half-landings. At three of the houses the pediments are decorated with cut-brick ornament, and a bold modillion cornice and frieze of terracotta* (for the most part now painted over) tie the houses together at both front and rear. At roof level Nos. 2 and 4 have similar but not identical gables while Nos. 6, 8 and 10 have dormer windows with projecting semi-pyramidal hoods. (No. 4 has a twenty-one-foot frontage and No. 6 twenty-two-foot but Daws thought them of equal value as No. 4 had the 'better top floor'.[268]) The rear elevations to the communal garden are fully embellished and have bay windows on the lower floors.

These arresting designs were not repeated, and the differences even from house to house within this group are characteristic of the variety introduced into the development as a whole. Nos. 1-7 (odd) opposite, which were erected at about the same time in 1886, are three-storey houses with wider frontages and dispense with projections at front and back. All of the remaining houses have three main storeys, basements and attics, and enclosed porches with arched openings to the street, some with decorated brick panels at the sides and others cement rendered. Nos. 9-29 (odd) also have deep projections at the front containing four storeys, with some inevitably clumsy joins where they meet the main front wall, but in the other houses such projections are more conventionally placed at the back.

Symmetry is, in general, eschewed, although Nos. 31-44 (consec.) form a nearly symmetrical terrace with two slightly projecting, gabled end houses framing three groups of four houses. The outer groups have sash windows with segmental heads dressed with red rubbed bricks, but the middle group is in a 'Jacobethan' style with stone mullioned-and-transomed windows and Dutch gables. A similar style to the latter but with variations in the gables was used on the middle group of houses in each of the other east-west ranges, namely Nos. 12-22 (even) and 9-19 (odd), and throughout the long north-south range consisting of Nos. 45-70 (consec.), although here further variety was introduced by providing sash windows set in stone or artificial stone surrounds for the upper storeys (Plate 59a).

The houses have been little altered externally but have inevitably undergone much internal change and modification. One small job is perhaps worth mentioning; in 1930 Sir Edwin Lutyens designed a new bathroom for the top of the rear extension of No. 50, probably for Sir Edward

James Reid, baronet, a director of Baring Brothers, who was shortly to take up residence here.[269]

The layout of Evelyn Gardens pleased contemporaries and near-contemporaries. Muthesius had this area specifically in mind when he commented that 'In this system of unbuilt-up garden squares the layout of London's residential quarter may almost be described as exemplary', and in 1906 A. E. Street thought that both in its general disposition and in its architectural features Evelyn Gardens was commendably superior to earlier work in the same neighbourhood.[270] Most of the occupants of the houses were evidently equally satisfied. Of the seventy families who first moved into the new houses, thirty-eight lived there for ten years or more and nineteen for at least twenty years.[91]

Occupants

The enumerators' books for the census of 1891 are not yet open for public inspection and so less is known about the first inhabitants of Evelyn Gardens than about those of earlier developments; but some information can be derived from directories. Several occupants can be identified as merchants with firms in the City, and a number belonged to the professions and the armed forces. The latter were represented by two generals, three colonels, a major and two captains. Those connected with the law included four barristers and three solicitors. Among the other occupants were a clergyman, an engineer and a surveyor (J. H. Clutton at No. 1). Charles Digby Harrod, the proprietor of Harrods, was the first occupant of No. 31 from 1888 to 1894, and Sir William Mackinnon, a surgeon-general to the army and honorary surgeon to Queen Victoria, who lived at No. 28, was pre-eminent in his profession.[271] Philip Norman, the joint editor of the *Survey of London* from 1909 to 1931, whose purchase of No. 45 has already been noted, lived there from 1890 until his death in 1931.

Brompton Road and Egerton Gardens Area

In the mid 1880's the Smith's Charity trustees decided not to renew the leases of Novosielski's houses in Michael's Place, Michael's Grove and Brompton Crescent for further short-term periods, but to demolish the houses and let the ground for building. In so doing they were making an investment for the future, as there was a loss of income when rack rents were exchanged for ground rents, albeit in this instance quite high ones. The largest piece of ground, comprising the present-day sites of Nos. 227-251 (odd) Brompton Road and all of Egerton Gardens except Nos. 1-7 (consec.) and 36-50 (even), was let under one building agreement dated 25 March 1886 at an ultimate ground rent (payable from 1891) of £1,425. At about the

---

*These are probably the houses for which Gibbs and Canning of Tamworth offered to deliver the terracotta cornice on site at six shillings per foot run.[267]

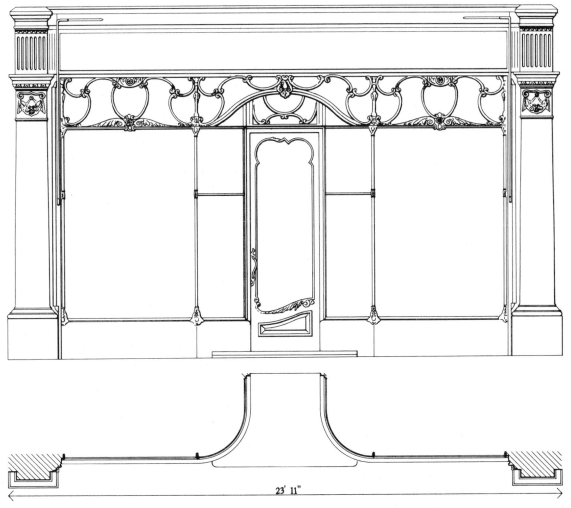

Fig. 33. No. 235 Brompton Road, shop front

same time the sites of Nos. 209–225 (odd) Brompton Road, Egerton Gardens Mews and Nos. 17 and 19 Egerton Terrace were taken under several separate agreements at a total ground rent of £642 per annum, while Crescent House was replaced by the large mansion called Mortimer House at a ground rent of £240. The houses at the eastern end of Egerton Gardens, Nos. 1–7 (consec.) and 36–50 (even), were erected under a separate building agreement in 1888 at a rent of £500. Finally Egerton Place and Nos. 4–28 (even) Yeoman's Row were built under another agreement of 1891 (modified in 1893) at £700 per annum.[272] The leasehold terms granted under these agreements ranged from ninety years in Egerton Gardens to ninety-nine years in Egerton Place and Yeoman's Row. Some eight-and-a-half acres of land were involved, and the total ground rent received (£3,507) was, at over £400 per acre, very substantially larger than the £75 per acre received on average from Freake's various takes. A higher sum was, however, to be expected from the redevelopment of an established area than from the opening up of new territory.

Nos. 209–251 (odd) Brompton Road and Egerton Gardens

The agreement of 25 March 1886 was with Alexander Thorn, builder, of Cremorne Wharf, Lots Road, Chelsea. In April Thorn applied to the Metropolitan Board of Works for permission to form a new street between Brompton Road and the street then still known as Brompton Crescent, and in June the course of this road and its name, Egerton Gardens (after the Honourable Francis Egerton, son of the first Earl of Ellesmere, one of the trustees), were approved.[273]

In the same month Thorn commenced building at Nos. 227–235 (odd) Brompton Road,[274] a group of ground-floor shops with three main storeys and high attics above decked out with characteristic 'Queen Anne' trimmings of gables, red brickwork with occasional lighter bands, ribbed chimneys, and round-arched and segmental-headed window openings, and sporting little semi-circular balconies in front of the central windows on the second floor (Plate 25a, fig. 33). Above the shops in Brompton Road these buildings were intended to provide very spacious single dwellings entered from Egerton Gardens, where the numbers 67-75 (odd) were assigned, but within a few years most of them were occupied as flats.[91]

Thorn was also involved in extensive building operations in Elm Park Gardens, Chelsea, and by 1887 he was apparently in financial difficulties. He entered into an arrangement with his creditors[275] whereby he divested himself of his responsibilities in the Egerton Gardens area to Matthews Brothers and Company, who were then building in Bramham Gardens. Nos. 229-235 Brompton Road were assigned to Matthews Brothers in the names of the company's partners, Andrew Rogers, Maurice Charles Hulbert and Henry Arthur Matthews, for £3,000 per house (sums which would indicate that they were then practically finished).[276] No. 227 had already been sold to Charles Leonard Hacking, an ironmonger,[277] hence the ceramic plaque with the initials CLH on the side of the building.

Building had also begun in 1886 at Nos. 209-225 (odd) Brompton Road, a range of shops with flats above. Here individual or pairs of buildings were erected under separate agreements, and the flats, which were given the collective name of Egerton Mansions, are approached from entrances between the shops in Brompton Road. They also consist, above the shops, of three storeys and attics with gables or prominent dormers but are treated in a mixture of more restrained styles than Thorn's houses, ranging from simple brick façades verging on neo-Georgian to neo-Elizabethan fronts with squared-off stone bays of a kind which were to become increasingly common along commercial street frontages.

Three of the lessees of the buildings in this range were the occupants of previous buildings on the site, namely Charles Patrick Smith, upholsterer, James Hume, baker, and Mrs. Caroline Corby, lodging-house keeper, while another, Charlotte Adele Jeffreys, was presumably related to Mrs. Harriet Jeffreys who also ran a lodging-house at the old No. 219.[278] Neither the new shops nor any of the flats above were, however, occupied by the lessees, all of whom apparently undertook the rebuildings as speculations. The builders were Smith for No. 209, G. and G. Green of Hackney (who submitted the lowest tender at £3,125 to execute a design by R. J. Worley[279]) at No. 211, Samuel Chafen of Rotherhithe for Nos. 213 and 215, and Mark Manley of St. Pancras for Nos. 217-225.[280] Manley was also the builder, at this time, of Nos. 17 and 19 Egerton Terrace.[281]

Further along Brompton Road the range begun by Thorn was completed in 1887-8 by the erection of Nos. 237-249 (odd) in a similar but simplified style retaining the same storey heights and gabled roofline (Plate 25a, *right*). The lessee here was William John Stuart of Thornton Heath, builder, but the notices to the district surveyor of the commencement of building operations were in the name of the local builders, S. and R. Cawley of Hornton Street.[282] As with the other buildings in this range, the

flats above the shops are entered from the rear in Egerton Gardens where they are numbered 53-65 (odd).

No. 251 Brompton Road, a sharply angled building on the south corner of the short street opening from Brompton Road into the middle of Egerton Gardens, was built by Matthews Brothers in 1889 for The Working Ladies' Guild which had been founded in 1877 'with the aim of helping "necessitous gentlewomen" and encouraging them to develop their own skills and sell their work'. The building, which has thin Ionic pilasters between large window openings and ornately decorated pediments, had a showroom on the ground floor and presumably workshops above. A handsome shop front originally stretched around both street frontages, surmounted by a coat of arms at the corner. The activities of the Guild were boldly advertised on the showroom windows and included art needlework, china painting, poker work, church work, tapestry repairs and the making of trousseaux, layettes and emigrants' and servants' outfits. The Guild's motto, 'Bear Ye One Another's Burdens', is carved in the pediment above the entrance from Brompton Road. The Guild retained the premises until 1958.[283]

In Egerton Gardens Nos. 17-25 (odd) had been begun by Thorn in 1886,[284] and have some features which are common with Nos. 227-235 (odd) Brompton Road, but, like those houses, they were handed over to Matthews Brothers for completion. No. 17 was let, on their direction, to Major-General Charles Edmund Webber, who was the first occupant to move into the street in 1887,[285] and Nos. 19-25 were let individually to Rogers, Hulbert and Matthews in the same year.[286] They then proceeded to build the remainder of Egerton Gardens with great despatch. By 1890 all of the houses were occupied with the exception of No. 50, which was taken in the following year.[287]

Maurice Charles Hulbert, who had recently joined the building firm as a partner, was an Associate of the R.I.B.A. and had latterly been in private practice as an architect.[288] It seems inherently probable that he was the architect of the houses in Egerton Gardens (Plate 60a, c) with the exception of No. 31, where another architect was certainly employed, and probably of Nos. 17-25, which seem to have been designed, at least in part, by an architect employed by Thorn. Hulbert was to design several buildings for Matthews, Rogers and Company (as Matthews Brothers were later called) on the Grosvenor estate in Mayfair, where he later proved himself to be an architect of some flair and distinction.[289] In Egerton Gardens, however, there is little evidence of a talent much above the average, and the rapid rate of occupancy may be testimony more to the appeal of Brompton as a residential quarter than to the attractiveness of Matthews Brothers' houses.

These have basements, three or, more usually, four main storeys and high attics behind gables of various shapes and sizes. Their red-brick façades, treated with a modicum of ornamental brickwork, are sometimes relieved by bands and voussoirs of Portland cement, and most of the houses have canted bays through two or three storeys. Although there is some repetition of house-types, and the terraces are tied together by continuous iron-railed balconies carried on large brackets, symmetry is carefully avoided. Nos. 18–50 (even) have their principal fronts on the south side overlooking the communal garden which serves all the houses (Plate 60a), and their street fronts are of a familiar 'back-to-front' kind with split storey levels. Some of the upper storeys have been disfigured by alterations and additions, and the brilliant-white painting of the cement work has produced a striped effect which was not intended originally, as early photographs testify.

No. 31 was designed by Thomas Henry Smith for Lieutenant-Colonel William Wetherly, the lessee and first occupant.[290] While retaining the storey heights and general disposition of its neighbours (Plate 60c), the house has some individual features including a tall stepped and scrolled gable, ornamental carving in brick and cement by Gilbert Seale and lead-quarry glazing by Campbell, Smith and Company. Inside, the principal feature was a large inner hall and a wide open-well staircase decorated in an early-seventeenth-century manner in dark wood with ornamental plasterwork. Like the majority of houses in Egerton Gardens, it has been turned into flats. No. 17, which is lower than its neighbours, having only two main storeys and a high double attic, also has several individual characteristics. As it occupies a prominent corner position next to Mortimer House, much attention is given to the side elevation, which has exposed chimney-stacks, ornamental brickwork, a shaped gable and an octagonal turret with a lead cupola at the rear.

Officers of the armed forces provided a substantial core of the first occupants of Egerton Gardens. Besides Webber and Wetherly there were three colonels, three majors, two captains and an admiral (Sir Michael Seymour at No. 1). Two barristers and a solicitor can also be identified although there may have been more, as can two stockbrokers and a civil engineer. Her Majesty's Consul-General in Bogota occupied No. 20 briefly, and there were several merchants. A more sizeable upper-class presence here than in Evelyn Gardens is reflected in a number of aristocratic residents, including members of the Cadogan family, a son of the ninth Earl of Galloway, the fourth Earl of Kenmare and the second Baron Romilly, who had only recently moved into No. 38 when a fire broke out there in 1891, killing this unfortunate peer and two of his servants.[291]

Egerton Place

The initial building agreement for the redevelopment of the site occupied by Novosielski's houses in Michael's Grove and the terrace immediately behind in Yeoman's Row was concluded on 24 June 1891 with Harold Malet, a retired colonel, who lived at No. 12 Egerton Gardens.[292] Malet, who was a friend of the architect

(Sir) Mervyn Macartney, 'had taste and knew people'. He was involved with Macartney, Reginald Blomfield, W. R. Lethaby, Sidney Barnsley and Ernest Gimson in the famous but short-lived design firm of Kenton and Company which was formed in February 1891 with Malet holding, 'as it were, a watching brief on the whole proceeding'.[293]

In August 1891 another new company, The Estates Improvement Company Limited, was formed with Malet as secretary, to carry out the building agreement. Among the subscribers were Macartney and his father-in-law, Charles Thomson Ritchie, later Baron Ritchie of Dundee, who was President of the Local Government Board and, as such, had been responsible for the Local Government Act of 1888. Other subscribers included Edward L. Tomlin of Angley Park, Cranbrook, a client of Macartney, and William Henry Collbran, a local architect, surveyor and house agent, who had designed blocks of shops and residential chambers in Earl's Court Road, Old Brompton Road and Gloucester Road.[294]

Early in 1892 Macartney applied to the London County Council on behalf of The Estates Improvement Company for permission to lay out a new street in the form of a tight, deep crescent off Michael's Grove to be called Egerton Place, and in May 1892 John Grover and Son of Wilton Works, New North Road, gave notice of their intention to build the first houses there.[295]

Nos. 1–7 (consec.) Egerton Place (Plate 60b, *left side*, fig. 34a) were built by Grover to Macartney's designs and at once introduced a higher quality of architecture to the generally undistinguished ensemble of the Egerton Gardens area. They have the usual four main storeys with basements and garrets characteristic of most other houses in the development, and are finished in costly two-inch bricks of red and orange, with copious brown stone dressings. Their decorative features are spare and refined — a bold but plain linking cornice in stone at third-floor level, stone doorcases with open segmental or triangular pediments, shallow canted stone bays, and rubbed brick dressings with keystones to other windows. The overall effect is of a suave neo-classicism well in advance of its time, exemplified particularly in the long flank frontage to Egerton Terrace of Nos. 1 and 2 with its central pedimented window at first-floor level.

Leases of all seven houses were granted by the Smith's Charity trustees in 1894, that of No. 3 to the house's first occupant, Sir Evan MacGregor, permanent secretary to the Admiralty, and the remaining six to shareholders in The Estates Improvement Company.[296] Nos. 3 and 7 were occupied in 1894, the latter by another son-in-law of Ritchie, Thomas Barclay Cockerton, a barrister, but either the rate of completion or of occupancy of the other houses was slower than that of the houses in Egerton Gardens. Nos. 1 and 2 were used successively as the company's office before attracting private residents in 1895 and 1896 respectively, and in the latter year Nos. 4, 5 and 6 were also inhabited for the first time. The occupants

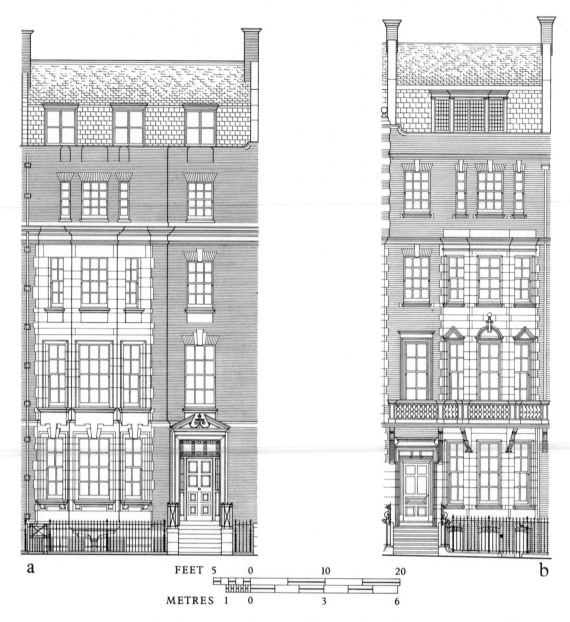

Fig. 34. Comparative elevations of houses in Egerton Place
a. No. 3, Mervyn Macartney, architect, 1894   *b.* No. 9, Amos Faulkner, architect, for W. Willett, builder, 1895

were, however, invariably people in high stations. Besides MacGregor and Cockerton, they included the Dowager Lady Lawrence, probably the widow of the first Baron Lawrence, at No. 5, Henry Arthur William Hervey, chief clerk of the Foreign Office, at No. 6, (Sir) Henry Fielding Dickens, Q.C., son of the novelist, at No. 2, and a stockbroker at No. 4.[297]

The original agreement with Malet had, for an unknown reason, been superseded by another in July 1893, and in November 1894 Malet obtained a licence from the trustees to allow William Willett of Sloane Gardens, Chelsea, to

take over the ground on which the southern half of Egerton Place was to be erected.[298] Willett's was an established building firm with its own architect, Amos Faulkner, and by the end of 1894 it had begun the construction of Nos. 8-13 (consec.) Egerton Place to Faulkner's designs[299] (Plate 60b, *right side*, fig. 34b). All six houses were completed and occupied by 1897.[91]

Faulkner retained the general storey heights of Macartney's houses and he completed No. 8 as a pair to No. 7 with common pediments over the doorcases and above the attic storey. There are differences, however, in the size of the window openings and the thickness of the glazing bars, and Faulkner could not resist the addition of a stone balcony in front of the central window on the first floor. The remaining houses broke from the original line of the crescent and progressively departed from Macartney's design by omitting the linking cornice and adding various features which placed the houses firmly in the context of the 1890's; balconies appeared of the type fashionable at this time, with stone balustrades carried on heavy brackets, and at No. 13 gables were given to both the front and side elevations. (No. 13 has been disfigured by the addition of a five-storey tower at the north-west corner to accommodate a staircase, carried out with the Smith's Charity trustees' consent as recently as 1960-1.[300]) A. E. Street commented in 1906 on the disparity between the two halves of Egerton Place and thought that the southern half which had been built by Willetts was 'anything but an improvement', a view with which one may certainly concur even though Street was writing in *The Architectural Review*, then under the editorship of Macartney.[301]

Nos. 4-28 (even) Yeoman's Row

The west side of Yeoman's Row between Egerton Gardens Mews and the present No. 28 was included in the ground taken under Malet's agreement and was intended to be used for stabling, one set of stables (which survive in a converted state) being quickly erected at Nos. 6-10 (even). In 1896, however, the remaining frontage was released by The Estates Improvement Company in a subsidiary agreement to William Henry Collbran, who had taken over from Malet as secretary of the company and was by then its principal shareholder.[294] Collbran erected one more stable and coach-house at No. 12[302] (rebuilt in 1957-8 to the designs of M. Howard-Radley[303]), but, even though the short Egerton Gardens Mews provided the only other stabling in the area, there seems to have been little demand for such buildings at a time when the practice of keeping one's own carriage in London was decreasing, and Collbran decided to utilise the remainder of the ground for studios.

In 1898 The Estates Improvement Company (then in voluntary liquidation) surrendered its remaining interest in the land, and the Smith's Charity trustees concluded a new building agreement with Collbran. Recognising an already existing state of affairs, this permitted the erection of studios or residential buildings provided that they were no higher than thirty-three feet (in effect three storeys) and that any windows at the rear were glazed with opaque glass unless they lit reception rooms, when clear glass was to be allowed. These and other specifications limiting the extent to which the windows could be opened were no doubt framed with the susceptibilities of the occupants of Egerton Place in mind.[304]

Collbran was granted leases of the main group of studios, originally designated Nos. 1-8 Egerton Place Studios but quickly renumbered 14-28 (even) Yeoman's

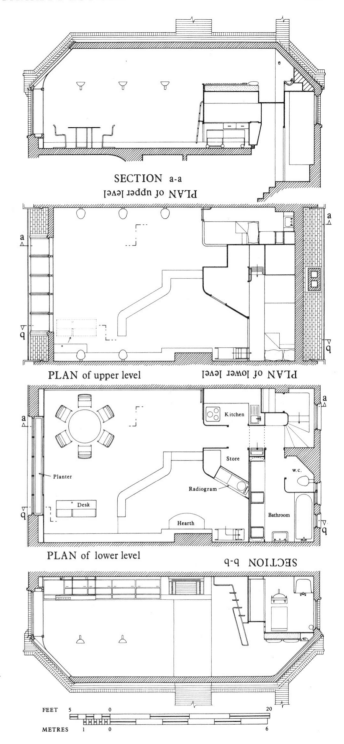

Fig. 35. No. 18 Yeoman's Row, plans and sections of flat. Based on original drawings by Wells Coates, architect, 1935

Row, in 1898-9,[305] but he promptly sub-let Nos. 14-22 to Charles E. Brassington of Camberwell, builder, who had erected the buildings.[306] No. 22 (Plate 25d) was designed by Alfred J. Beesley of Tufnell Park[307] in a simple red-brick manner with bay windows, a roof light and a pedimented brick-and-terracotta doorcase, but the author of the designs for No. 20 and the simpler group with large factory-style windows at Nos. 14-18 (Plate 25c) is not known.

Nos. 24, 26 and 28 (Plate 25b, d) were sub-let by Collbran to a trio of spinster artists, Ida Lovering, Emily McCallum and Sarah Vaughan, who jointly employed William Barber of No. 3 Brick Court, Temple, as architect: Brassington was the builder.[308] Barber employed a number of motifs in red brick and tile (to which weatherboarding has been added in an extension to the top storey of No. 26) and a variety of window openings in an exuberant manner no doubt thought appropriate for a residential studio. There is perhaps a hint, though, of the more serious-minded studio architecture of Philip Webb or E. W. Godwin at No. 24, but even this is more apparent in design than execution.

No. 4 Yeoman's Row, at the corner of Egerton Gardens Mews, which originally had a bicycle workshop on the ground floor and studios above, was erected in 1900-2 for Collbran by W. Mitchell and Son of Dulwich.[309]

In 1935 the architect Wells Coates, searching for a suitable 'pied à terre' which he could adapt to embody his ideas of 'planning in section', settled on No. 18 Yeoman's Row. As he had to share the building with other tenants the space available was limited and he created an ingenious flat on the 2:1 principle out of the top-floor studio, which measured some thirty-six by eighteen feet with a ceiling height of twelve feet (fig. 35). He double-glazed the large studio window and planted a 'window garden' between the two skins of glass. The main living space had a hearth-scene 'à la japonais' with matting and large cushions and easily moveable furniture elsewhere. The principal manifestation of Coates's ideas, however, was in the placing of a double-bed and a single-bed 'cabin' above the bathroom and kitchen respectively, with ladders for access. Part of the upper-level storage space could also be used as a projection room for films. A radio, which was uncased and had its chassis exposed, and a gramophone occupied a prominent place in an illuminated niche at the side of the hearth-scene to complete a highly personal interior. Apart from the war years, Coates lived here until 1955.[310]

Mortimer House

This large, detached mansion with spacious grounds at the southern junction of Egerton Gardens with Brompton Road (Plate 61, fig. 36) was built in 1886-8 for Edward Howley Palmer, a merchant with Dent, Palmer and Company of Gresham House, Old Broad Street, City, and a director and former governor of the Bank of England.[91] His father, John Horsley Palmer, had also been governor of the Bank.[311] Palmer's builder was William Goodwin of Hatton Garden,[312] but neither the identity of his architect nor the reason for his choice of name for the new house is known.

Since about 1881 Palmer had been living at Crescent House, which stood on the site of Mortimer House, and in 1885 or 1886 he had entered into an agreement with the Smith's Charity trustees to rebuild the mansion, paying a rent of £100 for the first year and £240 per annum thereafter.[313] Palmer had recently commissioned Richard Norman Shaw to design a house for him at No. 62 Cadogan Square and Shaw had exhibited his designs for that house at the Royal Academy in 1883,[314] but Palmer had either built it speculatively or decided not to live in it. The extent of his commitment to Mortimer House is also uncertain. In the lease of the house from the trustees to Palmer, dated 8 May 1889, he is described as of Mortimer House,[315] but except for 1892, when he is given as the occupant, the house is not entered in the directories, and by that date he also had another London home—an ordinary late-eighteenth-century terraced house at No. 16 Lower Seymour Street (now 126 Wigmore Street), St. Marylebone.[91] In 1896 he sold Mortimer House[316] and continued to live in Lower Seymour Street where he died in 1901 leaving effects of over £110,000.[317]

Largely secluded behind a high brick wall, Mortimer House exudes an air of mystery and surprise amid the surrounding terraces of South Kensington. Perhaps most surprisingly of all, it is still in private occupation. Its style is an amalgam of Tudor and Jacobean in red brickwork diapered with blue, with stone mullioned-and-transomed windows, a multiplicity of gables of various shapes, some of them stepped, crested with statuary of griffins or bears supporting shields, and clusters of tall, decorated brick chimneystacks. Inside there is a predictable eclecticism of style, ranging from Jacobean in the long hallway containing an oak open-well staircase with twisted balusters and wide handrail to Adamesque in the double drawing-room at the front. The fittings include fine marble chimneypieces in a late-eighteenth-century manner. A room on the first floor may originally have been used as a chapel. Several changes have been made to the decorative schemes since the house was built, some of them quite recently, and a long conservatory-cum-swimming-pool has been added to the west side of the house, where the detached stables (now converted into garages) with stepped gables and a turret with a conical roof are also situated.

Later Rebuildings

The first large block of flats to be erected on the Smith's Charity estate was Sussex Mansions, built in 1896-1900 to replace Sussex Terrace on the south side of Old Brompton Road. Constructed in three sections, the outer ones of five storeys and the centre of six, with shops on the ground floor, Sussex Mansions is in a minimal 'Queen Anne' style characteristic of the 1890's, with red-brick façades, decorative iron balconies and three small Dutch gables over the centre bays. The developer was William Henry Collbran, architect, who was at the same time building

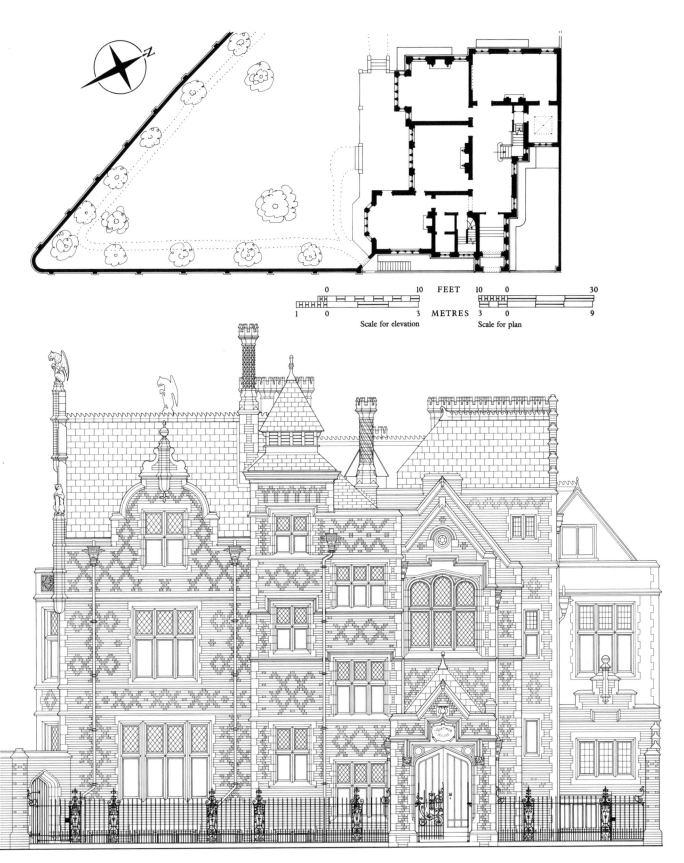

0   10   FEET   10   0   30

1   0   3   METRES   3   0   9

Scale for elevation   Scale for plan

Fig. 36. Mortimer House, Egerton Gardens, ground plan as built in 1886-8 and elevation to street

studios in Yeoman's Row (see above), and who may have provided the designs here.[318] Under a building agreement with the Smith's Charity trustees dated 14 December 1895 he paid an ultimate ground rent of £700 per annum; James Carmichael of Wandsworth was the contractor.[319]

In 1899 Collbran let part of the ground behind the flats to the National Telephone Company for a telephone exchange, which was built by William King and Son of Vauxhall Bridge Road. To the south of the exchange a 'Motor Car Warehouse' was erected in 1901 for the Locomobile Company of America.[320]

The buildings erected in and near Pelham Street as a result of the construction of the various railways which now form part of the London Underground system have been described on page 117. The present London Transport offices at Nos. 63-81 (odd) Pelham Street were originally built as a sub-station and workshops, with offices and a board room on the street frontage, for the Kensington and Knightsbridge Electric Lighting Company. The original design, of 1924-5 by C. Stanley Peach, was for a two-storey building in stone, and this was duly erected on land belonging partly to the Metropolitan District Railway and partly to the Smith's Charity estate. The main feature of Peach's design is a double-storey portico in antis with large square columns capped by palm-leaf capitals drawing their inspiration no doubt from Basevi's work nearby in Pelham Crescent. Two further red-brick storeys were added to the building in the 1950's by the successors to Peach's practice, Stanley Peach and Partners, and in 1975 the building was taken over by London Transport.[321]

Shortly after the completion of the original building the Kensington and Knightsbridge Electric Lighting Company found that it needed more land for its works, and in December 1930 it entered into a building agreement with the Smith's Charity trustees for the redevelopment of a large site on the north corner of Pelham Street and Fulham (now Brompton) Road. Peach drew up a scheme for the extension of the engineer's department on the ground floor with shops on the street frontages and the erection of flats, partly intended for the company's employees, above. In May 1933 he commented that 'The flats are intended to be fitted throughout with the most modern development of electricity. My clients hope to demonstrate on a large scale in these flats, that the use of electricity for labour-saving appliances, heating and lighting, is a practical and economical commercial proposition, even for small houses, and the size and accommodation of the flats has been carefully considered with this end in view.'[322]

In July 1933 the building agreement was assigned to a subsidiary company, Kenbridge Estates Limited, and the flats, named Crompton Court, presumably after R. E. B. Crompton, who was a pioneer in the development of the electrical supply industry, were virtually completed by April 1935. The builders were W. Moss and Sons Limited.[323]

Crompton Court is a six-storey block of flats (with additional penthouses on top) in red brick and cement. A wide opening at ground-floor level in Brompton Road allows access to the works behind, and the fenestration is given a horizontal emphasis by the unusual use of outside shutters.

A short distance to the north of Crompton Court another six-storey block of flats named St. George's Court was erected at the same time in a neo-Georgian style in red brick and stone with shops and showrooms on the ground floor. Together with a service station and garage called St. George's Garage, the building replaced the remaining houses of Onslow Terrace. The architects were Robert Angell and Curtis and the contractors were Sir Lindsay Parkinson and Company Limited.[324]

At the west end of Pelham Street, where the junction with the northward extension of Onslow Square forms an acute angle, seven houses which had been built by (Sir) Charles James Freake in the late 1840's were demolished for the erection of Malvern Court in 1930-1. Designed by H. F. Murrell and R. M. Pigott, Malvern Court has seven main storeys and an additional floor within the roof and is in a neo-Georgian style with multi-coloured red bricks, stone dressings including two canted stone bays on the main frontage to Onslow Square, and a tiled roof. The contractors were J. Knox and Dyke.[325]

Opposite to Malvern Court the demolition of Onslow Crescent for redevelopment in 1935 provoked an exchange of letters in *The Times*. Arthur Dasent, the author of several books on the history of London, who lived nearby in Cromwell Place, was particularly concerned at the loss of the garden enclosure in front of the houses in Onslow Crescent, remarking that 'not only was this unobtrusive Victorian crescent doomed to be blotted out but that its entire garden was marked out for destruction. And for what purpose, it may be asked, has this act been set in motion? It is to erect a huge cinema with rows of shops and towering flats, which, so far as I can gather, are not desired by anyone living in the immediate neighbourhood.'[326]

The cinema failed to materialize, and Melton Court, an eight-storey block of flats with ground-floor shops, was erected in 1936-8 under a building agreement of 23 July 1936.[327] The agreement was made with Edmund Howard of St. James's Street, 'architect', who was described as a man of 'substantial means', but the building, which is faced with brown bricks and cream-coloured stone or faience, was designed by Trehearne and Norman, Preston and Company. The contractors were Harry Neal Limited.[328] Most of the former garden enclosure was used by Kensington Borough Council to create the complex road junction between Old Brompton Road, Onslow Square and Pelham Street.

The building of Melton Court was intended to be followed by the further redevelopment of parts of Onslow Square and Gardens. The outbreak of the war of 1939-45 and the Smith's Charity trustees' subsequent change of policy in favour of the rehabilitation and conversion of the houses built by Freake has been described above (see page 112). In pursuit of this policy the unexpired leases of 154 houses and mews dwellings were acquired in 1949 from the Freake family for £110,000, a move thought advisable by the trustees as 'it would put us in closer touch with the occupiers at a time when the character of the Estate is changing and needs close attention if the property is not to deteriorate too badly'. [329]

Elsewhere on the estate, the present office of Cluttons, the estate surveyors, at No. 48 Pelham Street and the flats above numbered 42-46 (even) Pelham Street were built in place of numbers 44 and 46 Fulham Road (formerly Nos. 7 and 8 Onslow Place), which were destroyed during the war. The small neo-Georgian houses at Nos. 9-11 (consec.) Crescent Place also replaced war-damaged buildings in 1956.[330] In Yeoman's Row the houses which had been built in the 1840's on the site of Novosielski's Brompton Grange were in turn replaced in c. 1953 by a small three-storey red-brick block of flats numbered 38-62 (even).[331]* These modest and restrained rebuildings of the post-war period were all designed in the architect's department of Cluttons, headed by John V. Hamilton.

The policy of restoration and rehabilitation of the original nineteenth-century building fabric, coupled with piecemeal small-scale rebuilding instead of comprehensive redevelopment under building leases, bore fruit in the 1960's and 1970's as the rise in the income from rents outstripped inflation. In 1964 the total rental income amounted to £290,000; by 1977 this had been increased to £1,464,000, and when a further £440,000 received from interest on investments is added to this, the total income from the Kensington and Chelsea estate was little short of £2,000,000.[5]

*The site of the Metropolitan Police Traffic Wardens' Centre at No. 64 Yeoman's Row formerly belonged to the Smith's Charity estate but was purchased by the Receiver for the Metropolitan Police District under the Metropolitan Police Act of 1886. A small strip of the land was first sold in 1894 for an addition to the police station in Walton Street. The remainder of the plot was conveyed in 1907 and the present building was erected in 1909.[332]

CHAPTER VII

The Brompton Hospital Estate

This chapter describes the buildings of Brompton Hospital itself, and the area immediately to the west which was purchased by the governors of the hospital from the fifth Earl of Harrington in 1853 and on which Nos. 80-108 (even) Fulham Road, Nos. 9-17 (consec.) Onslow Gardens and the houses in Foulis Terrace, Neville Street and Neville Terrace were erected.

Brompton Hospital

The initiative for the foundation of the Hospital for Consumption and Diseases of the Chest came from a young solicitor, Philip Rose. Apparently a clerk in Rose's firm had fallen ill with tuberculosis but could not obtain admission to any of the general hospitals in London which, because of the long-lasting and frequently terminal nature of the illness, invariably had rules specifically excluding patients suffering from consumption. Accordingly, in January 1841 Rose, who was then only twenty-four years old, wrote a number of letters to friends and associates urging the need to remedy this situation. His brother-in-law, Dr. William Harcourt Ranking, who was physician to the Suffolk General Hospital, helped to draw up a prospectus, and at a meeting held in Rose's house in Hans Place in March of that year a resolution was passed to establish a special hospital for consumptive patients.[1]

The first hospital to cater largely for sufferers from tuberculosis and other chest illnesses was the Royal Sea-Bathing Hospital at Margate (originally the Margate Infirmary), which was founded in 1791. In London, however, the only special hospital for diseases of the lungs was the Infirmary for Asthma, Consumption and other Diseases of the Lungs (later the Royal Chest Hospital), which had been established in Spitalfields in 1814, but by the 1840's even this solitary institution had ceased for a while to admit in-patients.[2]

There was thus a *prima facie* need for a hospital for the treatment of a disease which was becoming increasingly widespread as the population of the metropolis increased, and at a public meeting held in May 1841 and attended by several prominent members of the medical profession Rose's venture was given enthusiastic support. Appeals to the Victorian philanthropic conscience proved successful and by March 1842 funds were sufficient to allow an out-patients' department to be opened in Great Marl-

borough Street, Westminster. Later in that year a ten-year lease was taken of a detached house in Smith Street, Chelsea, called the Manor House, which was adapted to receive the first in-patients by September 1842.[3]

Most admissions were made on the basis of letters of recommendation from governors or subscribers, but the medical staff were able to choose a small number of in-patients from among the out-patients being treated by them. The administration of the hospital was vested in a court of governors which met quarterly, a committee of management which met weekly and a number of specialist committees, especially the influential medical commitee. Rose was honorary secretary from the hospital's foundation in 1841 to his death in 1883. He was a personal friend and financial adviser to Disraeli, and, largely through the latter's influence, he was created a baronet in 1874.[4]

In 1843 the committee of management decided to enlarge the Manor House and held a competition for a suitable design. The competitors' instructions included directions from the medical staff that the wards were to be varied in size but should not contain more than eight beds, that they should open into corridors about nine feet wide and that they should be capable of being heated and ventilated without the use of open fires.[5]

A building committee was formed, but its early records have not survived and the precise sequence of events is unclear. The competition was advertised for September 1843[6] and the award of a prize of thirty guineas to an unnamed winner was recorded in the annual accounts.[7] This was evidently Frederick John Francis, the eventual architect of Brompton Hospital, who was later said to have been chosen 'out of above thirty competitors'.[8] By November, however, the building committee had decided that it was impracticable to extend the Manor House and, having resolved to seek a better site for a new building, asked 'Mr Francis . . . to enquire at the Office of Woods and Forests whether any suitable plot of Crown land might be obtained for building'.[9]

The site eventually acquired 'after much difficulty' was some three acres of land on the north side of the Fulham Road belonging to the Smith's Charity estate. It had formerly been part of the large nursery of William Malcolm and Company and was chosen partly because Brompton was considered to be one of the most salubrious neighbourhoods in the vicinity of the metropolis. The charity's trustees agreed to let the ground at a rent of £170 per annum with the understanding that they would sell the

Fig. 37. The Brompton Hospital estate. Based on the Ordnance Survey of 1862-72. The broken line marks the division between the areas purchased from the trustees of Smith's Charity (right) and the fifth Earl of Harrington

freehold to the hospital when its funds allowed.* The trustees insisted that their architect and surveyor, George Basevi, should not only approve the elevation and specifications of the hospital but also have the final word about the precise location of the building. He duly imposed a *cordon sanitaire*, about one hundred feet wide, between the eastern wing of the hospital and the boundary of the site on that side, thereby pushing the whole building over towards the western edge of its plot where the adjoining land did not belong to the Smith's Charity estate (see fig. 37). The hospital's governors later acknowledged that 'from the position of the ground and other circumstances, the Building was almost necessarily placed at one extremity of it. . . . Although this step seemed at the time to be a matter of necessity more than of choice, it was not done without deliberation.' The acquisition of the land to the west, which formed part of the Harrington-Villars estate, thereafter became a major objective of the governors.[10]

After these negotiations with Basevi (for which he was paid a fee of £36 15s.[11]), Francis's design was ready by 1 February 1844, when collectors' cards bearing an illustration of the proposed building were issued.[12] What relationship the final design (Plate 62a) bore to the scheme which had won the competition is not known, but the differences between the new site in Brompton and the old one in Chelsea suggest that substantial changes must have been made. The H-shaped plan which Francis adopted was a conventional one for hospitals erected on relatively restricted sites, and the Tudor style which he employed was also a familiar idiom for such institutions, and one moreover with which he had had some experience as a pupil of Thomas Hopper, the architect of a number of Tudor Gothic country houses.[13] Basevi also used Tudor Gothic for almshouses and similar buildings, but whether he had any influence on the appearance of Brompton Hospital must be conjectural. Francis, who, like Rose, was only in his mid-twenties at the time of this, his first major commission, went on to develop an extensive and successful practice in partnership with his younger brother Horace.[14]

The hospital had to be erected in stages as funds became available, and the first part to be built was the west wing and half of the central linking block, including the main entrance. A formal building agreement with the Smith's Charity trustees was drawn up, and a contract was made with the builders George and William Bird of Hammersmith to complete the initial phase of the building programme for £11,290. The foundation stone was laid by the Prince Consort amid elaborate ceremony on 11 June 1844.[15]

The west wing was completed in 1846 and the first patients were admitted in that year. A small gabled porter's

*The freehold was eventually purchased in 1868 for £6,500.

lodge was built to Francis's designs in the south-west corner of the grounds in the following year,[16] and in 1849-50 a chapel was erected to the north of the hospital, to which it was joined by a long corridor (see St. Luke's Chapel below). An Act of Parliament (passed in 1849) was needed to enable the chapel to be built, and the opportunity was taken to establish the hospital as a corporate body and obtain powers for it to buy land and grant long leases.[17]

The benefactor who paid for the chapel, the Reverend Sir Henry Foulis, baronet, thereafter played a major role in the affairs of the hospital. He was appointed a vice-president in 1849 and held the influential position of chairman of the committee of management from 1850 to 1875. Probably through his influence, his chosen architect for the chapel, Edward Buckton Lamb, was retained as architect for the completion of the main building in collaboration with Francis.

Plans for the east wing and the remaining half of the linking block were submitted by Francis and Lamb in 1850, but work was not begun until the following year when a contract to build the carcase of the extension at a cost of £5,500 was concluded with H. W. Cooper, builder, of St. Pancras.[18] Cooper completed the contract in 1853 but his tender for fitting out the building was too high and another builder, John Glenn of Liverpool Road, Islington, carried out this work for £4,854.[19] A kitchen and other offices were added at the rear of the linking block, and when the whole hospital was finally completed in 1854 it could accommodate 220 in-patients.[20]

In the building of the eastern half of the hospital Francis's design of 1844 was faithfully adhered to on the south front where the principal architectural effect was naturally concentrated (Plate 62a). Here the façade of red brick with blue-brick diapering is enlivened by prominent buttresses, a crenellated roofline and the plentiful use of Caen stone dressings in quoins, stringcourses, hood-moulds and, more extensively, in the three oriel windows which decorate the ends of the wings and the entrance tower in the centre of the linking block. The tower, which appears to have been modelled on the Founder's Tower at Magdalen College, Oxford, had a broad flight of stone steps leading up to the principal entrance at first-floor level. The steps have recently been removed, however, for the erection of a sun lounge which projects in front of the former main entrance. The picturesque asymmetrical turret with a squat crocketed spire on the west side of the tower contains a spiral staircase which originally provided access to the medical officers' rooms.

The east-facing façade of the later wing differs from the façade of the west wing in detail. The latter, which is now partly clad with Virginia creeper, has a narrow entrance bay flanked by octagonal piers, while the east wing has a wide projecting centre with a canted bay on each side of the entrance. The most prominent feature of the later wing, however, is a tower which was designed to house a ventilating shaft. It is treated with marked architectural effect and decorated with small-scale battlements and finials at the top and blind windows on its sides, those on the upper stages filled with carved heraldic shields. The latter were favourite sculptural devices of Lamb, whose experience with towers at his many churches probably led to his assumption of the principal role in designing this one.

The planning of the hospital reflects the wishes of its medical staff as expressed in the instructions to competitors in 1843 (fig. 38). The low ground storey was originally occupied by the administrative offices, laboratory, dispensary and museum, and by the waiting- and consulting-rooms for out-patients. The first and second floors, both fourteen feet high, contained the wards for female and male patients respectively. These wards, though varying in size, were intended to hold no more than eight beds, and open on to long corridors or galleries, ten feet wide, which can be used as day rooms. To protect the wards from cold winds the corridors are arranged so that they occupy the east side of each wing and the north side of the central block. Dormitories for nurses and servants were provided in attic rooms on the north side of the hospital, Francis and Lamb having been specifically ordered to construct a servants' staircase from which there would be no direct access to the ward floors.[21]

Much thought was given to the methods of heating and ventilating the wards and corridors so that an even temperature and constant supply of fresh air could be provided by artificial means, even though the wards were furnished with fireplaces. In the west wing the system used was one developed by Dr. Neil Arnott, a well-known physician and expert on heating and ventilation, whereby air warmed in a basement heating plant passed through openings in the walls and was eventually carried up to the roof. Difficulties in maintaining an even temperature were encountered, however, and when the east wing was built Messrs. Haden of Trowbridge were called in to provide the necessary equipment. Their method required the erection of a ventilating shaft rising some twenty-five feet above the roof, and it was the need to accommodate this shaft which led to the erection of the distinctive tower above the east wing.[22]

Victorian mechanical ingenuity extended beyond the provision of a flow of warm air to the wards, for a description of the hospital in the annual report for 1856 described enthusiastically how, 'The steam, which heats the water both in the Kitchen and the Baths attached to the wards, turns the spit, grinds the coffee, and raises the lift which takes up the Patients' meals hot from the Kitchen, as well as other necessaries; it also raises a lift for conveying those Patients to and from the galleries for whom exercise in the grounds is desirable.'

Inside the hospital there is understandably little in the way of decoration, Francis and Lamb having been specifically instructed in 1850 that there should be 'no cornice or moulding or any expensive decoration of any sort'.[23] Nevertheless the main open-well staircase behind the former entrance hall has a balustrade and plain columns of stone and a vaulted ceiling of stained and varnished wood with large carved angels on the bosses. The board room at the north end of the east wing has deep wooden beams with Gothic tracery and a simple stone chimneypiece.

In 1853 the governors purchased four acres of land on the west side of the hospital from the trustees of Lord Harrington. Most of this land was used for speculative house-building, which will be described below, but, as indicated earlier, a major reason for its acquisition had been the desire to provide extra space on the west side of the hospital. Accordingly half an acre was added to the hospital's grounds, which were laid out to Lamb's designs in 1854.[24]

In 1863 a report on the hospitals of the United Kingdom was submitted to the Medical Officer of the Privy Council by Dr. John Syer Bristowe, a physician at St. Thomas's Hospital, and Timothy Holmes, a surgeon on the staff of St. George's. Although the report generally favoured larger wards and natural ventilation in accordance with contemporary ideas on hospital design, its authors found much to praise at the Brompton Consumption Hospital, where 'the small wards and heating of the air seemed to us to be well adapted for the class of cases'. They praised the 'handsome' building and the ample grounds in which patients could take exercise, and were impressed with the general management and arrangement of the institution. The specialist nature of the hospital generally kept it immune from the changing currents of thought on hospital planning; the small wards were retained and it was not until the very end of the nineteenth century that fresh air from open windows was considered to be more beneficial than artificial ventilation.[25]

Few changes were made to the original building during the nineteenth century. In 1855 Arthur E. Robinson was appointed surveyor to the fabric, but the office was soon allowed to lapse.[26] The decay of the external stonework began to cause problems, however, and in the late 1860's David Brandon was consulted on such matters. In 1871 the stone chimneys on the west wing proved so defective that they had to be replaced with terracotta ones in an Elizabethan style, and the need to obtain proper estimates for such work prompted the committee of management to appoint a permanent architect. The post was offered to George Pownall, who had acted as the hospital's surveyor during building operations on its estate to the west, but he declined and recommended his son-in-law, Henry Arthur Hunt junior, who was duly engaged at an annual salary of twenty-five guineas.[27]

During his tenure as architect and surveyor, which lasted until 1881 when he resigned and was replaced by Lewis Karslake,[28] Hunt carried out a number of small works. In 1872 a subway was constructed under Fulham Road to link the main hospital building with a group of houses on the south side of the road (in the parish of Chelsea) which the governors had purchased; John Aird and Sons were the contractors at a price of £1,150.[29] Two years later the porter's lodge was rebuilt on a larger scale to Hunt's design in red brick with Portland stone dressings; the builder, whose tender was for £1,691, was the hospital's former surveyor, Arthur E. Robinson.[30] In 1876 Messrs. Haden were called in to improve the heating and ventilation of the west wing and they recommended the construction of an extraction shaft similar to that on the east wing. In order to save costs, however, Hunt was asked to design a smaller and less decorative tower, and the resulting unobtrusive addition was built in that year.[31]

A substantial bequest was made to the hospital in the early 1870's, and this enabled the governors to replace the houses on the south side of Fulham Road with one large building. In 1877 Hunt was asked to supply outline plans for the new building, but it was made clear to him that he would not necessarily be appointed as its architect. The committee of management was eventually asked to choose between three candidates, Hunt, Arthur Graham, who was recommended by Florence Nightingale, and Thomas Henry Wyatt. The choice fell on the last, no doubt because of his extensive experience in hospital design throughout the country.[32]

The instructions issued to Wyatt by the medical committee reflected the successful planning of the main hospital building, for he was asked to provide small wards, ideally holding five or six beds, and wide corridors, which, in the event, were similarly situated on the north and east sides of each ward. He was also given the general direction that 'The Style of Architecture should be not inharmonious with that of the existing Hospital, carried out with due regard to economy in material and construction'. He responded by submitting sketch elevations in both Elizabethan and Queen Anne styles and the latter was chosen; a narrow preference for terracotta over Mansfield stone for the dressings was also expressed. Higgs and Hill were the contractors and the foundation stone was laid by the Prince of Wales on 17 July 1879. T. H. Wyatt died in August 1880 and his son, Matthew Wyatt, who had already largely taken over his father's practice, replaced him as architect. The new building, or south block, was opened by the hospital's president, the fifteenth Earl of Derby, on 13 June 1882. The cost of the building was some £60,000.[33]

The south block of Brompton Hospital was originally an E-shaped building with its main front to Fulham Road and has a basement, four main storeys with an additional mezzanine floor in part of the tall ground storey, and extra floors within the roof. The style adopted by the Wyatts is a conventional Queen Anne in red brick with terracotta bands and dressings, sporting shaped gables at each end and a Dutch gable in the centre. Two octagonal turrets at the angles of the projecting centre bay, with two others at the rear, perform the same function as the towers on the earlier building in housing ventilating shafts. When opened the south block accommodated 137 in-patients, making Brompton Hospital, with over three hundred beds, by far the largest tuberculosis hospital in the country.[34]

In 1898-9 a nurses' home was erected behind the south block, facing Chelsea Square, to the designs of Edwin T. Hall. A long, shallow building, originally four-storeyed with additional rooms behind a large segmental gable in the centre, it is in a transitional style between Queen Anne and free classicism in red brick with Portland stone dressings

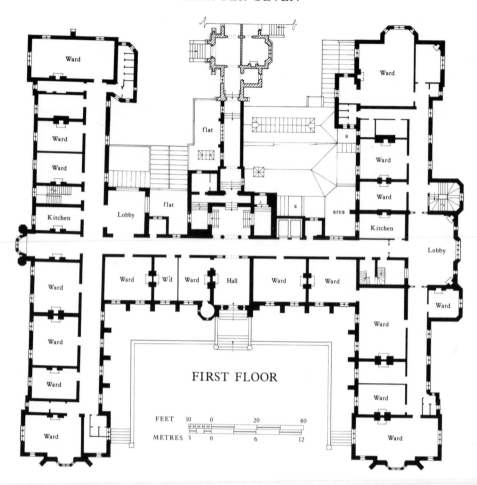

Fig. 38. Brompton Hospital, plans in 1931

and bays. The builders were Foster and Dicksee and the cost some £32,000.[35]

In the 1920's and 1930's some in-filling took place in the courtyards on the north side of the original building, but most additions were made on the south side of Fulham Road including an extension at the western end of the south block in a matching style and the construction of an extra floor within the roof of the nurses' home. The hospital's architects during this period were Alfred Saxon Snell and Phillips, who had a large hospital practice.[36]

When the National Health Service came into operation in 1948 Brompton was placed in the category of teaching hospitals and became the official centre in London for instruction in diseases of the chest. Most of the extensive building work which has taken place recently has been in connexion with this teaching role. Initially a single-storey building capable of enlargement was erected on the east side of Foulis Terrace (thereby encroaching on the open space which had been acquired at high cost in 1853) and opened on 26 October 1949 as the Institute of Diseases

of the Chest (now the Cardiothoracic Institute) of the University of London.[37] In 1958 a four-storey laboratory building was erected for the Institute at the northern end of this range.[38]

These building schemes were the work of Saxon Snell and Phillips, who also drew up designs for a further extension to the west of the south block in 1963, but in March 1964 the ill-health of the sole remaining partner, P. R. Rees Phillips, led to his resignation and the appointment of Adams, Holden and Pearson as architects to the hospital.[39] The latter completed the south block extension and undertook several additions to the Institute in phases during the 1960's. The work involved the addition of a second storey to the existing range along Foulis Terrace and the extension of the range to the south which necessitated the demolition of Hunt's lodge.* In 1966 Adams, Holden and Pearson also designed the obtrusive projecting sun lounge which was added to the centre of the main front at first-floor level, to the considerable detriment of Francis's original elevation.[41]

*A large bas-relief of the Good Samaritan which was carved by the sculptor James Havard Thomas above the entrance to the lodge in 1876 was, however, re-erected on a wall of the Institute near to a new porter's lodge.[40]

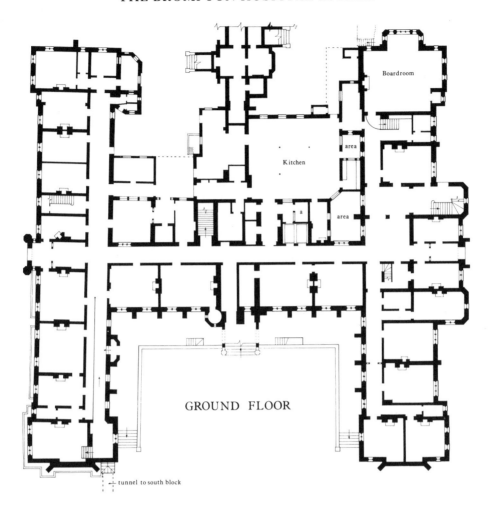

GROUND FLOOR

tunnel to south block

Further structures, generally of prefabricated materials, have been erected in various parts of the grounds in a manner now common in older hospitals, and at the time of writing (1982) the proposed construction of a new chest and heart hospital in Chelsea which would absorb Brompton Hospital makes the future of the building uncertain.

St. Luke's Chapel

The chapel attached to Brompton Hospital (Plates 62b, c, 63, figs. 39-40) was built in 1849-50 to the designs of Edward Buckton Lamb and enlarged in 1891-2 by the architect William White.

When Frederick Francis drew up plans for the hospital which was to be built on the new site at Brompton in 1844 he set aside a plot at the north end of the east wing for a chapel and made a drawing of his proposed design.[42] The building of the east wing had to be delayed because of lack of funds, however, and a ward in the west wing was fitted up as a temporary chapel, thereby depriving the hospital of much-needed bed space and making the provision of a permanent structure an urgent necessity.

The problem was resolved in 1849 when a new benefactor appeared in the person of the Reverend Sir Henry Foulis, ninth baronet, of Ingleby Manor, Yorkshire, prebendary of Lincoln and rector of Great Brickhill, Buckinghamshire. Foulis, who does not appear to have had any previous connexion with the hospital, offered to pay for the erection of a chapel as a memorial to his recently deceased sister, Sophia Frances Pauncefort Duncombe. He insisted on approving the design and arrangements for the chapel and chose E. B. Lamb as architect on the recommendation of Lady Frankland Russell, widow of Sir Robert Frankland Russell of Thirkleby, Yorkshire. The Frankland Russells, who were amateur stained-glass artists, had worked with Lamb on several churches in the North Riding, including All Saints, Thirkleby, which was being rebuilt at that time to his designs.[43]

An Act of Parliament was quickly obtained to allow the chapel to be built and consecrated and, as the governors had not yet purchased the freehold of the whole hospital site, to enable the Smith's Charity trustees to give the site of the chapel gratis to the hospital.[17] Hopkins and Roberts of Islington, who submitted the lowest tender at £1,613, were engaged as contractors, and the foundation stone was laid by Sir Henry Foulis on 30 August 1849. A separate contract was made with Samuel Pratt of New Bond Street,

FEET   10   0   30
METRES 3   0   9

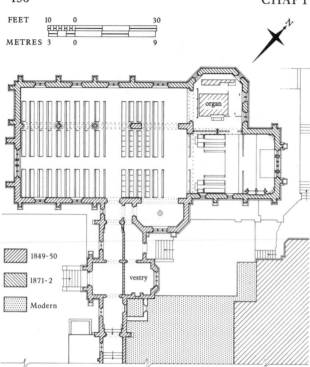

Fig. 39. Brompton Hospital Chapel, plan

1849-50

1871-2

Modern

organ

vestry

designer of wood carving, for executing the carved oak fittings, including the pews, stalls, pulpit, reading desk and altar table. Even with extras the cost was only some £2,500 for the chapel itself and a further £1,500 for the long range which connects it to the hospital. The completed chapel was consecrated on 27 June 1850.[44]*

In 1891 the hospital's committee of management decided to celebrate the fiftieth anniversary of the foundation of the institution by enlarging the chapel and, on the suggestion of a member of the committee, chose William White as architect. He virtually rebuilt the chancel, which was enlarged in breadth, length and height as well as by the addition of an organ chamber on the north side, and he also built an aisle on the north side of the nave, re-using the original stonework as far as possible. The contractor was B. E. Nightingale of Albert Embankment and the total cost was over £4,000. The much-altered chapel was re-consecrated on 22 October 1892.[45]

E. B. Lamb was described by Goodhart-Rendel, in a term that has passed into the language of architectural criticism, as a 'rogue-architect', by which he meant one who used traditional styles in a highly personal and idiosyncratic manner that defied both imitation and analysis.[46] Lamb's eclectic use of Gothic forms at a time when Pugin and the Camdenians were steering the Gothic revival into strictly confined channels made him in many ways the arch rogue. *The Ecclesiologist*, that organ of Gothic rectitude and ritualistic orthodoxy, could never come to terms with his quirky genius. It viewed Brompton Hospital chapel 'with a

feeling of sadness' that the munificence of Sir Henry Foulis had produced such a debased building,[42] failing to recognise that in Foulis Lamb certainly had an ally, and, moreover, one who no doubt felt that the broad evangelism implicit in his architect's approach to church architecture was appropriate for a congregation which would not for the most part be using the chapel from choice. Much of Lamb's work in the chapel has, however, been 'tamed' by White's alterations and by the removal of some of the decorative stonework, but what remains can be supplemented by early engravings and photographs of the exterior. Unfortunately, however, there is no record of the interior, and especially the chancel, as Lamb left it.

William White, on the other hand, was a member of the Ecclesiological Society and well-regarded in the 1850's and 1860's when his work was boldly innovative,[47] but by the time he was called upon to remodel the chapel he was in his sixties and had produced little of note for some years. His work there, though certainly worthy and producing a greatly increased sense of space, suffers in comparison with the exuberance of his predecessor's.

The chapel, which is faced with Kentish rag and Caen stone dressings, stands out in sharp contrast to the brick-faced hospital to which it is attached. Today it is largely hemmed-in by other buildings and the rationale for providing it with such an imposing appearance is not obvious, but when built it was surrounded on three sides by open fields and it was even raised on an artificial mound to make it more conspicuous, a reminder, no doubt, that the hospital was a fit object for Christian charity.

The chapel is connected to the hospital by a long, single-storey range which is faced with red brick at the hospital end and stone in front of the chapel. Here Lamb placed another short block crossways containing a gabled porch (now almost completely obscured), lobby and vestry-room. A bell-turret with an octagonal upper stage originally stood at the south-east angle of the two ranges but it has recently fallen victim to the persistent in-filling of the hospital's courtyards.

The west front of the nave in its original form (Plate 62b) well illustrated Lamb's style with its large five-light window, basically Perpendicular but decorated with crockets, ball-flowers and elaborate 'cuspy' tracery (to use Goodhart-Rendel's adjective), set closely between buttresses with crocketed pinnacles. Additional pinnacles broke through the steeply raking sides of the gable and a trio of smaller pinnacles crowned the apex, the middle one carrying a cross. The rectangular openings above the window originally contained the arms and crest of Sir Henry Foulis. Such intricate, not to say finicky, decorative stonework is particularly vulnerable to decay, however, and much of it has been stripped off the upper part of the front including all but the topmost pinnacle. White may have made some alterations in 1891-2 but more recent repairs have also taken their toll. The west front of the aisle which

*The outline plan of the chapel, as originally built, can be seen on fig. 37.

was added in 1891-2 respects Lamb's basic forms and has a two-light window set between buttresses, three tiny blind lancets at the apex of the gable, a cross above and crocketed pinnacles on each side.

The sides of the nave are separated into three bays by buttresses with crocketed pinnacles, and have two-light windows with complex tracery characteristic of Lamb and lozenge-shaped openings inset with quatrefoils interrupting the parapet above. (Although the north wall was moved several feet outwards to accommodate the new aisle, Lamb's decorative stonework and windows were carefully re-incorporated to match the south side.) The short transepts, which *The Ecclesiologist* contemptuously dismissed as 'paddle-boxes', were originally both five-sided but that on the north side is now flush with the aisle to the west.

The organ chamber, which projects slightly on the north side, is entirely the work of White, as for the most part is the three-bay chancel, the original chancel having been a bay shorter as well as narrower and lower. Some stonework was re-used and the five-light east window, more strictly Perpendicular in form than the west window, was reinstated in the new east wall, shorn of some of its more delicate tracery (Plate 62c). The two single-light windows on the south side of the chancel were preserved from the original structure, one of them having formerly been on the north side.

The roofs were slated by White, who added two copper-covered *flèches* over the nave (with a weather vane) and aisle respectively, Lamb's roofs having been tiled with diaper patterning.

The main approach to the interior of the chapel is from the first floor of the hospital (the lowest ward floor) through the linking range along a corridor which descends gradually until the chapel's outer appendages are reached. Here the flat ceiling of the corridor gives way to open-timber roofs, supported in the entrance lobby on corbels decorated with monograms of Lamb, Foulis, his sister and (Sir) Philip Rose, the hospital's honorary secretary. After the long cloistral approach the nave unfolds quite dramatically, its most arresting feature being an open-timber roof in which hammerbeams, arched braces with traceried spandrels arranged both crossways and lengthways, diagonal ties, struts and pendants vie with each other in a manner described by *The Ecclesiologist* as 'decidedly astonishing. . . . Such a chaos of carpentry so near our heads we have seldom seen.' Lamb was to produce even more remarkable displays in the vast timber roofs of later churches such as St. Martin, Gospel Oak, and St. Mary Magdalene, Croydon, but the effect in such a small chapel must have been even more startling before the north aisle was added and a solid wall pierced only by windows filled with stained glass enclosed the nave on that side. Now a stone arcade of wide arches carried on pillars of quatrefoil section with foliated capitals separates nave and aisle (Plate 63c).

White's chancel roof is placid by comparison and relies for effect on simple hammerbeams ornamented with large carved angels and heraldic shields, the latter probably re-used from the original roof (Plate 63b).[48]

Besides the roof of the nave, the main interest of the interior of the chapel lies in its fittings and stained glass. Most of the stained and varnished oak fittings designed by Lamb and made by Samuel Pratt remain and have been supplemented by others in a matching style. They include the pulpit, reading desks, altar table, altar rails, low chancel screen and the stalls and pews. The bench-ends are for the most part decorated with conventional fleur-de-lis poppyheads but are occasionally embellished with the arms and crest of Sir Henry Foulis. The crest, consisting of a cross surmounting a crescent, is a ubiquitous feature of the chapel's decorations in wood, stone and tile. Its use was defended by Lamb as symbolising the triumph of Christianity over paganism, but *The Ecclesiologist* could not refrain from wondering what particular triumph of Christianity over Islam had taken place in Brompton. Some of the pews are provided with arm rests for the benefit of weaker patients, not, as was mischievously stated in some quarters, for the governors and subscribers.[49] A small stone font inset with painted ceramic panels of New Testament scenes in blue on gold, signed and dated 'J. Rochefort 1875', stands in the south transept.

The remodelled chancel incorporates Lamb's carved stone fittings including florid two-part sedilia with the usual cross and crescent motif (fig. 40), two canopied niches in the angles of the east wall which originally displayed the Ten Commandments, and an equally elaborate aumbry on the north side of the sanctuary. The mason who was paid extra for work on the sedilia was 'Mr Bellini', perhaps William Bellenie of Fisher Street, Red Lion Square.[50]

The chapel is particularly rich in stained glass, most of it donated by benefactors at the time of building and of Lamb's own designing. In 1849, on proposing that the west window should be filled with heraldry, he was asked to prepare a plan for all of the windows,[51] and his monogram appears on several, while others are sufficiently similar to be confidently attributed to him. Most of the designs, in bright reds and blues against backgrounds of yellow stain with scrolled patterns, illustrate New Testament themes, with a special emphasis on healing and ministering to the sick. In execution the figures are often naively treated, but the identity of the manufacturers is unknown. The west window is the most elaborate and, in the main lights, depicts the twelve apostles under canopies. The heraldry so much favoured by Lamb is used principally in the south transept window where the committee of management chose to honour Foulis by placing his arms and crest and those of his sister.[52] A small window in the entrance to the nave depicting the widow's mite has Lamb's monogram and a pair of dividers at the bottom, and was a gift of the architect himself.[53]

The glass in the north transept window, which takes St. Cecilia playing the organ as its theme (appropriately, as the

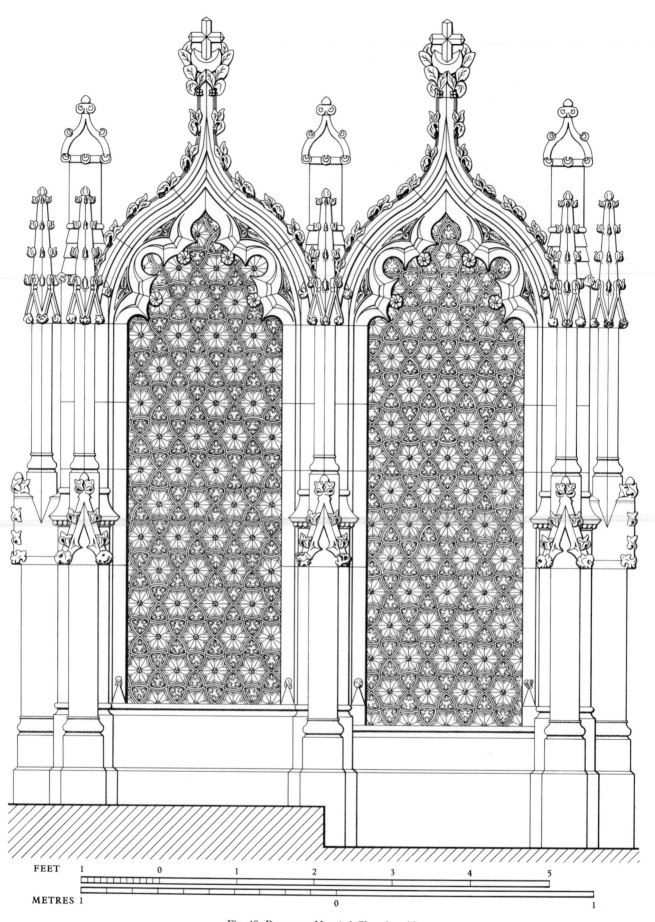

FEET 1   0   1   2   3   4   5

METRES 1   0   1

Fig. 40. Brompton Hospital Chapel, sedilia

organ originally stood in the transept), was presented and probably designed by Lady Frankland Russell. The window at the west end of the north aisle, which dates from 1892, was designed and made by A. L. Moore and Company of Southampton Row.[54] The east window, also originally filled with stained glass, is now mostly clear.

The Estate

The land which was purchased by the governors of the hospital from the trustees of the fifth Earl of Harrington in 1853 was the southern half of an irregularly shaped parcel of ground, about eight acres in extent, which lay on the east side of the lane variously known as Selwood, Sallad or Swan Lane. This eight-acre piece had formed a detached part of the large Harrington-Villars estate and had been divided, together with the remainder of that estate, between its aristocratic co-owners in 1851, the southern four acres devolving on Lord Harrington. The northern part, which had fallen to Baron Villars, had subsequently passed into the hands of the Commissioners for the Exhibition of 1851 who in turn conveyed it to the Smith's Charity trustees in exchange for other land (see page 103).

The whole eight-acre site has particular significance in the history of gardening. Here in the late seventeenth and early eighteenth century Richard Sel(l)wood ran a famous nursery, and in the mid eighteenth century, when the tenant was John or Jean Rubergall, it was noted for the cultivation of lettuces.[55] In 1789 William Curtis, the author of *Flora Londinensis* and the founder of *The Botanical Magazine*, took over from Rubergall as tenant and moved the botanical garden which he had opened in Lambeth in 1779 to this spot. The Brompton Botanic Garden, as it was known, covered about three and a half acres, almost exactly conforming to the area which is now occupied by the streets and houses on the hospital's estate, while the remaining four and a half acres to the north were used for experiments in agriculture. After Curtis's death in 1799 his partner William Salisbury kept the garden here until 1808 when he moved it to Sloane Street, Chelsea.[56] He continued to use the ground at Brompton for a nursery, however, until 1829 when he was succeeded there by David Ramsay, whose establishment was known as the Queen's Elm or Swan Lane nursery. Ramsay's son, David Allan Ramsay, was the tenant when negotiations were taking place between Lord Harrington's representatives and the hospital authorities, and after vacating the nursery he pursued a chequered career as a builder on the Ladbroke estate in northern Kensington.[57]

The governors of the hospital had cast anxious eyes on this piece of ground from the moment that they had acquired the site for their new hospital from the Smith's Charity trustees in 1844. Forced by the Charity's surveyor to build the hospital closer to the western boundary of their plot than they would have wished, they viewed 'the attainment of this additional land as an object of the deepest importance to the well-being of the [hospital]; whether it be considered merely as adding to the present recreation-ground for Patients, or for the more important purpose of preventing the close proximity of other buildings, or for a still more lasting object, of the allowing of a future extension of the Building in that direction'.[58]

After the partition of the Harrington-Villars estate in 1851 the hospital was under the impression that it had been promised first refusal of Lord Harrington's plot, but in the autumn of 1852 it was perturbed to learn that the Earl had concluded an agreement with the builder William Jackson to cover all of his estate with speculative housing, including the four acres in question. The surveyor George Pownall, who had previously warned the hospital that Lord Harrington's land was about to be offered for speculative development, was immediately authorized to treat with Jackson for the purchase of his interest and with Lord Harrington for the conveyance of the freehold. Pownall was in a good position to negotiate, for as surveyor to Baron Villars and H. B. Alexander and as agent for (Sir) Charles James Freake he was already much involved in the complex arrangements for the disposal of land in South Kensington which had followed the Great Exhibition of 1851.[59]

The precise area of the land was four acres and ten perches, and Jackson, on agreeing to relinquish his interest for £500 per acre, was promptly paid the requisite £2,031.[60] By February 1853 Pownall had concluded terms with Lord Harrington for the purchase of the freehold for £13,195 (£3,248 per acre), the Earl agreeing to wait three years for payment and in the meantime to receive interest at three-and-a-half per cent on the sum. A formal agreement to that effect was drawn up in May 1853, and the purchase money and interest were paid in full in April 1855 with the help of a loan of £9,000 from the hospital's honorary treasurer, John Labouchere, who was a partner in Williams and Deacon's Bank. As soon as the deed of sale had been signed a mortgage was arranged with three spinster sisters who were clients of the law firm of Philip Rose, the hospital's honorary secretary, to repay Labouchere's loan.[61]

In all the hospital had paid slightly over £16,000, or almost exactly £4,000 per acre, for the land, a sum which was higher, though not substantially higher in some instances, than the prices paid by the Commissioners for the Exhibition of 1851 to acquire their estate a little to the north.[62] Understandably, the governors felt called upon to include a long justification of the purchase in their annual report for 1853.

Once in possession of the land, and having set aside about half an acre to add to the grounds of the hospital, the committee of management sought to promote speculative building development on the remainder. By April 1853 (before the formal agreement with Lord Harrington had been signed) Pownall had prepared a scheme for letting the ground to Charles Delay of Lower Belgrave Place (now Buckingham Palace Road), builder, and a building agreement was drawn up in July. Delay, who had been the building lessee of No. 10 Beauchamp Place in 1844, when he was described as a plasterer,[63] was currently engaged in the building of the Oratory House in Thurloe Place as a sub-contractor of William Jackson and it seems likely that he was recommended by the latter. One of his sureties for carrying out his contract with the hospital was William Wright, manager to Jackson's brother, the contractor Thomas Jackson. The other surety was Charles Richardson of Paddington, a lime merchant.

The plan accompanying the agreement shows the present layout of streets on the estate, with a total of eighty-seven house plots marked out. No doubt this was merely meant to be a general guide as under the agreement Delay was required to build only sixty-nine houses and to finish the development within six years. He or his nominees were to be granted leases for terms equivalent to ninety-seven and three-quarter years from 24 June 1853 at a total ground rent for the whole area of £120 in the first year, rising to £700 in the fifth and succeeding years. The houses were to be built according to plans and elevations previously submitted to, and approved by, the hospital's architect and surveyor, that is Pownall, who was to be paid four guineas per house 'for his time and trouble in and about the arrangement of the Plans and the superintending the building of the several messuages'. A long schedule of building materials to be used included the stipulation that, apart from internal partitions where place bricks were permissible, the brickwork was to consist of well-burnt grey stocks; the scantlings of the timber were also specified.[64]

While Delay was preparing the ground and laying foundations, however, the committee of management had second thoughts about how much land they should incorporate into the grounds of the hospital and asked the builder what price he would accept for surrendering the eastern of the two blocks delineated on the plan, up to the street now called Neville Street. On being told that he would want £2,000 and a proportionate reduction in his ground rent, the committee resolved to re-acquire the ground. George Godwin senior, acting on Delay's behalf, sought to modify slightly the terms which the committee thought had been agreed, and angered them by a 'peremptory' letter demanding that the revised terms should be accepted at once. They refused, and later attempts by Godwin to be more conciliatory failed, the committee taking such umbrage over Godwin's tone that they resolved to have nothing more to do with the matter and ordered Delay to proceed with his contract forthwith. In the event Godwin had done his client no favour and the stoppage of building works while negotiations were proceeding may have contributed to difficulties which Delay subsequently encountered. The involvement of Godwin in this affair, however, raises the possibility that he may have designed the houses in Fulham Road and Foulis Terrace which were built under the agreement with Delay.[65]

Delay commenced building in earnest in November 1853 along Fulham Road, where the houses were originally named Rose Terrace after (Sir) Philip Rose.[66] The first block to be built, Nos. 80-92 (even), included the Rose public house, for which Delay sought a licence in February 1854.[67] In March of that year he applied to the hospital for mortgages, 'the Committee having kindly offered to assist him with advances', and £3,000 was lent in the name of the Reverend Sir Henry Foulis, the chairman of the committee of management.[68] A further £1,500 was borrowed on a mortgage of the Rose public house to a client of Rose's law firm.[69] All seven houses, which, apart from the Rose, had shops on the ground floor, were completed and occupied by the end of 1855.[70]

In April 1855 Delay, who had established himself as the proprietor of the Rose public house, thus combining the callings of speculative builder and licensed victualler in a manner by no means uncommon in the mid nineteenth century, began building in Foulis Terrace, which was so named after Sir Henry Foulis.[71] In July of that year, however, his existing building agreement was replaced with a new one, partly because the hospital had now completed the purchase of the freehold of the land but mainly because Delay wanted some of the provisions modified. On reflection the committee of management probably thought that their treatment of him in the autumn of 1853 had been rather harsh and they extended the time limit for completion of the development by eighteen months, granting at the same time an initial period at a peppercorn rent. The new agreement also contained a clause allowing Delay to erect a church or chapel in lieu of some of the houses, a necessary stipulation for he had already received a request to make a plot available for a chapel and had obtained the committee's approval. The schedule of materials was shorter, one change requiring external walls, where not stuccoed, to be faced with malms.[72]

The mid 1850's were troublesome years for builders, and the easing of the conditions of his contract was probably designed to tide Delay over a period of financial stringency, but by January 1856 Pownall was having to urge the committee to grant him further assistance 'in the unfavourable state of the money market'. 'I believe', he wrote, 'that but for the unforseen difficulties which the State of Public affairs has brought on all speculations similar to that under consideration, Mr Delay would have had no difficulty in obtaining the necessary funds to carry on his Building operations from the ordinary sources, but with the high interest which money now bears, a preference is given to other and more available security's [sic] and he has had and still has difficulty in obtaining sufficient funds to carry on the speculation with advantage to himself or to the Governors of the Hospital, who considering the high price they have given for the land are greatly interested in getting the property covered with Buildings and the ground rent secured at as early a period as possible.' The committee accordingly resolved to lend Delay a further £5,000, making £8,000 in all, and were told that this sum, together with £2,000 from one of

Rose's clients, would enable him to finish the houses in Foulis Terrace and Fulham Road.[73] Williams, Deacon and Company lent £5,000 to the hospital to cover the advance to Delay, both transactions being at the same rate of interest of six per cent.[74]

Delay was further helped by the purchase of No. 14 Foulis Terrace for £950 by the hospital as a residence for its chaplain,[75] and the remaining houses in the terrace and Nos. 94–108 (even) Fulham Road were begun in 1856.[76] In the autumn of that year, however, the development received a serious set back when Delay became insane and was confined in the Grove House Asylum at Bow.[77] He died a year later, in August 1857.[78]

Delay's widow, Ellen, and his clerk of works, Robert Wright, struggled on with the speculation. They found it difficult to dispose of any of the houses in Foulis Terrace and placed the blame on the unpleasant sight of male patients exercising in the hospital grounds opposite, 'walking up and down smoking and expectorating'. They requested that the west side of the hospital should be used by the female patients, who would presumably behave with more decorum, but had to repeat the complaint several times before the committee of management took action.[79] In 1858 six of the houses in the street were leased to John William Sanders of Guilford Street, St. Pancras, builder, who was presumably called in to assist with the development.[80] None of the houses in Foulis Terrace (with the possible exception of the chaplain's house) were occupied before that year.[70]

Early in 1859 Ellen Delay asked the committee of management to accept the rent which had been reserved to date — some £440 — instead of the higher rent which was then due under the building agreement and to postpone further the date when the full rent of £700 would be due, 'in consideration of the unprecedented difficulties which have attended the working out of this contract and the severe losses that both she and her late husband have sustained'. The committee were sympathetic and Philip Rose in reply suggested that Mrs. Delay might like to give up the undeveloped part of the land which she held under the agreement. She readily consented, and in return for the hospital remitting an outstanding mortgage debt of £2,200 and paying her £200, she also surrendered her interest in four houses in Fulham Road, Nos. 96, 98, 102 and 104, which had not yet been let.[81] The hospital soon found a purchaser who was prepared to pay £650 for each of these houses, but after some legal difficulties had arisen, he was eventually granted long leases at rents of £60 per annum per house.[82]

The houses in Foulis Terrace were all taken by 1860, but some of the houses and shops in Fulham Road were not occupied until 1861.[70]

The undeveloped ground was let within a short time of its surrender by Mrs. Delay. The builder who took it over

was Thomas Stimpson of Brompton Row, Brompton Road, a carpenter by trade.[83] He agreed to build at least fifty houses at an ultimate ground rent (after five years) of £260 per annum, thus making up the £700 which had been anticipated under the original agreement with Delay. As before, Pownall was to approve the elevations, and brief general specifications were appended to the building agreement.[84]

Stimpson was fortunate in taking over the speculation during an upturn in the building cycle when demand was high and credit plentiful, but he was also assisted by a loan of £2,000 from the hospital.[85] The building agreement was signed in November 1859 and by May 1863 he had been granted leases for a sufficient number of houses to secure the whole of the ground rent of £260 for which he was liable. Under the terms of the agreement he was entitled to receive any subsequent leases at a peppercorn rent, but he proposed that another £100 in ground rents should be created in return for a payment to him of a sum equivalent to twenty years' purchase, namely the £2,000 which he owed to the hospital. The committee agreed, the remaining leases were granted by mid 1864 at ground rents amounting to £100, and his debt was cancelled.[86] Stimpson built forty-nine houses in all in Neville Street, Neville Terrace and Onslow Gardens, the shortfall being accounted for by the erection of a school behind Onslow Chapel, and only one of the houses appears to have been still unoccupied at the end of 1865.[70] The reason for the street name Neville is not known, but it does not appear to have had anything to do with the hospital.

The first lessees of the individual houses in Neville Street and Neville Terrace included a number of persons connected with the building trades, nearly all with local addresses in Brompton and Chelsea, who were evidently assisting Stimpson with the development. They were George Brown, plumber and builder; Henry Joseph Chappell, smith; Charles Dunning, carpenter and builder; James Edwards, builder; Thomas Emery, plumber; William Morgan of Albert Terrace, Knightsbridge, builder; Christopher Richard Surrey, builder; John Henry Surrey, builder; George Taylor, ironmonger; and Thomas Tozer of Crescent Mews, Belgrave Square, builder.[87]

The leases of Nos. 9–16 (consec.) Onslow Gardens* were divided between Alfred Williams of Pelham Street, who initially described himself as a builder and later as architect and surveyor, and Thomas Wyatt of Maddox Street, Mayfair, and later Sydney Street, Chelsea, architect and surveyor.[88] No. 16, of which Williams was the lessee, was sold in 1864 for £2,250 to the two daughters of William Makepeace Thackeray, who had had to move out of their father's house at No. 2 Palace Green after his death on Christmas Eve 1863.[89] Alfred Williams, who was for some time assistant district surveyor and later district surveyor for South Kensington, took up residence himself

---

*These houses were briefly known as Nos. 1–8 Onslow Gardens but were renumbered almost immediately when the first houses were erected on the part of Onslow Gardens which belongs to the Smith's Charity estate.

in 1865 at No. 17 Onslow Gardens (formerly No. 15 Neville Terrace), where he shared an office with the then district surveyor, T. L. Donaldson, their former premises having been in Pelham Street on the site of the present London Transport offices. Williams was not the first lessee of No. 17, however.

By 1863 the hospital was receiving the full ground rent of £700 which Pownall had thought that the estate would bear. In addition it had obtained an extension to its grounds which he considered to be worth £100 per annum, and if this is added to the £700, the governors had paid almost exactly twenty years' purchase for Lord Harrington's land. This was by no means an excessive rate, especially as the hospital had a valuable reversionary interest in the houses which had been erected. Despite the delay in the completion of building development, the hospital had, indeed, fared rather well from its investment in contrast to the sad fate of the first developer.

The houses built under the auspices of firstly Delay and secondly Stimpson fall into two groups, the earlier houses having fully stuccoed façades and the later ones grey brick with stucco dressings. Of the first group, the two terraces at Nos. 80-108 (even) Fulham Road, which have three storeys above ground-floor shops, have been greatly mutilated, only the Rose public house retaining an impressive display of dressings with faceted quoins, elaborate architraves to the windows and a bracketed cornice.

Foulis Terrace consists of a symmetrical group of fourteen houses, each originally of four main storeys (the additional storeys at Nos. 10 and 11 dating from 1875[90]), with Doric porches and standard Italianate features above. The balconies at first-floor level have iron railings which are identical in pattern to those used by C. J. Freake on the neighbouring Smith's Charity estate. Inside, according to a description in 1858, the houses had a dining-room and library on the ground floor, two drawing-rooms on the first floor and five bedrooms and a dressing-room on the top two floors.[91]

The houses built under the agreement with Stimpson display a number of variations on the Italianate theme. Nos. 9-16 (consec.) Onslow Gardens are divided by Neville Street into two groups of four tall, impressive four-storey houses, in which the bold Tuscan porches, well-spaced window-openings with wide architraves, prominent stringcourse at third-floor level and crowning entablature with dentil cornice and guilloche-band frieze convey an air of solid prosperity (Plate 64b).

The houses in Neville Street are much smaller, the majority having only three storeys above basements, and the decorative motifs are more crowded. Each side of the street consists of a terrace of thirteen houses in which the three houses in the centre and two at each end are advanced slightly from the general building line. On the east side Nos. 1-2 at the south end and Nos. 12-13 at the north end have an additional full storey above the cornice, but on the west side the symmetry is rather surprisingly destroyed by the omission of the extra storey

from Nos. 25-26. The addition of attic storeys with dormer windows to some of the other houses commenced as early as 1871 when it was stated that 'any addition to the houses in Neville Street will be for the interests of the Hospital'.[92]

In Neville Terrace the house fronts are less standardised and display an almost playful combination of decorative motifs (Plate 64c), perhaps the result of an attempt to produce a foil to the dour and at that time unfashionable late-Georgian houses of Selwood Terrace opposite. At the south end of the terrace No. 1 and the entrance bay of No. 2 share a wide gabled façade which is set back, presumably to avoid encroachment on the view of the Onslow Chapel to the south. Alterations were soon made to several of the houses. No. 17 Onslow Gardens (originally No. 15 Neville Terrace) was raised by a storey in 1872 and further altered in 1875, and extra storeys were also added to No. 8 in 1878 and No. 4 in 1885, although the hospital's architect, Lewis Karslake, did say of the latter addition that it would be 'a decided improvement as regards the interior of the house but will damage the general appearance of the Terrace'.[93]

The census of 1871 was the first to be taken after all of the houses on the estate had been completed.[94] Apart from the shops with living quarters above in Fulham Road, which are perhaps best placed in a separate category, there are sixty-three houses in Foulis Terrace, Neville Street, Neville Terrace and the small part of Onslow Gardens which belongs to the estate. Three of these houses were being looked after by caretakers on the night of the census while awaiting new occupants, and of the other sixty, nine were used as lodging-houses (seven of them in Neville Street) and No. 13 Onslow Gardens housed a girls' boarding-school. The remaining fifty houses had 284 occupants, of whom 107 were servants, an average of 5.68 persons (including 2.14 servants) per house. The biggest households were in Onslow Gardens, where three of the resident families each had five servants. The total number of occupants in the nine lodging-houses was sixty-three, an average of exactly seven per house; most of the lodgers described themselves as annuitants or shareholders. Some even had their own servants, but in six of the lodging-houses only one general servant attended to the needs of everybody else.

Apart from the three caretakers, nine lodging-house keepers and headmistress of the girls' school, there were fifty householders, of whom seventeen lived off the proceeds from rents, government funds, stocks and shares or annuities. This large rentier element was, however, actually outnumbered by those belonging to the professions, who totalled twenty-two. They included four solicitors, three barristers, three retired army officers, three music teachers (all living in Neville Terrace), two clergymen (the chaplain of Brompton Hospital and a curate of Holy Trinity, Brompton), a civil engineer, an artist, an artistic repairer (from the South Kensington Museum), a physician, a dentist, an architect and surveyor (Alfred Williams at No.

17 Onslow Gardens), and an 'editor and journalist' (Leslie Stephen, who was living at No. 16 Onslow Gardens with his first wife, Harriet Marian, the daughter of William Makepeace Thackeray, and her sister, Anne, later Anne Thackeray Ritchie). Nine of the householders were connected with commerce and industry—two merchants, a 'warehouse man', a linen manufacturer, a commercial traveller (who was not present on the night of the census but whose wife described his occupation in those words), two builders (Thomas Stimpson at No. 1 Neville Street and Christopher R. Surrey at No. 10 Neville Terrace), an upholsterer and a retired contractor. The remaining two householders were clerks in the civil service.

In Fulham Road all but one of the houses (No. 96) were occupied by the families and assistants of the proprietors of the ground-floor shops. The households were generally small with one, or sometimes two, servants, and in some instances none at all. The exceptions were a draper who occupied three of the houses and had fourteen assistants living-in as well as four servants, and the publican of the Rose who had three servants. Two of the houses were divided, the other occupants being an annuitant and a shareholder, and the head of the household which occupied the premises above a lock-up wine shop at No. 96 also derived his income from dividends. In all there were ninety-nine occupants of the fifteen houses, of whom eighteen were servants and eighteen more were shop assistants.

The expansion of the hospital since the war of 1939-45 has led to the adaptation of several houses on the estate to provide services for the hospital or accommodation for its staff, while other houses have been let on a short-term basis so as to be available for similar uses in the near future. In Neville Terrace, however, houses have continued to be let on long leases or sold freehold, a policy first introduced in 1979, amid the uncertainties brought about by leasehold reform legislation and when attempts to sell houses on eighty-year leases were proving unsuccessful.[95] The governors have used the proceeds from the sale of houses in Neville Terrace to purchase property in King's Road, Chelsea, adjacent to the site of the proposed new chest and heart hospital, for much the same reasons that induced their predecessors to buy the land adjacent to Brompton Hospital some 130 years ago.

Onslow Chapel, Neville Terrace

This chapel (now demolished) was built in 1856 for an interdenominational congregation which had been meeting for some years in the former premises of the Western Grammar School on the site of the present No. 2 Alexander Place (see page 85). The first minister, the Reverend John Bigwood, was a Baptist, and the chapel quickly became known as the Onslow Baptist Chapel.

The chapel was a substantial building finished in Kentish rag with Bath stone dressings and was later described as 'one of those early attempts of the Nonconformists to establish a better style of architecture in their buildings for public worship' (Plate 64a). The towers with octagonal open belfries and spires which flanked the west front were conspicuous landmarks in the district before many of the surrounding houses and churches were built. The interior had a western gallery and an unusual arched ceiling divided into compartments by beams and intersecting ribs with enriched bosses at their main junctions. The architect was William Mumford and the builder was Thomas Rudkin of St. Giles in the Fields. A large hall which served as a schoolroom and lecture-hall was erected in 1862 behind the chapel, facing Neville Street.

The contract price for the chapel was £2,369 and the entire cost was estimated at the time of building to be about £3,500. The cost of the hall was said at the time of opening to be £900, but in 1872 it was stated that about £6,000 had been spent on both structures. A lease of the chapel site was granted by the governors of the hospital in 1856 at a ground rent of £42 per annum, and another lease of the hall was granted in 1862 at a further annual rent of £10.[96]

The chapel continued to be used until shortly after the war of 1939-45, but after standing empty and decaying for some years it was demolished in 1961.[97]

The Ware Estate

This estate, which is slightly under four acres in extent, comprises Selwood Terrace, Selwood Place, Elm Place, Lecky Street (formerly Elm Mews), Regency Terrace and Nos. 110-132 (even) Fulham Road (formerly Elm Terrace). Apart from some recent rebuilding in its southern part, it forms an enclave of small-scale late-Georgian houses amidst the predominant Italianate and Queen Anne of this area of South Kensington. As a compact and separate unit of land-ownership, which actually remained in copyhold tenure of the manor of Earl's Court until after building had commenced, it was ideally suited for suburban development during the last great Georgian building boom of the 1820's.

The copyhold ownership of the estate had passed through various hands in the seventeenth and eighteenth centuries, but for much of that period the land appears to have been farmed by tenants in conjunction with the neighbouring Brompton Heath on the Smith's Charity estate.[1] From 1802 to 1823, however, it was held separately by Francis Shailer, a market gardener, whose neat

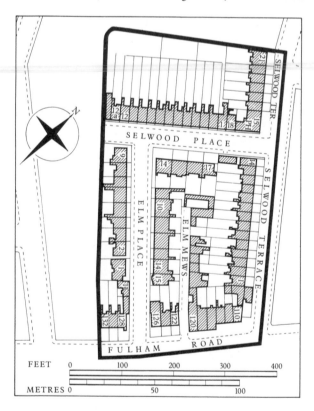

Fig. 41. The Ware estate. Based on the Ordnance Survey of 1894-6

smallholding, surrounded by hedges, is clearly delineated on the map of Kensington published by Thomas Starling in 1822 (Plate 70a).[2] In 1823, perhaps at the termination of a twenty-one-year lease to Shailer, the copyhold ownership was put up for sale.[3]

The purchaser was Samuel Ware, a successful and by then prosperous architect whose best-known works in London are the Burlington Arcade and the remodelling of Burlington House in Piccadilly.[4] On entering into possession of the land Ware informed the Kensington Turnpike Trust of his intention to build there and suggested that the trustees might like to take the opportunity to widen Fulham Road and Selwood Lane, both of which came under their jurisdiction.[5] Selwood Lane, which formed the eastern boundary of Ware's holding, linked Fulham Road with Old Brompton Road and was named after Richard Sel(l)wood, the former owner of a nursery which had been established on the eastern side of the lane at the end of the seventeenth century. It was also sometimes known as Sallad Lane, which was no doubt a corruption of Selwood Lane, or Swan Lane after the Swan tavern which stood on the north side of Old Brompton Road immediately opposite to the entrance to the lane. As well as purchasing land from Ware, the turnpike trustees decided to straighten the lane by buying further land on the east side, then in the joint ownership of John Lewis Fleming and the fourth Earl of Harrington and in the occupation of William Salisbury, nurseryman.[6] The straightened road was called Selwood Lane on the large-scale Ordnance Survey map published in 1867, but when shortly afterwards houses were built along the portion north of the Ware estate they were numbered in the complex of streets named Onslow Gardens and the name Selwood Lane dropped out of use. In the southern part of the street the terraces of houses on each side have retained their original names of Selwood Terrace and Neville Terrace, and thus this section of the street has two official names.

Ware must have quickly obtained a promise from the lord of the manor, Lord Kensington, to enfranchise the copyhold, for by 1825 he was granting long leases of building plots. The actual enfranchisement of all the land except, for some unknown reason, the site of No. 21 Selwood Terrace, took place in November 1827 and cost him £1,000;[7] the plot on which No. 21 stands was enfranchised in 1861 for £53.[8]

Building appears to have begun simultaneously in Selwood Terrace, on the north side of Selwood Place, and in

Fulham Road where the houses stood opposite to Queen's Elm and were given the name of Elm Terrace. Three builders were involved, Samuel Archbutt of Coleshill Street (now Eaton Terrace) on the boundary of Chelsea and Belgravia, Christopher Surrey of Pond Place, Chelsea, and James Ardin of Caroline (now Donne) Place, Chelsea. Archbutt and Surrey worked in partnership and were granted the southern of two large plots, while Ardin had that to the north, the boundary between their respective 'takes' being between Nos. 9 and 10 Selwood Terrace, the differences in the fronts of which are still very noticeable.

With one exception, Ware proceeded in the normal manner at this early stage of the speculation, granting leases of individual houses to the builders or their nominees, or entering into agreements to grant such leases. The leases were usually for eighty-one years from midsummer 1824, or for equivalent shorter terms if they began at a later date, but there were several variations and not all the leases expired at the same time. The exception to this pattern was the south-eastern corner house, No. 1 Elm Terrace, which was renumbered as 110 Fulham Road in 1866 and has now been demolished. Here Ware paid £50 to the turnpike trustees for the toll house which had previously stood upon the site, and after taking it down he let the new house (the building costs of which he probably paid himself) to its first occupant, a baker, for twenty-one years at a rack rent.[9]

Apart from Surrey and Ardin, only two of the lessees are known to have been builders. They were William Huckel the elder and younger of Duke Street, St. James's, who were granted leases of Nos. 19 and 20 Selwood Terrace in 1825.[10] Most of the remaining lessees were the first occupants of the houses, but some also had wider interests in the estate. Stephen Harrison, originally of Walham Green, esquire, was granted leases of five houses in Selwood Terrace including No. 14, where he lived briefly in 1826-7, and No. 8, to which he then moved,[11] and William Barber of Chelsea, gentleman, who was the lessee of three houses, lived at No. 2 Selwood Terrace.[12]

By the end of 1825 Nos. 1 and 2 Elm Terrace, Nos. 12, 13 and 16 Selwood Terrace and No. 1 Selwood Place had been completed and occupied, the last by James Ardin himself. In the following year the remaining four houses in the eastern part of Elm Terrace up to Elm Mews and all of Selwood Terrace with the exception of the Anglesea public house and No. 21 were completed. The Anglesea was leased in 1827 but does not seem to have opened until 1829, while No. 21 was not built until 1829 on the piece of ground which then still remained copyhold.[13]

Building along the north side of Selwood Place proceeded more slowly. Nos. 2-6 were occupied by the end of 1826, No. 7 in 1827, Nos. 8, 9 and 10 in 1828, No. 11 in 1829 and Nos. 12 and 12A (originally numbered 13) by 1831. No. 18, which was added to the eastern end of the terrace, was built by 1831 on ground originally leased with the Anglesea.[14]

On the south side of Selwood Place, the site of Nos. 14 and 15 was not part of Ardin's 'take' and these houses belong chronologically and stylistically to the later development of Elm Place which will be described below. Nos. 16 and 17 were built on a plot which was leased to Ardin in 1829 but the houses themselves were not erected until 1834.[15]

The houses in Selwood Terrace have two storeys above a semi-basement and are standard examples of late-Georgian speculative housing (Plate 65c). Nos. 1-9 (consec.), for which Archbutt and Surrey were responsible, have channelled stucco at ground-storey level, uncomfortably narrow arched doorcases, and sunk brick panels above the first-floor windows, while Ardin's houses have plain brick façades. Inevitably several have been altered, especially by the addition of an extra storey, and Nos. 4, 6 and 21 have been more thoroughly Victorianised. The Anglesea public house has an attractive stuccoed façade (Plate 66a) but has been so extensively altered inside that few original features survive.

The terraced houses on the north side of Selwood Place built by Ardin have three storeys without basements, their stock-brick façades, well-proportioned window-openings with slightly curved heads and honeysuckle-patterned iron window guards providing a handsome though conventional appearance (Plate 65a). The distinguishing features of these houses, however, are the stuccoed doorcases, which have shouldered architraves and prominent hood-moulds. Similar doorcases are found in Elm Place (fig. 42), where Ardin was not apparently involved, and their use may indicate a more direct contribution by Ware to the design of these houses than in Selwood Terrace. All of the houses except Nos. 18, 1-3 and 8 now have channelled stucco on the ground floor, but at No. 4 the stucco was added during recent restoration. Other alterations include the addition of extra storeys to Nos. 7 and 10.

Nos. 16 and 17 on the south side of Selwood Place, which were also built by Ardin, form a pair of two-storey 'cottages' with an overhanging eaves cornice. Both houses have been extended at the sides. The Studio, which is situated to the east of No. 17 and has a large bracketed doorcase, a tall studio window and an asymmetrically placed gable, was originally built as a stable and coach-house behind No. 14 Selwood Terrace in 1829. It was later converted into a workshop and was probably given its present form in c. 1909, when William Bateman Fagan, a sculptor, took up residence.[16]

In Elm Mews (now Lecky Street) some five small cottages were interspersed with stables and workshops, one of the latter being a carpenter's shop belonging to Christopher Surrey.[17] All have now been demolished.

Archbutt and Surrey having quickly finished their part of the initial development, Archbutt retired from the scene. He had not been granted any leases of the completed houses and was apparently left with no interest in the estate. Ardin was still engaged in building Selwood Place, and so Ware seems to have relied entirely on

Christopher Surrey for the development of the remaining vacant rectangular plot in the south-western corner of his estate.

A new road, Elm Place, was laid out along the middle of the plot to link Fulham Road with Selwood Place, leaving room for two groups of three houses to face Fulham Road on each side of its entrance. In May 1827 Ware entered into a conventional building agreement with Surrey for the construction of the western group, originally Nos. 10-12 Elm Terrace and later Nos. 128-132 (even) Fulham Road,* and for the granting of eighty-one-year leases to Surrey or his nominees.[18] Four months later, on Surrey's direction, Ware granted such a lease of the central house and the site of No. 1 Elm Place, which was included in Surrey's ground, to William Bushell, a pianoforte-maker, who eventually took up residence at No. 1 Elm Place.[19]

In June 1828, however, Ware and Surrey sold their respective freehold and leasehold interests in Surrey's plot, subject to the lease already granted and to an agreement to let No. 12 Elm Terrace for three years. The purchaser was William Bristow of Fulham Road, Chelsea, gentleman, perhaps the nurseryman who was a partner with Samuel Harrison (see page 60).[18] The eastern trio of houses, formerly Nos. 7-9 Elm Terrace and later Nos. 122-126 (even) Fulham Road, now demolished, were also sold freehold by Ware in August 1828 to Richard Foster of Limehouse, a schoolmaster.[20]

Of these six houses in Fulham Road, the surviving group at Nos. 128-132, which was completed in 1828-9, is a good example of the kind of terraced housing which was springing up in the late-Georgian period along the major thoroughfares leading out of London. The houses have three full storeys above basements, with channelled stucco at ground-floor level and exposed stock brickwork above, round-headed doorcases, wrought-iron window guards of the same pattern as those in Selwood Place, and a bold stringcourse below the third-storey windows.

The freehold sales of the two plots in Fulham Road occurred at about the same time as Ware was mortgaging the whole estate in July 1828 to Robert Langford of Covent Garden, a solicitor, for £3,000 with an option to borrow further sums up to £10,000.[21] In March 1829 he also sold the freehold of another plot, this time on the north side of Selwood Place and comprising the sites of Nos. 9-12A, to James Ardin the builder.[22] The desire to obtain a large amount of capital, which is implied by these transactions, may have been the result of a wish on Ware's part to take a more direct financial involvement in the speculation than hitherto. In this context the absence of any record of building leases of all but four of the houses in Elm Place (and two of those were granted ten years after building) may be an indication that the houses there were built directly for Ware by Surrey at the former's expense. Of the four exceptions, the site on which No. 1 was erected

had already been leased in 1827, Nos. 2 and 3 were belatedly leased to Surrey in 1843 for eighty-one years from 1834, and only at No. 10 was a similar lease granted, to Surrey's nominee, at the time of building in 1836.[23]

The original houses in Elm Place were completed between 1830 and 1836[14] and, apart from No. 1, form a homogeneous group. They are two-storeyed houses, faced with channelled stucco at ground-floor level and stock brick above, and have a continuous moulded stucco parapet. Nos. 2-9 (consec.) on the west side form a symmetrical terrace of three-bay double-fronted houses interspersed at Nos. 4 and 7 with two-bay houses which project slightly from the general building line (fig. 42). A similar pattern is followed on the east side, where Nos. 10 and 13 are the projecting, narrower houses, but here the shortness of the range does not allow for strict symmetry (Plate 65b). The appearance of these neat, small houses is given added character by the use of doorcases with shouldered architraves similar to those in Selwood Place. Here each door has a small rectangular fanlight above it, the transom between them being sometimes embellished with egg-and-dart moulding (fig. 42). In contrast to the other houses, No. 1 has an arched doorcase, a smoothly rendered façade and projecting eaves.

Nos. 14 and 15 Selwood Place, which were built by Surrey in 1834-5 but not leased to him until 1843,[24] are virtually identical to the houses in Elm Place, apart from the addition of a bay window to No. 15.

Selwood Lodge, a two-storey stucco-fronted house to the north of No. 10 Elm Place, was built by Christopher Surrey in 1842-3 as his own residence. It was leased to him together with Nos. 14 and 15 Selwood Place in 1843 and he lived there until his death in 1865.[25] The site of No. 15 Elm Place was originally occupied by a two-storey shed which Surrey used as a carpenter's shop, and the present house was built in 1886 by his son, Christopher Richard Surrey.[26] Formerly a dour, brick-faced house with two tall storeys and a mansard-roofed attic, typical of the 1880's, it was substantially altered in c. 1962, when a new entrance to Lecky Street was made on its south side, and is now stuccoed and white-painted.

On the west side of Elm Place, No. 1A (originally called Alpha Cottage), which is of a similar, though not identical, appearance to the main group of houses in the street, was built in c. 1860 on the curtilage of No. 128 Fulham Road and first occupied, from 1860 to 1865, by John Liddell, an architect who was employed by the Science and Art Department on the design of several of its monumental buildings in South Kensington.[27] No. 1B, to the south of No. 1A, was formerly an outbuilding of No. 128 Fulham Road and has recently been converted into a separate house; it differs from No. 1A in that its upper storey is rendered.

Samuel Ware maintained a close control over the estate, applying in 1839, for instance, to the Westminster Com-

---

*No. 128 Fulham Road, which has recently been restored, is now numbered as 1c Elm Place, but in this account its former number is used.

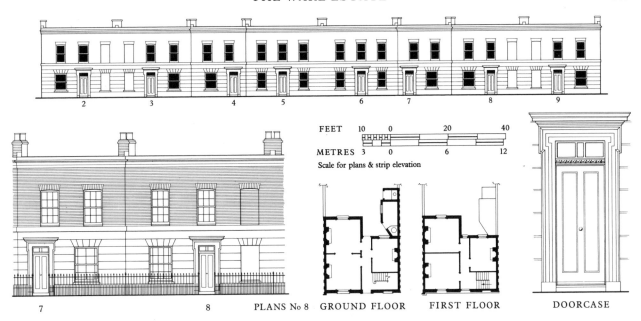

Fig. 42. Nos. 2-9 Elm Place, plans, elevations and detail of doorcase. Christopher Surrey, builder, 1830-3. Back addition on plan restored from lease-plan in Middlesex Deeds Registry

missioners of Sewers for the construction of sewers in place of the cesspools with which the houses were originally provided.[28] He died in 1860 with effects of 'under £60,000' and by his will the estate was entailed on his nephew, Charles Nathaniel Cumberlege, and his descendants on condition that they adopted the surname and arms of Ware.[29]

From the evidence of the census enumerators' books the houses were respectably tenanted in the nineteenth century despite their small size and, to Victorian eyes, unfashionable appearance. In 1871, for instance, only three of the sixty-six inhabited houses were occupied by more than one family, although at seven others there were lodgers or boarders. Excluding visitors, there were 291 occupants in the sixty-six houses (an average of 4.4 per house). At forty-two of the houses there was one servant living-in and at five more there were two servants; in Elm Place only two of the houses were without at least one servant in residence on the night of the census. The householders' occupations ranged from the building trades to marshal and chief constable of the City of London. A number lived on private incomes, while others were clerks, tradesmen, commercial travellers or small-scale manufacturers, such as bootmaker, harness-maker and pianofortemaker. Persons who belonged to the professions included three music teachers, two doctors, a naval lieutenant, a journalist, an auctioneer, a surveyor and an architect (Zephaniah King at No. 3 Selwood Terrace).[30]

Although it cannot boast of many famous inhabitants, this small area does have associations with two outstanding English novelists. Charles Dickens lodged here in the summer of 1835 in order to be near his future wife,

Catherine Hogarth, who lived in York Place on the south side of Fulham Road. In a letter written in June of that year he gives his address as 11 Selwood Terrace, but, confusingly, some other letters of about that time are headed simply 'Selwood Place'.[31] D. H. Lawrence stayed at No. 9 Selwood Terrace for about six weeks in the summer of 1914 and it was while he was living here that he married Frieda von Richthofen at South Kensington Register Office in July.[32]

The estate remained in the ownership of the Cumberlege-Ware family until after the war of 1939-45. At that time it included all of the houses which had been built under Ware's auspices with the exception of Nos. 128-132 Fulham Road and the adjoining buildings on the west side of Elm Place up to and including No. 1, which had been sold to William Bristow in 1828, and Nos. 9-12A Selwood Place, which had been sold to James Ardin in 1829. The freehold of the ground on which Nos. 122-126 Fulham Road stood, which had also been sold in 1828, must have been re-purchased in the meantime.

In 1949 a small company, Ware Estates (Kensington) Limited, was formed to take over the management of the estate, but shareholding was restricted largely, or perhaps wholly, to members of the family. In 1960, however, the company went into voluntary liquidation after having sold the estate to Shop Investments Limited for £394,862 net, the proceeds from the sale being distributed among the shareholders.[33]

The new owners decided to carry out some redevelopment and began in Lecky Street where in 1960-2 the existing dilapidated and war-damaged buildings were demolished and five two-storey neo-Georgian houses were built in their place.[34] A new entrance was made into Lecky Street from Elm Place, and this made possible the rebuilding of the frontage to Fulham Road between Selwood Terrace and Elm Place as one composition. Plans for this were drawn up in 1963 and the resulting neo-Georgian terrace was built in 1964-6. It consists of ground-floor shops with three-storey houses above, which are entered from an upper level at the rear and have been given the separate name of Regency Terrace. The company's architect for these schemes was Raymond J. Sargent.[35]

Plans for the erection of further buildings at the rear of the houses on the north side of Selwood Place were thwarted in 1964 when the demolition of No. 4 Selwood Place, which was necessary to provide access to the ground at the rear, was prevented by the vigilance of nearby residents and the prompt action of the London County Council in serving a building preservation order on the owners.[36]

CHAPTER IX

Roland Gardens

Roland Gardens and its adjacent mews, now called Roland Way, were laid out for building in 1870 upon the site of the Eagle Lodge estate, which had hitherto been held by copyhold tenure of the manor of Earl's Court (fig. 43). The developers were Charles Aldin, senior, a very successful speculative builder with many years' experience of house-building in the nearby Queen's Gate Gardens area, and his two sons, Charles and William, who took over the business after their father's unexpected death in 1871. The development got off to a brisk start, with more than half the length of the road built up by 1874, but it then faltered for several years and was not finally completed until about 1893.

This chapter also describes the history of a small rectangle of freehold land which was situated between part of the Eagle Lodge estate and Old Brompton Road. This was sometimes known as the Brompton Cottage estate, and here in 1873-4 the Aldin brothers built six houses called Roland Houses, none of which now survives.

The Eagle Lodge estate consisted of some five acres held in 1651 by Francis Dyson, who also had another small copyhold property nearby, beside the Fulham Road. These two holdings remained in the same succession of owners until 1823,[1] when they were both put up for sale by auction.[2] The purchaser of the land at Fulham Road was the architect Samuel Ware, who at once began to develop it (see Chapter VIII). The Eagle Lodge estate was bought by John Gostling, esquire, who was admitted as its customary tenant soon afterwards.[3]

The sale particulars of 1823 describe the estate as having a 'truly pleasant and healthy' situation, and as 'affording an opportunity rarely to be met with for erecting two villas or continuous rows of houses.' There was also 'a large Dwelling-House and various out-buildings and Erections'.[2] Gostling appears to have lived here in 1824,[4] but by the following year he had let the house to the engineer Samuel Brown, while he himself moved to Highbury House in Islington.[5] When Brown took up residence there was a very large increase in the rateable value of the house,[4] perhaps reflecting substantial building work, or even complete rebuilding. In this connexion it may be significant that the house was not (so far as is known) called Eagle Lodge before 1825.[6]

Particulars of 1841 show that Eagle Lodge stood in the north-east corner of the estate, its north wall flush with Old Brompton Road and its privacy protected by a high wall which was pierced by two pairs of gates. It was a square two-storey house with its principal entrance in the centre of the west front, which faced a long range of coach-houses and stables. The drawing-room and dining-room on the south front looked out over well-planted pleasure grounds and shady gravel walks, and there was also a large greenhouse. Upstairs there were six bedrooms.[7] No illustration of the house has been found.

Samuel Brown, a cooper by training, has been described as the 'father of the gas engine'. It was during his residence at Eagle Lodge, from 1825 to 1835, that he developed 'the first gas engine that unquestionably did actual work and was a mechanical success', and in the grounds here he set up two engines for demonstration purposes.[8] In 1830 Gostling granted him a sixty-year lease (back-dated to 1825) of both house and estate at a rack rent of £200 per annum. In 1831 Brown mortgaged the property for £1,000, and in 1836, soon after his departure from Eagle Lodge, he assigned all his interest to his mortgagee, whose executors offered the lease for sale by auction in 1841.[9] The name of the purchaser is not known.

After Brown the next occupant of Eagle Lodge was Alfred Bunn, who lived there from 1836 to 1839.[4] He was then the sub-lessee and manager of Drury Lane Theatre, but in 1839, when his arrears of rent on the theatre amounted to over £12,000, he was forced to resign, and in 1840 he was declared bankrupt.[10]

On the night of the census of 1851 Lady Wombwell, wife of Sir George Wombwell, third baronet, was living here with her six-year-old son, her lady's maid, six other servants and a coachman.[11] Later occupants included Tom Taylor, dramatist and editor of *Punch*, 1855-8, and Alexander Redgrave, formerly chief government inspector of factories, 1859-67.[4]

Meanwhile mechanical and industrial activities had not come to an end with Brown's departure in 1835, for in 1837 a sawmill had been established in the grounds, the first proprietors being William and Thomas Pye. The mill stood at the western side of the estate, out of sight of Eagle Lodge itself, upon a long strip of land between Thistle Grove and the modern Roland Way which is now occupied by a garage. In addition to the mill itself, which contained a fifteen-horse-power steam-engine and other machinery, there was a dwelling-house, counting-house, smithy, and cart sheds and stables. Under a sub-lease of 1839 Messrs. Pye also held all the southern half of the estate, now described as a paddock, the pleasure grounds of Eagle Lodge being thereby much reduced in size.[12]

The sawmill closed in 1855.[4] In 1860 John W. Roberts converted the mill building into a 'racket court', and in the census of 1861 he described himself as 'proprietor of the West London Cricket Ground', which now occupied the whole of the paddock in the southern part of the estate. At about the same time the grounds of Eagle Lodge were still further diminished by the formation of a bowling green near the racket court.[13] In 1865 Roberts was succeeded by E. Jones, under whose management this little recreational centre appears to have continued until the building of Roland Gardens began in 1870.[4]

The half-acre rectangle of freehold land situated between the north-west part of the Eagle Lodge estate and Old Brompton Road has its own separate history. At the beginning of the eighteenth century it was one of several scattered properties in Kensington owned by Henry Hassard (or Hazard), who died in 1706.[14] At about that time a dwelling called Brompton House stood here, and by 1718 this had been divided into three separate messuages.[15] Hassard's property in Kensington descended through his daughter to the Reynell family[16] and was subsequently acquired by Isaac and Thomas Preston[17] (see page 23), who in 1748 sold Brompton House to Joseph Colebourne of Exeter Street, Strand, a shoemaker. One part of the building was then used as a public house called the Red Lion.[18] At some stage, probably towards the end of the eighteenth century, Brompton House was pulled down and the dwelling later called Brompton Cottage built on the site. The latter was centrally placed in its well-planted grounds, which included a hot-house, greenhouse and gardener's cottage. For some years before 1818 it was occupied by a doctor of medicine.[19] In 1838 it was bought by Hugh Stark,[20] later clerk and assistant secretary of the Board of Control.[21] Previously he had lived from 1819 to 1838 at a house in Thistle Grove (now No. 58 Drayton Gardens), of which he had been the first occupant. He remained at Brompton Cottage until his death in 1857.[22]

By the mid 1860's the Eagle Lodge and Brompton Cottage estates had become virtually an island of undeveloped land surrounded by the advancing tide of bricks and mortar; and during the great flood of building which then extended throughout London, speculators began to interest themselves in its future. After the death in 1857 of Hugh Stark his administrators sold his little estate in 1864 to James Waller, an associate of the redoubtable builder and developer Charles Freake,[23] from whose leaseholdings on the Smith's Charity estate to the east it was separated only by the grounds of Eagle Lodge. Three months later Waller reconveyed the property to Freake.[24]

It seems probable that Freake also intended to acquire the larger Eagle Lodge estate, which would have brought nearly all the land on the south side of Old Brompton Road as far west as Thistle Grove within his control. But events turned out differently, for after the death in 1865 of William Gostling (who in 1842 had succeeded his father John Gostling as the copyhold owner[25]) the Eagle Lodge estate was sold in November 1869 by the representatives of the Gostling family to Thomas Henry Scarborough, a

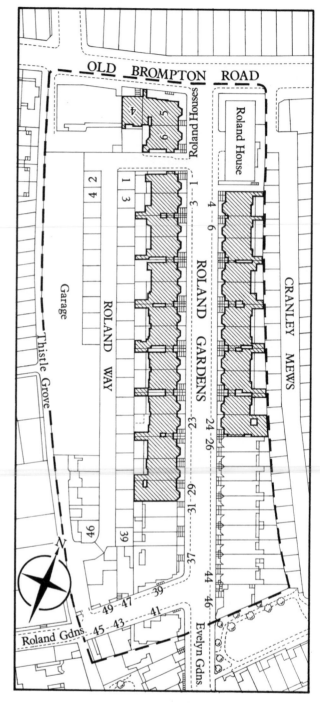

Fig. 43. Roland Gardens. Site plan based on the Ordnance Survey of 1949-63, and plans, elevation and detail of typical houses (hatched on site plan) built by C. Aldin and Sons, 1871-3

solicitor of Spring Gardens, Westminster, who seems to have been speculating on his own account.[26] Soon afterwards Scarborough was negotiating with Charles Aldin, who like Freake was one of the great moguls of the Victorian building world in South Kensington, and by July

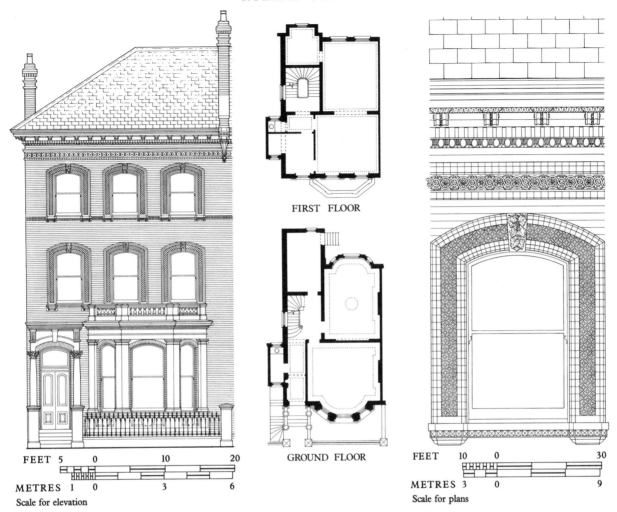

FIRST FLOOR

GROUND FLOOR

FEET 5 0 10 20

METRES 1 0 3 6

Scale for elevation

FEET 10 0 30

METRES 3 0 9

Scale for plans

1870 the future development of the Eagle Lodge estate had been substantially determined.

This was to be Aldin's last speculation, for he died in 1871, aged fifty-one or fifty-two. His *magnum opus*, the building of some two hundred large houses and almost as many mews dwellings within the rectangle bounded by Queen's Gate Terrace, Gloucester Road, Cromwell Road and Queen's Gate, was now nearing completion, and despite the adverse turn which the tide of building in London took in 1868-9, he was probably on the lookout for land.[27] In June 1870, accordingly, he obtained the approval of the Metropolitan Board of Works for the layout (substantially as later built) of the Eagle Lodge estate,[28] and on 19 July he agreed with Scarborough to take some two thirds of it for immediate development.[29]

By this agreement Aldin was to take ninety-nine-year leases from Christmas 1869 of almost all the land on the west side of Roland Gardens and the east side of Alveston Mews (now Roland Way) at a rent of £540 per annum commencing at midsummer 1871. For three years from the date of the agreement he was to have the right to buy the freehold of practically all of this land if he so wished, and Scarborough also agreed to sell Aldin the freehold of

all the ground on the west side of Alveston Mews and of the future sites of Nos. 47 and 49 Roland Gardens.[29] On the same day Scarborough was admitted as copyholder of the manor of Earl's Court, and immediately mortgaged the estate for £15,000.[30] In December 1870 he purchased the enfranchisement for £1,906.[31]

In January 1871 Scarborough sold the freehold of the rest of the estate, comprising the east and south sides of Roland Gardens, in several interspersed lots, two to D. H. Serrell, another solicitor well versed in land speculation, and the rest to Aldin.[32] Six months later Aldin bought Serrell's portion, and a few days later he exercised his right to purchase the freehold of the lands comprised in his original agreement of 19 July 1870 with Scarborough.[33] Thus by the end of July 1871 he had acquired the freehold of the whole of the Eagle Lodge estate; but within less than ten days of doing so he died at his house at Clapham Park, leaving effects valued at about £160,000.[34]

By this time building was already in full swing. In the layout plan which he had submitted to the Metropolitan Board of Works in June 1870 Aldin had proposed the street names Eagle Lodge Gardens and Mews, but the Board had substituted the names Roland Gardens and

Alveston Mews (the latter changed to Roland Mews in 1921 and to Roland Way in 1936):[35] the reason for the Board's choice of names is not known. By February 1871 he had constructed nearly a quarter of a mile of sewers,[36] and by the time of his death he had by a series of mortgages raised capital of over £13,000 on the security of his Eagle Lodge property, much of it evidently arranged by the solicitor D. H. Serrell.[37] In October 1871 work was sufficiently advanced for his two sons, Charles and William Aldin, who with W. G. Logan, the trustee of their father's will, were carrying on the business, to request the Kensington Vestry to erect lamp-posts for the lighting of Roland Gardens.[38]

This first phase of building continued until the end of 1873, much of the work being no doubt directed from the dwelling-house and office and later the works built by the Aldins on the long strip of land between Thistle Grove and Alveston Mews. Theirs was one of the firms singled out for attention in the building strike of summer 1872, but it does not seem seriously to have hampered progress.[39] By late 1873 Nos. 2-24 (even) on the east side of Roland Gardens, Nos. 1-23 (odd) on the west side, and some of the adjacent stables and coach-houses in Alveston Mews had all been built or at least started.[40] The careful design of these houses (Plate 69c, fig. 43) suggests the hand of a competent architect, but who he was is not known. Built in stock brick, they are very different from Aldin's houses in the Queen's Gate Gardens area, being arranged in pairs with mirrored plans, except No. 2, a detached house. Their three main storeys are surmounted by an over-hanging *cornicione* old-fashioned in style but up-to-date in materials, being composed of cut and moulded brick with a possible admixture of terracotta. The upper windows have flat surrounds in a criss-cross pattern also in moulded brickwork, and strong keystones with several patterns of foliage carving. Stucco appears only on the doorcases and the broadly projecting ground-floor bay windows. No secondary staircase for servants' use was provided, though at the time of the census of 1881 there was an average of nearly five domestics resident in each house.[41] In the attic storey there was a single large top-lit room, presumably intended as quarters for female servants.*

Fourteen of these twenty-four houses were occupied in 1873, but the others were not all taken up until five years later. This disappointing response may have been due to a glut on the house market after the boom years of the 1860's; alternatively the eccentric planning whereby such large houses enjoyed no back staircase may have put off potential customers. Many of those house-hunters who did become residents in this part of Roland Gardens

originally took their houses on twenty-one-year leases, but in nearly all cases where information is available the freeholds had by 1881 been sold by the Aldins, most of the purchasers being the resident at the time of each sale.[43]

In 1872, when the Aldins' first phase of building in Roland Gardens was well under way, C. J. Freake evidently decided that the Brompton Cottage property, which he had purchased in 1864, was no longer of any use to him. In 1871 Brompton Cottage itself had been occupied by one of his own employees, the architect and surveyor Henry E. Cooper;[44] but in April 1872 Freake sold the house and its half-acre curtilage, not (as might have been expected) to the Aldins but to two other important builders in South Kensington, William Corbett and Alexander McClymont,[45] the developers of Redcliffe Square and many of the surrounding streets. Corbett evidently regarded this purchase as a business success, for he celebrated it (and the conclusion of several other favourable deals of about this time) by the gift of an épergne to Mrs. McClymont on the occasion of her birthday; but in June 1872 Corbett was happy to comply with Mr. Aldin's wish that no more trees should be cut down at Brompton Cottage, and the quite close relation-ship known to exist between Corbett and Charles Aldin, junior, suggests that Corbett and McClymont may have been acting on behalf of the Aldins in the purchase of this little estate.[46] At all events they sold it in May 1873 to the Aldins, to whom it must have been a valuable acquisition rounding off their speculation in Roland Gardens.[47]

Brompton Cottage provided the Aldins with the site for another six houses in essentially the same style as those already built in Roland Gardens, but here all joined together in a single clumsy block and having ungainly dormer windows instead of top-lit attics. Four of the houses had their entrances in Old Brompton Road and two in Roland Gardens, the whole block being known as Roland Houses and independently numbered 1 to 6. All six houses were said to be 'in course of erection' in August 1873, when the Aldins mortgaged the whole site to the architect and surveyor, George Pownall,[48] and one house at least was ready to be let to its first occupant, an official at the Foreign Office, in October 1874. Tenants had been found for all the other five before the end of 1878.[49]

The Aldins did not start to build any more houses during the years 1874-7, but in 1878 work on three, Nos. 25-29 (odd) Roland Gardens, was begun.[50] Of these, only No. 25 was in occupation by the time of the census of 1881, the returns for which therefore relate only to Nos. 1-25 and 2-24 Roland Gardens, 1-6 Roland Houses and most of the coach-houses and stables in Alveston

---

*The interior decoration of the houses includes one remarkable display at No. 6, where the floors of the entrance hall and former study are paved with copies of Roman mosaics. Between the front door and the outer hall is the 'Cave Canem' from Pompeii; in the outer hall are 'Spring', from Cirencester (now in the Corinium Museum), and 'Winter', from the villa at Bignor, Sussex; in the inner hall are 'Autumn' and 'Summer', from Cirencester, and in the study 'The Rape of Ganymede', from Bignor.[42] The walls of the hall and staircase-well are lined with ceramic tiles in browns, mauves and gold, which have grotesque panels in Renaissance style. The outer hall has a ceramic fireplace on its north side, and a mosaic ceiling, of which the predominant colours are blue and gold. Stylistically all these decorations seem to date from the 1880's or '90's.

Mews. Twenty-one of these houses were in substantially normal occupation on the night of the census, and their heads of household included two major-generals, two civil engineers, and one East India broker, shipowner, accountant, wine merchant and lime merchant. There were also five female heads of household, all living on income from dividends, annuities or landed property. The average number of residents in each house was just over nine, of whom (as previously mentioned) nearly five were servants. Inhabitants of note included Philip Frederick Rose, son of the founder of Brompton Hospital, later second baronet (at No. 6 Roland Gardens), George Willoughby Hemans, civil engineer (at No. 11), and Oliver Ormerod Walker, M.P. for Salford 1877-80 (at No. 22). In Alveston Mews all the occupied premises were inhabited by coachmen and their families except No. 40, where there was an engine driver.[51]

During the boom years in metropolitan house-building in the mid 1870's the Aldins' energies were diverted to an altogether unexpected project — the construction of a rink for the current craze of roller-skating upon (approximately) the sites later occupied by Nos. 40-46 and 37-49 Roland Gardens (see Plate 71b). An open-air rink was opened on 22 April 1876, followed a few months later by a covered rink and ancillary buildings designed by Thomas W. Cutler, architect (whose later works included the Kursaal at Ramsgate and a huge hotel at Folkestone). In October *The Kensington News* welcomed 'the erection of a handsome and commodious covered building', which was open at stated times and days either to subscribers and invited guests or to the general public. Facilities included a 'well lighted warm and comfortable' ladies' room, reading room and smoking room; a band played under the direction of the organist of St. Stephen's, Gloucester Road; and such was 'the careful supervision exercised that, on the public, as well as on members' days, ladies may safely visit the rink in the evening as during any other portion of the day.'[52]

This incongruous undertaking only survived until 1881,[53] and the premises must have been demolished soon afterwards.

During the lifetime of the skating rink the only new houses to be built in Roland Gardens were Nos. 25-29 (odd), begun (as previously mentioned) in 1878. They were slow to let, No. 27 remaining unoccupied until 1883 and No. 29 until 1884.[54] They were also the last to be built in the original style, for in 1882 the Aldins adopted a new design, which was first used at Nos. 26-32, begun in that year.[55] Nos. 34-38 followed in 1883 and Nos. 40-44 in 1884.[56] On the west side Nos. 31-35 were begun in 1883 and Nos. 37 and 39 in 1887.[57] These two facing ranges of narrow-fronted red-brick houses have four storeys and pedimented dormer windows in the attics. The tall first-floor windows open on to a continuous balcony with an iron railing, and are ornamented with triangular or segmental-headed pediments of cut brick.

The east side of Roland Gardens was completed by the building in 1883-5 by Aldins[58] of No. 46, the southern side of which overlooks the enclosure at the rear of a range of houses in Evelyn Gardens on the adjoining Smith's Charity estate. The roughly triangular site had been sold by the Aldins in March 1883 to (Sir) Peter Le Page Renouf, the Egyptologist, oriental scholar and theologian.[59] The house was designed for him in the Tudor Gothic style reminiscent of a Victorian country vicarage, and has a prominent corner tower capped by a small spire (Plate 69d). It is built of red brick with stone dressings (now painted), and was occupied by Renouf until his death in 1897. His widow and his daughter continued to live there for many years; the house is now occupied as St. Teresa's Home. The name of Renouf's architect is not known, but the striking similarity between No. 46 Roland Gardens and Parmiter's School, Bethnal Green, of 1885-7, designed by T. Chatfeild Clarke, suggests that they may have been by the same hand; and it may be significant that Renouf's many varied activities included the post of H. M. Inspector of Schools for the Bethnal Green area.[60]

The building of Nos. 26-44 and Nos. 31-39 Roland Gardens in a new style, starting in 1882, coincided with the introduction of a new partner to the firm. This was Eli Plater, hitherto the Aldin brothers' works manager,[61] who in 1882 was admitted to a partnership for seven years, the firm's name being changed to Aldin and Plater.[62] At first the new houses had been quickly occupied (for example Nos. 26-32),[54] but due to a general fall in metropolitan demand in the early 1880's [63] takers for the others were to prove more difficult to find, and the firm was therefore evidently short of capital. This (reinforced, perhaps, by the new partner's influence) seems to be the reason why in August 1883 the Aldin brothers and Logan (the trustee of their father's will) conveyed all the remaining undeveloped land, the houses then in course of erection but not yet disposed of, and the firm's workshops in Alveston Mews and a number of stables there, to Coutts' Bank, of which Logan was an employee.[64]

This conveyance was evidently in effect a form of mortgage, for between October 1883 and August 1887 Coutts' Bank leased Nos. 31-39 and 38-44 Roland Gardens, as each house was completed, to the Aldins and Plater for ninety-one-year terms;[65] and between 1884 and 1894 the bank sold the freeholds either to the Aldin brothers or to Plater or to their nominees.[66]

The only land still undeveloped was situated on either side of the short east-west arm of Roland Gardens, and in 1889-90 this was sold by the bank in three lots to the firm or its nominee. The first of these conveyances was to Sir Philip Frederick Rose, second baronet, who was then living at No. 6, and with whom Aldin and Plater had a contract to build No. 41 Roland Gardens.[67] The firm began work in 1889[68] and Sir Philip moved in late in the following year.[54] This large red-and-stock-brick house in

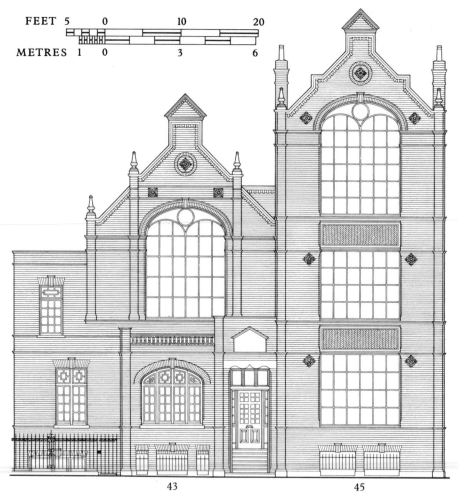

Fig. 44. Nos. 43 and 45 Roland Gardens, elevation. J. A. J. Keynes, architect, 1891-2

the Queen Anne manner is set askew on its irregularly shaped corner site. Its principal entrance was originally on the north side but is now on the east side, which is surmounted by a shaped gable. The name of the architect is not known.

The rest of the land on the south side of Roland Gardens — now the site of Nos. 43 and 45 — was sold in 1889 by Coutts' Bank to Aldin and Plater. After obtaining a licence from the London County Council for the erection of 'private Studios for Painters' the firm in turn sold the site to John Angell James Keynes, a local architect and surveyor.[69] Two sets of studios with large north-facing windows were built here in 1891-2 to Keynes' designs (fig. 44); the builders were Clarke and Company of Gledhow Terrace.[70] Artists who soon afterwards took studios here include Ada Freeman Gell (sculptress), Paul Fordyce Maitland and George Sauter.[54]

On the north side of Roland Gardens Keynes was probably also the architect of Nos. 47 and 49, two undistinguished red-brick houses in the Queen Anne manner. In 1890 the site was sold by Coutts' Bank to the

Aldin brothers, who leased it to Keynes in 1892.[71] The builders were Sherries and Company of Chelsea.[72] Subsequently Keynes brought an action against the Aldins' successors in title claiming rights of passage along Alveston Mews at the rear.[73]

The development of the whole estate was now complete, having been spread over some twenty years. Its integration with the streets of the adjoining Smith's Charity estate to the south and east had been achieved in 1886, when Aldin and Plater had agreed to pay C. A. Daw and Son, the developers of the contiguous land to the south, one hundred pounds for the right to join the south end of Roland Gardens with Evelyn Gardens.[74] Vehicular communication westward to Drayton Gardens was not, however, achieved until 1927, when the London County Council ordered the removal of a dwarf wall extending across the junction of the western arm of Roland Gardens with Thistle Grove.[35]

The completion of development was very soon followed by the collapse of the firm responsible for it. At the end of 1889 the partnership between the Aldin brothers and Eli Plater had been dissolved, several thousand pounds being owed to the latter, and George Davies, a surveyor who had been employed by the firm for over twenty years, was admitted a partner in lieu of Plater.[75] But both the Aldins had died soon afterwards, neither having reached the age of fifty, William in 1892 and Charles in 1894. Davies then found that 'through the complications which had arisen in consequence of the death of his partners, the business had become crippled for want of capital', and that there were unsecured liabilities of over £11,000. He therefore filed his petition in bankruptcy. During his examination he later stated that 'The business had been profitable throughout, but the drawings had exceeded the profits made.'[76]

By 1897 the Aldins' works in Alveston Mews had been taken over by the important building firm of Leslie and Company,[35] later to be the contractors for several institutional buildings in South Kensington, including the Science Museum.[77] Aldin Brothers and Davies, as the firm had been recently known, nevertheless survived at its original address in Queen's Gate Gardens until 1926, latterly sharing these premises with Leslie and Company. In the 1960's this last firm gave up its London address, but it still exists at Darlington.

The outward appearance of the Aldins' estate has not changed greatly since the 1890's except on the Old Brompton Road frontage. There No. 2 Roland Gardens, a northward-facing detached house with a large front garden, was demolished in 1935 for the building of Roland House, a nine-storey block of flats designed by Wimperis, Simpson and Guthrie and completed in 1936; the contractors were Gee, Walker and Slater.[78] In 1937-8 Nos. 1-3 Roland Houses suffered the same fate when Brew Brothers, motor engineers in Roland Way since 1920, built a five-storey block of car showrooms and offices upon the site. The architects were Wallis, Gilbert and Partners and the contractors Leslie and Company.[79] Nos. 4-6 Roland Houses were demolished in 1981, and their site is now (1982) vacant. In Roland Way many of the original coach-houses and stables survive, and some of them still have their round-headed doors.

CHAPTER X

The Day Estate in Drayton Gardens

For more than two hundred years the Day family has owned land in Old Brompton on both sides of Old Brompton Road, but only the southern portion of the estate is described here. This area, formerly a three-acre field called Rosehall or Rose Hawe, is now occupied by Nos. 1-39 (odd) and 4-56 (even) Drayton Gardens, Nos. 135-157 (odd) Old Brompton Road, Nos. 10-13 Thistle Grove and a few properties on the east side of Cresswell Place (fig. 45). The history of the other part of the Day family's land, on the north side of Old Brompton Road, which was customarily known as the 'six acres', and which now comprises Hereford Square, Brechin Place, Rosary Gardens and Wetherby Place, will be described in volume XLII of the *Survey of London*.

The two parts of the estate have been in common ownership since at least the seventeenth century, when the land was (and remained until 1835) copyhold of the manor of Earl's Court. In the 1530's Rosehall had been in the tenure of one Thomas Thatcher and subsequently of his son, John (d. 1558), who owned a substantial copyhold estate in the vicinity but not, it seems, the piece known as the 'six acres'.[1] By 1661, however, both Rosehall and the 'six acres' were among a small group of copyhold properties held by James Dyson, and by 1666 these two alone had descended to his son Francis.[2] Thereafter they remained in the ownership of the Dysons until the early eighteenth century, when they passed into other hands.[3]

The Day family first secured an interest in the property in 1743. This was through the marriage of Benjamin Day, the son of a successful worsted weaver in Norwich, to Ann Dodemead, daughter and co-heir of Walter Dodemead, esquire, of St. Paul's, Covent Garden,[4] who had acquired the property in 1735 by foreclosing on a mortgage.[5] A fellow-parishioner of the Dodemeads in Covent Garden, Day was a mercer by trade, with a shop or warehouse at the north corner of Tavistock Street and Charles (now Wellington) Street, which doubtless afforded a London outlet for the family business in Norwich.[6]

On the death of Walter Dodemead in 1744 Ann Day and her two sisters, Elizabeth Brent and Susanna Vincent, became the joint owners of their father's lands.[7] But in 1753 Ann and Susanna surrendered their share to Elizabeth, who died in 1755 leaving the property to her husband, Thomas Brent, with the proviso that if he died childless it should pass to her nephew, James Frapwell Day, the second son of Benjamin and Ann Day.[8] And this

is what eventually happened, though it was not until 1772 that James Frapwell Day came into his inheritance following the death of his uncle's brother, the Reverend William Brent, who had been left a life-interest by Thomas Brent's will.[9]

From James Frapwell Day, who died unmarried in 1819,* the estate passed to a nephew. He was James Day of Horsford near Norwich,[10] who in 1835 purchased the enfranchisement of the copyhold tenure from Lord Kensington, the lord of the manor of Earl's Court.[11]

The present proprietors of the estate (now by a number of sales considerably reduced in size) are the direct descendants of James Day (see fig. 46). He died in 1875, and by his will placed the estate in the hands of trustees until all the children of his son, Gerard, should come of age. It then passed to his eldest grandson, Herbert Allen Day, who later achieved local fame as a socialist and philanthropist in Norwich,[12] and it is now owned by two of the latter's grandchildren.

Fig. 45. The Day estate in Drayton Gardens. Based on the Ordnance Survey of 1949-63

*His will nevertheless includes a small bequest to two daughters.

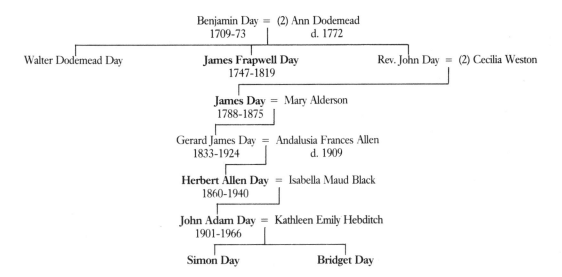

Fig. 46. Abridged pedigree of the Day family, showing the owners of the Brompton estate in bold.

In the 1820's and '30's Rosehall, the three-acre field on the south side of Old Brompton Road, was used as a market garden, Henry Kennett, William and William Thomas At(t)wood being successive tenants of it.[13] After a period of relative quiescence in building activity in London, there were signs in the early 1840's of a revival, and this evidently encouraged James Day to think about developing his property. By the summer of 1843 Rosehall, though still under cultivation as a market garden, was already being classified by the Tithe Commissioners as 'Building Ground',[14] and in January 1845 Day concluded an agreement to let the ground to two speculators. These were Joseph Dunning of York Street, Foley Place, St. Marylebone, and William Ward of Northampton Road, Clerkenwell.[15] In the agreement they are both described as builders, but it is as architects, with an address in Hanover Chambers, Buckingham Street, Adelphi, that they appear both in directories and in the early leases soon to be granted.

Dunning, who was then aged about thirty-one, had been involved professionally in the development of the Norland estate in northern Kensington since 1841. There he had at first worked as an assistant to the architect Robert Cantwell, before assuming an independent role as surveyor to several of the principal developers — a function he continued to perform until at least 1851. As a speculator he built more than twenty houses on part of the estate in Portland Road in the mid 1850's.[16] In 1861 he was practising his profession from lodgings at No. 7 Barkham Terrace, Southwark; ten years later he was still at the same address, having in the meanwhile (it seems) married his landlady.[17] Of Ward's career, either before or after his involvement with the Day estate, nothing is known.

Under the terms of their agreement with Day, Dunning and Ward were required to construct a new road down the middle of the site, from north to south, build fifty-seven houses and complete the whole development within seven years.[15]

At its southern end the new road was to link up with an existing road, then called Thistle Grove, which extended northward from the Fulham Road as far as the southern boundary of Day's property (see page 166). In this way a new thoroughfare was to be opened between Old Brompton Road and the Fulham Road. But instead of a single name being adopted for the whole street, as is now the case, the longer, southern section continued to be known as Thistle Grove while Day's portion was originally called Drayton Grove.* This dual nomenclature survived until 1865, when the Metropolitan Board of Works abolished the name Drayton Grove, and for nearly twenty years the entire road, newly renumbered from south to north, was called Thistle Grove. It was renamed Drayton Gardens in 1884 and given its present sequence of house numbers in 1894. In 1907 the name Thistle Grove was revived, being applied (very confusingly) to the old pathway formerly called Thistle Grove Lane which runs parallel to and east of Drayton Gardens.

The development of Rosehall took place under the overall supervision of Day's surveyor, the local architect John Blore (1812-82), of Michael's Place, Brompton, who provided the layout plan and designed all the houses. These he grouped into three terraces of unequal length, one facing Old Brompton Road, and two in Drayton Grove. Each terrace is basically symmetrical, consisting mainly of three-storey houses over basements with one or more four-storey houses as a centrepiece (Plate 67, fig.

*Drayton Grove evidently derived its name from the village of Drayton near Norwich. In 1839 one of James Day's brothers owned land there, and a few years earlier James Day himself had occupied a house in the vicinity known as Drayton Lodge.[18]

47). Executed in stock brick with copious stucco dressings, Blore's designs are in an orthodox late-Georgian manner, showing little to justify the later assertion of *The Building News* (echoed by the architect himself) that 'the style adopted is Italian'. The dressings of the doorcases, however, seem distinctively Victorian, those in Old Brompton Road by reason of the console brackets supporting the straight hood-moulds, and those in Drayton Grove by reason of the Doric pillared porches.[19]

Blore's authorship of the design is avowed by an inscription incised into the front of No. 151 Old Brompton Road which reads J. BLORE ARCH 1846.

For supervising the construction of the houses Blore was to be paid a fee of £3 per house by the developers.[15]

As soon as the houses were covered-in Dunning and Ward could apply to Day for a grant of a ninety-nine-year lease for each house or group of houses. The individual ground rents were not specified in the agreement but they were to be apportioned in such a way as to produce after five years a total annual ground rent for the whole site of £110 (equivalent to just over £36 an acre). The houses were to be occupied only as private dwellings, and the leases granted by Day contained restrictive covenants forbidding the premises to be used for any trade, sale or exhibition, manufactory, lunatic asylum or any other business 'except surgeon, apothecary, sculptor, artist or seminary for young ladies'.[20]

Road-building and sewer-laying occupied the developers during the spring and summer months of 1845, and house-building did not begin until September.[21] The first to be completed were the nine houses fronting Old Brompton Road between Thistle Grove Lane and Drayton Grove (Plate 67b, fig. 47). Now numbered 135-151 (odd) Old Brompton Road, they were originally known as Drayton Terrace, a name that can still be seen cut into the stucco of the pedestal-course below the first-floor windows of Nos. 135 and 151. All nine houses were leased in February 1846 to Dunning and Ward, who immediately mortgaged them for £1,000.[22] Apart from what is now No. 135 they were all occupied by the end of 1848.[23]

At the time of the census of 1851, when six of these nine houses were still in the hands of their first occupants, the heads of household included a professor of music, a solicitor, an upholsterer, a lodging-house keeper and two clerks, one of them the chief clerk in the office of Cox and Company, the bankers. The total number of people then living in Drayton Terrace was fifty-three, of whom twelve were servants. In 1861 the number of resident servants was still twelve and the total number of inhabitants forty-six. The heads of household then included a sculptor, Felix Miller, at what is now No. 147 Old Brompton Road, and a market gardener, Henry Atwood, at No. 149.[24]

In Drayton Grove* (Plate 67b, c) building started at the north end of both sides of the street in the summer of 1846, and by December twelve houses there were ready to be leased to Dunning and Ward.[25] These are now Nos. 1 and 3 Drayton Gardens, on the east side, and Nos. 4-22 (even) on the west. Also leased at the same time was the Drayton public house at the west corner with Old Brompton Road. This had been the subject of a separate agreement with Day in August 1846, whereby Dunning and Ward were allowed to substitute a public house for the dwelling house originally intended here. The building had to be erected in accordance with plans prepared by Blore, and the ground rent was to be £10.[26] It was first occupied in the second half of 1847, at least as early as any of the houses in Drayton Terrace.[23]

The original Drayton public house has been demolished and no illustration of it is known. But a plan shows a rather narrow building with a porticoed entrance on the north side opening on to a carriage drive into Old Brompton Road. On the western side of the site a private roadway gave access to a coach-house and stables behind Nos. 4 and 6 Drayton Gardens.[27]

All the leases granted by Day in 1846 had been made direct to Dunning and Ward, and the houses had evidently been built under their auspices by building contractors employed by them. This method of working came to an end, however, in the spring of 1847, when building operations all over the country were badly disrupted by a short but very severe financial crisis. In Drayton Grove work on three houses which Dunning and Ward had started in September 1846 was suspended,[28] and for several years building here was at a complete standstill. Unlike many of their contemporaries, however, (including the developer of Hereford Square on Day's other Brompton property) they avoided bankruptcy, but only by mortgaging most of their interests in the development to provide security for their creditors.[29] One of these mortgages was to a builder, William Thomas of Princes Street, Lambeth,[30] who had probably built the houses concerned — Nos. 1 and 3 and 4-22 Drayton Gardens — but had not yet been paid.

After the crisis of 1847 Dunning and Ward took no more leases, which were thereafter granted (sometimes at their nomination) to the individual builders. As owners of the building agreement of 1845 they were still involved in the development, but they ceased to employ building contractors on their own behalf.

In 1849, when the worst effects of the crisis had passed, building work was resumed in Drayton Grove. But only five houses were erected (now Nos. 5-13), and they probably included one or more of the three previously suspended. All five were either built or completed by William Thomas, to whom the leases were granted, at Dunning and Ward's request, in November 1849.[31]

*Throughout this account, unless otherwise stated, Drayton Grove is used to distinguish the Day portion of Drayton Gardens, irrespective of date, but the house numbers are the present ones.

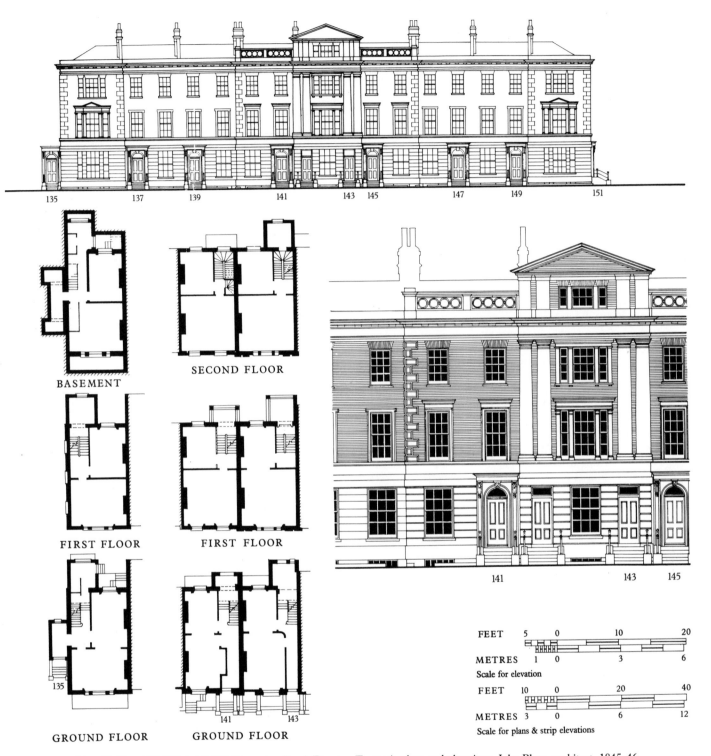

FEET 5 0 10 20
METRES 1 0 3 6
Scale for elevation

FEET 10 0 20 40
METRES 3 0 6 12
Scale for plans & strip elevations

Fig. 47. Nos. 135-151 (odd) Old Brompton Road (Drayton Terrace), plans and elevations. John Blore, architect, 1845-46

Only twenty-seven houses, including the Drayton public house, had so far been completed on the estate. But Dunning and Ward's agreement with Day of 1845 required the erection of fifty-seven houses by January 1852, and in March 1851, when fulfilment of this condition was clearly proving impossible (no building

having taken place since 1849), Day granted them a three-year extension. Dunning and Ward agreed to a small increase in the total ground rent. Most of this increase was appropriated to four additional houses, to be built at the north end of Thistle Grove Lane on a vacant site at the back of some of the houses at the north end of Drayton Grove.

Originally called Drayton Villas and now numbered 10-13 Thistle Grove, these four additional houses were erected in 1852-3 by Frederick Detheridge Davies of Schofield Place, Brompton, builder, and leased, in December 1852, to John Carter of King's Road, Chelsea, grocer.[33] Designed by Blore,[34] they consist of two pairs of unpretentious semi-detached villas in greyish brick with stucco dressings. Each pair is two storeys high over a semi-basement, and is flanked by narrow recessed wings which contain the entrances. The latter are dressed with Roman Doric doorcases. In 1861, when only two of the four houses were still in the hands of their original occupants, none of the families living in Drayton Villas employed any servants. No. 10 was then a lodging-house, and No. 11 was shared by a joiner and a house painter and their families.[35]

Meanwhile in Drayton Grove another four houses were started in 1852, the first to be built there since 1849. These are now Nos. 24 and 26 (on the west side), and Nos. 37 and 39 (on the east). The former pair were built by Edmund Mesher of Blenheim (now Astell) Street, Chelsea, to whom they were leased in December 1852,[36] and the latter pair by Stephen Peirson of Elm Tree Cottage, Old Brompton,[37] a builder also working on the adjoining Gunter estate, where several houses on the west side of Gilston Road and the south side of Tregunter Road were built by him in the early 1850's.[38]

In the following year another builder in Tregunter Road, Henry John Clarke, erected six more houses in Drayton Grove, at the south end of the west side. These are now Nos. 46-56 (even). Clarke later had the misfortune to become bankrupt and for a few months in 1863-4 he was confined to a debtor's prison. In letters to the builder Edmund Mesher, to whom he had assigned a number of his houses in Drayton Grove in trust for his children, Clarke attributed his predicament to a breach of trust or embezzlement ('I cannot say which') by his father, 'whoom [sic] I have employed for some time past to do my business and keep my books'. He warned Mesher against allowing his father to collect any of the rents from Drayton Grove, and concluded his letter with a bitter postscript: 'See what depravity drink has brought on in him even imbecility'.[39]

Despite the efforts of Mesher, Peirson and Clarke the development was again behind schedule, and when Dunning and Ward's three-year extension expired in January 1855 twenty houses in Drayton Grove still remained to be built. Both terraces were punctuated by unsightly gaps caused by the builders having been allowed to leapfrog the intended four-storey centre houses, none of which had yet been started, and to work northwards from the south end. Surprisingly, these gaps do not seem to have deterred prospective inhabitants, the 'detached' portions being occupied just as quickly as the rest of the terraces.[23]

Having again failed to complete the development on time, Dunning and Ward applied to Day for another extension, pointing out, no doubt, that the building industry was once more going through a period of difficulty; and in November 1855 Day granted them a further three and a half years, again in exchange for a small rise in the ground rent to take account of the increased value of the plots still to be built.[40] When this second extension expired in January 1858, however, not a single new house had been erected; and thereafter Dunning and Ward do not appear to have taken any further part in the development.

The two terraces in Drayton Grove were eventually completed between 1858 and 1863 by one of the original builders engaged on them, William Thomas, then operating from York Road, Lambeth,[41] and by another builder not previously involved in this development, Evan Evans of Stanley (now Alderney) Street, Pimlico. Thomas was responsible for the west side, where the houses were leased in 1859 and 1862 (Nos. 28-36 and 38-44 even respectively),[42] while Evans took the east side, the houses here being leased in 1861 (Nos. 31-35), 1862 (Nos. 27 and 29) and 1863 (Nos. 15-25).[43] Most of these houses were occupied within a year or two of the lease being granted.[23]

The long time over which the terraces were built, and the difficulties under which the builders had laboured, seem not to have caused any major disruption of Blore's intended scheme, and the last houses to be erected are accordingly in a belated style for their date. In 1858 *The Building News* carried a short article about the development in Drayton Grove drawing attention to the central block of three four-storey houses in the western terrace (then being completed internally) which it thought 'renders the range more effective'.[44] It did not, however, comment on the disturbing effect of the off-centre portico at No. 30, the central house, which is otherwise distinguished from the rest of the terrace by its completely stuccoed façade and three tiers of triple windows (Plate 67a). Here, as elsewhere, Blore was prepared to sacrifice strict symmetry to the needs of a conventional terraced-house plan with a hallway and staircase on one side. According to the same article the living-rooms in each house were on the ground floor while the floors above were occupied by bedrooms, an arrangement, which, if accurately reported, was highly unusual in the 1850's in houses of this size, where the first floor was generally given over to one or more drawing-rooms.

Nothing is said about the internal finishing of the houses, but in *c.* 1864 a bill for redecorating the dining-room at No. 46 included painting and graining all the woodwork and wainscot and varnishing the same with a good oak varnish, and papering the walls with a satin paper and borders.[45]

The pattern of occupation in Drayton Grove as shown by the census returns of 1851 and 1861 is, not surprisingly, very similar to that already described in Drayton Terrace. In both 1851 and 1861 the average size of households was just over five and the average number of servants in each household just over one. In 1851, when all but one of the seventeen completed houses in Drayton Grove (Nos. 4-22 and 1-13) were in normal occupation, the heads of household included two naval officers, two annuitants, and one merchant, a clerk in the Foreign Office, a solicitor, a hosier and glover, a landed proprietor, a proprietor of mines and an animal painter (Edward Webb at No. 22). By 1861 the number of completed houses had risen to thirty-four, of which thirty-three were in normal occupation. The heads of household in that year included five fundholders, five clerks, three proprietors of houses and three lawyers, two clergymen and two engineers, and one accountant, annuitant, hotel keeper, lodging-house keeper and landed proprietor. The largest single household in 1861 was not at one of these houses but at the Drayton public house, where lived the publican, his wife, their seven children and five servants, making a total of fourteen.[46]

From 1873 until 1881 No. 9 Drayton Gardens (then No. 80 Thistle Grove) was the home of Alan Cole, younger son of Sir Henry and a senior official in the Science and Art Department.

Since the completion of the development in the mid 1860's only one of the original buildings has been demolished. This was the Drayton (now Drayton Arms) public house at No. 153 Old Brompton Road, which was rebuilt in 1891-2 to the designs of Messrs. Gordon, Lowther and Gunton of Finsbury Circus, surveyors, the contractor being J. Anley of Dalston Lane.[47] In sharp contrast to the grey brick and stucco of the adjoining terrace, the Drayton Arms displays chiefly a buff-coloured terracotta, flamboyantly decorated with Renaissance-style figures and motifs in high relief, interspersed with some red brickwork (Plate 68a). The adjacent building, incorporating two shops at Nos. 155 and 157 Old Brompton Road, shows the same materials, with less terracotta, and is part of the same redevelopment.

The overall appearance of the terraces remains generally good in spite of many small but often disfiguring alterations, of which the most intrusive are changes to the roof-line. As early as 1860 there was a proposal to raise the roof at No. 26 Drayton Grove, which Blore at first resisted, even though the addition was to be largely hidden behind a balustrade (now removed), as it would, in his opinion, 'disturb the uniformity and symmetry of the range of buildings in its outline next the sky as seen from the opposite side.' After modifications, however, 'which will in a great measure remove my objection', he allowed it to go ahead.[48] In the 1880's and '90's W. H. Collbran, Blore's successor as surveyor to the estate, permitted a number of roofs to be raised at Drayton Terrace but insisted that the work should be carried out in a uniform manner.[49]

In more recent years the problem of car-parking in Drayton Gardens, particularly for the houses on the east side, which have no rear access for vehicles, has led to the destruction of some of the front gardens to make parking sites or ramps down to basement garages. In the early 1970's the Greater London Council attempted to stop this practice as 'detrimental to the design of the terrace as a whole', but was overruled by the Secretary of State for the Environment.[50]

In Cresswell Place a number of former stables have been turned into dwelling houses. When first built none of the houses on the west side of Drayton Grove, whose gardens extended back to Cresswell Place (then Bolton Mews), were provided with stables; but by 1894[51] some had been erected at the back of Nos. 26-34 (even), and these were subsequently converted into two houses, numbered 43 and 44 Cresswell Place. No. 43 received its present form in 1973-4 (Nicholas Johnston, architect).[52] Further north at No. 50 a stable block rebuilt for the Drayton public house in 1891-2 was converted into a dwelling house by John G. Rutter and Company of Pall Mall, architects, in 1933.[53] No. 38 Cresswell Place was originally built in 1903 as a studio for the landscape artist Fanny S. G. Nathan.[54] The adjoining studio over a double garage at No. 37 dates from 1969-70 (W. R. Siddons and Associates, architects).[55]

CHAPTER XI

Little Chelsea in Kensington

This chapter is chiefly concerned with the Fulham Road (on its north side) between Thistle Grove and Redcliffe Gardens. Something is also said of the history of the ownership of the areas extending back from this frontage, but the buildings behind the Fulham Road are discussed only where the history of their development is related to that of the buildings fronting on that road.

This part of Fulham Road traverses what was formerly an old settlement called Little Chelsea, which lay also on the south side of the road in the parish of Chelsea proper. Why a settlement grew up at this particular part of the road is not known, or at what date. The first known references are in the early seventeenth century. In 1618 the parish register of Kensington records the burial of the child of a resident at 'lytle Cheley [sic] in this parish',[1] and in 1625 an alehouse at Little Chelsea was giving trouble to the magistrates.[2] (This alehouse, run by a Thomas Freeman, was probably near what is now the southern end of Drayton Gardens.[3]) In the hearth-tax lists of the early 1670's houses here in Kensington, some of them substantial, number perhaps about twenty-three (of which at least a few had evidently been built together in the 1650's) and in Chelsea perhaps eight. Titled names occur, with Sir John Griffin at a house near the southern end of Seymour Walk and Sir James Smith in Chelsea, but the area seems quite early to have had the mixed character it retained into the nineteenth century. For much of its history sizeable houses in private occupation by people of note were mingled with cottage terraces, lodging-houses, private mad-houses and, especially, the schools or academies that gathered here. One school at least was located near the later Nos. 252 and 254 Fulham Road in 1703,[4] and by the 1840's a traveller passing westward along the Fulham Road noted at Walnut Tree Walk (Redcliffe Gardens) the last of a sequence of schools, 'the unceasing work of education . . . appearing here for the first time to terminate'.[5]*

The houses on the north and south sides of the road together made a little hamlet of their own, separated by fields from the small towns of Chelsea and Kensington and the other hamlets of Brompton and Earl's Court. The road to Fulham was its high street and in 1671 was called 'Little Chelsey streete'.[6] Its isolation in 1680 is illustrated by the correspondence of John Verney (later Lord Fermanagh), who lived for a time, with his wife, in his father-in-law's house at the later Nos. 252 and 254 Fulham Road. He 'commuted' to his merchant's office in the City but had an unpleasant choice of transport: 'by land tis unsafe for Rogues, and by water tis cold besides a good walke in ye dirt and darke (if not rain) from Greate to little Chelsey'.[7] In 1712 the residents seem to have succeeded in obtaining an order from the magistrates in petty sessions for a watch or policing service at Little Chelsea independent of the watch provided by the two parishes, 'which is on both sides remote'.[8]

Little Chelsea in Kensington exemplified how the mixed social character of a group of houses strung along one of the highways out of London did not necessarily presage rapid decline. Salway's limpid and precise drawing of 1811 (Plate 72) delineates weather-boarded cottages, shops, builders' premises and schools in this part of Fulham Road, but also houses occupied by wealthy retired tradesmen, rentiers and office-holders, with poplars blowing in their front gardens and the orchards and nursery-grounds of south-west Brompton behind them. People of some standing still lived here in the 1870's.

'Little Chelsea' continued as a description of this area into the 1850's,[9] but went out of use when it became joined to the streets behind that were being laid out, mostly under the ownership of James or Robert Gunter, in the 1850's and 1860's.

The most substantial houses in the late seventeenth century were the one already mentioned near Seymour Walk, another near the south-west end of Redcliffe Road (approximately at Nos. 202-210 even Fulham Road) and an irregular row westward from what is now Hollywood Road to the Servite priory at No. 264 Fulham Road. Most of this row survived, if heavily reconstructed, into the 1870's. Some late seventeenth- or mid-eighteenth-century features remain, in the priory house at No. 264, and at the adjacent No. 262A. Much hereabouts is now an open, low-built no-man's-land occupied as dairy depot, primary school and postal and telecommunications premises. At the south-west corner of Hollywood Road five houses survive from the 1790's and 1800's (Plate 75e), and this is also the earliest date of surviving buildings further east, where the seventeenth-century developments were in any case less substantial. Here the chief features are Seymour Walk (Plate 74), a nearly complete survival of the 1790's-to-1820's, and Drayton Gardens and Thistle Grove, where a

---

*The house-numbers in Fulham Road used in this chapter are generally the modern ones. For Nos. 252-264 the numbers are based on those in use in *c.* 1870 and are shown on fig. 55 (page 185).

few houses date from the time of first laying-out (Plate 66b). This was in the second decade of the nineteenth century — a comparatively active building-period in this little neighbourhood.

Nothing of a distinctive identity can now be discerned in the 'Little Chelsea' area, and it was, in fact, from an early date fragmented in its ownership and development as well as in its social character. In Kensington it consisted of properties that, probably grouped in two or three units of ownership by the mid seventeenth century, were further divided before the second phase of gradual development from the 1790's onward. These later units of building-ownership were, when acquired for development, still mainly agricultural or horticultural, and extended longitudinally to the fields behind. The pre-building use was often intensive, in gardens and orchards, and the holdings seem to have had no extensive fronts to this part of the Fulham Road.

The history of ownership in the seventeenth century is not certain or complete. The allegiance to the manor of Earl's Court, which survived in the fields to the north as copyhold tenure into the nineteenth century, was here in rapid process of extinction. The alehouse near the eastern end of the area excited the attention of the manorial authorities by its illicit ninepins in the 1670's,[10] but otherwise the owners of property in Little Chelsea at that period figure only (and for the last time) as defaulters from their manorial obligations.

To deal first with the ownership at the eastern end of Little Chelsea, here a property-holding fronted on the Fulham Road between what are now Thistle Grove and Holmes Place (F on fig. 48), but also had a frontage to Fulham Road further west, at what is now the eastern corner of Hollywood Road (B on fig. 48). This property of some eighteen and a half acres was part of the land in Kensington and Chelsea bought in 1599 from Sir Robert Cecil by the second Earl of Lincoln and sold in 1651 by his grand-daughter and her husband, Sir Arthur Gorges, to Sir Michael Warton of Beverley in Yorkshire. The residential heart of the property had been in Chelsea, where Gorges and the Earl of Lincoln had both had big houses. In 1651 the Kensington part was described as ten acres of arable called Windmill Hill, another four acres of arable adjacent, and four acres in (a field called) Coleherne.[11] Warton's property passed to his grandson, also Sir Michael, who on his death in 1725 left it, with very extensive lands elsewhere, to his three married daughters.[12] In 1774 the representatives of these three joint interests agreed to a partition, confirmed by an Act of Parliament in the following year.[13] By this the eighteen and a half acres in Kensington, then worth about £100 per annum, came, with other land in Chelsea and Fulham, to Sir James Pennyman, sixth baronet, of Ormesby Hall, Yorkshire, M.P. for Beverley and the grandson of one of Sir Michael's sons-in-law. He sold the property in 1781. A small area, now mostly covered by the western part of the ABC cinema site (c on fig. 48), was bought by a coach-maker.[14] The purchaser of much the greater part (F and B less c on fig. 48) was the builder, Henry Holland,[15] but he seems not to have developed it significantly, and after his death his sons Richard and Henry (the architect) sold it in 1786.

Most of the area northward of the Thistle Grove-Holmes Place frontage (Fb, d and e on fig. 48) was sold to a purchaser living on the Chelsea side of the road, John Groves, gentleman,[16] although the Holmes Place area itself (a on fig. 48) (less the actual passageway at the southern end of what is now Gilston Road) was sold to the Jeffery Holmes who gives it its name.[17] Further west, next to the present Hollywood Road (B on fig. 48), the purchaser was a coal merchant.[18] Some buildings had stood on most of these frontages in the seventeenth century and although they were of no great consequence these sales did not presage immediate and significant rebuilding. Holmes put up three new but humble houses and Groves probably half a dozen — soon to be pulled down themselves. The first deliberate piece of redevelopment of any quality was in 1811, when Groves's son, possibly encouraged by the building of Seymour Walk, laid out the southern two-thirds of Drayton Gardens (then called Thistle Grove, d on fig. 48), selling the frontages, however, in freehold plots to give a much more diversified effect than in Seymour Walk. Perhaps Groves hoped to carry the road through to the Old Brompton Road, on another man's property, but this did not happen until the 1840's.

In 1812-13 Groves sold the western part of his land in two lots (e and b on fig. 48), the smaller portion, fronting Fulham Road between the present Nos. 152 and 176 (b on fig. 48), to an auctioneer. Here, soon after Drayton Gardens was laid out, humble late-eighteenth-century leasehold properties were extended, equally humbly, only to be replaced by more solid but unaspiring buildings (which partly survive) after further divisions of the freehold in 1846. The Hollywood Road corner-site remained garden ground with an 1820 villa at its southern end: the latter became a hospital in the 1850's and the whole was absorbed into the street-developments on the Gunter estate in the 1860's (see pages 179, 239).

West of the property sold to Groves and Holmes in 1786, it is likely that the ownership of a three-and-three-quarter-acre rectangle of land (E on fig. 48) in the seventeenth century followed that of a more westerly piece of property (A on fig. 48) from a Thomas Maundy to the Middleton family (see below). Here that family retained it until it passed to a Gloucestershire family in 1807. They sold it, not radically redeveloped, in 1859. The purchaser, the architect George Godwin (here acting as initial landowner), then subjected it to the spread of house-building which was transforming the hinterland to the north under the guidance of his own hand as estate surveyor to other owners.

The area between what are now Nos. 212 and 226 Fulham Road (D on fig. 48) seems to have belonged to Sir

THISTLE GROVE

THISTLE GROVE

DRAYTON GARDENS

CRESSWELL PLACE

PRIORY WALK

HARLEY GARDENS

MILBORNE GROVE

GILSTON ROAD

CAVAYE PLACE

ABC Cinema

Onslow Court

Drayton Court

Priory Mansions

Warner House

Holly Mews

Garage

Cinema

Grove Court

Donovan Court

Bolton Studios

PH

REDCLIFFE ROAD

FULHAM ROAD

SEYMOUR WALK

ROAD

CATHCART

HOLLYWOOD ROAD

FAWCETT STREET

Hollywood Court

Cecil Court

Fawcett Court

Servite Primary School

PO

BARKER ST

Ch. of Our Lady of Seven Dolours

St Mary's Priory

REDCLIFFE GARDENS

METRES 0 100 200 300

FEET 0 100 300

N

Fig. 48. The 'Little Chelsea' portion of Fulham Road, with former property divisions shown by heavy and dotted lines. Based on the Ordnance Survey of 1949–62

James Smith, of the 'Chelsea' portion of Little Chelsea, at some time before 1682, and was bought from him by a Covent Garden grocer, Charles Morgan, who died in that year. One big house stood at the southern end of garden ground at least sometimes in commercial cultivation, and here it was a sale to a local builder in 1790 that initiated house-building on the street frontage and then the building of Seymour Walk northward, latterly under another owner, in the first two decades of the nineteenth century (see page 176).

The early ownership of the small late-developed area to the west, at Nos. 228-234 (even) Fulham Road (C on fig. 48), is not known.

West of what is now Hollywood Road there took place an important early development (A on fig. 48). This seems to have included the sites of Nos. 240-264 (even) Fulham Road, but may also have affected a detached piece to the east at E. This property in the 1640's was mostly in the hands of the Reverend William Hobson, Rector of St. George's, Southwark, until his sequestration, while a smaller portion was in the hands of his younger brother, Robert Hobson, who took his degree of doctor of medicine in 1659 and died, aged forty-two, in the same year.[19] They were sons of Lancelot Hobson, a successful glazier and prominent parishioner in Southwark, who was for many years wholesale agent for Sir Robert Mansell, the glass-making monopolist. Hobson sent his sons to Cambridge and in 1639 had the satisfaction of seeing William's return to Southwark as rector and his marriage to a distant relation of Lord Keeper Coventry. Lancelot Hobson died a few months later.[20] He was possessed of substantial property in Kensington, or, if dispossessed, only in favour of his children. Unfortunately, its location and extent are not precisely known. In his will, dated in December 1639,[21] he speaks of a messuage and lands lately purchased by him which he had made over so that they would come to his sons William (the greater part) and Robert (the lesser) on his death. Presumably this was distinct from another property in Kensington which two months earlier he and William had settled on a son of Lord Coventry and a gentleman of Leatherhead, Thomas Rogers, in consideration of the impending marriage between William and Rogers's sister Margaret.[22] Her interest, however, only became effective, for her own life, if she outlived William (which she did not), subsequently to revert to William's heirs. This property consisted of a 'lane or drove' which can be identified with Walnut Tree Walk (later Redcliffe Gardens), leading north from the Fulham Road to twelve acres of arable and pasture called Little Coleherne (G on fig. 58 on page 196); another half acre of arable and pasture; and two houses. One was a 'Great mansion house' with its appurtenances, inhabited by a Charles Thynne, esquire, (who perhaps died in 1652[23]) and the other a house with garden and court and 'greate hall which formerly went with the next adjoining

house' occupied by a merchant, Edward Somner. The 'Little Coleherne' property was west of Walnut Tree Walk near its northern end, but the other Hobson property was probably further south, as some of the land sold by Gorges to Warton in 1651 mentioned above was said to abut southward and westward on land of Mr. Hobson.[24] The part of Lancelot Hobson's property that came to the younger son Robert certainly included a house on the site later marked by Nos. 240-248 (even) Fulham Road, where Robert was perhaps living in 1655.[25] That the southern boundary of the Hobson family's land lay along this part of Fulham Road also appears from subsequent events. In 1661 William Hobson became D.D. and was presented by St. George's Chapel, Windsor, to the vicarage of Twickenham, but in his will made in 1665 (a confused and confusing document) he spoke of his estate as 'contracted lately through God's providence' and of the lessening of it by a son's 'miscarriage'.[26]* Perhaps for that reason he broke an entail on his property[26] and in 1664 (according to a recital in a deed of 1671) sold a big house here, later numbered 252 and 254 Fulham Road. Other property of unknown extent was included in this sale. The purchaser was the son of one of his Twickenham parishioners, in trust for another, Henry Middleton. Joined with Hobson as a party in the sale was a Thomas Maundy and his wife.[28]

Maundy had already appeared on the scene a few doors to the west in or before 1659, when he mortgaged another big house, at what is now the Servite priory at No. 264 Fulham Road, to a gentleman of the Middle Temple. Maundy then described it as the westernmost of his 'New Buildings', recently erected. The identity of this Thomas Maundy will be reverted to later, with the evidence of a likely connexion with Henry Middleton, the beneficial purchaser in 1664. It is sufficient to note here that documents relating to the period around 1666-74 associate Henry Middleton, or a sister (or sister-in-law) of his, with each of the five houses at the sites later numbered 240-264 (even) Fulham Road; and that further east, probably at a house on the site later Nos. 202-210 (even, E on fig. 48) Maundy's name occurs as hearth-taxpayer in 1662-71 and Middleton's family as the freeholders so late as the 1800's (see page 174). Probably, therefore, this (discontinuous) frontage was all part of the original Hobson family's property, in which Maundy had a building-interest and which then passed to Middleton.

By 1669 some other part of the Hobson property, perhaps lying back from the road and regarded as a freehold tenure of the manor of Earl's Court, had been sold to Doctor John Whitaker.[29] In 1675 Henry Middleton owned thirteen acres of freehold in Kensington.[30] This may well have included former Hobson land. Middleton and trustees for him sold one big house (that later numbered 252-254 Fulham Road) in 1671 (see page 184) and evidently his family retained only

---

*One son, Lancelot, was perhaps the man shipping tin to London in 1669: another was perhaps John Hobson, consul at Venice *c.* 1654-70.[27]

the most easterly house at the later Nos. 202-210 (even) Fulham Road long in its ownership.

The 'New Buildings' for which Maundy was responsible, seemingly in the 1650's, are of uncertain extent eastward from No. 264. In the 1660's four big houses stood to the east of the latter. The easternmost of these, however, (at the site later numbered 240-248 even) was subsequently said to have been built by Henry Middleton where Robert Hobson's house had stood,[31] so it is doubtful whether Maundy's work extended there: nor is it known whether he developed only unbuilt land. The mansion of Charles Thynne and the evidently oldish house of Edward Somner in 1638 may well have stood on or near this Fulham Road frontage of the Hobson property.

As an early developer here Maundy's identity challenges conjecture, which is best made by reference to the likely identity of the Henry Middleton to whom at least some of the property passed. Middleton was a parishioner of Twickenham, where he had a brother-in-law, Edward Birkhead, who died in 1662. Edward's son William was Middleton's trustee in the purchase of 1664, and Edward's widow Ellen lived in one of the Little Chelsea houses about 1666-74, giving Middleton lodgings with her.[32] It seems very probable, therefore, that Henry Middleton and Edward Birkhead were the men of those names who had been colleagues as Serjeants at Arms under Charles I and the Commonwealth and who (for example) bore their maces at the proclamations in London and Westminster of Cromwell as Lord Protector in 1653.[33] That Henry Middleton was in fact a Serjeant at Arms is made more probable by the bequest of plate by one of his neighbours at Little Chelsea, who was also party to the purchase of a house there from him in 1671, to a friend he calls 'Serjeant Middleton'.[34] Thomas Maundy, therefore, would seem likely to be the goldsmith of that name who provided the Serjeants at Arms Birkhead and Middleton with their maces, in the supply of which he was given a monopoly by Parliament in 1649. This goldsmith was, in fact, the maker of the 'bauble' derided by Cromwell. Additionally, many corporations had their maces made by him.[35] The goldsmith's success in his trade might well have given him resources for investment: he is, indeed, found buying church property at Plymouth in 1650.[36] Whether there was a personal association between Hobson and Maundy is not known. The inclusion of Maundy's and Hobson's wives as parties to the sale of 1664 hints that there may have been.[28]

Another Twickenham-and-Southwark family, called Potkins, seems to have taken one of the Little Chelsea houses, perhaps at No. 264 Fulham Road, by 1666.[37]

Henry Middleton, himself son of a goldsmith, Sir Hugh Middleton, became the founder of a family widely propertied in America and Barbados (as well as, later, in Suffolk). It was especially prominent in South Carolina, where Henry's son became a member of the Council and his grandson Governor.[38]

To the west a small strip of ground (z on fig. 48) was probably part of the Walnut Tree Walk property of the Hobsons, with rather indeterminate limits bordering that drove-way. Its history was something of an epitome of Little Chelsea — humble late-seventeenth-century development ancillary to garden grounds, late-eighteenth-century genteel occupation, enhancement in Regency times, schoolmistressly occupation in the early Victorian period, and then absorption into the operations of a mid-Victorian building firm.

Southern Drayton Gardens and Thistle Grove Area

Drayton Gardens southward of Nos. 39 and 56 has a much more varied appearance than that part owned by the Day family to the north (see page 156), essentially because this southern portion was sold off by its owner in the early nineteenth century for development by numerous individual freeholders. The area described here also comprises, south of the line indicated, the west side of Thistle Grove and the east side of Cresswell Place, and also Fulham Road between Thistle Grove and Cavaye Place.

This long but comparatively narrow piece of ground (d on fig. 48) was part of the twelve acres of land, extending northward from a frontage between Thistle Grove and Holmes Place and formerly belonging to Sir Michael Warton, that was sold in 1786 by Richard and Henry Holland (see page 163). The new owner, who was associated in the purchase with a bricklayer, Thomas Moseley of Woolwich, was John Groves, gentleman, of Chelsea Park — a large house with grounds, south of the Fulham Road on the site of Elm Park Gardens.[16] Some four or five small houses had stood here in the seventeenth century, probably including one of Little Chelsea's first alehouses (see above). Groves evidently rebuilt them as half a dozen small houses, called Groves' Rents, but these were pulled down in 1810 by his son George Groves,[9] and it was the latter, then of Bristol, esquire, who laid out the southern two thirds of Drayton Gardens and short cross-streets in 1811-12.[39]

In his *Description of Chelsea* published in 1810 Thomas Faulkner noted 'a new street in building' at Little Chelsea, 'which, when finished, will open a direct communication with Earl's Court; an improvement much wanted'.[40] It is not clear whether this already refers to Groves's new road, or to Seymour Walk. In any event Groves's road continued to end abruptly against the undeveloped land of the Day family until an extension to Old Brompton Road known as Drayton Grove was made on that estate in the 1840's.

Groves's road was immediately known as Thistle Grove.[9] In 1865 that name was extended northward, replacing Drayton Grove, and in 1884 the whole street was renamed Drayton Gardens. In 1907 its former name Thistle Grove was, confusingly, given to the old footpath extending behind its east side, formerly distinguished as Thistle Grove Lane.

At its southern end Groves's property was narrower than throughout most of its length by reason of Sir James Pennyman's sale in 1781 of what is now the western part of the ABC cinema site.[14] In 1812 and 1813 Groves disposed of the western part of his inheritance to James Gunter (the Milborne Grove, Harley Gardens and Gilston Road area[41]) and Charles Harwood (the Cavaye Place area[42]). This left an area reckoned as about six and a quarter acres for the 'Drayton Gardens' development.

Here Groves departed from the method usual in central London, that is, granting building leases, and instead sold off the property fronting his road in lots. His layout plan envisaged some sixty of these, but the sales were actually made in larger units numbering thirty-five in all. They were effected in the years 1811-15.[43]

Only four significant sale prices are known.[44] This very slight evidence suggests they may have been calculated, for the greater part of the road's length, at rates between about £1 13s. and £2 4s. per foot of frontage, according to the depth of plot. If so, Groves's sales perhaps yielded him something of the order of £3,800.

The purchasers numbered twenty-five, of whom eleven were building tradesmen.* The fourteen others included six 'gentlemen' or 'esquires', a baker, a cordwainer (with whom a cheesemonger was associated in the purchase), a farrier, a harness-maker, a soda-water-manufacturer, a stable-keeper, an upholsterer and a victualler.

Of these, the ratebooks suggest that only the carpenter Cumming and three of the other purchasers actually occupied the houses (numbering perhaps forty-three) built on their plots.

At least two building leases were granted by purchasers to Thomas Ivey of Little Chelsea, plumber — one in 1817 by the landed confectioner James Gunter[45] and one in 1821 by the representatives of the builder Engleheart, who was then deceased.[46]

Three houses appear in the ratebooks in 1814, and by 1820 the development was more or less complete (except, perhaps, for three houses on the site of No. 49 added about 1825[9]). In Drayton Gardens itself only two or three rather doubtful vestiges of this early phase seem to survive.

The layout originally gave two more cross-roads on the west side than at present, north of Nos. 58 and 100 respectively and opposite two openings on the east side. Groves sold their intended sites in 1815 to the adjacent landowner, James Gunter, and probably neither was ever made.[47]

Some residents were John Burke, the originator of the *Peerage*, in 1825-31 (at No. 88), Captain (Sir) T. L. Mitchell, the Australian explorer, in 1826 (No. 83), Douglas Jerrold, the writer, in 1834-6 (near Nos. 80 and 82), the watercolourist William Cowen in 1843-60 (near Nos. 60-68 even) and the literary divine, the Reverend W. H. Brookfield, in 1858-60 (No. 63).[48]

The first building period showed a varied type of development, with big or biggish detached houses in gardens, semi-detached houses of medium and small size, and a few short runs of terraces. On the west side most houses stood forward on or near the street frontage but sometimes presented only a back-front to the street, facing westward over their garden.[49] On the east side some stood back where their plots abutted on Thistle Grove (Lane). In 1829 Faulkner called it all 'pleasantly situated'.[50]

It is possible that the author of the layout was the architect and surveyor William Inwood (c. 1771-1843), who in 1835 gave evidence about rights of way with reference to the private cross-roads originally intended and said he had 'been for some time the surveyor to the said estate'.[51]

Towards the south-east end of Drayton Gardens the 'back-frontages' now numbered 9A-F Thistle Grove seem to retain some early if altered work. (Nearby, at the southern junction of Thistle Grove with Roland Gardens, are two fluted cast-iron bollards with, on one of them, the parish mark and date KP 1844.)

Further south, behind Nos. 91-97 (odd) Drayton Gardens, a row of small terrace houses, grouped four, three and two, actually fronts eastward as **Nos. 1-9 (consec.) Thistle Grove**, and here the original buildings survive largely unchanged in their pleasantly modest outward appearance (Plate 66b).

Of these, the central group, Nos. 5-7, was built on a plot of land granted by Groves in 1812 to the plumber John Holroyd in association with the glazier Richard Cobbett (both of Great Scotland Yard),[52] and the southern group, Nos. 1-4, on a plot granted by Groves to Holroyd in 1814 as a trustee for Joseph Stutely the younger, a bricklayer with an address near his and Cobbett's.[53] It is doubtful, however, whether Holroyd, Cobbett and Stutely were the builders, as work on these seven house-sites did not proceed immediately, and in 1816 the sites of Nos. 5-7 were sold by Holroyd and Cobbett to a cornchandler in Chelsea, William Johnson.[54] He subsequently put a surviving tablet at the northern end of No. 7 to record his ownership and dated it 1816, but his three houses do not appear in ratebooks until 1820: for many years they were called Johnson's Place.[9] The sites of Nos. 1-4 had similarly been sold by Stutely and Holroyd, in 1818, to a

*These were William Blake of Little Chelsea, bricklayer; John Cumming of Swallow Street, St. James's, carpenter or builder; George H. Engleheart of Shepherd Street, Mayfair, builder; Thomas Flack of Little Chelsea, bricklayer; Thomas C. Green of Millbank, painter; John Holroyd of Great Scotland Yard, plumber; John Jones of Tothill Street, plumber; Joseph Stutely the younger of Northumberland Street, St. Martin in the Fields, bricklayer; Robert Todd of David Street, St. Marylebone, bricklayer; James Watts of Horseferry Road, builder; and William Wright of Carnaby Street, smith. Two other building tradesmen occur as trustees for purchasers — Richard Cobbett of Great Scotland Yard, glazier (for Holroyd) and George Warren of Grosvenor Street, Mayfair, carpenter (for Todd).

Thomas Thwaites of St. Pancras, but a solicitor living in Queen Anne's Gate, John Robinson, was a party to the sale and a few weeks later witnessed a 999-year lease of the site to William Blake of Little Chelsea, bricklayer. (Blake had already acquired the site of No. 65 Drayton Gardens for building.)[55] By 1819 Blake had bought Nos. 3 and 4 Thistle Grove,[56] and in 1820, when Nos. 1 and 2 also appear in the ratebooks, assigned his long lease to Robinson.[57] The latter's name was for some years given to these four houses[9] and is commemorated by the tablet lettered ROBINSONs PLACE 1820 surviving on No. 1. Blake may well have been the builder of Nos. 1-4 as well as of Johnson's Nos. 5-7: in 1820 he began to build extensively on the Lee estate in the Clareville Grove area of Old Brompton, where he evidently had a connexion with Johnson as some houses built by him about 1830-2 there were called Johnson's Cottages, seemingly after William Johnson or his son Thomas.[58] That Blake was sponsored in Thistle Grove by Johnson and Robinson together is perhaps hinted at by Johnson's taking the newly built No. 3, one of Robinson's houses, evidently for a relation.[59] In

their simple way the houses in the Clareville Grove area and here resemble each other.

The site of Nos. 8 and 9 Thistle Grove was sold by Groves to Robert Todd, a bricklayer of St. Marylebone, with whom a carpenter, George Warren, was associated in the transaction.[60] This was in 1811, but the two houses facing Thistle Grove do not appear in occupation until 1828.[9]

At the back of Nos. 5-7 Thistle Grove, abutting on Drayton Gardens, Johnson built a warehouse, coach-house and stables. On his death he left this portion, unlike the three dwelling houses, to his son Thomas, also a cornchandler, who in 1840 had the present semi-detached pair of westward-facing houses, **Nos. 93 and 95 Drayton Gardens,** built on the site (fig. 49). He set out this fact and his ownership on two surviving stone tablets, one at each gate.[61] (His neighbouring owner at No. 91, G. H. Rodman, had also fixed two small stone tablets, which similarly survive, dated 1817 and 1816, at his north and south boundaries.)

The only likely remains of the first building period in

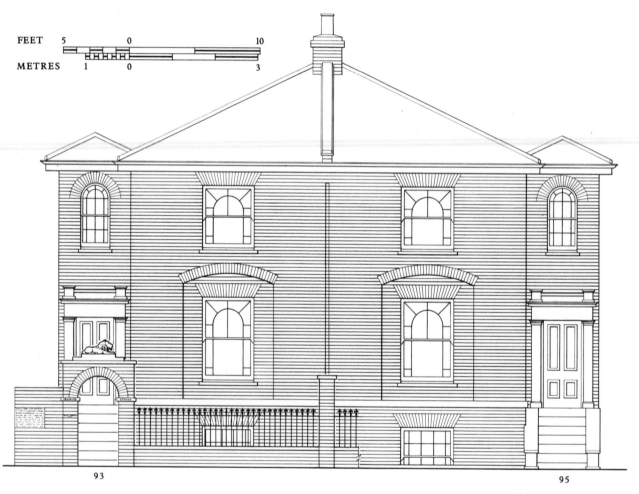

Fig. 49. Nos. 93 and 95 Drayton Gardens, elevation, 1840. Wall and gate in front of No. 95 not shown

Drayton Gardens itself are at **Nos. 58, 61 and 102**, which perhaps retain some original fabric of 1819, 1826 and 1817 respectively.[9] At **No. 63** what may be a rebuilding of about 1854[9] survives with its outer bays strangely visible behind a later block of flats.

Otherwise the present appearance of Drayton Gardens dates from *c.* 1878 onwards. At **Nos. 71-77 (odd)** (W. Toten, builder) and **60-68 (even)** (C. Hunt, builder) short rows of uniform, medium-sized terrace-houses date from 1878-9 and 1882 respectively.[62] The former development included **Holly Mews** at the back.

A more attractive and ambitious group, on a piece of ground owned by Robert Gunter, was built in 1885-9 at **Nos. 76-86 (even) Drayton Gardens**, with stable buildings (now converted) at **Nos. 18 and 21-22 Cresswell Place** behind them (Plate 69a, b, fig. 50). Although terrace houses they are quite large and picturesquely designed. Nos. 76-78 and 84-86 Drayton Gardens and the converted stables in Cresswell Place are similar in their tile-hung Surrey style, and were leased in 1885-6 to William Knight, builder, of Sussex Place, except for No. 86 Drayton Gardens, where the lessee was the builder, Edward Deacon, senior, of Milborne Grove. Deacon was in 1889 the lessee of the intervening Nos. 80-82, which are of slightly different style.[63] The architect of Knight's buildings in Cresswell Place was H. Phelps Drew, whose work here was publicized by *The Building News*. For one year at that time, in 1886, he shared Knight's address in Sussex Place (now part of Old Brompton Road), and it may therefore be surmised that the connexion extended to his designing at least Knight's Drayton Gardens houses also. But if so *The Building News* does not mention the fact.[64] The possibility that Robert Gunter's surveyors, George and Henry Godwin (the former of whom died in 1888), had a hand in these houses, cannot be wholly ruled out, but it would be a surprising extension of the styles sponsored by them on his property further west in the previous decades.

The first occupant of No. 86 Drayton Gardens, in 1888, was Sir Evan MacGregor, the Admiralty administrator, and of No. 82, in 1891, the scientist, the eighth and last Earl of Berkeley.[65]

Thenceforward the story is chiefly of blocks of flats, which characterize this part of Drayton Gardens more than surrounding areas. The existence of single house-sites here of a size large enough to accommodate a worthwhile development doubtless encouraged this tendency. The first block of flats was at **No. 57**, built, to a modest height, in 1886, followed by the taller **No. 55** of *c.* 1887. These were erected on sites recently bought by an architect, John Halley, with the backing of a stockbroker in Glasgow, R. H. Fraser, the two being 'joint adventurers' in the undertaking, for which Halley was probably, therefore, the architect.[66] Thereafter the blocks of flats were bigger. **Nos. 49-51, 53 and 59** (J. Norton, architect, Plate 68c, d)[67] and **No. 63** (front building) and **Priory Mansions** (C. J. C. Pawley, architect, Plate 68b) date from 1894-8,[68] and

Drayton Court (also Pawley) and **Grove Court** (probably A. Blackford, architect) from 1901-2.[69] There seems to have been some interest on the part of architects in sites here merely as investments. Nos. 55 and 57 were bought in 1893 by the architect Arthur Cawston,[70] and at Drayton Court the owner with whom Pawley agreed in 1901 to take from her a ninety-nine-year building lease at £230 per annum was the wife of the architect W. H. Collbran. She had bought the site, occupied by a large house in its garden, in 1897 for £5,800, whereas in 1844 it had sold for £1,600.[71] The pleasant rebuilding in 1901-2 of No. 89 — set back from the street front and in 1980 largely concealed by the building of No. 87 — was carried out for its owner and occupant, the architect F. E. Williams, who remained here until his death in 1929.[72] Whether or not he designed this rebuilding he did design (as of Williams and Cox) the projecting central bay added in 1922.[73] The same firm designed the three plain neo-Queen Anne houses at **Nos. 70-74 (even)**, built in 1925-6.[74] (These occupied a site that had stood vacant since the demolition in the 1880's of Grove Lodge, a long low house with rooms ranged all to face westward over its garden, where a large vinery was built, probably in 1863-4.[75]) At the same period (1926-7) a single house was built at **No. 100** (E. Schaufelberg, architect),[76] but more blocks of flats followed, all in 1933-5 — **No. 88** and **Warner House, Priory Walk** (Austin Blomfield, architect),[77] **Onslow Court** (J. Stanley Beard and Clare, later Beard and Bennett),[78] and **Donovan Court** (Ward, Hoare and Wheeler).[79]

In recent years some small houses have been built on street-frontages where the existing houses lay back from the street, for example at **No. 97c** (1958, Anthony Mauduit, architect), **No. 97** (1970, Lincoln and Miller, architects, project architect R. N. D. Kidd[80]), and **No. 87** (1980-1, C. J. G. Guest, architect[81]). At **No. 25 Cresswell Place** the garage-and-studio-flat dates from 1970 (Douglas Norwood and Associates, architects).[82]

The commercial garage at **Nos. 67 and 69 Drayton Gardens** was established, at No. 69, in 1910 and rebuilt in 1963 (T. W. Saunders, architect). It includes the former site of a chapel erected at No. 67 by J. Williamson, builder, in 1881 for a congregation of Baptists, which remained there until *c.* 1940.[83] The **Paris Pullman Cinema** was established at No. 65, as the Radium Picture Playhouse, in 1910-11 by the conversion of a 'gymnasium or school of arms', previously (from 1890) a dancing school.[84]

The unsightly **Nos. 134-140A (even) Fulham Road** were built as Elm Park Parade in 1888, on a site occupied since 1828 as a doctor's surgery and residence (one of the numerous houses in Brompton that took 'Grove' into its name). The freeholder was Arnold Gabriel of Bayswater, evidently a property speculator, and the building lessee William Mitchell of Kilburn, a civil engineer:[85] the architect is not known. The **ABC cinema** (Plate 73a) was built partly on the site of Nos. 106-110 (even) Drayton Gardens and extends in its western half as far as Cavaye Place over

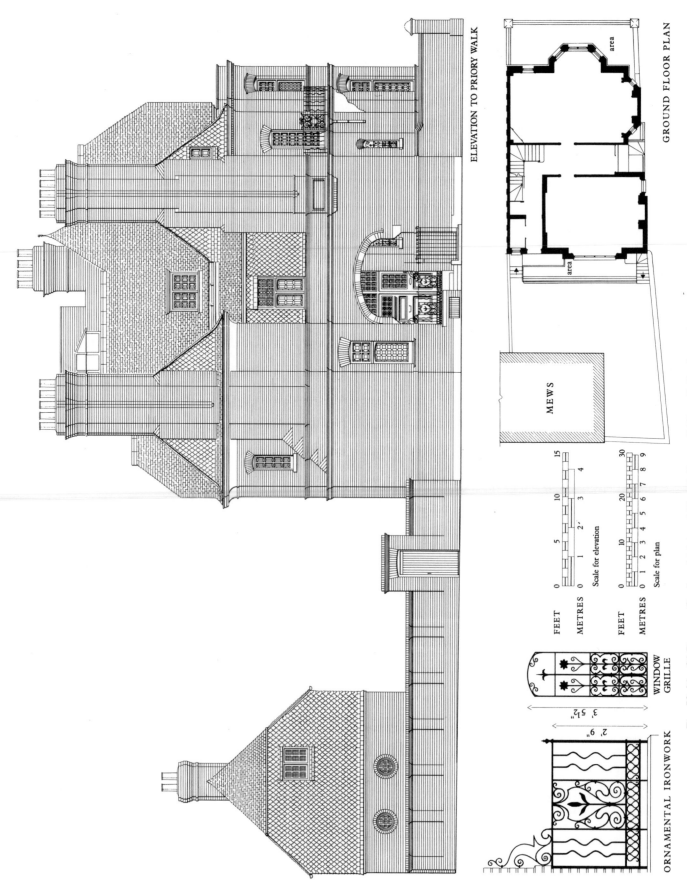

ELEVATION TO PRIORY WALK

GROUND FLOOR PLAN

MEWS

area

area

FEET
METRES   Scale for elevation

FEET
METRES   Scale for plan

WINDOW
GRILLE   3' 5½"

ORNAMENTAL IRONWORK   2' 9"

Fig. 50. No. 86 Drayton Gardens (right) and No. 18 Cresswell Place (left), plan and elevations to Priory Walk, 1885-6

the site of a development older than Drayton Gardens called Schofield Place; that is, westward of the main area described above. It was built and opened in 1930 as the Forum cinema. The architects for H. A. Yapp, the owner of this and other Forum-cinema sites, were J. Stanley Beard and Clare.[86]

Schofield Place

The western part of the ABC cinema site (c on fig. 48) obliterated a small area that had probably not been radically reconstructed since an early date. In 1781 it belonged to Sir James Pennyman, who in that year sold it to Robert Sc(h)ofield, a coachmaker. A row of three houses, later called Schofield Place, stood well back from the road, and there was also a carpenter's and wheeler's shop on the ground.[87] Buildings in this area had been occupied since the late seventeenth century.[88] Salway's view of 1811 (Plate 72) shows the houses with what looks like a canopied entrance to the premises of William Toby, a broker.[89] In 1830 Schofield's son sold the property to a flock manufacturer: the site then included a mill and mill-houses.[90] There had been a flock factory here, probably at the rear of the site, since at least 1811, and it was succeeded by a dye works in 1848 until c. 1916.[91]

Cavaye Place and Nos. 152-176 (even) Fulham Road

The name Cavaye Place has since 1937 denoted both a right-angled street leading northward from the Fulham Road and a larger rectangular area into which that street opens at the end of its western arm, and which also communicates at the south-west corner with Fulham Road through an archway (fig. 51). Before 1937, however, the area of Cavaye Place and the properties fronting Fulham Road immediately to its south had formed two distinct parts with separate building histories since their first development in the 1780's and 1790's. The eastern included the present Nos. 1-3 and 24-28 (consec.) Cavaye Place and Nos. 152-156 (even) Fulham Road; and the right-angled street, then called Clifton Place, was a cul-de-sac closed at the western boundary of Nos. 3 and 24 by the backs of buildings in the western part, then called Chelsea Grove. When the two parts were united in 1937-8 they were given their present name to commemorate a former Mayor of Kensington, Major-General W. F. Cavaye.[92]

Despite this separate development the whole area discussed here was in a single freehold ownership during its early building phase and until 1846, when sales made by the then owner inaugurated in both parts a new phase of building or rebuilding, some of which survives.

Until 1784 the whole area shared the history of the land to the east — that is, ownership by Sir James

Pennyman, sixth baronet, as successor to the heirs of Sir Michael Warton (d. 1725), and sale in 1781 to the Fulham builder, Henry Holland.[93] It was at that time largely undeveloped in building except for one or two houses and an alehouse in Fulham Road described as 'new' in 1768[94] and formed part of an area of a little over six acres, probably (as later) nursery ground, in the occupation of a James Russell. In 1784, however, Holland leased the one acre now under discussion for sixty-one years to James Naunton, a Chelsea victualler probably at the Goat in Boots on the opposite side of the Fulham Road. (Naunton also owned property a little further west.)[95]

The history of the freehold is that two years later, in 1786, after Holland's death, his sons sold it, together with larger areas to the north and east, to John Groves of Chelsea Park, and that Groves's son George, at the time he was beginning to develop Drayton Gardens, sold it in 1813 to an auctioneer of Grosvenor Row, Charles Harwood, whose representatives retained it until 1846.[96]

When Naunton had received his lease in 1784 the site contained a wheeler's or wheelwright's shop, which stood near the east end, probably at the approximate site of No. 154 or 156 Fulham Road. The other features were 'three small gardens', a bowling green and a skittle ground.[97] These last were in the western part, and the open area which still partly survives commemorates them. So too, perhaps, does the lower ground level here than in the right-angled roadway to the east. In view of Naunton's trade, the bowling green and skittle ground were perhaps associated with a public house, and then with the 'new room' built about 1791, which seems soon to have become known as a 'ball room'.[42] The latter was probably on the site of the present No. 4 Gilston Road.

In 1793 Naunton sub-leased this little suburban Cockaigne for £150 to the owners of the Stag brewery at Pimlico, John Elliot and Sir John Call, who promptly leased back to him a strip fronting Fulham Road, where

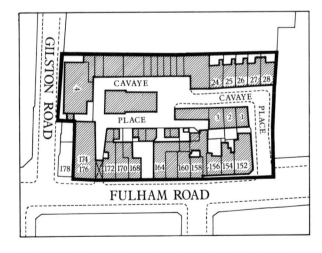

Fig. 51. Cavaye Place, Fulham Road. Based on the Ordnance Survey of 1949-63, with modern street numbers

Naunton built in 1793-5 a terrace of eight small weather-boarded cottages called Bowling Green Row.[98] He himself now had premises there.[99] The row is shown, on the present sites of Nos. 158-170 (even) Fulham Road, in Salway's view of 1811 (Plate 72).[89] By then, however, more changes were commencing in this western part of the area. In 1810 the then owners of the Stag brewery sub-leased the bowling green and its surroundings to Christopher Fryer of Little Chelsea, builder.[100] In 1810-11 Fryer built some twenty-five small, brick, tile-roofed terrace cottages chiefly on the north and south sides of the bowling green, called Fryer's Grove.[101] It was also presumably he who in c. 1810-11 built the stuccoed brick houses at what are now Nos. 174 and 176 Fulham Road, which are shown brand-new in Salway's view, together with No. 178 to the west on an adjacent freehold property, which was evidently built at the same time (see below).[102] Then in 1812-13 Naunton's son-in-law, John Eaton of Hammersmith, painter and glazier, rebuilt half of Bowling Green Row in brick.[103] If this was 'improvement' it was not very decisively so, as in 1813 what was probably the old 'ball room' nearby was leased to soap-boilers.[104]

To continue with the history of this part, in 1846 James Savage of North Cheam, Surrey, gentleman, as executor of Charles Harwood's will, sold it (as he did also the smaller eastern part). The sites of Nos. 174 and 176 Fulham Road were bought by Edward Gingell of Barretts Court, St. Marylebone,[105] an appraiser who was at that time building further west in the Fulham Road. He pulled down Fryer's houses and built the two present houses in 1847.[106] The rest of this western part was bought by another active Kensington builder, Stephen Bird.[107] He promptly, in 1846-7, rebuilt Bowling Green Row as Clifton Terrace,[108] and of these houses Nos. 170 and 172 Fulham Road survive. The architect was John Blore (Plate 73c).[109]

Bird also did at least a little building or rebuilding in the former Fryer's Grove behind, by then renamed Chelsea Grove.[110] Here an infants' school for the new church of St. Mary, The Boltons, was built in 1848-9 on a central island site. It was probably unelaborate but was designed by that church's architect, George Godwin.[111] The school and adjacent master's house survived, latterly in other use, until the 1960's. In 1878 the school, as St. Mary's National Girls', Infant and Sunday School, was transferred, until 1939, to a new and larger building at a site, bought from Bird for £1,300, on the west side of Chelsea Grove with a frontage also to Gilston Road. The builder, at a tender of £2,447, was B. E. Nightingale of Lambeth and the architect Joseph Peacock.[112] This survives as No. 4 Gilston Road. It is a symmetrical building in a residually Gothic style which, despite unsympathetic alteration, repays attention as a good example of Peacock's vigorous and not unsophisticated architecture (Plate 95). To the front there is a buttressed centrepiece which rises to a sharp gable breaking into a high hipped roof; at the back, too, is a prominent central gable, here projecting and serving the staircase, as ranks of ascending lights reveal. All round the

school, the upper-floor windows cut curiously into the cornice. The roof is now pantiled, the stonework all painted, and there are some regrettable additions at the rear.

By the end of the century Chelsea Grove was the part of south-western Kensington to be most decidedly identifiable as an abode of poverty on Charles Booth's map of London's poor and rich.[113] In 1935 the borough of Kensington declared it a Clearance Area, and in 1936 made a Closing Order for the demolition of the houses. The north side was rebuilt in c. 1938 as garages and studios (H. J. F. Urquhart, architect).[114] These have recently been demolished, and the area is now dominated by the large block built with a recessed street frontage at Nos. 158-168 (even) Fulham Road in 1972-4 (architects, Turner Lansdown Holt and Partners).[115]

To revert to the smaller eastern part of Cavaye Place, the wheelwright's shop of 1784 was still in the same use in 1807,[116] and it is probably the southern end of this long wooden building that is shown by Salway in 1811 immediately east of Bowling Green Row.[89] Eastward again was a straight cul-de-sac (later called Farmer's Place) leading to six small cottages on its west side built in the 1790's.[9] By 1846 the southern end of the wheelwright's shop was a public house, the Builders' Arms, and the small irregular timber buildings shown by Salway in 1811 east of the entrance to Farmer's Place were a cooperage and a baker's shop.[117]

In 1846 this little rectangle of land was bought from James Savage, as Harwood's executor, by a poulterer in Knightsbridge, William Aley or Ayley,[117] who completely changed the layout. A new street, soon called Clifton Place, was made along the eastern boundary, turning west to butt against the back of Chelsea Grove. Nos. 152-156 (even) Fulham Road were built in 1849-50, No. 152 as a public house, the Clifton Arms, which it remained until 1971. The builders were E. Underhill and his successors, Seal and Jackson, of King's Road, Chelsea.[118] In 1853 Nos. 1-3 (consec.) Cavaye Place were erected by Edmund Mesher, builder, of Chelsea.[119] The architect of these old-fashioned-looking buildings was again John Blore.[109] It was as late as 1863-4 that Nos. 24-28 (consec.) Cavaye Place were erected by George Symons of Brompton, builder, in the simplest (and even more outdated) of styles: this was under eighty-year leases from F. W. Aley and A. C. C. Beer or Bere of Thurloe Place, gentlemen:[120] the architect is not known. The Metropolitan Board of Works limited their height to the width of the roadway, that is twenty-two feet, and rejected Symons's request to build Nos. 27 and 28 higher 'having regard to the close proximity of the surrounding Houses, and to the Street being without a second entrance.'[121] As a result, these little houses are now dominated by the unpleasingly bare and high brick wall of the ABC Cinema, which extends along the whole of the north-south roadway on its east side. All these buildings in Cavaye Place and Fulham Road survive, Nos. 24-28 Cavaye Place with 'jalousies' added in 1938 (Plate 73b).[122]

Nos. 178-188A (even) Fulham Road, Holmes Place and Nos. 3, 3A, 5 and 5A Gilston Road

This small area is of mixed and rather undistinguished character, reflecting a fragmented historical development that is complicated out of proportion to the interest of the buildings upon it (fig. 52). Originally the area was part of the Warton family property and in 1781, like the land to the north and east, was sold by Sir James Pennyman to the builder Henry Holland[15](see above). Four brick houses already stood on or near the Fulham Road frontage (approximately on the sites of the later Nos. 182-188 even Fulham Road) and may have dated from or been enhanced in *c.* 1776-7.[9] Richardson's map of Chelsea in 1769 and ratebooks suggest there were buildings here before then. These four houses can be seen on Salway's view of 1811, together with a fifth, corner, house at the east end, which may have been reconstructed in 1781-2[9] and occupied a site, later numbered 180 Fulham Road, now mostly taken into Gilston Road (Plate 72). The fact that the westernmost pair of the group (later Nos. 186 and 188) had previously been one house, as a deed of 1786 states, is discernible.[89] (The same may, apparently, be true of the easternmost pair.) Also conspicuous is the adjacent gateway to the east, where the southern end of Gilston Road now opens from the Fulham Road and which led to the nurseries owned at the time of Salway's view by William Pamplin and earlier, in the 1780's, by James Russell.[123]

The greater part of this piece of property, extending north to include the later sites of Nos. 3 and 5 Gilston Road, was taken out of the larger area held by the Holland family in 1786, when Richard and Henry Holland (the elder Henry's sons) disposed of it by sale. The purchaser was a Jeffery Holmes of Kensington, later described as a 'gentleman'.[124] Holmes's acquisition included, on the east side of the passageway northward, the site of **No. 178 Fulham Road** (F on fig. 52), which was then a garden and was built upon in 1810-11, probably by the builder Christopher Fryer (see above). This house may survive in the present building after alteration in 1848.[102] Holmes did not, however, acquire an east-facing house or cottage on the western side of the passageway, approximately on the northern part of the present corner site, the passageway itself, or a small plot on its east, now numbered 2 Gilston Road. This part (D on fig. 52) continued to be held by the owner of the nursery to the north.[17] The nurseryman Pamplin's name on the overthrow of the gateway as shown in Salway's view proclaims this ownership.

In 1789 Holmes made an agreement with a carpenter, Henry Hicks of Marshall Street, Carnaby Market, by which Hicks was to construct three houses standing back

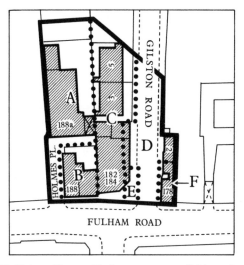

Fig. 52. Holmes Place, with former property divisions shown by dotted lines. Based on the Ordnance Survey of 1949-62

behind the Fulham Road frontage, on the north side of what became known as Holmes Place. They were built by 1790 and leased to Hicks in that year, together with the two rather older houses (formerly one) on the sites of Nos. 186 and 188 Fulham Road (then called Nos. 1 and 2 Holmes Row) (A and B on fig. 52). A witness to these transactions was the surveyor and architect, George Cloake, of St. Martin('s) Street, Leicester Fields, and another was John Field, carpenter, of King Street, Seven Dials.*[126]

In 1812 the house or cottage on the west side of the passageway, the passageway itself, and the small plot on its east (D on fig. 52) were bought, as part of the larger area of nursery ground to the north, from George Groves (see page 167) by James Gunter.[41] In 1851 his son Robert Gunter had a house called Bolton (or, briefly, Gilston) Lodge erected by the Islington builder John Glenn on the site of the cottage and another smaller building put up on the small plot on the opposite side of the passageway. A plan submitted by Glenn to the Metropolitan Commissioners of Sewers suggests that these buildings, joined by quadrant walls to a perhaps improved or regularized version of the old gateway, may have been intended as a somewhat formal 'entrance' to Robert Gunter's newly building Gilston Road and The Boltons beyond.[127] In the event the gateway seems to have disappeared.[128] Bolton Lodge, however, (on a site now obliterated by a widening of Gilston Road) was occupied from 1860 to 1871 by Robert Gunter's land agent, James Knowles, esquire, who also, or perhaps primarily, operated from Gunter's house, Wetherby Grange, in Yorkshire.[129]

In 1821 Holmes's heirs sold off, to Luke Flood of Chelsea, esquire, the two houses on the corners of the opening northward (the sites of No. 178 and the former

*Parties involved in mortgages by Hicks of this property in 1790 were John Feast of Cheshunt, Hertfordshire, carpenter, Jacob Holme of Warwick Street, St. James's, Westminster, timber merchant and Thomas Mann of Jermyn Street, bricklayer.[125]

No. 180 Fulham Road, E and F on fig. 52);[130] and in 1865 the sites of Nos. 182 and 184 Fulham Road and their northern hinterland (C on fig. 52) were sold to Robert Gunter's son Robert.[131] On this hinterland, north-west of Bolton Lodge, he had a pair of east-facing semi-detached houses, Nos. 3 and 5 Gilston Road, erected in 1871 by the builders Benjamin and Thomas Bradley.[132] (The Bradleys, who had taken building leases from him ten years before, in Harley Gardens and Milborne Grove, had their own premises close by, at No. 180 Fulham Road, from 1860 to 1893.[133]) Nothing is known of the authorship of this pair of houses, belatedly completing the development of Gilston Road, unless they are supposed to be an uncharacteristic work of Robert Gunter's surveyors, George and Henry Godwin. In 1974 demolition of these houses was begun, but after the intervention of the Borough they were rebuilt in 1980 behind the existing elevations as four 'town houses' numbered 3, 3A, 5 and 5A Gilston Road.[134]

In Fulham Road the five houses at Nos. 180-188 each contained a shop where the tenants from 1861 to 1888 were very stable. For twenty-eight years the quintet of happy families — Mr. Bradley's the builder, Mr. Floyd's the grocer, Mr. Wayt's the fishmonger, Mr. Chapman's the bootmaker and Mr. Padbury's the fruiterer — remained unchanging.[133]

Robert Gunter acquired in 1881 Holmes Place itself and its three houses (A on fig. 52).[135] These were rebuilt in 1902 by Frederick Humpherson, sanitary engineers, for their own premises, and survive as No. 188A Fulham Road. This shows no sign of the influence of Walter Cave, who about that time became Gunter's surveyor.[136] Nos. 186 and 188 Fulham Road (Plate 73d) are of uncertain date and may represent a late-nineteenth-century heightening and refacing of an older building. Robert Gunter extended his Fulham Road frontage when he bought the lease of No. 178 and the former No. 180 in 1887, subsequently acquiring the freeholds.[137] At the corner of Gilston Road the present Nos. 182 and 184 Fulham Road were rebuilt to designs by Gale, Heath and Sneath, architects, for W. H. Cullen, grocers, in 1936-7, when most of the site of No. 180 Fulham Road was taken for widening the southern end of Gilston Road and setting back the building line at this corner.[138]

Nos. 190-210 (even) Fulham Road, and Redcliffe Road and Bolton Studios

The buildings and layout of this area of some three and three quarter acres, which extends northward from Fulham Road the length of Redcliffe Road, date entirely from 1860 onwards (E on fig. 48). There were houses on and near the frontage to Fulham Road, however, in the seventeenth century, and although the history of the area before the 1770's is obscure at least one of the early houses

was well-inhabited and substantial. It is shown in Salway's view of 1811 (Plate 72) situated west of what is now Redcliffe Road behind a garden of ornamental trees and shrubs, with a flat front towards Fulham Road seemingly of late-seventeenth or early-eighteenth-century date.[89] A list of fixtures in 1776 tells us it then had four rooms on each of its two main floors over a basement, six garrets in the roof, and two staircases. The best staircase was of wood, and was decorated with 'History Painting' and 'Architraves painted to imitate Purple Marble'. All the rooms were panelled, some with 'small' or 'square' work, but in two rooms the panels were by then papered over. Some rooms had chimneypieces of various marbles — Dove, Plymouth, purple or white-and-veined — and some chimneypieces had 'tabernacle frames over them'. At the 'Top of the House' was 'an Alarm Bell with a Rope to the Bottom'.[139] In the previous year, 1775, it had been briefly occupied by the head of the Anglo-American family which had earlier owned a larger area hereabouts. This occupant was William Middleton (1710-75), a native of South Carolina, whose father had been Governor of the province and whose family was extensively landed both in North America and in the county of Suffolk. William died in the same year 1775, and his younger son Thomas, to whom he left the Little Chelsea property, disposed of the house on lease in 1776, being then resident at Charleston. (A month or two later his cousin Arthur was a signatory of the Declaration of Independence.)[140] The Middletons' ownership of this piece of property probably went back to the 1660's (see page 165), but the big house was generally occupied by others, although John Harwood, doubtless the Middletons' wealthy relation by marriage, was there from 1710 to 1724 or later.[88] In 1765-6 it was the residence of Admiral Richard Tyrrell,[88] and earlier occupants included the fourth Baron Berkeley of Stratton in the period c. 1732, 1736-7,[141] Edward Fowler, Bishop of Gloucester, in 1707-10, and Admiral the Marquess of Carmarthen (later second Duke of Leeds) in 1704-7.[88] In 1698-c. 1704 the occupant was a Mr. Chauvil or Chauvin — possibly related to the Mrs. Chauvin who in 1707 kept a ladies' boarding school of good standing at Chelsea.[142] In 1695-7 the resident was Sir Edward Ward, Chief Baron of the Exchequer.[88] In 1693-4 it was Henry Webb, esquire,[143] and before that a Mr. or Mrs. Webb were assessed here back to 1673.[144] In c. 1662-71 the occupant[145] can be identified with the Thomas Maundy who a little earlier had had a range of brick houses built further west and joined in the sale of property in that area in 1664 to William Middleton's great-grandfather, Henry (see page 165).

After the Middletons' disposal of the house in 1776 the ratepayers for many years were women. Possibly it was occupied as a school from that date, and probably was so from 1793. In that year Sarah Cannon, who certainly conducted a ladies' boarding school here in the early nineteenth century, entered into occupation until the year 1826.[146]

In 1807 the representatives of Thomas Middleton's heirs sold the large house and the whole area to Samuel Batchellor of Hamswell House, Gloucestershire, gentleman.[147] East of the house smaller dwellings had stood on the property since the late seventeenth century.[88] Salway's view of 1811[89] shows that by then, as well as the low 'school-house' added to the side of the old residence, some shops had been built out in front of two (united) houses on what is now the Fulham Road east of Redcliffe Road. Eastward again, next to Holmes Place, stood the gable-ended precursor of the present King's Arms, a public house under that name since at least 1760.[148] Northward lay a nursery garden previously of Daniel Grimwood and then of Henry Shailer.[149] By 1835 building and subdivision had placed more shops on the front curtilage of the former two houses,[150] but no major rebuilding had been accomplished when the Batchellors sold the whole area in March 1859.[151]

The purchaser, however, was the younger George Godwin, architect, editor of *The Builder*, resident in Alexander Square, and surveyor to Robert Gunter. The latter's estate had recently been developed to the east and north of the property here discussed and on Godwin's ground development proceeded without delay, in buildings which still stand on the site. It had, indeed, already started at the time of the sale to him, with the making of foundations at the south-east end of the plot.[151] Early in 1860 Godwin obtained sanction from the Metropolitan Board of Works for the road he had laid out northwards from Fulham Road through the centre of his ground and was allowed to name it Redcliffe Road.[152] This was doubtless in reference to the church of St. Mary Redcliffe at Bristol, which he had restored, and was a name thereafter taken up for wide use hereabouts. At its northern end the road was blocked until Cathcart Road was made here a few years later.

The first buildings to be completed were on a plot at the southern end of the east side of the new road, where Godwin granted ninety-nine-year building leases in May and November 1861 to Edwin Curtis, senior, of Bayswater, builder, who erected the two houses at **Nos. 1A and 2A Redcliffe Road, houses over shops at Nos. 192-200 (even) Fulham Road and the King's Arms public house at No. 190 Fulham Road:**[153] all these survive (Plate 73d). (The King's Arms perhaps had its present ground-floor front added in 1890, when work was done under one of the most prolific of public-house architects, H. I. Newton, to a tendered price of £2,030.[154])

Despite Godwin's connexion with these buildings they show no architectural ambition or individuality. Godwin soon disposed of the rest of his property on both sides of the intended road. Nevertheless, what was then built on that property — houses lining Redcliffe Road and five others over commercial premises extending westward along the Fulham Road — show such architectural similarities to houses of the 1860's nearby, where Godwin's authorship as architect can be postulated, that

his hand must be detected here. The absence of his stylistic fingerprints from the buildings mentioned above that were directly leased by him is an unexplained curiosity.

In February 1860 Godwin sold the land on the west side of the intended road and the large old house, which since 1832 or earlier had been an asylum for destitute females and known as the Manor House,[155] to the Reverend G. F. Ballard, a Father of the Oratory.[156] Ballard wished to transfer to the house St. Philip's Orphanage for boys, which he had established late in 1857 in Chelsea.[157] Just as the Oratorians' architect, J. J. Scoles, and Godwin had both been concerned in the Oratorians' purchase of their site at Brompton in 1853, so Scoles was the intermediary in Father Ballard's purchase here and was a party to the sale by Godwin. The remainder of the east side of the intended street Godwin sold in May 1861 to S. R. Lewin,[158] who was partner with others of his family in Lewin and Company, solicitors, of Southampton Street.

It is likely that Lewins were involved in the whole development, presumably as a source, direct or indirect, of finance. One of their clerks witnessed Godwin's leases to Curtis. They promptly became Father Ballard's mortgagees (in the person of S. R. Lewin's father, Robert) on the west side of the road — ultimately for £4,200 or more:[159] it is perhaps significant that in 1851 S. R. Lewin had acted as solicitor for a more famous Oratorian, Newman, in the Achilli trial.[160] And the builders who in turn bought the sites on which the Redcliffe Road houses were built in 1861-6 were probably already their clients.

These were William Corbett and Alexander McClymont, both in 1861-2 living at addresses in Winchester Street, Pimlico, the former as an accountant, the latter as a builder and estate agent.[161] The link thus made between Godwin as architect and surveyor, Corbett and McClymont as builders and Lewin and Company as their lawyers was to be important in the creation of the south-west part of Kensington in the years 1861-78.

In the course of 1861-3 McClymont bought the sites of **Nos. 1-12 Redcliffe Road** and Corbett those of **Nos. 13-32** on the east side from S. R. Lewin, and McClymont the sites of **Nos. 34-57** on the west side from Father Ballard and Robert Lewin.[162] Each then cross-leased sites to the other,[163] and the resultant terraces of houses, newly built in these years, are virtually uniform (Plate 87a). One differentiation, however, is that on the east side the houses have paired porches and on the west side splay-sided bay windows at basement and ground level. The details resemble those on houses being built in 1862-3 by other builders at Nos. 9-14 Harley Gardens on Robert Gunter's estate, where Godwin was surveyor (Plate 84c). Elongated and heterodox console-brackets are conspicuous features of the stucco dressings which dominate the grey-brick fronts, and are very characteristic of Godwin hereabouts.

On the west side of Redcliffe Road Father Ballard retained the area south of No. 57 for his St. Philip's

Orphanage, conducted independently but with the consent of the Oratorian Congregation, until 1865.[155] In 1861 it housed seventy-two boys.[164] For its last two years at least it was run as an 'Industrial School'[165] and in 1863 a school wing was added to the front of the Orphanage, probably by James Matthews, builder.[166] Ballard left the Oratorian Congregation in 1864-5[167] and in 1865 moved the Orphanage to Kingsbury.[168] In 1865-6 he and Robert Lewin sold the site, already being redeveloped as the surviving **Nos. 58-66 (consec.) Redcliffe Road** and **Nos. 202-210 (even) Fulham Road**, to Corbett or McClymont, who again cross-leased plots in their accustomed way.[169] The five houses over a bank and shops in Fulham Road were at first named Spencer Terrace, presumably after Spencer Robert Lewin.[170] Four of them, Nos. 204-210, are virtually identical in elevational treatment with the houses over shops built in 1865-6 at Nos. 270-296 Fulham Road by Corbett and McClymont on an estate (R. J. Pettiward's) which seems to have been under Godwin's architectural influence.

Most of the sites in Redcliffe Road were soon conveyed back by Corbett and McClymont, doubtless by way of mortgage, and subject to their leases to one another, to G. F. Ballard or E. H. Ballard (also a sometime Oratorian Father) or to a Lewin (Henry, S. R., or T. E.).[171]

Corbett's later testimony, speaking of Nos. 1-14 Redcliffe Road, was that Corbett and McClymont were here (as was not invariably the case with their undertakings) the actual builders.[172]

Corbett was himself the first occupant of No. 14 Redcliffe Road from 1863 to 1869, latterly under the designation of builder.[173] McClymont occupied No. 22 in 1865-6 and then the large house at the northernmost end of the same east side, called Cathcart House, from 1867 to 1878.[155] (This last house was denuded of its trimmings in 1947-8 after war-damage.[174] For its site, which had a separate history from that of the rest of the road, see page 212.)

The leasehold and freehold properties owned by Corbett and McClymont in the road were held by them individually, and probably in part for that reason their ownerships survived the bankruptcy that overtook them in 1878. In the following year Corbett retained enough interest in the value of property there to wish to sell to sitting tenants rather than investors and to have houses painted uniformly.[175]

Redcliffe Road had originally been quite rapidly occupied, virtually all its houses being taken by 1866 (or, at the south-west end, 1868).[155] Its social composition was, however, very mixed, and in 1871 no fewer than twenty-one of the houses were in multi-occupation, six being in the hands of lodging-house keepers.[176] In 1881-93 a resident at No. 20 was Alan Cole, a senior officer of the Science and Art Department and son of Sir Henry Cole, who commented in 1881 on the 'Quaker like decoration' of his son's house.[177] Herbert Gribble, architect of the Oratory, lived at No. 64 from at least 1883, dying there in

1894.[178] In 1892, however, the Post Office Directory had begun to notice the 'apartments' in the road and by 1895 listed nine of these.[133] In the later 1920's and 1930's the west side in particular was largely devoted to 'apartments' and to houses divided as 'studios'. The artist Edward Bawden was one of the occupants of Holbein Studios at No. 52 in 1929-33 and Eric Ravilious of another there in 1930-1.[133]

Comparatively little radical change has been made in the outward aspect of the houses, although the numerous alterations made incident to repair and conversion show how little their architecture has been admired. Post-war rebuildings include Nos. 33 and 34 (with No. 1 Cathcart Road, Richard Pollock, architect) and No. 37 (Kenneth R. Smith, architect) — both in 1951-2, after war-damage.[179] (For Redcliffe Road see also pages 239-40.)

Bolton Studios

Behind the east side of Redcliffe Road a strip of land extending along all its length and adjacent on the east to the back of the properties in Gilston Road was separately granted in 1863 by S. R. Lewin to Corbett (the southern two thirds) and McClymont (the northern third): McClymont and Corbett were respectively second parties to the conveyances. Right of access south of No. 1 Redcliffe Road was also granted.[180] In 1883 the long line of Bolton Studios was begun here. The district surveyor named the 'builder' (here evidently signifying the sponsor of the enterprise) as C. Bacon of Bognor. This was doubtless the sculptor Charles Bacon, who in 1884-6 had an address at the adjacent No. 5 (now 17) Gilston Road, whence access was also provided to the studios by what is now the main (but inconspicuous) entrance at No. 17A Gilston Road. Bacon's tenure was by virtue of a lease granted him in 1884 by a Henry Pritty, gentleman, of No. 7 Redcliffe Road. After a pause, work was recommenced in 1887, when the 'builder' was named as C. Irvine Bacon, who appears at the same address, No. 17 Gilston Road and in Bolton Studios in the late 1880's.[181] These strangely hidden-away studios came into use in the years 1885-90. An early occupant, in 1889-91 at No. 14, was Alfred Sassoon, sculptor, probably the father of Siegfried.[133]

Seymour Walk and Nos. 212-226 (even) Fulham Road

The long cul-de-sac of Seymour Walk is one of the few late-Georgian survivals on the north side of the Fulham Road in Kensington, and the earliest part of it dates from the last years of the eighteenth century. Before then its site was an enclosure of walled ground extending northward for some three acres, with a substantial house upon it near the Fulham Road. This house probably existed so early as *c.* 1664, in the tenure of a Doctor John Whitaker until *c.* 1666-70, when he moved to another house nearby. In the years *c.* 1670-73 the house was rated to 'Sir John Griffin' and in 1674 was in the occupation of Sir John Rolles, Knight of the Bath. By 1681, to 1685, the occupant was John Lister, esquire, and in 1686-9 John Creed, esquire.[182]

Some time before 1682 this property seems to have been purchased from the Sir James Smith who lived on the other side of the road in Chelsea by a grocer in Covent Garden, Charles Morgan, who was also acquiring land to the north about the same time. He died in that year and in 1691 the future Seymour Walk property was in the hands of his two brothers, John and Thomas Morgan, later described as of Marlborough in Wiltshire. In 1698 a lease was held by Peter Lavigne, grocer or perfumier, who had been servant to Charles Morgan, inherited his shop in Covent Garden and been servant also to one of the surviving Morgan brothers. He proceeded to treat with them for the purchase of this property on behalf of a sub-tenant, Gibbons Bagnall, who was using it for 'planting of Greens', and of their more extensive property to the north on his own behalf. He bought the whole in 1699 for £1600 and found this Little Chelsea part of it sufficiently attractive to ignore the arrangement to resell the house and three acres for £400 to Bagnall. Lavigne and Bagnall were men of substance enough to be able to make their meeting-places 'at Tunbridge Wells upon ye Walkes' and for Bagnall subsequently to bring a Chancery suit against Lavigne. The latter was evidently successful as he continued to occupy the house from 1700 to 1711.[183] From 1712 it was, as a 'mansion house', in the occupation of a Peter Latouche, gentleman. In 1730 James Latouche bought the freehold for £735 from William Blackmore of Covent Garden, gentleman, and his wife Elizabeth, Blackmore's tenure in succession to Lavigne perhaps having a similar origin to Sir Richard Blackmore's at Coleherne House (see page 200). The family of Latouche (or de Latouche) lived here until 1789.[184] Then in January 1790 they sold this small estate to a local man, Francis Mayoss,[185] and it was he, variously described as brick-maker, builder and gentleman, who began to develop the southern end of this land in building which partly survives today.

Mayoss promptly made a mortgage of all the property to a Hugh Jones of St. Pancras, gentleman. (It was subsequently transferred to a well-known doctor, Samuel Foart Simmons.)[186] By November 1790 Mayoss had built a small two-storeyed house or shop at what is now No. 212 Fulham Road. This he leased to a glazier, David Williams of Chelsea.[187] (The present **No. 212 Fulham Road** is a rebuilding of 1889-90.[188]) By 1792 Mayoss had put up a building also at what is now No. 214 Fulham Road on the opposite corner of the off-centre street-opening northward and had named the latter Seymour Place.[189] By 1794, if not before, the building at No. 214 was a public house called the Somerset Arms,[190] a name obviously suggested by the Somerset dukedom of the

noble family of Seymour. Salway's view of 1811 (Plate 72) shows a rather striking building with three large round-headed windows closely grouped on the first floor, and amply glazed 'shop windows' on the ground floor.[89] The Somerset Arms (now **The Somerset**) was rebuilt in a plainish manner in 1881 by W. E. Williams, architect, and Robert Mair, builder — both specialists in public houses.[191]

By 1793 six more small houses or shops had been built westward (in modern terms **Nos. 216-226 even Fulham Road**), of which one probably survives vestigially at No. 226 and the rest were rebuilt in 1962 (G. D. Fairfoot, architect). Salway shows Nos. 216-220 with different elevations (of the simplest kind) from those of Nos. 222-226, and perhaps intended from the beginning to have shop fronts. For the first few years these houses in Fulham Road were known as Mayoss's Buildings or Mayoss's Rents, although Mayoss had sold-off the sites of Nos. 224 and 226 in 1792. This had been to John Terry of Wimbledon, described as a gentleman but in fact a bricklayer, who by 1797 had died bankrupt: his trustee and co-partner in the purchase was a 'surveyor', James Johnson or Johnstone of St. Marylebone.[192] Another building tradesman was Philip Seymour, also a bricklayer, who was the first occupant of No. 222 in 1794.[193]

There is no evidence that this Seymour played such an important part in the development as to have given Seymour Walk its name. A possible alternative derivation is from the William Seymour, gentleman, of Margaret Street, St. Marylebone, who witnessed the deed of sale of Mayoss's dwelling-house in 1795 and was therefore perhaps a source of money.[194]

In the parish ratebooks the houses in Fulham Road are called Seymour Row from 1826 to 1866. Seymour Walk is called Seymour Place from 1819 to 1834, when all the west side and the east side northward to No. 34 was renamed Somerset Place and the east side northward of No. 34, where the houses were slightly higher rated, Seymour Terrace.[9] All was officially renamed Seymour Place in 1866 and Seymour Walk in 1938.

At the same time as his development in Fulham Road Mayoss built dwelling houses of greater consequence behind that frontage: first (in modern terms) **No. 1 Seymour Walk**, which he himself occupied in 1793, and **No. 3** attached to it, whither he removed in the following year; and then a house on the opposite side of Seymour Walk at the site of No. 4, which was first occupied in about 1803.[195] In *c.* 1794-7 the occupant of No. 1 was Hugh Lloyd and his wife Mary, *née* Moser, the Royal Academician and flower painter.[196] From 1801 to 1805 the ratepayers at No. 3 were successively the Honourable Arabella and the Honourable Catherine Fermor.[9] Both Nos. 1 and 3 survive, although altered — the former probably most materially in 1864-6.[9] No. 3 has a good wrought-iron gate of eighteenth-century date on its north side, hung between modern piers (fig. 53).

Further from Fulham Road Mayoss built two houses at

the sites of the later Nos. 7 and 9 in about 1805, selling them a little later to Thomas Whitford, a plasterer, of Titchfield Street.[197] In the meantime Mayoss and his mortgagees, among whom was the adjacent landowner, James Gunter of Berkeley Square, had been selling off the properties Mayoss had developed, and by 1807, when he was described as of North End, Fulham, had disposed of all south of the present Nos. 11 and 14.[198] More importantly, in 1806 he and Gunter also sold all the land northward.[199] This was undeveloped except for two houses on the approximate sites of Nos. 16-18A, but the purchaser was a man of property, Thomas Chandless of York Place, Portman Square, and the construction of a street of houses northward was continued, to end in a cul-de-sac, by him. The 'jink' in the layout, to give access to the Fulham Road eastward of the main line of the street, had already been established by Mayoss.

Between 1807 and 1811 Chandless granted leases, generally for some ninety-nine years, to a number of building tradesmen. Apart from Mayoss himself at one site,[200] lessees were William Allen and William Brace of Chelsea, bricklayers,[201] John Beedle of Sloane Street, Chelsea, painter,[202] John James of Kensington, painter and glazier,[203] Thomas Johnson of St. Marylebone, builder,[204] Thomas Nutt of Buckingham Place, Fitzroy Square, stonemason,[205] John Souter, bricklayer, and Samuel Symons of Chelsea, carpenter.[206] An assignee of Mayoss's site in 1809 was John Vale of Shepherd's Market, builder. Nutt, who built at least nine houses, was bankrupt by 1811.[207] It seems clear that by these leases the houses were carried north as **Nos. 22-58 (even)** on the east side to the full extent of the property and as **Nos. 11-27 (odd)** (only) on the west.[208] The slight setting back of the building line to accommodate areas in front of the basement windows and the introduction of first-floor iron balconies, which characterize the houses northward of Nos. 25 and 34 do not betoken any break in the chronology of development (Plate 74).

Chandless himself evidently provided some of the builders' capital, as a number of the leases were accompanied by mortgages back to him.

A comment by Thomas Faulkner in 1810 on a 'new street in building' at Little Chelsea, which he expected would be carried north to Earl's Court, has already been noticed (see page 166). If he meant Seymour Walk, and not the incipient Drayton Gardens, he was overlooking the obstacles presented by the various freehold ownerships subsisting in 1810 northward of Seymour Walk, which has remained emphatically a cul-de-sac.

In 1824 the property passed to Chandless's son, Henry Gore Chandless,[209] a young man with experience of property dealings in northern Kensington.[210] In *c.* 1829-30 two minor in-fillings were made with small houses at **Nos. 14** and **20**.[9]

South of Chandless's property the present No. 5 was built in its spacious curtilage about the same time for first occupation in 1829.[9]

Seymour Walk, particularly in its more northern part, was very slow to attract residents and cannot have been accounted a success in its early days. In 1827 almost all of the houses north of No. 13 and eight of those north of No. 36 seem to have been empty. Only in the 1830's did it gradually fill up with ratepaying occupants.[9]

In 1843 the owner of the house on the site of No. 4 sold it to its occupant, William Long, a builder (who a few years earlier had erected Nos. 20-30 even Clareville Grove, Kensington[211]). It was therefore probably Long who built the present **Nos. 10 and 12** at the northern end of the garden of No. 4 in *c.* 1845.[212] At the same time a house

Fig. 53. Gateways at Nos. 2 (bottom) and 3 (top) Seymour Walk, as in 1941

was built at **No. 2** which is also probably that surviving.[9] A wrought-iron gate of the eighteenth century now gives admission to the front garden (fig. 53). Long built two houses at Nos. 6 and 8 in 1855.[213]

In 1869-70 Chandless replaced the two houses at Nos. 16 and 18 by four new ones (**Nos. 16, 16A, 18, 18A**),[9] but it was 1889-90 before he extended the western range northward with ten new houses, **Nos. 29-47 (odd)** (Plate 74b). The builder was Thomas William Haylock of Ebury Street, who was associated at Nos. 29 and 31 with William Henry Newson of Pimlico Road, timber merchant. Two of Haylock's mortgagees (each for two houses) were a Charles Saunders, esquire, of Shepherd's Bush (conceivably the surveyor of that name who had an office in Gloucester Road) and the Fourth Grosvenor Mutual Benefit Building Society.[214] Unlike the earlier houses they are of only two main storeys but are raised above higher-rising basements and set back behind wider areas. Nos. 29-35 (odd) have only a little Victorian detailing but Nos. 37-47 have more to show of their period, particularly in their shaped gables. The architect is not known.

In 1904 the builders William Willett erected **No. 3A** as 'St. Dunstan's Studio' on a vacant site, to designs by the architect C. H. B. Quennell. The owners and first occupants were the metal-workers Omar Ramsden and Alwyn Carr:[215] the former made the cross and candlesticks for the altar of St. Mary, The Boltons.

At the northern end of the west side **Nos. 49-53 (odd)** were built in 1964-5 (architects, Cotton, Ballard and Blow).[216]

The social character of Seymour Walk was very mixed. An 'academy' or school was established at one of the bigger houses, No. 1, from 1821 until c. 1939, and in the 1820's and 1830's the smaller houses had a sprinkling of 'poor', 'very poor' and 'run' noted against them in the parish books by the rate collectors. Douglas Jerrold lived at No. 46 in 1832-4.[155] The Reverend Elias Huelin (whose son was latterly headmaster of the Western Grammar School in North Terrace) occupied No. 24 in 1838-68: he owned adjacent houses also, and when he died aged eighty-four in 1870, murdered by an employee at a house he owned in Chelsea, was described as a 'French protestant clergyman, assistant chaplain at the Brompton Cemetery . . . , the owner of considerable house property'.[217]

In 1848 there was a jeweller at No. 36, a ladies' school at No. 26, and a builder at No. 4 (which was later occupied for many years by chimney-sweeps). There was also an 'architect' (George Howard) at No. 27 in 1846-58. Other architects were J. W. Maye at No. 40 in 1852-6, John Butler at No. 38 in 1858-69 (before moving to Redcliffe Gardens) and W. H. Lamborn at No. 15 in 1870-84. In 1913-14 there were builders or building tradesmen at Nos. 8, 21, 49 and 56, artists at Nos. 3A, 5 and 9, and a lady doctor at No. 2.[155]

Except for post-war buildings at **Nos. 4-8 (even), 7-11,** 15 and 49-53 (odd), Seymour Walk retains much of its old appearance, and in 1980 numbered a duke among its residents.

Nos. 228-234 (even) Fulham Road

Four houses and shops comprising the present Nos. 228-232 Fulham Road and a demolished building numbered 234 were built in 1865-6. The application to the Metropolitan Board of Works was made by A. B. Smith, a builder of hot-houses who had premises east of Thistle Grove.[218] Since about 1833 the site, which extended backward for some 390 feet to comprise about an acre, had been occupied successively by William Foy and his son Henry Francis Foy, the owners of a school at No. 1 Seymour Walk, which in its rear premises abutted on this plot. Smith's application was on behalf of H. F. Foy, who in 1866 acquired the freehold.[219] Latterly there had been a house on the Fulham Road frontage, converted from a coach-house and stables built here in about 1810 by the occupant of No. 266 Fulham Road, who held the acre plot from 1808 to 1824. In 1805 and 1806 it had been held successively by the ladies who ran a girls' school at No. 264 Fulham Road. It is first recognizable in the ratebooks, as walled-in garden ground, in 1795, when it was owned by a Robert Robinson.[220]

At the northern end of the site a 'warehouse' was built in 1880 to the design of Owen Lewis, architect, and first occupied by the Salutaris Water Company.[221] British Telecommunication's Chelsea Telephone Service Centre was built, as the present No. 234 Fulham Road, at the rear of Nos. 228-232, in 1970-5 (architects, C. Frank Timothy Associates) and opened in 1976.[222]

Nos. 236A-D Fulham Road and Brompton Cottages at No. 1C Hollywood Road

In 1971-2 dwellings over shops were built at the east corner of Fulham Road and Hollywood Road (architects, Ian Fraser and Associates, renamed Turner Lansdown Holt and Partners) and numbered as above. Brompton Cottages, at first-floor level, are approached by steps from Hollywood Road. The ground floor was converted for use as a branch of Barclays Bank in 1976-7 (architects, Paton Orr and Partner).[223]

Previously, the site had been occupied by three houses over shops, numbered 236, 238 and 238A Fulham Road. They were built in 1869 under ninety-nine-year leases granted by James Gunter to William Corbett or Alexander McClymont which ran from Christmas 1863,[224] like the leases of the adjacent houses in the newly built Hollywood Road laid out by Corbett and McClymont on the line of Hollywood Grove. They marked the only place where

James or Robert Gunter's building campaigns in Kensington reached the Fulham Road.

Prior to 1725 a piece of property of some three and a half acres, extending northward from this narrow Fulham Road frontage to a boundary between the present Cathcart and Tregunter Roads, was owned, like a larger area further east, by Sir Michael Warton and ultimately was sold by Sir James Pennyman to the builder Henry Holland in 1781 (see page 163). At that time the property was occupied by Henry de Latouche, the owner of the Seymour Walk area.[15] Like the other parts of the former Warton property, it was sold by Holland's sons in 1786, here with a house on the site. The purchaser was William Virtue of Chelsea, coal merchant.[18] For a year or two it was held under Virtue by a gardener prominent hereabouts, James Shailer, and then from 1790 by a Chelsea gardener, William Knapp, under a thirty-one-year lease from Virtue (by then designated gentleman).[225] This required Knapp to build a house on the land, which he did, but the property, unlike the former Latouche property to the east, was not developed as a building site. From about 1797 Knapp was succeeded by another gardener, John Gre(a)sley, and he by another, William Warner, in about 1807-8. Occupiers called Lyons succeeded him, c. 1809-18, and then a long occupation followed by another prominent market-gardening concern under members of the Poupart family, from about 1820 into the 1860's.[9]

Meanwhile the freehold had been sold in 1806 by Virtue to Philip Gilbert of Cockspur Street, goldsmith,[226] by whose family it was retained until 1864.

It was probably in c. 1820 that the southern part of the area was appropriated for a detached house standing back from the Fulham Road in its garden, and called Hollywood Lodge or House.[227] This was seemingly in private occupation until 1852, when it was taken on lease by the recently founded Free Cancer Hospital (now the Royal Marsden Hospital), and opened in November for in-patients. It needed keen search in various towns before the committee of the Cancer Hospital could 'ferret out' the previous tenant, who had been 'sold up' owing back-rent, but in other respects the house was satisfactory, 'solid and square built', with seventeen rooms, of which all except the topmost had gas laid on. The proximity to the Brompton Hospital for consumption was thought advantageous. Some fifteen or sixteen patients were accommodated here. The committee hoped to extend the hospital for sixty patients, to plans made by one of its members, the architect David Mocatta, and was only deterred by doubts about the title of the landlord, the Reverend Edward Gilbert, who sought his health away from his Northamptonshire parish at various towns in France. Thence he wrote in 1856 that his lawyer had 'left England for America under very unpleasant circumstances' and with one moiety of Mr. Gilbert's title technically in question. By 1857 the committee had decided to buy instead a freehold site in Chelsea opposite the Brompton Hospital and in 1862 a new hospital was opened there to replace

Hollywood Lodge.[228] In 1866-8 the latter was the 'Redcliffe Estate Office' in the occupation of the builders Corbett and McClymont.[155]

This was a consequence of the sale of the freehold of Hollywood Lodge and its site and of the Pouparts' land to the north in 1864 by the representatives of the Gilbert family to James Gunter of Earl's Court, whereby the area on the the east side of Hollywood Grove was brought into the building schemes going forward on the latter's property and that of his brother Robert. (A small 'peninsula' on the north-east side of the land discussed here, now the eastern end of Cathcart Road, was excluded from this sale, see page 212).[229] As elsewhere on the Gunters' property it was Corbett and McClymont who laid out the road (Hollywood Road) in 1864[230] and took many of the building leases from 1865 onwards. By 1869 the road was completed (at its south-eastern end by other builders) and Corbett and McClymont replaced the former Hollywood Lodge by the former Nos. 236, 238 and 238A Fulham Road.

(For Hollywood Road see also page 239.)

Nos. 240-248 (even) Fulham Road and the west side of Hollywood Road south of Fawcett Street

Nos. 240-244 (even) Fulham Road and the adjacent Nos. 246 and 248 are groups of three and two plain houses over shops built in c. 1790-1 and c. 1801-2 respectively (Plate 75e). The whole rectangle bounded on the west by the Servite school, on the north by the block of flats at the corner of Fawcett Street and Hollywood Road and on the east by Hollywood Road has, however, a longer history of occupation, although none of it is hinted at by the appearance of the present buildings northward of the old houses in Fulham Road. These are mainly the late-nineteenth- and twentieth-century structures put up for the purposes successively of a riding school and livery stables established in 1883 and a depot of United Dairies (now Unigate) which replaced them in the 1920's.

It was evidently in the 1660's that a sizeable brick house was built here, standing well back from the Fulham Road, by the Henry Middleton who in 1664 bought the adjacent house westward.[31] The house may be that occupied by a Katherine Henry in c. 1662-4.[231] It is said, however, to have been built where a house occupied by Robert Hobson, a physician (who died in 1659), had formerly stood.[31] This was probably the house where Hobson was living, in the Kensington part of Little Chelsea, in 1655.[232] He was, like his brother William Hobson, a freeholder in this neighbourhood in succession to their father Lancelot, who probably had not acquired the land before the 1630's (see page 165). The age of Robert Hobson's house is not known: conceivably it was one of the two houses that already stood on the property in 1639 in the occupation of Charles Thynne and Edward Somner and was of an age to invite rebuilding by Middleton.

Subsequently occupants of Middleton's house[233] included Sir Robert Williams (?second baronet, of Penrhyn, Carnarvonshire, died 1680),[31] Captain Wild (1681-2), and Colonel (?John, later Lieutenant-General) Titcomb (1683-4).[234] In 1685-93 the ratepayer was Sir John Ernle, knight, who was James II's Chancellor of the Exchequer during the early years of his occupation of the house. He was succeeded by John Lefevre (1694-1707), and Captain Richard Newton, perhaps of the East India Company (1707-35).[234]

In 1744 the house was sold by Newton's executors to Michael Duffield of St. George the Martyr, Holborn,[31] who thereafter used it for one of the two private lunatic asylums he maintained in Little Chelsea on each side of the Fulham Road. Said to have been a Yorkshireman and to have recruited many of his staff from Leeds, Duffield and (from 1761) his son or grandson continued here until c. 1768. (For a few weeks in 1754 he accommodated Alexander Cruden, compiler of the Biblical concordance, in one of his houses, which resulted in some publicity unfavourable to Duffield.)[235]

In about 1768 the younger Duffield contracted to sell all this site to Thomas Main, gentleman, who lived at the house later numbered 260 Fulham Road.[236] It was 1779, after Main's death, before this is known to have resulted in a sale, by Duffield to Main's daughter,[237] but in November 1768 Main had sufficient lien on the property to agree to make a sixty-one-year lease of it to a building tradesman, Joseph Perkins, a painter who was also of St. George the Martyr, Holborn — a lease that was evidently executed.[238] It may be, therefore, that an advertisement Main had published in February 1768 refers to this site although it speaks of his tenure as freehold.[239] The land on offer was certainly in approximately this part of the Fulham Road. Main described it as 'A Freehold Piece of Ground, whereon is proposed to be built a certain Number of Houses, at a Village called Little Chelsea, in the Parish of Kensington, in the Road leading to Fulham, two miles from Hyde Park Corner, where the road is new making, and will be watered and lighted, being a very pleasant Situation, and in a good Neighbourhood'. If this was the site discussed here it is noteworthy that Main does not mention any big old house still standing on it. Instead he catalogues a mass of building material lying on the site. That this was not the debris of the old house is presumably shown by his description of it as 'almost new'. It consisted of 'good grey Stock Brick Work and plain Tiling, Lead Gutters, Pipes, Hips to Roofing, Lead Flats, Cisterns and Sinks; good Fir Roofing; Girders and Joysts; Dove, Sienna and white and veined marble Chimney Pieces, and slabs, and carved Ornaments; Purbeck and Portland Paving, Stone Coping, Necks, Balls, Plinth and Window Stools; clean Deal and second best dowled Floors; Dado Base and Imposts and oval flat Pannel, and square Work Wainscotting; two Inch

Deal Ovola six pannelled, and other Doors and Door Cases, with very good Town-made Locks, Keys and Bolts, very good Window Frames, Sashes and Crown Glass.' All this was 'near sufficient to compleat the intended Buildings' according to 'a Plan' kept by a lawyer in Staple Inn. The nature of the proposed development is indicated by his hint to prospective lessees: 'Middle sized Houses are much wanted on the Spot'.

Despite Main's lease to Perkins it is doubtful whether much new building was done here. Perhaps two houses, sometimes occupied as three, were built on the east side in about 1771, backing (not fronting) on what is now Hollywood Road.[240] Probably, however, the big house remained, the chief use of the site from 1770 being not for 'middle sized' housing but for the accommodation of a private military academy mainly in one large building.

The owner was Lewis Lochée, a Brabanter and native of Brussels, and the author of books on military science and education published between 1773 and 1780, wherein he describes himself as 'Master of the Military Academy at Little Chelsea'.[241] By 1776 he had had a building added on the east or 'Hollywood Road' side of the main house — probably a riding house. In that year he took a fourteen-year sub-lease of the site at £85 per annum.[242] Two years later he bought the assignment of Perkins's long lease,[243] and in 1781, the year after his naturalization as a British subject,[244] the freehold from Main's heirs.[245] Lochée's acquaintance extended to James Boswell, who brought General Paoli to see the academy in 1778.[246] His writings were respectfully noted in the Gentleman's Magazine,[247] which in 1780 said that 'for the encouragement of his institution, an annual pension for life has been settled upon him by his Majesty's order'.[248]

In 1780-1 Lochée could afford to buy neighbouring 'investment' property to the west and north. Additionally he acquired important properties on the south side of the Fulham Road in Chelsea, including Stanley House. Perhaps because of his status as an alien or newly natural-ized subject an intermediary and trustee for him was John Payne, Chief Accountant at the Bank of England, publisher, and friend of Johnson.[249]

According to Thomas Faulkner in the 1829 edition of his history of Chelsea the grounds of the academy 'were laid out as a regular fortification and were open to view'.[250] In 1784 Blanchard and Sheldon made use of the grounds for a balloon ascent watched by 'persons of the first fashion' and many others, to the detriment of the surrounding fields, where 'a general devastation took place in the gardens, the produce being either trampled down or torn up. The turnip-grounds were totally despoiled by the multitude.'[251] An engraved illustration of the ascent gives incidentally one of the two known views of the academy (Plate 75 a, d). The other, a watercolour in Kensington Public Library, is on paper watermarked 1831, when the academy had long ceased to exist, but is endorsed with an indecipherable reference to the year 1782, and if not a fanciful reconstruction might derive from an original of that year.[252] In neither view is the building easy to date, but in each a late-seventeenth-century origin looks possible. They agree in showing a plainish three-storeyed building nine bays wide, with a central entrance and above it a round-headed, statue-filled niche replacing the central first-floor window. The 1784 view shows the building as a double-pile, with the front hipped roof rising above the parapet. This roof is not, however, visible in the '1782' view. That, for what it is worth, shows a straight unelaborated finish to the façade, whereas the 1784 view shows a pediment over the central three bays. This pediment could, indeed, be of the 1780's, and put up at the same time as the riding house was rebuilt and the rateable value raised just at that period, about 1784.[9]*

In 1789-90 Lochée involved himself in the nationalist revolt in his native Brabant against the Austrian government, and raised a 'Belgic Legion' to fight under his command, with some British names among its officers. He was active also in the internecine enmities of the insurrectionists, but died in 1791 in unknown circumstances at Lille, whither many Belgians of his way of thinking had withdrawn after the suppression of the rising. His death, as one who had 'formerly kept the Royal Military Academy at (Little) Chelsea', was noted in English periodicals.[254]†

The academy had probably come to an end about 1788 or 1789. From the latter year, when Mrs. Lochée was the ratepayer, until c. 1800 the property is difficult to identify in rate- or tax-books, although it is mentioned as the 'late military academy' in 1795.[9] In the period 1796-99 a Mrs. Hatfield or a Mrs. La Croix may have been ratepayers,[258] possibly on behalf of the 'committee of the infant asylum' that was said to occupy the former academy in 1800.[259]

Perhaps to supply the place of the academy as a source of income, in c. 1790-1 the Lochées had three houses built for occupation by tradesmen at the south-east corner of the site, as the surviving **Nos. 240-244 (even) Fulham Road** (Plate 75e). Early occupants were the plumber,

Thomas Ivey, at No. 240 (1802-12), a baker at No. 242 (1793-1801) and a chemist at No. 244 (1810-11).[260] At about the same time three other houses to the north, backing on a passageway called Verney Row that became the southern end of Hollywood Road, had probably been built (unless they were rebuildings of houses built c.1771).[9] In 1797 and 1798, however, Lewis Lochée's widow and son, while retaining most of the investment property nearby, which remained in the family until 1836, sold off the military academy and all the site discussed here, in three parts. One was Nos. 240-244 Fulham Road (fig. 54),[261] and another (C on fig. 54) was the most important of the house-properties backing onto Verney Row. This house (a on fig. 54) was later called Grove House or No. 1 Hollywood Grove (see below).[262]

The third and largest part (A on fig. 54) was the site of the former military academy itself with its frontage to Fulham Road and also the other two properties in Verney Row. This (with other ground northward, B on fig. 54) was sold to J. S. Wells, a grocer in the City, and G. H. Kirton, gentleman, of Whitechapel.[263] They, in 1800, sold the former academy to Samuel Butler of Little Chelsea and William Butler of Moorfields, both builders.[264] In 1802 the Butlers also bought from Kirton and Francis Mayoss of Little Chelsea, builder, the two Verney Row properties.[265] Mayoss had from 1790 onwards been developing the southern end of Seymour Walk nearby, and his mortgagee there, Doctor Simmons, is said to have had, at an unspecified time, a lease also of the site discussed here.[263] Probably Mayoss and Simmons had had a tentative interest in making a similar development northward from the Fulham Road, but there is no evidence whether it was Mayoss who had built Nos. 240-244 Fulham Road or the 'Verney Row' houses in 1789-91. Samuel Butler had witnessed the Lochées' sale of the former houses in 1797, and therefore may have been concerned in their building.[261] It was doubtless Butler

---

*The nineteenth-century inscription endorsed on the watercolour which refers to the year 1782 also says of the statue in the niche, 'the figure over the Door is the Duke of Marlborough in character of Mars cost in Italy 800£ by subscription of the Gentleman Students: it now stands although a very fine piece of Sculptor little Noticed in Marlborough Square on Chelsea Common'. According to correspondents of *Notes and Queries* in 1890 and 1908 it was removed from Marlborough Square (off Cale Street) in c. 1885, and by 1908 had been sold by Crowthers.[253] The present whereabouts of the statue, if it survives, is not known.

†Lochée's son John (b. 1776) became an auctioneer in Covent Garden and committed suicide in 1815, when the *Gentleman's Magazine* in its obituary spoke of his father's 'unfortunate and premature death . . . at the head of a body of insurgents in Brabant'.[255] This elaboration of the plain contemporary death-notices was carried further in 1829 when Thomas Faulkner (b. 1777) included in the edition of his history of Chelsea published in that year another, and very strange, version of the elder Lochée's end. 'Mr Lochée . . . unfortunately engaged in the revolutionary troubles which agitated Flanders in the year 1790, and being taken prisoner by the Austrians, was condemned to be hanged; he, however, obtained permission to come to England, to settle his affairs, upon condition of leaving his only son as an hostage; and upon his return to the Continent he suffered the punishment of death. His son, a school-fellow of mine, afterwards married a daughter of Mr. King, an eminent book auctioneer, of King Street, Covent Garden, and, lamentable to relate, fell by his own hands.'[256] (Faulkner had not included this story in the 1810 edition of his history, to which John Lochée had himself subscribed.) Both these versions, of 1815 and 1829, perhaps originated in the excitable mind of John Lochée and seem to be contradicted by the contemporary bare reports of the elder Lochée's death not in the Austrian domains but in France.

In this account Lewis Lochée is treated as the same man throughout, from his appearance as a ratepayer in 1770 to his death in 1791, and this follows Faulkner. T. C. Croker (1798-1854) in his *A Walk from London to Fulham*, originally published in *Fraser's Magazine* in 1845 (volume XXXI) says, however, that the founder of the Military Academy died on 5 April 1787 and was succeeded by his son of the same name.[257] No confirmation of this has been found and it is probably a mistaken reference to the death of a John Louis Lochée of Little Chelsea, buried at Kensington on 10 April 1787 aged thirty-one, whose relationship to the founder of the academy is not known.

who proceeded to build the surviving **Nos. 246 and 248 Fulham Road** on part of the southern frontage of his property in 1801-2 (Plate 75e).[9] He was probably the first occupant of No. 248. The building line of Nos. 246 and 248 is set back from that of the slightly earlier Nos. 240-244, permitting a small window to look west from the flank wall of No. 244. Later occupants of No. 246 were H. G. Rowley, c. 1843-60, and Victor Barthe, c. 1868-70, both teachers of music, and J. B. Comley, sculptor, in 1884-93.[133]

Samuel Butler evidently also occupied the major, rearward, part of his site as a builder's yard and premises, where he was succeeded by Frederick Butler, also a builder, and probably his younger brother, until 1817.[266] Salway's view in 1811[89] (Plate 72) shows Nos. 240-248 Fulham Road and the entrance to the builder's yard immediately to the west, but throws no light on what lay behind or whether the old academy building still survived. The date of its disappearance is uncertain but it may already have been demolished, as the two (lesser) Verney Row houses probably had been by 1802.[9]

In 1817-18 a brewhouse replaced the builder's premises[9] and henceforward this greater part of the site was in the hands of brewers, being known, at least so early as 1823,[267] as the Hollywood Brewery. From 1847 the owner of the brewery here was John Bowden until he or a

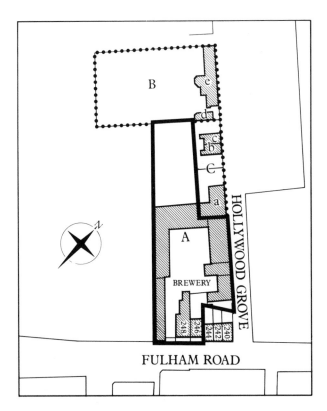

Fig. 54. Nos. 240-248 (even) Fulham Road and the south-west end of Hollywood Road, showing former property divisions. Based on the Ordnance Survey of 1862-72

successor of the same name removed it to the King's Road, Chelsea, in 1880-1.[268] In 1882 J. W. Butler and his brother, F. Hedges Butler, wine merchants, of No. 155 Regent Street, sold off the entire site, excluding Nos. 240-244 Fulham Road, which had been separately owned since their sale by the Lochées in 1798, but including the whole property northward in Hollywood Road,[269] part of which (C on fig. 54) had been brought back into the Butlers' ownership since its sale in 1797 (see below). The enhancement of the value of the site since the 1790's appears in the advance of the total selling price from some £985 in 1797-8 to £7,150 in 1882. In the following year the purchaser, Charles Bickers, gentleman, of No. 256 Fulham Road, sold an eighty-year lease at £400 per annum for £1,000 to J. A. Preece, a jobmaster in Paddington, who was obliged to spend at least £2,000 in new buildings and promptly had a riding school erected on the north-west part of the site.[270] In 1890 a forbidding range of buildings, labelled **Grove House,** in **Hollywood Road** opposite Nos. 13-27, was put up for him as a 'carriage warehouse and factory' (between a and d on fig. 54):[271] the architect is not known.

In 1924-5 the riding school and livery stables of J. A. Preece and Sons, who latterly included Motor Carriage Company in their title, were converted for use as a milk-distributing depot by United Dairies Limited, who bought the site (A and C on fig. 54), but again not Nos. 240-244 Fulham Road, for £8,300 in 1930.[272]

When the range labelled Grove House was built in Hollywood Road in 1890 the house sometime called Grove House or No. 1 Hollywood Grove immediately to its south (a on fig. 54), which had been built (or possibly rebuilt) about 1790 (see above), was again rebuilt or radically recast in the same style as the range to the north. Originally it had perhaps been in brief use as a boarding school run by a Mrs. Heath in 1790.[9] Having been sold by the Lochées in 1797[262] it was bought back into the main Butler property by James Butler, wine merchant, in 1859.[273] It was sometimes occupied in connexion with the brewery, and then in c. 1853 to 1868 by the Reverend F. C. Goodhart, minister of Park Chapel in Chelsea.[274] In 1908-12 it was used by the Territorial Army.[133]

The 1890 range covers the site of two short-lived houses, Nos. 2 and 3 Hollywood Grove (b and c on fig. 54), which were built in 1849 on the northern curtilage of No. 1 when that house was in the ownership of Edward Gingell, an appraiser active in building development in this neighbourhood.[275] They were probably demolished about 1878. No. 3 was occupied by G. V. McLellan, architect and surveyor, in 1877-8.[133]

These former houses in the southern part of what is now Hollywood Road were from 1838 until 1866 regarded by the rate collector as being in Hollywood Grove,[9] a name which continued in use in the *Post Office Directory* until 1881.[133] Earlier, from about 1797 to about 1818, this passageway from Fulham Road northward into the fields was named in the ratebooks Verney Row.[9] The passageway existed as a lane since at least 1746,[276] and must in fact have been known as Verney Row soon after that date as it took its name from some five and a half acres of garden and orchard to which it led, lying around what is now the junction of Oakfield Street and Cathcart Road, and which from 1746 to 1759 were owned by the Earls Verney (see below). The origin of the name Hollywood (applied by Salway to Nos. 240-244 Fulham Road in 1811) is not certainly known. It is said, however, that the Butler family which owned the freehold of most of this area from 1800 had a house of that name in Norwood or Sydenham.[277] Here, in and about the Fulham Road, it had a perplexingly wide application. On this Kensington side of the road it extended, until 1866, to include all of the five houses now known as Nos. 240-248 (even) Fulham Road,[133] but it was also applied in directories from 1845 or earlier until 1862-3 to a range of houses on the opposite side of the road in Chelsea and (as Hollywood Place) to another range further west on that side of the road. The name Hollywood House was also applied confusingly. In 1852 and 1866 it was given to the house on the east corner of Hollywood Grove and Fulham Road, which was sometimes also called Hollywood Lodge.[278] On Greenwood's map of Chelsea in 1830 and in directories of *c.* 1845-62 it is given to a house (No. 383) on the south side of the Fulham Road at a site now taken into that of St. Stephen's Hospital. And in Kensington it was applied to a house on the west side of Hollywood Grove or Road, immediately north of the area discussed above, and now replaced by flats called Hollywood Court, Cecil Court and Fawcett Court.

This last-mentioned site (B on fig. 54), which comprises also a frontage to Fawcett Street, has an obscure history before the 1790's. It was evidently part of the property that passed into the tenure of the owner of the military academy, Lewis Lochée, between 1770 and 1781, and by 1797 'the remaining part of the Riding house of the said late Military academy', most of which extended southward, stood upon it.[262] Evidently in 1798 the ground was, like that of the academy itself, sold to a City grocer, J. S. Wells, and is first identifiable in the ratebooks in that year, in the occupation of a gardener, John Gresley,[9] as a yearly tenant. In 1803 it was called The Grove, had fruit trees on it, and a 'cart house' which, from its position, can probably be identified with the riding-house remnant (d on fig. 54). A later occupant is said to have found 'the entire skeleton of a horse' somewhere on this site.[279] Wells and others sold it in 1803 to Robert Sproule of Queen's Elm, Chelsea,[280] and it was he who had the substantial house later called Hollywood or No. 4 Hollywood Grove built here in about 1810 (Plate 75b; e on fig. 54)[155] In 1823 Sproule's son and others sold the house (then evidently called Grove Cottage) to Giles Newton, gentleman, for £1,005.[281] From 1825 the ratepayer was a Captain Nisbet and this family remained here, latterly in the person of a master mariner, Captain Edward Parry Nisbet, until 1899 (General Charles Grant also appears here in directories

1888-99).[282] In 1866 (by which time additions had been made to the house since 1823[128]) Fawcett Street was laid out on its north side. Alterations were also made to the house by the architect C. Fitzroy Doll in 1872.[283] (Fitzroy Doll, as it happens, was later, from 1893 until his death in 1929, possessed of ownership rights in the adjacent properties to south and west, as one of the nephews of Charles Bickers of No. 256 Fulham Road.[284]) In 1902-5 the flats called Cecil Court (now **Hollywood, Cecil and Fawcett Courts**) were built on the site, with their long frontage to **Fawcett Street**. The architect was C. J. C. Pawley. The rents ranged from £80 to £140 per annum for three-to-five-room flats: each flat additionally contained a servants' bedroom and water closet.[285]

Nos. 252-264 (even) Fulham Road

Westward of the Unigate site so far as St. Mary's Priory at No. 264 Fulham Road is another area where the first pattern of development has been made difficult to recognize. In the 1650's or 1660's, four substantial houses were built here, set back from the road in approximate alignment with the first house on the Unigate site: the present No. 262A and the rearward priory house at No. 264 still occupy part of this line. It seems they were erected at the instigation of Thomas Maundy (later described as of Little Chelsea, gentleman, but see page 166), as his 'New Buildings', probably in the 1650's. From east to west one of these four houses stood, detached, on the site of the later Nos. 252 and 254, with its curtilage extending over the future site of No. 256; the second occupied the site of the sometime No. 258, the third that of the sometime Nos. 260 and 262, and the fourth that of St. Mary's Priory at No. 264 (fig. 55).

The occupation of most of the area is now divided, in a way which largely ignores the old property divisions, between the Servite Fathers and the Post Office.

The former Nos. 252-256 (even) Fulham Road

A large single house, later divided into **Nos. 252 and 254 Fulham Road,** was sold by the Thomas Maundy mentioned above to Henry Middleton, and to others in trust for him, in 1664.[28] The purchaser had a lien on other properties nearby and further east his family retained its ownership for many years (see pages 166, 174). In 1666 the house was occupied by a Mr. De Visscher, merchant — doubtless the William De Visscher, of Dutch extraction, who died in 1669 and was the father-in-law of James Boevey, an owner of property nearby.[286] Middleton himself occurs as occupant in *c.* 1670-1,[287] but in 1671 he sold the property, for £350, to Ralph Palmer of Kensington, gentleman.[28] In 1666 and 1670 Palmer had occupied the house next door, at what was later No. 258, and subsequently he owned both freeholds, together with a five-and-a-half-acre piece of orchard and garden to the north (see page 198 and L on fig. 58). Henceforward Palmer and his descendants or their representatives occupied this house (the later Nos. 252-254) and let or sub-let the other (No. 258).

Ralph Palmer (1636-1716), the eldest son of a gentleman of property at Royden in Essex, lived here contentedly until his death,[288] undisturbed by the proximity of a school and an inn.[289] In 1679 he urged upon his future son-in-law the attraction of suburban owner-occupancy 'in any airy place, for its a fine thing to sett [*sic*] rent free'.[290] His fifteen-year-old daughter Elizabeth (worth upward of £3,000 in dowry) was in that year courted by John Verney, eldest son of Sir Ralph Verney of Claydon House, Buckinghamshire, and himself a merchant in the City. Later that year John wrote to his father: 'Mr Palmer I take to be an open Ingenious person of a mechanick humour, being a neate contriver, and keeps his house and Gardens very well. . . . The first time I was there Mr P. shewd me his Garden and other out parts of his house: yesterday he carryd me about within which is all very gentile and neate.'[291] The following year John and Elizabeth married.[292] Elizabeth died in 1686 but the subsequent correspondence between Ralph Palmer and John and Sir Ralph Verney testified to a continuing friendship.[293] In 1712 Ralph Palmer's son, also Ralph, reported to a younger Verney 'We are very fine at Chelsea, ye front of our house is new pointed and rubd all with red brick, and ye remayns of ye old dead Phillarea taken quite away . . .'.[294] On the elder Ralph Palmer's death in 1716 the property passed to this younger Ralph (1668-1755), who continued in the house.[295] (In 1700 he had married Catherine, the daughter of Sir John Ernle, who had lived next door to the east in 1685-93.[296]) The flourishing state

of his garden is suggested by a gift in 1720 to his nephew at Claydon, Ralph Verney, second Viscount Fermanagh, to whom he sent '3 of my best Layers of ye Burgundy grape, which upon a South wall I dare say will produce as delicious black grapes as ever you'l eat'.[297] (Lord Fermanagh had been born in his grandparent Palmer's house here and was about taking a house across the road in Chelsea.[298]) Ralph Palmer, a barrister and littérateur, retained the house until 1746, when he sold it and the later No. 258, together with the five and a half acres of orchard ground to the north, to this same nephew — by then created Earl Verney.[276] Evidently Lord Verney lived in the house until his death there in 1752, when it passed to his son Ralph, second Earl Verney — initially, however, in trust for the second Earl's sister, wife of Bennet Sherard, third Earl of Harborough.[299] Lord Harborough occupied, or had lately occupied, the house in 1759. In that year, however, (Lady Harborough being dead) the second Earl, as empowered by his father's will on a younger sister's consent, sold the two houses and orchard land. The buyer was a spinster, Diana Robson, of St. George's, Queen Square, Holborn — the same parish, it so happens, as that of Michael Duffield, the asylum-keeper next door to the east.[300] She occupied the house later Nos. 252 and 254 until 1775.[9] In June 1781 (being then of Belmont, Hillingdon) she sold the properties to John Payne, chief accountant at the Bank of England, doubtless in trust for Lewis Lochée, the flourishing proprietor of the military academy next door, to whom Payne transferred them a month later.[301] Lochée proceeded in 1781-2 to divide the big old Palmer-Verney house into two, subsequently numbered 252 and 254.[9]

Little is known of the later history of the fabric of these houses, or how much, if any, of their original structure survived into this century. Salway's view of 1811 (Plate 72) shows the old house, of indeterminate age, in its divided occupation, the easternmost bay of No. 252 looking like an addition and the westernmost bay of No. 254 hidden behind a poplar tree. The main gate, hung between substantial piers, is shown serving No. 254 and supplemented by a less assuming gate to No. 252.[89] This main gate survives (see below).

At **No. 252 Fulham Road** the occupant in 1801-7 had been James Windsor, 'notary and agent to army hospitals',[302] and in 1809-10 Philip Gilbert, goldsmith and freeholder nearby. At the time of the Salway view the house was in the hands of a school proprietor, Ann Rishforth — the low building on the east being perhaps a schoolroom.[303] It is likely this use, so characteristic of Little Chelsea at that time, continued in 1812-31 under Ann Anderson, as it did in 1832-53 under Elizabeth Read.[155] In 1836 the representatives of the Lochée family sold what was then the two semi-detached houses, Nos. 252 and 254, to William Rogers of Islington, gentleman (and the five and a half acres of orchard ground to Robert Gunter), and in 1853 Rogers sold them off separately. No. 252 (called Tavistock House from about 1858) was bought

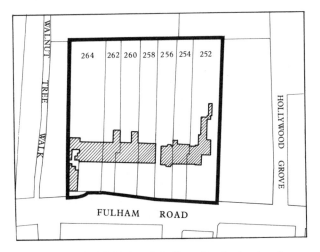

Fig. 55. Nos. 252-264 (even) Fulham Road, showing former site divisions. Based on the Ordnance Survey of 1862-72

by Messrs. Jackson, furniture dealers at the site of what are now Nos. 304A-306B (even) Fulham Road, for £1,100.[304] From 1864 to 1870 the occupants were Maull and Polyblank, latterly Henry Maull and Company, photographers.[133] In 1871 Frederick Jackson sold the house at the greatly enhanced price of £3,500 to Charles Bickers, gentleman, of No. 256 Fulham Road:[305] Bickers, with wealth evidently arising from the family's grocery business in Berkeley Square, also acquired over the years adjacent properties to this one.[306] Dillon Croker noted the house's degraded state in 1872, with a 'sand for sale' notice outside,[307] but the social switchback of the houses hereabouts then seems to have gone up and in 1879 Bickers let No. 252 at £150 per annum, with its stables, coach-house, conservatories and greenhouses, to H. A. Coventry, a cousin of the ninth Earl of Coventry. (He was also a rather distant relation of one of the Servite Fathers a few doors along the road.) The landlord's fixtures included a speaking-tube from the first-floor landing to the kitchen 'with mouth pieces and whistles complete', and 'about 750 red edging tiles for borders' in the garden.[308] Coventry stayed here until 1887.[133] The next occupant was Jonathan, or Ion, Pace,[308] the stained-glass artist responsible for most of the windows in the Servite church, who carried on his trade here and built a two-storeyed 'studio' in the front garden, numbered 252A, in 1888.[309] He remained here until 1901, when he was succeeded in 1902-4 by William Morris and Company, also stained-glass artists.[133] (They were unconnected with the firm founded by the poet and socialist.) By 1906 the old greenhouses in the garden were dilapidated and from about that time the premises were mostly in divided occupation by tradesmen until 1927.[310] Bickers's heirs then sold them at a further enhanced price of £7,500 to a bootmaker, plumber and watchmaker as trustees of the Eleusis Club.[311] This, formerly a political club founded by the Chelsea section of the Reform League in 1868, had for most of its former existence been in the King's Road, and removed here until 1936, when it returned to Chelsea.[312] The rearward, eastern, part of No. 252 (perhaps in origin a school-room addition) was converted into a club-room, and in 1931 a free-standing concert-hall was built by the club in the back garden (E. Meredith, architect). In c. 1935 the club sold the premises to the Servite Fathers at No. 264.[313] They returned them to their old school use. The former studio (latterly a shop) in front at No. 252A was demolished and the rearward, eastern, part converted in 1936 to an infant schoolroom for the opening of the Servites' school there in 1937 (architect, E. A. Remnant).[314] The demolition of the main house at No. 252, to give open access to an intended new school at the rear, was delayed by difficulty over the party wall with No. 254, but was carried out between 1939 and 1950.[315] The new school buildings were constructed at the rear in c. 1960 to the designs of E. A. Remnant on a site extending also over the former rearward curtilage of Nos. 254-260 (even). They incorporate in their eastern wing at No.

252 the former concert-hall of 1931 and the former club-room converted in 1936.[316]

On the street front the iron gates hung between brick piers have been moved here from a position a little westward, where they originally gave access to the old Palmer-Verney house and later to the western part of the divided house at No. 254. If Salway's view of 1811 can be trusted, the stone balls were added between that date and 1845.[317]

No. 254 Fulham Road was the western half of the old Palmer-Verney house after its division into two by Lewis Lochée in 1781-2 (fig. 55 and see above). It survived until c. 1962 and a photograph of the exterior in its last days, featureless as the nineteenth-century stucco was, would not be inconsistent with an early, perhaps seventeenth-century, origin for the basic fabric.[318] In 1791-3 it was occupied by Lochée's widow.[9] Like No. 252 it was bought from the Lochées by William Rogers in 1836, at which time it was conducted as a boys' boarding school by David Hooke, who occupied it from 1823 to 1842.[319] This use continued in 1843-51 under Mrs. Elizabeth Corder, perhaps the wife of Covent Garden's former and rather questionable vestry clerk, James Corder.[320] In 1853, again like No. 252, the house was sold by Rogers, the purchaser at £1,180 being Charles Bickers, gentleman, of Sloane Street (see above).[321] The house continued as a school under C. J. Sayer (1852-5) and James Watkins (1856).[133] By 1846 it was known as Bolton House.[322] From 1858 or 1859 to 1872 the occupant was Samuel Cundey, a clothier,[323] during which period, in 1862, the western part of the grounds of this house was utilized to build an entirely new, semi-detached, house, No. 256 (see below). In 1881 Bickers let No. 254 for fourteen years at £100 per annum as a private residence to the titular Maharajah of Lahore, Duleep Singh, who specifically undertook not to use it as a school, lunatic asylum or lodging house.[324] Being in financial difficulties, partly caused by architectural extravagance at Elveden Hall in Suffolk, the Maharajah moved from Claridge's, 'withdrawing himself from society in order to live within his means'. But this was to No. 53 Holland Park, and it is not clear what use he made of No. 254, which from 1883 is listed in the Post Office Directory in other hands.[325] In 1889-90 the occupant was a surgeon, and in 1891-1902 a dentist.[133] In 1899 Bickers's heir sold the freehold, including No. 256, for the sum, greatly advanced upon that paid by Bickers in 1853, of £8,925.[326] The purchaser was the Postmaster General, who had a branch Post Office established at No. 256. Subsequently for many years to 1934 No. 254 was occupied by Madam Violet Violette, cakemaker.[133] In 1940 the semi-derelict house and site, together with the back part of the site of No. 256, was sold by the Postmaster General to the Servite Fathers, who required it to facilitate the demolition of No. 252 for their intended school site.[327] It was, however, the early 1960's before No. 254 was itself demolished and its site, less a strip on the west side returned to the Post Office in 1962,[328] incorporated into that of the school.

No. 256 Fulham Road was built on a site that until *c.* 1861 was part of the garden on the west side of No. 254 and was owned from 1853 by Charles Bickers as part of the curtilage of that house. He then, during the occupation of No. 254 by Samuel Cundey, had a new house built here, called Hertford House. It was attached on one side to No. 254. The first occupant in 1862-7 was Robert Lemon, archivist and senior clerk in the State Paper Office.[329] From 1868 to 1893 it was occupied by Charles Bickers himself and then by his widow until 1898.[133] In the following year it was bought (with No. 254) by the Postmaster General and a branch Post Office was established here in about 1901.[133] The house was demolished when the present office, completed in 1965,

was built (planning architect for Ministry of Works, E. T. Sargeant, supervising architect, J. Russell[330]).

The former No. 258 Fulham Road

The present Nos. 258 and 258A Fulham Road and the eastern half of the entry named Barker Street occupy the southern part of the site of one of the two houses — the more westerly — owned in the seventeenth and eighteenth centuries by the Palmer and Verney families (fig. 55). Until 1836 that house shared the history of ownership of the more easterly house that was later divided as Nos. 252 and 254. Although thus associated with the detached house eastward, No. 258 was physically itself the easternmost of a 'terrace' of (originally) three big or biggish houses, of which the westernmost was latterly

Fig. 56. Fulham Road, gateway formerly to No. 254, as in 1942

numbered 264 (see below), and all of which were probably erected in the 1650's. No. 258 can be first identified in 1666 and 1670-1 in the occupation of a Mr. Palmer, doubtless the Ralph Palmer who thereafter occupied the eastern house and who seems to have been succeeded here in *c.* 1671-3 by Henry Middleton.[331] Later occupants,[332] as tenants or sub-tenants of Palmer, included Charles Knipe, perhaps the poet, by 1681 until 1686,[333] a Mr. Gibbons and family in 1687, and the painter John Riley in 1688-90.[334] From 1691 to 1701 the house was occupied by Sir Bartholomew Shower, who had been Recorder of London under James II.[335] Another lawyer, a Richard Minshull, took it in 1706, but in *c.* 1714 assigned his lease to an alehouse-keeper nearby, who let it in lodgings. This seems to have been less regretted by the Palmers than it might have been in a later age, as their relations sometimes stayed there.[336] As owner of the house Ralph Palmer insured it in 1708, when a 'summer house' was specified among its appurtenances.[337] This was an object of pride to the younger Ralph Palmer, newly succeeded in 1716, who spoke of it to his nephew Ralph Verney as 'a Noble Room 16 foot high and as wide standing by it self in the Garden'. He was repairing the dwelling house, preparatory to letting it for private occupation, 'for no body will take it without being [*sic*] put in thoro repair, Its a pretty place, and I hope I shall not let it under 35£ per annum, it has 5 rooms of a floor and closets to every one, with a neat one over the porch and a pretty ground to it, both Garden and Orchard, stabling for 3 or 4 horses, a Coach house, and special Cellars'. He was thankful the outgoing alehouse-keeper had left the wainscotting and marble hearth-stones behind as landlord's fixtures. By an outlay of £100 Palmer hoped to increase his rental by £20 a year. A German, perhaps of George I's court, had been to view it.[338] A relation took the house for a year or two and was 'so good a Tenant as to wainscot 2 Rooms', but then ran away from his wife[339] and Palmer probably had to wait for the long-term tenant he wanted until 1719, when it was taken by a John Stockwell, 'first Clerk in Mr Smith (ye Teller's) office who marryd Smith the Organ maker's widow worth 4000 to him'.[340] The name of Stockwell continues here until at least 1752.[341] In the later 1750's the Spanish consul is said to have occupied the house.[300] Like Nos. 252 and 254 ownership passed to Miss Robson in 1759,[300] and to Lewis Lochée in 1781.[301]

Salway's view in 1811 (Plate 72) shows the house (recently in the occupation of a wine merchant off the Strand[342]) west of a row of poplars, and bearing signs of its basic unity having at some time been divided into two parts of two and three bays wide: nothing in its known history, however, explains this.[89] The house was then occupied by Jos. Silver, perhaps recently a jeweller in Hatton Street, Holborn. His successor, in 1812-24, was an Elizabeth Baird, whose name is doubled with others in the ratebooks and who may be the lady of that name who had owned a 'carpet warehouse' in Leicester Square in

1800.[343] After another female ratepayer in 1825-6 the house was taken in 1826 by Mrs. Mary Fleming, who ran it as a small private lunatic asylum. (In 1844, by which time it was called Warwick House, there were five female inmates, two of them suicidal.)[344] Mary Fleming bought the house from the Lochées in 1836,[345] and it was retained until her daughter sold it in 1860 to another owner-occupier, seemingly for private occupation.[346] His heirs sold the house, together with the former No. 260 on its western side, to a builder in 1876.[347] This part of the old Palmer-Verney property was then completely redeveloped in a scheme that took in also the site of No. 260.

Nos. 258, 258A, 260 and 260A Fulham Road and Barker Street

The purchaser in April 1876 of the old houses at Nos. 258 and 260 (for the latter of which see below) was Thomas Hussey of Kensington High Street, builder,[347] who had recently embarked on a greater enterprise that became Albert Hall Mansions.[348] In the course of 1877-8 he replaced the two houses in their gardens by a terrace of four houses over shops on the street frontage, now numbered Nos. 258, 258A, 260 and 260A Fulham Road, with a passageway in the centre leading to a cul-de-sac of twenty-four mews behind.[349] Initially this was called Hussey's Mews.[350] Immediately on his acquisition of the two old houses Hussey had raised mortgages on each of them, that upon No. 258 yielding him £3,000.[351] The principal mortgagee here, and perhaps Hussey's legal adviser, would seem to have been Charles Mylne Barker, a solicitor in the firm of Barker and Ellis of Bedford Row. His clerk witnessed various of Hussey's title-deeds, others of his surname took mortgages from Hussey of parts of Hussey's new buildings here in 1877, and at the end of that year the mews was renamed Barker's Mews.[352]

C. M. Barker appears not, however, to have been the sole contributor to the loan of £3,000 on the security of No. 258 Fulham Road.[353] Another party to the deed was J. R. Tweddale of Cambridge Street, Hyde Park, esquire. But named first in the deed was a famous man of letters, whose respect for C. M. Barker is evidenced in an undated testimonial to the wisdom of his advice. This was Tweddale's cousin-once-removed, John Ruskin.[354] A year or so later, when Hussey's buildings were getting under way, Ruskin exposed his own financial affairs to the members of his Guild of St. George in Letter LXXVI of *Fors Clavigera*. Out of respect for 'honesty through Frankness' he there set out the disposal of his fortune and the current state of his affairs. He did not mention his investment in the Fulham Road, unless it was comprised under 'Herne Hill leases and other little holdings — thirteen hundred [pounds]', but spoke of the liquidation in the previous year of old and ill-judged investments in mortgages, and this may explain his possession of funds available for a (perhaps small) investment here on C. M. Barker's advice.[355] Ruskin's responsible attitude to his properties is very marked at that time. The appearance of Hussey's four houses at Nos. 258-260A Fulham Road (first occupied in 1880), whose architect has not been uncovered, cannot have pleased him — if, indeed, he saw them. Nor can the extensive use of the mews behind — purportedly livery stables — as dwellings. Whether or not by reason of any disquiet on Ruskin's part, the mortgage to which he was a party was liquidated in 1880.

By 1881 all twenty-four units in the mews were used as dwellings, housing 173 persons. Nine of these dwellings were in occupation by more than one family. Half were occupied by tenants unconnected with the work of the mews, including a number of 'labourers' and 'gardeners'.[356] By 1885 the cul-de-sac was known as Barker Street instead of Barker's Mews (Plate 75c).[357] Some rearrangement to group pairs of stables as dwellings seems to have taken place in the late 'eighties.[358]

In 1892 the works and sanitary committee of the Kensington Vestry asked Hussey to fill-in sunken dung pits in front of the stables but in 1895 permitted him to retain some or all of them.[359] Four years later half the individual dwellings were registered as lodging-houses.[360] In 1902 Charles Booth identified Barker Street as one of the three areas of poverty in the part of Kensington described in this volume west of Thistle Grove, it being then used as tenements inhabited by artisans and labourers.[361] The following year Hussey wanted to put up a water closet on the public way at the top of the street but was prevented by the Borough.[362] A few years later one side of the street was turned from lodging-houses into small 'flats' — two on each floor of the eight three-storeyed houses on the west side.[363] Hussey seems to have retained his ownership and in 1927 he or his successor of the same name, an estate agent at Hyde Park Gate, sold some or all of the street to trustees for a private purchaser.[364] The up-dating of Charles Booth's survey in 1930 found the inhabitants of Barker Street hovering at the poverty line.[365] The next year Kensington's Medical Officer of Health made a damning report on it to the Public Health Committee, mentioning the lack of light and air, the bad design of water closets, the broken paving and the appearance of neglect: all the premises, now renumbered as sixteen, were occupied by the working classes, although seven still had their ground floors used as stables or storage-places. Partly because of pressure from the parochial authorities of St. Mary, The Boltons, the Borough made a Clearance Order on Barker Street in 1934, confirmed by the Minister of Health after an appeal by the owners.[366] The properties there were demolished by the latter part of 1937 and a Closing Order made by the Kensington magistrates in 1938.[367] After its acquisition by the Servite Fathers the northern part was taken into the site of their new school but in 1940 the southern part was sold by them to the Postmaster General (in exchange for No. 254 Fulham Road, see above), and is used by the Post Office in connexion with its sorting office at No. 256 Fulham Road. It is now barely recognizable as an entity,

but the name Barker Street is still set up in the passageway between Nos. 258A and 260 Fulham Road.

The former No. 260 Fulham Road

The western half of this Barker Street development had previously been occupied by a terrace house probably built (unless merely recast) in 1711-12 (fig. 55). That would in turn have been a rebuilding (or recasting) of the eastern half of a larger house which had extended also over the site of No. 262 (now 262A).[88] Nineteenth-century plans suggest that it and No. 262 had a common origin with Nos. 258 and 264 and therefore probably in the 1650's. The large house is tentatively recognizable in taxbooks in 1666-74 in the occupation of widow Birkhead[368] — that is, of Ellen (d. 1679 or 1680), widow of Edward Birkhead and sister or sister-in-law of Henry Middleton, whose daughter Mary had in turn married her cousin, Ellen's nephew, William Birkhead of Lambeth, in 1664.[369] Alderman Robert Clarkson, evidently a propertied Bradford clothier, occupied the house in 1681 until his death in 1695-6, when he left it to his descendants.[370] Later occupants were Lady Sedley or Sidley in 1703-4, and Colonel Greenfield in 1707-11.[88] The house was then divided or rebuilt as two — the different window-spacings in the two parts as shown by Salway in 1811 rather suggesting a rebuilding. In 1712 it and No. 262 (now 262A) were both in one ownership, by Jacob Davison of Covent Garden, mercer,[371] who lived in this house, as did his heirs until the late 1750's, when it was taken by Thomas Main, gentleman, who bought it in 1765 and remained until 1772.[372] It was from this house that he advertized a freehold building site hereabouts to let or sell in 1768 (see above).[239] His library included a 'large Folio Book of Gardening' and 'two sets of fine prints unglazed'.[373] By the 1840's the house was called Amyot House, after the family occupying it from 1800 to 1845. Part of the premises was separately occupied in 1862-3 by the sculptor J. E. Boehm, and from 1869 by teachers of French,[155] until all was demolished by Hussey in 1877 (see above).

No. 262A Fulham Road (formerly 262)

This house (fig. 55), standing back behind a shop, engages the eye of the bus-passenger by a pompous cemented upper part of nineteenth-century date. Structurally, however, it is probably a house of c. 1711-12, conformably with the appearance of the brick back-front, where segmental-headed windows are set in wooden flush frames. Before 1711 it shared the history of No. 260, as part of a large seventeenth-century house. Probably then rebuilt, the first occupant thereafter, until c. 1719, was Huntley Bigg, doubtless the scrivener who had involved himself in property dealings in Westminster in the 1690's.[374] In 1769 Francis Darius Landumiey, an 'operator for the teeth', bought the house for £700 from the owner of this and the house to the east, and lived here until 1779.[375] In 1780 (being then of St. George's, Hanover Square) he sold it to a trustee for Lewis Lochée (for whom see above), but for only £550.[376] In 1789-91 it was a school conducted by a Miss Edmonds.[9] Lochée's heir resold it for £450 in 1803.[377] The poet and placeman William Boscawen lived here in 1807-11.[378] From 1862 to 1868 the house (called Mulberry House since the 1840's) was in divided occupation.[133] In 1869 a branch of the London Suburban Bank was established here and it was probably then that a one-storey addition was built on the forecourt (architect, Charles Sewell):[379] possibly the cementing of the upper part of the front of the house itself, occupied by the bank manager, was done at that time. The bank soon went, in 1871, and was succeeded in 1876 by a branch Post Office until c. 1901, when it moved to No. 256.[133] The premises subsequently served as the parochial hall of the Servite Church next door at No. 264, and when that function was removed to a free-standing temporary hall built behind the old house in 1925 the front premises on Fulham Road, now numbered 262, became the offices of estate agents. The parish hall was rebuilt in 1962-4 (Archard and Partners, architects) adjacent to the back of the old house, now numbered 262A.[380] This is occupied as flats in connexion with the Servite priory, and contains few if any old interior features.

No. 264 Fulham Road: the Church of Our Lady of Seven Dolours and St. Mary's Priory of the Servite Friars

The church and priory occupy the site of a single dwelling-house and its garden, the church occupying the former back garden, the priory the front garden and the old house itself, and the entrance tower and covered approach to the church the site of ancillary buildings and garden west of the old house (figs. 55, 57).

The original house here, according to a recital in 1783 of a mortgage dated 1659, was the westernmost of an unspecified number of houses called the 'New Buildings' of Thomas Maundy. In 1659 it was said to be of brick and to have been lately erected.[381] The existence so late as the 1870's of a sequence of four oldish houses extending from No. 264 eastward to No. 252 (interrupted only by the recent No. 256) suggests these were, at least in part, vestiges of Maundy's 'buildings', while Maundy's apparent occurrence as an occupier even further east, at what is now the west side of Redcliffe Road, in c. 1664-71 has been noted above, as has his likely identity with a goldsmith and macemaker. In 1659, when he mortgaged the house at No. 264 to Edward Barrington of the Middle Temple, gentleman, he was described as gentleman, of Little Chelsea.[381]

Henry Middleton, whose name is of frequent occurrence hereabouts, was said in 1713 to have been sometime the owner.[382] The house is perhaps first tentatively identifiable in hearth-tax books in 1666,[383] and 'Mr Middleton' was probably taxed for it in c. 1673.[384] The Charles Knipe who later lived at No. 258 was perhaps here in c. 1674.[385] By 1681 the occupant was Nicholas Staggins, Master of the King's Music, until his death in 1700.[386] In 1746 the house was bought for £320 by Robert Griffin, possibly the 'usher to the king' who died in 1765.[387] When he entered the house new buildings added to the old are mentioned.[387] In 1783 the house was sold again for £1,000.[388] From at least 1794 it was a school, run by Miss Ann Amelia Steers until c. 1804 and then by Ann Rishforth until 1810.[389] Salway indicates it in 1811 largely concealed behind trees in the front garden, where a coach-house is shown on the west side (Plate 72).[89] A Chelsea grocer, perhaps retired, was there in 1812-19.[390] From 1836 the house, called Heckfield Lodge, was occupied by Henry Milton, esquire, of the War Office, who bought it in 1839 and was succeeded in the ownership in 1850 by his son John, also of the War Office. John was later accountant general of the Army, and knighted. His mother occupied the house, which in 1868 attracted the attention of potential purchasers.[391]

Since then much has happened to the site but the house is an interesting survivor as part of St. Mary's Priory. Inside it has late-seventeenth- or early-eighteenth-century features and keeps much of the old plan, with a central compartment for the wooden staircase. This has a heavy, moulded closed string, plain newels and handrail, and turned balusters that have perhaps been renewed. A number of the rooms have plain marble chimneypieces, plain high panelling and dado rails and box cornices. All the ceilings are plain.

The Church of Our Lady of Seven Dolours and St. Mary's Priory of the Servite Friars (Plates 76-7, fig. 57). The potential purchasers of Heckfield Lodge in 1868 were members of the Order of the Servants of Mary, commonly called Servites.[392] It had been in 1864 that the first Servite friars had come to establish themselves in England, in the persons of two Italian priests sent from Rome to support the missionary work of a small convent in Cale Street, Chelsea. Their Order, originating in the thirteenth century at Florence, was then almost unknown in England. In 1867 they were given a parish, hitherto part of that of the Oratory and including south-western Kensington. This they served from converted houses in Chelsea, first in Park Walk and then, in 1868, in Netherton Grove. There they had a school adjacent, on part of the present site of St. Stephen's Hospital.[393]

It is significant of the vitality of the few early Fathers, and perhaps also of the assimilative characteristics of mid-Victorian London, that the Order — wholly foreign as it was, unlike the English converts at the Oratory — was able to establish itself quickly, and in 1868 was seeking a site for a permanent church.

An attempt was then made to buy Heckfield Lodge at No. 264, which was in fact only to be acquired for that

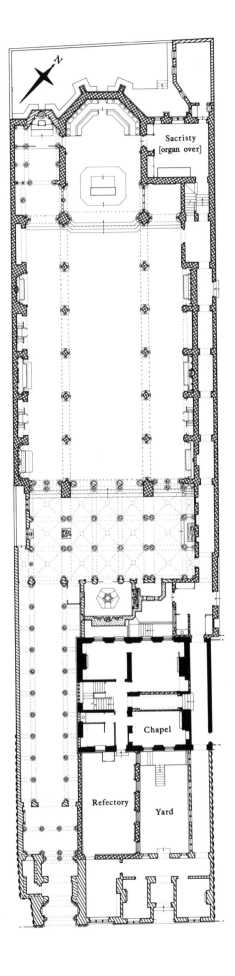

purpose some five years later. The negotiations in 1868 proved abortive, perhaps because an ill-chosen intermediary was used. Doctor John O'Bryen, a physician living in Drayton Gardens (at what is now the back building of No. 63),[133] had been employed in acquiring the school in Chelsea, to avoid anti-Catholic feeling.[394] At Heckfield Lodge, O'Bryen had evidently hoped to buy the house on his own account — at £2,250, however, not Milton's asking price of £3,000. According to Father Bosio, the Superior of the Servites, O'Bryen therefore agreed to treat for the house on their behalf, and came to an agreement for it at £2,750. Then, however, he asserted (according to Father Bosio) that the house must remain his own as Milton would not conclude the sale if the site was to be used for a Roman Catholic church. Father Bosio had employed another agent, who also approached Milton, and told Father Bosio that O'Bryen's statement was untrue. With the help of Father Knox at the Oratory an indignant letter was composed (and presumably dispatched) to O'Bryen, threatening him with recourse to 'the law' or the invocation of local opinion if he tried to conclude the sale on his own behalf.[395] What then happened is not known, but the house was still on offer five years later, and in May 1873 the Fathers decided to buy it. One of them seems to refer to it as 'that house which O'Brien [sic] had bought for us',[396] but O'Bryen was not a party to the sale, which was made in August directly to Father Bosio by Milton and his mortgagees.[397] It is also not known why the purchase price should have risen steeply, to £4,200.[398]

In the autumn of 1873 the architect for the new church was chosen. He was the Roman Catholic, Joseph Aloysius Hansom (1803-82). At that time he was working with his son Joseph Stanislaus Hansom, who assumed control of the firm in 1880[399] and was responsible for the important later stages of the work here in the 1880's and 1890's. J. A. Hansom was evidently chosen at least in part for his recent work on churches at Arundel, Manchester and Boulogne, and his designs then being executed for St. Aloysius's Church at Oxford.[400] It was his first church in London.

A temporary iron church was provided, in front of Heckfield Lodge, by Samuel Dyer, 'portable house builder' of the Euston Road.[401]

The permanent church, placed behind Heckfield Lodge, which was adapted for use as the priory and extended forward in a refectory wing, was built in 1874-5 by G. H. and A. Grimwood of Upper Charlton Street,

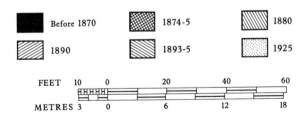

Fig. 57. Church of Our Lady of Seven Dolours, and St. Mary's Priory, No. 264 Fulham Road, plan

Fitzroy Square. The clerk of works was Condy. The contract price was £5,240, although the Fathers cautiously provided for calling a halt, if needs be, at £2,850.[402] Father Bosio had the reputation of keeping a keen watch on the builders' work and charges: nevertheless in 1875 he was complaining that the actual cost had risen to £9,000.[403]

The materials are stock brick with external dressings in Ham Hill stone, and internal dressings in Corsham Down stone, except for the pillars of the nave, which are of 'Freeman's Cornish granite' with polished shafts. Minton's encaustic tiles were laid in parts of the church.[404]

The original dedication of the church, at the laying of the foundation stone by Cardinal Manning in 1874, was to the Sacred and Sorrowing Hearts of Jesus and Mary,[405] but it immediately became known as Our Lady of Seven Dolours.[406]

The style of the church (Plates 76a, b, 77b) is Early English, although incorporating some features, such as the Decorated choir windows, the 'strainer arch' on the (liturgically) 'south' side of the sanctuary, and the choir-stalls, designed to look like later work.

The interior decoration was chiefly in the hands of Thomas Orr and Company, 'church furnishers and embroiderers' of Baker Street.[407] The altar of the Lady Chapel was carved by 'Mr Farmer', perhaps of Farmer and Brindley.[408] Most of the glazing, probably plain, was provided by J. J. Boyce, 'window lead maker' of Great Titchfield Street,[409] although the Lady Chapel had a window painted by a friend of the Fathers, Lord Charles Thynne,[404] and the central window at the (liturgically) 'East' end was soon filled with stained glass made by Clayton and Bell to designs by W. Tipping of Edith Grove, Chelsea.[410] G. M. Hammer, 'school furnisher' of Blue Anchor Lane and the Strand, provided benches, stalls and confessionals to Hansom's designs.[411] At the opening it was commented that the Fathers looked to Rome and Munich for some of the decorative fittings or devotional aids.[404] But over the years much has also come from craftsmen nearer home in Chelsea and the Fulham Road.

A notable contribution to the interior, in progress in 1876, was made by one of the Fathers, Piriteo Simoni, an artist, who designed and painted the altar of the Seven Founders (now the altar of Our Lady) with panels skilfully executed in a thirteenth-century Italian style.

The church was described in *The Builder* at its opening in September 1875 but without evaluative comment.[412] *The Tablet* said 'the front elevation is bold and effective, and the interior devotional and thoroughly church-like in composition and details, yet devoid of gloom'.[404]

The next major work was the building of a new block for the priory on the Fulham Road frontage (joined to the old house behind by the plain, recently constructed refectory wing), together with a street entrance to the approach leading to the church. This was done in 1880, to designs by J. A. Hansom and Sons and under the supervision of

Joseph Stanislaus Hansom (Plate 76d). A new contractor was chosen, Frank Wilkins of the Fulham Road, at a price of £1,580 (final cost, £1,620). Iron gates were provided by John Hardman and Company of Birmingham. It was probably at that time that W. H. Palmer, 'architectural sculptor' of Flood Street, Chelsea, carved the west front of the church, now largely concealed by the later narthex.[413] Inside, an organ was provided by another local firm, that of Henry Jones of the Fulham Road, replacing a temporary instrument supplied by them.[414]

The new buildings were greeted by *The Building News* as a 'welcome addition to this part of the Fulham Road', although it regretted that they were overtopped by the houses and shops immediately to the west[415] — a disadvantage made less apparent when a tower was added fifteen years later. *The Building News* did not comment on the choice of a late Gothic style for the domestic front of the priory in conjunction with the Early English style of the church and gateway — a deliberate contrast found also in J. Stanislaus Hansom's design for the Servites' church and monastery at Bognor, begun in the following year.

In 1882-3 important interior additions were made by the installation of a polychrome stone pulpit and a great pinnacled High Altar in Caen stone, alabaster and marble, both designed by J. Stanislaus Hansom. The cost was said to be about £1,000. *The Builder* and *The Building News* both described the work and the former gave a large illustration of the High Altar, which rose thirty-eight feet six inches above the nave floor at its central flèche (Plate 76b). The carving on the High Altar was by Richard Boulton of Cheltenham, and the tabernacle (now removed to the chapel of the Blessed Sacrament) by George Hardman of the Fulham Road. The main constructional work, however, was by George Porter, designated 'sculptor', of King's Road, Chelsea.[416] Of this only the altar table itself partly survives.

The work of adding to and enriching the church continued in 1890 with the reconstruction and enhancement of the Lady Chapel (now the chapel of the Blessed Sacrament) in a Decorated style to J. Stanislaus Hansom's designs on the (liturgically) 'north' side of the sanctuary (Plate 77c). The builder was again Porter, at a cost said to be £1,115.[417]

The Fathers perhaps liked employing local men and Porter was retained as contractor for the last great work, undertaken to Hansom's designs in 1893-5. This was the raising of a Perpendicular bell-tower over the entrance, which was itself dressed with a battlemented Perpendicular porch, and the construction of a covered, Early English approach to the church (Plate 77a) via a new, large, Early English narthex. This is separated by an arcade, opened in the pre-existing 'west' front, from the nave, which is at a higher level and approached by steps. This spatial sequence is now the most characteristic and telling feature of the church (fig. 57).

At the same time stained-glass windows were provided by Jonathan (or Ion) Pace, nearby at No. 252 Fulham

Road, at a cost of some £1,039, and the organ was enlarged by Henry Jones. The bronze statue of St. Peter in the narthex (copied from that in the Vatican) is by Paul H. Brondreth (at £135), and four statues in stone were provided for unknown positions by Vincent Biglioski, sculptor, of Upper Cheyne Row, Chelsea (at £89). The bells, by Mears and Stainbank, cost £636. The total outlay, variously stated at £10,132 or £12,000, was defrayed, as some earlier costs had been, by Charles Robertson, a stockjobber of Begbroke, Oxfordshire.[418]

Porter had tendered at £4,804 for his part of the work, but was eventually paid £6,291.[419] The employment of a man not very experienced in contracting for a large work as a general builder and without the use of either a clerk of works or properly made-out bills of quantities led to difficulties. Porter in fact charged too little. In Hansom's view 'he evidently had not the slightest conception of the way he had cheated himself; and it remained for me to point out to him how several items in his estimate meant nothing but absolute loss to him'. Being told this by Hansom, the Prior, Father Appolloni, instructed him to increase the payment to Porter to cover the work actually done. Sadly, this good thought led to trouble, and the Fathers became involved in a disagreement with Hansom when he charged a quantity surveyor's fee for the extra calculation thus necessitated. The matter had to be sent for arbitration to a past president of the Royal Institute of British Architects, J. Macvicar Anderson, who pronounced a compromise judgement.[420] This dispute did not, however, prevent Porter's employment in the following year, 1896, on work of unknown extent,[421] or Hansom's employment to design the tomb of Father Appolloni himself on his death in 1900.[422]

A total departure from the prevailing style of the church was made in 1925, when the impressive green and gold marble baptistery was opened off the 'west' side of the narthex, designed in an Arts-and-Crafts Lombardic-Byzantine style (Plate 77d). The octagonal bronze font is said to have been 'the gift and work of two convert artists, Miss Baker and Miss Brown', the former perhaps the Miss Alice Baker, artist, who is found at that time at No. 125 Cheyne Walk.[423] Unfortunately the designer of the baptistery scheme as a whole (and presumably of the small war memorial in the same style) is not known.

Preparatory to the consecration of the church, which did not take place until 1953, the sanctuary was extended further towards the nave.[424]

Subsequent changes have been rather by removal than addition. Externally, important alterations were made in 1962 when the top of the bell-tower, the dressing of the gateway, and the front of the priory were all divested of architectural features (architects, Archard and Partners). At the time the tower was said to have become dangerous in its upper parts and the stonework of the Priory window-dressings to have passed beyond repair.[425] The effect has been to make the Fulham Road front look of a more meagre and earlier Victorian period than 1880-95

(Plate 76c). Even greater has been the change inside brought about by the removal in 1974 of the polychrome pulpit and of the greater part of the High Altar. This had completely screened the apsidal end of the sanctuary and its destruction was intended to conform with the changes of liturgical practice that followed the Second Vatican Council of 1962-5.

Some features of the church are :

Narthex : tomb of the second Prior, Father Appolloni (1838-1900) with marble Pietà carved by J. W. Swynnerton; bronze figure of Our Saviour by Mayer and Company of Munich, 1872. *Magdalene altar* : marble relief by J. W. Swynnerton, 1895. *Founders' chapel* : carved and painted retable by Stufflesser family; frescoes by Father Simoni; the altar has been removed, together with panels painted by Father Simoni which were moved here from the present Lady Altar in 1952. *St. Joseph's altar* : painted panels signed by Leopoldo Galli, Florence (evidently replacing paintings by Guido Guidi); statue of St. Joseph by Mayer and Company of Munich. *Chamber organ* by James Davis of Francis Street (now Torrington Place, where Davis was in *c.* 1809-24[426]).

Nos. 266 and 266A Fulham Road and Nos. 1-11 (odd) Redcliffe Gardens

Between the Servite church and priory at No. 264 Fulham Road and the corner with Redcliffe Gardens the history of the site before 1681 is uncertain (z on fig. 48). It was probably part of the Hobson property which in 1639 included the rather indeterminate breadth of the droveway of Walnut Tree Walk on the line of Redcliffe Gardens. From 1681 to 1710 the land was owned as garden or orchard ground by a John Frank, who was said to have built the house and two cottages which stood upon it. The property passed, evidently as freehold, to his widow and then to his son John, a joiner.[427] In 1735 a slip of ground on the west was added, by lease from Daniel Pettiward of Putney, esquire:[428] the deeds relating to the property suggest its abutments to west and south, on the lane and high road, were not precisely established. The freehold, after passing through various hands (in 1750, for example, being sold for £300[429]), was bought in 1802 by Alexander Ramsay Robinson, esquire,[430] a landowner elsewhere in the parish.[431] The occupant of the house since 1797 had been a George Burley, probably a lawyer, who remained until 1824.[432] The rateable value rose greatly in 1808 and Salway's view of 1811[89] (Plate 72) may show a new or much renovated house. In 1835 Miss Mary Ann Foy, doubtless a relation of the schoolmaster in Seymour Walk, took the house (called Burley House) for a girls' boarding school, which she conducted until 1865-6.[155]

The making of Redcliffe Gardens northwards from Fulham Road by the building firm of Corbett and McClymont had already begun and the first houses to be built by them there were already just completed on the opposite side of the road on Pettiward land. The freeholders here followed suit. Burley House was demolished and in 1868 Robert Tetlow Robinson of Dieppe and Lucy Margaret Robinson of Bayswater granted leases (effectively for ninety-eight years) to Corbett and McClymont of newly completed houses over shops at Nos. 266 and 266A Fulham Road (in May) and to Corbett or McClymont individually of houses at Nos. 1-11 (odd) Redcliffe Gardens (in November).[433] In their usual way

Corbett and McClymont were each parties to the individual leases to the other. In Redcliffe Gardens the existence of No. 264 required them to plan wider and shallower houses than usual.

In 1960-2, after a fatal fire, Nos. 266 and 266A Fulham Road were reconstructed (Stewart and Shirley Thomson, architects), with a steel-framed concrete staircase at the north end in Redcliffe Gardens, expressed externally in narrow-coursed, vitrified engineering bricks.[434]

CHAPTER XII

The Boltons and Redcliffe Square Area

Westward of the properties in Drayton Gardens and south of the Old Brompton Road an area extending to Brompton Cemetery comprises some ninety-three acres which in 1800 were almost entirely unbuilt upon. To the southward the area was bounded, east of Walnut Tree Walk on the line of Redcliffe Gardens, by the properties fronting Fulham Road which constituted part of the small township of Little Chelsea, while beyond Walnut Tree Walk the unbuilt area extended south to Fulham Road itself. The only important part affected by residential use was the three acres or so of mansion and garden at Coleherne House, a substantial dwelling house since the seventeenth century. Between about 1802 and 1845 some eight acres more, near the Old Brompton Road, were devoted to nine villas or 'cottages' and their gardens or pleasure grounds. All but one lay east of Coleherne House. These were mostly built, about the same time as some villas north of the Old Brompton Road, on part of the property recently acquired by a successful Mayfair confectioner, James Gunter, and it was on the large remainder of his property, descended to his son Robert, that the spread of building began in about 1850 which over the next twenty-five years or so covered almost all the area with streets of houses (Plates 70b, 71b).* Beginning in the east it extended westward, and after Robert's death in 1852 largely on properties either inherited or bought for the purpose by his two sons, Robert and James. Their tenures were separate, and they granted their leases individually, but were advised by the same lawyer and surveyor. The earlier, and perhaps more attractive, part of the development, westward so far as The Little Boltons, was entrusted to various building-lessees. After 1863 the work was almost entirely in the hands of the firm of William Corbett and Alexander McClymont. They had already done work in the southern part of this area a year or two before under other owners, and were to do so also in the extreme west and south-west, particularly on the land of the Pettiward family. Their work on the estates of the two Gunter brothers and on those of other owners is not distinguishable.

This lack of co-extension between the units of land-ownership and of significant building-ownership makes it desirable to discuss this area as a whole. So, too, does the comparatively unhistoric nature of the largest element in the land-ownership pattern, that of the Gunters, where various properties were brought together piecemeal between 1801 and 1866 and subjected to a common process of development.

Altogether, on the eighty-two acres or so largely developed between 1850 and 1876 (including a small area built-over in the 1880's), some 1,100 houses, two churches, ninety or so mews premises and five public houses were built, and the greater part of this survives today. Of these 1,100 houses, some 670 were built on the Gunters' properties, and some 220 on the land of R. J. Pettiward. About 750 were built under leases or (in 76 instances) conveyances to Corbett and McClymont, and another 180 or so under leases to other building tradesmen evidently nominated by them. The most active period for the granting of leases of newly completed carcases of houses was 1866-9. In those four years 542 leases or conveyances were granted, all but 28 being to Corbett and McClymont or their nominees (fig. 64 on page 213).

The property of the Gunter family also extended north of the Old Brompton Road, where James Gunter's purchases had slightly antedated those to the south. Corbett and McClymont also operated north of the road, conspicuously if not very extensively. This area will be described in volume XLII of the *Survey of London*.

The line of this part of Old Brompton Road had from an early period been a property division. The area here discussed (fig. 58) was, as to the greater part of it, called Coleherne (or a variant of this), which as a place-name existed so early as 1430.[1] A portion of some fifteen or sixteen acres, immediately south of the line of the road and bounded to east, south and west by Coleherne, was separately distinguished as Goodwin's Field (C and H on fig. 58), a name already applied to it in the 1530's.[2] In the sixteenth century all was regarded as part of the manor of Earl's Court. Goodwin's Field remained largely or entirely copyhold land until acts of enfranchisement in 1809 and 1864,[3] but Coleherne seems to have lost its manorial status by or before the early eighteenth century. From at least the early seventeenth century the area was sub-divided into enclosures, and some of it from earlier. The history of its tenure before the period of building does not emerge at all completely from the records, however, partly because the closes are mostly identified in documents only by their extent and at any given time there was more than one 'four-acre' or 'eight-acre' close, and partly because their tenants' names also afford very uncertain identification

---

*Tabulated information about the present buildings in this area (and in the part of Fulham Road discussed in Chapter XI) will be found on pages 237-40.

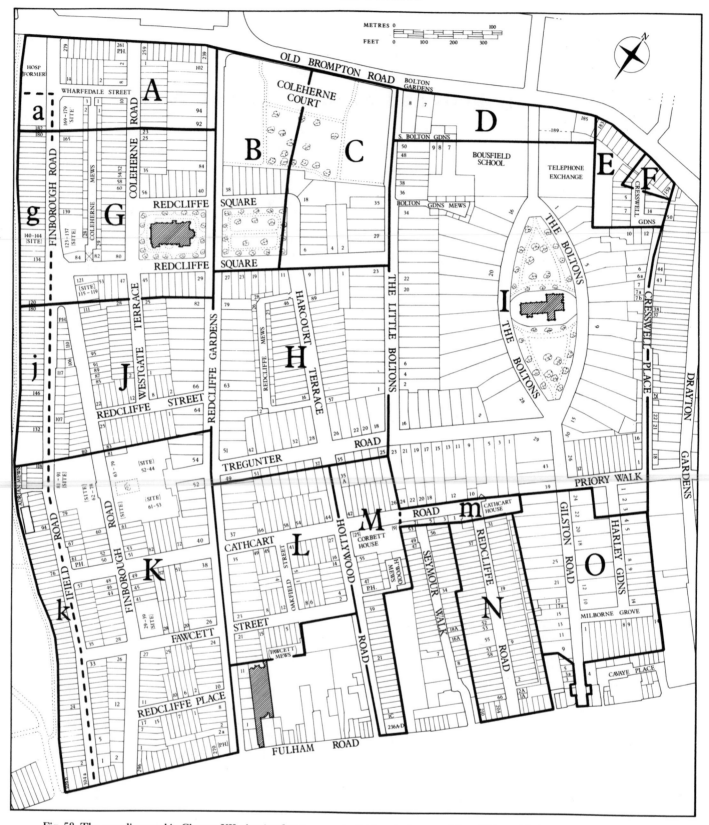

Fig. 58. The area discussed in Chapter XII, showing former property divisions by heavy and dotted lines, with the present street layout and house numbers. Based on the Ordnance Survey of 1949-72

when, as is usual, the tenants are known to have had a number of holdings in the vicinity.

The earliest map of the whole area in any detail is so late as 1822. Starling's map of that year (Plate 70b) shows the intensive development of Little Chelsea to the south, the beginnings of more luxurious building on the north side, and between them the rectangular or squareish enclosures of garden ground, market gardens and nurseries.

Landownership to the Early Nineteenth Century

To deal first with the ground landlordship until the early decades of the nineteenth century, a start may be made with the areas C, E, F, G, H and I on fig. 58 in 1715. They were then owned by a Peter Lavigne, grocer or perfumier of Covent Garden (who also owned the future site of Seymour Walk in Little Chelsea, see page 177). The western part, C, G and H (of which C and H constituted Goodwin's Field) he had bought (like the 'Seymour Walk' site) from two brothers, John and Thomas Morgan of Marlborough, Wiltshire — C and H at least in 1699. The earlier history of G is not known except in so far as it seems to have been the property which before 1639 had been acquired by the Southwark glazier, Lancelot Hobson (see page 165), and then and subsequently bore the name Little Coleherne. Goodwin's Field (C, H) had been inherited in 1699 by the Morgans under the provisions of the will of their brother Charles Morgan (d. 1682), also a grocer of Covent Garden, who had bequeathed his shop there directly to Lavigne, formerly his 'servant'.[4] Morgan had bought Goodwin's Field in 1680 from a William Chare who in turn had inherited it, by the custom of the manor of Earl's Court, as the youngest son of a John Chare.[5] The latter had bought it in 1641 from mortgagees of Samuel Arnold,[6] one of a family widely propertied in the vicinity of Earl's Court. (Earlier, in the 1530's to 1550's, Goodwin's Field had been owned by a family called Thatcher.[7]) One of Samuel Arnold's mortgagees in 1641, Francis Dyson, was in that year the owner of land to the east, probably identifiable with E, F and I.[6] (This was part of the rather straggling area, extending also south and west of Goodwin's Field, called Great Coleherne.) Whether that land followed the same line of descent as the western part to Lavigne is uncertain.

All this property of Lavigne's passed on his death in 1717 to his widow[8] and then in 1719 to their daughter, at that time also a widow, who promptly sold it to Edward Williams, described as of the Customs House, gentleman. What he paid for Goodwin's Field (C, H) is not known but the other parts (G, E, F and I) cost him £1,688.[9] After Williams's death in 1752 his son, also Edward Williams, of the Inner Temple, leased and then, in the following year, sold Goodwin's Field to trustees for the banker George Campbell, head of the firm that was to become Coutts.[10] Campbell, like subsequent owners of Goodwin's

Field, lived here, in Coleherne House (at the north-west corner of B). The history of the tenure of this old house is distinct from though often parallel to that of the adjacent Goodwin's Field, and the discussion of it is deferred. After Campbell's death in 1760 his trustees, in 1761, sold Goodwin's Field to the bearer of a name that became locally important — William Boulton, esquire, of Frith Street, Soho.[11] Like the elder Williams he was a public official, being one of the Clerks of the Roads in the Post Office. This was at that time a lucrative situation (by reason of its perquisites rather than its salary), and Boulton's nephew, the diarist William Hickey, calls him 'very rich'.[12] Boulton paid the trustees £1,220, but it is not clear whether this was only for Coleherne House, which he bought at the same time.[13] The land to the east (E, F and I) and west (G) remained in the Williams family until the 1790's. In 1796 William Boulton, the elder Boulton's son, bought E, F and I, and thus acquired, though only for a short time, the area that still (it seems) commemorates his name.[14] This part of Great Coleherne was now called Home Field — a confusing change of name particularly as at about the same time Goodwin's Field itself became known as Coleherne. The following year G was temporarily separated from this property-holding by its sale to Thomas Smith of Chelsea, gentleman,[15] elsewhere a developer, who left it unbuilt upon.

Some eight years later, in 1805, Smith and his mortgagees sold this land, G, to James Gunter of Berkeley Square, confectioner.[16] Gunter already had property north of Old Brompton Road and was acquiring other lands south of the road. In 1807 he bought E and I, but not the small plot F, from William Boulton (who had renamed himself William Boulton Poynton) and others.[17] Boulton Poynton had already sold F, in 1805, to a Samuel Babb, as the site for a genteel 'cottage'.[18] If James Gunter wanted to acquire a continuous holding east-to-west he was frustrated when in 1808 Boulton Poynton sold his third property, Goodwin's Field (C, H), to a goldsmith in Cockspur Street, Philip Gilbert, perhaps for £3,234.[19] Gilbert had already bought garden ground at M, extending to the Fulham Road, in 1806[20] (see below and page 180), but his family, although it retained these properties into the 1860's, was another, like the Morgans, Lavignes, Williamses and Boultons, to acquire substantial holdings here and then pass from the scene without leaving much trace in building.

Adjacent to the old Lavigne corpus of property at its northern end were two other pieces of ground that came to James Gunter at this time (fig. 58). At A the land had passed into his ownership in 1801 from the representatives of a John Mears, late of St. Margaret's, Westminster, gentleman, deceased.[21] It had been bought in 1755 by a farmer, John Mears, from a mason, Robert Hardcastle of Lambeth, who in the same year had himself bought it from the Rector of East Barnet, Samuel Grove.[22] Grove's ownership seems to have derived from the acquisition of a mortgage interest, perhaps of only part of the property, in

1737.[23] The mortgagor at that date, a 'yeoman', William Clarke, evidently derived his own lien on the land in part from a ninety-nine-year lease granted to an Edward Clarke in 1676 by a John Arnold.[24] In 1641 the land was in the hands of William Arnold, one of Samuel Arnold's mortgagees in Goodwin's Field.[6]

At D hardly anything is known of the ownership before its sale to James Gunter in 1811 by representatives of the Pettiward family, of Suffolk and Putney. Their ownership went back at least to Walter Pettiward, who died in 1749, but its origin is unknown, although elsewhere in south-west Kensington Pettiward ownership can be traced back to the 1640's. In 1811 Gunter acquired this well-placed two-acre rectangle under the name of Glassington Close or (as in 1753) Long Close.[25]

Southward from I on fig. 58 James Gunter extended his easterly holding just (and only just) to Fulham Road by the purchase of O in 1812.[26] At that time the vendor, George Groves, was laying out other property of his to the east as Thistle Grove (now part of Drayton Gardens, see page 166). Perhaps Gunter contemplated following suit, but did not do so, contenting himself with investments in house-sites in Thistle Grove. This plot (O) had come to Groves's father, John Groves, in 1786 by purchase from the sons of the builder Henry Holland, who had acquired it in 1781 from a beneficiary of the partition of the extensive property of the Warton family. Its descent, which is touched upon on page 163, went back to a purchase from Sir Arthur Gorges in 1651.

The Warton property in Kensington was not compact, and the awkwardly shaped piece M shared this line of descent down to ownership by the Hollands. They sold it to a William Virtue of Chelsea in 1786 and he to Philip Gilbert in 1806.[27] Like the Gilbert property northward it awaited purchase by others in the 1860's to be covered with houses.

Immediately west of O at N a mainly unbuilt property with an old house on its Fulham Road frontage also changed hands about that time, in 1807. It then passed to a Gloucestershire family called Batchellor from representatives of the Middleton family whose ownership went back to the seventeenth century and perhaps derived from the Hobson family already mentioned.[28] Of the properties so far dealt with this is the first never to pass into Gunter ownership, and the account given of it in the chapter on Little Chelsea would suffice (pages 174-6) were it not that the circumstances of its laying out, chiefly as Redcliffe Road, when it came to be sold by the Batchellors in 1859 brings it also within the scope of this chapter (see below).

At L the ground had in the early nineteenth century been held by the owners of the two houses at what were later Nos. 252-258 (even) Fulham Road since at least Ralph Palmer's tenure in the late seventeenth century (see page 185). Nothing is known of the earlier history of the

ground, or of the house upon it, unless the latter can be identified with the house of eleven hearths, otherwise difficult to locate, which in c. 1662-6 was in the possession of James 'Bovey'[29] — probably a member of the Boevey family whose chief property was on the south side of the Fulham Road in Chelsea.* In c. 1670 the occupant of that 'Bovey' house was Doctor John Whitaker until c. 1701, when other members of his family succeeded him until 1724 or later.[32] Charles Boyle, later fourth Earl of Orrery, soldier, author and patron of science, was born at Doctor Whitaker's house in 1674.[33] In 1784 James Gunter, in one of his earliest ventures in property in this area, acquired a mortgage interest from Lewis Lochée, to secure a loan of £700, but the Gunters did not acquire the freehold until 1836, when the Lochée family sold the ground to James Gunter's son Robert — his only purchase in this area and at that time isolated from his father's acquisitions.[34]

The large plot of ground at K on fig. 58, now virtually indistinguishable in appearance from the rest of the area subjected to the operations of Corbett and McClymont, has a quite different history of ownership from the lands so far mentioned. It is still in part owned by the Pettiward family and was so at least as early as 1753.[35] As at D, however, it is uncertain whether that ownership extends, like the Pettiwards' former tenure of the adjacent ground westward described on page 241, back to the mid seventeenth century.

The last plot on fig. 58 of which the ownership needs to be indicated is J. Together with K, L and I it was generally considered part of Great Coleherne, whereas G to the north was Little Coleherne. Like Goodwin's Field (C, H) its tenure at the beginning of the nineteenth century was still as copyhold of the manor of Earl's Court (being enfranchised only in 1867[36]). It was then in the ownership of the Hillersdon family who acquired it about 1794, evidently from a descendant of the Henry Marsh of North End, Fulham, who had bought it in 1641 from Samuel Arnold.[37]

The Use and Occupation of the Land

Despite such instances of long tenure, this diversity of ownerships in the area as a whole shows that it did not lie undeveloped in building because it reposed in the hands of one or a few ancestral proprietors with, perhaps, greater interests elsewhere. A sufficiently active picture emerges of land-transfers between men seemingly of a type to foster building development when that promised well. But the occupation of the land remained overwhelmingly agricultural or horticultural. By the time of the Tithe Commissioners' tabulation of the whole area in 1843 the part not taken as the sites of villas was shown to be divided into

---

*Their residence, rebuilt as Shaftesbury House, was that later occupied by Narcissus Luttrell, who in 1716 was evidently aggrieved not to be granted the lease of at least part of this ground.[30] Conceivably he had some 'historic' reason to hope it would again 'go with' the Chelsea house.[31]

some seventy acres of market gardens and ten acres of grassland or paddock.[38] The earlier picture is more variegated. Towards the south end of Goodwin's Field a gravel pit is mentioned in 1753,[39] and the right to excavate gravel was reserved by the ground landlord a few years later.[11] In 1808 land in this vicinity was said to be on lease of recent date for the purpose of extracting gravel.[40] A few years previously, in 1802, the farming tenant of area K on fig. 58 was also licensed by the owner to dig for gravel.[41] Brick earth had been dug at an unknown date in the part of area G where St. Luke's Church, Redcliffe Square, was built in 1872, when the old excavations impeded the laying of its foundations.[42] Some five acres of the area I were arable in about 1720,[43] and were probably still so in 1807.[17] Part of C and H was arable in 1748,[44] and rye grew there in 1808.[45] In 1746 the area L was described as 'planted with Walnut Trees, Mulberry Trees, Apple Trees and other fruit Trees'.[46] The walnut trees in particular were a landmark and presumably account for the name of Walnut Tree Walk, on the line of Redcliffe Gardens, which existed as a 'lane or drove' in 1639,[47] a 'warple' in 1753,[48] a 'footpath or bridle way' in 1797,[15] and a 'bridle or carriage way' in 1805.[16] This orchard at L is shown on the Ordnance Survey map surveyed in 1865, at the moment of its supersession by houses.[49] At the beginning of the nineteenth century another orchard, of cherry trees, was at D-E on fig. 58. Starling also shows the eastern limb of M and the south-west part of K as orchard in 1822 (Plate 70b).

Some of the 'gardens' here were or had been nurseries rather than market gardens. In the 1780's nurseries at O and N respectively (fig. 58) were conducted by James Russell and Daniel Grimwood (see pages 173, 175), the latter, at least, a notable name in the propagation of the rose, like his successor here in c. 1807-19, Henry Shailer.[50]

A comparison of Starling's map of 1822 with the tithe map of 1843 suggests the growing ascendancy of market gardening. At areas G and H pasture was seemingly changed to that use, and the nursery garden at O just mentioned seems similarly to have been taken by James Gunter's son Robert into his market garden at I (fig. 58).

In 1843 the agrarian occupants of the land were five.[38] Robert Gunter occupied his own land at A, G, I and O as part of the market-gardening enterprise which attracted the attention of contemporaries by its business-like progressiveness:[51] he himself lived and had extensive holdings north of the Old Brompton Road. At L the occupant under him was James Broadbent, probably dwelling in the house mentioned above as perhaps Doctor Whitaker's (or its successor), which stood in what is now the roadway of Fawcett Street, near Nos. 6-8. It was approached from Fulham Road via the precursor of Hollywood Road, called Hollywood Grove. At J the occupier of the land under John Hillersdon was William Atwood. At N John Rubergall had a small holding under Edward Batchellor and probably lived in one of the houses near its southern end in

the area discussed on page 175.[52] The fifth was the market gardener John Poupart, with a name later well known at Covent Garden, who occupied H and M under the Gilberts and K under the Pettiwards. He, too, lived here, in the small unpretentious farm-house near the south-east corner of K shown by Salway in 1811 (Plate 72).[53] Salway depicts a barn behind it, and in front a wooden fence that announces the lapse to rusticity after the front garden-walls and gate-piers of Little Chelsea. It stood near the present No. 2A Redcliffe Gardens and perhaps dated from the late 1780's.[54] Apart from this house, the only buildings of any note in the fields in the 1840's seem to have been a cottage at the south-west corner of H on fig. 58 (near the present No. 49 Redcliffe Gardens), James Broadbent's house, and some farm buildings erected by the go-ahead Robert Gunter at what is now the south end of the carriageway of Coleherne Road, seemingly between the dates of Starling's map of 1822 and Greenwood's of 1827. Away in the south-west corner of K, however, in the angle of Honey Lane and Fulham Road (now approximately the site of Nos. 304A-306B Fulham Road), a furniture dealer's establishment, run by a family called Jackson, was set up in 1812 and survived until the building wave of the sixties.[55]

Coleherne House to 1815

Having brought some aspects of the ownership and use of the area forward to the early nineteenth century it is convenient to revert to an area notably different from the rest — Coleherne House and its immediate grounds (B on fig. 58). (The house was sometimes called Coleherne Court, but is here called House throughout to distinguish it more readily from the blocks of flats which occupy its site.) Here at the beginning of the nineteenth century the old mansion was occupied by the family owning Goodwin's Field and had gardens that extended eastward across the northern part of C on fig. 58 to a shrubbery or 'garden walk' extending down what is now the west side of The Little Boltons. Here in 1808 the widowed Mrs. Boulton could perambulate.[40] Like Coleherne House itself but unlike most of the intervening garden this strip was a little piece of freehold, having at an earlier date been the 'headland' of the ploughed land to the east.[39] Part of the garden was shaded by the 'lofty brick walls' mentioned in particulars of the property, and a 'well stocked' fishpond extended east-west across the garden.[56]

Unfortunately, little is known of the house itself. Eighteenth-century title-deeds begin the descent of ownership with the occupation by the physician-poet Sir Richard Blackmore, whose tenure can be traced back from 1721 to 1705 or 1706.[57] His poetical works passed swiftly into 'silence and darkness', and Blackmore, 'being despised as a poet was in time neglected as a physician', which perhaps accounts for his vacating the mansion when he did.[58]

A large house existed in this vicinity before then, however, and can doubtless be identified with the same site. This was the house 'at Cold Hearne' which first occurs in the records in 1647 as the place of baptism of two sons of the Parliamentarian John Lambert, being the house of his father-in-law Sir William Lister.[59] In 1653[60] and (seemingly) 1665[61] 'Colehearne house' was occupied by a James Floyde, esquire, and then by a Doctor Ford in 1666.[62] The house can probably be traced forward to occupation by the pioneer journalist Henry Muddiman in c. 1673-1691,[63] being perhaps divided and shared with a Doctor Huybert. Later, this seems to be the house for which Peter Lavigne, the well-propertied Covent Garden grocer already encountered, was assessed by the parish for himself or a tenant in 1696-1701,[57] and the house of Lavigne, known as Coleherne House,[64] can certainly be identified as a piece of property with Blackmore's house, as it was Lavigne's son-in-law who sold the latter house in 1723, after Blackmore's tenancy had ceased.[65] (That Blackmore should have been Lavigne's tenant is consistent with the interest that a William Blackmore of Covent Garden had in another piece of Lavigne's former property in 1730.[66] See page 177.)

The only certain view of Coleherne House is a nineteenth-century photograph showing the staircase compartment[67] (Plate 78b). This gives a glimpse of early-Georgian-looking plasterwork (rather like that, for example, at No. 43 King Street, Covent Garden, of 1716-17). In other respects, however, the view would not preclude an earlier date for the house.

Coleherne House itself seems to have been freed from manorial status by or before the 1720's and thereafter changed hands as freehold. Its curtilage (the eastern and southern parts of area B on fig. 58) remained copyhold, however, until enfranchisement in 1864.[36] The purchaser from Lavigne's son-in-law in 1723 was Thomas Morgan of Lincoln's Inn, esquire, of the family that had earlier owned much land here. Since Blackmore's residence in the house it had been occupied by a Thomas Morphey or Morphew, esquire,[68] but in c. 1724-36 Morgan was the ratepayer.[69] In 1735 Morgan conveyed the house to another lawyer of Lincoln's Inn, Walter Gibbons, in trust himself to sell it on Morgan's death,[70] and in 1739 the latter and Morgan's son sold it to a Sibilla Egerton, spinster, of Soho, who was soon said to be in occupation.[71] The occupant was said to be a Catherine Hays in 1749, when Sibilla and her husband, Sir Francis Eyles Stiles, sold it to another unmarried lady in Soho, Ann Walwood or Watwood.[72] She sold it in 1751 to the banker George Campbell.[73] The ownership was thus reunited with that of the adjacent Goodwin's Field for the first time since Lavigne's ownership of the site. It was therefore presumably about this time that the gardens were extended eastward and the fishpond made. Campbell occupied the property until his death in 1760, and in 1761 it passed like Goodwin's Field into the ownership and occupation of William Boulton and his family.[74] In 1810 Boulton's son,

William Boulton Poynton, sold it to Philip Gilbert,[75] who had recently bought Goodwin's Field from him, and for the next five years Gilbert himself lived there.[54]

Coleherne House and Hereford House 1815-99

The subsequent history of areas B and C on fig. 58 is carried through here to the end of the century, before reverting to the history of the larger area about 1810. Philip Gilbert's abandonment of Coleherne House in 1815 was the result of his building a second large house on the east side of the extended garden, to which he moved in that year.[54] This was Hereford House, which in views of subsequent date looks much later than 1815 — a high block flanked by big staid conservatories and with the appearance of a Victorian idea of the architecture of the reign of George I[76] (Plate 78a). The fact that young Beatrix Potter in 1883 called it 'the red house' also suggests drastic revision since 1815[77] — perhaps in 1871.[78] The Gilberts vacated the house in 1838, and some later occupants were Charles Dance, son of the architect George Dance, burlesque-writer, and clerk in that 'Temple to the Genius of Seediness', the Insolvent Debtors' Court (1841-5); Lady Hotham, life tenant of the Pettiward estate nearby (1846-56); Benjamin Lumley, theatrical manager (1857-9); and Dion Boucicault, a more flamboyant figure of the same type (1861-3).[79] In 1864 representatives of the Gilbert family sold the house, with Coleherne House, to the younger James Gunter,[80] at the same time as Goodwin's Field.

Coleherne House on its vacation by the Gilberts had been occupied by, among others, Lady Georgiana Ponsonby (1816-34), W. J. N. Neale, judge and author (1849, 1851), Thomas Dyke Acland (1850), and Andrew Wynter, physician and essayist (1858-63).[81]

A perplexing circumstance is the lack of any apparent division between the gardens of Coleherne House and Hereford House as they are shown on the Ordnance Survey map surveyed in 1865.[82] The houses were then and always had been occupied by separate families. The arrangement has a long-established look, but perhaps was a very short-lived state of affairs brought about by Dion Boucicault in 1863 when he occupied Hereford House and had the lease also of Coleherne House, which was empty in that year.[83] (The same map shows that the fishpond no longer existed although its site was discernible.)

The double site of Coleherne House and Hereford House had been advertised in 1863 as 'Building Land . . . for an important building operation in first-class residences',[84] and the first effect of James Gunter's purchase of it was to bring this ground within the scope of Corbett and McClymont's schemes for their leasehold building estate. A plan of 1866 shows that they then hoped to carry the line of Hollywood Road and Harcourt Terrace northward to Old Brompton Road between the gardens of the two houses and at the same time build over at least the

Coleherne House site.[85] The line of road was marked out on the ground,[86] but Corbett and McClymont became bankrupt in 1878 and the Coleherne site remained undeveloped. The strip of intended road was evidently let on short lease by James Gunter to William Corbett, who in 1879-80 kept it as garden ground. He was at that time very hopeful of getting an extension of his tenure to the end of the century.[87] If he did so it would at least partly explain why it was not until about 1900 that the redevelopment of the sites of the two houses was taken in hand.

Meanwhile the two houses survived. Hereford House was occupied in 1865-9 by an Adam Spielman and in 1872 by a Leopold Seligman into the 1880's.[54] By 1896 it had declined to use as the home of a rather blue-blooded ladies' cycling club, where races were held on Saturday afternoons. 'The track is a miniature Olympian, composed of wood with trellis-work sides. It forms a circle round the grounds, running over two artistic bridges.'[88] In c. 1899-1900, however, Hereford House was demolished to make way for the flats of Coleherne Court.

Coleherne House had its longest occupancy under James Gunter's ownership, when from 1865 to 1898 it was the home of Edmund Tattersall, head of the bloodstock auctioneers.[89] It, too, was demolished in c. 1899-1900.

Villa-building near Old Brompton Road, c. 1802-44

The erection of Hereford House about 1815 was part of a significant development in that neighbourhood. This was the building of villas near but generally not fronting the south side of Old Brompton Road (fig. 59). Respectable houses of the kind called 'small' were already stretching out along the winding, leafy road from Old Brompton towards Earl's Court and extending westward the spacious, sequestered suburban development that already characterized Old Brompton.

In the area under discussion a lead was given at Hawk Cottage, built for occupation by Samuel Babb about 1802-4 at F on fig. 58 and sold to him by W. Boulton Poynton in 1805.[90]

More significant was the building of White Cottage in c. 1809 at what was later the south-west end of South Bolton Gardens. This was on the land (I on fig. 58) bought by James Gunter two years before and was evidently part of the same campaign in which he built a number of villas (one for his own occupation) between c. 1805 and 1813 on the opposite side of Old Brompton Road a little further west. Its positioning vis-à-vis Mr. Pettiward's cherry orchard (at D on fig. 58) — soon to be bought by James Gunter but not yet his property — and the eastern shrubbery of Coleherne House's grounds (at C) adumbrated the northern end of what later became The Little Boltons and the western end of the road later called South Bolton Gardens. The house was subsequently known as Rathmore Lodge at No. 10 South Bolton Gardens. (The name White Cottage was later applied to a quite different house on the north side of South Bolton Gardens, behind Nos. 5 and 6 Bolton Gardens.) The first occupant was John Fermor, until 1830.[91]

For his next house, Cresswell Lodge, James Gunter went to the other side of his 1807 purchase, at E on fig. 58. There in 1809 he made a building lease to a bricklayer with whom he was similarly associated on the other side of Old Brompton Road, James Faulkner of Jermyn Street,[92] who in 1810, when he subscribed to Thomas Faulkner's history of Chelsea, described himself as 'bricklayer to her Royal Highness the Princess Charlotte of Wales'.[93] (Later he subscribed also to Faulkner's history of Kensington, in 1820.) James Faulkner very soon sub-leased the property to a local builder, William Blore, a carpenter in Knightsbridge.[94] Blore seems to have mortgaged his leasehold interest back to James Gunter, who was probably financing the building of the house, and when Blore became bankrupt his assignees and Faulkner returned the leasehold interest to Gunter in 1812.[95] In the following year Gunter leased the newly built house, with additional land to the west and north, to its first occupant.[96] He was William Cresswell of Belgravia, probably an elder brother of the judge, (Sir) Cresswell Cresswell.[97] An advertisement of the house for sale in 1820 noticed its extensive aviary and conservatory, the 'high condition' of the plantations and the 'particularly beautiful and diversified views' enjoyed from the house. Its appearance can be judged in an undated lithograph, perhaps of the 1840's (Plate 78c). This shows the severest style of the Regency set off by rustic verandahing and an elaboration of sun-shades and trellis-work around the great west-facing bow, evoking the fierce suns of a still crescent empire rather than umbrageous Brompton.[98] Lady Groves lived there in 1831-4 and the Reverend T. S. Evans in 1835-40 but by 1842 it was a ladies' school.[55]

After James Gunter's death his son Robert had Osborn House, still surviving at No. 7 South Bolton Gardens, built eastward of White Cottage in a plain late-Georgian manner. The first occupant was a Jacob Jones in 1821. The name of the house derives from the residence of Sir John Osborn, fifth baronet, in 1826-47.[54]

The identity of South Bolton Gardens as a residential road between The Little Boltons and the northern limb of The Boltons (Plate 79a) has now been destroyed by the post-war construction of the Bousfield School, converting the road into a cul-de-sac. Originally the sequence of villas was extended eastward, after a rather long interval, by the building of Bladon Lodge in 1836 under a building agreement concluded the previous autumn by Robert Gunter with the first occupant, Martin Bladon Edward Hawke Nixon, who lived there intermittently until 1859.[99] It was again a plain house, facing south over a large garden, with a central bow to light the drawing-room (Plate 99a).

A more highly wrought attempt at architectural effect followed two years later, when Sidmouth Lodge was built east of what is now the northern limb of The Boltons.

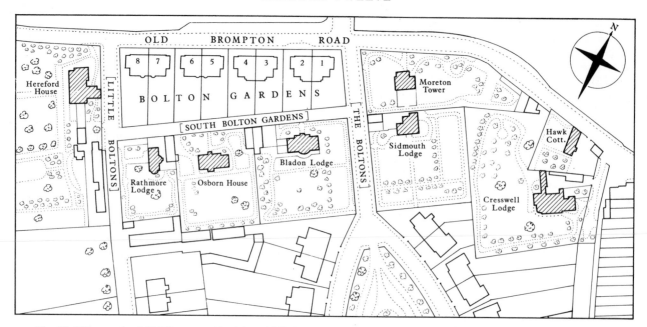

Fig. 59. Villas south of Old Brompton Road in *c.* 1865. Based on the Ordnance Survey of 1862-72, with modern road names

Again Robert Gunter's lease, in March 1838, was to the first occupant, Captain Samuel Lyde.[100] He was presumably a sometime resident at Sidmouth as his son had been born there.[101] Lyde occupied the house from 1839 to 1848.[54] Like Bladon Lodge, it was south-facing. The façade was carefully composed in a neo-Greek style, with a grave and narrow entrance between Ionic columns *in antis* (Plate 78d).[102]

The cherry orchard between the new road and Old Brompton Road had been Gunter property since 1811. In 1840 the western part was taken by Philip Conway of Earl's Court as a nursery and florist's establishment, which continued until the site was given over in 1862 to the building of Nos. 1-8 Bolton Gardens. The eastern part was leased to the occupant of Bladon Lodge in 1839 as an additional garden.[103]

In 1842 Robert Gunter completed this sequence south of Old Brompton Road when he had a 'cottage' built north of Sidmouth Lodge, for yearly letting.[104] A Mrs. Russell was the first tenant in 1843-5, succeeded by Lady Malcolm (1845-9) and the Reverend Hogarth J. Swale, the first incumbent of St. Mary, The Boltons (1849-52).[54] It was dignified by the name Moreton Tower.

An outlier of this development was the villa built a year or two later on Robert Gunter's land abutting on Old Brompton Road at the north-west corner of A on fig. 58. Here it originally had a roadway on its west side, the northern end of Honey Lane, until this was supplanted in the 1860's by a new road, Finborough Road, which joined Old Brompton Road east of the villa. Another plain house, called Brecknock Villa by 1851 and later Walwyn House, it was built in *c.* 1842 under a lease from Robert Gunter to a John Evan Thomas. He was possibly the sculptor, a native of Brecknockshire. Perhaps because of its remote situation

adjacent to a cemetery it did not 'go' very quickly. Its first occupant, briefly, in 1847 was the keeper of a menagerie, Bryan Helps.[105] (For the later history of this site see page 231.)

The Estate of Robert Gunter the Elder and Younger, to 1864: The Boltons Area

In 1819 James Gunter had died, leaving his son Robert a life-interest in his estate, which on Robert's death was to pass to the latter's eldest son. Robert was empowered to grant ninety-nine-year building leases, a right fortified by a private Act of Parliament in 1820.[106] So far as this part of Kensington was concerned, the property that had come into Robert's hands was an area of land at D, E, I and O (fig. 58), with a separate, less extensive, rectangle further west at A, G. The former area was particularly useful, being partly developed in villas at its northern end, immediately adjacent to the new Thistle Grove (now part of Drayton Gardens) on its east, and having access both to Old Brompton Road and to Fulham Road — this last, however, being limited at the junction with Fulham Road to little more than the width of the communicating entrance-way itself.

Robert Gunter lived at Earl's Court Lodge (at what is now the northern corner of Earl's Court Road and Bolton Gardens) from his father's death until his own in 1852.[55] In 1831 his eldest son, also Robert, was born, and in 1833 his second son, James. In 1836 Robert senior bought the plot L on fig. 58, in which the Gunters had long had a mortgage interest[107] (see page 198). Apart from some villa-building mentioned above, Robert Gunter's venture into estate development in this locality seems to have begun on his property in Chelsea, where in 1845-7 he had what is now the northern end of Sydney Street built between Fulham Road and Cale Street.[108] It is wholly in the late-Georgian tradition of urban building, with terraces of flat-fronted houses in stock brick over stuccoed ground storeys. Two architects figured among his building lessees there, in 1845-6: W. W. Pocock and George Godwin the younger. George Godwin the elder, also an architect, had a lease a few years later.[109]

On Robert Gunter's Kensington property the important one of these names was the younger George Godwin's. In 1846 Robert Gunter made his will, in which Godwin was named as one of the executors and one of the guardians of Robert Gunter's daughter (the latter provision being later changed). In 1851 a codicil to the will specifically authorized Godwin to receive his professional fees as architect from the trustees of Robert's estate despite Godwin's status as executor.[110] This was very much to the point, for by 1851, and still more by the time of Robert Gunter's death in the following year, important building operations were in progress on the large easternmost portion of Robert's estate, in a different manner from that of Sydney Street and doubtless showing George Godwin's hand as designer. They were essentially in the suburban mode of Thistle Grove, with a layout generally permitting front gardens before the houses.

The scheme was evidently settled in outline by May 1849. It comprised a vesica-shaped layout of facing crescents (The Boltons), joined to Old Brompton Road by an extension of the roadway serving South Bolton Gardens and to Fulham Road by a new long road (Gilston Road), with side roads corresponding to Tregunter Road, Priory Walk and Milborne Grove[111] (fig. 58). The centre of the vesica was to be a plantation divided into two by the site of a church. In May 1849 Godwin set the whole enterprise moving by intimating Robert Gunter's intention to the Commissioners for Building New Churches, and soon a church of his designing, with an out-of-town air about it, was being raised, in advance of the houses themselves. This is described on pages 232-4.

House-building 1850-2: Methods and Personnel

The houses built on the estate in 1850-2 were confined to Robert Gunter's property lying east of the line of what is now the roadway of The Little Boltons and (after a turn of that boundary eastward along the south side of properties in Tregunter Road) the line of Bolton Studios so far south as No. 5 Gilston Road. The work proceeded fairly rapidly and by the time of Robert Gunter's death in October 1852 the houses that were sufficiently completed to be made over to their building lessees constituted the eastern crescent of The Boltons, most of the south side of this part of Tregunter Road, most of Gilston Road, most of Milborne Grove, the north-east end of Harley Gardens, and Priory Walk.

The procedure was generally by the normal granting of leases to building tradesmen or, sometimes, to their nominees. The latter were often intending occupants. In two respects particularly Robert Gunter's practice was to be followed until almost the whole ground on his sons' estates was covered a quarter of a century later. A separate lease was granted of every house-plot, and no period of a year or two's peppercorn rent was conceded to the lessee. As in Sydney Street, Chelsea, the term granted was generally eighty-one years, and that remained the usual term in this part of the estate under his successors until the early 1860's. Initially the term ran from 1850 but ultimately the terms of the leases, which from the 1860's became almost always ninety-nine years, gave expiry-dates extending from 1931 to 1984.

House-building began in the summer of 1850. One of these first operations was, as it happens, apparently at least a partial exception to the leasing-procedure referred to above. This was the building of the terrace of houses at Nos. 1-12 Priory Walk and No. 26 Gilston Road (Plate 84a). Eight of these were begun in July and September 1850 by a builder, Robert Trower, who had an address in Chelsea and had participated in the building of Sydney Street.[112] The district surveyor's returns which record the work at Priory Walk describe him as 'owner' as well as 'builder' but no building leases to him have been found. Something also delayed the progress of the work. It was 1853, after Robert Gunter's death, when Trower began the remaining houses,[113] and there were then only five of these, to make a total (including the westernmost now numbered 26 Gilston Road) of thirteen, although in 1851 Godwin had applied to the Metropolitan Commissioners of Sewers on Gunter's behalf for leave for Trower to lay drains from fourteen houses here.[114] In 1854 it was necessary for Trower to rebuild Nos. 7 and 8[115] and by January 1855 Godwin as supervising architect had to invite tenders 'for completing houses in Priory-grove' (as Priory Walk was called until 1938). One of the other builders active nearby, Charles Delay, submitted the lowest tender of £2,259.[116] The only instance of a lease to a building tradesman in this terrace had occurred in December 1854, when trustees for the younger Robert Gunter's estate granted one eighty-one-year lease, of No. 12, to Patrick Buckley, a plumber and glazier of Brompton.[117] These houses came into occupation in 1855-7. The earliest resident, at No. 12, was an architect, J. H. Strudwick.[55]

Elsewhere in the streets developed in the elder Robert's lifetime, in 1850-2, leases were granted, and predominantly to, or with the participation of, building tradesmen. There were ten of these. Unlike John Glenn of Islington, who, as well as working on St. Mary's Church, did two estate buildings directly for Robert Gunter at the bottom of Gilston Road, all of the ten had addresses in this part of south-west London. The most important lessee, in terms of the sites committed to him, was H. W. Atkinson of Chelsea, builder, whose role as lessee in the eastern crescent of The Boltons must be noticed separately below. Three other Chelsea builders were John Atkinson and Daniel Tidey (a bricklayer), who participated in the leasing

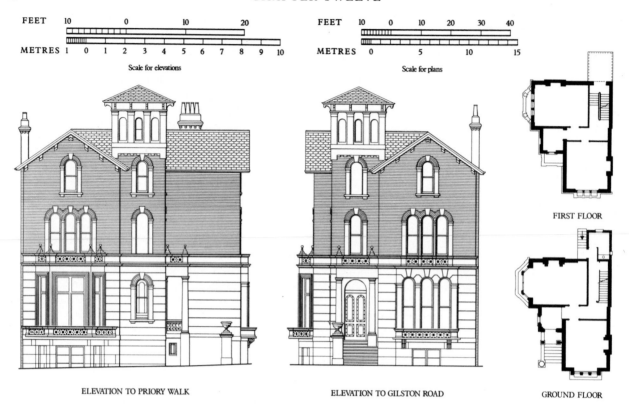

FEET 10 0 10 20   FEET 10 0 10 20 30 40

METRES 1 0 1 2 3 4 5 6 7 8 9 10   METRES 0 5 10 15

Scale for elevations   Scale for plans

FIRST FLOOR

ELEVATION TO PRIORY WALK   ELEVATION TO GILSTON ROAD   GROUND FLOOR

Fig. 60. No. 24 Gilston Road, plans and elevations as in 1970. William Harding, builder, 1852

of Nos. 21 and 23 Gilston Road to the first occupants in 1851,[118] and Thomas Eames, who in 1852 received the leases of Nos. 14 and 16 Gilston Road (and in 1854, after the elder Robert Gunter's death, was a party to those of Nos. 10, 12, 41 and 43).[119] Pimlico supplied H. J. Clarke (later a bankrupt) at Nos. 13-23 (odd) Tregunter Road[120] and Charles Delay at Nos. 13-19 (odd) Gilston Road[121] in 1851-2. Each was a participating party to the leases, which in Gilston Road were granted to a 'gentleman' and an 'esquire' buying two houses apiece doubtless as an investment, and in Tregunter Road were made to four of the first occupants, two of whom also bought an adjacent house. James Bonnin, junior, of Alfred (now Alexander) Place, who participated in the leases of Nos. 3 and 4 Harley Gardens (Plate 83b) in 1851 to the first occupants (that at No. 3 being J. S. Quilter, an architect)[122] and who took the leases of Nos. 1 and 3 Tregunter Road in 1852,[123] was son of a notable builder in Kensington. Thomas Holmes, a party to the leases of Nos. 1-8 Milborne Grove to a baker in Pimlico and a widow in Brompton (neither of whom were buying for occupation), had an address in Hereford Square.[124] A third very local man was Stephen Peirson of Elm Cottage, Old Brompton, who built at least eight houses in Gilston Road, probably Nos. 25-39 (odd, Plate 83d), in 1850-1.[125] He participated in 1851-2 in the leasing of Nos. 25-35, mostly to non-occupants,[126] and was also joined with John Atkinson or Daniel Tidey as a party to

the leasing of Nos. 21 and 23.[127] In 1853 he took three leases in Sydney Street, Chelsea.[128] More significant in that respect was the builder William Harding, of North End, Fulham, the recipient or nominator of leases at Nos. 18-24 Gilston Road (Plate 83c, fig. 60) and Nos. 1 and 2 Harley Gardens (Plate 83a) in 1851-2. He had in 1846-51 been the building lessee on Robert Gunter's land in Chelsea, at the Gunter Arms public house and other properties nearby on the south side of the Fulham Road and in Gunter Grove and Edith Grove, where George Godwin's hand is evident as architect.[129]

Generally the evidence of the building leases and that of the district surveyor's returns agree on the identity of the builder. An exception is that the fifteen leases of the chief houses of this early development, on the eastern side of The Boltons, were all made with H. W. Atkinson as the sole participating builder,[130] whereas the district surveyor's returns seem clear that the eight houses begun in February 1851 were divided four and four between him and the builder Daniel Tidey, and that of the remainder, begun in August, Atkinson was responsible for four and Tidey for three.[131] Atkinson was at that time in a comparatively small way of business, employing only four men and living in Cheyne Walk with only one servant. Tidey employed fourteen men, but lived in a house in Elystan Street that he shared with another couple, where one young servant looked after his family of nine.[132] He had some sort of hand in Nos. 21 and 23 Gilston

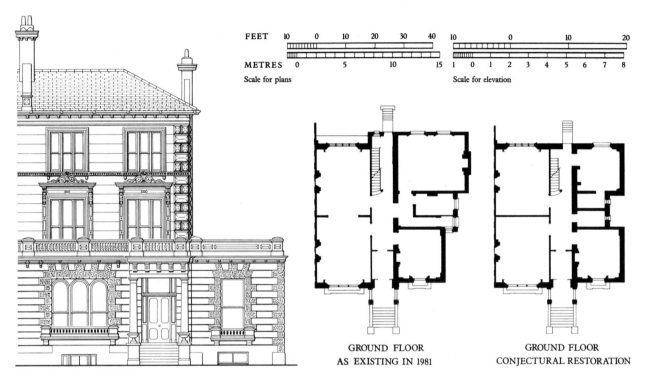

FEET 10 0 10 20 30 40 10 0 10 20

METRES 0 5 10 15 1 0 1 2 3 4 5 6 7 8

Scale for plans Scale for elevation

GROUND FLOOR
AS EXISTING IN 1981

GROUND FLOOR
CONJECTURAL RESTORATION

Fig. 61. No. 12 The Boltons, plans and elevation. H. W. Atkinson, building lessee, 1851

Road,[133] and later, before the common fate of bankruptcy befell him, ventured largely in building at Belsize Park and Chalk Farm.[134]

From what has been said of the transmission of leases direct to 'lay' purchasers it is apparent that this undertaking of Robert Gunter was in general a success (unless the uncertain evidence of Priory Walk is taken as an exception). This is also suggested by the fairly short interval of a year or two between the completion of the houses in carcase and the filling-up of the streets with ratepaying occupants. The designation of such owner-occupiers as are known smacks of respectability — 'esquires', 'gentlemen', architects, doctors, a jeweller, as well as the spinster and widow. One of the earliest, and longest staying, was John Wilkinson, senior partner in Sotheby's and book-auctioneer, who was at No. 1 Harley Gardens from 1851 until his death in 1894.[79] Another was Wilkinson's friend, the scholar and bibliophile, J. O. Halliwell-Phillipps, who was at No. 11 Tregunter Road from 1856 until his death in 1889.[79] A younger brother of George Godwin, James Godwin, an artist, was at No. 23 Tregunter Road from 1854 to 1876.[135]

The house-types chosen represented the 'mix' that was to prevail over the whole area. There were comparatively modest-sized houses in terraces (at that stage all arranged with mirrored plans), a very few detached houses, and a great emphasis on semi-detached houses often of large size. The layout of streets was, with one great exception, conventional, and this continued to be so as the network spread westward. Apart from one late instance at Moreton

Gardens, the arrangement so popular in Kensington, of a communal ornamental ground behind the houses, called 'Gardens', was not adopted on this side of Old Brompton Road. The architecture, generally less harsh than it became in the western streets, was also more frequently screened and ameliorated by the greenery of front gardens. The possible intention in 1851 to give Robert Gunter's estate a perceptible 'entrance' from Fulham Road has been noticed (see page 173). Gilston Road, which forms the approach thence to the centrepiece of this part of Robert Gunter's estate, still retains in a higher degree than some other streets the dignity formerly given it by solid balustraded front-garden walls and handsomely rusticated gate-piers (Plate 79b).

The Boltons

The centrepiece is The Boltons. The plan was submitted to the Commissioners of Sewers by George Godwin on Robert Gunter's behalf in March 1850, when it showed one more house on the western side than was built.[136] The name Boltons was used by Godwin but seems not to occur before 1850-1, when it was applied in that form to the houses now so called and to the immediately surrounding area, which was also known as Bolton's Field or Bolton's Estate.[137] It presumably referred back to the family of Boulton from whom James Gunter had acquired the land.

The eastern crescent, as has been seen, was erected in 1851-2 by the builders H. W. Atkinson and Daniel Tidey. These big houses (Plates 81, 82a-c, fig. 61)

constituted the boldest venture of Robert Gunter's enter-prise here, which was considered, as Godwin himself witnessed a quarter-century later, 'uncertain in its results'.[138] Doubtless for that reason Gunter, exception-ally, conceded to Atkinson his first two years' tenure at half the ground rent of £15 a house.[139] As it happens, this crescent was quickly successful in attracting occupants. The western crescent did not, however, follow until after Robert Gunter's death, when in 1856 an important trans-action introduced to the Gunters' estates a builder who was to become one of South Kensington's bigger oper-ators. In August of that year the younger Robert Gunter agreed to lease a large area to John Spicer, a builder in Pimlico. It embraced not only the western crescent of The Boltons but also the north side of Tregunter Road so far west as The Little Boltons and the east side of The Little Boltons (then called Tregunter Grove) so far north as the grounds of White Cottage (later Rathmore Lodge).[140]

The western crescent (Plates 80, 82d, figs. 62, 65f) was leased to Spicer as he finished the houses, working from north to south, between 1857 and 1860.[141] They were a little slower to be taken than the houses in the eastern crescent, although substantially similar to them.[54] In neither crescent, so far as the lease-plans show, were all the ground floors identically arranged, but one general difference between the sides was that in Spicer's houses the ground floors were planned so that the staircase compartment was not aligned on the front door, as it was in the houses in the eastern crescent (figs. 61-2). The planning of some of Spicer's houses here followed a lead given in Gilston Road.

Another difference was that at three of his pairs of houses on the west side Spicer carried the outer bays up to the full height of the house, instead of leaving them as one-storey wings. Nos. 20-25 thus form more massive six-bay blocks than the other pairs of houses in either crescent (Plate 80a, b). Most of the one-storey wings in both crescents have, however, been heightened by a storey, some in very recent times.

The eastern crescent filled up in 1852-4, the western in 1858-65.[54]

The first occupants were very respectable if not remarkable. Two army officers (one of whom was to have a command in the suppression of the Indian Mutiny), an artist (Charles Vacher at No. 4), an amateur artist and author (John Hughes, father of Thomas, the author of *Tom Brown's Schooldays*, at No. 7), a ship-owner, a landowner, a notable physician (Benjamin Golding, founder of the Charing Cross Hospital, at No. 28), the editor of the *Art Journal*, Samuel Carter Hall, at No. 21, a clergyman at No. 18, and Mrs. Gunter herself, the elder Robert's widow, at No. 16, indicate the tone.[142]

Godwin later said that the first houses in 'Boltons' were sold in the early doubtful days for so little as £1,350, which by the mid 1870's had risen to £3,000.[138] Prices at the end of the fifties are indicated by the £2,200 paid for No. 28 in 1859,[143] the £2,280 for No. 20 in 1861,[144] and the £2,300 for No. 7 in 1858.[145] The last was then valued at £175 per annum if let at a rack rent. A sale advertisement of that year details the attractions of this 'Villa Residence, elegantly finished, and in a most delightful situation'. One was the privilege of admission to the 'select Promenade and Ornamental Pleasure Grounds' in the centre, adjacent to the church, for which the ground landlord added £2 to the ground rent. The elevation was 'neat and pleasing', with plate glass in the windows. Water was laid on as high as the top (second) floor, and there was a 'Well of capital Spring Water' in the basement. Water closets were pro-vided at that level and on the ground and first floors. As usual the butler's bedroom was in the basement but his pantry was on the ground floor. The outbuildings, abutting on Cresswell Place, included 'a large Room used for Gymnastics'.[146] The auctioneers were, however, unable to speak, as they would have done a few years later, of the access to underground railway stations, and the previous occupant, John Hughes, writing as one of the pioneer residents in The Boltons about 1853 had humorously referred to it as 'this wild back-settlement, 2 miles beyond Hyde Park Corner . . . I consider myself, for all social purposes, as living in the country, out of the pale of the Red Book'.[147] But The Boltons achieved and has maintained a steadily respectable social level. So much so, indeed, that when in 1937 a telephone exchange was about to be built in the northern limb of The Boltons Sir Ronald Gunter's solicitors pleaded (unavailingly) with the Postmaster General to put it somewhere else, 'where the staff of a Telephone Exchange would mingle unobtrusively with the normal type of foot-passenger.'[148]

A notable feature of The Boltons is its shape. Facing crescents can be found on Horwood's map of London in the 1790's — generally, however, with roads traversing them. A very humble precursor of the vesica shape with a planted centre was The Oval at Hackney but on a very much smaller scale than The Boltons, and with terrace houses. In The Boltons the houses, with the exception of Nos. 15 and 28 at the southern end (and disregarding Nos. 29 and 30 which are not historically part of The Boltons) are semi-detached. They demonstrate, like some of the houses in Kensington Palace Gardens of a few years earlier, the high social and economic level at which this arrangement was acceptable.

Another remarkable feature of The Boltons is the spaciousness of the whole layout, where twenty-eight houses with their private and communal gardens (the latter admittedly accommodating a church) occupy some eleven and a half acres. On a map the contrast with the comparative density of the surrounding streets is very noticeable. Much of this is due to the size of the back gardens: it is a private type of suburbanism different in effect from the Gunters' 'Gardens' north of Old Brompton Road and those on the Smith's Charity estate.

The exteriors of the houses, of a distinctly worldly cast, except perhaps for the plain relaxed villa at No. 28, present the usual contrast to the style of the accompanying church

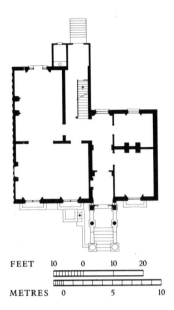

FEET 10   0   10   20

METRES 0   5   10

Fig. 62. No. 18 The Boltons, plan as originally built. John Spicer, builder, 1857

(Plates 80-1, fig. 61). Discounting later alterations, the pairs of houses are three storeys high under the over-hanging eaves of a shallow slated roof and each house is two bays wide with a slightly recessed one-storey wing (or, at Nos. 20-25, three bays wide). The entrance, dressed with a Roman Doric portico, is placed at the outer bay of each house in the eastern crescent; and in the western crescent is either placed in the one-storey wing or (at Nos. 20-25) grouped with the adjacent entrance in the centre of the block. Fully stuccoed in front, the houses have the separate elements of the façade strongly stressed. The first-floor windows are surmounted by elaborately brack-eted straight hood-moulds crowned with crestings of scrolls and acanthus leaves, and the corners of each main block are accentuated by heavily faceted quoins.

In their general composition as stuccoed semi-detached houses under eaves-cornices and with slightly recessed wings the houses in The Boltons resemble a run of houses begun about 1847 at Ealing, on the north-east side of the road called The Park, on the estate of General Sir Edward Kerrison of Oakley Park in Suffolk.[149] Two of these in particular, Nos. 21 and 22 (both now altered), had additionally distinctive cresting on the hood-moulds of the ground-floor windows and accentuated quoins that especially call to mind similar features at The Boltons.[150] Good evidence indicates that George Godwin had a hand in the design of these houses and tried there some ideas used at Brompton. This is strongly suggested by the close conformity of the ground-floor plans of some of the houses in The Park to those of houses in and around The Boltons[151] and is virtually established by the identity of office-style in the draughtsmanship of lease-plans for Ealing and Brompton.[152]

The treatment of the interiors in The Boltons, so far as

what survives can show us, was less assertive than that of the façades. The plans made no great visual feature of the staircase and allowed the large reception rooms to create the chief effect. The walls, ceilings and chimneypieces were not very greatly elaborated, each being supplied with adequate, conventional, but by no means consistent, adornments from a mixed menu of 'florid Classic' and 'after Owen Jones'. The occupants' furniture, soft furnishings, mirror-ware and china were evidently depended upon further to heighten the 'tout ensemble'. Probably the best 'period' interior surviving in The Boltons is at No. 12, where the double drawing-rooms on the main floor have painted doors, gilded cornices, and pretty 'aesthetic' tiles in the fireplaces which reveal that the scheme of decoration dates probably from around 1880 (Plate 82a-c, fig. 61).

In 1858 a resident at No. 9 The Boltons, J. Keating, employed an architect, Thomas Burton, to design or perhaps only to supervise the building of two villas for him, evidently as a speculation, in the immediate neighbour-hood. They were quite substantial, for the lowest tender for the work from builders was at £3,150.[153] Where they were is uncertain.

Architects and Builders

Nevertheless, the probability is that all the houses here in The Boltons and adjacent streets were designed by George Godwin as architect and surveyor to Robert Gunter and later to his two sons Robert and James. From at least the later 1860's, when the work had moved westward, George Godwin was joined by his younger brother Henry, who continued for at least a little while as the Gunters' surveyor or 'agent' after George Godwin's death in 1888.[154] Henry, however, only came of age in 1852, when George Godwin was thirty-seven, and this first phase of the work here in the early and mid fifties is perhaps likely to have been in the elder brother's hands alone.

A view of the 'styles' employed in these streets in and around The Boltons gives a rather bewildering impression of the shuffling and dealing-out of architectural motifs, defeating the question whether particular groups of houses compared with each other are 'like' or 'unlike'. This characteristic, if it can be so called, of mixed motifs and an ambiguity of effect continued in all the later work hereabouts under the 'Godwin' auspices, and not only on the Gunters' estates.

Here in the fifties, with a greater number of building tradesmen taking leases than later, it is evident that their areas of activity had for the most part little significance in the distribution of stylistic devices. One important and distinctive motif at that period, for example, was the peculiar form of curved hood-mould over segmental-headed window-openings, which occurs at the end pavilions of Priory Walk (Robert Trower, Plate 84a), Nos. 3 and 4 Harley Gardens (James Bonnin, Plate 83b) and

FEET   10   0   10   20   30

METRES   1   0   1   2   3   4   5   6   7   8   9   10   11

a

b

Nos. 9 and 11 Gilston Road (Thomas Holmes), as well as in the work of other builders at the Gunters' Edith Grove, Gunter Grove and Netherton Grove in Chelsea. Holmes's work at Nos. 9 and 11 Gilston Road does not resemble his houses at Nos. 1-8 Milborne Grove; nor does Thomas Eames's in Gilston Road at Nos. 10 and 12 resemble his other houses there at Nos. 14, 16, 41 and 43. Eames's No. 10 is, however, in the same Cheltenham-Swiss-Italianate style (otherwise very little used in the whole area) as William Harding's detached houses at Nos. 22 and 24 Gilston Road (Plate 83c, fig. 60). These last have a grouping of triple round-headed windows with prominent keystones in common with Harding's semi-detached houses at Nos. 1 and 2 Harley Gardens (Plate 83a), but this in no way makes the Gilston Road houses resemble the late-Georgian 'stock-brick-box' style of the pair in Harley Gardens. For a stronger hint at the insignificance, stylistically, of the

identity of the building lessee in this eastern part it is necessary to look forward a few years to the leases granted in 1861-3 to local builders, Benjamin and Thomas Bradley, of contiguous plots at Nos. 9-14 Harley Gardens and Nos. 9-14 Milborne Grove (Plate 84c).[155] (Subsequently, the Bradleys built Slaidburn Street in Chelsea for the younger Robert Gunter.[156]) At the Harley Gardens houses, which were separated from the earlier-built houses in Harley Gardens by a vacant site and from the Bradley's Milborne Grove houses by the width of a roadway, a fiercer and more up-to-the-minute type of detailing was used than at the existing houses in either street. But for the new Milborne Grove houses, which immediately adjoined the existing terrace at Nos. 1-8, the urbane style of those houses was continued. That this discrimination was at George Godwin's prompting as the younger Robert Gunter's architect seems to be shown by the resemblance of the

Fig. 63. Elevations of houses built on the estates of Robert and James Gunter.
a. No. 7 Harley Gardens, 1867   *b.* No. 36 Tregunter Road, 1865   *c.* No. 20 Tregunter Road, 1865   *d.* Nos. 10-16 (even) Tregunter Road (type), 1859

motifs used at Nos. 9-14 Harley Gardens to those being employed at the same time in the work of different builders on a different property at Redcliffe Road (Plate 87a), where Godwin as the instigator of that undertaking was the connecting link with Harley Gardens.

The correctness of the simplest and most obvious hypothesis regarding the source of the tantalizing mix of styles in this whole area—that it originated in the Godwins' office throughout—is supported by the similarity of draughtsman's style in the ground-floor plans on the leases memorialized in the Middlesex Deeds Registry. That some, and therefore presumably all, of these were in physical fact supplied by the Godwins is shown in the later correspondence of the builders Corbett and McClymont, which speaks of parchment leases being sent to the Godwins' office for plans to be drawn upon them.[157] The same office-style of plan occurs on the leases granted by

George Godwin to a builder, Edwin Curtis, on his own freehold in Fulham Road and Redcliffe Road (see page 175).

House-building 1852-63

To revert to Robert Gunter the elder, at his death in October 1852 the estate which had come to him from his father, James, passed to trustees for his eldest son Robert, then about twenty-one, and the property he had himself bought, at L on fig. 58, was bequeathed for the second son James, who came of age two years later.[110] Both sons were destined for military careers, in the Dragoon Guards, and in 1854-6 both fought in the Crimean War. In 1854 Robert, by a deed to which his brother James was a witness, barred the entail of his estate, and in the same month conveyed it in trust to James and the brother of their step-mother, W. E. Maude. In 1856 James, Maude and the family's solicitor, J. L. Tomlin, conveyed it back to Robert, who in turn conveyed it to Tomlin to his, Robert's, own use. In 1858 James similarly conveyed all his land in trust to Robert and Maude, and they reconveyed it in 1862.[158] This was not the last of the legal to-and-froing, which did not, however, affect the brothers' separate equitable ownership of their properties. Since 1854 both had been advised by a solicitor, J. L. Tomlin (in succession to J. L. Wetten), who handled their affairs throughout the long campaign of building development, himself lived in Bolton Gardens from 1866, and acquired freehold property hereabouts in his own right. The dealings of Robert and James at his guidance are, in the absence of evidence to the contrary, suggestive of a co-operative relation between the fraternal property-owners.

In 1857 building had advanced enough for Robert to raise a mortgage of £10,000 on his property, redeemed in the same year, and then later in the year no less than £56,000 on the security of land north and south of Old Brompton Road. (Part of this mortgage was paid off in 1868 and the rest in 1878.)[159] In 1857 he moved from Earl's Court to Wetherby Grange in Yorkshire. There he was a prominent landowner, colonel commandant of a Yorkshire regiment, and from 1884 Conservative Member of Parliament for the Barkston Ash division.[160]

The continuation of the elder Robert's development has already been touched upon. At Nos. 5-11 (odd) Tregunter Road Peirson had the leases in 1853-4 of four houses filling-in between Bonnin's and Clarke's.[161] His houses 'went' decidedly quicker than Bonnin's had done. (One difference was that his houses were planned in the traditional London way in so far as they had a long entrance-and-staircase-compartment on one side and on the other front and back reception rooms which could communicate, whereas Bonnin had placed his staircase compartment between the front and back rooms.) In 1854 Eames or his nominees had leases of Nos. 10, 12, 41 and 43 Gilston Road.[162] At Nos. 9 and 11, where Holmes had had a lien on the latter site in 1852,[163] the leases were made in 1855 to a 'laceman' in the City, who was the first occupant of No. 9.[164] In the same year the detached house at the south-east end of Tregunter Road, now numbered 29 The Boltons, was leased to its first occupant:[165] the builder employed by the lessee was Walter Taverner of Bayswater.[166] B. and T. Bradley's work finishing Milborne Grove with Nos. 9-14 in 1861-2, and adding to Harley Gardens with Nos. 9-14 in 1862-3 has been mentioned above. (Later, in 1867, the gap in Harley Gardens, hitherto occupied by an additional garden to a large house, The Grove, at No. 98 Drayton Gardens, was filled by two builders involved in the works then going forward further west, Thomas Hussey and Thomas Huggett, both of Kensington.[167] The two pairs of semi-detached houses built by them at Nos. 5-8 Harley Gardens are in a more full-blooded Victorian manner than the houses around them, with features suggestive of Redcliffe Square (Plate 86a, fig. 63a).

John Spicer, Builder

The largest work of continuation, however, was the building of the north-east end of Tregunter Road and the east side of what is now The Little Boltons (formerly Tregunter Grove) by John Spicer, on the western part of the large property agreed in 1856 to be leased to him for his side of The Boltons. At the south end, Nos. 2-16 (even) Tregunter Road (Plate 83e, fig. 63d) and Nos. 2 and 4 The Little Boltons were leased to Spicer or his nominees in 1857-9.[168] Nos. 6-20 and 22-36 (even) The Little Boltons followed in 1862 and 1864 (Plate 85b).[169] At No. 36 The Little Boltons, a detached house near the north end, Spicer let (or rather sub-let) the house to the first occupant, in 1866, for £125 per annum.[170] All these houses of Spicer's were occupied fairly promptly.[54] The first residents on this side of The Little Boltons included two clergymen, a lady of title, a barrister, a government clerk, a civil engineer, a brewer, a West India merchant, at least one man of no profession, and a 'dealer in fancy goods'.[171] They were provided, by Godwin and Spicer, with some of the least elaborated house-fronts in the neighbourhood. Only the eaves-brackets, here and at Nos. 2-16 (even) Tregunter Road, catch the eye.

In 1859-66 Spicer also received leases for Bolton Mews, now Bolton Gardens Mews — rather squeezed-in, to the curtailment of the gardens of Nos. 16 and 17 The Boltons.[172]

Much later, in 1883, when George Godwin in his capacity as editor of The Builder published Spicer's obituary, he spoke of him with great respect.[173] Just conceivably, and exceptionally, the architectural sobriety which characterized Spicer's work here at this time, once he had done with The Boltons, in some way reflects his influence in a matter of design.

This aspect of Spicer's house-building is even more noticeable in the next major undertaking of Robert Gunter on his property east of The Little Boltons. This was the building of eight large houses on a detached site fronting Old Brompton Road at Nos. 1-8 Bolton Gardens, where Spicer was granted leases in 1863-4 (Plate 79c, fig. 65a).[174] Their rectitude of composition is by no means characteristic of Godwin, however appropriate for houses whose first occupants included a solicitor, two barristers and a senior civil servant. The arrangement was perfectly normal, as four pairs of semi-detached houses facing the road, with ample gardens behind each. They looked across the road, however, to a large planted enclosure, leased by Robert Gunter to Spicer, and thus formed part, both in name and in the minds of the house's occupants, of the greater portion of Bolton Gardens which was laid out by Spicer in the course of the next few years on the northern part of Gunter's estate, to be discussed in volume XLII of the Survey of London.[175] These were some of the 'best' houses in the area. In 1870 they were assessed appreciably higher for rating purposes than the houses in The Boltons — perhaps, however, chiefly because they were newer.

The first occupant at No. 1 was the colonial civil servant and economist, Sir Louis Mallet. An even more significant token of approbation was given by the residence here of J. L. Tomlin, Robert Gunter's own lawyer, who moved to a new house at No. 5 from St. James's Street in 1866. (It is perhaps a sign of a confidential relationship between Tomlin and Spicer that when two years later the former set up in a new office at No. 9 Old Burlington Street Spicer's son, himself a solicitor, moved to the same address from the City and stayed there for some three years.) At No. 4 Bolton Gardens the first occupant was Albert Silber, a manufacturer of lamps and patent gas-burners.[81] Mallet paid £3,370 for the lease of his house, and the barrister Rupert Potter £3,700 for his next door at No. 2.[176] This latter house was also the residence of the owner of the most famous name in Bolton Gardens, Peter Rabbit, whose mistress, Beatrix Potter, was born there in 1866 and remained until her marriage in 1913.[177]

The site of Nos. 1-6 Bolton Gardens is now taken into that of the Bousfield School. No. 8 retains the tactfully unobtrusive westward extension given it in 1876 by the architect E. N. Clifton.[178]

Occupants in 1871

The census of 1871 gives a comparative view of some of the streets so far discussed, in the heyday of southern Kensington.[179] In The Boltons the 26 houses in 'normal' occupation on the night of the census contained in all 87 members of the owners' families, outnumbered by the 97 servants (including in the latter two governesses). Among the servants were four butlers and two coachmen. Five heads of households were widows, five were merchants, active or retired, and two clergymen. The others whose designation is known included one industrialist (a brick-maker), a civil engineer, two landowners, a house-property owner, a shipowner and broker, a magistrate, a retired servant of the East India Company and an artist.

On the eastern side of The Little Boltons the 16 houses in normal occupation accommodated 57 members of the 'family' and 48 servants, including one butler and two governesses but no coachmen. Four heads of households were widows, two were barristers, two active or retired merchants, one an industrialist (a brewer), one a 'dealer', one a clerk in a public office, one a civil engineer, one was of no profession, two were architects and one was a professor of music. (One of the architects, William Harvey, aged thirty, had a family of six brothers and sisters living with him.)

In Gilston Road 27 houses had a lower ratio of servants again, accommodating 94 'family' and 53 servants, including one butler and no governesses or coachmen. Two of the houses had lodgers in them. Otherwise the type of occupant was rather similar. The largest single class of head of household was again the widow (five). There were two army officers (one a lieutenant-general), again one industrialist (a bootmaker), two merchants and

one civil engineer. There were two architects. Four declared themselves 'of no profession', 'independent', or 'gentleman'. There were two surgeons (one retired from the East India Company), a stockbroker, a ship and insurance broker, a 'mercantile clerk', and a thirty-two-year-old 'student at law'. There was again a slight representation of the humanities with an author and botanist (Robert Fortune) at No. 9. At No. 13 the owner was secretary to a goldmining company and at No. 43 a restaurant proprietor.

At the 12 terrace houses in normal occupation in Priory Walk the situation was rather different. There 55 'family' lived with 16 servants, although this ratio was distorted by the unusual establishment at No. 7, where the head, a professor of fencing, had nine of his family living with him and no servants at all. Apart from four female heads of households Priory Walk seems to have attracted the 'clerk' — doubtless of the top-hatted Victorian rather than the billycock-hatted Edwardian status.

In none of these streets was any house in the occupation of more than one family.

Testimony, of a kind, to the respectability of this area in 1871 is the presence at No. 14 Harley Gardens in 1870-2 of 'Sir Roger Charles D. Tichborne', that is, Arthur Orton of Wapping, who was then pursuing his sensational claim to the baronetcy until its collapse in court in March 1872. He and his family of five occupied the house with a young lady's-companion, a butler, a nurse and three other servants. The 'Claimant' was 'bravely championed by the tradespeople in the neighbourhood'.[180]

The Estates of James Gunter the Younger and Robert Gunter the Younger, and others, 1864 to 1878: the Redcliffe Estate of Corbett and McClymont, Builders

The leasing of Nos. 1-8 Bolton Gardens to Spicer was concluded in March 1864. In November ten new houses were leased to their builders on the south side of Tregunter Road and the north and south sides of Cathcart Road, extending those streets a little westward. The lessor was Robert Gunter's younger brother James and the lessees, together or individually, were William Corbett and Alexander McClymont, builders.[181] With these trans-actions an expansion of the building activities of the Gunter brothers was initiated. James Gunter was then about thirty-one and like his elder brother a captain in a regiment of the Dragoon Guards. He ultimately rose to the command of the Fourth or Royal Irish Dragoon Guards and retired as a major-general in 1887. He had seemingly shared his brother's home at Earl's Court Lodge for a time, and for many years after Robert's removal to Wetherby in 1857 continued to be designated as 'of Earl's Court' in title-deeds. He does not figure there in directories, however, conceivably because he used his step-mother's house at

No. 16 The Boltons as his *pied à terre*. In the 1880's he is described as of Boston Hall, Tadcaster, Yorkshire, where he was a rider to hounds and in steeplechases. He married in 1891 and died in 1908.[182]

The ensuing development differed from the earlier by being carried out more extensively on the property of James than of Robert Gunter (so far as the area south of Old Brompton Road is concerned) and by being placed almost entirely in the hands of Corbett and McClymont, except in so far as they brought in what George Godwin called 'some few undertenants' in the persons of other local builders. Corbett and McClymont seem to have been in a sense the motivating force and their wave of building flowed uninterruptedly over the adjacent land of R. J. Pettiward (at K on fig. 58), the small property of the Robinsons at the south-east end of Redcliffe Gardens (see page 194) and two other properties, those of J. L. Tomlin at a, g (fig. 58), and of members of their own firm of solicitors, Lewins of Southampton Street, at j, k.

They named all their large leasehold property here the Redcliffe Estate and publicized it under that designation, regardless of the various ground landlords' boundaries, or the minor sites of subordinate builders (fig. 64).

At the same time Corbett and McClymont were working on Robert Gunter's estate at Fulham and on other estates in and out of London.

The evidence of the buildings themselves is conclusive that the kind of house they put up on the 'Redcliffe Estate' was more or less unaffected by the freehold boundaries across which they operated. In Redcliffe Gardens, for example, the ranges between Fawcett Street and Tregunter Road are similar on both sides (and similar to some of Corbett and McClymont's houses in Avenue Elmers at Surbiton), although on the east the freeholder was James Gunter and on the west R. J. Pettiward (Plate 88b). That the designs all came from the office of George and Henry Godwin seems probable. The scattering and mingling of architectural detail throughout the area suggests this. So does the evidence of the lease of one building erected on the Pettiward estate, the former Redcliffe Arms public house at No. 268 Fulham Road. All the other Pettiward leases have only block plans on them, but there the room-plan was given and it is drawn in the 'house-style' attributable to the Godwins' office.[183]

The westward spread of building by the Gunter brothers in 1864 was dependant on the purchase of the land (B, C, H, M on fig. 58) that had been acquired at the beginning of the century by Philip Gilbert and that separated the land already built upon around The Boltons from the inherited lands of James Gunter at L and of Robert Gunter at A, G.

In March and April 1864 James Gunter bought the requisite land from the widow of the Reverend Edward Gilbert, in whom Philip Gilbert's property had become vested.[184] The piece of three and a half acres that had not yet been freed from its copyhold status had been enfranchised by Mrs. Gilbert in February for £948.36

James Gunter paid her £15,810 for the area B, C, with Coleherne House and Hereford House standing upon it, and £15,500 for the piece H, M, less the eastward limb of M at m (fig. 58).[184]

This latter piece, which hitherto had followed the same line of descent as the rest of M, had been sold by Mrs. Gilbert and her mortgagees in the previous month, January 1864. The purchaser was Spencer Robert Lewin, a partner in the firm of solicitors in Southampton Street already mentioned.[185] The property lay across the head of two streets, the well-established Seymour Walk, which remained a cul-de-sac, and Redcliffe Road, to which it was to give outlet at the northern end. This latter road had just been completed (except at its south-west end), the last conveyances of the new houses there having been made two months before, by Lewin himself and his father Robert Lewin. The making of this road has been described on pages 175-6. Its significance here is that it had brought together in one enterprise the Gunters' architect, George Godwin, the Lewins' firm, and the builders Corbett and McClymont. Unusually, the undertaking had concluded with the grants of the freehold tenure of the houses to Corbett and McClymont. At plot m (fig. 58) the same procedure was followed, and soon, in April 1864, S. R. Lewin, for an unknown consideration, granted the eastern part to McClymont and the western to Corbett.[186] On the eastern extremity of his plot McClymont built Cathcart House, finishing the east side of Redcliffe Road, for his own occupation (see page 176). Cathcart Road was laid out along the north side of the strip of ground, giving Redcliffe Road westward communication with the streets to be built on the Redcliffe Estate. On its south side Corbett just had room for four houses, one completing the sequence on the west side of Redcliffe Road, and three, double-fronted but shallow, facing Cathcart Road (Nos. 1-7 odd Cathcart Road). On the north side of the road lay the back gardens of Nos. 9-23 (odd) Tregunter Road on the separate property of Robert Gunter.

Nos. 1-7 (odd) Cathcart Road (Plate 84b) came into occupation in 1865-6.54 At No. 7 the first occupant from 1865 to 1868 was an architect employed at South Kensington by the Science and Art Department, John Liddell,[187] who moved here from Elm Place during his brief period of hopeful prosperity before sinking to the obscurity in which he eked out his resources by acting as occasional draughtsman to, among others, Corbett and McClymont.[188]

Despite the immediate proximity to Redcliffe Road, where the development was closely associated with Godwin, and where some of the characteristic architectural features of the Redcliffe Estate are on display, the houses built on Corbett's freehold in Cathcart Road, although by no means beyond Godwin's stylistic vagaries, are more in the manner of some of the houses at Corbett and McClymont's starting point in Pimlico.

Perhaps because Robert and James Gunter's advisers were finding it better to work through one or two lessees,

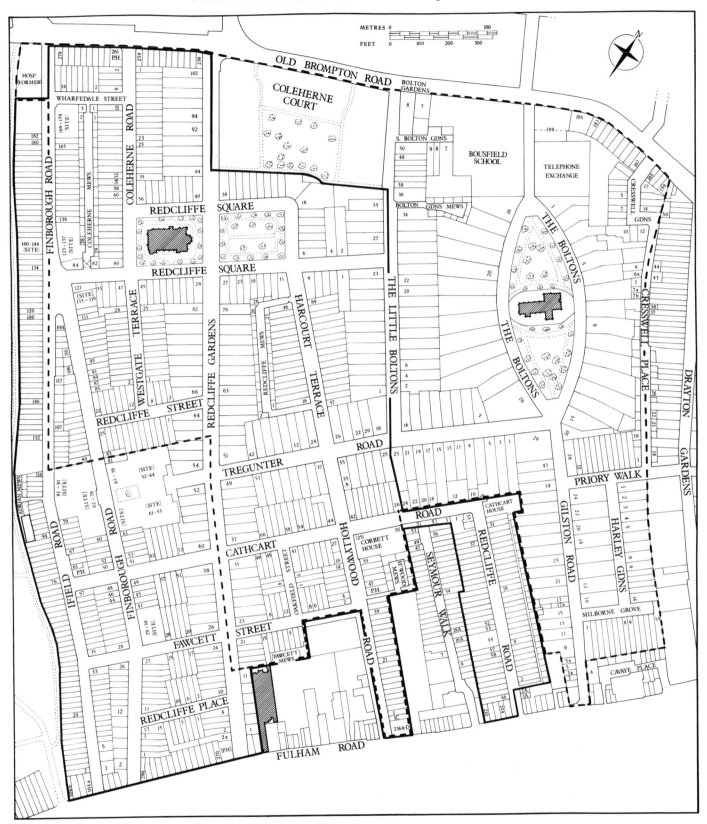

Fig. 64. The area discussed in Chapter XII, showing the boundaries in *c.* 1870 of the freehold estates of Robert and James Gunter (broken line) and the leasehold Redcliffe Estate of Corbett and McClymont, builders (solid line), with present street layout and house numbers. Based on the Ordnance Survey of 1949-72

and because Godwin was pleased with Corbett and
McClymont's work in Redcliffe Road, they had the chief
role henceforward south of Old Brompton Road, just as
John Spicer was given a large 'take' north of that road.

Layout and Progress

As has been seen, the expansion westward into the new
territory began promptly, with a few houses at Nos. 25
and 27 Tregunter Road and Nos. 26-32 (even) and
9-15 (odd) Cathcart Road in 1864 (the last now replaced
by part of Corbett House). Generally, Corbett and McClymont worked from the south-east part, around the lower
half of Hollywood Road, westward and northward. This
was a natural progression which also accommodated the
fact that the piece of property west of Walnut Tree Walk at
J on fig. 58 was acquired only in June 1866, when Robert
Gunter bought it for £8,500 from J. G. Hillersdon of
Wexham, Berkshire, as copyholder of the manor of Earl's
Court.[189] In April 1867 Gunter paid £2,228 to enfranchise this plot of seven and a quarter acres.[36]

This completed the Gunters' major freehold purchases
in the area here dealt with. The site of Hawk Cottage was
bought in the following year and small properties were
acquired at the bottom of Gilston Road and in Holmes
Place in 1865 and 1881 (see pages 174, 229). In 1877
Robert Gunter wisely ignored a suggestion, made by
Corbett via Tomlin, that he should buy the freehold of the
land already developed at Nos. 1-14 Redcliffe Road.[190]

A factor in the progression of Corbett and McClymont's
work, slightly modifying its south-to-north tendency, was
evidently a wish to see the two main-road frontages quickly
occupied, so that the two ranges at Nos. 239-259 and
261-279 (odd) Old Brompton Road were built as part of
the campaigns of 1866-8, slightly before other 'northerly'
areas and at about the same time as the development of the
southern frontage at Nos. 266-306B (even) Fulham Road
in 1865-9. In view of the age-old liking of London builders
for making taverns the first structures to be put up on their
building-sites it is not perhaps surprising that the public
houses (five in number) erected on the Redcliffe Estate
were either, like the Hollywood Arms, in areas of naturally
early development, or built a little before most of the
surrounding houses. The latter is also true of two sites, at
the south side of Wharfedale Street (in lieu of the site of
the Coleherne Arms) and the north-west corner of Redcliffe Mews, which were originally meant to accommodate
public houses (Plates 85c, 92a).

The layout of streets, submitted in its southern part by
Corbett and McClymont to the Metropolitan Board of
Works from the Redcliffe Estate Office at No. 2A
Redcliffe Gardens in April 1864 and approved by the
Board in June, was straightforward.[191] It already proposed
a network of streets over both the Gunter and Pettiward
properties. The main lines of communication ran north
and south. Hollywood Road and Harcourt Terrace were to
continue the line of Hollywood Grove (and in 1866 were

still intended to traverse the land now covered by
Coleherne Court to meet Old Brompton Road[192]).
Redcliffe Gardens was a widening of the existing Walnut
Tree Walk. At the extreme western margin of the area
Honey Lane skirted the boundary of Brompton Cemetery
from Fulham Road to Old Brompton Road. Corbett and
McClymont obtained permission to close this so far north
as the line of Tregunter Road, and to replace it by Ifield
Road a house-plot's width to the east.[191] Robert Gunter's
acquisition of plot J on fig. 58 in 1866 allowed the rest of
Honey Lane to be closed, and Ifield Road and Finborough
Road proceeded northward. In 1866 the proposal was to
make the northern third of this route, after the junction of
the two roads, prolong the direction of Finborough rather
than of Ifield Road,[192] but this was soon changed and a
full depth of house-plot was thus obtained on the west side
of the road. Behind Ifield Road on its west side Adrian
Mews preserves the name which, in the form Adrian
Terrace, was borne by this part of Ifield Road until 1909.
It represents a portion of what Corbett and McClymont
called 'the old Cart Road' of Honey Lane.

A plan of the layout intended in summer 1866 differs
from what was built chiefly in the northward extension of
the line of Hollywood Road, the construction of streets of
houses on the northern part of the site of Coleherne
House, and the positioning of Redcliffe Square on the
southern part of that site and westwards — that is, one
'block' northward of its actual location. A church
adumbrating St. Luke's, Redcliffe Square, is shown but is
placed further south, at the southern corner of Redcliffe
Street and Redcliffe Gardens.[192]

Setting aside the 62 house-sites that had been granted
to Corbett and McClymont in 1861-4 in Redcliffe Road
and Cathcart Road and the 14 more made over to them in
Redcliffe Road and Fulham Road in 1866 (see pages 175-6,
212), the numbers leased to them in the years 1864 to
1876 south of Old Brompton Road were 827 houses and
some 72 mews premises, including in this number 156
houses and 22 mews leased to other builders at their
nomination. Additionally a run of 25 houses and 5 mews at
Nos. 70-118 (even) Ifield Road were granted by S. R.
Lewin in 1868 direct to other builders but in every other
respect were integral parts of the Redcliffe Estate and were
advertised as such by Corbett and McClymont.

This whole west side of Ifield Road and its continuation
as Nos. 120-194 (even) Finborough Road was, however,
rather distinctive in the history of its freehold ownership.
In July 1867 R. J. Pettiward and his trustees, with whom
Corbett and McClymont had already come to some
agreement concerning the disposal of his freehold land (K
on fig. 58), conveyed the strip west of Corbett and
McClymont's intended road, the future sites of Nos.
2-118 (even) Ifield Road and Nos. 304A-306B Fulham
Road (k), at the request of Corbett and McClymont to
Henry Lewin, who was the head of their firm of
solicitors.[193] The following month, August 1867, Robert
Gunter conveyed the adjacent strip northward (j) at the

west side of his newly acquired plot J, where Nos. 120-180 (even) Ifield Road were to be built, to Corbett and McClymont, who in February 1868 conveyed it to Henry Lewin's brother Robert.[194] In June 1869 Robert Gunter conveyed the northernmost section, south of Brecknock House, at the future site of Nos. 120-194 (even) Finborough Road (a, g, on the west side of his inherited property A, G on fig. 58) to Corbett and McClymont: in August they conveyed it away, again to one of the men of business they were constantly dealing with, Gunter's own solicitor, J. L. Tomlin.[195] In each case the beneficiary of the grant proceeded to make building leases to Corbett and McClymont or (in the limited instance noted above) to builders doubtless associated with them. (In the southernmost section these leases were made by S. R. Lewin as the trustee, and successor at Messrs. Lewin, of his uncle Henry.[196]) Corbett and McClymont's handling of the legal and financial interests in their properties was not simple or easily intelligible, but this conveyance-and-lease-back arrangement may have been merely some kind of remuneration for professional services. If so, it was in one of the least choice, but perhaps in one of the 'safer', parts of their estate.

The numbers of houses leased to Corbett and McClymont or their nominees in each year, generally betokening the numbers roofed-in during that year, rose from 12 in 1864 to 156 in 1867: the most active period was the four years 1866-9, when 524 house-sites were leased, the number falling to 7 in 1876.[197] The last ones to be leased, in 1872-6, were, with the exception of Nos. 72-82 (even) Finborough Road, all in the vicinity of Redcliffe Square. (This last period of Corbett and McClymont's activity also encompassed their only substantial ventures north of Old Brompton Road, with the houses over shops westward from No. 232 Old Brompton Road round the corner into Earl's Court Road in 1875-6 and the big houses at Nos. 198-224 Old Brompton Road ('Bolton Gardens West') in 1876-8.)

The totals given here comprise under 'Corbett and McClymont' leases granted to each individually, with the other a consenting party, and to both of them.

The number of houses built by Corbett and McClymont in 1871-7 was much greater than the number built by any other firm within the area of the district surveyor for South Kensington in the ten years 1871-80, even though the period 1871-7 was past the peak of Corbett and McClymont's activity.[198]

This surge of building ended with the bankruptcy of Corbett and McClymont in 1878 with liabilities of some one-and-a-quarter million pounds. The little that can be said about the way they conducted their business and its bearing upon their failure will be reverted to below, but it may be noted here that so far as the ground landlords' estates were concerned the bankruptcy might well have been much worse timed, as in the event the fields had just been safely covered with houses.

Corbett and McClymont, Builders, and Others

When William Corbett and Alexander McClymont had first worked in southern Kensington, at Redcliffe Road in 1861, both were living as 'esquires' at houses in Winchester Street, Pimlico.[135] The former, born in London, was aged thirty and the latter, born in Scotland, aged thirty-four. Both were married, with a child or children.[199] McClymont had a builder's and estate agent's office in St. George's Road, where he was also manager of the National Savings Bank.[135] Corbett at that time described himself in title-deeds, significantly, as an accountant and continued to do so until 1863, changing in 1864 to McClymont's designation of 'builder'.[200] He had probably begun his working life as a clerk in the solicitor's office of Messrs. Lewin,[201] and if so this, too, would have been significant. Lewins were to be much involved in Corbett and McClymont's work, giving them, especially in the person of William Corbett, access to the wide borderland where legal and financial expertise (or the assumption of such) overlapped.

In 1863 Corbett moved to No. 14 Redcliffe Road as its first occupant and in 1865 McClymont to No. 22 in the same street.[54] For the next thirteen years both lived on their Redcliffe Estate (Corbett for longer), success enabling each to take a larger house. McClymont in 1867 moved to one of the estate's few detached houses, Cathcart House, newly built at the top of Redcliffe Road, and Corbett in 1870 to a new house at No. 35 The Little Boltons (semi-detached from the house of one of the firm's backers, the banker W. G. Logan, at No. 33).[54] In 1871 each had two female servants living in. McClymont at least (then aged forty-four) additionally employed a coachman, stable boy and gardener.* In 1871 Corbett's elder son, W. G. Corbett, aged seventeen, was still at school.[204] In 1874 the younger daughter seems to have gone away to school. By 1878 both sons (aged twenty-four and twenty-one) were working for their father: they called their parents 'Pater' and 'Mater'.[205]

The firm's offices were in Fulham Road just east of Hollywood Road from 1866 to 1869. In the latter year they were moved permanently to No. 2A Redcliffe Gardens: for a year or two the firm also had an office at No. 259 Old Brompton Road.[55] In 1866 the site of No. 2A Redcliffe Gardens had been briefly in use as a 'Bowling Saloon' with 'Billiard Rooms' over it, in connexion with the newly established Redcliffe Arms next door at the corner of Fulham Road. That year the Metropolitan Fire Brigade considered taking the site for a fire station. Corbett and McClymont would have welcomed this but when the brigade did not do so converted the premises

---

*At that time two other natives of Scotland called McClymont were lodging with a builder's foreman at No. 153 Finborough Road, David, aged thirty-four, himself a builder's foreman, and Robert, thirty, an 'architect's assistant'.[202] They were probably relations of McClymont's.[203]

into their offices.[206] In 1870-2 No. 2A Redcliffe Gardens also accommodated an office of T. E. Lewin, brother of S. R. Lewin and a member of Corbett and McClymont's firm of solicitors: since 1866 or 1867 he had lived on their estate in a detached house at No. 18 Tregunter Road.

As a building firm Corbett and McClymont attracted some attention for the modernity of their methods. Steam-powered joiner's machinery, supplied at a cost of about £1,000 by Samuel Worssam and Company of Chelsea, was used from at least 1867 and was fully described by George Godwin in a leading article in *The Builder* the following year, with a relish for the great economies in labour it effected.[207] The plant was then apparently on the Redcliffe Estate, but by 1872 the main works had been moved (probably in 1871) to buildings erected for Corbett and McClymont near Lillie Bridge in Fulham, at the corner of Seagrave and Merrington Roads.[208] From about 1870 they also had a workshop at No. 26 Redcliffe Mews (Plate 92a).[209]

One feature of their work that was praised by their friend *The Builder* was their roofing. The tops of some houses were sealed by two or three courses of plain tiles laid in cement over arched wooden ribs, the whole then being rendered and cemented to give the house an impermeable (if very heavy) roof, slightly convex in section, that was thought resistant to fire. This kind of roof survives quite extensively, particularly in the streets of smaller houses. The earliest are some of 1862 in Redcliffe Road. Conceivably others survive unrecognizably under orthodox roofs. Some are also to be found on the Gunter estate in Chelsea, at the south-east end of Edith Grove. But, as *The Builder* commented, 'good workmanship is necessary'.[210]

Relations with the workmen were not always good, and Corbett and McClymont held out longer than most firms against their men's demands in the strike in 1872 before a compromise was made. McClymont was reported in *The Building News* as asserting the firm's determination not to be bound to a set rate of pay but to observe differentials for superior skill. Furthermore (McClymont said), 'it should be understood the firm did not occupy the position of ordinary builders or contractors who regulated their prices by the ruling or standard wages of the day, but more resembled an independent gentleman employing workmen to build on his own land. No matter what he paid he could get no more than a certain rent for his houses, and was fully justified in purchasing his labour cheap if he could, without reference to the custom or regulations of the trade. . . . [Since 1862] they had got around them a great body of workmen whom they were now sorry to part with, but whom they had never ceased to classify or pay according to merit and ability.'[211]

The workmen — or the joiners at least — were, as the true-blue Corbett said, 'mostly Liberals!!' and enough of them were employed in the 'large joiners Shop' at Lillie Bridge in 1874 to make it worthwhile for a prospective Parliamentary candidate to come and harangue them in

the Conservative interest.[212] In 1872 and 1878 some 500 men were employed.[213] That Corbett and McClymont's establishment was extensive is suggested by Corbett's comment to an employee on his property at Westgate in Thanet, whom he instructed to use a work-diary or day-book — 'I have diaries used by all my leading men in Town and they are found very useful'.[214]

Not all the work on the Redcliffe Estate, however, was done by Corbett and McClymont themselves. They built the roads and sewers,[215] but were inclined to make a 'selling-point' of the fact that, for example, Nos. 1-7 (odd) Cathcart Road and the houses in Redcliffe Road (on their own freehold) had been built by them.[216] They subsequently employed at least two local builders to do repairs on their estate.[217] And at some sites, particularly in the years 1865-8, they arranged for other builders to receive the leases to which they were entitled by their agreements with the ground landlords. The most extensively involved was a local builder, John Beale, who was a nominee for leases of house-sites from 1864 to 1868,[218] (as well as being lessee from Robert Gunter in Fernshaw Road, Chelsea, in 1863 and 1865),[219] and was marked 'bankrupt' in the ratebooks in 1869.[220] By 1868 bankruptcy had also overtaken the builder A. M. Greig,[221] who came from Pimlico and was nominee for leases in 1864[222] and 1866.[223] Other nominees were William Forster and Joseph Temple of Paddington (1865-6),[224] John Gibbings of Chelsea (1865-6),[225] Thomas Hussey and Thomas Huggett (1865),[226] Frederick Saunders (1865),[227] and George Smith of Pimlico (1865-6).[228] Rather later Jeremiah Little had a substantial 'take' as nominee in Redcliffe Gardens (1869) and Coleherne Road (1872-3).[229] Gibbings, Greig and Saunders are also known to have been sub-lessees from Corbett and McClymont.[230] So were other builders — R. G. Sharpin, for example, (1867),[231] George German of Pimlico (1868),[232] and Richard Fitt of Pimlico (1868),[233] who also worked for Corbett at Westgate. Doubtless there were other sub-leasing builders whose names are not known.

Generally the areas of these 'subsidiary' builders do not coincide perceptibly with significant 'breaks' in the handling of the houses. The division between Beale's and Little's houses at Nos. 23 and 25 Coleherne Road is noticeable but there is four years' difference of date and doubtless a change of intention on the part of Robert Gunter's surveyor between them. Little's adjacent houses facing Redcliffe Gardens seem more coarsely detailed than the similar houses in the same street south of Redcliffe Square, perhaps by Corbett and McClymont themselves. This is explicable in the light of Corbett's own words in 1879. He was describing how the work had been carried on at another part of Robert Gunter's estate, in Fulham: 'Mr Tomlin (Col. Gunter's solicitor) and Mr Godwin his Surveyor hold a set of elevations and specifications; and it was understood that when we had built a house, other houses that might be built afterwards, were to be similar to that already built; therefore any house in St

Oswald's Road would be a pattern house, for those to be erected'.[234] This time-worn procedure would account for some variations over and above the brisk diversity of the Godwins' taste.

Architects and Architecture

That taste was seemingly for harsher motifs brought together in a more random manner than in most of the pre-1864 work. It is, however, foreshadowed in the houses in Redcliffe Road and Harley Gardens of 1861-3. It may be that the influence of Henry Godwin, who was thirty-four in 1865 to his brother's fifty, was taking effect. The contrast is marked in The Little Boltons — on the east side Spicer's plain and mild houses of 1858-64 and on the west Corbett and McClymont's of 1867-8, still plainish but square-jawed and raw-boned (Plate 85a, b). Ruthless chamfering did what was desired there, but elsewhere a gaunt effect was more simply achieved by misproportioning, as at the forbidding houses, Nos. 2-26 (even) Finborough Road. Opposite, at Nos. 1-7 (odd) and No. 17 Redcliffe Place, the lavishing of unsightly motifs on the high stock-brick hulk of the ordinary London terrace does at least powerfully evoke what 'London' in its western reaches means to many dwellers in bedsitting-rooms (Plate 92c, d). In the smaller cross-streets such as Fawcett Street or Wharfedale Street the more subdued use of the repertory of motifs is less unpleasing (Plate 85c). The two terraces of shops at Nos. 239-279 (odd) Old Brompton Road (1866-8, Plate 89d) have the gawky appeal of 'down-market' quasi-Gothicizing (rarely used hereabouts) and are quite different from Corbett and McClymont's other ranges over shops west of Redcliffe Gardens, which at Nos. 270-296 (even) Fulham Road (Plate 89b) repeat something of the style of Nos. 204-210 Fulham Road. And where the miscellany of stylistic devices is employed without inhibitions, on public houses such as the Hollywood Arms (1865) and Coleherne Arms (1866), the effect is, in its way, invigorating (Plate 89a, c). Redcliffe Square, built so far as its characteristic parts go in 1869-76, is an undiluted example of one version of the Godwins' mixed 'style', illustrated and published under their names (Plates 90-1, 96a, 108, fig. 68). Here the vivacity of detailing at one time extended to the mansard roofs, where the zinc flashing was originally cut into the form of acanthus leaves and the use of two tones of slate gave a polychromatic effect.

If the 'Corbett and McClymont' phase of building in this area is harder on the eye than are the earlier, eastern, streets it is partly because the arrangement less frequently permitted the front gardens which in those streets by their lushness happily recall Brompton's horticultural fame. Nor was this yet quite the period when trees were commonly planted in London streets (unlike Westgate, where in 1877 Corbett was planning to plant many poplars and sycamores[235]).

George Godwin's magazine The Builder in March 1868 named him and Henry as the architects on the Redcliffe Estate for the Gunter brothers and Messrs. C. Lee and Sons as architects for 'the freeholder of another part of the estate'.[207] This presumably meant R. J. Pettiward's property at K but, as has been seen, there is no perceptible all-over difference in the mixture of styles on his and the Gunters' land. Neither The Builder nor The Building News mention work for Pettiward in their obituaries of Charles Lee in 1880.[236] The stress in the obituary in The Builder then lay on Lee's career as a surveyor. Perhaps that was chiefly his role here.

The relations of the Godwins with Corbett and McClymont seem, so far as the perhaps obscuring evidence of Corbett's business-letters shows, to have been formal and distant, with Tomlin normally an intermediary. George Godwin certainly, however, and perhaps Henry also, was involved with the firm's work as an investor. In 1872 Corbett and McClymont repaid £800 which George Godwin had lent them and one of the Godwins still had an involvement as to £500 in 1878.[237] George also bought some improved ground rents — of six houses in The Little Boltons in 1867, for example,[238] and of five houses in Hollywood Road in 1868,[239] as well as at least one house in Ifield Road.[240]

Corbett and McClymont did employ an architect of their own. He was F. Nesbitt Kemp, who on his death was said by The Builder, in a not wholly accurate obituary, to have been 'responsible for the layout of large areas in Kensington, including Redclyffe-square [sic]'.[241] This statement was made, however, in 1939, and although Kemp had by then begun practice 'over 70 years ago' that can hardly have been appreciably before 1869, and he does not occur in the Architect's, Engineer's and Building Trades Directory of 1868. Possibly he set up with his elder brother Alfred as architect in Lincoln's Inn Fields in 1869.[135] The stylistic tone of the Redcliffe Estate was by then established, and some of the Redcliffe Square houses must have already been designed. In 1871 Kemp, then aged twenty-four and the son of a bill-broker, was living in his parents' house at No. 12 Finborough Road.[242] By 1873 he had a professional address at Corbett and McClymont's Redcliffe Estate office at No. 2A Redcliffe Gardens, whence he applied to Kensington Vestry, seemingly in his own right as architect, to erect Nos. 280 and 282 Earl's Court Road, which were then being constructed by a builder, Edward Francis.[243] Although off the Redcliffe Estate, they are rather in its manner. After Corbett and McClymont's bankruptcy in 1878 Kemp, called by Corbett in 1880 'our late Architect', drew some room-plans of 'Bolton Gardens West' for them, to help sales. He had previously had the working drawings of these houses in his room at Corbett and McClymont's offices.[244] But it may be that here, as was evidently the case in Redcliffe Square, his role was that of setting-out or site architect, not designer. In 1881 he developed an estate of small houses around Dancer Road, Fulham,[245] in a blunt 'red-brick'

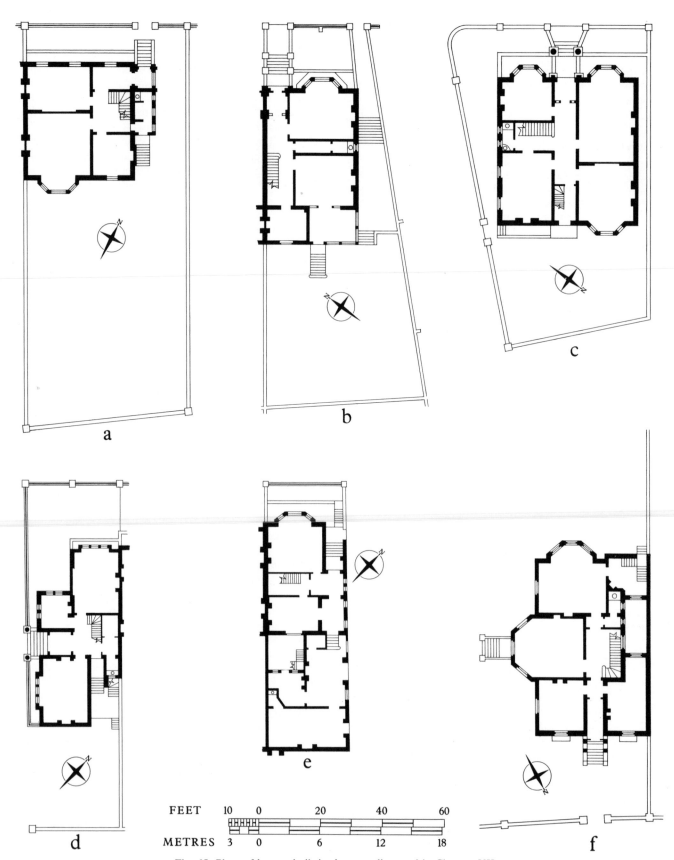

Fig. 65. Plans of houses built in the area discussed in Chapter XII.
a. No. 5 Bolton Gardens, 1863. *Demolished*   *b.* No. 1 The Little Boltons, 1866   *c.* No. 51 Redcliffe Gardens, 1871   *d.* No. 35 Tregunter Road, 1866   *e.* No. 27 Cathcart Road, 1864   *f.* No. 28 The Boltons, 1859

FEET 10 0   20   40   60
METRES 3 0   6   12   18

manner which has no affinity with that of the Redcliffe Estate beyond its striving for variety.

At Westgate William Corbett employed C. N. Beazley as his architect. It seems certain, however, that although later, in 1882-96, Beazley lived at No. 32 Harcourt Terrace[135] he had nothing to do with the Redcliffe Estate as architect. This seems negatively apparent from Corbett's letters. Further, in 1870 Corbett invited him and a Westgate landowner to come up from Thanet to view the firm's workshops and then go down to see their operations at Surbiton, which suggests that Beazley was not very familiar with what was going on in and around London.[246] A reference by Corbett in 1878, addressing the Royal Insurance Company, of which he had long been an agent, to 'my old friend Mr Chas N. Beazley the architect, whose name has come several times before you in connection with the Westgate on Sea Estate' similarly seems to make it unlikely he had also been known in the context of Kensington.[247] Beazley's houses for Corbett at Westgate have little or nothing of the Redcliffe Estate about them stylistically.

Only at one place is there any hint of the possible adjustment of the range of 'styles' of the house-exteriors in connexion with a known architect. This is at Nos. 20 and 22 Tregunter Road — houses in a slightly different manner from their neighbours, not least in their display of 'red' brick (Plate 86d, fig. 63c). There Corbett and McClymont's nominee for the lease in 1865 was an architect, J. H. Strudwick, who had been a resident in Priory Walk and became the first occupant of No. 20 Tregunter Road.[248]

House Plans and Types

If the architecture of this swathe of building is not attractive the arrangement of individual houses, so far as the Godwins' ground-floor lease-plans indicate, was sensible and sometimes ingenious.[249] Extending the view back to include the houses built before 1864, one or two points appear. In the smaller terrace houses the number where the front and back rooms are shown intercommunicating is notable. This was made possible because in these houses the staircase was almost always given its traditional position at the rear of the entrance hall. Fewer front and back rooms are so connected in the semi-detached houses, perhaps because borrowed light from one room to the other seemed less necessary.

Throughout all the houses three rooms on the ground floor was the general rule. Some small sites had only two rooms, but in the earlier part of the development, in the 1850's, two-roomed ground floors also occur even in uncramped semi-detached houses: in Gilston Road and Harley Gardens, for example, less need seems to have been felt to contrive a third room than in the streets of ten or fifteen years later. At the big terrace houses in Redcliffe Square the third, rear, room was an important apartment, often the full width of the house and lit from the garden or,

where a corner location gave side light, extending over most of the available space at the back. Only a very few houses had more than three ground-floor rooms. Two or three corner houses in Redcliffe Square had four, and Nos. 16 and 17 The Boltons six (unless some of these were service areas).

About a quarter of the Redcliffe Square houses generally conformed to old town-house practice of the grander sort in having two staircases (fig. 68) — a very unusual provision in the area occurring elsewhere, so far as the lease-plans show, only at the detached house, No. 51 Redcliffe Gardens (fig. 65c).

The difference in the management of the staircase between the east and west sides of The Boltons has been noticed. In the semi-detached houses generally the placing of this feature varied. Sometimes the usual terrace-house entrance-cum-staircase hall was retained, more usually on the 'outer' side of the house than against the party wall. The arrangement on the west side of The Boltons was partly adumbrated in Gilston Road, where, for example, the plan of Nos. 18 and 20, built by William Harding in 1852, is very close to what Spicer built on a larger scale and with a very different stylistic dress, at Nos. 18 and 19 The Boltons in 1857.[250]

Most of the plans and all the 'semi-detached' plans seem to show water closets on the ground floor. Only smaller terrace houses in the western streets and in Milborne Grove seem to be without them.

These plans were presumably in general not much susceptible of modification, although in 1871 at No. 32 Coleherne Road Corbett and McClymont may have adjusted the plan for the lessee and occupant, a dilettante-architect, A. H. Edmonds.[251]

At No. 44 Cathcart Road, a corner house, the arrangement was conceivably adapted to the needs of the first occupant, a surgeon. A distinct rear room is provided, with separate access from the side road.[252] Other houses, like some on the west side of The Boltons or Nos. 1 and 2 Harley Gardens look as if they might have been arranged with a 'professional' man in mind or at least a 'man of business', having smallish rooms set off to one side of the entrance hall away from the larger reception rooms, as if for the conduct of business or to serve as waiting rooms. At No. 27 Cathcart Road, finished in 1866, the single-storey, top-lit rear building opens, as at No. 44 opposite, to Hollywood Road: here, however, as the building lease states, it was 'intended to be used as Studios'[253] (Plate 84d, fig. 65e). It is separately numbered as 16 Hollywood Road and was indeed first occupied by a sculptor, Morton Edwards, until he became bankrupt in about 1870.[54]

A top-lit rear room was provided also at No. 19 Redcliffe Square, but there it was perhaps a billiard-room[254] (fig. 68).

Another Victorian amenity, the conservatory, seems to be supplied in the ground-floor plans of a number of houses, some of modest size, over a range of years. They

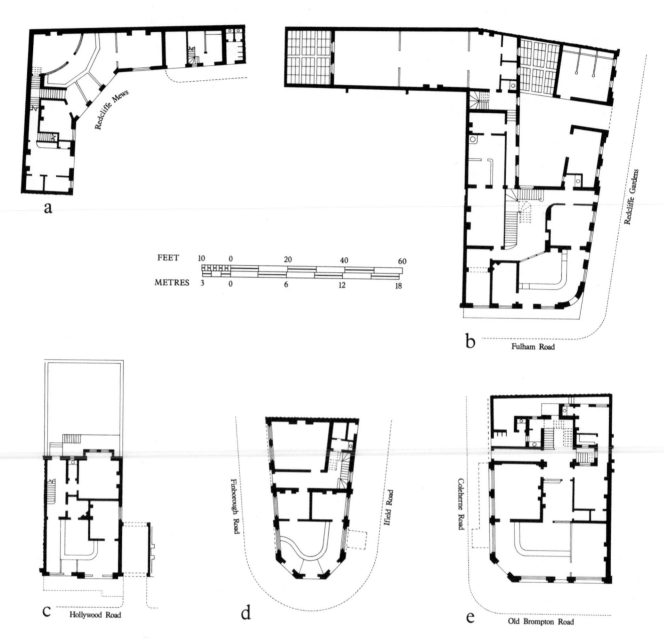

Fig. 66. Plans of public houses built or proposed on the Redcliffe Estate, 1865-8.
a. Harcourt Arms, Redcliffe Mews. *Not established.* *b.* Redcliffe Arms, Fulham Road   *c.* Hollywood Arms, Hollywood Road
d. Finborough Arms, Finborough Road   *e.* Coleherne Arms, Old Brompton Road

are probably discernible on plans of Nos. 1 and 2 Harley Gardens (1851), Nos. 18 and 20 Gilston Road (1852), Nos. 13 and 14 Milborne Grove (1862), Nos. 9-13 (consec.) Harley Gardens (1863), Nos. 45-49 (odd) Cathcart Road (1866), Nos. 1-27 (odd) The Little Boltons (1866-7, fig. 65b), and Nos. 92 and 94 Redcliffe Gardens (1869).[255]

As to the general types of house built by Corbett and McClymont, these continued the existing pattern: very few

detached houses, and many semi-detached. The proportion of terrace houses was, however, higher than before, as the more westerly streets brought a rather humbler client within the aim of the Redcliffe Estate. One departure was that, whereas the terraces built in the 1850's and early 1860's were all set out as pairs of houses with mirrored plans, Nos. 9-25 (odd) Cathcart Road of 1864-5 introduced the terrace of identically planned houses here, and thereafter Corbett and McClymont (or the Godwins) used that arrangement as freely as the other. It was used in Redcliffe Square (and at the big houses of Bolton Gardens West on the north side of Old Brompton Road).

Shops and Public Houses

One type of building shown on the plans for the Redcliffe Estate not represented in the earlier phase is the purpose-built shop. This was not an elaborate matter, the planning being little more than the inclusion of a wide, flat shop window and second entrance, and (sometimes) the omission of the partition between front and back rooms. On the Gunter and Robinson estates the plans show shops intended from the first at Nos. 106-116 (even) Finborough Road (1868-9), Nos. 236-238A (even) and Nos. 266 and 266A Fulham Road (also 1868-9), Nos. 2-14 (even) and 47-55 (odd) Hollywood Road (1865), and at the two ranges originally called Coleherne Terrace (Nos. 239-259 odd Old Brompton Road, 1867) and Claro Terrace (Nos. 261-279 odd Old Brompton Road, 1866-8, Plate 89d).[256]

Most of these groups of shops included or were adjacent to public houses. There were none of these within the earlier-developed part of the Gunter estate, but their provision was important to Corbett and McClymont, who were permitted to erect six on their Redcliffe Estate — this presumably by agreement between the Gunters and R. J. Pettiward. In fact, Corbett and McClymont built, between 1865 and 1868, only five operative public houses — two on Robert Gunter's land (the Coleherne Arms, now The Coleherne, Old Brompton Road (Plate 89c), and Finborough Arms, Finborough Road), two on R. J. Pettiward's (the Ifield Arms, Ifield Road, and the former Redcliffe Arms, Fulham Road, Plate 89b), and one (the Hollywood Arms, Hollywood Road, Plate 89a) on James Gunter's land. Corbett thought this a slenderer provision than on other estates of comparable population in London, which at least tended to make the five 'very valuable properties'.[257] Corbett and McClymont sold their lease of the Hollywood Arms in 1866 to a victualler from Southwark for £6,500. On a sale in 1872 the price was down to £6,000, but in 1894 the reduced term of the lease was bought by Watney and Company for £10,000.[258] The sixth of the prospective public houses, the Harcourt Arms, intended to be placed at Nos. 26 and 28 Redcliffe Mews (Plate 92a), was never opened. Corbett and McClymont used the premises as a workshop until their bankruptcy and thereafter James Gunter would not let them convert it to a tavern.[259] On the leases of public houses the ground-floor plans are drawn as carefully as those of dwelling houses, showing the bar arrangements (fig. 66). The Redcliffe Arms was an extensive establishment, with separate drinking-places besides the main bar (too spacious, perhaps, to be called snuggeries), and, initially, stabling, bowling saloon and billiard-room.[260] Separate drinking-rooms seem to have been provided at the Hollywood Arms and Coleherne Arms;[261] and at the

Finborough Arms and the abortive Harcourt Arms, in addition to these snuggeries, the main bar was divided in three with separate entrances.[262] Segregation was evidently desired even at the last of these, in what must have been intended wholly as a working-man's tavern.

Rents and Prices

The houses of the 'Corbett and McClymont' period were not, generally, designed for or taken by prospective frequenters of the 'Harcourt Arms'. There is an exception to be made to this, but most of the new streets initially attracted 'middle class' families. The well-informed Builder said in 1868 that the range of rents then current on the Redcliffe Estate was £50-£160 per annum.[207] By 1871 the big houses in Redcliffe Square were being built and in that year The Builder gave the range of rents as from £46 (a realistic figure, being the actual rent of No. 7 Cathcart Road in 1879[263]) to a perhaps unrealistic £600 per annum.[264] In 1872 Corbett and McClymont themselves advertised houses at £80 to £300 per annum[265] and in 1873 The Builder gave the range of rents as £50 to £400 per annum.[266] The rival Building News reported a visit of the Architectural Association to Redcliffe Square in the same year. The opinion (whether its own or the Association's) was that the houses 'while apparently well and substantially built, are somewhat meretricious in design, although by no means bad specimens of what wealthy people are content to pay from £200 to £300 a year for.'[267] Corbett himself put the range at £50 to £500 in 1877, the lower limit in Redcliffe Square being £170.[268] In 1878 one house, No. 27 Redcliffe Square, was let at £465 per annum.[269]

The asking-price for the long leasehold of this same large corner house in 1874 had been £6,000[270] and for the smaller No. 23 probably about £4,350.[271] In 1877 Corbett and McClymont claimed owners of their houses could obtain twenty-two and a half to twenty-five years' purchase of the improved ground rent when they sold them.[272] Other actual sale-prices are mostly known for the period of depression in the house-market that immediately followed: perhaps about £2,250-£3,350 in Redcliffe Square, £2,200-£2,900 in Redcliffe Gardens and £1,900-£2,000 in Tregunter Road or The Little Boltons. Houses in Redcliffe Road sold for £1,050 in 1879 and in Finborough Road for £530 in 1880.[273] At the time of Corbett and McClymont's bankruptcy in 1878 their houses were said to be valued as assets from £500 to £8,000 each.[274]

The range was thus wide, but did not reach quite down to the area of mass-demand. At the time of the bankruptcy and perhaps with reference to it The Estates Gazette said that the keenest demand was, rather, for houses letting at about £40 per annum.[275]

Occupants in 1871 and Later

The census of 1871 shows the modest and perhaps rather strained respectability of two ordinary streets within the

Redcliffe Estate.[242] At 25 houses in Fawcett Street 87 members of the 'family' were attended by 32 resident servants. None of the houses was in divided occupation, but one was run by a lodging-house keeper and four others had lodgers in them. At four houses resident servants were dispensed with — perhaps a better arrangement than at No. 19, where one young woman from Poplar served a family of ten. A stockbroker, a wine merchant (without a servant), a silk merchant, a bookseller, an art dealer, three annuitants (one of them a lady of twenty-nine with three servants), an officer's widow, six clerks or civil servants, a 'professor of languages', a twenty-two-year-old actress living with one servant, a dressmaker, an elderly man who gave his occupation as 'Navy Reserve' (and took in four lodgers) and a policeman made up the twenty household-ers whose designation was recorded.

In Finborough Road most of the 57 houses then in normal occupation were seemingly in the hands for which they were intended, but there are perhaps some signs of a misjudgement of the market. At the big houses, Nos. 2-14 (Plate 92d), the occupants included an artist and a manufacturer (each with two servants), a rentier (with three), a colonel in the army (two servants) and a bill-broker (one servant), but also a servantless dressmaker and three families in one house (No. 14). In all the houses 258 members of the 'family' were attended by 71 servants. Four houses were in divided occupation, five were run by lodging-house keepers, and twelve others had lodgers in them. Thirteen houses were without servants. At two houses a young female servant had ten of the family to look after. At the ten houses from No. 139 northward, all in undivided tenure, the householders gave their occupation as 'Parson (C. of E.)', surgeon, 'dividends', lodging-house keeper, secretary of Joint Stock Bank, colonel, 'boarding house', builder's foreman, clerk and hardware traveller. One of the bigger houses, No. 121 at the corner of Redcliffe Square (now neighboured by post-war flats of Kensington Borough), had not yet come into occupation, but when it did Charles Appleyard of Lincoln's Inn, esquire, had what sounds in an inventory of 1872 like a very respectable home there of a traditional kind. There was a servants' bedroom (with two beds), probably in the basement, a dining-room, library and boudoir (with a Kirkman piano in it) on the ground floor, a drawing-room and two bedrooms on the first floor, more bedrooms and a bathroom above, and a conservatory somewhere. All the reception rooms had Brussels carpets, and the main rooms furnishings and curtains en suite — in crimson rep downstairs, blue rep in the upstairs drawing-room and dimity in the bedrooms. The interior was shiny with a lot of mahogany, mirror-glass, china and glass ornaments and framed pictures. Outside there were 'fancy tile flower-boxes' at the windows.[276] Perhaps Mr. Appleyard felt his house was not really in Finborough Road at all, like the owner of another corner house at what was meant to be No. 73 in that road, who changed his address to No. 54 Tregunter Road.[277]

In the latter road the *Post Office Directory* in 1880 shows the houses of this phase seemingly filled up at a rather wealthier level, with one person of title and four army officers. That was the characteristic picture — two 'titles', three officers (one a major-general), a clergyman, a Q.C. and an architect in Redcliffe Gardens, for example.[135]

The architect was John Butler, architect to the Metropolitan Police, who was at No. 11 Redcliffe Gardens from 1870 to 1901, for many years with his son John Dixon Butler, who held the same position and continued there until 1907. Similarly at No. 62 Cathcart Road the archi-tect Thomas Verity was the first occupant in 1868 until his death in 1891, when his architect son Frank continued there for another year. Other first or early occupants of these houses were the architect Richard Popplewell Pullan at No. 87 Harcourt Terrace in 1877-80, the decorative artist Percy Macquoid briefly at No. 253 Old Brompton Road in 1876 and the chronicler of art, Algernon Graves, successively at No. 1 Redcliffe Place in 1871-2 and No. 51 Finborough Road in 1873-93. At the south end of Finborough Road the first occupant of No. 2 in 1869-70 was Arthur Hughes and an early occupant of No. 7 opposite in 1875-83 Richard Doyle, in grim-looking houses than which none could seem less suitable for the painter of 'April Love' and the illustrator of 'In Faery Land'.[135] Corbett and McClymont were not (any more than the Godwins) suppliers of 'the Artist's House'.

Builders as Landlords

Corbett and McClymont's attitude to their estate was in some respects, however, the opposite of perfunctory or uninvolved. They were willing to sell leaseholds (or free-holds where they had them), but the statements of house-values already noticed show how often the yearly lettable value was what mattered. Corbett and McClymont were the resident owners to a great many 'tenants'.[278] They kept a sharp eye on such things as the uniform painting of adjacent houses.[279] More than this, as extensive leasehold owners, there was, compared with many large builders' operations, a proprietorial element in their attitude, hinted at in McClymont's reference to the 'independent gentle-man'. After writing to Switzerland to entice a physician to take up residence in Redcliffe Square in 1877, Corbett confided to a friend, 'Entre nous there is a good opening for a "good Man". We have only really two good men on this large Estate.'[280] In 1874 he had felt able to assure a Conservative backer of the firm that 'the majority of our Tenants, to the number of I should think at least 600 will vote for Mr Gordon', the Parliamentary candidate for Chelsea. He added 'If all other districts are as Conser-vative as the "Redcliffe Estate" Mr Gordon's return is a certainty'.[212] Writing to congratulate William Gordon on his election he offered to help 'if at any time we can afford you any information relative to the neighbourhood'.[281] Corbett was involved with the Little Chelsea and West Brompton Benevolent Society,[282] bought his beer from the Hollywood Brewery[283] and used, among other banks, one on their estate at No. 202 Fulham Road, the London and South Western.[284] There was a note of pain in his comment when houses were being auctioned off after the bankruptcy: 'It is a cruel thing to see these sales carried out by auctioneers of whom we know nothing, and who do not take proper care of the premises'.[285] Corbett had attended divine service at the Park Chapel in Chelsea for some years, but this was pending the erection of the long-projected church of St. Luke's, Redcliffe Square, on their own estate.[286] When it was built he went there, would report an 'excellent Sermon' to his partner,[287] and was, with him, patron of the living for some eight or nine years.[288] This addition to the amenities of the estate was something in which Corbett and McClymont were, for good or ill, deeply involved. The financing of the work, which may have materially increased their troubles, is described, with the building of the church, on pages 235-6.

Unprospering West Brompton

The exception to the actual or pretended gentility of the Redcliffe Estate was Ifield Road. This was not particularly apparent in the outward aspect of the houses, comparatively small though they were (Plate 87d). But in its occupants the road was from the beginning mainly plebeian. A sprinkling of 'run', 'gone' and 'excused' in the ratebook for 1870 warns that Ifield Road was not the home of affluence, and the census of 1871 confirms this.[289] In 94 houses there were 29 servants, 797 members of the 'family' and 153 other residents. In most streets nearby the average number of occupants per house seems roughly proportionate to the average size of the house but in Ifield Road the density of occupation is noticeable, with ten or eleven persons per house whereas in Finborough Road, for example, where the houses are in general larger, the number was six or seven. Comparatively few of the Ifield Road houses were avowed lodging-houses, but this seems to have been because its social level was below that, with more than half the houses in divided occupation and lodgers frequent in working-class homes. At two houses, Nos. 74 and 85, there were 27 occupants, in four and five separate families respectively. The most noticeable feature of the population of the street was the proportion of heads of families who worked in the building trades — 66 out of 188 that are known. There were 21 who had work in transport old and new — six coachmen, two carmen, two cabmen, a cab-proprietor, two horsekeepers, three omnibus drivers or conductors, and five railway employees (two guards, a signalman, a clerk and a porter). Five were butlers or valets, but to households elsewhere. Mechanical technology accounted for only three — an engine-fitter, a gas-fitter and a hot-water engineer: another was a wire-worker. Only one was a 'professional man' — an architect, Augustus Dempster, who shared No. 71 with two other families (a railway guard's and a carpenter's) and himself took in four lodgers. Another architect lived in the street,

G. V. McLellan, as the son of an out-of-work tailor who took in a boarder and also shared No. 2 with a railway porter and a mason's labourer.

In 1902 Charles Booth noticed Ifield Road as one of the few exceptions to the generally decent level of prosperity in the area ('Some poor in Ifield Road, inhabited mainly by artisans and labourers') and marked it on his analytic map as 'poverty and comfort mixed'.[290] Its 'backwater' location, hemmed against the long wall of Brompton Cemetery, perhaps told against it — the same factor which has probably accounted for its very recent rise in the world.

The rate at which the Redcliffe Estate's houses were taken for occupation was satisfactory for some years. In 1871 *The Builder* said nearly all the completed houses were let.[264] This seems to be more or less borne out down to 1870 (after which the test can no longer be applied) by the comparison of the years in which house-carcases were leased and those in which rates were first paid. There is a tendency for the northern streets and northern ends of streets to 'go' a little slower. Harcourt Terrace of 1867-8 and Westgate Terrace of 1869-71 seem, on the less certain evidence of the *Post Office Directory*, to show a slowing-up, and this was conspicuously the case in Redcliffe Square, built 1868-76. (It was even more so with the houses of 1874-8 on the north side of Old Brompton Road.) It may have been Corbett and McClymont that *The Estates Gazette* had in mind when it said in 1878, a few days after their bankruptcy, that 'one firm of builders in the neighbourhood of Kensington have houses unlet on their hands to the value of £10,000 a year'.[275]

Thereafter the streets here, more than those in the earlier-developed part, evinced decline in the last decades of the century. It is particularly in the nineties that the change declares itself in the *Post Office Directory*, although this probably records belatedly an earlier change. In Coleherne Road, Fawcett Street, Redcliffe Road and Finborough Road particularly 'apartments' replace private residences and other households cease to be noticed at all. In 1902 Charles Booth thought the decline of parts of West Brompton could be ascribed to the fact already noted, that it was an area where the houses were built for a richer class than was becoming willing to inhabit them. It showed 'a failure on the part of ground landlords and builders to appreciate the economic strength of the classes who keep no servants and make no pretence to fashion, . . . amongst whom are to be found every year a larger proportion of the population. The mischief seems to be an inevitable consequence of the construction of property for which there is no sound demand . . .'[291]

Harcourt Terrace in 1900 had not, avowedly, succumbed to apartments, but had been slow to fill. One class for which this part of South Kensington seems to have gained rather than lost attraction was the officer of the armed services. In 1880 ten had lived in Tregunter Road and five in Westgate Terrace. By 1900 they were more noticeable in Harcourt Terrace (a general, two colonels, a major and a captain). It was evidently not the ramrod architecture of that street (more conventional than others on the Redcliffe Estate) which attracted them, as Redcliffe Square was also favoured, with seven officers.

The Methods and Bankruptcy of Corbett and McClymont

On 4 May 1878 Corbett and McClymont suspended payment. The immediate occasion seems to have been the maturing of certain promissory notes, perhaps in particular those of the incumbent of St. Luke's, Redcliffe Square (see page 236). The verdict of *The Building News* at the time on the general cause was simply that in South Kensington 'they have over-built'. It spoke of empty houses in one road 'which must have meant £200,000 lying idle'.[292] On 6 May *The Times* reported their joint liabilities as an estimated £1,300,000 and their separate liabilities as £65-70,000 (Corbett) and £45,000 (McClymont).[293] In February 1879 the Bankruptcy Court made an order for the payment of 2s. 6d. in the £ to creditors of the joint estate and 6d. in the £ to those of the separate estates.[294] Much of their property in London and elsewhere was sold off or passed into the hands of mortgagees, but some remained to them. Corbett moved to a narrower house at No. 57 Cathcart Road (Plate 87c) in autumn 1878 and McClymont (not too cast down by his misfortunes, however, to go to the 1879 Boat Race) moved to a house at No. 318 King's Road, Chelsea, where in 1881 he called himself a 'retired builder'.[295] Corbett obtained some income from a long-standing agency for the Royal Insurance Company, through which the insurance of all houses on the Redcliffe Estate had been effected.[296] The firm remained at No. 2A Redcliffe Gardens[135] administering what remained of its estate until the partnership was dissolved in *c.* 1880.[297] Alexander McClymont disappears from King's Road after 1882. (Someone of the same name, perhaps his son, was at No. 32 Cathcart Road in 1891-8.) Corbett moved in 1882 or 1883 to No. 2 Redcliffe Gardens, next to the firm's old office, where Corbett and Company continued until 1889 as 'builders', although seemingly not house-builders. William Corbett disappears after 1889 but his younger son, A. J. Corbett, kept the firm going in the late nineties and then moved with it to No. 19 Finborough Road until 1905.[135]

As has been noticed, in South Kensington Corbett and McClymont's houses had all been built by the time of the bankruptcy. Some finishing needed to be done, however, and much of this work seems to have fallen to Aldin and Sons. (One big house brought them a contract for £1,500.[298]) Corbett and McClymont's relations with rival building firms are not known. Corbett had sent a circular to Freake on behalf of at least one West Brompton charity[282] and dispatched one of his sons with a polite letter to Spicer asking him to subscribe to St. Luke's Church.[299] With Aldins the relations were closer, perhaps because of a common association with one of the bankers

at Coutts, W. G. Logan.[300] (Corbett interested Charles Aldin in his estate at Westgate, for which Aldin negotiated to supply him with bricks from a field at Slough, and where the younger Charles Aldin had a house.[301])

Something of the background of the bankruptcy is revealed in copies of William Corbett's office out-letters, which survive, with gaps, for the years 1870-80. Unfortunately, one of the gaps is from the end of March 1878 until the bankruptcy on 4 May. The light thrown on the firm's workings is further limited by a fact stated in one of Corbett's later letters — 'the practical part of our business was conducted by Mr McClymont'.[302]

Corbett's detachment from the building process seems to have been complete. His letters show little interest in the design or planning of the product his firm was offering. That this was more than scrupulosity in regard to his partner is suggested by the paucity of such references in the many letters concerned with his own estate at Westgate (where McClymont, however, did have some involvement). Nor did Corbett very much concern himself with salesmanship. The chief agents for the Redcliffe Estate seem to have been Rogers and Chapman of Gloucester Road. At least one general layout plan was publicized.[265] Particulars and room-plans of some big houses which Corbett and McClymont were especially anxious to be rid of were prepared for circulation in 1880, but Corbett's comment to the architect employed to make them that 'similar things I find have been prepared and distributed by some of the Builders of South Kensington for their large Houses'[303] suggests the firm had not been very forward in using this kind of inducement to customers.

The half of the firm represented by Corbett was concerned solely, it seems, with financial management and with the legal technicalities necessary to raise funds. In Corbett the accountant (or ex-accountant) and the lawyer both found a voice — he spoke in 1874 of his 'success in life' being 'mainly due to the *Legal* profession and my connection with it' and about that time he was joining the Temple Club.[304]

It was presumably Corbett who would have been concerned to determine the apportionment of the building leases between him, McClymont and both of them. Those individually granted were thereupon sub-leased by each to the other at an increased ground rent, thereby creating an 'improved ground rent', which could in turn be sold or mortgaged.[305] In June 1877 Corbett said they had sold upward of £200,000 of these.[306]

The prevailing rate of interest was one of Corbett's most anxious concerns. In November 1873, for example, he was deploring that 'Bank rate has today reached the enormous figure of £9 per cent'.[307] (The 'prevailing' rate of interest was not, however, as will be seen, a simple matter.) Its importance was, of course, in the effect it had on Corbett's main activity in the seventies, that is, raising money. If Corbett abjured McClymont's 'practical' concerns he often called on his partner to help obtaining new creditors or persuading old ones to provide more funds ('Will you

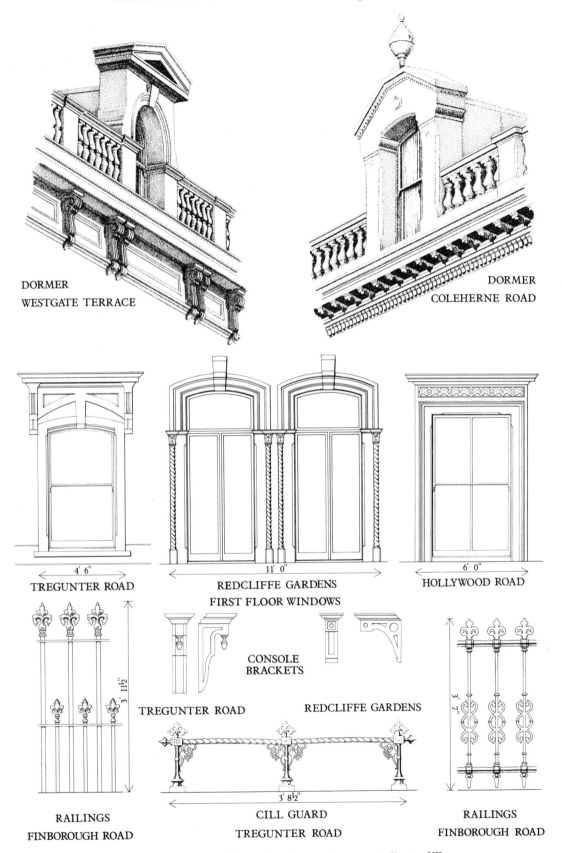

DORMER
WESTGATE TERRACE

DORMER
COLEHERNE ROAD

TREGUNTER ROAD
4' 6"

REDCLIFFE GARDENS
FIRST FLOOR WINDOWS
11' 0"

HOLLYWOOD ROAD
6' 0"

CONSOLE
BRACKETS

TREGUNTER ROAD   REDCLIFFE GARDENS

RAILINGS
FINBOROUGH ROAD
3' 11½"

CILL GUARD
TREGUNTER ROAD
3' 8½"

RAILINGS
FINBOROUGH ROAD
3' 7"

Fig. 67. Architectural details from the area discussed in Chapter XII

see Price and *get £2000 if you can*' (May 1874), 'I hope you have done some good today as to Cash' (June 1874), 'I hope you will do no end of good tomorrow *re funds* (July 1877)[308]. In 1873 Corbett and McClymont do not seem, in fact, to have had great difficulty in attracting creditors, who were 'very civil' or even 'very civil indeed'. (Later, they tended to be only 'pretty civil'.)[309] But the chase after funds was energetic. In February 1874, for example — 'I saw *Houseman, Jarrett, Weiss, Cole, Gabriel, Matthews, Ingpen and Griffith Davies* and *Lewin*; got on well at each place and must not grumble at the days work'[310] (a day, that is, at solicitors' offices, with one call on a bank manager). One morning in June 1877 Corbett went from Redcliffe Gardens to (another) bank manager in Old Brompton Road at 9 o'clock, then to the Gunters' lawyer Tomlin (perhaps at his house in Bolton Gardens rather than at his office in Old Burlington Street), then back to Redcliffe Gardens at 9.45 to see McClymont, then to another solicitor (presumably at his office in Storey's Gate rather than at his house in Bayswater), then back to Redcliffe Gardens to meet a third solicitor at 11.30.[311]

The sources of funds were various and numerous. Some money came from the Gunters via Tomlin, although in other respects the relations with the ground landlords seem to have been distant. In 1874 the firm had a loan from Robert Gunter, who declined, however, to advance a further £10,000 on a second mortgage, and Corbett was hopeful of getting £5,000 that James Gunter would shortly have for investment.[312] As has been seen, George Godwin was an investor on a modest scale. Some private backers occur. Lady Price, a widow, living in Lowndes Square, was mortgagee of some houses in The Little Boltons (from Spicer as well as from Corbett and McClymont) and Redcliffe Gardens.[313] An E. L. Price, colourman of Ebury Street, was also a backer, although a trade connexion is possible there:[314] Alfred Waterman of Gracechurch Street, timber merchant, and Henry Bingley, slate merchant, were also lenders.[315]

Insurance companies seem not to have been much used. The chief sources of money were solicitors and bankers, and nearly two dozen solicitors occur in this role. The firm of Lewin seems to have had an involvement at one time to the extent of £50,000.[316] How far solicitors' money was their own does not usually appear, although one, in Essex Street, held mortgages to secure £27,700 'of which about 3/4ths are Mr Cole's own money'.[317] The most important firm in some respects was Farrer, Ouvry in Lincoln's Inn Fields, whose contact with Corbett and McClymont was through a partner, W. J. Jarrett. Farrer, Ouvry's importance was largely due to the fact that they acted for Coutts and Company, a major source of funds. Coutts's contact with Corbett and McClymont was more directly through W. G. Logan. He, apart from being Corbett's next-door neighbour in The Little Boltons, was closely connected

with Thomas Logan and Company, wine merchants, in Buckingham Street, who supplied and perhaps ran the hotel at Corbett's Westgate, and was himself an interested resident there.[318] (Tomlin and the Lewins also had or took houses at Westgate.[319])

Coutts was not the only bank involved with Corbett and McClymont. The National Bank at Grosvenor Gardens, the Union Bank at Chancery Lane, and nearer home the London and Provincial in Old Brompton Road and the London and South Western in the Fulham Road were all used for loans. Their managers were important people to Corbett and McClymont. (The manager of the National Bank was given the free use of a house at Westgate at Christmas 1876.[320]) None, however, was so important as Coutts. The extent of Coutts's financial commitment does not appear, but in 1874 was sufficiently large for Corbett to be anxious to satisfy one of the partners that he was a sound man even in the matter of party politics.[212] And it was Coutts who were sufficiently involved to take active, if ineffectual, steps to protect their stake in the firm. In February 1878 they evidently asked an estate agent and surveyor to report on the firm's progress (perhaps in building at Surbiton) when another large loan was under discussion on the security of this new work. One of the partners was sufficiently concerned to go and see for himself. Corbett wrote to McClymont: 'From a whisper I heard I think Mr Ryder [later the fourth Earl of Harrowby, of Coutts] and Mr Jarrett [of Farrer, Ouvry] will be down when not expected. Pray keep a sharp look out and see that all outside is going on properly.'[321] Rather in the manner of an 'institutional shareholder' nowadays Coutts also put in an accountant to inspect the firm's books.[322] This was W. F. Marreco of Marreco and Gilbert, whose name introduces the final phase. In the same month the manager of the London and Provincial bank refused the offer of some property (probably at Westgate) as security for the continuation of a loan of £1,000. Corbett paid the loan off and closed the account with a dignified letter.[323] But the charge of debt could no longer be kept at bay and on 4 May 1878 Marreco exchanged his role as 'company doctor' for that of receiver for and manager of a firm in liquidation.

As to the cause of failure, Corbett wrote immediately afterwards to a solicitor who was one of the firm's creditors (perhaps with a touch of malice in the apparent naivety) that 'Messrs Coutts and Co. who have assisted us very largely, found great fault when they discovered we had been paying interest exceeding five per cent, but there were others besides yourself, to whom we had been paying a similar rate'.[324] It is evident from Corbett's letters that since at least the beginning of the year he had been striving hard to rearrange the firm's credit on the basis of long-term mortgages and that this conventional method had by no means been the staple of its borrowing.[325]

Fig. 68. Nos. 11-27 (odd) Redcliffe Square, site and house plans, elevations and details. George and Henry Godwin, architects, 1872-3

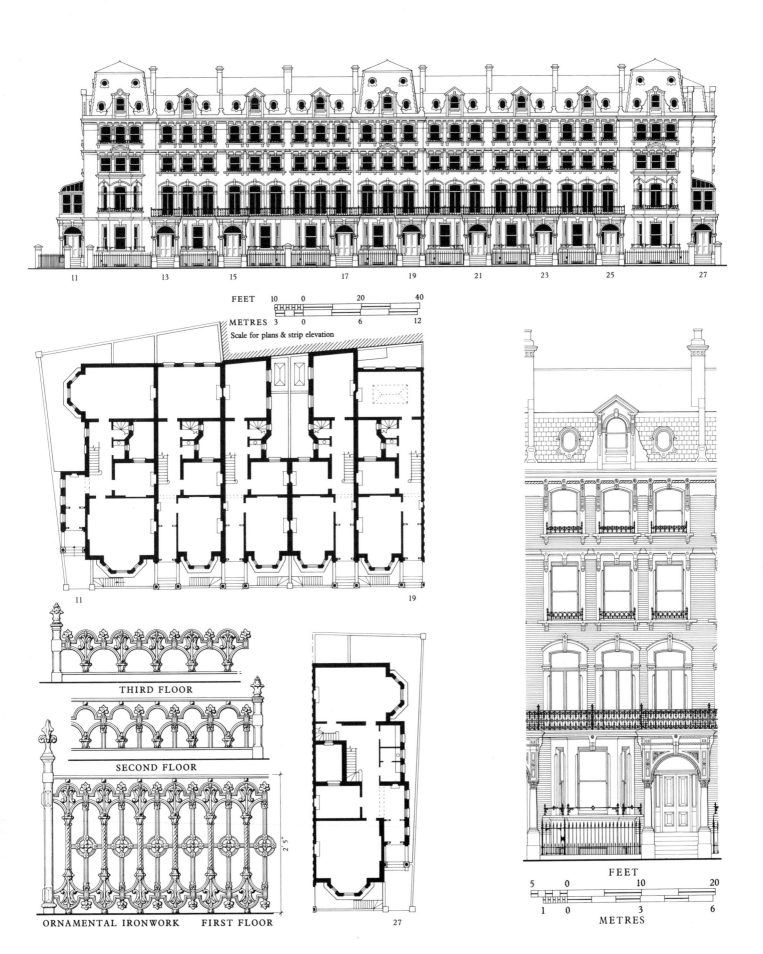

11 13 15 17 19 21 23 25 27

FEET 10 0 20 40

METRES 3 0 6 12

Scale for plans & strip elevation

11 19

THIRD FLOOR

SECOND FLOOR

2' 5"

ORNAMENTAL IRONWORK FIRST FLOOR

27

FEET

5 0 10 20

1 0 3 6

METRES

Much of the money had been raised not by first or second mortgages but by a complication of short-term loans, often on the security of the deposit of title-deeds and at a high rate of interest.[326] In January 1878, for example, he had to ask for £250 for three or four months at seven and a half per cent, but arranged for £2,000 on mortgage at four-and-a-half per cent.[327] As Corbett told his 'confidential clerk' in that month, with an eye to Coutts's investigation, 'every effort must be made to clear off temporary loans and make permanent mortgages'.[328]

The hazards of money-raising were increased by a falling-off in the demand for the wares Corbett and McClymont were offering and, probably, a rise in costs. In summer 1877 Corbett was complaining of the high cost of materials and labour.[329] The firm's obduracy against wage-demands has been noticed and possibly explains Corbett's dislike, expressed in 1875, of the London School Board and its 'mania' for building:[330] perhaps this spoilt the labour-market. And demand which in 1873 was still good was evidently declining in 1877.

Houses in a range on the west side of Redcliffe Square had, Corbett said, been valued at £3,000 when built in 1873 or 1875.[331] The asking price of one in 1877 was £2,625[332] and of another in 1880, after the bankruptcy, £2,250. (The offer of £1,600 for the latter brought Corbett as near as he came to boiling-point — 'Whoever makes this offer can be no well wisher to us or our Estate, in fact it is neither more nor less than an insult'.)[333] A house on the south side, valued at about £4,350 when built in 1874, was on offer at £3,350 in 1880.[334] (Even more difficulty was found with the big houses of 'Bolton Gardens West' on the north side of Old Brompton Road.)

A year after the bankruptcy the depression in the house market was such that Corbett was able to persuade the trustee for a bankrupt creditor that properties on the Redcliffe Estate which had been made security, by second mortgages, for £8,000 would not sell at auction even at their reduced estimated value of £4,800 and successfully offered £4,000 to discharge the mortgage. Characteristically Corbett and McClymont had to borrow £3,500 of this from another lawyer.[335] Elsewhere, the deeds of properties on which a customer of the Union Bank had advanced money had been lodged with the bank and then transferred, with the loan, to T. E. Lewin. But the brute fact was that in April 1879, as Corbett confessed, the properties were 'not of sufficient value to pay the amount due upon them'.[336] In these circumstances Corbett was at a loss: 'the sad misfortune which befell us', he wrote to W. G. Logan in May 1879, 'was from no fault of mine; and the most terrible depression of property which has happened, not only on our Estate, but also in the neighbourhood, I could not possibly avoid'.[337]

So far as Corbett's letters suggest, personal inadequacy (other than sickness — both he and McClymont had gout[338]) was probably not a major element in the failure. *The Builder* in 1870 had praised Corbett's 'energy and clear-headedness',[339] and his letters are lucid, measured

and concise. Neither he nor (so far as the letters suggest) his partner was idle. Corbett wrote twenty-nine letters, for example, on Boxing Day 1877[340] and sixty-one on 4 and 5 April 1879 (very few of them merely as routine).[341] And it is evident that in its complicated dealings the firm at least thought it knew what it was doing. Its straightforwardness is less easy to judge. After the bankruptcy Corbett was seemingly guilty of at least disingenuousness when in November 1879 he tried to sell No. 26 Redcliffe Mews to a fellow-builder with the prospect of its use as a tavern a week after he had told the Union Bank there was '*no chance whatever of a licence*'.[342]

The wide range of the partners' activities does not seem to have helped the firm. The Westgate estate was not greatly prospering in 1877 (and early in 1878 Corbett sold such of his land there as was still undeveloped). The firm had building interests on Robert Gunter's land in Fulham, and on other estates in Surbiton, Putney and Croydon.

To some extent the firm seems to have recognized the situation, if belatedly. There are signs of retrenchment in its activities in 1877.[343] But the leasehold system did not make this easy for builders who had to meet legal commitments in regard to their property, and this difficulty must have been greater for firms which, like Corbett and McClymont, had little or no business as contractors to fall back upon.

Perhaps in an attempt to move with the times, Corbett had been interesting himself early in 1877 in buying 'good Red Bricks'[344] — a commodity not much used on the Redcliffe Estate. This apparent recognition came too late to help there, where the firm was trying in the late seventies to dispose of houses built in strong versions of the 'style' of the late sixties. It was unfortunate for the firm that the phasing of the Redcliffe Estate, presumably in some measure at the behest of Tomlin and the Godwins, saddled it in a difficult market not with its more modest and muted houses but, in Redcliffe Square and on the north side of Old Brompton Road, with some of its biggest and least appetizing.

The Area after 1878

The failure of Corbett and McClymont in 1878 did not, at least immediately, lead to dereliction on the estate. Apart from the intimacy of Tomlin's knowledge of his neighbourhood on the Gunters' behalf, Corbett and McClymont retained enough interest in the area to control such matters as external painting, to look sharply after arrears of rent, to encourage one or two private schools to set up there, and to wish for any sales to be to owner-occupiers.[345] Other parts of their property passed to their banks — Coutts bought eighty-eight houses[346] (as well as acquiring a large interest at Westgate[347]) and the firm's former receiver, W. F. Marreco, himself picked up twelve houses in Ifield Road at £100 each.[348]

To the landlords Robert and James Gunter the ground

rents of all this property developed since 1850 were worth perhaps some £3,560 and £2,330 per annum respectively, for about sixty-three acres. The capital and reversionary value of the land, prospective upon the expiry of leases betwen 1931 and 1984, was, of course, enormously increased.

Moreton Gardens and Terrace and Cresswell Gardens

One area of house-building remains to be mentioned. In 1867 Robert Gunter bought Hawk Cottage, at the north-eastern boundary of his land south of Old Brompton Road (F on fig. 58 on page 196; fig. 59 on page 202), from the Atwood family of market gardeners.[349] This was not far from the builder John Spicer's houses in Bolton Gardens and before February 1875 Gunter had evidently come to an agreement with Spicer for the redevelopment of the site of Hawk Cottage and of Moreton Tower to its west and of Cresswell Lodge to its south. In that month he granted Spicer the leases of three newly built houses at the western end of the area.[350] Two were semi-detached and lay in the angle of Old Brompton Road and the northern limb of The Boltons (then named as part of Gilston Road). The more southerly house of this pair faced west to the latter roadway, and was designated No. 1 Moreton Gardens, and the more northerly, facing Old Brompton Road, was numbered 2 Moreton Gardens. Both were renumbered as 189 Old Brompton Road in 1937. The third, numbered 3 Moreton Gardens, was detached and faced Old Brompton Road to the east of No. 2, being redesignated No. 185 Old Brompton Road in 1937 (Plate 79d). Neither building is quite in the manner adopted for the Redcliffe Estate. Both are completely stuccoed in front. No. 189 attempts an un-Godwinian suavity in a rather French way, while No. 185 is a quite confident exercise in the Royal-icing-on-the-cake style.

The first occupant of the southern part of No. 189 (No. 1 Moreton Gardens) was Jenny Lind (Goldschmidt) from 1874 until her death in 1887.[351] The northern part (No. 2 Moreton Gardens) was first occupied, in 1877-88, by Sir Frederick Milbank, M.P., a noted game shot, who had previously lived at No. 5 Cromwell Gardens. In 1877 he had Morris and Company design him a stained-glass window here.[352] The semi-circular bow window on the west front was added by C. G. F. Rees, architect, in 1906.[353]

Spicer was then taken up with his activities north of Old Brompton Road, and the sequence of Moreton Gardens was not continued until after his death in 1883. What followed was more closely allied than anything hitherto built on the Gunters' estates south of that road to what was happening northward. Like much of the building there the work was done under leases granted by Robert Gunter to which G. J. Spicer, a solicitor and John Spicer's son, was a party evidently by right of an agreement to which his father had been entitled. The leases here were granted between May 1884 and September 1885.[354] They encompassed not only the extension of Moreton Gardens but the creation of a small new street opening off Old Brompton Road across the former sites of Hawk Cottage and Cresswell Lodge. Nine terrace houses were built eastward of No. 185 Old Brompton Road, called 4-12 (consec.) Moreton Gardens (since 1937 Nos. 167-183 odd Old Brompton Road). Between them and a further four houses called Nos. 1-4 Moreton Terrace (now Nos. 159-165 Old Brompton Road), which brought the development along Old Brompton Road to the eastern boundary of the Gunter estate, an angular road, Cresswell Gardens, was opened southward to connect with the northern end of Bolton Mews (now Cresswell Place). Four terrace houses were built on the east side of this street and nine on the west, the latter backing on the pleasaunce of Moreton Gardens itself. In that respect they are akin to the houses of the various 'Gardens' north of Old Brompton Road. To some of those they are allied also in their architecture. This is of 'Queen Anne' fashion, in yellow and red brick and terracotta, not noteworthy in itself but showing, like some of the houses to the north, the intrusion into the Gunters' estates of architects seemingly independent of the estate surveyor. Here the builders brought their own architect. They were the firm of John Matthews and Andrew Rogers, who were together or separately the recipients of or nominators for such leases (at Nos. 4-12 Moreton Gardens, now Nos. 167-183 odd Old Brompton Road) as were not made to G. J. Spicer himself. Their architect, who submitted the proposed layout to the Metropolitan Board of Works on their behalf in 1883, was Maurice Hulbert.[355]

Coleherne Court

After a lapse of years the next major building operation marked a complete break with the past. West of South Bolton Gardens the entire site of Coleherne House and Hereford House was devoted by General James Gunter not to a modernized version of the street layout of the Godwins' day but to a great aggregation of flats in three blocks, called Coleherne Court and built in 1901-4 (Plate 101b). The building-owner was Henry Bailey, an active intermediary in the construction of flats in other parts of Kensington, and the contractor T. W. Brown of Hornsey. The architect for the ground landlord was Walter Cave, who was then or soon became the Gunters' estate surveyor. Some role was also played on Bailey's behalf by the experienced architect of blocks of flats, Paul Hoffmann, who worked for Bailey elsewhere.[356] The flats were conventionally planned and commodious without being exceptionally large (five rooms, a servant's bedroom, domestic offices, two water closets and a bathroom), and at £130-£160 per annum were neither cheap nor extremely expensive.[357] Some twenty already appear as occupied in the *Post Office Directory* in 1903. The style shows an interesting application to a massive undertaking of a partly

Georgianized Arts-and-Crafts manner of the sort more usually employed for individual houses. The motifs are effectively distributed to avoid both monotony and over-busyness. The texture of careful brickwork, smooth ashlar and occasional sunny stone-carving is a kind of metaphor of the 'good manners' doubtless cultivated by the first occupants. Using similar, if richer, quasi-pediments as on the Gunter estate's humbler houses of this period in Fulham, the style externally is undoubtedly Cave's — not monumental, but quiet, cheerful, salubrious and sensible. Altogether Coleherne Court looks rather like what it is — the work of a slightly advanced gentleman-architect who had played cricket for Gloucestershire.[358]

The South Bolton Gardens Area

Meanwhile the area of villas around South Bolton Gardens (until 1906 named Bolton Gardens South) and the northern limb of The Boltons (Gilston Road until 1913) had become more emphatically separated from Old Brompton Road by the building of Nos. 1-8 (consec.) Bolton Gardens in 1863-4 and of Nos. 159-189 (odd) Old Brompton Road in 1875-85 (see pages 210, 229).

South Bolton Gardens by no means fell out of favour. In 1880 the thirty-six-year leasehold tenure of Bladon Lodge fetched £3,500 whereas in 1859 the fifty-nine years of the lease had sold for £2,310. In 1883 the former White Cottage, renamed Rathmore Lodge, was greatly extended for a banker, John Turnbull, by the architects Wallace and Flockhart.[359]

In 1901-4 Coleherne Court rose to the west, on the other side of The Little Boltons, and Sir Robert Gunter brought the style of the same architect to South Bolton Gardens when in 1903 Walter Cave designed two short terraces of houses to flank Osborn House, three to the east and two to the west. Those to the east were numbered 4, 5 and 6, Osborn House was numbered 7, and the two houses to the west 8 and 9. Cave exhibited the designs at the Royal Academy (Plate 101a). Each new house was planned 'with a view to combining a small bachelor's house with servants' accommodation and a large studio', and an alteration to a similar use by a not-impoverished artist was intended at Osborn House. In each house, including the latter as it was meant to be altered, the ground floor was to accommodate bedrooms and the first floor one large studio with a small 'model's room' off it or upstairs. Externally the new houses were to be in a Voyseyish Arts-and-Crafts suburban style, with very big studio windows divided by the unmoulded stone mullions and transoms favoured by Cave elsewhere, and placed under gables in the grey-green slated roofs. The elevations were rough-cast. Osborn House was to be altered externally, in an even more mixed vocabulary of architectural styles and with a more adventurous arrangement of window-openings. In the event Osborn House was not altered, but Nos. 4-6 and 8-9 were built in 1904-6 by F. G. Minter under leases granted in 1906 by the son of Sir Robert Gunter (d. 1905),

Sir R. B. N. Gunter.[360] A glimpse of the range Nos. 4-6 in an old photograph seems to show that these, at least, were built with smaller windows on the north side than originally intended.[361] All seem to have been disposed of quite quickly. At No. 8 the first occupant in 1906 was (Sir) William Orpen, who painted the *Hommage à Manet* there and retained the house as his studio until his death in 1931. In 1907-9 his friend, the dealer and art collector (Sir) Hugh Lane, also lived there.[362] Nos. 8 and 9 survive, as does Osborn House, but the site of Nos. 4-6 has been taken into that of the Bousfield School.

The next period of change was in the prosperous years of 1927-9. In 1918, after the rather abortive attempt by Sir R. B. N. Gunter (d. 1917) to auction off his estate in Kensington, representatives of the Gunter family had sold the freehold of Bladon Lodge, subject to a leasehold interest expiring in 1930, for £3,600. In 1927 a merchant banker living in Rutland Gate, C. L. Dalziel, contracted to buy it from the then owner for £14,000 and paid another £2,000 for the last three years of the lease.[363] He then employed Clough Williams-Ellis to extend the house in 1928 by adding wings to east and west, and to make a new entrance from South Bolton Gardens via a loggia and paved courtyard (Plate 99). The work received some publicity.[364] Bladon House was bombed during the war of 1939-45, and in 1947-8 proposals were made by Victor Kerr and Colbourn on behalf of A. E. Marples, and by Austin Blomfield on behalf of a client, for blocks of flats to be built here, but the site was already destined to become part of a school site.[365]

In 1929 Nos. 8 and 9 were altered and united by J. E. Forbes and J. Duncan Tate for the latter's friend, Sir William Orpen, who then held the lease of both houses. The work resembled, though with a more modernistic flavour, that at Bladon Lodge in so far as it showed a taste for loggias opening to formal courtyards with pools in them, and made gestures towards the Mediterranean (Plate 100). Similarly also, the publicity included an article in *Country Life*.[366]

In the same year the architect D. Barclay Niven designed a two-storeyed neo-Georgian house for his own occupation on the north side of South Bolton Gardens, behind No. 2 Bolton Gardens, called South Lodge.[367] This site has now been taken into that of the Bousfield School.

At Sidmouth Lodge Samuel J. Waring of Waring and Gillow (later Baron Waring) had contracted with Sir R. B. N. Gunter in 1917 to buy the house for £6,600. He did not do so and in 1920 sold his option at a profit of £900 to Doctor N. S. Mercer, physician, of Omaha, Nebraska. In 1926 Doctor Mercer turned himself into a property company, Realtor Securities Company Limited, and in 1930 it became known that he proposed to build a block of flats on the site, designed by J. Stanley Beard and Clare. Very widespread objections arose from neighbouring residents, directed at the local authorities. They were without effect upon the London County Council, but while they were still being voiced Doctor Mercer sold the site, in March 1931, to the Post Office. The price was £21,000. The intention of the Post Office was to use the site for the Frobisher (automatic) Telephone Exchange. This large but low-built and easily ignored building, now the Earl's Court Telephone Exchange, was erected in 1939 to designs made in the Office of Works.[368]

The last domestic buildings to be noticed are on the site of the former Rathmore Lodge. These are what is now No. 50 The Little Boltons (still called Rathmore Lodge), and the terrace of 'town houses' south of it, numbered 38-48 (even) The Little Boltons. They were built c. 1961-2 in a neo-Georgian style to designs by Stone Toms and Partners.[369]

A more notable work, changing the character of the area, is the Bousfield Primary School. The site of the school occupies that of Bladon Lodge and Nos. 4-6 South Bolton Gardens, the eastern part of the roadway of South Bolton Gardens, and the former Nos. 1-6 Bolton Gardens. All these sites were bought freehold by the London County Council in 1949-54, at a total cost of £23,800 for six lots. (The largest single price, £7,250, was paid for the smallest site, on the north side of South Bolton Gardens, occupied by the war-damaged remains of White Cottage.)[370] The school was built in 1954-6 for the London County Council to designs by Chamberlin, Powell and Bon (assistant-in-charge George Agabeg). The contractors were W. J. Marston and Son.[371] The low-built plan, the peep-holed brick walls along Old Brompton Road and The Boltons, the small watercourse boundaries and the paint-box colours are perhaps appropriate.

The Gunter Estates since 1905

Sir Robert Gunter (created a baronet in 1901) died in 1905, leaving some £650,000, of which about £35,000 was paid in estate duty. His brother James died in 1908.[372] In 1917 Sir Robert's son, Lieutenant-Colonel Sir R. B. N. Gunter, put the land in Kensington he had inherited from Sir Robert Gunter up for auction, together with other land so inherited in Fulham and Chelsea, at a reserve price of £500,000 for properties worth some £17,000 per annum in ground rents and some £1,900 per annum in rack rents.[373] The *Star* newspaper interpreted this as meaning that 'the great ground landlords of London think it wise to sell out lest after the war the unceremonious methods of the Defence of the Realm Act should be applied to ground rents,' and hoped that before the subsisting leases expired 'the London tenant and London ratepayer will have a look in.'[374] The auction was unsuccessful, by a little, in achieving the reserve price for the estate as a whole, and the subsequent bidding for smaller lots left several unsold. Sir R. B. N. Gunter died two months later, in August 1917.[375] In 1928 property in this area continued to be owned by Sir R. V. Gunter as descendant of Sir Robert Gunter and by Mr. R. G. Gunter as descendant of General James Gunter,[376] and the Gunter Estate still exists.

Inter-war Building

Building or rebuilding in this area between the wars of 1914-18 and 1939-45 was very scanty outside the area of South Bolton Gardens already described. One small development near that locality in 1937 was the building of three neo-Georgian houses at Nos. 10, 11 and 12 Cresswell Gardens to designs by Hoare and Wheeler.[377] This was on land at the back of Nos. 3 and 4 The Boltons. A little studio-building that still catches the eye was similarly erected at the back of No. 21 Tregunter Road in 1930 for the sculptor (Sir) Charles Wheeler, who at that time occupied the latter house, and survives as No. 22 Cathcart Road: the architect was possibly C. D. St. Leger.[378]

One considerable inter-war building was of quite different character. This was at the site of Walwyn House, formerly Brecknock Villa, in Old Brompton Road at the west corner with Finborough Road. In 1887 that house had been taken by the newly founded Jubilee Hospital, which maintained fourteen beds there. A private charitable institution, it catered solely for the 'sick and needy poor'. Nurses lived in houses in Finborough Road. The name was subsequently changed to the Fulham and Kensington General Hospital and in 1921 'Chelsea' was added.[379] In 1930 the old house was replaced by a new building, erected by Holloway Brothers at a tendered price of about £70,000,[379] to designs by Aston Webb and Son (that is, Maurice Webb). After renaming as the Princess Beatrice Hospital it was opened in 1932. This building represents, however, only two-thirds of the intended design, the southern wing never having been added. The six storeys above the lower ground floor included in 1932 private wards on the second floor.[380] In 1971-2 the hospital was converted to an obstetric unit and closed in 1978. In 1982 it was being altered and extended as 'single-person dwellings' for a housing association.[381]

Since 1945

Since the war of 1939-45 more new work has been done, partly on bomb-damaged sites. The Bousfield School has already been noticed. Some of the earliest post-war building was of public-authority housing in flats for the Royal Borough of Kensington. At the south-east corner of Cathcart Road and Hollywood Road Corbett House was built for the Borough in 1949-51 to designs by Gordon Jeeves.[382] Further west, in Finborough Road, blocks of flats were erected to designs by the Borough Engineer at Nos. 115-119 (odd) (1952-3, tender accepted at £10,875), Nos. 123-137 (odd) (1953-5, estimated cost £30,422 plus £2,600 for the site), and Nos. 169-179 (odd) (1955-6, tender accepted at £27,537).[383] At Nos. 140-144 (even) a block was built in 1955-6 for the Borough to similar designs by John Grey and Partners, who also designed the present Nos. 82 and 84 Redcliffe Square built in conjunction with Nos. 123-137 (odd) Finborough Road (final account for both £35,727).[384]

A more important development by the Borough was of five blocks in 1969-71 at a site of two and a quarter acres comprising what had been Nos. 63-79 (odd) and 62-78 (even) Finborough Road, Nos. 81-91 (odd) Ifield Road and Nos. 53-61 (odd) and 44-52 (even) Tregunter Road. In 1961 the Pettiward Estate had contemplated redevelopment in that area and in 1965 was given outline planning permission for five blocks rising to a maximum height of eight storeys.[385] In 1967, however, the Borough decided to buy out the Pettiward Estate's interest for £336,660, and in 1969 approved a scheme by Triad, Architects and Planners, for 126 flats of one to five rooms. This provided for 'a low-rise development having no lifts and a maximum "walk-up" of three floors'. The arrangement 'aimed at minimising the noise and disturbance likely to be caused by the heavy traffic in Finborough Road'. A tender was accepted at £663,187.[386] By 1973 occupants were petitioning the Borough for their windows to be double-glazed against the noise of traffic.[387]

A private block of flats, Finborough House (H. M. Grellier and Sons, architects), was put up in c. 1956-7 at Nos. 29-39 (odd) Finborough Road.[388]

New houses have already been mentioned in Redcliffe Road (1951-2, see page 176), The Little Boltons (1961-2, see page 231) and at the Fulham Road end of Hollywood Road (1971-2, see page 179). Others have included Nos. 81 and 83 Finborough Road (completed in 1958 by G. D. Fairfoot, architect[389]), No. 30 The Boltons (1958[390]), No. 35A Tregunter Road (1961, Daniel Watney, Eiloart, Inman and Nunn, architects[391]), the reconstruction of Hollywood Mews (1960-2, Diamond, Redfern and Partners, architects[392]) and an extension to No. 29 The Boltons (1971-3, City Design Group (A. V. Peel), architects[393]).

Some mews have undergone 'gentrification' by successive changes difficult to document. The most extensive have been in Cresswell Place, where, for example, the 1960's brought new houses at Nos. 6 and 6A in 1963 (Bruce Henderson-Gray, architect) and Nos. 7, 7A and 7B in 1969 (M. Howard-Radley, architect).[394]

Greater interest attaches to the succession of houses built at Nos. 10-20 and 24 (even) Cathcart Road between 1953 and 1972. Here the location offered the opportunity for a sequence of south-facing houses to be built where the back gardens of Nos. 9-23 (odd) Tregunter Road abut on Cathcart Road at its retired and leafy junction with Redcliffe Road. The earliest house was at the east end, where No. 10 was built in 1953-4 to designs by Neville Conder (Casson Conder Partnership).[395] No. 12 was built behind No. 11 and No. 13 Tregunter Road in 1956-7 to designs by Wallis, Gilbert and Partners, with an upper storey added to part of it in 1959 to designs by Anthony Mauduit, architect.[396] The next house westward, No. 18, was built behind No. 17 Tregunter Road in 1961 to designs by W. Paton Orr and Partner, with a second floor added in 1972-3 by Nerios Consultants Group, architects (Plate 101c).[397] The most recent dwell-

ing is at No. 20, where the architect C. J. G. Guest designed the glass-clad house for his own occupation which was built in 1972-5 behind No. 19 Tregunter Road and received considerable publicity here and abroad (Plate 101c). In *The Architectural Review* it was acclaimed in 1976 as evoking and excelling 'the early Le Corbusier, the brilliant liberator of the upper middle class'.[398] Westward of Sir Charles Wheeler's studio at No. 22 (see page 231) is No. 24, built behind No. 23 Tregunter Road to designs by Sir Hugh Casson (Casson Conder Partnership), with Timothy Rendle as associated architect, in 1959-61.[399] This also attracted attention. The representative magazine of the day, *House and Garden*, said in 1964 that it was designed as 'an ideal London *pied à terre* for a busy businessman — and his wife', who had left their children at 'the perfect family home' in Hampshire.[400]

The most recent history of this whole area has been chiefly marked by the steep rise in the value, monetary and otherwise, put upon its houses. In The Boltons, large as the houses already were, a number of their owners enlarged them in the 1960's and 70's — for example, at Nos. 6, 7, 11 and 27. Since 1970 an extensive territory around The Boltons has been a Conservation Area. Early in 1982 *The Daily Telegraph* reported that houses in The Boltons 'command the sort of prices which few Englishmen can now afford'.[401] Here and in neighbouring streets basements are converted into swimming-pools, and in The Little Boltons the seventy-two-year lease of the house vacated by William Corbett on his bankruptcy is offered for sale a century later at £625,000, with a eulogy of the Victorian interior plasterer's 'superb cornice work'.[402]

The Church of St. Mary, The Boltons

Built in 1849-50 to designs by George Godwin the younger, this church has since been variously altered, principally in 1871 and between 1952 and 1966 (Plates 93-4, fig. 69).

St. Mary's was the first 'ecclesiastical district' to be taken out of that of Holy Trinity, Brompton, to which in 1829 had been assigned much of the old Kensington parish south of the High Street and of Hyde Park. Like many Victorian churches, the impetus for its creation derived from a mixture of fervour for church extension and of desire to lend tone to a proposed estate development, in this case Robert Gunter the elder's. That the church should slightly precede the houses to be built around it was not unusual. The initial decision must have been taken by the vicar of Holy Trinity, the Reverend William J. Irons, in combination with Robert Gunter, who promised to give a site in the centre of the 'planted enclosure' planned for The Boltons. A sufficiently wealthy and 'energetic coadjutor' soon appeared in the person of the Reverend Hogarth J. Swale, the first incumbent of St. Mary's.[403]

In May 1849 George Godwin, acting as architect to the church and as estate surveyor for Robert Gunter, sent in plans to the Commissioners for Building New Churches

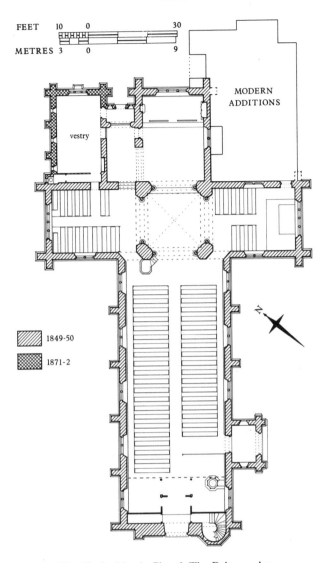

FEET 10 0   30
METRES 3   0   9

MODERN
ADDITIONS

vestry

N

▨ 1849-50

▦ 1871-2

Fig. 69. St. Mary's Church, The Boltons, plan

stretching west as far as Kensington Canal, east as far as Selwood Terrace, and north not far beyond the Old Brompton Road. For the people of this area, then estimated at 3–4,000 in number, the church offered 700 sittings rather than the 500 at first envisaged: of these, 200 were free.[408]

As completed, St. Mary's was rigidly cruciform in plan, having a central tower and strongly projecting transepts but no aisles. The only divergences from this shape were a south porch and a small vestry north of the chancel. This arrangement made its appearance unusual, not to say eccentric, in a London suburb. The reasoning behind this plan is unknown. It may represent an experiment on the part of Godwin, then aged thirty-four and already attracting attention as the energetic editor of *The Builder*. Godwin, a restrained advocate of Gothic for churches but never a dogmatist on stylistic questions, had not so far as is known built a new church before, though he did hold the important post of architect to the celebrated church of St. Mary Redcliffe at Bristol. He was therefore reasonably knowledgeable in matters of 'ecclesiology', and may well have had a specific mediaeval village church in mind when designing St. Mary's, particularly at this stage in the Gothic Revival, when precedent was much emphasized.

The aisleless plan with transepts also allowed all parts of the congregation to come reasonably close to the lectern and pulpit, even if it excluded those in the transepts from a sight of the altar. Additionally, this type of church contributed towards retaining some rural feeling in the neighbourhood. A possible model for the plan is Shottesbrooke Church in Berkshire, which attracted some attention in the 1840's and was closely followed in Benjamin Ferrey's country church at Penn Street, Buckinghamshire. The style of St. Mary's, however, is distinctly later than the Early English of Shottesbrooke and Penn Street.

St. Mary's was built of Kentish ragstone, with dressings of Bath stone from Combe Down and parapets and cornices of Caen stone. In style, the church generally follows orthodox Decorated models, with flowing tracery in all the windows, four competently detailed tower arches and some internal fittings of stone on fourteenth-century lines. But there are small touches of the individuality which became more marked in later Gothic works by George and his brother Henry Godwin. On the outside, the roofs are confined by parapets pierced with trefoils, while the west end is broken into by a blunt projection housing the stair to the gallery and by a sharply detailed bellcote (reduced from Godwin's first design). The tower, octagonal lantern and steeple (all designed in 1849 though not built until 1856) are of a Northamptonshire type: they have a heaviness as alien to earlier nineteenth-century church-building as to mediaeval tradition, although the conspicuous angels round the base of the spire are pleasantly distinctive (Plate 93).

Inside, there was originally no direct communication between the nave (necessarily broad, because there are no

with the news that Gunter wished to convey this site to them for a nominal £100, which he would then contribute towards the building work.[111] Next month Godwin published the design in his organ, *The Builder*,[404] and in August the foundation stone was laid.[405] In September Robert Gunter conveyed the site.[406] At the time of the consecration in October 1850 the church was finished except for the upper parts of the tower and spire, which were deferred for later completion. The expense was estimated at £6,000, most of which was given by Swale, with contributions from the Commissioners and other subscribers. The original contract for the nave was with James Barr, a plumber and glazier of Holborn, but, becoming bankrupt, he was succeeded during the course of the work by John Glenn, an Islington builder.[407] In December 1850 St. Mary's, West Brompton, (as the church was at first known) officially acquired a compact district

aisles) and the transepts. The nave itself has a rude braced collar roof resting on carved corbels representing the twelve apostles; the transepts have simple open roofs, but that in the chancel is boarded. As first completed in 1856, the tower was open up to the lantern stage. The walls throughout were rendered with lias. As for original fittings, there was an organ in the north transept, a stone pulpit and desk beneath the tower, and unusually elaborate sedilia (carved by Swales and Boulton, architectural sculptors of Lambeth) in the chancel (Plate 94a, c). The sedilia alone survive, along with the stone font, which at first stood in a central position at the west end. The tower and chancel floors were laid with Minton tiles, and there were simple painted decorations by W. H. Rogers against the east wall. Of stained-glass windows four were already in place at the time of consecration, two in the chancel and one in the nave by Powells, and one in the north transept by O'Connor: the east window, an Ascension scene by Hardman, followed shortly afterwards.[409]

Since Godwin's original arrangements conformed with the low-church school of Anglican worship, that easily provoked journal, *The Ecclesiologist*, pronounced them 'not what we should have expected from the Vicar of Brompton, the services being read from a desk of stone in the lantern. The chancel is filled with stall-like seats of deal, and there are sedilia in the sanctuary. We were, we own, not a little scandalized to see a central block of inferior free seats up the middle of the nave. Really Mr Irons ought not to have sanctioned such an outworn corruption in 1850. . . . Neither can we approve of the plan. The cruciform church without aisles, with clustered lantern-piers, and the desk and pulpit in the lantern, and a door in one of the transepts, is an auditorium disguised, rather than a place of collected worship: — the congregation being divided into three perfectly distinct bodies, (arranged on the radiating principle), of which the largest is entirely invisible to the two smaller ones, who sit facing each other like adverse squadrons, — the pulpit and desk forming the centre of radiation, and the altar standing quite out of sight of the two minor congregations.'[410]

Subscriptions for completing the tower and steeple of St. Mary's were opened in October 1854. The work, under Godwin's supervision, was undertaken by the well-known builder George Myers in the latter half of 1856 at a cost of approximately £1,000.[411] Further alterations were made, according to the church guide, in 1865, when G. E. Street was brought in to move the organ to a gallery, still in the north transept.[412] From about this time the churchmanship at St. Mary's became perceptibly 'higher'. A new vicar, William Thomas Du Boulay, who served here between 1868 and 1909, redecorated the chancel in 1870 and moved the choir hither from the west gallery, so that the stalls extended into the space under the tower. William Pepperell, visiting the church in 1871 after this rearrange-

ment had been made, sourly noted the changed tenor of services under Du Boulay and complained that 'the whole aspect of things in the chancel looks towards Ritualism'.[413]* But the acoustics and aspect of the church remained unsatisfactory. In 1871-2, therefore, a large new north vestry was built, the organ was moved into the area taken up by the former vestry, the space under the tower was filled in with a groined vault of wood, and angled arches were contrived left and right of the western tower arch to connect the nave and transepts (Plate 94b). The architect for this work, records B. F. L. Clarke, was Joseph Peacock (who also designed the church school in Gilston Road a few years later, Plate 95), and the contractor was T. H. Adamson and Sons of Putney.[414]

Between 1867 and 1874 the parish of St. Mary's was reduced by the successive creation of districts for St. Peter's, Cranley Gardens, St. Augustine's, Queen's Gate, St. Jude's, Courtfield Gardens, and St. Luke's, Redcliffe Square. At about that time the church became generally known as St. Mary's, The Boltons rather than St. Mary's, West Brompton. Within the building, a new organ was acquired in 1881[415] and in 1882 and 1885 windows by Mayer and Company of Munich were installed.[416] Rather later, in 1902, the old deal seats in the nave were replaced with oak ones and side gangways were formed.[417] Inter-war changes to the fabric were not extensive, though as early as 1920 there was talk of whitening the walls and bringing the altar forward to a position under the tower, under the architectural direction of W. A. Forsyth.[418] Some small war memorials were erected, chiefly in the south transept, while in 1929 a curate undertook extensive diapering work throughout the church; of this, no trace remains.[419]

Major alterations were made to the interior of St. Mary's from 1952 onwards, following bomb damage and neglect during the war of 1939-45. Romilly Craze of Milner and Craze was appointed architect and in 1952-3 started on a scheme of pallid de-Victorianization. The High Altar was brought forward to a position under the eastern tower arch, the old chancel became a Lady Chapel, and the south transept was rearranged. A new pulpit, lectern, stalls and communion rails were installed, mainly made of oak from previous fittings. At the same time the walls were whitewashed, the font was painted over, and much of the remaining painted glass was removed from the windows. In 1954 a new east window designed by Margaret Kaye was put in at a cost of £2,000. A little later, in 1959-60, a new organ was erected in the west gallery and the old space north of the chancel was converted into a chapel by David E. Nye and Partners, architects. In 1964 a further large coloured window with 'mosaic' patterns was installed at the west end by Messrs. Harper and Hendra. Finally, in 1965-6 Romilly Craze built a two-storey church hall in stone, attached to the south side of the chancel and reached from the south transept.[420]

*The vicar, Pepperell also observed, had started a 'Guild of St. Michael' for local female domestic servants who agreed to give up fairs, races, dancing and music halls.

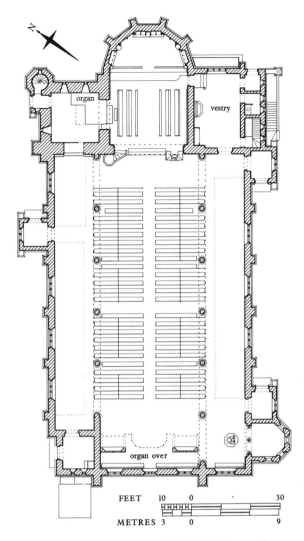

organ

vestry

organ over

FEET 10 0 · 30

METRES 3 0 9

Fig. 70. St Luke's Church, Redcliffe Square, plan

The Church of St. Luke, Redcliffe Square

This church, built in 1872-3 to designs by George and Henry Godwin, was the third and last of the Godwins' three churches on the Gunter estates in West Brompton and Earl's Court (Plates 96-8, 108, fig. 70), the others being St. Mary, The Boltons (1849-50) and St. Jude, Courtfield Gardens (1870).

As has been seen, a church had been envisaged by Corbett and McClymont to lend tone to their developments so early as 1866 and by March 1868 was destined for a location in Redcliffe Square.[207] In November 1869 they applied for a district which it might serve to be taken out of the parish of St. Mary, The Boltons.[421] A year later *The Builder* reported that George and Henry Godwin, whose St. Jude's, Courtfield Gardens, close by, was just being finished, had designed for Redcliffe Square a 'church of large size' which was shortly to be started.[422] This appointment proceeded directly from the Godwins' role as estate surveyors to the Gunter brothers in South Kensington and their more recent employment as

architects for Corbett and McClymont's houses in Redcliffe Square. Robert Gunter promised to give the site, whilst by an arrangement formalized in January 1871, Corbett and McClymont undertook to find the funds for a church to cost at least £6,000 and seating 900 persons.[423]

In the event money proved harder to obtain than at St. Jude's, where a single contributor paid for the church almost entirely. By the spring of 1871, the chief responsibility for fund-raising had been taken up by the first incumbent, the Reverend William Fraser Handcock, a clergyman of some private means. Previously vicar of St. Luke's, Cheltenham, Handcock brought with him from that parish not only a dedication for the new church but also a temporary wooden structure to serve until a permanent edifice could be funded and built. This wooden church, duly cased in iron at extra cost so as to conform with London building regulations, was put up on the site of the future Nos. 29-33 (odd) Redcliffe Square and opened in July 1871.[424]

The permanent St. Luke's was commenced in 1872, having by this time grown in ambition to 1,200 sittings and an estimated £17,000 in cost, of which £9,000 had been promised, mainly it appears by Handcock 'and his friends'.[425] Corbett and McClymont did not themselves undertake the building work, which was entrusted in two stages to Hill and Sons of Islington. The contract for the foundations proceeded from February 1872. Because the ground had previously been taken out to great depth for brick-earth, particularly under the position of the tower and chancel, and therefore had to be re-excavated and filled in with a deep bed of concrete, this expense amounted to the unusual sum of £1,732. Piers to support the nave columns were connected by brick arches, *The Building News* reporting: 'The church, in fact, stands upon a number of legs, and these legs have good shoes for them'.[426] The contract for the superstructure, valued at £13,409 but later increased, followed on from July 1872.[427] The total cost at the time of consecration in August 1873 was reckoned at £17,532, and the final number of sittings was between 900 and 1,000.[428]

St. Luke's today does not much differ from its state at the time of its completion in 1873. Like St. Jude's, Courtfield Gardens, it affords insight into the thinking which governed the planning and design of a moderately ambitious mid-Victorian Evangelical church in what, it was hoped, would be a prosperous London suburb. As regards ecclesiastical style, the Godwins (of whom Henry rather than his better-known and busier brother George was possibly the more active on this project) occupy a position halfway between such pioneers of 'advanced' church architecture as Street and Butterfield, who worked mainly for Tractarian clients, and men like Teulon, Lamb and Bassett Keeling, whose buildings were usually for the Evangelical wing of the church. All three churches built by the Godwins on the Gunters' estates were originally Evangelical in character and 'vigorous' in style, but at St. Luke's neither tradition was aggressively pronounced.

Thus the six-bay nave was broad and the chancel was comparatively short, and the design allowed for a future gallery at the west end. On the other hand, an apsidal east end was provided, the chancel was modestly raised, and the altar was the undivided focus of attention (fig. 70).

The interior of St. Luke's, with its strong distinction in height between nave and chancel, recalls the churches of Street (Plate 97). The nave arcade, of thirteenth-century character, rests upon columns formed from drums of Hollington stone. Above, the walls are of pink tuck-pointed bricks, relieved by lively patterns in several colours and pierced by lancet windows in the clerestory. Originally the brickwork was also exposed in the aisles, above the chancel arch and in the chancel, but these walls are now whitewashed. The roofs are all of open timber: the most elaborate is in the nave, where carved stone corbels carry arched braces with pierced panels, while each of the principals rises to an orthodox scissors truss. Where tracery appears, as in the aisles, the large west window and the sanctuary, it is geometrical. The tile floors which originally extended throughout the church, were supplied by Minton, Hollins and Company. There is much rich carving, notably round the chancel arch, where the angel corbels in Caen stone are handsome. Most or all of this was performed by Richard Boulton of Cheltenham, who also supplied the lectern, the reading desk which once stood centrally (both of 1873 and later amalgamated), the reredos, sedilia and connecting blank arcade in the apse (1874) and the pulpit (1876), all boldly figurative pieces in marble, alabaster and Caen stone.[429] Probably also by Boulton are the alabaster altar rails and bronze gates (1881 or shortly thereafter), the twelve stone statues of saints and Protestant divines fixed above the nave columns (the gift of Handcock, 1889), and the dramatic alabaster font, consisting of an angel holding a scallop shell — a copy of Thorvaldsen's Angel of Baptism in Copenhagen's Lutheran Cathedral (before 1889, Plate 98).[430]

The exterior of St. Luke's (Plates 96, 108), like that of many High Victorian churches, is broken somewhat affectedly into separate elements; nave, chancel, aisles, south vestry (with a choir vestry beneath), tower and porch are all strongly differentiated. At the south-west angle an attached baptistry with a tall eight-sided roof draws the attention. The tower rises over the north-east vestry to a tall lantern stage with geometrical windows, above which an octagonal steeple rises to 158 feet. The materials of the exterior are Kentish ragstone with Box-ground Bath dressings,[266] perhaps a curious choice considering that the interior is of brick. The roofs were originally in two tones, of grey and purple slates, but they are now of only a single hue.

How far the cost of this expensive church had outrun available funds appears from the correspondence of William Corbett. To get St. Luke's finished, Handcock had evidently issued promissory notes against loans on the guarantee of Corbett and McClymont. By the autumn of 1873, only a few months after the consecration and with money due to the builders, Corbett was having difficulty in amalgamating the loans and confessed to feeling 'very uncomfortable as to what is to be done'.[431] By the end of the year there was talk of the church changing hands,[432] but the immediate crisis passed, to recur in 1878, when Corbett and McClymont encountered difficulties and were declared bankrupt. Before they suspended payment in May 1878 there was a flurry of activity relating to St. Luke's. In January, Corbett reported to his solicitors that Handcock's notes 'are now causing us much trouble,' adding that 'some of the P. Notes are at high interest; as Clergymen's Bills are difficult to deal with.'[433] Soon afterwards Corbett strongly complained to Handcock that he had paid out £3,000 on these notes in the previous fifteen months and that 'there is now upwards of £12,000 running, and the various holders of P. Notes are objecting and making and raising difficulties as to the continuing of the loans.'[434] As a result of this Handcock spoke of retiring, as 'the debt on the Church was so large he could not cope with it.'[435] In the event this did not occur, Handcock remaining until 1892. But there is reason to suppose that Corbett and McClymont's failure in May 1878 was not unconnected with St. Luke's, for a bill of Handcock's was dishonoured immediately before they suspended payment. Over the ensuing eighteen months Corbett strove desperately to secure money from Handcock and his friends, but in the main his efforts appear to have been unfruitful.[436]

These events may help to explain why St. Luke's has not been greatly altered since its completion. As there appear to have been no proper endowments, the incumbent's income depended entirely upon pew rents, which declined as the district began to fall in tone from the Edwardian period onwards. A small church hall was built in 1896-7 to designs by one William Murray of Kingston Hill, on the site of three stables in Adrian Mews off Ifield Road.[437] But no vicarage was provided, a house in Redcliffe Square eventually being bought on lease in 1918. Thereafter the parish was often in financial difficulties.[438]

Within the church, the largest single alteration occurred at the west end, where in 1920 a large and elaborately carved organ case made by W. Aumonier was installed as a war memorial.[439] Later, in 1930, oak panelling was installed in the choir, small changes were made in the sanctuary, and a memorial chapel was formed at the end of the north aisle, all to designs by A. B. Knapp-Fisher.[440] Then in 1938 the tiling on the floors of the choir and sanctuary was replaced with marble under the supervision of J. Ernest Franck, architect.[441] The main post-war alteration has been the whitewashing of the aisles and chancel.

Among the few memorials, one of interest is a tablet with a portrait relief in the north aisle by E. E. Geflowski commemorating Ave Merwanjee Bhownagree (d. 1888). The original stained-glass windows in the apse, given by Robert Gunter, have now gone following war damage, but there is glass by Ward and Hughes in the lower lights at the west end (1880). The various later windows are of no special interest.

Existing Buildings

In the following table relating to surviving buildings the lessees are all builders or building tradesmen unless otherwise designated, and the dates are those of the grant of building leases to them, generally on the completion of the carcases of houses. The information is usually derived from the Middlesex Deeds Registry. Information about occupants is generally from ratebooks and directories. Reference to the sources of other information is only given when it is not given in the text above.

Adrian Mews
Name evidently given by W. Corbett, who used 'Adrian Square' on his estate at Westgate.
Leased S. R. Lewin to B. J. and W. J. Hudson, 1871.
St. Luke's Church Hall, 1896-7, W. Murray, architect.

Bolton Gardens, Nos. 7 and 8
Leased R. Gunter (II) to J. Spicer, 1863.
Westward extension of No. 8, 1876, E. N. Clifton, architect.

Bolton Gardens Mews
Leased R. Gunter (II) to J. Spicer, 1859 onwards.

The Boltons
Name presumably derived from former owners, the Boulton family. Northern limb named Gilston Road until 1912.
East crescent (Nos. 1-15) leased R. Gunter (I) to H. W. Atkinson, 1851-2 (D. Tidey associated builder), west crescent (Nos. 16-28) leased R. Gunter (II) to J. Spicer, 1857-60.
No. 7 restored as private house, 1972-5, Ewan Macleod, architect.
No. 9 decorated, 1887-91, C. S. Peach, architect.[442]
Nos. 20-23. Rearward extension for Franciscan Missionaries of Mary, 1966-7, John E. Sterrett and B. D. Kaye, architects.[443]
No. 29 erected by W. Taverner, builder, 1855: iron and glass entrance-way, 1879:[444] garage dormer window, 1960, H. O. Corfiato, architect:[445] southern extension, 1971-3, City Design Group, architects.
No. 30 built c. 1958.
Some occupants:
No. 11, Sir Robert Rawlinson, civil engineer, 1863-98.
No. 16, Madame Albani (Mrs. Ernest Gye), singer, 1879-98.
No. 21, S. Carter Hall, editor of *The Art Journal*, 1861-3.
No. 22, Brandon Thomas, playwright, 1900-4.
No. 24, W. S. Gilbert, dramatist, 1877-84.
No. 27, Sir F. C. Burnand, playwright and editor of *Punch*, 1892-1906.
No. 28, Benjamin Golding, physician, 1860-3.

Cathcart Road
No. 1, 1951-2, R. Pollock, architect.
Nos. 3-7 odd granted freehold, S. R. Lewin to W. Corbett, 1864.
Corbett House, 1949-51, G. Jeeves, architect.
Nos. 27 (including No. 16 Hollywood Road), 29-49 odd leased J. Gunter to W. Corbett and/or A. McClymont, 1866.
Nos. 51-59 odd leased R. J. Pettiward to Corbett and McClymont, 1867.
No. 10, 1953-4, Neville Conder (Casson Conder Partnership), architect.
No. 12, 1956-7, Wallis, Gilbert and Partners, architects (addition, 1959, Anthony Mauduit, architect).
No. 18, 1961, W. Paton Orr and Partner, architects (addition, 1972-3, Nerios Consultants Group, architects).
No. 20, 1972-5, Hon. C. J. G. Guest, architect.
No. 22, 1930, ?C. D. St. Leger, architect (addition, c. 1950, John Ware, architect).

No. 24, 1959-61, Sir Hugh Casson (Casson Conder Partnership), architect; Timothy Rendle, associated architect.
Nos. 26-42 even leased J. Gunter to W. Corbett or A. McClymont, 1864-5.
Nos. 44-52 even leased same (Corbett and McClymont parties) to G. Smith, 1865-6.
Nos. 54-58 even, 1953-4, R. Pollock, architect.[446]
Nos. 60-66 even leased J. Gunter (Corbett and McClymont parties) to G. Smith, 1865-6.
Nos. 72-82 even leased R. J. Pettiward to Corbett and McClymont, 1866-7.
Some occupants:
No. 31, Robert Kerr, architect, 1897/8-1904.
No. 62, Thomas Verity, architect, 1869-91, and Frank Verity, architect, to 1892.

Coleherne Mews
Leased R. Gunter (II), Nos. 1-4 and 6 (Corbett and McClymont parties) to J. Beale, 1866; Nos. 8-28 even, 5-29 odd, to W. Corbett or A. McClymont, 1868-9.

Coleherne Road
Named after Coleherne field or House.
Leased R. Gunter (II), Nos. 1-23 odd (Corbett and McClymont parties) to J. Beale, 1867-8; Nos. 25-35 odd to J. Little, 1872-3; Nos. 2-20 even to J. Beale, 1867; Nos. 22-34 even to W. Corbett or A. McClymont, 1871.
Dylan Thomas, poet, stayed at No. 21 in 1934.[447]

Cresswell Gardens
Named after Cresswell Lodge.
Nos. 1-9, 14-17 leased R. Gunter (II) to G. J. Spicer, solicitor (s. of J. Spicer), 1884-5, Matthews and Rogers, builders, Maurice Hulbert, architect.
Nos. 10-12 consec., 1937, Hoare and Wheeler, architects.

Cresswell Place
Named Bolton Mews until 1908.
Nos. 6, 6A, 1963, Bruce Henderson-Gray, architect.
Nos. 7, 7A, 7B, 1969, M. Howard-Radley, architect.
Nos. 18-22 consec., 1885, W. Knight, builder, H. Phelps Drew, architect.
No. 25, 1970, Douglas Norwood and Associates, architects.

Fawcett Mews and No. 1 Fawcett Street
Leased J. Gunter to Corbett and McClymont, 1865.

Fawcett Street
Hollywood, Cecil and Fawcett Courts, 1902-5, C. J. C. Pawley, architect.
No. 1 see Fawcett Mews.
Nos. 3-15 odd leased J. Gunter (Corbett and McClymont parties) to J. Gibbings, 1866.
Nos. 17-25 odd leased R. J. Pettiward to Corbett and McClymont, 1866 (sub-let to J. Gibbings).

Nos. 2-10 even leased J. Gunter (Corbett and McClymont parties) to J. Beale, 1866.

Nos. 12-18 even leased same to Corbett and McClymont, 1866.

Nos. 20-28 even leased R. J. Pettiward to same, 1867.

Finborough Road
Named after Pettiward estate at Finborough, Suffolk.

Nos. 1-27 odd leased R. J. Pettiward to Corbett and McClymont, 1866-8 (Nos. 1-19 sub-let to A. M. Greig: Nos. 21-27 ?built by J. Gibbings[448]).

Nos. 29-39 odd, Finborough House, 1956-7, H. M. Grellier and Sons, architects.

Nos. 41-49 odd leased R. J. Pettiward to Corbett and McClymont, 1868 (sub-let to J. Gibbings).

Nos. 51-61 odd leased same to W. Corbett, 1871.

Nos. 63-79 odd and 62-78 even, together with Nos. 81-91 odd Ifield Road and Nos. 53-61 odd and 44-52 even Tregunter Road, 1969-71, Triad, architects, for Royal Borough of Kensington and Chelsea.

Nos. 81 and 83, c. 1958 (completion architect G. D. Fairfoot).

Nos. 85-113 odd leased R. Gunter (II) to W. Corbett or A. McClymont, 1870-1.

Nos. 115-119 odd, 1952-3, R. B. K. Engineer's Department, architects.

No. 121 leased R. Gunter (II) to W. Corbett, 1870.

Nos. 123-137 odd, 1953-5, R. B. K. Engineer's Department, architects.

Nos. 139-167 odd leased R. Gunter (II) to W. Corbett or A. McClymont, 1869.

Nos. 169-179 odd, 1955-6, R. B. K. Engineer's Department, architects.

Nos. 2-60 even leased R. J. Pettiward to W. Corbett or A. McClymont, 1867-70.

Nos. 62-78 even see Nos. 63-79 above.

Nos. 80-116 even leased R. Gunter (II) to W. Corbett or A. McClymont, 1868-9, 1871-2.

No. 118 (Finborough Arms p. h.) leased same to Corbett and McClymont, 1868.

Nos. 120-138 even leased J. L. Tomlin to W. Corbett or A. McClymont, 1869-70.

Nos. 140-144 even, 1955-6, John Grey and Partners, architects, for R. B. K.

Nos. 146-182 even leased J. L. Tomlin to W. Corbett or A. McClymont, 1870-1.

Former Princess Beatrice Hospital, 1930-2, Sir Aston Webb and Son (Maurice Webb), architects. (Under conversion and extension, 1982.)

Some occupants:
No. 7, Richard Doyle, illustrator, 1875-83.
No. 51, Algernon Graves, chronicler of art, 1873-93.
No. 2, Arthur Hughes, artist, 1869-77.

Fulham Road, Nos. 134-306B even (including the part described in Chapter XI).

The part of Fulham Road in Kensington renumbered 1866 and Nos. 138-142B again 1894.

Nos. 134-140A, building lessee W. Mitchell, 1888.

ABC Cinema, 1930, J. Stanley Beard and Clare, architects.

Nos. 152-156, 1849-50, J. Blore, architect.

Nos. 158-168, 1972-4, Turner Lansdown Holt and Partners, architects.

Nos. 170 and 172, 1846-7, J. Blore, architect.

Nos. 174 and 176, 1847.

No. 178, ?1810, altered 1848.

Nos. 182 and 184, 1936-7, Gale, Heath and Sneath, architects.

Nos. 186 and 188, uncertain date.

No. 190 (King's Arms p. h.) leased G. Godwin to E. Curtis, sr., 1861 (ground-floor front, ?1890, H. I. Newton, architect).

Nos. 192-200 leased Godwin to Curtis, 1861.

Nos. 202-210 sold Rev. G. F. Ballard and R. Lewin to W. Corbett and/or A. McClymont, 1865.

No. 212, 1889-90.

No. 214 (The Somerset), 1881, W. E. Williams, architect.

Nos. 216-224, 1962-3, G. D. Fairfoot, architect.

No. 226, ?1793 (altered).

Nos. 228-232, 1865-6, building-applicant, A. B. Smith, hot-house builder.

Nos. 236A-D and Brompton Cottages at No. 1c Hollywood Road, 1971-2, Ian Fraser and Associates (Turner Lansdown Holt and Partners), architects: conversion for Barclay's Bank, 1976-7, Paton Orr and Partner, architects.

Nos. 240-244, c. 1790-1.

Nos. 246 and 248, c. 1801-2, ?S. Butler, builder.

No. 256, Post Office, 1965, planning architect for Ministry of Works, E. T. Sargeant, supervising architect, J. Russell.

Nos. 258-260A, 1877-8, T. Hussey, builder.

No. 262A (rear building) c. 1711-12, altered.

No. 264, Servite Priory buildings, J. A. Hansom and Son (J. S. Hansom), architects: Priory building, 1880: church entrance, 1880, altered 1893-5: tower, 1893-5. All altered 1962.

Nos. 266 and 266A leased R. T. and Lucy Robinson to W. Corbett and/or A. McClymont, 1868.

No. 268 (formerly Redcliffe Arms p. h.) leased R. J. Pettiward to Corbett and McClymont, 1865.

Nos. 270-304 leased same to same, 1865-7.

Nos. 304A-306B sold S. R. and R. Lewin to Rev. E. H. Ballard at nomination of Corbett and McClymont, 1869.

Gilston Road
Named after a home of the Gunter family in Breconshire.[449]
Renumbered 1912.

Nos. 3, 3A, 5, 5A leased R. Gunter (II) to B. and T. Bradley, 1871 (rebuilt behind façade, 1981).

Nos. 9 and 11 leased by J. Gunter and W. E. Maude, 1855 (in possession T. Holmes, builder, 1852).

Nos. 13-39 odd leased R. Gunter (I) 1851-2; Nos. 13-19 to nominees of C. Delay, Nos. 21 and 23 to nominees of J. Atkinson, S. Peirson and D. Tidey, and Nos. 25-35 to nominee of Peirson.

Nos. 41 and 43 leased J. Gunter and W. E. Maude (No. 41) and R. Gunter II (No. 43), 1854 (T. Eames, party): southern extension of No. 41, 1972, Edward Cullinan, architect.[450]

No. 4 (formerly St. Mary's School), 1878, Joseph Peacock, architect.

Nos. 10 and 12 leased J. Gunter and W. E. Maude to nominee of T. Eames, 1854.

Nos. 14 and 16 leased R. Gunter (I) to T. Eames, 1852.

Nos. 18-24 even leased R. Gunter (I) to W. Harding, 1852: porch at No. 24, 1971, A. and P. Smithson, architects.[451]

No. 26, c. 1850-3, R. Trower, builder.

Some occupants:
No. 9, Robert Fortune, botanist, 1857-80,
No. 27, Mrs. (latterly Lady) Irving, estranged wife of Sir Henry Irving, 1877-1908: also Henry Irving, junior, 1895-6 and Laurence Irving, 1898-1914.

Harcourt Terrace
For two or three years named Hollywood Road.

Leased J. Gunter to W. Corbett or A. McClymont, 1867-8.

Some occupants:
No. 87, R. Popplewell Pullan, architect, 1877-80.
No. 32, C. N. Beazley, architect, 1882-1896 or 1897.

Harley Gardens
Nos. 1-4 and 9-14 numbered as Harley Road until 1874.
Nos. 1-4 leased R. Gunter (I) 1851 to nominees of W. Harding (Nos. 1 and 2) and J. Bonnin, jr. (Nos. 3 and 4).
Nos. 5-8 leased R. Gunter (II) to T. Hussey and T. Huggett, 1867.
Nos. 9-14 leased same to B. and T. Bradley, 1862-3.
Arthur Orton, the 'Tichborne Claimant', lived at No. 14 in 1870-2 under the name of Sir Roger Tichborne, baronet.

Hollywood Mews
Originally leased J. Gunter to Corbett and McClymont, 1865, 1867. Converted 1960-2 by Diamond, Redfern and Partners, architects.

Hollywood Road
For the name see page 184.
East side:
No. 1C, see Fulham Road, Nos. 236A-D.
Nos. 1-55 odd leased J. Gunter, 1865; Nos. 1-15 to T. Hussey and/or T. Huggett (Corbett and McClymont parties), Nos. 17-27 to F. Saunders (Corbett and McClymont parties), Nos. 29-55 to W. Corbett and/or A. McClymont.
West side:
Grove House, 1890.
Hollywood Court see Fawcett Street.
Nos. 2-14 even leased J. Gunter, 1865; Nos. 2-6 to J. Beale (Corbett and McClymont parties), Nos. 8-14 to Corbett and McClymont.
No. 16 see Cathcart Road, No. 27.

Ifield Road
Named after Ifield, Sussex, where S. J. Lewin was Vicar. North of Tregunter Road and Adrian Mews (*q. v.*) named Adrian Terrace until 1909.
Nos. 1-79 odd leased R. J. Pettiward, 1866-8: Nos. 1-57, 63-79 to Corbett and McClymont; Nos. 59 and 61 to B. J. Hudson and/or W. Spires (Corbett and McClymont parties to lease): sub-lessees, 1867-8, R. Fitt (Nos. 1-5, 21-27), G. German (Nos. 7 and 9).
Nos. 81-91 odd see Finborough Road, Nos. 63-79.
Nos. 93-129 odd leased R. Gunter (II) to W. Corbett or A. McClymont, 1868.
Nos. 2-68, 72-118, 132-180 even leased S. R. or R. Lewin, 1869: Nos. 2-68, 132-180 to W. Corbett or A. McClymont; Nos. 72-118 to B. J. or W. J. Hudson or W. Spires.
No. 70 granted S. R. and R. Lewin to Corbett and McClymont, 1871.

The Little Boltons
Named Tregunter Grove or The Grove until 1939. Renumbered 1868.
Nos. 1-35 odd leased J. Gunter to W. Corbett and/or A. McClymont, 1866-8.
Nos. 2-36 even leased R. Gunter (II) to J. Spicer, 1858 (Nos. 2 and 4)-1864 (Nos. 22-36).
Nos. 38-50 even, *c.* 1961-2, Stone Toms and Partners, architects.
Osbert Salvin, naturalist, occupied No. 32 in 1866-74.

Milborne Grove
Nos. 1-8 leased R. Gunter (I) to nominees of T. Holmes, 1851-2.
Nos. 9-14 leased R. Gunter (II) to B. and T. Bradley, 1861-2.

Oakfield Street
Nos. 1, 3, 5 leased J. Gunter (Corbett and McClymont parties) to J. Beale, 1865.
Nos. 2, 4, 6 leased same to Corbett and McClymont, 1866.

Old Brompton Road, Nos. 159-279 odd
Renumbered 1937 and 1939.
Nos. 159-165 (formerly Moreton Terrace), Nos. 167-183 (formerly Moreton Gardens), 1884-5, Matthews and Rogers, builders, Maurice Hulbert, architect.
Nos. 185 and 189 (formerly No. 3 and Nos. 2 and 1 Moreton Gardens) leased R. Gunter (II) to J. Spicer, 1875: bay window at northern part of No. 189, 1906, C. G. F. Rees, architect.[452]
Bousfield Primary School, 1954-6, W. J. Marston and Son, builders, Chamberlin, Powell and Bon, architects.
(Nos. 7 and 8 Bolton Gardens see Bolton Gardens.)
Coleherne Court, 1901-4, T. W. Brown, builder, Walter Cave, architect, Paul Hoffmann, associated architect.
Nos. 239-259 (formerly Coleherne Terrace) leased R. Gunter (II) to W. Corbett or A. McClymont, 1867.
No. 261 (The Coleherne p.h.) leased same (Corbett and McClymont parties) to J. Beale, 1866.
Nos. 263-279 (formerly Claro Terrace) leased same to Corbett and McClymont, 1866-8.
Former Princess Beatrice Hospital see Finborough Road.
Jenny Lind (Mrs. Otto Goldschmidt) lived at No. 189 (southern part) in 1874-87.

Priory Walk
Named Priory Grove until 1938.
Builder R. Trower 1850, 1853.

Redcliffe Gardens
For the name see Redcliffe Road.
Nos. 1-11 odd leased R. T. and Lucy Robinson to W. Corbett or A. McClymont, 1868.
Nos. 13-79 odd leased J. Gunter to W. Corbett and/or A. McClymont, 1866 (Nos. 13-21) — 1873 (Nos. 77 and 79).
Nos. 2A, 2-58 even leased R. J. Pettiward to W. Corbett and/or A. McClymont, 1865 (Nos. 2A, 2-8) — 1871 (Nos. 54-58).
Nos. 60-82 even leased R. Gunter (II) to W. Corbett or A. McClymont, 1871-2.
Nos. 84-102 even leased same (Corbett and McClymont parties) to J. Little, 1869.

Redcliffe Mews
For name see Redcliffe Road.
Leased J. Gunter, 1865-70, to W. Corbett and/or A. McClymont or nominees (A. M. Greig at southern end).

Redcliffe Place
Named Clyde Street until 1938. For name Redcliffe see Redcliffe Road.
Leased R. J. Pettiward to Corbett and McClymont, 1866-7 (sublet to A. M. Greig).

Redcliffe Road
Presumably named by G. Godwin, who had restored the church of St. Mary Redcliffe at Bristol and designed other buildings in the Bristol area.

Nos. 1A, 2A leased G. Godwin to E. Curtis, sr., 1861.

Nos. 1-32 and Cathcart House sold S. R. Lewin to W. Corbett or A. McClymont, 1861-4 (Cathcart House altered 1947-8).

Nos. 33 and 34, 1951-2, R. Pollock, architect.

Nos. 35-36, 38-53, 57 sold Rev. G. F. Ballard and R. Lewin to A. McClymont, 1862-3.

No. 37, 1951-2, Kenneth Smith, architect.

No. 55, 1955 (as Metropolitan Police Married Quarters), Chief Architect and Surveyor, Metropolitan Police, architect.[453]

Nos. 58-66 consec., sold Rev. G. F. Ballard and R. Lewin to W. Corbett or A. McClymont, 1866.

Herbert Gribble, architect, lived at No. 64 in *c.* 1883-94.

Redcliffe Square

For name see Redcliffe Road.

Nos. 1-27 odd leased J. Gunter to W. Corbett and/or A. McClymont or nominees, Nos. 1-9 1868-9, Nos. 11-27 1872-3.

Nos. 29-53 odd leased R. Gunter (II) to W. Corbett or A. McClymont, 1873-6.

Nos. 2 and 4 leased J. Gunter to nominee of Corbett and McClymont, 1868.

Nos. 6-80 even leased same to W. Corbett or A. McClymont, Nos. 6-16, 1870, Nos. 18-48, 1873-5, Nos. 50-56, 1876, Nos. 58-80, 1873-5.

Nos. 82 and 84, 1953, John Grey and Partners, architects for R. B. K.

(Sir) Rider Haggard, novelist, lived at No. 24 in 1888-91.

Redcliffe Street

For name see Redcliffe Road.

Leased R. Gunter (II) to W. Corbett or A. McClymont, Nos. 1-17 odd, 1867, Nos. 19-25 odd, 1870, Nos. 2-22 even, 1869-70.

Austin Dobson, writer, lived at No. 10 in 1873-80.

South Bolton Gardens

No. 7, Osborn House, first occupied 1821.

Nos. 8-9 built 1904-6 (W. Cave, architect), recast 1929 (J. E. Forbes and J. Duncan Tate, architects).

No. 8 occupied as studio by Sir William Orpen, painter, in 1906-31 (also (Sir) Hugh Lane in 1907-9).

Tregunter Road

Named after a home of the Gunter family in Breconshire.[449] Renumbered east of Nos. 18 and 25 in 1867.

Nos. 1 and 3 leased R. Gunter (I) to J. Bonnin, jr., 1852.

Nos. 5-11 odd leased R. Gunter (II) to S. Peirson, 1853-4.

Nos. 13-23 odd leased R. Gunter (I) to nominees of H. J. Clarke, 1851-2.

Nos. 25 and 27 leased J. Gunter (Corbett and McClymont parties) to A. M. Greig, 1864.

Nos. 29-35 odd leased same to Corbett and McClymont, 1865-6.

No. 35A in Hollywood Road, 1961, Daniel Watney, Eiloart, Inman and Nunn, architects.

Nos. 37-51 odd leased J. Gunter (Corbett and McClymont parties) to J. Temple and W. Forster, 1865-6.

Nos. 53-61 see Finborough Road, Nos. 63-79.

Nos. 2-16 even leased R. Gunter (II) to J. Spicer, 1857-9.

Nos. 18-42 even leased J. Gunter, 1864-6; Nos. 20 and 22 (Corbett and McClymont parties) to J. H. Strudwick, architect, Nos. 24 and 26 to W. Corbett or A. McClymont, Nos. 28-34 (Corbett and McClymont parties) to J. Beale, No. 36 to nominee of Corbett and McClymont, Nos. 38-42 (Corbett and McClymont parties) to J. Beale.

Nos. 44-52 even see Finborough Road, Nos. 63-79.

Some occupants:

No. 3, Major (later Lt.-Gen. Sir) W. F. Butler and his wife, Elizabeth Thompson, battle-painter, 1878-80.

No. 11, J. O. Halliwell-Phillipps, bibliophile, 1856-89.

No. 21, (Sir) Charles Wheeler, sculptor, 1930-1941/3.

No. 4, F. R. S. Yorke, architect, 1937-40.

No. 14, Sir Charles Petrie, author, *c.* 1931-58.

Westgate Terrace

Named after W. Corbett's estate at Westgate, Thanet.

Leased R. Gunter (II) to W. Corbett or A. McClymont, 1869-71.

Wharfedale Street

Named after R. Gunter (II)'s property in Yorkshire.

Leased R. Gunter (II), with Corbett and McClymont parties, to J. Beale, 1866-8.

CHAPTER XIII

Stamford Bridge and the Billings Area

The small area (fig. 71) between the south side of Brompton Cemetery and Fulham Road consisted in the eighteenth century of a freehold estate in the possession of the Pettiward family and, at the south-western extremity, of half a dozen plots either in copyhold tenure or part of the waste ground of the manor of Earl's Court.

Until the middle of the nineteenth century the section of the Fulham Road west of what is now the southern entrance to the cemetery was sometimes, from its propinquity to Stamford Bridge, known as Bridge Street.[1] Stamford Bridge formerly traversed the common sewer known as Counter's Creek, a tidal tributary of the Thames which was one of the principal watercourses for the drainage of west London and which formed the boundary between the parishes of Kensington and Fulham. In 1824-8 the lower part of Counter's Creek was canalised and became known as the Kensington Canal; but after the canal had proved a commercial failure a railway line known as the West London Extension Railway was built along its course in 1859-63, the waters of the ancient sewer being diverted underground. The present brick Stamford Bridge was built in 1860-2 but has since been partly reconstructed.

In mediaeval times Counter's Creek had been known (with numerous variants) as Billingwell Dyche, which has been reliably thought to mean 'Billing's spring or stream'.[2] A map of 1694-5 in Kensington Central Library marks three fields beside the creek (all now part of Brompton Cemetery) as 'The Three Billins Wells', which may perhaps be identified with the 'medicinal spring at Earl's Court' mentioned by Thomas Faulkner in 1820 in his *History of Kensington*. Faulkner states that this medicinal spring 'still retains the name of Billings-well, from a former proprietor; this has been much frequented for its virtues, though now scarcely known in the parish'.[3] By the eighteenth century, however, the creek was known as Counter's Creek, this name evidently being taken from Counter's Bridge, which traversed the creek at the west end of Kensington High Street. The name, first recorded in the mid fourteenth century as Countessesbrugge, may have reference to Matilda, Countess of Oxford, who held the manor of Kensington at about that time, and who may have built or repaired the bridge.[4] 'Stamford Bridge' is evidently a corruption of 'Samfordesbrigge', several fifteenth-century examples of which are recorded, meaning 'the bridge at the sandy ford'.[5] The name is now widely used to denote the nearby Stamford Bridge Stadium, which stands on the west or Fulham side of the railway line and is the home of Chelsea Football Club.

The first building development within the area described in this chapter took place on the copyhold land at the south-western corner. In 1703 Matthew Child, who owned land at Earl's Court, was paying rates for a brewhouse[6] and in 1707 he was said to have a brewhouse at Little Chelsea.[7] This may refer to the brewhouse which stood somewhere on this copyhold land near Stamford Bridge and which was occupied from 1711 to 1719 by Mr. Nurse (or Nourse), from 1719 to 1724 by Mr. Turner, and thereafter for many years by Richard Osgood, brewer.[8] Between 1777 and 1784 the ratebooks show that another brewhouse known as Belchier's or Belcher's stood nearby, but neither of them is specifically mentioned after 1784, and by 1805 four houses had been built upon part of the site of Osgood's by John Jessopp of Waltham Holy Cross, gentleman.[9] These four houses may be those shown on Joseph Salway's drawing of 1811[10] (Plate 102a), the site of which is now occupied by the glum five-storey red-brick blocks of flats built in the mid 1890's and known as Mentone Mansions (architect, Alfred Burr) and Hereford House.[11]

In 1789 the house at the west corner of what is now Billing Road was for the first time licensed as a public house, known as the Black Bull (or sometimes as the Bull or Bull's Head).[12] In 1830 it was bought by the owners of the Stag brewery, Pimlico,[13] whose successors, Watney's, still own it. The present three-storey brick building (Plate 102c) dates from 1874,[14] and contains vestiges of the original Victorian bar furniture.

The Billings Area

In 1658 Sarah Pettiward, wife of John Pettiward, esquire, citizen of London, inherited four and a half acres of freehold land in Kensington from her father, Henry White of Putney, baker.[15] This small estate, situated near the south-west corner of the parish, and abutting on the copyhold and waste ground described above, remained in the possession of John and Sarah Pettiward's descendants until 1812, when it was sold for £500 to Charles Foster of Angel Court, Throgmorton Street, auctioneer,[16] who had recently purchased two small pieces of adjacent waste ground from Lord Kensington, lord of the manor of Earl's Court.[17]

In 1828 the opening of the Kensington Canal along the lower course of Counter's Creek temporarily enhanced the value of the adjacent land, and on 29 May 1830 Foster's

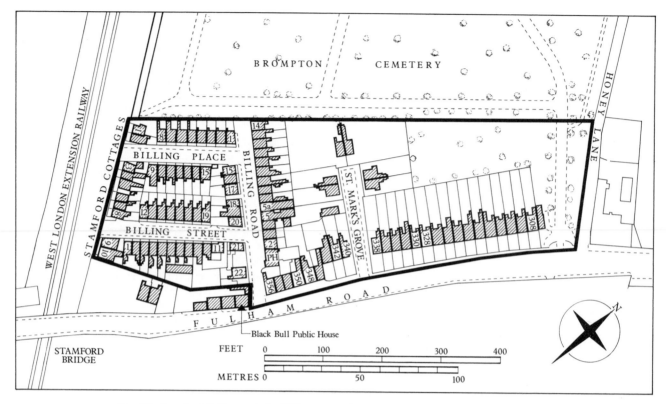

Fig. 71. Stamford Bridge and the Billings area. Based on the Ordnance Survey of 1862-72

widow granted a ninety-nine-year lease of her estate (then in the occupation of Samuel Poupart, gardener) to the chairman and deputy chairman of the Equitable Gas Light Company. The lessees paid £500 for the lease and undertook within five years to spend at least £2,000 on building; the rent was to be £80 per annum.[18]

The Equitable Gas Light Company was a very recently formed association (not yet incorporated by Act of Parliament) established for the purpose of supplying Westminster and the western suburbs of London with gas.[19] In the previous November its leaders had signed an agreement with Mrs. Foster for the lease of her land,[20] but very soon afterwards they decided instead to build their works in Westminster, a little to the west of Vauxhall Bridge;[21] and by January 1831 the company secretary was advertising the land at Stamford Bridge as to be let or sold.[22]

The disposal of this prematurely acquired property was, however, to take over twelve years. In 1835 Mrs. Foster's heir threatened to take legal action against the company for failure to fulfill the covenant to spend £2,000 on building within five years of the date of the lease,[23] and in 1836 the company therefore bought the freehold for £2,000.[24] In 1838 the whole estate was unsuccessfully offered to the West London and Westminster Cemetery Company for the very high price of £5,000,[25] later reduced first to £4,500 and in 1842 to £4,000; but the cemetery company refused to pay what it regarded as an extortionate price, and even rejected the gas company's offer to sell a small

part of the land for the formation of a central entrance to the cemetery from Fulham Road.[26] The best offer from other prospective purchasers was only £3,000, and in December 1842 the (now incorporated) gas company decided to put the whole property up for sale by auction in lots.[27]

The estate was divided into fifteen parcels, so arranged that only three, in the centre (now the sites of Nos. 330–342 even Fulham Road and the part of St. Mark's Grove behind them), had frontages to both the cemetery and to Fulham Road; and a very high reserve price of £1,300 was placed upon these three lots because it was thought that the cemetery company would have to buy them in order to obtain its much-needed access to Fulham Road.[28] In the event, however, the cemetery company outwitted the rapacious gas company, for at the auction in February 1843 one of its directors, John Gunter, had to bid only £475 to acquire the lot at the eastern extremity adjacent to Honey Lane, with a frontage of fifty-three feet to Fulham Road, and a piece of contiguous back land with a frontage to the cemetery.[29] Soon afterwards Gunter conveyed both parcels for the same price to the cemetery company, which thereby at last obtained an adequate, if off-centre, rear entrance from Fulham Road.[30]

Five other lots were sold at the auction. William Allen of Avery Row, St. George's, Hanover Square, plumber and glazier, paid £620 for four of them, now the site of Nos. 308–328 (even) Fulham Road.[31] The other lot, now the site of Nos. 350-356 (even) Fulham Road and Nos. 1-5 or 5A (consec.) Billing Road, was bought by Edward Gingell of Barrett's Court, St. Marylebone, appraiser, for £215.[32]

In May 1844 the unsold land was again put up for auction. Allen bought all the remaining ground east of Billing Road for £930 (now the sites of Nos. 330-348 even

FEET 5 0   10   20
METRES 1 0   3   6

Fulham Road, all of St. Mark's Grove and the east side of Billing Road to the north of No. 5 or No. 5A).[33] To the west of Billing Road, where the parcel bordering on the canal had been advertised as 'peculiarly desirable for the construction of a Wharf', Joseph Ball of the Queen's Arms, Newgate Street, tavern keeper, bid £700 (below the reserve price, yet nevertheless accepted); but when he found that owing to the towing path being on this side of the canal, the Kensington Canal Company would not permit a wharf there, the gas company had eventually to accept a price of only £600.[34] Thus the total yield from the sale of the whole estate amounted to only £2,840 — hardly more than half the original asking price of £5,000.

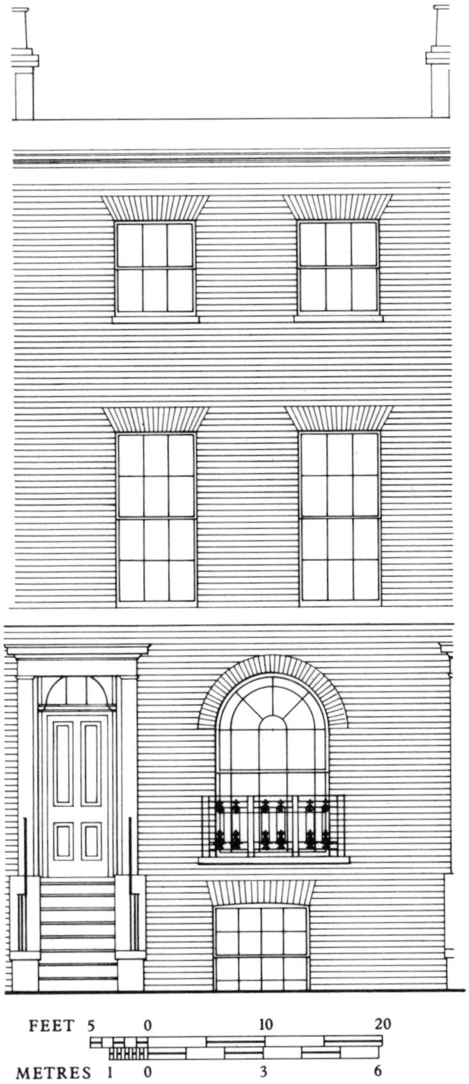

Allen lost little time in developing his land. On the eastern part of the site a long, symmetrical terrace of old-fashioned-looking houses (originally called Devonshire Terrace and now Nos. 308-328 even Fulham Road, fig. 72) was built under eighty-year leases granted by Allen in the latter part of 1844. The lessees were Robert Gunter of Old Brompton, esquire (Nos. 312, 326, 328),[35] Thomas Johnson of Little Chelsea, corn dealer (Nos. 308, 310),[36] Thomas Pocock of Bartholomew Close, City, gentleman (Nos. 322, 324),[37] William Toby of King's Road, Chelsea, bookseller (No. 314),[38] and John Tout of Medway Street, Horseferry Road, builder (Nos. 316-320 even).[39]

Devonshire Terrace was soon followed by another range, consisting of ten houses (originally known as St. Mark's Terrace and now as Nos. 330-348 even Fulham Road), divided in the centre by a road (St. Mark's Grove) which provided access to the land at the rear. Nos. 330-344 are in the same general manner as Devonshire Terrace but have more stucco ornamentation and only one instead of two windows in the upper storeys. At Nos. 340-344 single-storey shops have been built over the front gardens. The leases, all granted in 1844-6, were to George Baker of St. Mark's Terrace, gentleman (No. 332),[40] Thomas Johnson (No. 330),[41] Frederick Nicoll of Battersea, esquire (No. 340),[42] and John Tout (No. 338).[43]*At Nos. 342 and 344 Edward Gingell, the appraiser who had bought the lot adjoining Allen's land to

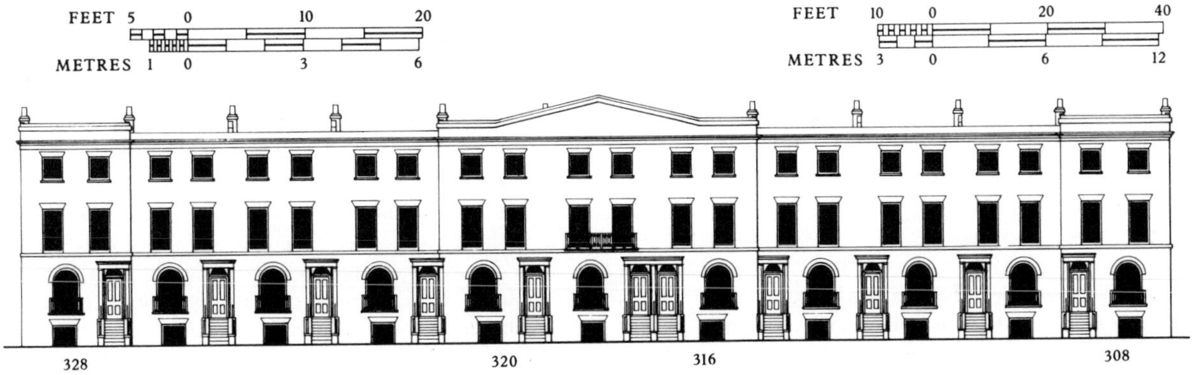

FEET 10 0   20   40
METRES 3 0   6   12

Fig. 72. Nos. 308-328 (even) Fulham Road (Devonshire Terrace), elevations, 1844

*The leases for Nos. 334 and 336 have not been found, but the lessee of No. 334 may have been William Benham of St. Mark's Terrace.[44]

the west, was the lessee.[45] In the latter part of 1844 he had started to build a range of four three-storey shops on his own land (now Nos. 350-356 even Fulham Road).[46] These had no front gardens and were built flush with the pavement, as also were Nos. 346 and 348 (the westernmost two houses on Allen's land), where Gingell was Allen's lessee[47] (Plate 102b).

St. Mark's Grove, the land behind Nos. 330-348 Fulham Road, was divided by Allen into six large plots upon which three pairs of semi-detached houses (all now demolished) were built. Allen's lessees were William Simon of Brewer Green, Westminster, builder (two houses, lease granted in 1846),[48] Frederick Cooper of Paulton Square, Chelsea, gentleman (one, leased 1845),[49] William Toby (one, leased 1844),[50] and Edward Gingell (two, 1852).[51] Another house, Grove Cottage (also now demolished), was later erected by Gingell behind Nos. 340 and 342 Fulham Road.[52]

In 1938 Kensington Borough Council bought the whole of St. Mark's Grove for the building of working-class flats, and all the houses were demolished in the following year. The Council also contemplated purchasing the adjoining area, now generally known as 'the Billings', but after the outbreak of war both schemes were suspended, and in 1945-6 eleven temporary bungalows were erected in St. Mark's Grove. In 1959-60 three four-storey blocks of flats for the aged were built here by the Council, to designs by the Borough Engineer, H. Burleigh.[53] In 1973-4 four small private houses having their access from St. Mark's Grove and known as Nos. 51-54 were built in the back gardens of Nos. 326-338 Fulham Road. The architects were Harry Spencer and Associates.[54]

Edward Gingell also became the owner of the whole of the range of small two-storey brick-fronted houses without basements on the east side of Billing Road (formerly St. Mark's Place or Road), having built Nos. 1-5 or 5A on his own freehold land[55] and acquired the remainder under leases of 1846 and 1852 from Allen.[56] All of them were occupied by 1848.[57] The public house at No. 1 was originally known as the Prince of Wales,[58] but by 1861 it was called the Bedford Arms. In c. 1966 its name was again changed to the Fox and Pheasant.[59] The angle in its frontage is probably the result of a dispute between Gingell and Allen about the line on which Billing Road was to be laid out.[60] (During this dispute Allen was described by the gas company's surveyor as 'the most unreasonable and litigious man I have had to deal with for some time.'[61]) At No. 5A there was originally a cowshed, used by the dairyman who occupied No. 5.[62]

Billing Road provided the only access to the little self-contained estate bought by Joseph Ball. This was soon to be covered with rows of small two-storey terrace houses with basements and, facing the canal, a group of eight cottages. Within a few months of his purchase of the ground in 1844 Ball was having sewers built, but by February 1845 he had evidently disposed of all of his land under an agreement with Christopher Crew, a Chelsea

bricklayer to whom or to whose nominees all Ball's building leases were subsequently granted.[63] The whole of this development, comprising some fifty-two houses, was completed by about 1856.[57]

The first range to be occupied (by 1848) was Nos. 1-8 (consec.) Stamford Cottages, whose tiny gardens fronted on the towing path of the canal. At Nos. 1 and 2 (which in 1982 are in course of having an additional storey built to designs by Anthony R. Harding), the lessee, nominated by Crew, was William Biscoe of Chelsea, gentleman:[64] at Nos. 3-5, the first of two groups of three cottages, the lessees (also nominated by Crew) were respectively Robert Cripps of Chelsea, gentleman, William Hooper, and John Ravenhill of the Royal Hospital, Chelsea, gentleman;[65] and at Nos. 6-8 (all built by Crew), Henry Martin of Battersea Bridge Road, tailor, who was evidently financed by the West London and General Benefit Building and Investment Society.[66] At Nos. 9 and 10 Stamford Cottages it was originally intended to build a public house,[67] and in 1846 the site was let to James Collis of Pitfield Cottage, Eltham, Kent, an architect who specialised in public houses and shops.[68] But this idea was soon abandoned and in 1852 (Collis's lease having presumably been cancelled) Christopher Crew took the ground and built Nos. 9 and 10 here.[69]

In Billing Place (until 1938 known as North Street) James Wormsley of Chelsea, builder, was the lessee for Nos. 1-8, all occupied by 1850[70] (Plate 103b) and William Tayler of Young Street, Kensington, builder, for Nos. 9-15, not all occupied until a little later[71] (fig. 73). Tayler also built the adjoining Nos. 15-17 Billing Road, while at Nos. 18-20 the lessees were respectively Thomas Gingell of Fulham Road, upholsterer, John Townsend of St. Mark's Terrace, and Joseph Stone, also of St. Mark's Terrace, grocer. All of these were occupied by 1852.[72] Further south, Christopher Crew took the sites of Nos. 21 (in 1849) and 22 (in 1855).[73]

In Billing Street (until 1938 known as South Street) all nineteen houses were occupied by 1854[57] (Plate 103a, fig. 73). On the south side the lessees were the St. Marylebone and Paddington Joint Stock Building and Trading Company (Nos. 1-3 consec.), William Bundey of Stamford Cottages, builder (Nos. 4-6), and Christopher Crew (No. 11 and at least one other).[74] On the north side they were Crew (Nos. 12-15, 18 and 19) and Edward Foster of Chelsea, builder (Nos. 16 and 17).[75]

The census of 1861 shows that the inhabitants of this little enclave (including the east side of Billing Road) were almost all working-class. The largest group of heads of household comprised those engaged in the building trades (bricklayer, carpenter, etc.), 21, followed by labourers and transport workers (bus drivers and conductors, cab or engine drivers, etc.), 14 each, laundresses, 9, and gardeners, 8. Many of the houses were evidently let out in lodgings, with the absentee owner paying the rates: cases in point are the builders Wormsley and Tayler in Billing Place, and Gingell on the east side of Billing Road. The

Fig. 73. Billing Road and Billing Place, typical elevations

total number of inhabitants in the 66 houses involved was 550, giving an average per house of 8.3. The highest number in any single dwelling was 18, at No. 1 Billing Street.[76]

By 1881 the situation had not greatly changed. Heads of household included 26 labourers, 23 engaged in the building trades, 14 in transport and 12 laundresses; and there were also four policemen and three grave-diggers, the last no doubt employed at Brompton Cemetery nearby. The total number of inhabitants had fallen slightly to 529 (average per house, 8.01). The highest number in any single dwelling was 17, at No. 9 Stamford Cottages.[77]

In his survey of living conditions in London, Charles Booth in 1902 placed the inhabitants of this little area in the category of 'Poverty and Comfort (mixed)'.[78] In 1929-30 his successor categorised them as 'skilled workers and others of similar grades of income'.[79] In more recent years this social ascent has continued with increasing rapidity, and in the late 1950's 'the Billings . . . started to become fashionable.' In 1962 a number of houses were being modernised and three quarters of them had 'elected to lose their humble past . . . Douglas Fairbanks' daughter has lived there; a peer has been seen looking over one of the properties. The Billings can be said to have arrived.'[80]

CHAPTER XIV

Brompton Cemetery

The origin of Brompton Cemetery, like that of Kensal Green, lies in the movement to remedy the shocking state of the overcrowded graveyards of the metropolis in the early nineteenth century.[1] Between 1832 and 1841 Parliament, in order to relieve this situation, authorized the establishment of half a dozen cemeteries near London by commercial companies. Of these the West London and Westminster Cemetery Company was one, and undertook to lay out a large new burial place at Brompton.

This company was incorporated by Act of Parliament in 1837, its self-styled 'founder' or 'projector' being Stephen Geary, architect and civil engineer.[2] In 1830 Geary had designed the monument to George IV at what later became known as King's Cross, and had taken out a number of patents for a variety of inventions. He also founded the London Cemetery Company, which had been incorporated in 1836, and was the architect of its cemetery at Highgate.[3] At Brompton he acted from 1837 to 1839 as architect to the West London and Westminster Cemetery Company.[4]

In August 1836 the provisional directors of this intended company were advertising for subscribers to a share-capital of £50,000,[5] and in February 1837 the Bill for the incorporation of the company was introduced in the House of Commons. One of its sponsors was Thomas Wakley, the medical reformer and M.P. for Finsbury, who provided similar support for several other cemetery company bills at about this time.[6] The Bill received the royal assent in July 1837 and nominated fourteen gentlemen to act as directors of the company. They were authorized to lay out a cemetery on forty acres of ground in Kensington, build chapels and catacombs, charge fees for burials, and raise a capital sum of not more than £100,000, of which half was to be obtained by the sale of two thousand shares at £25 each. In order to placate the metropolitan clergy (some of whom, being dependent in substantial measure for their income upon the revenues from burial fees, had petitioned against the Bill), the Act also required the company to pay a fee of ten shillings to the local incumbent upon the burial of any person removed from a parish within ten miles of the cemetery.[7]

The first meeting of the board of directors was held at the company's offices in Essex Street, Strand, on 20 July 1837. Only five of them attended, and after the election of the Honourable Edmund Byng as chairman, the only

significant items of business transacted were the appointment of a solicitor and a secretary, and of Stephen Geary as architect.[8] At the next meeting only three directors attended, and in the first few months of its existence attendance rarely exceeded four. Of these the most important were two barristers, Francis Whitmarsh and Sir Francis Knowles, both of whom had acted as Counsel for the company's Bill as it went through Parliament,[9] and both of whom acted successively as deputy chairman of the board. Half a dozen of the original directors never attended at all, and in August 1838 Byng, who had only been present at two meetings, resigned as chairman. By this time the bankers Messrs. Bouverie had been appointed treasurers to the company, and it was evidently to provide the board with more efficient leadership that the Honourable Philip Pleydell Bouverie, senior partner in the firm, was in the following month elected first to the board and immediately afterwards to the chairmanship.[10]

Efficient leadership was certainly needed, for the company at once ran into difficulties over the acquisition of the intended site of the cemetery. By its Act of 1837 the company was empowered to lay its cemetery out on some forty acres of land bounded on the north by Old Brompton Road, on the east by Honey Lane, on the south by Fulham Road and the lands of the Equitable Gas Light Company, and on the west by the Kensington Canal.[11] Most of this land (reputedly over thirty-eight acres of it) belonged to Lord Kensington,* but a small piece at the south end, fronting on to Fulham Road, had recently become the property of the gas company. During the progress of the cemetery company's Bill through Parliament the provisional directors had signed an agreement with Lord Kensington for the purchase of his land for £20,000, which was to be paid in seven instalments spread over three years. But after the first three instalments had been paid doubts arose about Lord Kensington's capacity to sell the land, his title to it having been severely limited by the marriage settlement which he had made for his heir in 1833. By mutual agreement the question was referred to the Court of Chancery and was not resolved until November 1838. The conveyance to the company was finally made in August 1839.[13]

The purchase of land from the Equitable Gas Company proved even more troublesome. The cemetery company had originally intended to buy the whole of the Equitable's

---

*This ground had since 1832 been on lease to John Shailer, a market gardener, who in 1836 had sub-let it to William Hosking (then the engineer of the Birmingham, Bristol and Thames Junction Railway) on behalf of the Pneumatic Railway Association.[12]

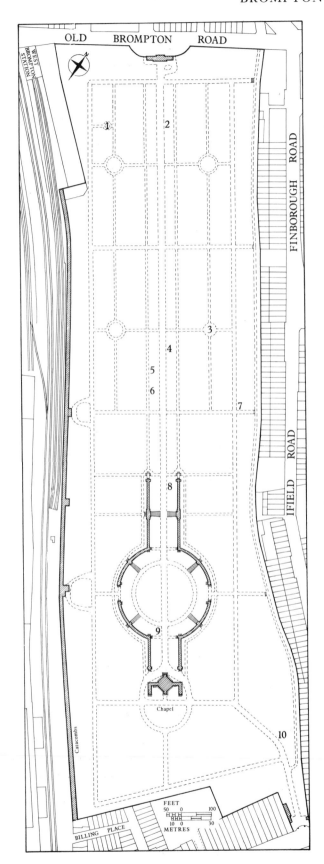

Fig. 74. Brompton Cemetery, plan. Based on the Ordnance Survey of 1949-63.
Location of some monuments mentioned in the text or illustrated:
1. Chelsea Pensioners; 2. Mrs. Pankhurst; 3. Earl of Kilmorey; 4. G. Godwin; 5. F. Leyland; 6. Val Prinsep; 7. J. Jackson; 8. Lt. R. Warneford, V.C.; 9. B. Roosevelt Macchetta; 10. R. Coombes

four-and-a-half-acre estate, with its long frontage to Fulham Road, but the price of £5,000 was considered to be too high, and the directors therefore decided to try to buy only a strip wide enough 'to make a handsome approach' to the cemetery from Fulham Road. Unsuccessful negotiations ensued, and in 1839 a makeshift entrance was made from the south end of Honey Lane instead.[14]

In 1843, however, the gas company put the whole of its estate up for sale by auction. Two lots were bought for £475 by John Gunter, now one of the directors of and eventually the largest shareholder in the cemetery company, to which he soon afterwards reconveyed them for the same price. An adequate entrance from Fulham Road was thus at last obtained.[15]

Until possession of Lord Kensington's land was obtained little could be done towards forming the cemetery. In November 1837 David Ramsay, a nurseryman of Brompton, was appointed 'landscape gardener and contractor', but he does not seem to have immediately been given any work to do;[16] and in March 1838 one shareholder, when pressed to pay the first call on the shares for which he had subscribed, complained that 'although a considerable time has elapsed since the passing of the Act, there are no visible signs of any proceedings to carry it into execution.' By this time the company was already 'considerably in Debt', a special board meeting was needed to discuss ways of 'getting rid of the remaining Shares', and by the end of 1838 only two of the original directors still bothered to attend meetings with any regularity.[17] This depressing start to its career was certainly one reason for the company's endemic financial problems.

In June 1838, when possession of Lord Kensington's land was (wrongly) thought to be imminent, the directors decided to hold a public competition for designs for the layout of and intended buildings in the cemetery, and offered a first prize of one hundred guineas. Stephen Geary, the company's architect, had already prepared designs, which he exhibited at the Royal Academy at about this time, and they were specifically stated to be eligible for the competition.[18] But when in September 1838 the directors serving on a special 'Committee of Taste' examined all the designs submitted, they awarded the first premium to an entry marked 'Windsor', which proved to be by Benjamin B. Baud. The second premium was won by Henry E. Kendall and Thomas Allom, and the third by Frederick Sang.[19]

Baud had been one of Sir Jeffry Wyatville's assistants in the rebuilding of Windsor Castle, where in 1824 George IV had authorized Wyatville to adopt the word 'Windsor' as his motto. Brompton Cemetery seems to have been Baud's only important independent work, and when he died in 1875, aged sixty-nine, a correspondent of *The Building News* wrote that he was 'now almost forgotten in the profession.'[20]

After some 'consultation with Practical Men' (from the evidence of the company's minutes, probably the architect John Shaw the younger), a full meeting of the directors confirmed the Committee of Taste's award of the first premium to Baud.[21] Geary's services as architect to the company were therefore no longer required, and in January 1839 he was told that his appointment would be cancelled unless he tendered his resignation.[22] He did so, but soon afterwards he claimed compensation of £498 as the 'Projector of the Company', and when this was refused he took the matter to court. Ultimately he seems to have been paid a very much smaller sum.[23]

In February 1839 Baud succeeded Geary as architect to the company, but there seems to have been some doubt about his capacity, for the directors decided to inquire from Wyatville 'as to the competency of Mr. Baud' to carry out the works now projected. Yet despite these reservations the directors also decided at the same meeting 'to adopt the General Design of Mr. Baud in its main elements and order of architecture . . . subject to any modifications in detail or extent that may seem expedient'; and shortly afterwards he was instructed to prepare estimates for a portion of his plans, the cost not to exceed £30,000.[24]

This first stage of building comprised the wall which was to enclose the whole cemetery and the lodge at the main entrance on the north side. Although the question of Lord Kensington's title to the site had been settled in November 1838, further disputes ensued about the precise acreage of ground involved, and work could not start until August 1839, more than two years after the passing of the company's Act.[25] The contractor for the wall on the east and south sides was John Faulkner, who had completed his work by the end of the year. The lodge, west wall and catacombs there (the last now partly removed), and the brickwork for the north wall were done by Messrs. Nowell, evidently the firm of Philip Nowell, mason to the Queen, of Grosvenor Wharf, Pimlico, and one of the contractors in the building of Belgravia. The ironwork in the north wall was by E. and R. Dewer. Extensive drainage works were also begun, and J. Finnemore (late gardener to Lord Ravensworth and the Marquess of Normanby) was appointed gardener.[26] In December 1839 J. C. Loudon was consulted about the trees and shrubs best suited for planting on the site.[27]

Baud's designs for the layout of the cemetery provided for a long carriage drive to lead from the entrance lodge straight down the middle of the site to an octagonal domed chapel near the south end. This drive was to be flanked in its northern half by an avenue of lime trees (which cost 1s. 6d. each and were planted in 1840[28]). In the southern half of the drive there were to be two parallel ranges of round-arched arcades, each with a central bell tower, and these arcades were to be continued into a 'Great Circle', at the east and west extremities of which there were to be two subsidiary chapels in the manner of Greek temples, one for the Nonconformists and the other for the Roman Catholics. At the south extremity of the 'Great Circle' two more parallel ranges of arcades led up to the principal octagonal chapel, the focal point of the whole cruciform design (Plate 105a, fig. 74).

This conception proved, of course, extremely expensive to realise, and the two subsidiary chapels were in fact never built. In the summer of 1840, however, Messrs. Nowell's tenders for the carcase of the principal chapel (which was to be faced with Bath stone) and for the two southern segments of the 'Great Circle' and the two bell towers were all accepted.[29] Levelling works, road-making and planting also proceeded, and it was in this scene of busy disorder that the cemetery was consecrated by C. J. Blomfield, Bishop of London, in June 1840. The first burial took place a few weeks later, the east end of the lodge having been fitted up as a temporary chapel.[30]

By this time money was short, and although it was decided to issue another thousand shares of £25 each, the company had nevertheless to resort in June 1840 to one of its directors, the local landowner Robert Gunter, for a short-term loan of £5,000 needed to pay Messrs. Nowell. The costly conditions laid down by the Westminster Commissioners of Sewers for the drainage of the cemetery were considered by the directors to be so unreasonable that they sought the advice of both George Gutch (who, as district surveyor for Paddington, was well versed in such matters) and of Counsel; but ultimately they had to acquiesce, leaving them with no remedy 'for what the Directors still feel to be an injustice'. Apart from a contract with Messrs. Nowell for the interior of the chapel, building work seems to have come to a halt.[31]

In the spring of 1841 there were 'Opposing opinions' among the directors about future policy. Some of them attributed 'the inadequate present success' of the cemetery to 'the disorder consequent on building', and urged that 'no further buildings are at present requisite', while others thought that 'the present incomplete execution of the designs has checked resort to the Cemetery.' At a special general meeting held in May to resolve the directors' differences, the shareholders were told that over £61,000 had already been spent, and that the capital so far subscribed fell short of expenditure already engaged for by some £2,640. Despite this depressing news the shareholders decided to press on, and by the end of June Messrs. Nowell's tenders for the completion of the arcades and the 'Great Circle', the completion of the interior of the principal chapel and the building of small wings on either side of it had all been accepted.[32]*

By early 1842 all this work had been completed.[34]

---

*In July E. and R. Dewer were instructed to supply two pairs of iron doors for two of the four entrances to the catacombs in the 'Great Circle', and presumably they also executed those for the other two entrances.[33]

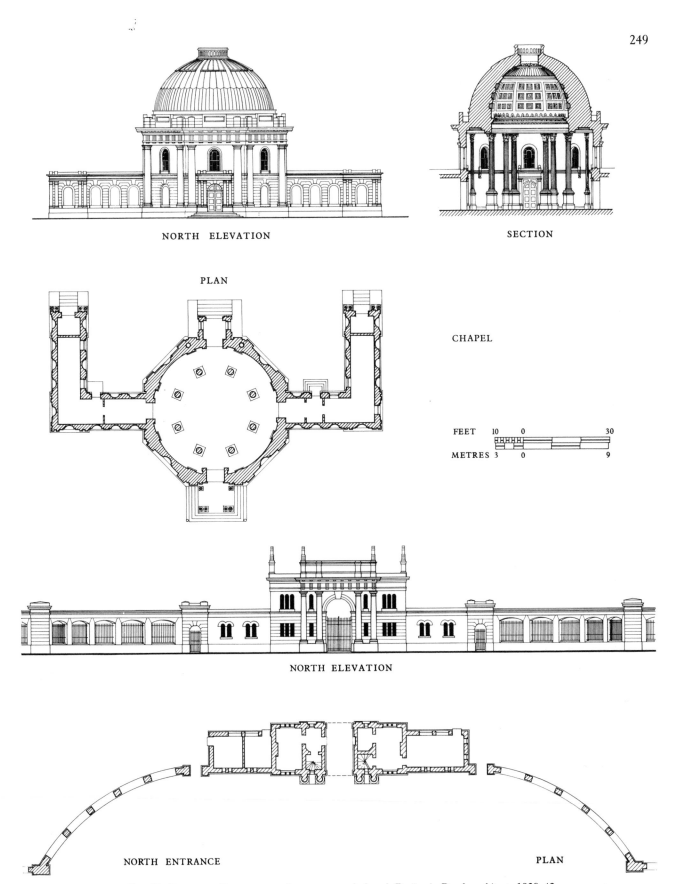

NORTH ELEVATION

SECTION

PLAN

CHAPEL

FEET 10 0 30

METRES 3 0 9

NORTH ELEVATION

NORTH ENTRANCE

PLAN

Fig. 75. Brompton Cemetery, north entrance and chapel. Benjamin Baud, architect, 1839-42

Apart from the two subsidiary chapels in the 'Great Circle', the only important omissions from Baud's original layout plans were thus the arcades which he had envisaged for the formation of a large courtyard in front of the principal chapel; but it may well be that in their continuous search for economy the directors had reduced the quality and embellishment of his first designs. *The British Almanac* criticised the open screen of segmental arches filled in with iron palisading which formed the north wall — 'If intended as decoration, arches of that form have no particular elegance to recommend them'; and the design of the entrance lodge, in the Italian Doric manner, was 'without any decided character'.[35] Today the impact of the long ranges of arcades and of the 'Great Circle' is greatly reduced by the tombstones and monuments which fill all of the space thus enclosed, and the octagonal chapel, despite its claims to be regarded as 'a chaste specimen of Palladian architecture', seems too small in relation to the dominant position allocated to it.[36] Notwithstanding their considerable cost, the cemetery's buildings seem, indeed, to have a somewhat meagre air (Plates 104-5, fig. 75).

The number of burials in the cemetery soon proved to be disappointingly small — 89 in 1841, producing gross receipts of only £800, and 285 in 1842, producing £1,350. Expenditure was therefore reduced to a minimum,[37] and (perhaps in consequence) there began early in 1843 a long dispute between Baud and the directors about the amount of the fees due to him.[38] In the autumn of the same year serious defects in the construction of the catacombs along the west wall were found to be due to the contractors' failure to follow the architect's specifications; but Nowell's, the firm involved, replied that Baud had passed their work.[39] At about the same time the acquisition through John Gunter of part of the Equitable Gas Company's ground provided access to Fulham Road, and in February 1844 the directors were considering a drawing submitted by a surveyor, Mr. Winterbotham, for a new entrance there.[40] In March Baud protested at the directors' employment of Winterbotham and reminded them that he had already supplied them with two designs for the lodge at the intended Fulham Road entrance; but by this time the directors had already decided to remove him from the office of architect. In April Baud (through his solicitor) demanded a special meeting of the directors to investigate any charges against him, but when this was held the directors confirmed their decision to dismiss him.[41] Subsequently he brought an action against the company claiming £4,000, his fees for the design of buildings not yet executed being the main item in dispute; but in 1846 the Court of Exchequer ruled against him, and although the company's legal expenses were heavy, Baud seems to have got nothing.[42]*

The small lodge at the Fulham Road entrance was designed and erected in 1844 by a builder, Mr. Dawson.

At the same time part of the wall on the south side of the cemetery were taken down and rebuilt to enclose the additional land recently acquired.[44]

Despite rigid economy the company's liabilities amounted in 1845 to nearly £22,000, and in that year the directors therefore obtained another Act of Parliament which authorized them to raise £21,731 by the sale of 3,477 new shares. These new shares were to be of the nominal value of £25 each, but at first they were to be sold for only £6 5s.; they were to confer the same rights as the old shares, and in the first instance they were to be offered to the existing shareholders.[45] By 1847 most of the liabilities had been paid off, and a dividend of two shillings per share was declared. Three years later, when the number of burials per annum had increased to over seven hundred, the dividend had risen to five shillings per share,[46] but this still only amounted to one and a half per cent upon the company's total outlay.[47]

By this time the appalling conditions prevailing both in the metropolitan graveyards and in those of many provincial towns had been grimly described to Parliament in 1843 by Edwin Chadwick, then the secretary of the Poor Law Commission, in his *Report on the Practice of Interment in Towns*.[48] But nothing had been done to remedy the situation when the cholera epidemic of 1849 (in which some 14,000 people had died in London alone) again raised the problem in urgent form. During the winter of 1849-50 Chadwick, now one of the members of the new General Board of Health, accordingly prepared another report which *inter alia* castigated the record of the metropolitan cemetery companies. They had 'effected no appreciable diminution of the existing evils'; there was not even one of them 'in which some of the worst of the old evils are not continued'; entombment (e.g. the provision of catacombs and family mausolea) as distinguished from inhumation was still encouraged; they had 'afforded no relief from the oppressive expense of funerals', nor had they 'effected the slightest improvement of any kind in respect to the interment of the poor.' And the report stated flatly that 'the interment of the dead is a most unfit subject for trading profit.'[49]

The Government's Metropolitan Interments Act of 1850, which was largely based upon the proposals contained in this report, provided a solution which would, if it had been fully implemented, have extinguished all the metropolitan cemetery companies. The Board of Health was empowered to provide new burial grounds in the metropolitan area, purchase the existing cemetery companies, and in due course close all the old insanitary and overcrowded graveyards. Funeral costs were to be regulated by a series of scales of fees to be promulgated by the Board, which was to make all contracts with the undertakers.[50]

The Board of Health soon found that none of the

---

*In his later years Baud 'did little besides some private business for a nobleman, but spent most of his days painting in oil or preparing drawings', while 'his evenings were frequently spent at the theatre'.[43]

cemetery companies was willing to sell its property voluntarily, and in March 1851 the Board finally persuaded its reluctant Treasury masters to sanction the compulsory purchase of all of them, but successively. The first two (and as events turned out, the only) purchase notices issued were in respect of the Brompton Cemetery and the London Cemetery Company's property at Nunhead; and in April Chadwick and the directors of the Brompton company agreed that the assessment of the price to be paid for that cemetery should be referred to an independent arbitrator.[51] (At this stage Chadwick was hoping to involve his friends Joseph Paxton and the émigré German architect Gottfried Semper in improving the Brompton Cemetery after its acquisition, but this was to come to nothing.[52])

The directors calculated that their total expenditure upon the cemetery amounted to £147,685,[53] (more than double that at Nunhead, the next most expensive cemetery for which figures are available[54]*), of which nearly £60,000 was attributed to the cost of Baud's elaborate buildings.[55] Fortified by the advice of (Sir) William Tite, the architect of the South Metropolitan Cemetery Company's Norwood cemetery, they decided that they were entitled to the sum actually expended by the company, to which 'lost interest may be added', and they therefore demanded £168,762.[56] The Board of Health, on the other hand, considered that with the exception of the General Cemetery Company at Kensal Green all the metropolitan joint-stock companies had 'as commercial undertakings ... been failures', the Brompton company (as previously mentioned) only paid a dividend equivalent to one and a half per cent upon capital outlay, and expenditure upon all 'such works as are deemed perfectly useless' was to be disregarded. It therefore offered only £43,836.[57]

The arbitration hearing took place in July 1851 before Mr. (later Sir) Barnes Peacock, Q.C., assisted by two professional men, one chosen by each party, the architect Philip Hardwick being the company's nominee.[58] Their award, announced in October, amounted to £74,921, and represented a considerable triumph for the now beleaguered Board of Health.[59]

Earlier in the year the Board had needed to raise a large capital sum to buy land at Abbey Wood, Erith, for its own proposed new cemetery. But the assurance companies to which it had applied for a loan had refused, principally because the Board's own life was statutorily limited to five years; and the Government refused to help by the issue of Exchequer Bills. The Government was in fact having second thoughts about the whole of Chadwick's grandiose scheme. In July, at the very time of the arbitration hearing, the Treasury had ordered the Board to abandon the purchase of the land at Abbey Wood and had inquired whether it was still 'possible to put an end' to the purchase of the Brompton and Nunhead cemeteries. By December the Government had decided to introduce a new interments Bill based on different principles from the Act of 1850, and the Treasury therefore instructed the Board to abandon the purchase of the two cemeteries 'if the parties consent thereto'.[60]

The directors of the Brompton Cemetery had, of course, been aware of the Government's change of position since at least October and had at first decided to await events. But after the Board of Health's request for the award to be set aside had been received a special general meeting of all the shareholders was held in January 1852. Some of the directors, and certainly the chairman, Pleydell Bouverie, proposed that the request should be accepted, but most of the shareholders thought otherwise, and by 122 votes to 54 they called upon the directors to enforce the award.[61]

Brompton was thus the only metropolitan cemetery company to be acquired by the Government, for the owners of the Nunhead Cemetery (who had demanded £99,000, been offered £40,000, and awarded only £42,000) agreed to forgo the arbitrator's decision.[59] The conveyance of the cemetery, from the West London and Westminster Cemetery Company to the Commissioners of Works and Public Buildings, was made on 5 November 1852.[62] By the time of the directors' final meeting, on 20 December 1854, all the shareholders had received a total of £11 9s. 5d. per share.[63] Thus those of them who only held the original £25 shares must have lost heavily, but those who had bought the new shares of 1845 at only £6 5s., or who held some of both issues, must have been well pleased to be rid of a property which had never yielded a dividend of more than 5s. per share and on which far too much had been spent on inessential building works.

By 1889 over 155,000 interments had taken place, and the question of closure was being considered.[64]

Brompton Cemetery is now managed by the Department of the Environment, and is closed for burials except where old graves can be re-opened.

The monuments erected in the cemetery display much of the wide range of Victorian and later tastes (Plates 106-7). John Jackson, the pugilist (d. 1845), had an altar-tomb with statues of athletes (now removed) at either end and surmounted by a couchant lion. Similar in conception is the monument to Robert Coombes, the champion sculler (d. 1860), which is surmounted by an inverted skiff. The second Earl of Kilmorey (d. 1880) is commemorated by a massive granite mausoleum in the Egyptian manner, designed by Messrs. Kendall and Pope.[65] George Godwin (d. 1888), architect and editor of The Builder, has a more modest and very much more pleasing monument which includes a portrait medallion attached to a column flanked by mourning female figures. Frederick Leyland (d. 1892), ship-owner and patron of the Pre-Raphaelites, has the finest tomb of all, designed by Sir Edward Burne-Jones.[66] An ancient Gothic sarcophagus in Sienese marble and

---

*No figures are available for the doubtless expensive cemeteries at Kensal Green or Norwood.

supported on eight squat pillars provides a very unusual monument for the artist Val Prinsep (d. 1904), Leyland's son-in-law. The suffragette leader Emmeline Pankhurst (d. 1928) has a Celtic cross with figures carved in relief in the manner of Eric Gill. Close to the western boundary of the cemetery a granite obelisk commemorates the graves of over two thousand pensioners from Chelsea Royal Hospital; and a separate enclosure nearby for other military graves contains a large memorial to the Brigade of Guards, erected in 1889.

Other notable people buried in Brompton cemetery include George Borrow, author; Sir Henry Cole, first director of the South Kensington Museum; Thomas Cundy (d. 1895), architect; Sir John Fowler, railway engineer; Sir Charles James Freake (d. 1884), the developer of a large part of South Kensington; Sir James Kay-Shuttleworth, educational pioneer; Samuel Smiles, author of *Self-Help*; and John Snow, the anaesthetist who discovered that cholera is water-borne. The ashes of Constant Lambert, composer, are also buried here.

APPENDIX

Actors, Musicians and Writers resident in Brompton between 1790 and 1870

The following list covers the general area of Brompton as understood in the nineteenth century, rather than the narrower area described in the present volume. Only writers connected in some way or other with the performing arts are included. The list has been compiled from a variety of sources, principally the *Post Office Directories*, the ratebooks, and T. C. Croker's *A Walk from London to Fulham* (1860). Original addresses are generally given; where the house survives with a changed address, the latter is supplied in brackets.

John Banim, dramatist and novelist. No. 7 Amelia Place, Brompton (Chelsea), 1822; No. 13 Brompton Lower Grove, 1822-4.

Elizabeth Billington, *diva*. No. 16 Michael's Place, 1792-3; No. 33 Michael's Place, 1805-7.

Dion Boucicault, actor and playwright. Hereford House, Old Brompton, 1861-3.

John Braham, singer. Brompton Grange, Yeoman's Row, 1830-42.

John Baldwin Buckstone, actor, manager and playwright. No. 2 Onslow Terrace, 1835-9; No. 6 Brompton Square, 1840-54.

Alfred Bunn, actor-manager. Eagle Lodge, Old Brompton, 1835-9.

Angelica Catalani, *diva*. The Hermitage, Yeoman's Row, 1811-14.

Louisa Simeon Chatterley (Mrs. Francis Place), actress. No. 15 Brompton Square, 1825-30; No. 21 Brompton Square, 1833-51.

Muzio Clementi, composer. No. 10 Brompton Lower Grove, 1826-8.

John Payne Collier, critic. No. 22 Brompton Square, 1839-43.

George Colman the younger, playwright. No. 22 Brompton Square, 1825-36.

Thomas P. Cooke, actor. No. 35 Thurloe Square, 1845-54; died at No. 37 Thurloe Square, 1864.

John Cooper, actor. No. 20 Pelham Crescent, 1860-7.

Charles Dance, burlesque writer. Hereford House, Old Brompton, 1841-5.

Mary Ann Davenport, actress. Died at No. 22 Michael's Place, 1843.

William Farren, comic actor. No. 23 Brompton Square, 1824-36, 1854-61; No. 30 Brompton Square, 1837-53.

Helen(a) Faucit (Lady Martin), actress. No. 23 Brompton Square, *c.* 1841; No. 31 Onslow Square, 1852-98.

Edward Francis Fitzwilliam, composer. No. 14 Brompton Square, *c.* 1853-6; No. 9 Grove (now Beauchamp) Place, 1856-7.

Fanny Elizabeth Fitzwilliam, actress. No. 6 Brompton Square, *c.* 1852-3.

Gerald Griffin, playwright, poet and novelist. No. 13 Brompton Lower Grove, *c.* 1824-5.

Anna Maria Hall, novelist, playwright and 'miscellaneous writer'. The Rosary, Old Brompton, 1839-49.

Augustus Glossop Harris, actor-manager. No. 9 (now No. 18) Pelham Place, 1852-63.

Charles Incledon, 'tenor vocalist'. No. 13 Brompton Crescent, 1802-11.

Douglas William Jerrold, playwright and wit. No. 6 Seymour Terrace (now No. 46 Seymour Walk), 1832-4; No. 11 Thistle Grove (demolished, site now in Drayton Gardens), 1834-6.

Robert and Mary Ann Keeley, actors. No. 19 Brompton Square, 1845-56; No. 10 Pelham Crescent, 1856 to 1869 (his death) and 1899 (hers).

James Kenney, playwright. No. 22 (now No. 20) South Terrace, 1847-9.

Henry Lazarus, clarinettist. No. 4 (until 1864 No. 2) Pelham Place, 1860-71.

Jenny Lind, *diva*. Clareville Cottage, Old Brompton, 1847-9; No. 1 Moreton Gardens (now part of No. 189 Old Brompton Road), 1875-87.

John Liston, comic actor. No. 40 Brompton Square, 1829-33.

Benjamin Lumley, theatrical manager. Hereford House, Old Brompton, 1857-9.

Gertrud Elisabeth Mara, *diva*. Hereford Lodge, Old Brompton, 1798.

Charles James Mathews, actor and manager. Gore Lodge, Brompton Park Lane, 1848-54; No. 25 Pelham Crescent, 1865-70.

Drinkwater Meadows, actor and manager. No. 6 Grange Villas (now No. 33 Egerton Terrace), 1846-66.

Arthur Murphy, author and playwright. No. 14 Queen's Buildings, 1800-5.

James Robinson Planché, playwright, librettist and herald. No. 20 Brompton Crescent, 1823-44; Michael's Grove Lodge, Grange Terrace (now No. 6 Egerton Terrace), 1845-52.

Jane Pope, actress. Died at No. 17 Michael's Place, 1818.

John Reeve, comic actor. No. 46 Brompton Row (now No. 170 Brompton Road), 1835-8.

George H. B. Rodwell, composer. No. 15 Brompton Crescent, 1829; No. 7 Brompton Square, 1829-32; No. 1 Alexander Square, 1832-3; No. 23 Brompton Row, 1833-6; No. 14 Brompton Row, *c.* 1842; No. 1 Thurloe Place West (now No. 18 Thurloe Place), 1844-7.

George Augustus Sala, scene-painter, minor dramatist and journalist. No. 1 Alexander Square, *c.* 1870-1.

John Palgrave Simpson, dramatist and novelist. No. 9 Alfred Place West (now Thurloe Street), 1850-87.

Richard J. Smith ('O. Smith'), comedian. No. 1 North Terrace, 1846-51.

Paul Spagnoletti, violinist. No. 21 Brompton Square, 1825-32; Queen's Buildings, 1832-4.

Lucia Elizabeth Vestris (Mrs. Charles Mathews), *diva* and manageress. Gore Lodge, Brompton Park Lane, 1848-54.

Frederick Vining, comic actor. No. 21 (now No. 5) Pelham Place, 1841-4.

James Vining, actor. No. 21 Pelham Crescent, 1847-9, 1852 and 1862-7. Also rated for No. 22 Brompton Square, 1849-51, 1856-7 and 1861; No. 59 Brompton Square, 1851.

Benjamin Nottingham Webster, actor, manager and playwright. 'No. 3 Brompton Road' (close to Brompton Park House), 1841-54.

Alfred Sydney Wigan, actor. No. 6 Michael's Grove, 1846-9; No. 13 (now No. 23) Pelham Place, 1849-52.

Edward Richard Wright, low comedian. Brompton Vale, 1840-3; Cromwell Lane, 1844-8.

Frederick Yates, actor-manager. No. 21 Michael's Place, 1842.

References

ABBREVIATIONS

A.E.P.	Alexander Estate Papers in the possession of Mr. Ian Anstruther
B.	*The Builder*
B.A.	Building Act case, Greater London Council
B.L.	British Library, Reference Division
B.N.	*The Building News*
Boase	Frederick Boase, *Modern English Biography*, 1965 ed.
B.R.	Building Regulations case, Greater London Council
C.C.	Archives of the Church Commissioners
Colvin	Howard Colvin, *A Biographical Dictionary of British Architects 1600-1840*, 1978
Corbett Letters	Letter books of William Corbett in Margate Public Library
D.N.B.	*Dictionary of National Biography*
D.S.R.	District Surveyors' Returns for South Kensington in Greater London Record Office. The year and number of each return are given
E.C.R.	Court Rolls of the Manor of Earl's Court in Kensington Central Public Library
Faulkner	Thomas Faulkner, *History and Antiquities of Kensington*, 1820
G.E.C.	*The Complete Peerage*, ed. G.E.C., 1910-59
G.L.C.	Greater London Council
G.L.R.O.	Greater London Record Office
H.B.	Historic Buildings Division, Department of Architecture and Civic Design, Greater London Council
H.L.R.O.	House of Lords Record Office
H.M.C.	Historical Manuscripts Commission
I.L.N.	*Illustrated London News*
K.P.L.	Kensington Central Public Library
L.C.C.	London County Council
M.B.W.	Metropolitan Board of Works, and its archives in Greater London Record Office
M.C.S.	Archives of the Metropolitan Commissioners of Sewers in Greater London Record Office
M.D.R.	Middlesex Deeds Registry in Greater London Record Office
Musgrave	*Obituary Prior to 1800 . . . compiled by Sir William Musgrave* (Harleian Society Publications, vols. XLIV-XLIX, 1899-1901)
N.R.A.	National Register of Archives
O.S.	Ordnance Survey maps of London, 5 feet to the mile
Pepperell	Rev. William Pepperell, *The Church Index: A Book of Metropolitan Churches and Church Enterprise. Part I. Kensington*, [1872]
P.O.D.	*Post Office Directories*
P.P.	*Parliamentary Papers*
P.P.R.	Principal Probate Registry, Somerset House
P.R.O.	Public Record Office
R.B.	Ratebooks in Kensington Central Public Library
R.I.B.A.	Royal Institute of British Architects
R.O.	Record Office
W.C.S.	Archives of the Westminster Commissioners of Sewers in Greater London Record Office

CHAPTER I (pp. 1-8)

Brompton Road: Introduction

1. M.B.W. Minutes, 22 May 1863, p. 500; 29 April 1864, p. 473: L.C.C. Street Naming Order no. 7820.
2. *Survey of London*, vol. XXXVIII, 1975, p. 59.
3. *Ibid.*, p. 4.
4. K.P.L., MS. 1211.
5. M.D.R. 1764/2/114.
6. *London and Provincial Directory*, 1827-8, *sub* Knightsbridge and Brompton.
7. National Society for Promoting Religious Education, file 3486.
8. *Fraser's Magazine*, vol. XXXI, 1845, pp. 1-16, 188-205, 330-42, 445-57. The text of these articles differs little from the essays as posthumously collected in 1860. A revised edition, enlarged by Beatrice E. Horne, appeared in 1896.
9. W. Carew Hazlitt, *The Hazlitts, Part the Second*, 1912, pp. 74, 97. This is an expansion of the account of Brompton which originally appeared in W. Carew Hazlitt, *Four Generations of a Literary Family*, vol. 2, 1897.
10. *The Times*, 22 Nov. 1836: Guildhall Library, La Pr W2/Kni.
11. *The Architectural Magazine*, vol. III, 1836, p. 327: G.L.R.O., MR/UP/172-3, 181, 204, 237: *Commons Journals*, vol. CI, 1846, p. 74.
12. *P.P.*, 1845, XXVII, *The Nineteenth Report of the Commissioners of the Metropolis Turnpike Roads North of the Thames*, p. 5; 1849, XXVII, *The Twenty-Third Report of the Commissioners*, *ut supra*, p. 5.
13. W. Carew Hazlitt, *The Hazlitts, Part the Second*, 1912, p. 74.
14. *B.* 3 Jan. 1852, pp. 11-12; 7 March 1857, p. 141; 6 April 1861, p. 235; 1 Feb. 1862, p. 82.
15. Pepperell, p. 15.
16. *B.* 22 March 1862, p. 212; 29 March 1862, p. 227: P.R.O., Ed. 28/15, no. 48: Kensington Vestry Minutes, 12 March 1873.
17. *The Chelsea Herald*, 30 Aug. 1884.
18. *B.* 20 Aug. 1859, p. 545.
19. *The Architectural Review*, vol. XVII, 1905, p. 251.
20. B.A. 102132: information kindly supplied by Mr. Dennis Marler of Capital and Counties Property Company Ltd.
21. B.A. 23847.
22. *Ibid.*, 5833.

23. *Ibid.*: *B.N.* 21 June 1895, pp. 875-6.
24. D.S.R. 1898/113.
25. *Ibid.*, 1898/121.
26. *Ibid.*, 1898/83.
27. *Ibid.*, 1899/23.
28. Kensington Vestry Minutes, 26 July 1899, p. 361.
29. *Ibid.*, 4 May 1898, p. 74.
30. D.S.R. 1899/109.
31. *Ibid.*, 1899/134.
32. B.A. 17280: D.S.R. 1899/147.
33. *B.* 6 Oct. 1860, p. 648: M.D.R. 1862/4/374.
34. B.A. 68569.
35. *Ibid.*, 16019.
36. *B.* 8 Dec. 1860, p. 792: M.D.R. 1861/16/344.
37. B.A. 58962.
38. *Ibid.*, 33173.
39. *Ibid.*, 64366.
40. *Ibid.*, 41334.
41. M.D.R. 1845/5/200.
42. B.A. 12546: D.S.R. 1897/123.
43. National Society for Promoting Religious Education, file 5755.
44. B.A. 101064.
45. B.R. 120320.
46. *The Architect and Building News*, 4 Oct. 1956, pp. 450-3.
47. B.A. 70237.
48. B.R. 9096.
49. *Ibid.*, 30523.
50. D.S.R. 1905/1210-12.
51. B.A. 56067: *The Architectural Review*, vol. 138, Nov. 1965, pp. 348-9.
52. B.A. 89241.
53. *Ibid.*, 74343.

CHAPTER II (pp. 9-32)

Brompton Road, South Side

1. E.C.R., 3 June 1766.
2. M.D.R. 1756/1/353.
3. Kensington Vestry Minutes, 11 March, 8 April 1756.
4. M.D.R. 1764/5/542-3; 1765/1/268-9.
5. *Ibid.*, 1764/2/273; 1765/2/404; 1765/4/38; 1765/6/411; 1766/5/244; 1766/7/311; 1767/5/104; 1767/6/92.
6. *Ibid.*, 1767/2/451.
7. *Ibid.*, 1764/4/186-7; 1772/2/526.
8. *Ibid.*, 1768/1/576-7.
9. *Ibid.*, 1768/4/57-60; 1769/7/292; 1770/3/494-5; 1770/6/55, 329.
10. *Ibid.*, 1766/7/494-6; 1766/8/701-4; 1767/1/52-4; 1767/5/207-10; 1767/7/171; 1770/3/51.
11. *Ibid.*, 1768/1/278-81; 1768/3/69-72.
12. *Ibid.*, 1768/7/92; 1769/5/418-19; 1778/3/10.
13. *Ibid.*, 1775/2/476; 1775/4/217; 1777/3/196-8.
14. R.B.
15. M.D.R. 1775/2/479; 1775/3/9; 1776/6/424; 1777/5/536; 1778/1/75.
16. Dorothy Stroud, *Henry Holland, His Life and Architecture*, 1966, pp. 43-9 and Plate 12.
17. M.D.R. 1781/2/377-8; 1783/2/303-6.
18. *Ibid.*, 1786/4/292; 1789/7/412.
19. *Ibid.*, 1789/7/288, 298, 361.
20. *Ibid.*, 1789/7/287, 289; 1790/4/317-18; 1790/5/45-9, 281-3; 1791/3/74-6; 1791/8/2; 1791/9/11-12; 1791/10/286-7; 1792/6/47; 1793/4/179; 1796/5/616; 1797/3/398.
21. *Ibid.*, 1809/8/216; 1810/1/748; 1810/2/656, 715; 1810/9/248; 1830/7/707: R.B.
22. Pepperell, p. 55.
23. T. C. Croker, *A Walk from London to Fulham*, 1860, pp. 25-6.
24. *Ibid.*, pp. 25-30: R.B.
25. *B.* 20 Aug. 1859, p. 545.
26. E.C.R., n.d. 1842, 8 Feb. 1842, 4 Jan. 1843.
27. P.R.O., C16/18/F18, para. 75, answer of Tennant in Ford *v.* Tennant.
28. *Ibid.*, C16/18/F18, paras. 5-8, Ford's bill of complaint in Ford *v.* Tennant: M.D.R. 1842/2/161.
29. P.R.O., C16/18/F18, para. 22, answer of Tennant in Ford *v.* Tennant.
30. *Ibid.*, J57/3771, p. 49, certificate of 1881: M.D.R. 1919/21/182, first schedule, part II.
31. P.R.O., J4/4377/677, affidavit of John Goddard, 1892.
32. E.g. M.D.R. 1842/4/107-15; 1842/5/718-25.
33. P.R.O., J4/3500/1061, affidavit of William Watkins, 1888; J15/1889, f. 446; J15/1891, f. 1525.
34. P.P.R., 1892/288 and 1906/805, wills of John Goddard I and II.
35. P.R.O., J15/1273/1258, order of 29 April 1876.
36. *Ibid.*, J15/2021, ff. 1582, 1583.
37. *Ibid.*, J15/1949, f. 1647; J15/1985, f. 1198; J15/2018, f. 20; J15/2025, f. 651; J15/2051, f. 326; J15/2051, f. 579 (orders): M.D.R. 1895/7/651; 1897/29/822.
38. M.D.R. 1898/26/7.
39. *Ibid.*, 1898/26/510, 712; 1919/21/182.
40. *Ibid.*, 1889/9/837.
41. M.D.R. 1892/37/502; 1894/31/686: Chelsea Vestry Minutes, 9 Oct., 6 Nov. 1894; 19 Feb. 1895: P.R.O., BT31/15408/41731.
42. M.D.R. 1889/16/152: Kensington Vestry Minutes, 12 Dec. 1888, p. 307.
43. Kensington Vestry Minutes, 25 April 1894, p. 87; 9 May 1894, p. 130: B.A. 8533.
44. M.D.R. 1898/27/632.
45. B.A. 5833: *B.N.* 21 June 1895, pp. 875-6.
46. *Dekorative Kunst*, XI, 1902-3, p. 211: photographs kindly supplied by the Kodak Museum.
47. T. C. Barker and Michael Robbins, *A History of London Transport*, vol. II, 1974, pp. 57, 82, 109-113: B.A. 21974.
48. B.A. 33228: *B.N.* 11 Dec. 1903, p. 793: *Who's Who in Architecture*, 1914, *sub* Harber: *P.O.D.*
49. B.A. 32391.
50. Ibid., 23847.
51. Ibid., 21864: D.S.R. 1903/23.
52. B.A. 27281.
53. Kensington Borough Council Minutes, 24 Nov. 1903, p. 23: D.S.R. 1903/174; 1904/698-705; 1905/1637-9.
54. B.A. 62446: D.S.R. 1903/69, 452: *The Architects' Journal*, 14 May 1930, pp. 739-40.
55. G.L.R.O., SBL 1034, pp. 204, 236; 1015, pp. 154, 443; 1031, p. 50.
56. Records of C. A. Daw and Son Ltd., in-letters, box 15A, letters from Slade, 8, 20 Feb. 1894.

57. D.S.R. 1893/87-9, 120-1, 150, 196-7; 1894/86-7; 1895/ 1-4: Daws' Records, in-letters, box 15A, Slade, 30 Aug., 4, 13, 16 Oct. 1893; 14 Jan., 20 Feb. 1894.
58. Daws' Records, unlabelled ledger 1877-1910, ff. 134, 171.
59. B.A. 7183.
60. Daws' Records, in-letters, box 8, Grove, 1891.
61. *Ibid.*, in-letters, box 8, Grove, 1891; box 12, Marshall, 1891; box 17A, Voysey, 1891.
62. *Ibid.*, in-letters, box 10A, Knight, 1893-6.
63. D.S.R. 1892/55-9, 169; 1894/157-60.
64. Daws' Records, unlabelled ledger, 1877-1910, ff. 134, 171-2.
65. *The British Architect*, 9 Feb. 1894, p. 93.
66. *Ibid.*, 18 March 1892, p. 208.
67. *Ibid.*, 9 Feb. 1894, p. 93: D.S.R. 1892/79-80.
68. *The British Architect*, 18 March 1892, p. 208.
69. *P.O.D.*
70. *B.* 29 Aug. 1896, p. 171.
71. D.S.R 1893/154: *P.O.D.*
72. P.P.R., 1906/805, will of John Goddard II.
73. M.D.R. 1907/17/103; 1909/3/764; 1919/21/182.
74. *Ibid.*, 1923/17/816.
75. P.P.R., 1953, will of John Goddard III.
76. *The Times*, 31 Jan. 1956.
77. Information kindly supplied by Mr. Dennis Marler.
78. R.B.: *P.O.D.*
79. *Harrods: A Story of British Achievement 1849-1949*, 1949, pp. 10-11: Tim Dale, *Harrods: The Store and the Legend*, 1981, pp. 5-6.
80. Harrods Archives 1/10, extract from *The Harrodian Gazette*, 1916.
81. Dale, *op. cit.*, pp. 6-8: *P.O.D.*
82. Harrods Archives 1/10, copy of letter from H. D. Harrod.
83. *Ibid.*, 1/10, particulars of 1934: *Harrods: A Story of British Achievement*, p. 17.
84. *The Chelsea Herald*, 30 Aug. 1884: *Harrods: A Story of British Achievement*, p. 16.
85. *Harrods: A Story of British Achievement*, p. 20: *The Chelsea Herald*, 8 Dec. 1883; 30 Aug. 1884.
86. *The Chelsea Herald*, 8 Dec. 1883.
87. *Ibid.*, 30 Aug. 1884: Dale, *op. cit.*, pp. 9-12.
88. *B.* 22 Oct. 1881, p. 531: R.I.B.A. Library, Fellowship nomination papers of Alfred Williams, 9 April 1888.
89. *The Chelsea Herald*, 30 Aug. 1884: Dale, *op. cit.*, pp. 12-15.
90. Harrods Archives 1/10, misc.: Dale, *op. cit.*, pp. 16-19.
91. Harrods Archives 1/10, notes from directors' reports, 1890-4.
92. Dale, *op. cit.*, p. 17: P.R.O., BT31/15408/41731.
93. Chelsea Vestry Minutes, Oct. 1894-Feb. 1896, *passim*.
94. G.L.R.O., SBL 1034, pp. 204, 236.
95. *Ibid.*, SBL 999, p. 136; 1015, pp. 154, 443; 1018, pp. 295-6; 1031, p. 50: P84/TRI2/128 (Holy Trinity Church, Brompton, Church Council Minutes), Nov. 1892.
96. Cadogan Estate Office, Minutes, *passim*: *P.O.D.*
97. Chelsea Vestry Minutes, 9, 30 July 1895.
98. L.C.C. Minutes, 15 Nov. 1892, p. 1058.
99. *B.N.* 8 Aug. 1917, p. 119: *P.O.D.*
100. D.S.R. 1894/121-2.
101. L.C.C. Minutes, 8 Oct. 1895, p. 876: D.S.R. (St Luke's, Chelsea), July 1895-Jan. 1896: Chelsea Vestry Minutes, 10 Dec. 1895; 4 Feb. 1896.
102. Kensington Vestry Minutes, 24 March, 28 July 1897: *The British Warehouseman*, Nov. 1898.

103. Harrods Archives 1/10, misc. correspondence: G.L.R.O., SBL 999, p. 136.
104. Harrods Archives 1/10, notes from Directors' Reports: B.A. 19208: D.S.R. 1901/95.
105. Harrods Archives 2/2, *The House that Every Woman Knows*, 1909.
106. B.A. 19208, 21169: D.S.R. 1902/69, 178; 1904/38, 222, 239-46: *The Studio*, vol. 29, 1903, p. 117.
107. B.R. 1926: B.A. 32615, 37248.
108. B.R. 1926: B.A. 32615, 32708, 37248, 37914: Harrods Archives 2/5, *The Wonderful Development of Harrods during Twenty-One Years*, 1911: Daws' Records, agreement with Harrods of 23 March 1911: *The Harrodian Gazette*, 1913, p. 116.
109. G.L.R.O., LP/1/138, evidence of Richard Burbidge on London Building Acts (Amendment) Bill, 1905, q. 5860.
110. Harrods Archives 1/10, notes by Joseph Appel, 1906.
111. B.A. 32615, 32708, 37114, 37248, 37914, *passim*.
112. *Ibid.*, 32708 (Feb. 1914): G.L.R.O., LP/1/138, qq. 5863-5, 5895-5923.
113. Harrods Archives 1/10, notes by Joseph Appel, 1906.
114. Deryck Abel, *The House of Sage 1860-1960*, [n.d.], p. 19.
115. *The Studio*, vol. 29, 1903, p. 117.
116. G.L.R.O., LP/1/138, q. 5869: Harrods Archives 1/10, statement of annual profits, and notes by Joseph Appel, 1906.
117. B.A. 27281.
118. L.C.C. Minutes, 20 Feb. 1912, p. 399: Harrods Archives 1/ 10, notes from Directors' Reports: Dale, *op. cit.*, p. 42.
119. L.C.C. Minutes, 22-23 Dec. 1908, p. 1526: Harrods Archives 1/10, House Architect's Memorandum, 1943: B.R. 1926.
120. B.A. 37248.
121. B.R. 1926: B.A. 32615: *The Architectural Review*, vol. LXX, Nov. 1931, pp. 137-8.
122. Abel, *op. cit.*, p. 21.
123. B.R. 1926: Harrods Archives 1/10, House Architect's Memorandum, 1943.
124. M.D.R. 1923/17/816.
125. Dale, *op. cit.*, pp. 50-7.
126. P.R.O., PROB 11/487/63, will of Henry Hassard; C105/5: M.D.R. 1718/6/39; 1729/5/378-9: K.P.L., MS. 1211.
127. M.D.R. 1740/2/224-5; 1744/3/136; 1746/1/564-5.
128. *Ibid.*, 1763/1/512-15, 520.
129. Charles Humphries and William C. Smith, *Music Publishing in the British Isles*, 1970, p. 297.
130. M.D.R. 1764/2/329-31.
131. *B.* 15 Dec. 1860, p. 807.
132. M.D.R. 1801/3/743.
133. *Ibid.*, 1818/3/809.
134. *Ibid.*, 1825/5/369; 1826/1/464; 1830/5/11; 1831/3/ 378; 1834/3/637: K.P.L., MSS. 533-8.
135. M.D.R. 1843/2/355; 1843/7/154; 1843/8/67; 1843/ 9/738; 1860/1/804.
136. Colvin, *sub* Hopper: Gilbert Herbert, *Pioneers of Prefabrication*, 1978, p. 111.
137. K.P.L., MS. 2356: M.B.W. 2504.
138. *B.* 6 Oct. 1860, p. 648: M.D.R. 1862/4/374.
139. M.D.R. 1861/2/623-4; 1861/8/724; 1861/10/30.
140. *B.* 8 Dec. 1860, p. 792: M.D.R. 1861/13/88-91; 1861/16/ 344-7.
141. *B.* 15 Dec. 1860, p. 807.
142. M.D.R. 1861/17/646-9; 1863/5/260: K.P.L., MS. 921.

143. M.D.R. 1863/5/229-30: *Survey of London*, vol. XXXVII, 1973, p. 53.
144. M.D.R. 1863/21/772-6; 1864/5/57; 1865/7/888; 1865/9/214; 1865/15/499; 1865/19/155, 423; 1865/21/812; 1865/23/700; 1865/25/278 (all leases); 1865/8/384; 1865/10/528; 1865/11/526; 1865/12/401; 1865/15/1023 (freehold conveyances).
145. *Ibid.*, 1874/11/995.
146. *P.O.D.*: P.R.O., RG 10/49, ff. 55-61.
147. M.D.R. 1871/18/607-8.
148. *Evening Standard*, 25 March 1974.
149. K.P.L., press cutting in file *sub* Beauchamp Place.
150. *Evening Standard*, 29 Nov. 1972.
151. M.D.R. 1763/2/63-4.
152. *Ibid.*, 1761/1/256; 1768/5/94: K.P.L., MS. 1211.
153. K.P.L., MS. 5017: P.R.O., PROB 11/1243/180.
154. W. Keith Neal and D. H. L. Back, *The Mantons: Gunmakers*, 1967, pp. 125-213.
155. *Ibid.*, pp. 182-213.
156. M.D.R. 1825/2/444: K.P.L., MS. 5017: P.R.O., C13/1811/25, J90/533.
157. M.D.R. 1825/13/458.
158. Neal and Back, *op. cit.*, p. 190.
159. M.D.R. 1825/13/650-1; 1826/1/351-3; 1826/3/284-5; 1826/9/224-5: K.P.L., MS. 5017.
160. P.R.O., J90/533; C13/1811/25.
161. *Ibid.*, C13/1811/25: M.D.R. 1831/7/379-81: K.P.L., MS. 5017.
162. M.D.R. 1836/5/301.
163. K.P.L., MS. 5017.
164. D.S.R. 1845/440-1.
165. *Ibid.*, 1850/26-7.
166. M.D.R. 1844/8/47, 130, 291, 711, 1001; 1844/9/119, 345; 1844/10/870; 1845/1/894-5; 1845/2/598, 1003; 1845/3/847-8; 1845/5/317; 1845/7/145; 1845/8/776; 1845/9/298; 1845/10/143, 243-4; 1846/2/987-9; 1846/3/525: K.P.L., MS. 5017.
167. Kensington Vestry Minutes, 5 Oct. 1864: *P.O.D.*
168. P.R.O., RG 10/49, ff. 61-9.
169. K.P.L., MS. 5017-18.
170. B.A. 58962.
171. M.D.R. 1761/1/256; 1769/1/504.
172. *Ibid.*, 1768/5/94: *Survey of London*, vol. XXXVIII, 1975, pp. 17-18.
173. K.P.L. MS. 1138.
174. M.D.R. 1764/2/114, 290-2: K.P.L., MS. 1138.
175. M.D.R. 1765/4/609.
176. *The World*, 17 May 1791: T. C. Croker, *A Walk from London to Fulham*, 1860, pp. 45-7.
177. *The World*, 17 May 1791: *D.N.B.*
178. M.D.R. 1793/6/412: *D.N.B.*
179. M.D.R. 1805/3/234.
180. *The Autobiography of William Jerdan*, 1853, vol. IV, p. 252: Croker, *op. et loc. cit.*
181. Croker, *op. et loc. cit.*: R.B.
182. M.D.R. 1766/1/328; 1766/7/134; 1767/3/52; 1767/7/153; 1769/3/203; 1770/2/170; 1771/5/143.
183. *Ibid.*, 1769/3/349.
184. R.B.: M.D.R. 1771/5/143: Croker, *op. cit.*, p. 44 (which, however, assigns Andrews to No. 10 rather than No. 9 Brompton Grove, probably in error).
185. R.B.: *Dizionario Biografico degli Italiani*, vol. 22, 1979, p. 266.
186. Croker, *op. cit.*, p. 47.
187. K.P.L., GC 2418 (lithograph of The Hermitage).
188. M.D.R. 1766/2/231; 1766/4/291; 1766/6/360.
189. Croker, *op. cit.*, p. 48.
190. K.P.L., pencil sketch of Yeoman's Row, *c.* 1888.
191. M.D.R. 1766/4/291; 1768/4/224: R.B.: G.L.R.O., MR/LV/8/65.
192. M.D.R. 1766/2/189, 232-4, 493-9.
193. *Ibid.*, 1771/6/431-2.
194. D.S.R. 1879/72-5: M.D.R. 1881/9/41.
195. *Burke's Peerage*, *sub* Dyer.
196. M.D.R. 1864/14/558.
197. R.I.B.A. Library, transcripts of autobiography of W. W. Pocock by Miss M. A. Powel. Selections relating to Ovington Square and Gardens were published in *The Times*, 29 Nov. 1960.
198. M.D.R. 1845/3/922-3; 1845/5/200.
199. R.I.B.A. Library, autobiography of W. W. Pocock, *ut supra*: M.D.R. 1845/4/902-3; 1845/5/996.
200. M.D.R. 1846/12/718; 1847/2/234-5; 1847/6/642; 1847/7/468; 1848/1/56; 1848/5/671: D.S.R. 1846/191-3, 334-5, 406-7; 1847/1-2, 236-7, 291-2, 300-1; 1848/80-1, 92.
201. M.D.R. 1845/4/900-1; 1845/5/126-7, 230-1; 1845/9/593-7; 1846/1/824: D.S.R. 1845/367-9.
202. M.D.R. 1846/1/391-5; 1846/6/685-7; 1846/7/840-7; 1846/11/186-8; 1847/7/484; 1847/8/277-8; 1848/9/183-4; 1849/1/114; 1849/2/236; 1849/4/921; 1849/7/205-6; 1849/9/617; 1849/10/887; 1851/1/584; 1851/2/499, 510-11; 1851/9/969-70; 1852/16/295-9; 1854/9/557.
203. R.I.B.A. Library, autobiography of W. W. Pocock, *ut supra*: M.D.R. 1845/5/126-7, 230-1; 1846/1/644-6; 1846/8/253-6.
204. R.I.B.A. Library, autobiography of W. W. Pocock, *ut supra*: G.L.R.O., MBO/DS/29, *passim*: Dorothy Stroud, *The South Kensington Estate of Henry Smith's Charity: Its History and Development*, 1975, p. 73.
205. K.P.L., MS. 2409.
206. M.D.R. 1848/3/22; 1849/2/811.
207. P.R.O., HO 107/1469, ff. 202-7.
208. *P.O.D.*: Algernon Graves, *The Royal Academy of Arts: A Complete Dictionary of Contributors . . . 1769 to 1904*, 1905-6, *sub* Long and Middleton.
209. M.D.R. 1854/4/387.
210. R.I.B.A. Library, autobiography of W. W. Pocock, *ut supra*: M.D.R. 1867/19/59-64; 1867/21/582-8; 1868/12/320-5, 336-7; 1868/14/955-74; 1868/22/985-6.
211. B.A. 33173, 64366.
212. *Ibid.*, 41334.
213. R.I.B.A. Drawings Collection, Clough Williams-Ellis drawings (RAN 32/K/3). Drawings of 1886 by George Aitchison also in this collection, once thought to be for the interior decoration of No. 18 Ovington Square, are now believed to be for No. 1 Grosvenor Crescent.
214. B.A. 100863: *House and Garden*, Feb. 1960.
215. P.R.O., HO 107/1469, ff. 209-23, 227-38.
216. *Ibid.*, RG 11/43, ff. 102-20.
217. K.P.L., valuation note books, 1890-1.
218. *Ibid.*, 1905-6.
219. Kensington Borough Council Minutes, 25 Oct. 1938, p. 502.
220. B.A. 68726-9.
221. *Ibid.*, 68731: *The Architect and Building News*, 14 Oct. 1938, p. 52.

222. B.A. 102365.
223. *The Sunday Times*, 7 Dec. 1958.
224. G.L.R.O., MR/PLT 4889-4938.
225. Croker, *op. cit.*, pp. 75-6.
226. P.R.O., MAF9/167/7359.
227. M.D.R. 1854/16/761.
228. R.B.: B.L., Add. MS. 31326 (Salway's plan).
229. K.P.L., D/5/341, xiii: G.L.R.O., MR/PLT 4924-31: R.B.
230. R.B.: M.D.R. 1826/4/259; 1828/2/547-8.
231. M.D.R. 1831/6/429.
232. B.R. 161875.
233. R.B.: *P.O.D.*: P.R.O., HO 107/1469, ff. 260-2.
234. P.R.O., PROB 11/1800/342: M.D.R. 1847/2/768; 1854/16/761.
235. M.D.R. 1867/8/1041.
236. D.S.R. 1871/283-5.
237. *Ibid.*, 1871/170, 407-8.
238. *P.O.D.*: B.R. 7504.
239. Surrey R.O., 367/13/48: D.S.R. 1936/1008.

CHAPTER III (pp. 33-49)

Brompton Road, North Side

1. Estate plan and sale particulars of 1759 in K.P.L. 12423 (extra-illustrated copy of Faulkner): M.D.R. 1717/1/200-2.
2. List of possessions of Sir William Blake at his death, in extra-illustrated copy of Faulkner in B.L. (pressmark L.R.271.c.3), between pp. 440 and 441.
3. Faulkner, p. 433: E.C.R., 19 Jan. 1747.
4. M.D.R. 1717/1/202-3.
5. *Ibid.*, 1717/1/200-3; 1717/3/255-6: G.L.R.O., C/96/47.
6. *Transactions of the Huguenot Society of South Carolina*, no. 57, 1952, p. 26.
7. *The Gentleman's Magazine*, vol. iii, 1733, p. 607.
8. M.D.R. 1761/3/452.
9. Henry George Davis, *The Memorials of the Hamlet of Knightsbridge*, 1859, p. 146.
10. Estate plan and sale particulars of 1759 in K.P.L. 12423: M.D.R. 1717/1/200-2.
11. M.D.R. 1757/4/453; 1758/3/376: sale particulars in K.P.L. 12423.
12. *Transactions of the Huguenot Society of South Carolina*, no. 57, 1952, pp. 27-8.
13. *Ibid.*, p. 29.
14. St George's Hospital Archives, Deeds, bundle no. 3A, deed of 12 May 1778, Ann Moreau and Elisha Biscoe.
15. Charleston District Will Book A, pp. 405-6, and Inventory Book A, pp. 250-1, kindly communicated by South Carolina Department of Archives and History.
16. M.D.R. 1760/2/55-60: G.L.R.O., C/96/47.
17. M.D.R. 1801/6/20; 1808/1/674; 1817/5/485: G.L.R.O., C/96/46-7, 49, 58-60.
18. G.L.R.O., C/96/55, 57, 59, 61: M.D.R. 1803/7/753; 1808/1/674; 1817/5/485.
19. See e.g., M.D.R. 1820/1/319-20; 1824/11/738: *Survey of London*, vol. xxxv, 1970, p. 56.
20. M.D.R. 1817/5/486; see also M.D.R. 1821/6/220; 1822/1/751.
21. K.P.L., MS. 16794: G.L.R.O., C/96/58-60, 66.
22. G.L.R.O., C/96/66, 68-71; M.D.R. 1825/1/475-6: K.P.L., MSS. 16794-16821.
23. M.D.R. 1760/2/153-4.
24. *Ibid.*, 1762/3/259-61; 1776/1/516-17.
25. *Ibid.*, 1778/2/327-8; 1793/3/229; 1795/3/300: date of 1780 on gutterhead of No. 62 Brompton Road, photograph of 1902 in Westminster City Library, Buckingham Palace Road, E138: R.B.
26. M.D.R. 1793/3/226-31; 1795/3/300; 1796/1/492, 497-8: R.B.
27. T. C. Croker, *A Walk from London to Fulham*, 1860, p. 38.
28. M.D.R. 1841/7/732, 737: National Society for Promoting Religious Education, file 3486.
29. G.L.R.O., Y/SP/84/1/A-F: *B.* 4 Jan. 1845, p. 7.
30. National Society for Promoting Religious Education, file 3486: K.P.L., MS. 6436: *B.N.* 1 Sept. 1893, p. 293: *P.O.D.*
31. *B.* 11 Nov. 1921, pp. 636, 640, 642.
32. *Ibid.*, 17 Nov. 1888, p. 368: K.P.L., MS. 13711.
33. *B.* 30 July 1910, p. 128: *P.O.D.*
34. Kensington Vestry Minutes, 29 July 1896, p. 321: D.S.R. 1896/111-12.
35. B.A. 90262, 113962.
36. *Ibid.*, 88025: *The Architectural Review*, vol. 121, Jan. 1956, p. 28.
37. B.A. 100934.
38. *B.* 14 Nov. 1958, p. 817.
39. Sale particulars of 1759 in K.P.L. 12423.
40. M.D.R. 1760/2/81.
41. John Chancellor Covington Smith, *Pedigree of the Family of Biscoe*, 1887.
42. M.D.R. 1757/4/453; 1758/3/376.
43. *Ibid.*, 1765/3/449: K.P.L., MS. 916.
44. M.D.R. 1766/2/317, 338-9; 1766/3/217, 409-13; 1766/5/127-8, 268, 420; 1766/6/580-2; 1766/7/608-10; 1766/8/16-21; 1767/1/25, 27, 235-40, 251; 1767/3/295-6; 1767/5/76-7; 1767/9/440; 1768/2/425-8; 1768/5/454, 490-5; 1768/6/88-90, 235.
45. E.g. M.D.R. 1766/2/340; 1766/3/450-4; 1766/5/421; 1766/8/22.
46. M.D.R. 1766/2/317; 1777/1/208.
47. *Ibid.*, 1767/1/235-40; 1768/5/454, 490-5; 1768/6/88-90, 235: K.P.L., MS. 916.
48. M.D.R. 1766/8/16-19; 1767/3/295-6; 1767/5/76-7; 1767/9/440; 1768/2/425-8.
49. *Ibid.*, 1771/3/100; 1772/6/469.
50. K.P.L., MSS. 6282-8.
51. M.D.R. 1870/10/398-9: *B.* 5 Dec. 1868, p. 885: K.P.L., MS. 6284.
52. *B.* 10 Oct. 1903, pp. 358-9: *B.N.* 23 Oct. 1903, p. 547: B.A. 22347.
53. D.S.R. 1905/1210-12.
54. *Architectural Design and Construction*, vol. 5, 1935, p. 272: B.A. 34454.
55. *The Shoe and Leather Record*, 13 Feb. 1931, p. 35: *The Cabinet Maker and Complete House Furnisher*, 3 Jan. 1931, pp. 17, 19: *The Architectural Review*, vol. 69, Feb. 1931, p. 43: *Architectural Design and Construction*, vol. 7, 1937, p. 278: Sherban Cantacuzino, *Wells Coates*, 1978, pp. 42-3: *Wells Coates, Architect and Designer*, 1979 (exhibition catalogue), pp. 12, 22-3.
56. G.L.R.O., P84/TRI2/135: M.D.R. 1769/1/487.

57. Pepperell, p. 29.
58. R.I.B.A. Drawings Collection, X5/4 (Dove Brothers drawings).
59. G.L.R.O., P84/TRI2/136/2.
60. Pepperell, pp. 29-30.
61. *The British Architect*, 24 May 1878, p. 240: R.I.B.A. Drawings Collection X5/4 (Dove Brothers drawings).
62. Letter and drawing communicated by Mr. Nicholas Bonham, Dec. 1980.
63. R.B.: Royal Institution, Rumford Papers, solicitor's bill (undated).
64. Royal Institution, Rumford Papers, letters, 1798-1802: Sanborn C. Brown, *Benjamin Thompson, Count Rumford*, 1979, ch. 21.
65. Brown, *op. cit.*, pp. 240-1: M. A. Pictet in *Bibliothèque Britannique (Sciences et Arts)*, vol. 19, 1802, pp. 386-91: Thomas Webster, *An Encyclopaedia of Domestic Economy*, 1844, p. 88: *The Collected Works of Count Rumford*, ed. Sanborn C. Brown, vol. 3, 1969, pp. 358, 363-5.
66. *Bibliothèque Britannique, loc. cit.*
67. Dartmouth College Library, U.S.A., Rumford Papers, inventory of No. 45 Brompton Row, 1802.
68. *The Collected Works of Count Rumford, loc. cit.*
69. Royal Institution, Rumford Papers, letters, 1802-3.
70. *Ibid.*: R.B.
71. Auction notice in Count Rumford's house, Woburn, Mass., kindly communicated by Miss Louisa Chafee.
72. M.D.R. 1824/11/145; 1824/12/1110.
73. *Ibid.*, 1826/8/587-90.
74. *Ibid.*, 1826/9/507.
75. *Ibid.*, 1826/2/464; 1827/3/315-16; 1827/6/716; 1827/7/9; 1827/10/703; 1828/2/60, 114; 1828/4/461; 1828/6/292; 1828/8/760; 1828/9/284; 1829/1/578; 1829/2/232, 539, 683, 767; 1829/3/278; 1830/6/597, 712; 1830/7/470; 1833/3/518; 1836/1/263.
76. *Ibid.*, 1829/2/539, 683; 1830/7/471.
77. *Ibid.*, 1829/2/683; 1829/3/583.
78. *Ibid.*, 1830/4/211.
79. B.A. 55271.
80. M.D.R. 1774/7/359; 1781/1/271.
81. D.S.R. 1873/344-52; 1875/19-24, 317-19.
82. M.B.W. contract no. 476.
83. M.D.R. 1808/2/591; 1808/8/240; 1809/1/576; 1809/5/675; 1813/1/184; 1814/3/381; 1814/4/194.
84. St George's Hospital Archives, Weekly Board Minutes, 23 Jan., 8 Feb., 29 May 1895: D.S.R. 1895/80.
85. M.D.R. 1777/1/208.
86. E.C.R., 19 Jan. 1747.
87. London Oratory, MS. A/1/3: M.D.R. 1808/6/390; 1812/8/374: C.C., file 20637.
88. M.D.R. 1812/8/374; 1812/9/933.
89. *Ibid.*, 1762/3/164; 1808/6/390; 1812/8/374.
90. *Ibid.*, 1821/9/495; 1822/2/629.
91. P.R.O., PROB 11/1821/150.
92. W.C.S. 66, p. 543.
93. *P.O.D.*: M.D.R. 1819/6/593; 1819/8/129; 1822/8/135-9: Westminster City Library, Buckingham Palace Road, Grosvenor Board Minutes, vol. 8, ff. 133, 353, 417, 480.
94. M.D.R. 1821/9/495; 1822/2/629.
95. *Ibid.*, 1823/3/300.
96. *Ibid.*, 1823/4/666; 1823/5/43, 46, 114, 149, 755-7; 1823/6/616; 1823/7/81, 446, 810; 1823/9/21, 68, 668, 736-7; 1823/10/983; 1824/3/780; 1824/5/79, 83, 791; 1824/8/32, 765; 1824/11/510, 512; 1825/2/798; 1825/4/532, 676; 1825/5/194; 1825/13/649, 850.
97. *Ibid.*, 1822/2/629; 1823/9/668, 736-7: R.B.
98. M.D.R. 1823/5/149, 756; 1823/7/446; 1824/5/791; 1825/4/676; 1826/5/151.
99. *Ibid.*, 1826/10/24; 1837/1/393; 1839/3/18.
100. E. Beresford Chancellor, *The History of the Squares of London*, 1907, pp. 291-4.
101. R.B.: *P.O.D.*: P.R.O., HO 107/1469, f. 51.
102. W.C.S. 70, pp. 280, 286; 178, p. 414; 179, pp. 34, 263.
103. *Ibid.*, 69, p. 14; 236, petition of 15 Sept. 1825.
104. 5 Geo. IV, c. 108, local and personal.
105. M.D.R. 1826/3/449; 1826/5/151; 1826/10/24; 1828/9/140; 1829/5/269; 1830/2/316-17; 1831/3/147; 1839/3/18: G.L.R.O., O/169/1: R.B.
106. M.D.R. 1824/6/301; 1830/4/211; 1832/4/619; 1839/2/317; 1842/4/1004; 1842/5/330, 388; 1843/8/540.
107. W.C.S. 71, p. 265: M.D.R. 1832/4/619: *P.O.D.*
108. M.D.R. 1832/4/619-22.
109. W.C.S. 187, p. 33: R.B.
110. M.B.W. 213, presented papers for meeting of 4 Feb. 1856.
111. *The Times*, 4, 7 March 1842.
112. M.D.R. 1837/1/393; 1838/2/514; 1838/3/258.
113. *Ibid.*, 1832/4/623; 1839/2/317; 1850/1/712.
114. Guildhall Library, MS. 8733/8, p. 139.
115. M.D.R. 1839/3/18.
116. *The Times*, 20 Jan. 1849.
117. *Ibid.*, 4, 7 March 1842: M.D.R. 1842/4/1004; 1842/5/330, 388; 1842/7/415; 1842/8/134, 312-13; 1843/8/540.
118. *The Times*, 19 Aug., 2 Dec. 1848; 20 Jan. 1849.
119. R.B.: P.R.O., HO 107/1469, f. 51: M.D.R. 1849/7/247; 1850/3/429; 1850/8/280; 1851/7/20.
120. P.R.O., J121/162: P.P.R., probates of wills of Mary Farlar (1860) and John Farlar (1864), and administration of effects of William Farlar (1875).
121. M.D.R. 1849/10/1178.
122. Drawing exhibited at Fine Arts Society Gallery, 1981.
123. *B.* 24 May 1856, p. 290; see also *B.* 14, 21 Jan., 11, 18, 25 Feb., 18 March 1854, pp. 18, 30, 36, 78, 90, 102, 142.
124. M.D.R. 1854/1/698; 1855/4/404-5.
125. *B.* 24 May 1856, p. 290.
126. P.R.O., HO 107/690/11, ff. 5-13.
127. *The Autobiography of Francis Place*, ed. Mary Thale, 1972, pp. 258, 267-9, 273: R.B.
128. H.B., Blue Plaque file 1259.
129. L.C.C. Minutes, 14 Jan. 1890, p. 11: K.P.L., applications to Vestry from L.C.C., no. 483: P.R.O., BT31/4359/28315.
130. M.B.W. 1793, f. 339: D.S.R. 1881/233: *B.* 21 Nov. 1885, p. 716.
131. B.A. 21974: D.S.R. 1906/806-9.
132. B.A. 31123.
133. H.B. files.
134. B.R. 156927.
135. B.A. 48311.
136. St. George's Hospital Archives, Misc. Deeds, abstract of title (*c.* 1800): C.C., file 20637, abstract of title, *c.* 1825.
137. St. George's Hospital Archives, Weekly Board Minutes, vol. 5 (1746-9), pp. 101, 220, 317, 350, 353, 360; vol. 6, *passim*.
138. Kensington Vestry Minutes, March-May 1823: C.C., file 20636, letter from Rev. Thomas Rennell, 1 April 1823.

139. C.C., files 20636, 20637, 44080, *passim*; Commissioners for Building New Churches, Minute Book 16, p. 138.

140. St. George's Hospital Archives, Weekly Board Minutes, March-April 1825.

141. C.C., file 44080.

142. *The Gentleman's Magazine*, vol. C, 1830, p. 580: C.C., file 44080.

143. *The Gentleman's Magazine*, vol. C, 1830, p. 579.

144. *Ibid.*, p. 580.

145. C.C., file 44080: *The Gentleman's Magazine*, vol. C, 1830, p. 579.

146. G.L.R.O., P84/TRI2/127, Nov. 1830.

147. *B.* 21 May 1843, p. 181; see also *B.* 22 April, 3 June 1843, pp. 129, 212: M.B.W. 213, *loc. cit.*: G.L.R.O., P84/TRI2/127, May 1843.

148. *B.* 31 Oct. 1863, p. 777: Pepperell, p. 15: *The South London Press*, 26 Oct. 1872, p. 5.

149. G.L.R.O., P84/TRI2/128, May 1879.

150. *Ibid.*, June-Dec. 1879: R.I.B.A. Drawings Collection, 05/1 (Dove Brothers drawings and specification): *The Kensington News*, 28 June 1879, p. 2.

151. G.L.R.O., P84/TRI2/128, May 1880-Nov. 1882: R.I.B.A. Drawings Collection, 05/1 (Dove Brothers drawings).

152. G.L.R.O., P84/TRI2/128, May 1884-Nov. 1886, April 1891.

153. *Ibid.*, P84/TRI2/129, May 1901, March 1905-Nov. 1906: *B.* 14 April 1906, p. 414.

154. G.L.R.O., P84/TRI2/129, Nov. 1903.

155. *Ibid.*, Feb., May 1904, May 1906, March-Dec. 1914, May 1927.

156. *Ibid.*, Nov. 1910, March, Nov. 1913.

157. G.L.R.O., P84/TRI2/72-5, 78; P84/TRI2/129, Nov. 1917, Feb., Oct. 1919, May 1923, April 1924, May 1926, April 1928: dates *in situ*.

158. Information kindly supplied by Vicar and Churchwardens of Holy Trinity, Brompton.

159. National Society for Promoting Religious Education, file 3486, report of 1936: Pepperell, p. 15: D.S.R. 1841/224: information kindly supplied by Vicar and Churchwardens of Holy Trinity, Brompton.

160. Harvey Hackman, *Wates's Book of London Churchyards*, 1981, p. 71.

CHAPTER IV (pp. 50-57)

The London Oratory of St. Philip Neri and the Church of the Immaculate Heart of Mary

1. *The Tablet*, 26 April 1884, p. 645.

2. [Fr. R. F. Kerr], 'The Oratory in London', in *Oratory Parish Magazine*, Jan. 1924, pp. 437-42.

3. London Oratory, Congregation Minutes (1850-1900), Sept.-Oct. 1852; MS. vol. of 'Various memoranda relating to the London Oratorian history', pp. 142f. (journal of Fr. Gordon).

4. Kerr, *op. cit.*, pp. 439-41: *The Letters and Diaries of John Henry Newman*, vol. XV, ed. C. S. Dessain and V. F. Blehl, 1964, p. 167 and note.

5. London Oratory, Letters, vol. 25, ff. 35-6; Fr. Kerr's anno-

tated copy of 'The Oratory in London', vol. 1, p. 170 (Faber to Whitty, 23 Dec. 1852).

6. *Ibid.*, MS. A/1/3.

7. Faulkner, p. 615.

8. Information kindly supplied by Fr. Richard Price.

9. London Oratory, Congregation Minutes, *ut supra*; MS. A/1/4; MS. declaration of trust, 29 May 1854: M.D.R. 1852/16/341; 1854/8/260: *B.* 11 Dec. 1852, pp. 779-80; 20 May 1871, p. 384.

10. London Oratory, General Congregation, Minutes, 7 May 1853: M.D.R. 1854/2/420: Kerr, *op. cit.*, April 1924, p. 502.

11. Kerr, *op. cit.*, April, May 1924, pp. 502, 517-18: *The Letters and Diaries of John Henry Newman, ut supra*, p. 364 and note.

12. London Oratory, General Congregation, Minutes, 21 April 1853; MS. A/1/5: G.L.R.O., MBO 31, pp. 134, 230; MBO 32, p. 169: Kerr, *op. cit.*, May, June 1924, pp. 518, 541.

13. London Oratory, plan, 2 Oct. 1852: G.L.R.O., MBO 31, case 1841; MBO 165, case 1486.

14. London Oratory, MS. vol. of 'Various memoranda . . .', p. 142f. (journal of Fr. Gordon, 26 July 1853); General Congregation, Minutes, 19 Aug. 1853.

15. E. Yates, 'Then and Now' (copy in Victoria and Albert Museum Library, MS. 86 HH Box 1).

16. London Oratory, General Congregation, Minutes, 7 Oct. 1853; MS. A/1/11: Kerr, *op. cit.*, June 1924, p. 541: *The Tablet*, 17 Dec. 1853, p. 803.

17. Information kindly supplied by Dr. J. M. Robinson.

18. *I.L.N.* 1 April 1854, p. 290.

19. *The Tablet*, 17 Dec. 1853, p. 803: *I.L.N.* 1 April 1854, p. 290.

20. London Oratory, Letters, vol. 30, no. 25.

21. *The Freehold Land Times, and Building News*, 15 Aug. 1854, p. 292.

22. London Oratory, Letters, vol. 20, no. 29.

23. *Ibid.*: *Survey of London*, vol. XXXVIII, 1975, pp. 56-7.

24. London Oratory, Congregation Minutes (1850-1900), 19 March 1853.

25. *Ibid.*; Auditor's Report Book 1851-64 (18 Feb. 1855).

26. Kerr, *op. cit.*, Nov. 1926, p. 208.

27. London Oratory, Letters, vol. 20, no. 32.

28. *Ibid.*; Auditor's Report Book 1851-64 (18 Feb. 1855).

29. *The Tablet*, 17 Dec. 1853, p. 803: *I.L.N.* 1 April 1854, p. 290: *British Almanac for 1855. Companion*, p. 220: London Oratory, Auditor's Report Book 1851-64 (18 Feb. 1855).

30. London Oratory, Fr. Kerr's annotated copy of 'The Oratory in London', vol. 1, p. 216; folder, 'New Church 1880-1884'.

31. *Ibid.*, General Congregation, Minutes, 7 Oct. 1857, 5 Jan. 1858: Kerr, *op. cit.*, Dec. 1924, pp. 661-2: *B.* 8 May, 24 July 1858, pp. 323, 501: *B.N.* 9 July, 17 Sept. 1858, pp. 696, 930 (where, on p. 696, the method of lifting the roof off is described).

32. O.S. sheet VI/100, 1862-7.

33. *The Architect*, 19 Jan. 1878, p. 34.

34. London Oratory, General Congregation, Minutes, 7 Oct. 1857.

35. *Ibid.*, 6 June, 23 Oct. 1871: R.I.B.A. Drawings Collection, J. H. Pollen, vol. II, pp. 69, 81, 83, 85, 87: Kerr, *op. cit.*, June 1926, p. 108: Anne Pollen, *John Hungerford Pollen*, 1912, p. 376.

36. London Oratory, General Congregation, Minutes, 24 May 1872: Kerr, *op. cit.*, June 1926, p. 108.

37. Kerr, *op. cit.*, Nov., Dec. 1926, pp. 209, 225: Arundel Castle Muniments, MS. 2082.

38. London Oratory, General Congregation, Minutes, 17 May 1875.

39. *Department of Science and Art, Directories*, 1870-5.

40. James Fergusson, *History of the Modern Styles of Architecture*, 2nd ed., 1873, vol. II, Appendix, pp. 569-74.

41. London Oratory, General Congregation, Minutes, 18 Oct. 1875.

42. *Ibid.*, Congregation of Deputies, Minutes, 4 June 1875.

43. *Ibid.*, MS. vol. of 'Various memoranda . . .', p. 220 (journal of Fr. Keogh): Kerr, *op. cit.*, Feb. 1927, p. 21.

44. London Oratory, Prefect of Edifices, Church Building Account: *The British Architect*, 25 May 1877, p. 316.

45. *B.N.* 3, 10 March 1876, pp. 218, 262.

46. Kerr, *op. cit.*, Feb. 1927, p. 22: *B.N.* 28 June 1878, p. 643: *B.* 18 May, 15 June 1872, pp. 396, 472: Boase: R.I.B.A. Library, WeS/1/10.

47. London Oratory, MS. vol., 'Various memoranda . . . ', p. 219 (journal of Fr. Keogh).

48. *Ibid.*, p. 379 (note by Fr. Kerr).

49. *Ibid.*, Congregation of Deputies, 12 Nov., 16, 21 Dec. 1877: Kerr, *op. cit.*, Feb. 1927, pp. 23-5: *The British Architect*, 25 Jan. 1878, p. 49.

50. London Oratory, *Instructions for Architects offering designs for the new Church of the Oratory*.

51. *Ibid.*, General Congregation, Minutes, 22 May 1878.

52. *Ibid.*, Report, 19 June 1878, in folder 'New Church 1880-1884'.

53. *Ibid.*, Gribble's explanation of his design, 1 May 1878, in folder 'New Church 1880-1884'.

54. *Ibid.*, General Congregation, Minutes, 24, 26 June 1878.

55. *The British Architect*, 28 June 1878, pp. 300-1: *The Architect*, 6, 13 July 1878, pp. 15, 27 (corresp.): *B.N.* 19 July, 9 Aug. 1878, pp. 69, 146-7 (corresp.): *B.* 27 July, 3 Aug. 1878, pp. 789 (corresp.), 817 (corresp.).

56. *The Architect*, 6, 13 July 1878, pp. 15, 27.

57. *The British Architect*, 28 June 1878, pp. 300-1: *B.N.* 28 June 1878, pp. 643-4: *B.* 29 June 1878, pp. 665-6.

58. *The British Architect*, 28 June 1878, pp. 300-1.

59. London Oratory, General Congregation, Minutes, 26, 27 June 1878: *B.* 29 June 1878, pp. 665-6.

60. London Oratory, General Congregation, Minutes, 25 Oct. 1878, 7 May 1879.

61. *Ibid.*, 2 Oct. 1878.

62. *B.N.* 2 May 1879. Cf. south elevation and cross-section by 'D.O.M.' in possession of the architects to the Oratory, Carden, Godfrey, MacFadyen and Sturgis.

63. London Oratory, General Congregation, Minutes, 25 June, 23 Sept. 1879.

64. *B.* 17 Feb. 1883, p. 225.

65. *Ibid.*: *B.N.* 12 Dec. 1879, p. 719.

66. London Oratory, Prefect of Edifices, Church Building Account (total to 31 Dec. 1885).

67. *Ibid.*, photograph album in Library, p. 23: Kerr, *op. cit.*, Sept. 1927, p. 159: information kindly supplied by Mr. E. R. C. Holland, H.M. Consul General at Alexandria.

68. London Oratory, MS. vol. of 'Various memoranda . . .', p. 222 (journal of Fr. Keogh).

69. Herbert Gribble, 'How I Built the Oratory' in *Merry England*, 1885, vol. V, p. 260.

70. *B.* 3 July 1880, p. 33.

71. *The Tablet*, 19, 26 April 1884, pp. 630, 645.

72. *B.* 17 Feb. 1883, p. 225.

73. *Ibid.*, 5 Jan. 1895, p. 13.

74. Gribble, *op. cit.*, pp. 260-72.

75. *B.N.* 2 May 1884, p. 692: *The Architect*, 13 Dec. 1894, p. 378: London Oratory, Specification of Works, 1879.

76. London Oratory, Specification of Works, 1879.

77. *B.N.* 30 Sept. 1881, p. 426.

78. Printed précis of Minutes of Science and Art Department, 13 Dec. 1886: 34th. *Report* of Department, 1887, p. xxvi.

79. *B.* 29 June 1878, p. 665.

80. Gribble, *op. cit.*, p. 272.

81. London Oratory, General Congregation, Minutes, 23 Dec. 1881, 5 Jan., 22 Feb. 1882; MS. vol. of 'Various memoranda . . .', p. 92 (journal of Fr. Gordon): *B.N.* 20 Jan., 3 March 1882, pp. 91, 283: *B.* 11 March 1882, p. 279; 22 Dec. 1894, p. 458.

82. London Oratory, General Congregation, Minutes, 20 May 1885.

83. *Ibid.*, memorandum by J. H. Pollen, May 1885, in folder, 'New Church 1880-1884': R.I.B.A. Drawings Collection, J. H. Pollen, vol. II, pp. 81, 85, 87.

84. London Oratory, General Congregation, Minutes, 20 Jan., 16 May, 27 June 1888 *et seq.*: Fr. E. Kilburn, *A Walk Round the Church of the London Oratory*, 1980 ed., p. 19.

85. London Oratory, General Congregation, Minutes, 28 May, 3 June, 10 Dec. 1890.

86. *Ibid.*, General Congregation, Minutes, 3 July, 15 Aug., 22, 29 Dec. 1891, 4 May 1892.

87. *Ibid.*, Congregation of Deputies, Minutes, 14 Aug. 1893; General Congregation, Minutes, 31 Oct. 1893; elevation signed by Gribble, n.d.; elevation signed by Shaw, Sept. 1893: *Guide to the Oratory*, ed. H. S. Bowden, 1893, p. 3: *R.I.B.A. Journal*, 3rd. series, vol. II, Dec. 1894, p. 128.

88. Arundel Castle Muniments, C 591.

89. London Oratory, Prefect of Edifices, Church Building Account.

90. *Ibid.*, General Congregation, Minutes, 10 June, 23 Nov. 1896, 28 April, 13 Oct. 1897: D.S.R. 1891/57.

91. K.P.L., applications to Vestry from L.C.C., no. 693.

92. Gribble, *op. cit.*, pp. 268-9: London Oratory, Gribble to Fr. Gordon, 20 Sept. 1882, 21 March 1883 in folder, 'New Church 1880-1884'.

93. Kilburn, *op. cit.*, p. 11.

94. London Oratory, General Congregation, Minutes, 4 July 1894; elevation by Sherrin, 1894.

95. ' "Architects I have known": The Architectural Career of S. D. Adshead', ed. Alan Powers, in *Architectural History*, vol. 24, 1981, pp. 110-11.

96. London Oratory, General Congregation, Minutes, 30 Oct. 1895: *The Times*, 16 July 1896.

97. London Oratory, General Congregation, Minutes, 4, 18 Jan. 1911; plans and elevations by Stokes, Oct. 1910, April 1911: *B.* 10 Dec. 1910, p. 719.

98. London Oratory, General Congregation, Minutes, 27 April 1910: Kerr, *op. cit.*, May, June 1925, pp. 85, 101.

99. Information kindly supplied by the Fathers of the Oratory.

100. *B.* 15 March 1884, pp. 386-7.

101. In possession of the London Oratory.

102. London Oratory, General Congregation, Minutes, 5 June 1895: Kilburn, *op. cit.*, p. 14: V. Suboff, 'Giuseppe

Mazzuoli' in *Jahrbuch der Preussischen Kunstsammlungen*, vol. 49, 1928, pp. 37, 47.

103. London Oratory, General Congregation, Minutes, 30 Sept. 1884, 15 June 1885, 1 July 1889, 7 May 1890: *Guide*, 1893, *ut supra*, *passim*.

104. London Oratory, General Congregation, Minutes, 19 Oct. 1927 to Oct. 1932; memorandum by Fr. Superior in MS. vol. of 'Various memoranda...', pp. 300-5; typescript by Formilli in folder 'New Church 1880-1884'; coloured photograph of Formilli's perspective (proposed): *Who Was Who 1941-50*: P.O.D.

105. *Oratory Parish Magazine*, Sept. 1928, p. 179.

106. London Oratory, Gribble's explanation of his competition design, 1 May 1878, in folder 'New Church 1880-1884'; General Congregation, Minutes, 19 May 1879.

107. Unless otherwise stated the information is taken from the 1980 edition of Fr. Kilburn's *A Walk Round the Church of the London Oratory*.

108. London Oratory, design by Webb, Oct. 1935.

109. Drawing by Scoles in possession of Carden, Godfrey, Macfadyen and Sturgis.

110. *The Tablet*, 19 April 1884, p. 630.

111. London Oratory, General Congregation, Minutes, 20 Oct. 1897, 14 Dec. 1898: R.I.B.A. Drawings Collection, U/6.

112. London Oratory, letters, vol. 18, no. 41; Fr. Kerr's annotated copy of 'The Oratory in London', vol. 1, p. 214: Thieme u. Becker, *Lexikon...*, vol. XXXII (1938).

113. *B.N.* 19 May 1882, p. 615.

114. London Oratory, General Congregation, Minutes, 25 June, 2 July 1890; estimate, n.d., in folder 'New Church 1880-1884': *Guide*, 1893, *ut supra*, p. 23.

115. London Oratory, General Congregation, Minutes, 26 Jan. 1927.

116. *Ibid.*, 25 May, 2 Oct. 1901; MS. A/6/12.

117. *Guide*, 1893, *ut supra*, p. 27.

118. London Oratory, General Congregation, Minutes, 22 April 1885.

119. *Ibid.*, 20 Jan., 16 May, 27 June 1888 *et seq.*

120. *Ibid.*, 23 Jan. 1924, 29 April 1925: *Oratory Parish Magazine*, 1927, p. 50.

121. J. Mordaunt Crook, *William Burges*, 1981, p. 396, note 30: London Oratory, MS. vol. of 'Various memoranda...', p. 221 (journal of Fr. Keogh)

122. London Oratory, MS. vol. of 'Various memoranda...', p. 375 (notes by Fr. Keogh): *The Tablet*, 5 April 1884, p. 551: information and photographs kindly supplied by Dr. A. H. Jenniskens of the Gemeentelijke Archiefdienst Maastricht: F. X. De Feller, *Itinéraire ou voyages...*, Liège, 1820, vol. 2, p. 176.

123. *Guide*, *ut supra*, 1893, p. 55.

124. London Oratory, General Congregation, Minutes, 30 Sept. 1884.

125. *Ibid.*, drawings by D. Stokes, Aug. 1936.

126. *Ibid.*, General Congregation, Minutes, 12 Nov. 1879; MS. vol. of 'Various memoranda...', p. 223 (journal of Fr. Keogh): *B.* 15 March 1884, pp. 386-7.

127. Kerr, *op. cit.*, May 1927, p. 79.

128. G. B. Carboni, *Le Pitture e Sculture di Brescia*, 1760, p. 89: Carmela Tua, 'Orazio Marinali e i suoi fratelli', in *Rivista D'Arte*, vol. XVII, 1935, p. 310.

129. Carboni, *op. et loc. cit.*: Thieme u. Becker, *Lexikon...*, vol. XXIX (1935): C. Semenzato, *La Scultura Veneta Del Seicento e Del Settecento*, 1966, p. 89: Kilburn, *op. cit.*, p. 24.

130. Carboni, *op. et loc. cit.*: Kilburn, *op. cit.*, p. 24.

131. *The Times*, 26 April 1884: *Guide*, *ut supra*, 1893, p. 66: P.O.D.

132. *B.N.* 12 Oct. 1883, p. 586: *B.* 15 March 1884, pp. 386-7.

133. *Oratory Parish Magazine*, Sept. 1970, p. 2.

134. London Oratory, General Congregation, Minutes, 9 Oct. 1918: *Oratory Parish Magazine*, March - Dec. 1921.

135. H. M. Gillett, *The Story of the London Oratory Church*, 1934, p. 50.

136. Information kindly supplied by Fr. Manus P. Keane, S.J.

CHAPTER V (pp. 58-86)
The Alexander Estate

1. A.E.P., box 3, bundle 15, deed of settlement, 28 Sept. 1830.

2. Dorothy Stroud, *The Thurloe Estate South Kensington, an account of its origins and development*, 1965 ed., pp. 5-6.

3. *Survey of London*, vol. XXXVIII, 1975, p. 8.

4. List of possessions of Sir William Blake at his death, in extra-illustrated copy of Faulkner in B.L. (pressmark L.R.271.c.3), between pp. 440 and 441.

5. A.E.P., box 3, bundle 15, copy of will of Anna Maria Brace.

6. *Ibid.*, box 3, bundle 15, copy of will of Harris Thurloe Brace.

7. *Survey of London*, vol. XXXVIII, 1975, pp. 10-11: Stroud, *op. cit.*, p. 28.

8. A.E.P., box 1, bundle 16, land tax redemption contract, 22 June 1799.

9. John H. Harvey, 'The Nurseries on Milne's Land-Use Map', in *Transactions of the London and Middlesex Archaeological Society*, vol. 24, 1973, p. 186.

10. K.P.L., MS. 1040.

11. John H. Harvey, *op. et loc. cit.*: K.P.L., MS. 94: G.L.R.O., B/HRS/44, 49.

12. G.L.R.O., B/HRS/51.

13. *Ibid.*, B/HRS/40.

14. Peregrine Bingham, *New Cases in The Court of Common Pleas*, vol. IV, 1838, pp. 799-800.

15. P.R.O., B4/45, H148.

16. R.B.

17. M.D.R. 1786/1/461.

18. A.E.P., box 2, bundle 13, sale particulars of 1808; lease and release of 4/5 Oct. 1808: M.D.R. 1808/9/696.

19. G.L.R.O., MR/LV *passim*: M.D.R. 1747/2/545; 1749/1/103-4; 1758/3/610; 1786/1/461.

20. Guildhall Library, MS. 8674/5, p. 244, no. 16290: G.L.R.O., MR/LV/3/95; 5/17: G.L.R.O., MR/LV *passim*: K.P.L., MS. 94.

21. Stroud, *op. cit.*, pp. 11-12.

22. K.P.L., Kensington Turnpike Trust, Committee Minutes, 28 June 1824: A.E.P., box 2, bundle 13, lease of 22 Dec. 1825: M.D.R. 1825/10/77.

23. *The Land and Building News*, 1 Sept. 1855, p. 1071: Colvin.

24. A.E.P., box 2, bundle 13, lease of 4 Feb. 1856; agreement of 28 July 1879: M.D.R. 1856/2/601: *The Land and Building News*, 1 Sept. 1855, p. 1071: *B.* 20 Sept. 1879, p. 1065.

25. *B.* 3 Oct. 1874, p. 828.

26. *Ibid.* (illus.): K.P.L., watercolour of Hoop and Toy by T. H. Shepherd.

27. R.B.: G.L.R.O., MR/LV/7/46; MR/LV, 1760-75 *passim*.

28. A.E.P., box 1, bundle 1, agreement of 9 July and lease of 31 Dec. 1844.
29. Bingham, *op. et loc. cit.*: A.E.P., box 1, bundle 17, agreement of 14 June 1826.
30. P.R.O., HO 107/690/10, f. 59.
31. Chelsea Library, Hans Town ratebook, June 1806; parish ratebook, Midsummer 1806.
32. M.D.R. 1809/2/11; 1810/2/656, 715; 1810/5/706-7; 1810/6/116, 839; 1810/8/7, 457.
33. Chelsea Library, Hans Town ratebook, June 1810.
34. *Holden's Triennial Directory*, 1816-17.
35. M.D.R. 1820/2/326; 1820/3/54-5; 1821/1/395; 1821/2/216.
36. *Ibid.*, 1825/7/86-7: R.B.
37. P.R.O., B4/51, B15: G.L.R.O., KBG 12, pp. 318-19.
38. P.R.O., B4/51, B389.
39. K.P.L., Kensington Turnpike Trust, Committee Minutes, 28 June 1824: *Underhill's Triennial Directory*, 1822-24.
40. A.E.P., box 2, bundle 7, lease of 25 May of No. 1 Alexander Sq.
41. *Ibid.*, box 1, bundle 17, agreement of 14 June 1826: Bingham, *op. cit.*, pp. 800, 806: M.D.R. 1836/1/347.
42. M.D.R. 1830/1/201; 1833/5/1.
43. This and the following paragraphs are based on the building agreement, A.E.P., box 1, bundle 17, agreement of 14 June 1826.
44. Ashley Barker, 'Nineteenth century estate development in South Kensington' in the *Annual Report* of The Kensington Society, 1967, p. 25: Stroud, *op. cit.*, p. 14.
45. W.C.S. 182, pp. 36, 114-15.
46. A.E.P., box 3, bundle 11, lease of 11 Jan. 1827.
47. *Ibid.*, box 3, bundle 11, lease of 7 April 1827; agreement of 19 Dec. 1863: P.R.O., HO 107/690/10, f. 47: R.B.
48. A.E.P., box 3, bundle 11, leases of 13 Feb., 25 April 1827.
49. *Ibid.*, box 3, bundle 11, leases of 13 Feb., 12 April 1827: M.D.R. 1827/2/128, 165: P.R.O., HO 107/690/10, f. 48.
50. M.D.R. 1828/1/695-6.
51. *Survey of London*, vol. XL, 1980, p. 66.
52. M.D.R. 1828/7/95; 1830/8/463.
53. A.E.P., box 3, bundle 8, lease of 13 Aug. 1830.
54. M.D.R. 1828/7/31.
55. A.E.P., box 2, bundle 7, leases of 25 May, 14 July, 1 Sept., 18 Oct. 1827.
56. *Ibid.*, box 3, bundle 8, lease of 19 Sept. 1827: Anthony King, 'Architectural journalism and the profession: the early years of George Godwin', in *Architectural History*, vol. 19, 1976, p. 35.
57. *P.O.D.*
58. King, *op. cit.*, p. 35: M.D.R. 1889/31/262-3: *P.O.D.*
59. P.R.O., HO 107/1469, f. 282.
60. H.B. file 2881.
61. M.D.R. 1827/8/295, 339; 1828/1/693.
62. *Ibid.*, 1827/8/339; 1828/1/693.
63. *Ibid.*, 1828/4/390; 1828/7/704, 705, 720; 1828/9/119; 1829/7/147; 1830/1/188: R.B.
64. A.E.P., box 1, bundle 11, leases etc. of No. 19: Hertfordshire R.O., D/E Lt/T105, leases etc. of No. 18.
65. Hertfordshire R.O., D/E Lt/T105, sale particulars of No. 18, 1854.
66. M.D.R. 1828/9/119.
67. *Ibid.*, 1830/1/201.
68. *Ibid.*, 1830/6/101-2; 1830/9/404-5.
69. *Ibid.*, 1830/7/540; 1831/5/633; 1831/7/112; 1832/8/273.
70. *Ibid.*, 1828/9/119; 1830/1/201.
71. *Ibid.*, 1831/5/4-6; 1831/8/592; 1832/2/471-2; 1832/5/438; 1832/7/731: R.B.
72. M.D.R. 1831/8/592; 1832/2/473: R.B.
73. Surrey R.O., 367/11/2, pp. 265-6
74. Stroud, *op. cit.*, pp. 16-17.
75. M.D.R. 1832/7/631: R.B.
76. A.E.P., box 2, bundle 11, lease of 9 Sept. 1833: M.D.R. 1833/6/572-3.
77. R.B.: M.D.R. 1834/4/600; 1834/6/451.
78. M.D.R. 1833/3/566; 1833/7/635.
79. *Ibid.*, 1833/3/566: R.B.
80. R.B.: P.R.O., HO 107/690/10, f. 49.
81. M.D.R. 1833/5/1; 1834/7/40; 1834/8/269; 1835/3/449.
82. *B.* 25 May 1861, p. 359: *P.O.D.*
83. P.R.O., HO 107/690/10, ff. 47-53.
84. W. Carew Hazlitt, *The Hazlitts, Part the Second*, 1912, p. 22.
85. P.R.O., HO 107/690/10, f. 52: R.B.
86. *P.O.D.*: Algernon Graves, *The Royal Academy of Arts: A Complete Dictionary of Contributors . . . 1769 to 1904*, 1905-6, *sub* Gribble.
87. P.R.O., HO 107/1469, f. 283.
88. R.B.: T. C. Croker, *A Walk from London to Fulham*, 1860, pp. 73-4.
89. Bingham, *op. cit.* pp. 799-800, 807.
90. M.D.R. 1828/9/119; 1836/1/686: R.B.
91. Malcolm Seaborne, *The English School, its architecture and organization, 1370 - 1870*, 1971, pp. 182-3: Brian Simon, *The Two Nations and the Educational Structure 1780 - 1870*, 1974, p. 115.
92. *The Morning Post*, 19 June 1835, p. 3.
93. *Ibid.*: Rules of the Western Grammar School, Brompton, [n.d.], copy in B. L., pressmark 8304.bbb.1.(1): W. W. Pocock, *In Memoriam William Fuller Pocock*, p. 36: M.D.R. 1827/7/732; 1828/9/119.
94. *The Quarterly Journal of Education*, vol. IV, no. VII, 1832, p. 183: Rules of the Western Grammar School, ut supra.
95. *The Times*, 13 Feb. 1838, p. 7.
96. Rules of the Western Grammar School, Brompton, ut supra, and 1831 ed. with mss. alterations in archives of King's College, London: King's College, letters "W" 1833-7; Council Minute Books, 1829-36.
97. Rules of the Western Grammar School, Brompton, 1831 ed., *ut supra*.
98. Bingham, *op. cit.* pp. 799-813: *The Law Journal Reports for 1839*, n.s. VIII/I, pp. 53-9.
99. M.D.R. 1839/8/425.
100. R.B.: W. T. Whitley, *The Baptists of London*, [*c.* 1929], p. 163, no. 161: P.R.O., HO 107/690/10, f. 49.
101. P.R.O., RG 9/21, f. 48.
102. Seaborne, *op. cit.*, p. 137: B.A. 58936.
103. *P.O.D.* and local directories: P.P.R., index to wills 1917 *sub* Huelin: General Register Office, Death Registers, Dec. 1917; *The Architectural Review*, vol. LV, 1924, p. 86.
104. W.C.S. 79, pp. 66-7.
105. *Ibid.*, P38/1209: H.L.R.O., Minutes of evidence to Select Committee of the House of Lords on Metropolitan Railway (Notting Hill-Brompton Extension) Act, 1864, p. 144.
106. *B.* 21 Nov. 1846, p. 553.
107. M.D.R. 1842/8/479: A.E.P., 3/12, leases of 13-15 Thurloe Place, 30 Nov. 1842, 29 May 1843.
108. *P.O.D.*: M.D.R. 1839/5/511-12; 1841/1/22-5.

109. *Survey of London*, vol. xxxvii, 1973, p. 296: Day Estate Papers, articles of agreement, 14 June 1845.
110. M.D.R. 1841/1/792: P.R.O., C14/1065/W12: P.R.O., HO 107/690/10, f. 50; HO 107/1469, f. 272.
111. P.R.O., B4/51, G90, H131.
112. P.R.O., HO 107/1480, f. 832; PROB 11/2139, ff. 194-5.
113. *Ibid.*, HO 107/1472, f. 133: D.S.R. 1851/74-7, 351-4.
114. A.E.P., box 3, bundle 14, leases of 20 Feb., 24 Dec. 1841, 31 Jan. 1842, 30 Jan. 1843; box 1, bundle 11, lease of 25 Nov. 1840: *P.O.D.*: W.C.S. 80, pp. 331-2.
115. A.E.P., box 3, bundle 14, leases of 25 Nov. 1840, 24, 27 Dec. 1841: M.D.R. 1841/2/557-8; 1841/5/733, 735; 1842/2/273, 275.
116. M.D.R. 1842/2/338.
117. W.C.S. 82, p. 373.
118. A.E.P., box 3, bundle 14, lease of 31 Jan. 1843: M.D.R. 1842/3/811; 1844/4/242-3: P.R.O., PROB 11/1983,ff. 367-8: General Register Office, Death Registers, July-Sept. 1843.
119. A.E.P., box 2, bundle 11, lease of 9 Oct. 1841; box 3, bundle 14, lease of 1 March 1844.
120. W.C.S. 79, p. 155.
121. A.E.P., box 2, bundle 6, leases of 3 Dec. 1840, 15 Feb., 8 March, 7 Aug. 1841; box 2, bundle 6, assignment of 24 March 1888; box 3, bundle 11, leases of 30 Oct., 10 Nov. 1841: M.D.R. 1841/7/995.
122. A.E.P., box 2, bundle 6, leases of 21 June, 30 Oct. 1841, 15 Feb. 1842.
123. *Ibid.*, box 2, bundle 6, leases of 15 Jan., 10 Feb. 1842.
124. R.B.: P.R.O., HO 107/1469, f. 286.
125. A.E.P., box 1, bundle 11, lease and memo of 30 Nov. 1842.
126. *Diagrams of the Parish of St. Mary Abbotts*, 1847, p. 173.
127. M.D.R. 1850/11/608-9.
128. *B*. 25 Oct. 1845, p. 511.
129. M.D.R. 1841/7/11; 1843/5/43-4, 48, 51, 53, 56.
130. *Ibid.*, 1841/7/12; 1842/5/105, 107; 1842/5/353; 1842/8/136, 138, 140-1; 1843/7/464.
131. *Ibid.*, 1841/7/13; 1842/5/106, 108, 354; 1842/8/137, 139, 142; 1843/7/465.
132. *Ibid.*, 1842/1/893; 1842/6/135; 1843/4/597.
133. A.E.P., box 3, bundle 13, lease of 12 May 1843.
134. M.D.R. 1843/7/591; 1844/4/269 (recital), 270-1; 1845/4/75, 116; 1846/4/387-9: A.E.P., box 3, bundle 13, leases of 3 Aug. 1843, 18 April, 17 Dec. 1844, 10 March 1845.
135. A.E.P., box 3, bundle 13, leases of 11 Feb., 12 May, 28 Aug. 1843, 5 Dec. 1844.
136. *Ibid.*, box 3, bundle 13, leases of 21 Dec. 1843, 1 March, 31 Aug. 1844, 22 Sept. 1845, 25 May 1846.
137. *B*. 4 Nov. 1843, p. 475.
138. W.C.S. 82, pp. 493-4.
139. A.E.P., box 3, bundle 13, leases of 20 Jan., 7 Sept. 1844, 19 April 1845: R.B.
140. A.E.P., box 3, bundle 13, lease of 29 Sept. 1845.
141. D.S.R. 1845/143.
142. A.E.P., box 3, bundle 13, lease of 7 Jan. 1846.
143. M.D.R. 1843/6/956-7; 1843/8/427-8; 1844/4/957-9; 1844/5/916, 921; 1844/6/682; 1844/8/126-7; 1845/1/920: W.C.S. 82, p. 219.
144. Cf. photographs of 1856, Plate 43b, and *c*. 1861, Victoria and Albert Museum, Guard Books, no. 2428, reproduced in *Survey of London*, vol. xxxviii, 1975, Plate 7a.
145. Victoria and Albert Museum, Guard Books, no. 9770,

146. P.R.O., HO 107/1469, ff. 268-77.
147. A.E.P., box 3, bundle 13, assignment of 27 Oct. 1845 endorsed on lease of 20 Jan. 1844.
148. *Ibid.*, box 3, bundle 13, letter of H. B. Alexander to Mrs. Smith, 18 June 1846, attached to lease of 20 Jan. 1844.
149. R.B.: *D.N.B.*
150. *D.N.B.*
151. *P.O.D.*: *B*. 2 Nov. 1872, p. 860.
152. Victoria and Albert Museum Library, Sir Henry Cole's diary, 18 Nov., 22 Dec. 1873, June 1874: *Survey of London*, vol. xxxviii, 1975, p. 115: *P.O.D.*
153. A.E.P., box 3, bundle 12, leases of 7, 30 Nov. 1842, 29 May 1843: M.D.R. 1842/8/479: R.B.
154. A.E.P., box 3, bundle 12, assignments of 6 May and 1 July 1843 endorsed on leases of 30 Nov. 1842: P.R.O., HO 107/1469, f. 267.
155. See photograph of construction of the South Kensington Museum, April 1856, in Victoria and Albert Museum, neg. no. 80119.
156. A.E.P., box 3, bundle 12, lease of 10 July 1843: R.B.
157. O.S. sheet VI/100, cf. eds. publ. 1872 and 1895: *Twenty-Third Annual Report of Kensington Vestry*, 1878-9, pp. 55-6.
158. A.E.P., box 3, bundle 12, leases of 10 July, 7 Oct. 1843: M.D.R. 1843/8/24-5; 1843/9/449-50; 1844/2/154-7.
159. D.S.R. 1846/353-8: M.D.R. 1847/7/266; 1847/5/150-2.
160. R.B.: P.R.O., HO 107/1469, f. 278: Allan J. Hook, *Life of James Clarke Hook, R.A.*, vol. 1, 1929, p. 76.
161. *B*. 21 Nov. 1846, p. 553: H.L.R.O., Minutes of evidence to Select Committee of the House of Lords on Metropolitan Railway (Notting Hill-Brompton Extension) Act, 1864, p. 146.
162. M.B.W. 213, presented papers for meeting of 4 Feb. 1856.
163. *Ibid.*: D.S.R. 1846/353-8: A.E.P., box 3, bundle 12, leases of 4 June 1847: R.B.: P.R.O., HO 107/1469, f. 278.
164. W.C.S. 84, p. 76.
165. R.B.: K.P.L., valuation note books, 1880-1, Alfred Place West.
166. D.S.R. 1845/275-80, 347-9: M.D.R. 1845/11/492-5; 1846/2/773, 968-70; 1846/6/525-6; 1846/7/946.
167. R.B.: *P.O.D.*: P.R.O., HO 107/1469, f. 287: *The Diaries of Lewis Carroll*, ed. Roger L. Green, 1953, p. 35 and *passim*: *The Times*, 23 Jan. 1982, p. 9: *D.N.B.*
168. M.D.R. 1846/2/522-3, 773-8; 1846/6/391, 524: R.B.
169. M.D.R. 1846/9/721-4; 1847/6/307; 1848/8/903.
170. *Ibid.*, 1845/2/120-2: A.E.P., box 3, bundle 11, leases of 23 Jan., 2 May 1845: R.B.
171. R.B.: P.R.O., HO 107/1469, f. 288: *D.N.B.*
172. M.D.R. 1846/4/449-54; 1846/6/14: R.B.
173. D.S.R. 1846/144-9: A.E.P., box 3, bundle 11, leases of 29 Aug., 21 Sept., 7 Dec. 1846: M.D.R. 1846/9/678.
174. M.D.R. 1846/12/268-73.
175. A.E.P., box 3, bundle 11, assignment of 31 Dec. 1846.
176. This and the following paragraphs are based on the accounts published in *B*. 21 Nov. 1846, pp. 553-4, and *I.L.N.* 21 Nov. 1846, p. 330: *The Times*, 11 Nov. 1847, p. 6f.
177. P.R.O., B4/51, H131: A.E.P., box 3, bundle 11, leases of 13 Dec. 1847: M.D.R. 1847/12/184; 1851/3/272: R.B.
178. *The Times*, 11 Nov. 1847, p. 6f.
179. R.B.: P.R.O., HO 107/1469, ff. 289-92.
180. R.B.: P.R.O., RG 9/21, f. 71: *P.O.D.*: Arundel Castle

Manuscripts, 15th Duke's Corresp., letter of J. S. Hansom, 5 July 1888.

181. 27 & 28 Vict., c. 291, local and personal: 27 & 28 Vict., c. 321, local and personal; C. Baker, *The Metropolitan Railway*, 1951, p. 9: John R. Day, *The Story of London's Underground*, 1963, pp. 20-22: Charles E. Lee, *100 Years of the District*, 1968, pp. 8, 10.

182. H.L.R.O., Minutes of evidence to Select Committee of the House of Lords on Metropolitan Railway (Notting Hill-Brompton Extension) Act, 1864, pp. 110, 177: *Survey of London*, vol. XXXVIII, 1975, p. 65.

183. H.L.R.O., Minutes of evidence to Select Committee, *ut supra*, pp. 149-50.

184. *Survey of London*, vol. XXXVIII, 1975, p. 65: H.L.R.O., Minutes of evidence to Select Committee, *ut supra*, p. 118.

185. A.E.P., plan of property sold for the railways; box 2, bundle 16, conveyance of Nos. 1-11 Thurloe Sq.: M.D.R. 1870/5/1042.

186. 27 & 28 Vict., c. 321, local and personal, clause 23.

187. A.E.P., box 2, bundle 16, conveyance of Nos. 1-11 Thurloe Sq.

188. *B.N.* 26 Jan. 1866, p. 57: *B.* 27 Jan. 1866, p. 68.

189. *B.* 27 Jan. 1866, p. 68.

190. Plans of South Ken. Stn. in possession of London Transport, D/109.

191. G.L.R.O., MDR 1/1, March 1867, March 1868: plans of South Ken. Stn. in possession of London Transport, D/109: John R. Day, *The Story of London's Underground*, 1963, p. 21.

192. Charles E. Lee, *The Metropolitan District Railway*, 1956, p. 3.

193. *B.N.* 24 March 1871, p. 237: G.L.R.O., MDR 1/2, March 1871: Lee, *op. cit.*, 1956, p. 5.

194. M.B.W., file 27519.

195. Alan A. Jackson and Desmond F. Croome, *Rails Through the Clay*, 1962, pp. 42, 71, 72, 108, 114.

196. Plans of South Ken. Stn. in possession of London Transport, D/109: *R.I.B.A. Journal*, 3rd series, vol. XVII, p. 176: *B.* 18 Dec. 1909, p. 678: *P.O.D.*

197. Stroud, *op. cit.*, p. 26n.

198. M.B.W., file 27519: D.S.R. 1880/104-8, 234-6: M.D.R. 1881/17/785-9; 1881/24/882-4.

199. M.D.R. 1889/31/261: *B.* 29 Sept. 1888, p. 240: D.S.R. 1888/261.

200. D.S.R. 1885/53, 'in progress' until March 1887.

201. K.P.L., applications to Vestry from M.B.W., no. 375.

202. M.D.R. 1870/5/1042.

203. H.L.R.O., Minutes of evidence to Select Committee of the House of Lords on Metropolitan Railway (Notting Hill-Brompton Extension) Act, 1864, pp. 10-11, 99.

204. O.S. sheet VI/100, 1872: M.B.W., file 22098.

205. K.P.L., applications to Vestry from M.B.W., no. 8.

206. L.C.C. Minutes, 15 Jan., 2 April 1895, pp. 11, 15, 306.

207. K.P.L., applications to Vestry from M.B.W., no. 8 : M.B.W., file 22098: *P.O.D.*

208. M.B.W., file 22098: M.B.W. Minutes 2 Feb. 1877, p. 206.

209. K.P.L., postcard no. 702.

210. *Ibid.*, applications to Vestry from M.B.W., no. 351: D.S.R. 1883/218-20.

211. L.C.C. Minutes, 2 June 1891, p. 565: *P.O.D.*

212. B.A. 28926.

213. P.R.O., BT31/16905/75129: T. C. Barker and Michael Robbins, *A History of London Transport*, vol. II, 1974, pp. 70-4 *passim*.

214. K.P.L., oversize sequence, KQ 173-197.

215. B.A. 36111: D.S.R. 1910/255.

216. B.A. 36111: D.S.R. 1922/877.

217. O.S. sheet VI/100, 1894-6: *23rd Annual Report of the Kensington Vestry*, 1878-9, p. 55: H.B., Report on Cabmen's Shelters, 6 June 1973.

218. B.A. 28926: D.S.R. 1910/24; 1915/69.

219. B.A. 53009: D.S.R. 1926/211, 334.

220. P.R.O., BT31/16905/75129.

221. Nigel Playfair, *Hammersmith Hoy*, 1930, p. 241.

222. A.E.P., box 3, bundle 12, leases of 10 July, 30 Nov. 1843: *P.O.D.*

223. Nigel Playfair, *op. cit.*, p. 242.

224. *Ibid.*: Giles Playfair, *My Father's Son*, 1937, pp. 16, 55.

225. *The Architectural Review*, vol. LV, 1924, pp. 86-9; vol. LX, 1926, pp. 252-3: *The Architect's Journal*, 3 Feb. 1926, pp. 212-13.

226. Giles Playfair, *op. cit.*, p. 55.

227. D.S.R. 1922/423-5.

228. Giles Playfair, *op. cit.*, p. 17.

229. *The Architectural Review*, vol. LV, 1924, pp. 86-9.

230. Giles Playfair, *op. cit.*, p. 56: Nigel Playfair, *op. cit.*, p. 241.

231. B.A. 58936.

232. Kensington Borough Council Minutes, Nov. 1926-Nov. 1927, p. 418.

233. A.E.P., box 2, bundle 12, agreement of 14 March 1927: D.S.R. 1927/289, 327-9, 967-9: *P.O.D.*

234. A.E.P., box 3, bundle 13, leases of 1 May 1848, 12 June 1858.

235. D.S.R. 1927/206.

236. B.A. 58936: General Register Office, Index to Consular Deaths 1926-30, *sub* Selby.

237. *The Architect and Building News*, 8 Jan. 1932, pp. 78-82: *Architecture Illustrated*, July 1931, pp. 12-14: David Braithwaite, *Building in the Blood*, 1981, appendix 1 (1928); D.S.R. 1928/329.

238. *P.O.D.*: *Who Was Who, 1929-1940.*

239. W. T. Whitley, *The Baptists of London*, [c. 1929], p. 163, no. 161: R.B.

240. P.R.O., HO 129/1, no. 34.

241. *B.* 20 Dec. 1856, p. 682.

242. P.R.O., RG 9/21, f. 48.

243. *P.O.D.*: Kitty Shannon, *For My Children*, 1933, p. 15.

244. D.S.R. 1929/339: copy of lease of 29 Dec. 1929 in possession of present occupant: *P.O.D.*

245. 'No. 14 Alexander Place, Thurloe Square, . . .', in *Country Life*, 26 April 1930, pp. 619-20.

246. A.E.P., box 1, bundle 1, lease of 18 May 1926 to Huggins and Co.: B.A. 57383: B.R. 100077: D.S.R. 1927/311.

247. B.A. 57383.

248. A.E.P., box 3, bundle 13, lease of 30 Sept. 1844.

249. B.A. 86677.

CHAPTER VI (pp. 87-129)

The Smith's Charity Estate

1. *Survey of London*, vol. XXXVIII, 1975, pp. 15, 55-6.

2. William Bray, *Collections Relating to Henry Smith Esq. Some Time Alderman of London; The Estates by him given to charitable uses; and the Trustees appointed by him*, 1800: Joseph Gwilt, *Evidences relating to the Estate of Henry Smith Esquire*, 1828:

Charles Perkins Gwilt, *Notices relating to Thomas Smith of Campden, and to Henry Smith, sometime Alderman of London*, 1836: Dorothy Stroud, *The South Kensington Estate of Henry Smith's Charity: Its History and Development*, 1975, pp. 5-12.

3. P.R.O., PROB 11/153/1.
4. 12 Geo. III, c. 90, private.
5. Charity Commissioners, file 230102.
6. P.R.O., C54/3995, nos. 3-4.
7. E.C.R., 12 July 1664.
8. Faulkner, p. 432.
9. Inquisition post mortem in P.R.O., C142/480/114, transcribed in extra-illustrated Faulkner in B.L. (pressmark L.R.271.c.3), between pp. 440 and 441.
10. P.R.O., PROB 11/338/43.
11. *Ibid.*, PROB 11/501/111.
12. *Ibid.*, C33/550, ff. 1151-5.
13. M.D.R. 1749/3/348-9: *Survey of London*, vol. XXXVIII, 1975, pp. 17-18.
14. P.R.O., C33/550, ff. 1151-5: M.D.R. 1760/4/464.
15. P.R.O., C33/550, ff. 1151-5: R.B.
16. M.D.R. 1785/3/266; 1785/5/207.
17. Colvin: *Survey of London*, vol. XXIX, 1960, pp. 231-41.
18. K.P.L., MS. 144: M.D.R. 1789/2/334-5; 1789/6/320-3; 1790/1/490-1; 1790/5/370-1.
19. M.D.R. 1793/5/800; 1796/2/326.
20. K.P.L., MS. 5023.
21. M.D.R. 1796/3/400.
22. T. C. Croker, *A Walk From London to Fulham*, 1860, p. 50.
23. R.B.
24. Croker, *op. cit.*, p. 67.
25. M.D.R. 1789/2/333-4; 1789/6/320, 322; 1790/1/490; 1790/5/370.
26. P.R.O., B4/23, C205.
27. M.D.R. 1790/9/202; 1790/10/278; 1792/1/800.
28. *Ibid.*, 1790/10/275; 1791/1/180; 1791/3/356; 1792/1/795; 1793/2/603-4.
29. *Ibid.*, 1787/5/65; 1790/2/141; 1805/4/233.
30. *Ibid.*, 1792/3/722; 1792/4/480: *The World*, 31 Jan., 7 Feb. 1793: R.B.
31. M.D.R. 1793/5/749-66: R.B.
32. M.D.R. 1802/5/564-6: R.B.
33. Anna Sutton, *A Story of Sidmouth*, 1959, p. 23.
34. P.R.O., PROB 11/1259/269.
35. M.D.R. 1796/2/326: R.B.
36. M.D.R. 1813/4/204.
37. *D.N.B.*
38. M.D.R. 1803/5/485.
39. *D.N.B.*: R.B.: Surrey R.O., 367/7/35, 38, 54 (2 March 1831): Osbert Wyndham Hewett, *Strawberry Fair: A Biography of Frances, Countess Waldegrave 1821-1879*, 1956, p. 6: Barry Duncan, *The St. James's Theatre. Its Strange and Complete History*, 1964, p. 67.
40. P.R.O., C13/2401, Atty. Gen. v. Griffith; C33/550, ff. 1151-5.
41. *Ibid.*, PROB 11/1403/25; C13/2406, Atty. Gen. v. Griffith.
42. Report appended to William Bray, *Collections, ut supra* (ref. 2) in G.L.C., Greater London History Library (pressmark 20.29 SMI), pp. 6-7.
43. John H. Harvey, 'The Nurseries on Milne's Land-Use Map' in *Transactions of the London and Middlesex Archaeological Society*, vol. 24, 1973, p. 185: *Plan of . . . Kensington*, published by Thomas Starling, 1822.

44. Harvey, *op. cit.*, p. 186.
45. M.D.R. 1800/2/327-8: G.L.R.O., Acc. 8/32f., bundle of deeds and papers relating to Gibbs's nursery.
46. Faulkner, pp. 23-4: Harvey, *op. cit.*, p. 187: information kindly supplied by Dr. J. M. Robinson from a forthcoming study of farm buildings.
47. Surrey R.O., 367/7/35, 36: G.L.R.O., TA9.
48. P.R.O., C13/2401, Atty. Gen. v. Griffith.
49. K.P.L., 362.209 COW: *P.P.*, 1844, vol. XVIII, no. 1, *Statistical Appendix to Report of Metropolitan Commissioners in Lunacy*, p. 88: Surrey R.O., 367/7/39 (May 1850).
50. Stroud, *op. cit.*, p. 66, n. 17.
51. Surrey R.O., 367/7/39.
52. K.P.L., MS. 166: H.B., notes on draft building agreement of 24 Aug. 1822 formerly in R.I.B.A. Drawings Collection, present whereabouts unknown: M.D.R. 1824/7/167; 1825/3/45; 1825/7/87.
53. K.P.L., MS. 166: R.B.
54. *The Graphic*, 30 March 1872 (cutting in K.P.L.): Mrs. Hamilton King, *Letters and Recollections of Mazzini*, 1912, pp. 37-8, 88: *Mazzini's Letters to an English Family*, ed. E. F. Richards, [n.d.], vol. III, p. 16.
55. M.B.W., case 32884: M.D.R. 1889/4/51-6: D.S.R. 1883/308-13: H. J. Dyos, *Victorian Suburb. A Study of the Growth of Camberwell*, 1966, pp. 127-35.
56. M.D.R. 1825/7/86-7: R.B.
57. Surrey R.O., 367/7/54, p. 24; 367/7/63, 12 May 1847: K.P.L., 711.5 SMI, K69/380.
58. Colvin.
59. Surrey R.O., 367/11/1, pp. 505-6; 367/11/2, pp. 70, 263.
60. *Ibid.*, 367/11/2, pp. 265-6.
61. *Ibid.*, 367/7/54, 9 March, 27 Aug. 1830, 2 March 1831.
62. *Ibid.*, 367/7/36, at rear.
63. M.D.R. 1832/4/126-7; 1834/6/583-99; 1845/2/751-3.
64. *Ibid.*, 1845/2/754-6.
65. P.R.O., B4/45, H148.
66. R.I.B.A. Drawings Collection, Basevi drawings, E6/1, 7-15.
67. Surrey R.O., 367/11/3, pp. 32, 34.
68. K.P.L., MS. 1284: R.I.B.A. Drawings Collection, Basevi drawings, counterpart agreement of 1 June 1833.
69. Surrey R.O., 367/7/56, Feb. 1834.
70. *Ibid.*, 367/7/56, Sept. 1835: G.L.R.O., Acc. 8(1).
71. R.I.B.A. Drawings Collection, Basevi drawings, counterpart agreement of 21 Oct. 1838.
72. Surrey R.O. 367/7/39: H.B., notes on draft building agreement of 25 July 1843 formerly in R.I.B.A. Drawings Collection, present whereabouts unknown.
73. M.D.R. 1835/4/365.
74. *Ibid.*, 1835/7/450-1; 1836/1/685; 1837/4/132.
75. Surrey R.O., 367/7/61, 1 May 1843.
76. W.C.S. 79, pp. 354-6, 397-8.
77. P.R.O., B4/49, J70: M.D.R. 1842/3/443.
78. M.D.R. 1842/3/441-2: W.C.S. P38/1210.
79. K.P.L., applications to Vestry from M.B.W., nos. 334, 335: M.D.R. 1884/26/714-17.
80. P.R.O., HO 107/690/10, f. 59: R.B.
81. M.D.R. 1840/3/654; 1842/2/214.
82. *Country Life*, 28 Nov. 1957, pp. 1156-7: *House and Garden*, Sept. 1961: D.S.R. 1888/26.
83. M.D.R. 1843/5/98-100; 1843/6/165; 1844/3/922; 1844/4/201; 1845/3/381: W.C.S. 80, p. 250; 81, p. 193.
84. M.D.R. 1834/3/104; 1839/7/536; 1845/2/57-61; 1846/

7/389: P.R.O., HO 107/690/10, f. 55.

85. M.D.R. 1845/8/500: W.C.S. 83, pp. 104, 194: Surrey R.O. 367/7/62, 1 May 1844; 367/7/63, 13 May 1846.

86. M.D.R. 1839/9/345, 363; 1840/7/797; 1843/1/864; 1843/3/833; 1843/8/503; 1844/6/348; 1844/7/1002; 1844/9/424; 1844/10/736; 1845/7/704; 1846/2/288; 1847/6/769; 1849/4/256.

87. *Ibid.*, 1833/7/611; 1836/7/313; 1837/4/86; 1837/5/750; 1839/7/223; 1840/2/253: R.B.: P.R.O., HO 107/690/10, f. 56; HO 107/1469, f. 309.

88. M.D.R. 1836/1/223: Hertfordshire R.O., D/ECh/T232: R.B.

89. M.D.R. 1836/1/685; 1836/7/125-6; 1838/2/733; 1838/4/103-4; 1838/5/562-3; 1839/7/134-6; 1839/9/362-5; 1840/7/113-16, 711; 1842/6/638; 1843/4/464-5, 973-4.

90. K.P.L., MS. 16981: P.R.O., PROB 11/2107/136; PROB 8/243, Abbot and Abbot, Feb. 1850.

91. *P.O.D.*

92. Surrey R.O., 367/7/25, f. 60.

93. M.D.R. 1847/11/682.

94. *Ibid.*, 1835/8/123: Hertfordshire R.O., D/ECh/T232.

95. *B.N.* 21 June, 26 July 1861, pp. 534, 632.

96. Dorothy Stroud, *The Thurloe Estate South Kensington, an account of its origins and development*, 1965 ed., pp. 16-17.

97. R.I.B.A. Library, transcripts of autobiography of W. W. Pocock by Miss M. A. Powel.

98. K.P.L., applications to Vestry from M.B.W., no. 21.

99. G. W. Playfair, *My Father's Son*, 1937, p. 17.

100. Philip Tilden, *True Remembrances*, 1954, pp. 83-6.

101. P.R.O., HO 107/690/10, ff. 56-60: *D.N.B.*

102. P.R.O., HO 107/1469, ff. 308-16.

103. Croker, *op. cit.*, pp. 79-80: Henriette de Witt, *Monsieur Guizot in Private Life 1787-1874*, 1880, p. 256: *Lettres de M. Guizot à sa Famille et à ses Amis*, ed. Henriette de Witt, 1884, p. 251: General Register Office, death certificate of Elizabeth Sophie Guizot, 1848.

104. *D.N.B.*: *P.O.D.*

105. *P.O.D.*: *The Life of Charles James Mathews*, ed. Charles Dickens, 1879, vol. II, p. 212.

106. *P.O.D.*: R.B.: *D.N.B.*

107. Surrey R.O., 367/7/36: M.D.R. 1832/2/417; 1832/6/431; 1833/2/287, 423: *B.* 4 Sept. 1875, p. 791: P.R.O., B4/45, R109: R.B.

108. M.D.R. 1842/6/936: R.B.

109. H.B., notes on draft building agreement of 25 July 1843 formerly in R.I.B.A. Drawings Collection, present whereabouts unknown: Surrey R.O., 367/7/25, ff. 55-9.

110. Surrey R.O., 367/7/25, ff. 55-9: M.D.R. 1845/10/330; 1848/6/345-51, 542-55, 853-7.

111. M.D.R. 1844/6/390; 1844/9/957-8; 1845/5/895-6; 1845/7/794-6; 1845/8/674.

112. *Ibid.*, 1844/7/651.

113. P.P.R. 1862, will of Stephen Phillips.

114. M.D.R. 1845/7/445-53: R.B.

115. P.R.O., HO 107/1469, f. 256.

116. M.D.R. 1846/10/911-12.

117. *Ibid.*, 1846/10/904-8, 910; 1846/11/320-2.

118. *Ibid.*, 1844/6/390, 554, 745; 1844/7/103, 105, 438; 1844/9/958; 1845/1/919; 1845/4/577; 1845/5/291, 344-5; 1845/8/86-7; 1845/11/133-4.

119. *B.* 25 Oct. 1845, pp. 510-11: Surrey R.O., 367/7/63, 12 May 1847.

120. *B.* 21 Nov. 1846, p. 562: John Summerson, *The Architectural Association 1847-1947*, 1947, pp. 3-4, 8-9: *Survey of London*, vol. XXXVI, 1970, pp. 237-8; vol. XXXVIII, 1975, pp. 269, 270: R.B.: P.R.O., HO 107/1469, f. 249.

121. P.R.O., HO 107/1469, ff. 252-7.

122. K.P.L., MS. 412.

123. P.R.O., HO 107/1469, ff. 258-60: Surrey R.O., 367/11/6, f. 387.

124. Tilden, *op. cit.*, p. 86.

125. P.R.O., B4/51, B15.

126. G.L.R.O., KBG 12, pp. 318-19.

127. Information kindly provided by the State Library of South Australia.

128. P.R.O., B4/51, B389.

129. G.L.R.O., KBG 12, *passim*.

130. Surrey R.O., 367/7/38.

131. *Survey of London*, vol. XXXVIII, 1975, pp. 262, 285-93, 301, 303-4; vol. XL, 1980, pp. 120, 126, 127, 144, 151.

132. M.D.R. 1826/3/225.

133. *Ibid.*, 1830/4/799-801.

134. *Ibid.*, 1839/1/636.

135. *Ibid.*, 1839/2/49-51; 1839/7/389.

136. *I.L.N.* 11 May 1844, p. 300.

137. W.C.S. P29/915.

138. *Ibid.*, P43/1401.

139. H.B., notes on draft building agreement of 13 April 1844, formerly in R.I.B.A. Drawings Collection, present whereabouts unknown.

140. K.P.L., 711.5 SMI, K69/375.

141. Surrey R.O., 367/7/32.

142. D.S.R. 1845/343-6.

143. R.B.: *P.O.D.*

144. M.D.R. 1811/10/611; 1854/1/550: 16 and 17 Vict., c. 23, private.

145. C. E. Hallé, *Notes from a Painter's Life*, 1909, pp. 5-6: *Survey of London*, vol. XX, 1940, p. 18.

146. *The Architect*, 22 Oct. 1870, p. 238: *P.O.D.*

147. D.S.R. 1871/182-4, 225, 424-33.

148. *Survey of London*, vol. XXXVIII, 1975, pp. 3, 7, 55-6: P.R.O., MAF11/107/867: Victoria and Albert Museum Library, Sir Henry Cole's diary, 25 Jan., 28 April, 10 June 1876.

149. D.S.R. 1883/225-32, 347-50.

150. P.R.O., HO 107/1469, f. 330.

151. *Survey of London*, vol. XXXVIII, 1975, p. 288: *The Times*, 9 Oct. 1884, p. 5: P.P.R. 1885, will of C. J. Freake, and index to wills *sub* Freake.

152. *B.* 21 Dec. 1867, p. 929.

153. W.C.S. 83, p. 402; P47/1588.

154. M.D.R. 1846/7/134: D.S.R. 1871-81 *passim*: *Survey of London*, vol. XXXVIII, 1975, p. 219: P.P.R. 1885, will of C. J. Freake.

155. M.D.R. 1856/4/117-18: *Survey of London*, vol. XXXVII, 1973, pp. 64, 75, 76, 118.

156. K.P.L., applications to Vestry from M.B.W., nos. 206, 215.

157. *P.O.D.*: D.S.R. 1883/225-32, 347-50: *The Architect*, 19 Feb. 1886, p. 109 and illus.

158. *The Architect*, 1 May 1891, p. 264: M.B.W., case 6273.

159. R.I.B.A., application for A.R.I.B.A., 12 Jan. 1880: P.R.O., RG 10/52, f. 74.

160. *Survey of London*, vol. XL, 1980, p. 127.

161. P.R.O., RG 10/52, f. 74: M.B.W. Minutes, 27 Sept. 1872, p. 325.

162. Westminster City Library, Buckingham Palace Road, rate-

books of St. George's, Hanover Square: M.D.R. 1846/7/134: *P.O.D.*: R.B.

163. R.B.: P.R.O., HO 107/1469, f. 248.
164. Barry Supple, *The Royal Exchange Assurance. A History of British Insurance 1720-1970*, 1970, p. 321.
165. M.D.R. 1839/7/389; 1839/8/702.
166. G.L.R.O., BRA 686/1.
167. Royal Exchange Assurance Corporation, Committee of Treasury Minutes, 31 July 1839.
168. Hermione Hobhouse, *Thomas Cubitt Master Builder*, 1971, p. 337.
169. *Survey of London*, vol. xxxviii, 1975, pp. 269, 271, 282, 299, 307.
170. Royal Exchange Minutes, 11 Feb., 1 April, 22 July 1846.
171. *Ibid.*, 20 Oct. 1852.
172. *Ibid.*, 21 Dec. 1853: Gordon N. Ray, *Thackeray. The Age of Wisdom 1847-1863*, 1958, p. 224: M.D.R. 1863/8/487.
173. Supple, *op. cit.*, p. 323.
174. Royal Exchange Minutes, 24 Aug. 1853.
175. *Ibid.*, 18 Sept. 1867.
176. *Survey of London*, vol. xxxviii, 1975, pp. 291, 298.
177. M.D.R. 1847/3/18-29.
178. *Ibid.*, 1854/5/416-19: Royal Exchange Minutes, 14 Sept. 1853: *B.* 3 June 1865, p. 403.
179. Gloucestershire R.O., D1388 SL1/119.
180. Royal Exchange Minutes, 1852-61 *passim*.
181. *Ibid.*, 22 May 1861.
182. *Ibid.*, 11 Aug. 1858.
183. *Survey of London*, vol. xxxviii, 1975, p. 291.
184. D.S.R. 1847-9 *passim*.
185. Surrey R.O., 367/11/6, p. 26.
186. *P.O.D.*: Surrey R.O., 367/11/6, p. 216.
187. *B.* 25 Oct. 1845, pp. 510-11.
188. D.S.R. 1845/343-6.
189. *Ibid.*, 1871/464: K.P.L., applications to Vestry from M.B.W., no. 28.
190. M.D.R. 1884/19/156-67.
191. *Ibid.*, 1849/8/952: *The Estates Gazette*, 15 June 1870, p. 284.
192. M.D.R. 1873/24/178.
193. General Register Office, birth certificate of Edwin Landseer Lutyens.
194. Stroud, *The South Kensington Estate of Henry Smith's Charity*, pp. 58-61.
195. *The Letters and Private Papers of William Makepeace Thackeray*, ed. Gordon N. Ray, vol. iii, 1946, pp. 311-12.
196. Gordon N. Ray, *Thackeray. The Age of Wisdom 1847-1863*, 1958, p. 392.
197. Margaret Leicester Warren, *Diaries*, privately printed, 1924, vol. ii, pp. 125, 185, 228.
198. P.R.O., RG 10/52, ff. 14-55.
199. Surrey R.O., 367/11/6, f. 872.
200. Boase: R. Webber, *The Early Horticulturalists*, 1968, pp. 156-9: P.R.O., RG 10/52, f. 56: M.D.R. 1873/16/930; 1875/14/449: *P.O.D.*
201. Surrey R.O., 367/13/97, 100.
202. *Ibid.*, 367/11/6, p. 306: C.C., file 23744: M.D.R. 1861/1/838.
203. C.C., files 18530, 23745.
204. *B.N.* 17 June 1859, p. 554.
205. *British Almanac for 1861. Companion*, p. 232.
206. Derek Taylor Thompson, *The First Hundred Years. The Story of St. Paul's Church Onslow Square 1860-1960*, 1960, p. 3:

C.C., file 18530.
207. Pepperell, pp. 17-18: C.C., file 18530.
208. Thompson, *op. cit.*, pp. 7-12.
209. Pepperell, p. 17.
210. Thompson, *op. cit.*, pp. 9-10: G.L.R.O., records of St. Paul's Church, book titled 'Notes', pp. 28-31, 48, 61, 65.
211. G.L.R.O., St. Paul's Church records, minutes of Parochial Church Council dated 23 March 1936 and Faculty dated 23 Jan. 1936.
212. C.C., file 23744: G.L.R.O., St. Paul's Church records, 'Notes', p. 4.
213. G.L.R.O., St. Paul's Church records, 'Notes', pp. 9a, 60m, 95.
214. *St. Paul's Church Magazine*, May 1970.
215. Thompson, *op. cit.*, p. 9: Pepperell, p. 17.
216. C.C., file 41286.
217. Surrey R.O., 367/11/7, p. 483: C.C., file 41286.
218. C.C., files 33341, 41286: Pepperell, p. 18.
219. *B.* 13 July 1867, p. 509.
220. *Survey of London*, vol. xl, 1980, pp. 126-7, 144.
221. Victoria and Albert Museum Library, Sir Henry Cole's diary, 24 July 1869, 23, 29 Dec. 1870, 24 Jan. 1871.
222. Sir Reginald Antrobus, *St. Peter's Cranley Gardens 1867-1940. Seventy Years in a West London Parish*, [1940], p. 7: *Burke's Peerage*.
223. W. S. Swayne, *Parson's Pleasure*, 1934, p. 187.
224. Antrobus, *op. cit.*, pp. 9, 11: *The Times*, 15 June 1907 (cutting in C.C., file 41286): *The Chapel of the Holy Spirit in The Church of St. Peter's, Cranley Gardens, S.W. Notes Descriptive of the Chapel, its Furniture and its Principal Features*, [1909] (copy in K.P.L.): St. Peter's Church Council Minute Book 1919-30, pp. 70, 120 (presently kept with the records of St. Mary, The Boltons).
225. Information kindly supplied by Mr. A. D. R. Caroe.
226. *The Times*, 9 Dec. 1966: *St. Peter's Church Cranley Gardens, S.W.7* (parish magazine), Jan. 1967.
227. *St. Peter's Parish Magazine*, vol. xi, 1906, p. 241: Martin Harrison, *Victorian Stained Glass*, 1980, pp. 65-6, 67-8.
228. Pepperell, p. 18.
229. Faculty of 29 Jan. 1900 originally among the records of the church, whereabouts now unknown.
230. St. Peter's Church Council Minute Book 1919-30, p. 70.
231. *Ibid.*, pp. 70, 108: Antrobus, *op. cit.*, p. 11: job-sheets in the possession of Messrs. Caroe and Martin: Pepperell, p. 18: D.S.R. 1922/525.
232. *The Chapel of the Holy Spirit, ut supra.*
233. E. H. Pask, 'The Organ at St. Peter's, Cranley Gardens, Restored' in *The Organ*, vol. xxxix, no. 153, July 1959, pp. 1-11.
234. Antrobus, *op. cit.*, p. 8: *St. Peter's Parish Magazine*, vol. vii, 1902, pp. 8-9, 59, 81, 164: *P.O.D.*
235. *Clarion. The Magazine of St. Mary The Boltons*, February 1973, August 1975.
236. M.D.R. 1870/5/172; 1871/15/621: Charles E. Lee, *The Metropolitan District Railway*, 1956, p. 5: G.L.R.O., MDR 1/1, Aug. 1867; MDR 1/2, March 1871.
237. M.D.R. 1870/13/920: M.B.W., case 26010: D.S.R. 1879/80-2.
238. Alan A. Jackson and Desmond F. Croome, *Rails Through the Clay*, 1962, pp. 41-2, 70-3, 82, 94, 108, 114: Charles E. Lee, *The Piccadilly Line*, 1973, pp. 9-16.
239. Stroud, *The South Kensington Estate of Henry Smith's Charity*, p. 62.

240. B.A. 24385: *P.O.D.*
241. P.P.R. 1885, will and codicils of Freake.
242. M.D.R. 1890/5/700.
243. Records of C. A. Daw and Son Ltd., letter book 1879-89, 9 Oct., 3, 9 Nov. 1885; in-letters, boxes 3 and 4, letters from Burrows and Barnes, and Chinnock, Galsworthy and Chinnock.
244. *Ibid.*, letter book 1879-89, 28 April 1888.
245. *Ibid.*, ledger with family dates in back; information kindly provided by Major A. F. Daw: *P.O.D.*: M.D.R. 1862-72 *passim, sub* Daw.
246. Daws' Records, in-letters, box 3, Burrows and Barnes, 29 Jan. 1886.
247. D.S.R. 1886/110-14, 162-7.
248. *Ibid.*, 1887/115, 141-4, 197-8, 292-8.
249. *Ibid.*, 1888/118-21, 159, 232-7; 1889/57-9, 127-31.
250. Daws' Records, in-letters, box 1, Barnes, Pears and Ellis: D.S.R. 1890/28-32, 204-7; 1891/68-72; 1892/60-5; 1893/33-8.
251. Daws' Records, register of mortgages.
252. *Ibid.*, deed for consolidating mortgages of 28 Dec. 1893.
253. *Ibid.*, letter book 1879-89, 29 April, 16 June, 7 Nov. 1887; register of mortgages.
254. *Ibid.*, letter book 1879-89, 19 Dec. 1887, 22 March 1888.
255. *Ibid.*, letter book 1894-8, 12 July 1895.
256. *Ibid.*, letter book 1879-89, 28 April 1887.
257. *Ibid.*, letter book 1889-94, 2 May 1893.
258. *Ibid.*, letter book 1879-89, 21 April 1888.
259. *Ibid.*, in-letters, box 13A, Norman.
260. *Ibid.*, unlabelled ledger 1877-1910.
261. *Ibid.*, in-letters, box 17B, Trollope, 29 Jan. 1894.
262. *Ibid.*, unlabelled ledger 1877-1910, ff. 133-4, 171-2.
263. *Ibid.*, in-letters, box 17A, Voysey, 4 July 1891.
264. *Ibid.*, in-letters, box 4, Chinnock, Galsworthy and Chinnock, 5 Jan. 1886.
265. *Ibid.*, in-letters, box 13A, Norman; box 17, Tarbutt.
266. *Ibid.*, letter book 1889-94, 10, 31 May 1893.
267. *Ibid.*, in-letters, box 8, 5 July 1886.
268. *Ibid.*, letter book 1879-89, undated letter of Nov. or Dec. 1886.
269. B.A. 66386: *P.O.D.*
270. Hermann Muthesius, *The English House*, English ed., 1979, p. 140: *The Architectural Review*, vol. XIX, May 1906, p. 204.
271. Boase.
272. Surrey R.O., 367/7/33, 42.
273. M.B.W. Minutes, 7 May, 4 June 1886, pp. 864, 1057.
274. D.S.R. 1886/145-9.
275. M.D.R. 1887/20/922.
276. *Ibid.*, 1887/16/194-7.
277. *Ibid.*, 1886/28/384-5.
278. *Ibid.*, 1887/13/578-9; 1887/18/308; 1887/26/846; 1889/4/794: *P.O.D.*
279. *B.* 7 Aug. 1886, p. 222.
280. D.S.R. 1886/160, 210, 215, 236, 242, 262-3, 274-5.
281. *Ibid.*, 1886/363-4.
282. M.D.R. 1888/24/983-9: D.S.R. 1887/131-7.
283. M.D.R. 1889/9/626: *Annual Report of the Working Ladies' Guild, 1978-9*, p. 4: K.P.L., photograph K63/519.
284. D.S.R. 1886/155, 179-82.
285. M.D.R. 1887/25/592.
286. *Ibid.*, 1887/23/787-90.
287. D.S.R. 1887-9 *passim* : *P.O.D.*

288. *R.I.B.A. Journal*, 3rd ser., vol. XXXIV, p. 698: *P.O.D.*
289. *Survey of London*, vol. XL, 1980, pp. 17, 187, 188, 196, 213, 219, 229, 263.
290. M.D.R. 1888/33/169: *B.* 14 July 1888, p. 29 and illus. between pp. 28 and 29.
291. *P.O.D.*: *Daily Graphic*, 25 May 1891 (cutting in K.P.L.).
292. Surrey R.O., 367/7/33, f. 33.
293. W. R. Lethaby, Alfred H. Powell and F. L. Griggs, *Ernest Gimson. His Life and Work*, 1924, p. 6, and Reginald Blomfield, *Memoirs of an Architect*, 1932, p. 76 (references kindly supplied by Mr. Alan Crawford): P.R.O., BT31/5001/33484.
294. P.R.O., BT31/5134/34652.
295. L.C.C. Minutes, 22 March, 3, 31 May 1892, pp. 241, 382, 384, 508: D.S.R. 1892/85-7: K.P.L., applications to Vestry from L.C.C., nos. 545-6.
296. M.D.R. 1894/15/61; 1894/31/532-6; 1894/33/228.
297. *P.O.D.*: *D.N.B.*: *Burke's Peerage*: *Who Was Who 1929-1940*.
298. Surrey R.O., 367/7/33, f. 51; 367/13/67.
299. D.S.R. 1894/169-74.
300. B.R. 5983.
301. *The Architectural Review*, vol. XIX, May 1906, p. 200.
302. M.D.R. 1897/7/279.
303. B.A. 64109.
304. Surrey R.O., 367/13/67.
305. M.D.R. 1898/12/819-23; 1899/27/385-7.
306. *Ibid.*, 1898/22/534-5; 1899/33/631-6: D.S.R. 1897/122, 148; 1898/32, 156, 178.
307. K.P.L., applications to Vestry from L.C.C., no. 714.
308. M.D.R. 1898/9/627; 1898/14/866; 1898/20/639: B.A. 12224: K.P.L., applications to Vestry from L.C.C., no. 708: D.S.R. 1896/165-7.
309. D.S.R. 1900/135.
310. *The Architectural Review*, vol. LXXXII, Aug. 1937, pp. 51-8: Sherban Cantacuzino, *Wells Coates*, 1978, pp. 75-8.
311. *D.N.B.*: *Burke's Peerage*, 1908 ed.
312. D.S.R. 1886/150; 1887/318.
313. Surrey R.O., 367/7/42.
314. Andrew Saint, *Richard Norman Shaw*, 1976, p. 425.
315. M.D.R. 1890/3/729.
316. *Ibid.*, 1896/26/414.
317. P.P.R. 1901, will of E. H. Palmer.
318. *B.* 4 Jan. 1902, p. 13.
319. Surrey R.O., 367/7/65, f. 39: D.S.R. 1896/102; 1897/49; 1898/194.
320. M.D.R. 1899/16/817: K.P.L., applications to Council from L.C.C., no. 806: D.S.R. 1899/101; 1901/70.
321. B.A. 40954: Surrey R.O., 367/13/75: B.R. 1958.
322. B.A. 40954.
323. Surrey R.O., 367/13/75: D.S.R. 1933/686.
324. B.A. 40954: D.S.R. 1934/696.
325. *B.* 4 Sept. 1931, p. 395: B.A. 66257.
326. *The Times*, 25, 27, 31 July 1935.
327. Surrey R.O., 367/18/89.
328. D.S.R. 1936/1381.
329. Surrey R.O., 367/13/47.
330. Charity Commissioners, file 230102/62.
331. B.A. 82434.
332. Charity Commissioners, file 230102/30: Surrey R.O., 367/13/136: D.S.R. 1909/293.

CHAPTER VII (pp. 130-143)

The Brompton Hospital Estate

1. Maurice Davidson and F. G. Rouvray, *The Brompton Hospital. The Story of a Great Adventure*, pp. 5-8: S. C. Hall, *Retrospect of a Long Life: From 1815 to 1883*, 1883, vol. I, pp. 417-19: P. J. Bishop, 'The History of the Brompton Hospital' in *Transactions & Studies of the College of Physicians of Philadelphia*, vol. 1, no. 2, Sept. 1979, p. 172: Boase: Brompton Hospital, volume entitled 'Miscellaneous Papers' *passim*.
2. G. Gregory Kayne, *The Control of Tuberculosis in England Past and Present*, 1937, pp. 24-32: *Survey of London*, vol. XXVII, 1957, pp. 143-4.
3. Davidson and Rouvray, *op. cit.*, pp. 7-12.
4. *Ibid.*, pp. 33, 50: Boase.
5. Brompton Hospital, 'Miscellaneous Papers', p. 189.
6. *B.* 16 Sept. 1843, p. 392.
7. Annual Report (*Hospital for Consumption and Diseases of the Chest*) for 1844.
8. *I.L.N.* 16 March 1844, p. 172.
9. Brompton Hospital, Committee of Management, Minute Book 1, pp. 82-3.
10. Surrey R.O., 367/13/45: Brompton Hospital, Building Committee Minute Book 1850-1883, pp. 23-5: Annual Report for 1853.
11. Annual Report for 1845.
12. Brompton Hospital, 'Miscellaneous Papers', p. 195.
13. Colvin.
14. *B.N.* 23 Oct. 1896, p. 589.
15. Surrey R.O., 367/13/45: Brompton Hospital, deeds, bundle 1, box 1, contract of 21 Oct. 1845: Davidson and Rouvray, *op. cit.*, pp. 38-45.
16. Annual Reports for 1846 and 1847.
17. 12 & 13 Vict., c. lxxx, local and personal.
18. Brompton Hospital, Building Committee Minute Book, pp. 1-18 *passim*; deeds, bundle 2a, box 1, contract of 2 Aug. 1851.
19. *Ibid.*, Building Committee Minute Book, pp. 50, 51, 78, 86.
20. Davidson and Rouvray, *op. cit.*, p. 49.
21. Brompton Hospital, Building Committee Minute Book, pp. 8-9: Annual Report for 1856.
22. Davidson and Rouvray, *op. cit.*, pp. 46, 49: Brompton Hospital, deeds, bundle 18, box 2, contract of 15 Sept. 1853.
23. Brompton Hospital, Building Committee Minute Book, p. 10.
24. *Ibid.*, Committee of Management, Minute Book 3, pp. 22, 29-30.
25. *P.P.*, 1864, vol. XXVIII, *Sixth Report of the Medical Officer of the Privy Council, 1863*, pp. 500n., 502, 721-2: Barbara Duncum, 'The Development of Hospital Design and Planning' in *The Evolution of Hospitals in Britain*, ed. F. N. L. Poynter, 1964, pp. 217-19: Davidson and Rouvray, *op. cit.*, p. 49.
26. Brompton Hospital, Committee of Management, Minute Book 3, p. 157.
27. *Ibid.*, Committee of Management, Minute Book 6, pp. 99, 110-11, 113, 115, 126.
28. *Ibid.*, Committee of Management, Minute Book 8, pp. 15, 20.
29. *Ibid.*, Committee of Management, Minute Book 6, pp. 187, 190, 297.
30. *Ibid.*, Committee of Management, Minute Book 6, pp. 378-9, 395-6, 400: K.P.L., 362.19 BRO/C.
31. Brompton Hospital, Minutes of Sub-Committees 1867-1887, p. 146.
32. *Ibid.*, Building Committee Minute Book, p. 87.
33. *Ibid.*, Building Committee Minute Book, pp. 87-200 *passim*: *B.* 22 Nov. 1879, pp. 1293-5; 17 June 1882, p. 747: Davidson and Rouvray, *op. cit.*, p. 71.
34. Kayne, *op. cit.*, pp. 52-4.
35. *B.* 29 Oct. 1898, p. 395; 19 Aug. 1899, p. 178.
36. B.R. 104409: Davidson and Rouvray, *op. cit.*, pp. 119, 122.
37. Davidson and Rouvray, *op. cit.*, pp. 134-5: B.R. 104409.
38. B.R. 104409: Brompton Hospital, Board of Governors' Minutes, 2 Oct. 1956-4 March 1958, pp. 62, 69, 78.
39. B.R. 104409: Brompton Hospital, Board of Governors' Minutes, 1 Nov. 1960-3 Dec. 1968, p. 204.
40. Brompton Hospital, Committee of Management, Minute Book 6, p. 487; Book 7, pp. 29, 41: information kindly supplied by Fiona Pearson of the National Museum of Wales.
41. B.R. 104409: Brompton Hospital, Board of Governors' Minutes, 1 Nov. 1960-3 Dec. 1968, pp. 223, 299-300, 340, 379.
42. *The Ecclesiologist*, n.s., vol. VIII, 1850, pp. 195-6.
43. Brompton Hospital, Committee of Management, Minute Book 1, pp. 478-9: *The British Almanac for 1850. Companion*, pp. 231, 234: Nikolaus Pevsner, *The Buildings of England. Yorkshire. The North Riding*, 1966, pp. 351, 364-5, 452, 455, 456.
44. Brompton Hospital, Committee of Management, Minute Book 1, p. 502; deeds, bundles 1 and 2a, box 1, contracts of 10 July 1849 and 12 March 1850: Annual Reports for 1850 and 1851: *B.* 10 Aug. 1850, pp. 377-9.
45. Brompton Hospital, Committee of Management, Minute Book 9, pp. 490, 494, 495, 504, 544; Book 10, pp. 33, 106, 257-8; deeds, bundle 18, box 2, faculty of 14 Oct. 1891: *B.* 9 April 1892, p. 294.
46. *R.I.B.A. Journal*, 3rd series, vol. LVI, 1949, pp. 251-2.
47. Stefan Muthesius, *The High Victorian Movement in Architecture 1850-1870*, 1972, pp. 42-4, 53, 54-5, 76-83, 90-3: *Survey of London*, vol. XXXVII, 1973, pp. 317-20.
48. Brompton Hospital, Building Committee Minute Book, p. 13.
49. *B.* 10 Aug. 1850, pp. 377-9; *The Ecclesiologist, loc. cit.*: Rev. John Hanson Sperling, *Church Walks in Middlesex*, 1853, Additional Particulars, p. 27.
50. Brompton Hospital, Committee of Management, Minute Book 2, pp. 98, 101: *P.O.D.*
51. Brompton Hospital, Committee of Management, Minute Book 2, p. 32.
52. *Ibid.*, Committee of Management, Minute Book 2, p. 63.
53. Annual Report for 1850.
54. Brompton Hospital, Committee of Management, Minute Book 10, pp. 108, 110.
55. M.D.R. 1731/3/285-6; 1732/3/118: G.L.R.O., AM/PW/1720/139; AM/PW/1729/155: R.B.: T. C. Croker, *A Walk from London to Fulham*, 1860, pp. 89, 105: W. Hugh Curtis, *William Curtis 1746-1799*, 1941, p. 86: G.L.R.O. Map Collection, JK 1861.

56. R.B.: *Survey of London*, vol. XXIII, 1951, pp. 16-17: Dr. [R. J.] Thornton, *Sketch of the Life and Writings of the Late Mr. William Curtis*, [1806], pp. 23-30: *The Subscription Catalogue of the Brompton Botanic Garden, For the Year 1790* (B.L. pressmark 988.b.33 1-9): Curtis, *op. cit.*, pp. 84, 86 (where, however, the location of the garden is wrongly given): *The Gentleman's Magazine*, vol. LXXX, pt. II, Aug. 1810, pp. 113-14.

57. R.B.: Brompton Hospital, Committee of Management, Minute Book 2, pp. 79, 82, 83: *Survey of London*, vol. XXXVII, 1973, pp. 7, 8, 221, 225, 232, 233, 239, 250, 253, 254, 256, 257.

58. Brompton Hospital, Committee of Management, Minute Book 1, pp. 117, 359: Annual Reports for 1849 and 1853.

59. Brompton Hospital, Building Committee Minute Book, p. 25; Committee of Management, Minute Book 2, pp. 329, 331, 345: Annual Report for 1853: *Survey of London*, vol. XXXVIII, 1975, pp. 54, 55, 57, 58.

60. Brompton Hospital, Committee of Management, Minute Book 2, pp. 349, 351, 367: Annual Report for 1853.

61. Brompton Hospital, Committee of Management, Minute Book 2, p. 365; Book 3, pp. 103, 106, 181: Annual Report for 1853: P.R.O., C54/14814/1: M.D.R. 1856/1/148: *P.O.D.*

62. *Survey of London*, vol. XXXVIII, 1975, pp. 54-8.

63. M.D.R. 1844/8/291.

64. Brompton Hospital, deeds, bundle 17, box 2, agreement of 28 July 1853; Committee of Management, Minute Book 2, p. 370.

65. *Ibid.*, Committee of Management, Minute Book 2, pp. 394, 395, 397-8, 400, 401-3, 406-7.

66. D.S.R. 1853/289-95.

67. Brompton Hospital, Committee of Management, Minute Book 3, pp. 6, 12.

68. *Ibid.*, Committee of Management, Minute Book 2, p. 403; Minute Book 3, pp. 13, 29-30: M.D.R. 1855/5/605.

69. Brompton Hospital, deeds, bundle 17, box 2, mortgage of 9 May 1856.

70. *P.O.D.*

71. D.S.R. 1855/66-71.

72. Brompton Hospital, deeds, bundle 17, box 2, agreement of 19 July 1855; Committee of Management, Minute Book 3, p. 116.

73. *Ibid.*, Committee of Management, Minute Book 3, pp. 208-10.

74. *Ibid.*, Committee of Management, Minute Book 3, pp. 238-9, 269.

75. *Ibid.*, Committee of Management, Minute Book 3, p. 259: P.R.O., C54/15275/7.

76. *The Land and Building News*, 29 Nov. 1856, p. 874.

77. P.R.O., C211/31, 20 Vict. 1856/7, no. 39.

78. *Ibid.*, C54/15275/7.

79. Brompton Hospital, Committee of Management, Minute Book 3, pp. 346-7, 353, 406: *B.N.* 22 Jan. 1858, p. 91.

80. M.D.R. 1858/12/476-81.

81. Brompton Hospital, Committee of Management, Minute Book 3, pp. 556-7; Book 4, p. 2.

82. *Ibid.*, Committee of Management, Minute Book 4, pp. 99-100, 108.

83. M.D.R. 1863/6/3.

84. Brompton Hospital, Committee of Management, Minute Book 4, pp. 29-31, 34; deeds, bundle 5, box 3, agreement of 24 Nov. 1859.

85. *Ibid.*, Committee of Management, Minute Book 4, pp. 99-100.

86. *Ibid.*, Committee of Management, Minute Book 4, p. 425; Book 5, p. 120.

87. M.D.R. 1860/10/633-4; 1860/15/809-10; 1861/15/905; 1862/7/107, 174; 1862/14/331; 1862/19/341, 1213-14; 1863/13/977; 1863/19/731-2, 734; 1864/7/955, 958.

88. *Ibid.*, 1862/6/741-2; 1862/15/919; 1862/19/542; 1863/13/495-6; 1863/20/77-8.

89. MS. journal of Anne Thackeray Ritchie, April 1864 (in possession of, and inspected by kind permission of, Mrs. Belinda Norman-Butler).

90. Brompton Hospital, Committee of Management, Minute Book 6, p. 503.

91. *B.N.* 22 Jan. 1858, p. 91.

92. Brompton Hospital, Committee of Management, Minute Book 6, p. 114.

93. *Ibid.*, Committee of Management, Minute Book 6, pp. 199, 535-6; Book 7, p. 225; Book 8, pp. 487-8.

94. P.R.O., RG 10/52, ff. 42-51.

95. Brompton Hospital, Estates Sub-Committee Minutes, 1975-9 *passim*.

96. *Ibid.*, deeds, bundle 18, box 2, agreement of 15 Jan. 1856: *The Land and Building News*, 1 March, 15 May, 22 Nov. 1856, pp. 117, 239, 850: *B.* 20 Dec. 1856, p. 682: *B.N.* 3 Oct. 1862, p. 264: Pepperell, p. 30: M.D.R. 1857/3/63; 1863/5/898.

97. *P.O.D.*: Brompton Hospital, Board of Governors' Minutes, 1 Nov. 1960-3 Dec. 1968, pp. 73-4.

CHAPTER VIII (pp. 144-148)

The Ware Estate

1. K.P.L., index to court rolls of the manor of Earl's Court, *sub* Parsons, Keightley, Maule and Torrane: R.B.

2. R.B.: G.L.R.O., MR/PLT 4912-29: Faulkner, p. 15.

3. *The Morning Herald*, 18 April 1823.

4. Colvin: *Survey of London*, vol. XXXII, 1963, pp. 407-12 *passim*, 422, 424, 425, 429, 430-4.

5. K.P.L., MS. 58/7012, p. 225.

6. *Ibid.*, MS. 58/7024, ff. 60, 71, 74, 75: M.D.R. 1826/5/50-1.

7. M.D.R. 1827/10/179.

8. P.R.O., MAF9/167/3280.

9. K.P.L., MS. 58/7024, f. 71: M.D.R. 1828/6/754; 1836/5/651.

10. M.D.R. 1826/1/359.

11. *Ibid.*, 1825/9/482; 1826/9/649: R.B.

12. M.D.R. 1825/13/246; 1826/3/708: R.B.

13. R.B.: M.D.R. 1833/4/468.

14. R.B.

15. M.D.R. 1829/3/339: R.B.

16. M.D.R. 1842/5/590: K.P.L., valuation note books, 1900-1, 1905-6, 1910-11: *Kelly's Kensington ... Directory ... For 1910*.

17. R.B.: M.D.R. 1829/7/489: P.R.O., RG 10/52, f. 72.

18. M.D.R. 1828/7/274.

19. *Ibid.*, 1827/8/580: R.B.
20. M.D.R. 1829/3/162.
21. *Ibid.*, 1828/6/754: *P.O.D.*
22. M.D.R. 1829/3/171.
23. *Ibid.*, 1836/5/651; 1843/6/745.
24. R.B.: M.D.R. 1843/6/744.
25. P.P.R. 1865, index to wills, *sub* Surrey.
26. M.D.R. 1843/6/745: D.S.R. 1886/205.
27. *P.O.D.*: *Survey of London*, vol. XXXVIII, 1975, pp. 88, 90, 142, 144, 183, 184, 192, 193, 205.
28. W.C.S. 78, pp. 45, 46, 101.
29. P.P.R. 1865, will of Samuel Ware and index to wills.
30. P.R.O., RG 10/52, ff. 69-74.
31. William J. Carlton, 'An Early Home of Dickens in Kensington', in *The Dickensian*, vol. LXI, 1964, pp. 20-5.
32. H.B., Blue Plaque file 1064.
33. Companies Registration Office, file 474656.
34. B.A. 102529: B.R. 16011.
35. B.R. 127049.
36. *The Times*, 23 Jan. 1964: H.B., file 623.

CHAPTER IX (pp. 149-155)

Roland Gardens

1. K.P.L., index to court rolls of the manor of Earl's Court, *sub* Parsons, Keightley and Torrane.
2. *The Morning Herald*, 18 April 1823.
3. E.C.R., 1842.
4. R.B.
5. M.D.R. 1836/5/170.
6. A. K. Bruce, 'Samuel Brown and the Gas Engine', in *The Engineer*, 6 Sept. 1946, pp. 214-15: *The Mechanics' Magazine, Museum, Register, Journal, and Gazette*, 28 July 1832, pp. 274, 276.
7. K.P.L., 01894 (sale partics. of Eagle Lodge).
8. Bruce, *op. cit.*: R.B.
9. K.P.L., 01894: M.D.R. 1836/5/170-2.
10. *Survey of London*, vol. XXXV, 1970, pp. 24-5.
11. P.R.O., HO 107/1469, f. 348.
12. K.P.L., 01894: R.B.
13. R.B.: P.R.O., RG 9/22, ff. 55-6: O.S. sheet X/9, 1865-7.
14. P.R.O., PROB 11/487/63.
15. M.D.R. 1718/6/39.
16. P.R.O., PROB 11/487/63; C105/5: M.D.R. 1718/6/39.
17. M.D.R. 1744/3/136.
18. *Ibid.*, 1748/3/119-21.
19. *Ibid.*, 1813/4/485-6; 1819/1/399.
20. *Ibid.*, 1838/3/160.
21. P.R.O., HO 107/690/10, f. 25.
22. *Ibid.*, PROB 6/233, f. 300: M.D.R. 1862/4/584: R.B.
23. P.R.O., PROB 6/233, f. 300: M.D.R. 1864/12/311.
24. M.D.R. 1864/15/828.
25. E.C.R., 13 Sept. 1842.
26. K.P.L., MS. 13825, schedule, deeds of 16 Nov. 1869.
27. *Survey of London*, vol. XXXVIII, 1975, pp. 269, 271, 282, 285: Francis Sheppard, Victor Belcher and Philip Cottrell, 'The Middlesex and Yorkshire deeds registries and the study of building fluctuations', in *The London Journal*, vol. 5, 1978, p. 183.

28. M.B.W. Minutes, 24 June 1870, p. 687; M.B.W., case 15206.
29. M.D.R. 1870/24/513.
30. *Ibid.*, 1871/16/243: K.P.L., MS. 13825, schedule, deeds of 19 July 1870.
31. P.R.O., MAF9/167/9798.
32. M.D.R. 1871/2/503, 526.
33. *Ibid.*, 1871/16/243; 1871/18/201, 572.
34. P.P.R., 1871, C. Aldin's will, and index to wills *sub* Aldin.
35. M.B.W., case 15206.
36. K.P.L., Vestry Works Committee Minutes, vol. 7, p. 36.
37. M.D.R. 1871/2/527; 1871/16/244-6; 1871/18/202, 204; 1873/16/27; 1874/11/692.
38. K.P.L., Vestry Works Committee Minutes, vol. 7, p. 291.
39. D.S.R. 1871/244: M.D.R. 1883/26/798; 1892/22/676: *B.N.* 19 July 1872, p. 54.
40. D.S.R. 1871/39-40, 188-91, 244, 410-11; 1872/14-15, 91-4, 171-2; 1873/119-20, 157-8.
41. P.R.O., RG 11/48, ff. 56-9.
42. J. M. C. Toynbee, *Art in Roman Britain*, 1962, Plates 210-12, 218, 224.
43. M.D.R. 1872-81, *passim*.
44. P.R.O., RG 10/52, f. 74.
45. M.D.R. 1872/8/613.
46. Corbett Letters, II, 723, 943; III, 207.
47. M.D.R. 1873/9/981.
48. *Ibid.*, 1873/18/991.
49. *Ibid.*, 1878/12/418: *P.O.D.*: P.R.O., RG 11/48, ff. 62-3.
50. D.S.R. 1878/29-31.
51. P.R.O., RG 11/48, ff. 59-63.
52. K.P.L., applications to Vestry from M.B.W., no. 137: *The Kensington News*, 22, 29 April, 14 Oct., 4 Nov. 1876: D.S.R. 1876/60, 400.
53. *P.O.D.*: P.R.O., RG 11/48, f. 63.
54. *P.O.D.*
55. D.S.R. 1882/45-8.
56. *Ibid.*, 1883/104-9; 1884/216-18.
57. *Ibid.*, 1883/104-9; 1887/151-2.
58. *Ibid.*, 1883/306.
59. M.D.R. 1883/11/129.
60. *Committee of Council on Education: Report*, 1883-4, p. 197.
61. A.E.P., box 1, bundle 15, letter from Aldin and Sons, 17 Sept. 1875.
62. K.P.L., MS. 16426.
63. Sheppard, Belcher and Cottrell, *op. cit.*, p. 202.
64. M.D.R. 1883/26/797-9: K.P.L., MS. 13821/3.
65. M.D.R. 1884/17/1003-6; 1887/25/849-50: K.P.L., MSS. 13821/3, 13822, 16430.
66. M.D.R. 1884/20/581; 1884/25/780; 1890/3/208; 1890/17/1088; 1890/19/963: K.P.L., MSS. 13821/3, 13825, 13827.
67. M.D.R. 1889/30/739: K.P.L., MS. 16427.
68. D.S.R. 1889/213.
69. M.D.R. 1889/31/991; 1891/29/514.
70. Records of C. A. Daw and Son Ltd., in-letters, box 13A, letters from P. Norman, 19, 27 Sept. 1891: D.S.R. 1891/95.
71. M.D.R. 1890/19/962; 1892/22/675-6.
72. D.S.R. 1892/95-6, 117-18.
73. M.B.W., case 15206: P.R.O., J54/1004, 1897, K, no. 483.
74. Daws' records, in-letters, box 1, Aldin and Plater, 25 June 1886.

75. K.P.L., MSS. 16427, 16431: *The Kensington News*, 28 July 1894.
76. *The Kensington News*, 28 July 1894: *The Times*, 26 July 1894.
77. *Survey of London*, vol. XXXVIII, 1975, pp. 121n., 244, 254, 261.
78. B.A. 70663.
79. B.R. 107159.

CHAPTER X (pp. 156-161)

The Day Estate in Drayton Gardens

1. E.C.R., 20 April 1554, 16 May 1558.
2. *Ibid.*, 5 Dec. 1661, 5 April 1666.
3. P.R.O., C7/562/17: E.C.R., 4 May 1704, 8 Jan. 1704/5.
4. Family tree of Day family in possession of Mr. Simon Day: Walter Rye, *Norfolk Families*, 1913-15, pp. 156, 157: M.D.R. 1740/3/244: E.C.R., 16 May 1744.
5. E.C.R., 4 Dec. 1735.
6. Westminster City Library, Buckingham Palace Road, rate-books of St. Paul's, Covent Garden, Tavistock Street, 1740 *et seq.*; H 805 (Vestry Minutes), 1 May 1755: G.L.R.O., E/BER/CG 180/16.
7. P.R.O., PROB 6/120, f. 142: E.C.R., 16 May 1744.
8. E.C.R., 1 Sept. 1753, 19 June 1755.
9. *Ibid.*, 3 Jan. 1772.
10. G.L.R.O., P 87/MRY/61, p. 284: P.R.O., PROB 11/1622/512.
11. Day Estate Papers (at Messrs. Church, Adams, Tatham and Co., 23 and 25 Bell Street, Reigate, Surrey), indenture of enfranchisement, 30 Nov. 1835: M.D.R. 1835/8/181-2.
12. P.P.R. 1875, will of James Day, proved 4 Aug.: Rye, *op. cit.*, p. 158.
13. R.B.: Day Estate Papers, indenture of enfranchisement, 30 Nov. 1835.
14. G.L.R.O., TA9, schedule.
15. Day Estate Papers, articles of agreement, 7 January 1845.
16. *Survey of London*, vol. XXXVII, 1973, p. 280.
17. P.R.O., RG 9/334, ff. 115-16; RG 10/609, district 14, f. 7.
18. Information from the Tithe map of Drayton (1839), kindly supplied by the Norfolk County Archivist: Day Estate Papers, lease of 25 Nov. 1834 (of Hereford Lodge, Old Brompton Road).
19. M.B.W. 213, presented papers for meeting of 4 Feb. 1856: *B.N.*, 22 Oct. 1858, p. 1044.
20. Day Estate Papers, articles of agreement, 7 January 1845; leases of Drayton Terrace and Drayton Grove.
21. W.C.S. 84, pp. 302, 337-8: D.S.R. 1845/357-366.
22. Day Estate Papers, leases of Drayton Terrace 4 Feb. 1846: M.D.R. 1846/2/334-342.
23. R.B.
24. P.R.O., HO 107/1469, ff. 368-9; RG 9/22, f. 56.
25. D.S.R. 1846/253-262: Day Estate Papers, leases of Drayton Grove, 8 Dec. 1846: M.D.R. 1846/12/328-337.
26. Day Estate Papers, articles of agreement, 29 Aug. 1846: M.D.R. 1846/12/327.
27. M.D.R. 1846/12/327.
28. D.S.R. 1846/323-5.
29. M.D.R. 1847/5/67; 1847/10/496; 1854/7/204.
30. *Ibid.*, 1847/10/496.
31. D.S.R. 1849/156-9: Day Estate Papers, leases of Drayton Grove, 10 Nov. 1849: M.D.R. 1849/10/242-246.
32. Day Estate Papers, articles of agreement of 4 March 1851, endorsed on agreement of 7 Jan. 1845.
33. *Ibid.*, lease of Drayton Villas, 20 Dec. 1852.
34. M.B.W. 213, *loc. cit.*
35. R.B.: P.R.O., RG 9/22, ff. 55-6.
36. D.S.R. 1852/272-3: Day Estate Papers, lease of Drayton Grove, 20 Dec. 1852.
37. D.S.R. 1852/151-2.
38. Day Estate Papers, leases of Drayton Grove, 28 Feb., 26 July 1853.
39. P.R.O., J90/1233, correspondence of H. J. Clarke, 1863-4, and deed of settlement, 22 Jan. 1858
40. Day Estate Papers, articles of agreement of 8 Nov. 1855, endorsed on agreement of 7 Jan. 1845.
41. M.D.R. 1855/8/453.
42. Day Estate Papers, leases of Drayton Grove, 18 Feb., 12 March, 2 Aug., 13 Dec. 1859, 12 May, 29 July, 7 Aug. 1862.
43. *Ibid.*, leases of Drayton Grove, 30 Dec. 1861, 13, 24 May 1862, 17 Jan., 20 Feb., 2 March, 3 July 1863.
44. *B.N.* 22 Oct. 1858, p. 1044.
45. P.R.O., J90/1233, bill for work done at No. 23 Drayton Grove (46 Drayton Gardens) *c.* 1864.
46. *Ibid.*, HO 107/1469, ff. 370-2; RG 9/22, ff. 57-60.
47. K.P.L., applications to Vestry from L.C.C., no. 510: Day Estate Papers, packet of deeds etc. *re* the Drayton Arms: D.S.R. 1891/84-6.
48. Day Estate Papers, letters and memo of Oct. and Nov. 1860, enclosed with lease of 20 Dec. 1852.
49. *Ibid.*, consents to make alterations enclosed with the leases of Drayton Terrace.
50. H.B., Report, 8 Jan. 1973, EP 752.
51. O.S. sheet X/9, 1894-6.
52. B.R. 156993.
53. Day Estate Papers, plans for conversion of No. 50 Cresswell Place, 1933, in packet of deeds etc. *re* Drayton Arms.
54. *Ibid.*, consent to erect studio, 3 March 1903, with lease of 29 July 1862 for 42 Drayton Gardens.
55. B.R. 151465.

CHAPTER XI (pp. 162-194)

Little Chelsea in Kensington

1. St. Mary Abbots Church, burial register, 4 Sept. 1618 (John, son of Robert Sewell).
2. *Middlesex County Records*, ed. J. C. Jeaffreson, vol. III, 1888, p. 161.
3. K.P.L., index to court rolls of the manor of Earl's Court, *sub* Freeman; MSS. 58/5630, 63/1379: P.R.O., E179/143/370; E179/252/32, book 40.
4. B.L., Verney Papers, microfilm, M636/52, Ralph Palmer to Lord Fermanagh, 30 Nov. 1703.
5. T. C. Croker, 'A Walk from London to Fulham' in *Fraser's Magazine*, vol. XXXI, 1845, p. 334.
6. P.R.O., C54/4312, no. 12.
7. Verney Papers, microfilm, M636/34, John Verney to Sir Ralph Verney, 30 Sept. 1680.

8. *Ibid.*, M636/55, Ralph Palmer jr. to Lord Fermanagh, 18 Nov. 1712.
9. R.B.
10. K.P.L., index to court rolls of manor of Earl's Court, *sub* William Freeman.
11. P.R.O., C54/1634: G.L.R.O., BRA 203/162: *Survey of London*, vol. IV, 1913, pp. 11, 22, 38, 43.
12. P.R.O., PROB 11/602/76.
13. 15 Geo. III, c. 49, private.
14. M.D.R. 1781/3/25.
15. *Ibid.*, 1781/3/117.
16. *Ibid.*, 1786/5/431-2.
17. *Ibid.*, 1786/2/560.
18. *Ibid.*, 1786/2/38.
19. J. and J. A. Venn, *Alumni Cantabrigienses*, and *The Book of Matriculation and Degrees . . . in the University of Cambridge from 1544 to 1659*, 1913, p. 350: Manning and Bray, *History of Surrey*, vol. III, 1814, p. 640.
20. P.R.O., C54/2846, no. 10; C54/3193, no. 28: *Cal. S. P. Dom. 1637-1638*, pp. 153-4: Eleanor S. Godfrey, *The Development of English Glassmaking 1560-1640*, 1975, pp. 89, 90, 129: *Burke's Peerage* (1923 ed.) *sub* Coventry.
21. P.R.O., PROB 11/182/3.
22. *Ibid.*, C54/3193, no. 28.: *A Calendar of the Marriage Licence Allegations in the Registry of the Bishop of London*, ed. Reginald M. Glencross, 1937, vol. 1, 1597 to 1648, p. 193.
23. P.R.O., PROB 11/223/164.
24. G.L.R.O., BRA 203/162.
25. M.D.R. 1744/3/506: *The Parish Register of Kensington 1539-1675*, ed. F. N. Macnamara and A. Story-Maskelyne, 1890, p. 125.
26. P.R.O., PROB 10/100G (original will). It is extracted largely, from the registered copy, in *Surrey Archaeological Collections*, vol. IX, p. 302n.
27. *Cal. S. P. Dom.*, *passim*.
28. P.R.O., C54/4312, no. 12.
29. E.C.R., 22 April 1669.
30. Faulkner, p. 432.
31. M.D.R. 1744/3/506.
32. P.R.O., PROB 11/309/142; PROB 11/362/2; C54/4312, no. 12: G.L.R.O., MR/TH/6: *The South Carolina Historical and Genealogical Magazine*, vol. 1, no. 3, July 1900, p. 228n.
33. *Cal. S. P. Dom. 1637-38*, pp. 1, 39; *1638-39*, p. 16; *1651*, p. 49; *1651-52*, p. 163; *1653-54*, pp. 293, 299, 322; *1655*, p. 210; *1655-56*, pp. 125, 281-2, 317; *1659-60*, pp. 240, 596: *Cal. Procs Committee for Compounding 1643-1660*, index *sub* Birkenhead or Birkhead, Edward: *Cal. Procs Committee for Advance of Money 1642-1656*, pp. 906, 1071, 1094, 1332: *Commons Journal*, vol. V, p. 466: *H.M.C. Laing MSS.*, vol. I, 1914, p. 249: *H.M.C. 7th Report*, 1879, p. 84a: G. E. Aylmer, *The State's Servants 1649-1660*, 1973, pp. 66, 99: P.R.O., C54/3385, no. 25.
34. P.R.O., PROB 11/352/115.
35. Llewellyn Jewitt, *The Corporation Plate and Insignia of Office of the Cities and Towns of England and Wales*, ed. W. H. St. John Hope, 1895, vol. I, pp. xlvi-xlvii, li, 28, vol. II, pp. 21, 97-8: Sir Ambrose Heal, *The London Goldsmiths 1200-1800*, 1935, p. 203: Maj.-Gen. H. D. W. Sitwell, 'Royal Serjeants-at-Arms and the Royal Maces' in *Archaeologia*, vol. CII, 1969, pp. 213-20: *Cal. S. P. Dom. 1651*, p. 551; *1655*, pp. 61, 122, 608: Lt.-Col. P. F. Thorne, C.B.E., *The Mace in the House of Commons*, House of Commons Library

Document No. 3, 1971, p. 6: information kindly supplied by Sir Peter Thorne, Serjeant at Arms, and by Mr. David Beasley of the Goldsmiths' Company.
36. P.R.O., C54/3551, no. 19.
37. *Ibid.*, E179/252/32, book 40; C5/540/29 and 30: G.L.R.O., MR/TH/6.
38. *Miscellanea Genealogica et Heraldica*, ed. J. J. Howard, 3rd. ser., vol. II, 1898, p. 272: *The South Carolina Historical and Genealogical Magazine*, vol. 1, no. 3, July 1900, pp. 228-62.
39. M.D.R. 1811/8/259; 1812/9/33.
40. Thomas Faulkner, *An Historical and Topographical Description of Chelsea and its Environs*, 1810, p. 421.
41. M.D.R. 1812/9/33.
42. *Ibid.*, 1813/7/757.
43. *Ibid.*, see index 1811-15 *sub* Groves.
44. *Ibid.*, 1813/4/260; 1813/6/23; 1814/5/287; 1814/6/347.
45. *Ibid.*, 1817/6/275.
46. *Ibid.*, 1821/4/401.
47. *Ibid.*, 1816/5/598: K.P.L., MS. 15265.
48. R.B.: *D.N.B.*: Faulkner, *Description of Chelsea, ut supra*, 1829 ed., vol. I, p. 150: T. C. Croker, *A Walk from London to Fulham*, 1860, p. 94.
49. M.D.R. 1878/23/88.
50. Faulkner, *op. et loc. cit.*
51. K.P.L., MS. 15265.
52. M.D.R. 1814/1/544-5.
53. *Ibid.*, 1815/6/474.
54. *Ibid.*, 1816/3/482.
55. *Ibid.*, 1815/6/354; 1818/5/8; 1818/7/60.
56. *Ibid.*, 1819/7/20.
57. *Ibid.*, 1820/1/778: R.B.
58. *Survey of London*, vol. XXXVIII, 1975, pp. 19-24.
59. M.D.R. 1819/7/183: R.B.
60. M.D.R. 1814/1/546-7.
61. *Ibid.*, 1838/2/620: R.B.
62. D.S.R. 1878/258-61; 1882/307-11: M.B.W. Minutes, 28 June 1878, p. 990; 9 Aug. 1878, p. 302: K.P.L., applications to Vestry from M.B.W., no. 219; valuation note books.
63. M.D.R. 1885/20/465; 1885/23/491; 1885/31/275-6; 1886/2/195; 1886/25/1054-5; 1889/13/409; 1889/17/492; 1889/19/655: D.S.R. 1885/40-1; 1886/140-1; 1883/157-8: K.P.L., applications to Vestry from M.B.W., no. 368; valuation note books, 1885-6, 1890-1.
64. *B.N.* 28 Oct. 1887, pp. 669-70: *P.O.D.*
65. *P.O.D*: *D.N.B.*
66. D.S.R. 1885/40-1; 1886/140-1, 183: M.D.R. 1885/10/534; 1885/31/539; 1887/1/631; 1887/3/5; 1888/24/326; 1888/28/758-60.
67. L.C.C. Minutes, 15 Nov. 1892, p. 1057; 28 Feb. 1893, p. 203; 1 May, 11 Dec. 1894, pp. 479, 1292; 13 April, 1, 28 June, 20 July 1897, pp. 430, 647, 698, 850: D.S.R. 1894/74; 1897/120; 1898/34.
68. B.A. 75345: L.C.C. Minutes, 2 Oct. 1894, p. 941; 2 April 1895. p. 307; *P.O.D.*: D.S.R. 1894/163; 1895/125; 1896/95: N.R.A., Catalogue of MSS. of Wadham College, Oxford, item 66.
69. L.C.C. Minutes, 29 March 1898, p. 382; 30 April 1901, p. 513: D.S.R. 1901/29, 89; 1902/64: *B.N.* 12 Sept. 1902, p. 363: *P.O.D.*: B.A. 13203.
70. M.D.R. 1893/9/780-2.
71. K.P.L., MSS. 15270, 15290, 15292.
72. D.S.R. 1901/118: *P.O.D.*

73. B.A. 50377.
74. *Ibid.*, 33302: D.S.R. 1925/571-3.
75. M.D.R. 1878/23/88: R.B.: K.P.L., valuation note books, No. 9 District, 1885-6, 1890-1.
76. B.A. 56585: D.S.R. 1926/355.
77. B.A. 73670: B.R. 106392.
78. B.R. 106394.
79. *Ibid.*, 105475.
80. B.A. 88184: B.R. 105475: information kindly supplied by Mr. Anthony Mauduit and by Mr. Peter Watson.
81. B.R. 114889: information kindly supplied by the Hon. C. J. G. Guest.
82. B.R. 151371.
83. *Ibid.*, 57117: *P.O.D.*: W. T. Whitley, *The Baptists of London 1612-1928*, [n.d.], p. 169: D.S.R. 1881/230.
84. B.R. 57117 (elev. of chapel): B.A. 36854: *P.O.D.*: L.C.C. Minutes, 1911, pt. 1, index *sub* Theatres.
85. M.D.R. 1887/8/1016; 1888/23/242-3; 1890/12/269: D.S.R. 1888/8-12: R.B.: *P.O.D.*
86. B.A. 61374: L.C.C. Minutes, 3 June 1930, p. 1031: David Atwell, *Cathedrals of the Movies*, 1980, p. 109.
87. M.D.R. 1781/3/25 (this wrongly orientates the plot).
88. K.P.L., MSS. 58/5630, 63/1379.
89. B.L., Add. MS. 31326.
90. M.D.R. 1830/5/690.
91. R.B.: *P.O.D.*: O.S. sheet X/19, 1894-6: D. Lysons, *The Environs of London*, vol. VI, 1811, p. 214: Faulkner, *Description of Chelsea, ut supra*, 1829 ed., vol. I, p. 150.
92. Kensington and Chelsea Public Libraries, *Kensington and Chelsea Street-Names. A Progress Report*, 1968, p. 8.
93. M.D.R. 1727/3/30; 1781/3/117.
94. R.B.: T. Richardson, 'Plan . . . of Chelsea', 1769, reproduced in *Survey of London*, vol. IV, 1913, Plate 2.
95. M.D.R. 1795/2/24, 97: R.B.
96. M.D.R. 1786/5/431-2; 1813/7/757.
97. *Ibid.*, 1795/2/24.
98. R.B.: M.D.R. 1795/2/25, 96.
99. M.D.R. 1795/2/97.
100. *Ibid.*, 1810/7/111; 1813/3/134: Hurford Janes, *The Red Barrel. A History of Watney Mann*, 1963, pp. 59, 61, 71.
101. R.B.: M.D.R. 1813/7/757.
102. R.B.: B.L., Add. MS. 31326.
103. M.D.R. 1813/3/631.
104. *Ibid.*, 1814/1/169.
105. *Ibid.*, 1846/2/458.
106. R.B.: D.S.R. 1847/276-7.
107. M.D.R. 1846/3/122.
108. D.S.R. 1846/185-8, 227, 229, 242-3, 290: R.B.
109. M.B.W. 213, presented papers for meeting of 4 Feb. 1856.
110. D.S.R. 1847/53-4: R.B.
111. G.L.R.O., MBO 72, ff. 297f.: *The Architect's, Engineer's and Building-Trades' Directory*, 1868, p. 113.
112. D.S.R. 1878/60: M.D.R. 1877/27/437; 1878/30/807; 1878/34/909: National Society for Promoting Religious Education, file 2567: T. F. Gibbs, *St. Mary Boltons 1850-1964*, [n.d.], p. 17.
113. Charles Booth, *Life and Labour of the People in London. Third Series. Religious Influences, 3, The City of London and the West End*, 1902 ed., following p. 135.
114. Royal Borough of Kensington Minutes, 1935-8 *passim*: B.R. 110728
115. B.R. 150491.
116. M.D.R. 1807/3/395-6.

117. *Ibid.*, 1846/1/387.
118. R.B.: D.S.R. 1849/134; 1850/162-3: *P.O.D.*
119. R.B.: D.S.R. 1853/153-4.
120. R.B.: M.D.R. 1864/2/888-90.
121. M.B.W. 5455.
122. Kensington Borough Council Minutes, 14 Dec. 1937, p. 34.
123. M.D.R. 1781/3/117; 1813/7/757: R.B.
124. M.D.R. 1786/2/560; 1790/7/327.
125. *Ibid.*, 1790/3/163; 1790/8/145-6; 1791/6/441.
126. *Ibid.*, 1790/3/162; 1790/7/327-8: G.L.R.O., Acc. 240/ 14.
127. D.S.R. 1851/190-1: M.C.S. 291/638.
128. O.S. sheet X/19, 1868.
129. *P.O.D.*: M.D.R. (e.g.) 1864/10/138-41.
130. M.D.R. 1821/2/568.
131. *Ibid.*, 1866/3/21.
132. *Ibid.*, 1872/3/797: D.S.R. 1871/299-300.
133. *P.O.D.*
134. H.B., file 6158.
135. M.D.R. 1882/21/356.
136. *P.O.D.*: D.S.R. 1902/17.
137. M.D.R. 1887/20/163: K.P.L., *Particulars of Sir Nevill Gunter's Portion of the Gunter Estate*, 11 June 1917.
138. B.A. 77016.
139. G.L.R.O., Mddx. records, Acc. 1347/3.
140. *Ibid.*: R.B.: K.P.L., MS. 63/1379: G.L.R.O., MR/PLT: P.R.O., PROB 11/1011/351: *South Carolina Historical and Genealogical Magazine*, vol. 1, no. 3, July 1900, pp. 233-4 (date of death of William Middleton wrongly stated): W. A. Copinger, *The Manors of Suffolk*, vol. 2, 1908, p. 295: Christopher Hussey, 'Shrubland Park, Suffolk, I' in *Country Life*, 19 Nov. 1953, p. 1656.
141. K.P.L., MSS. 58/5630, 63/1379: P.R.O., PROB 11/707/43.
142. *Verney Letters of the Eighteenth Century*, ed. Lady Verney, 1930, vol. I, p. 101.
143. K.P.L., MSS. 58/5630, 63/1379: Corporation of London R.O., Assessment Box 42.21, 1693/4.
144. K.P.L., MSS. 58/5630, 63/1379: P.R.O., E179/143/370: G.L.R.O., MR/TH/40.
145. P.R.O., E179/252/32, book 40; E179/253/30: G.L.R.O., F98; MR/TH/3, 12.
146. R.B.: Holden's and Underhill's triennial directories, 1805-7, 1817-19.
147. M.D.R. 1807/8/57.
148. R.B.: G.L.R.O., MR/LV/7/46.
149. M.D.R. 1807/8/56; 1814/5/638; 1815/3/145: R.B.
150. M.D.R. 1835/7/142.
151. *Ibid.*, 1859/5/721.
152. M.B.W. 2527.
153. M.D.R. 1861/7/1001-5; 1861/15/843-4.
154. *B.* 25 Jan. 1890, p. 70: Mark Girouard, *Victorian Pubs*, 1975, pp. 103-4, 107.
155. R.B.: *P.O.D.*
156. M.D.R. 1860/3/501.
157. London Oratory, *St. Philip's Orphanage, Report*, 1858; volume of 'Various Memoranda', p. 189 (MS. notes by Fr. Kerr).
158. M.D.R. 1861/7/562.
159. *Ibid.*, 1860/3/502; 1861/14/162; 1863/5/920; 1865/7/485.
160. *The Letters and Diaries of John Henry Newman*, ed. C. S. Dessain and V. F. Blehl, vol. XIV, 1963, index *sub* Lewin, S. R.

161. *P.O.D.*: M.D.R. 1862/12/425-32.
162. M.D.R. 1861/15/534-9; 1861/17/1180-5; 1862/5/894-9; 1862/12/425-32; 1862/16/767-72; 1863/4/812-16, 827-30; 1863/7/298-302; 1863/9/318-22; 1863/21/453, 455-8. Some original deeds in K.P.L., MSS. 2228-33.
163. M.D.R., e.g., 1862/12/425-38; 1862/16/767-78.
164. P.R.O., RG 9/22, ff. 6-7.
165. *Catholic Directory*, 1863-5.
166. O.S. sheet X/19, 1868: M.B.W. Minutes, 20 March 1863, p. 311.
167. London Oratory, Letters, vol. 24, ff. 68-70.
168. *Catholic Directory*, 1866: *Victoria County History of Middlesex*, vol. v, 1976, p. 87.
169. M.D.R. 1866/13/1022-48. Some original deeds in K.P.L., MSS. 1263, 2234-7, 2239-43.
170. M.D.R. 1866/13/1031-5.
171. *Ibid.*, 1862/12/497-502; 1862/16/779-82, 840-1; 1863/4/822-6, 835-8; 1863/7/308-12; 1863/9/351-5; 1863/21/465-70; 1866/19/100: K.P.L., MSS. 2227, 2229, 2231, 2233, 2238, 2244.
172. Corbett Letters, VIII, 79; XXI, 267.
173. R.B.: M.D.R. 1866/13/1022-5.
174. B.R. 100555.
175. Corbett Letters, XVII, 215; XXI, 88, 262, 336, 363, 530, 538.
176. P.R.O., RG 10/54, ff. 5-12.
177. *P.O.D.*: Victoria and Albert Museum Library, Sir Henry Cole's diary, 3 April 1881.
178. *B.N.* 27 April 1883, p. 548: *R.I.B.A. Journal*, 3rd ser., vol. II, 1894-5, pp. 128-9.
179. B.A. 25310: B.R. 6853.
180. M.D.R. 1863/4/108; 1863/21/471-2.
181. D.S.R. 1883/94; 1885/35; 1886/320; 1887/282-90: M.D.R. 1884/13/734: *P.O.D.*: Rupert Gunnis, *Dictionary of British Sculptors 1660-1851*, *sub* Bacon, Charles.
182. K.P.L., MS. 63/1379: P.R.O., E179/143/370: G.L.R.O., MR/HT/3, 12, 40, 45, 93.
183. P.R.O., C5/589/12; C7/30/109: K.P.L., MSS. 58/5630, 9035.
184. *Ibid.*: R.B.: M.D.R. 1715/4/80; 1730/6/231-3.
185. M.D.R. 1790/1/333-4.
186. *Ibid.*, 1790/1/335; 1794/5/616.
187. *Ibid.*, 1790/10/27: B.L., Add. MS. 31326.
188. D.S.R. 1890/15: the building itself is dated 1889.
189. M.D.R. 1792/8/895.
190. *Ibid.*, 1794/6/192.
191. *B.* 5 Nov. 1881, p. 592: D.S.R. 1881/322.
192. M.D.R. 1792/3/567-8; 1797/4/130: R.B.: B.L., Add. MS. 31326: B.A. 103244.
193. M.D.R. 1799/2/148: R.B.
194. M.D.R. 1796/1/15.
195. R.B.: G.L.R.O., MR/PLT: M.D.R. 1796/1/15.
196. Algernon Graves, *The Royal Academy of Arts: A Complete Dictionary of Contributors . . . 1769 to 1904*, 1905-6, *sub* Lloyd and Moser: *D.N.B.*
197. R.B.: M.D.R. 1808/1/476.
198. M.D.R. 1792/3/567-8; 1794/6/192; 1796/1/15; 1803/2/98; 1803/4/81; 1805/1/481; 1808/1/476.
199. *Ibid.*, 1807/2/664.
200. *Ibid.*, 1808/7/786.
201. *Ibid.*, 1808/2/340.
202. *Ibid.*, 1808/1/631.
203. *Ibid.*, 1810/9/916.
204. *Ibid.*, 1811/2/394.
205. *Ibid.*, 1808/7/432; 1811/10/604.
206. *Ibid.*, 1808/1/627, 629.
207. *Ibid.*, 1809/3/773; 1811/9/516.
208. R.B.: *Plan of . . . Kensington*, published by Thomas Starling, 1822.
209. P.R.O., PROB 11/1670/267.
210. *Survey of London*, vol. XXXVII, 1973, p. 77.
211. M.D.R. 1839/5/56, 695.
212. R.B.: M.D.R. 1844/1/164.
213. R.B.: D.S.R. 1855/226, 228.
214. M.D.R. 1890/8/274-9; 1890/18/381-3; 1890/26/17-18: D.S.R. 1889/247-56: *P.O.D.*
215. B.A. 23990: D.S.R. 1904/41: *P.O.D.*
216. B.A. 84090.
217. *Ibid.*: *Annual Register*, 1870, Chronicle, pp. 47, 95.
218. R.B.: *P.O.D.*: M.B.W. 1786, no. 618: M.B.W. Minutes, 10 Nov. 1865, p. 1231.
219. R.B.: M.D.R. 1851/4/336; 1866/5/732-3: M.B.W. Minutes, 10 Nov. 1865, p. 1231.
220. R.B.: G.L.R.O., MR/PLT: M.D.R. 1805/1/481.
221. D.S.R. 1880/167: *P.O.D.*
222. B.R. 73146, plan roll 1812: *P.O.D.*
223. B.R. 73146.
224. M.D.R. 1869/18/674-6.
225. *Ibid.*, 1797/4/518; 1806/5/285: R.B.
226. M.D.R. 1806/5/392.
227. R.B.: *P.O.D.*: *Diagrams of the Parish of St. Mary Abbotts*, 1847.
228. R.B.: *P.O.D.*: Royal Marsden Hospital, Committee Book and Sub-Committee Book.
229. M.D.R. 1864/6/680.
230. M.B.W. 6500.
231. P.R.O., E179/253/30: G.L.R.O., F98; MR/TH/3.
232. *The Parish Register of Kensington 1539-1675*, ed. F. N. Macnamara and A. Story-Maskelyne, 1890, p. 125.
233. G.L.R.O., MR/TH/40, 45, 93: P.R.O., E179/143/370: K.P.L., MSS. 58/5630, 63/1379.
234. *Musgrave.*
235. R.B.: ratebooks of Chelsea parish: P.R.O., PROB 11/868/315: Alexander Cruden, *The Adventures of Alexander the Corrector*, 1754 (B.L. pressmark 1415.f.40(1)).
236. R.B.: M.D.R. 1798/3/499.
237. M.D.R. 1780/1/265.
238. *Ibid.*, 1773/3/275; 1779/2/577.
239. *The Public Advertizer*, 25 Feb. 1768.
240. R.B.: M.D.R. 1797/3/785.
241. R.B.: Lewis Lochée, *An Essay in Military Education* (1773), *A System of Military Mathematics* (2 vols, 1776), *An Essay on Castrametation* (1778), *Elements of Fortification* (1780): 20 Geo. III, c. 39, private: J. A. Houlding, *Fit for Service, The Training of the British Army 1715-1795*, 1981, pp. 220, 253-4.
242. M.D.R. 1776/4/259: watercolour in K.P.L.
243. M.D.R. 1779/2/577.
244. 20 Geo. III, c. 39, private.
245. M.D.R. 1781/3/31-2; 1798/3/499.
246. *Boswell in Extremes, 1776-1778*, ed. C. M. Weis and F. A. Pottle, 1971, p. 306.
247. *The Gentleman's Magazine*, e.g., vol. XLIII, 1773, p. 390.
248. *Ibid.*, vol. L, June 1780, p. 284.
249. Archives of St. Mary's Priory, Fulham Road, leases and

releases, 26-27 Jan. 1780, Landumiey to Payne, 29-30 May 1780, Payne to Lochée: M.D.R. 1780/2/491-2; 1781/3/170-1, 294-5; 1790/8/150: *Survey of London*, vol. IV, 1913, p. 44: W. Marston Acres, *The Bank of England From Within 1694-1900*, 1931, vol. I, pp. 257-8: *D.N.B. sub* John Payne.

250. Faulkner, *Description of Chelsea, ut supra*, 1829 ed., vol. I, p. 139.

251. *The Gentleman's Magazine*, vol. LIV, pt. 2, Oct. 1784, pp. 792-3.

252. Engraving entitled 'Grand Aerostatic Balloon', published by R. Wilkinson, 1784: watercolour in K.P.L.

253. *Notes and Queries*, 7th. ser., vol. X, p. 214; 10th. ser., vol. X, p. 493.

254. *The Gentleman's Magazine*, vol. LXI, pt. 1, June 1791, p. 588: *The Times*, 29 June 1791: Lewis Lochée, *A Monsieur Le Baron Schonfelt*, Lille, 1790; *Au Président du Congrès*, 1790; *Relation de ce qui c'est passé le 18 Mai entre les Autrichiens et les Patriotes*, 1790 (B.L. pressmark 8079.e.25 (1, 3 and 4)); *Observations sur La Révolution Belgique . . .*, 2nd. ed., Lille, 1791, pp. 48-50 (B.L. pressmark 1608/4882): *Revue de Belgique*, vol. LVII, 15 Sept. 1887, pp. 69-70.

255. *The Gentleman's Magazine*, vol. LXXXV, pt. 2, Dec. 1815, p. 572.

256. Faulkner, *Description of Chelsea, ut supra*, 1829 ed., vol. I, pp. 139-40.

257. T. C. Croker, *A Walk from London to Fulham*, 1860, p. 119.

258. R.B.: G.L.R.O., MR/PLT.

259. M.D.R. 1800/2/172.

260. R.B.: trade directories.

261. M.D.R. 1805/3/570.

262. *Ibid.*, 1797/3/785.

263. *Ibid.*, 1798/3/499.

264. *Ibid.*, 1800/2/172.

265. *Ibid.*, 1802/1/185.

266. R.B.: information kindly supplied by Messrs. Hedges and Butler.

267. *The Morning Herald*, 9 July 1823 (advert.).

268. R.B.: *P.O.D.*: Hurford Janes, *The Red Barrel. A History of Watney Mann*, 1963, p. 159.

269. Unigate Properties Ltd., conveyance, 21 April 1882, Butler to Bickers: information kindly supplied by Messrs. Hedges and Butler.

270. Unigate Properties Ltd., leases, 13 Feb. 1883, Bickers to Preece: D.S.R. 1883/93.

271. D.S.R. 1890/141.

272. *P.O.D.*: B.A. 39861: Unigate Properties Ltd., agreement, 30 Sept. 1925; conveyance, 10 Nov. 1930, Doll to United Dairies.

273. M.D.R. 1859/11/362.

274. *P.O.D.*: Boase.

275. *P.O.D.*: R.B.: D.S.R. 1849/19-20: M.D.R. 1849/2/584.

276. M.D.R. 1746/2/467-8.

277. Information kindly supplied by Messrs. Hedges and Butler.

278. Royal Marsden Hospital, Sub-Committee Minutes, 29 June, 20 July 1852: M.D.R. 1866/5/732.

279. T. C. Croker, *A Walk from London to Fulham*, enlarged by Beatrice E. Horne, 1896, p. 143.

280. M.D.R. 1803/6/551.

281. *Ibid.*, 1823/5/301.

282. R.B.: *P.O.D.*: P.R.O., RG 9/22, ff. 15-16; RG 10/54, f. 28.

283. R.I.B.A. Library, Fellowship nomination papers, C. F. Doll, 6 May 1901.

284. Unigate Properties Ltd., conveyance, 19 Sept. 1899, between members of the Doll family: Post Office, Conveyancing Dept., box 537 (1), copy will of Charles Bickers.

285. *P.O.D.*: L.C.C. Minutes, 5 May, 28 July 1903, pp. 666, 1363: D.S.R. 1902/102, 109-10: K.P.L., leasing particulars, n.d. (K 4678/B).

286. P.R.O., C54/4312, no. 12; PROB 11/330/104; E179/252/32, book 40.

287. G.L.R.O., MR/TH/12.

288. P.R.O., E179/252/30, book 40; E179/253/30; PROB 11/286/26; PROB 11/550/35: G.L.R.O., MR/TH/3, 12, 93.

289. B.L., Verney Papers, microfilm, M636/34, John Verney to Sir Ralph Verney, 21 Oct. 1680; M636/52, Ralph Palmer to Lord Fermanagh, 30 Nov. 1703.

290. *Ibid.*, M636/33, John Verney to Sir Ralph Verney, 4 Dec. 1679.

291. *Ibid.*, M636/33, John Verney to Sir Ralph Verney, 7 Nov., 10 Dec. 1679.

292. Randall Davies, *Chelsea Old Church*, 1904, pp. 208, 210, 212.

293. *H.M.C. 7th Report and Appendix*, 1879, pp. 403-509: *Verney Letters of the Eighteenth Century*, ed. Lady Verney, 1930, 2 vols. (originals on microfilm in B.L., M636/1-60).

294. B.L., Verney Papers, microfilm, M636/54, Ralph Palmer jr. to Hon. Ralph Verney, 29 May 1712.

295. P.R.O., PROB 11/550/35: K.P.L., MSS. 58/5630, 63/1379.

296. *Verney Letters of the Eighteenth Century*, ed. Lady Verney, 1930, vol. 1, p. 70.

297. B.L., Verney Papers, microfilm, M636/56, Ralph Palmer to Lord Fermanagh, 4 Oct. 1720.

298. *Verney Letters of the Eighteenth Century*, ed. Lady Verney, 1930, vol. 1, p. 91, vol. 2, pp. 79-80.

299. G.E.C.: P.R.O., PROB 11/798/311.

300. M.D.R. 1759/2/13-14.

301. *Ibid.*, 1781/3/170-1, 294-5.

302. R.B.: *London Directory*, 1795.

303. R.B.: *Holden's Directory*, 1799.

304. Archives of St. Mary's Priory, Fulham Road, grant, 11 July 1853, Rogers to Jackson: R.B.

305. Archives of St. Mary's Priory, Fulham Road, conveyance, 15 Aug. 1871, Jackson to Bickers.

306. *P.O.D.*: Post Office, Conveyancing Dept., box 537(1), copy will of Charles Bickers, 1889.

307. *The South London Press*, 17 Aug. 1872.

308. Archives of St. Mary's Priory, Fulham Road, lease, 29 Sept. 1879, Bickers to Coventry.

309. D.S.R. 1888/43: *P.O.D.*: M.B.W. Minutes, 2 March 1888, p. 407; 28 Sept. 1888, p. 449.

310. *P.O.D.*: archives of St. Mary's Priory, Fulham Road, lease, 30 Jan. 1906, Doll to Rhind.

311. Archives of St. Mary's Priory, Fulham Road, conveyance, 6 May 1927, Doll *et al.* to Tutt *et al.*

312. *P.O.D.*: information kindly provided by the secretary of the Eleusis Club and by Chelsea Reference Library.

313. B.R. 104425.

314. *Ibid.*: archives of St. Mary's Priory, Fulham Road, plans by E. A. Remnant, 1936: Post Office, Conveyancing Dept., box 537(1), correspondence 20 Aug. 1937.

315. Post Office, Conveyancing Dept., box 537(1), letter, 23 July 1938, E. A. Remnant to Office of Works: B.R. 104425: Ordnance Survey, 1:1250, 1950, plan TQ2677NW.

316. Archives of St. Mary's Priory, Fulham Road, plans, 1960: B.R. 104425.

317. B.L., Add. MS. 31326: *Fraser's Magazine*, vol. XXXI, March 1845, p. 333.

318. H.B. photograph.

319. R.B.: *Pigot's Directory*, 1832-4.

320. *P.O.D.*: P.R.O., HO 107/1469, ff. 330-435: *Survey of London*, vol. XXXVI, 1970, pp. 57-9.

321. Post Office, Conveyancing Dept., box 537(1), appointment and release, 11 July 1853, Rogers to Bickers.

322. *Diagrams of the Parish of St. Mary Abbotts, Kensington*, 1847.

323. R.B.: *P.O.D.*: P.R.O., RG 9/22, f. 16; RG 10/54, f. 38.

324. Post Office, Conveyancing Dept., box 537(1), 15 Oct. 1881, Bickers to Duleep Singh.

325. *P.O.D.*: Major Evans Bell, *The Annexation of the Punjaub and the Maharajah Duleep Singh*, 1882: *The Maharajah Duleep Singh and the Government*, privately printed, June 1884, p. 96 (B.L. pressmark 9057.b.15).

326. Post Office, Conveyancing Dept., box 537(1), conveyance, 25 Sept. 1899, Drew to Postmaster General.

327. *Ibid.*, box 537(1), conveyance, 9 July 1940, Postmaster General to McCarthy; correspondence, 20 Aug. 1937, 23 July 1938: B.R. 104425.

328. Post Office, Conveyancing Dept., box 537(2), 3 Jan. 1962.

329. R.B.: *P.O.D.*: *D.N.B.*: M.D.R. 1860/10/918.

330. Information supplied by London Postal Region, Post Office.

331. P.R.O., E179/143/370; E179/252/32, book 40: G.L.R.O., MR/TH/12, 40, 93.

332. P.R.O., E179/143/370: K.P.L., MSS. 58/5630, 63/1379.

333. Faulkner, p. 261: *Musgrave*.

334. K.P.L., MSS. 58/5630, 63/1379: B.L., Verney Papers, microfilm, M636/42, Ralph Palmer to John Verney, 11 Oct. 1687.

335. K.P.L., MS. 58/5630: *D.N.B.*

336. B.L., Verney Papers, microfilm, M636/53, Ralph Palmer jr. to Lord Fermanagh, 22 Oct. 1706; M636/55, same to Hon. Ralph Verney, 6 June 1715; M636/56, same to Lord Fermanagh, 28 Nov. 1716: *Musgrave*.

337. Guildhall Library, MS. 8674/6, p. 116.

338. B.L., Verney Papers, microfilm, M636/56, Ralph Palmer to Hon. Ralph Verney, 4 Oct., 8 Nov. 1716, 9 May 1717; same to Lord Fermanagh, 28 Nov. 1716.

339. *Ibid.*, Fra. Luttrell to Mrs Eliz. Baker, 12 May 1718; Ralph Palmer to Lord Fermanagh, 18 April 1719.

340. *Ibid.*, Ralph Palmer to Lord Fermanagh, 13 Aug. 1719.

341. K.P.L., MS. 58/5630: P.R.O., PROB 11/798/311.

342. R.B.: M.D.R. 1803/6/372.

343. Holden's directories, 1799-1807.

344. R.B.: *P.P.*, 1844, vol. XVIII, no. 1, *Statistical Appendix to Report of Metropolitan Commissioners in Lunacy*, pp. 4-11, 71.

345. M.D.R. 1836/6/793.

346. *Ibid.*, 1860/10/918.

347. *Ibid.*, 1876/10/295, 330.

348. Andrew Saint, *Richard Norman Shaw*, 1976, p. 195.

349. D.S.R. 1877/28-37, 174-87, 299-300, 364-7: K.P.L., MS. 58/19969, pp. 432, 500-1.

350. M.D.R. 1877/10/355.

351. *Ibid.*, 1876/10/296, 331.

352. *Ibid.*, 1876/10/330-1; 1877/10/355; 1877/13/979; 1877/17/384; 1877/24/341: Post Office, Conveyancing Dept., box 537(1), mortgages, 15 Oct. 1877, Hussey to Barker, 21 Dec. 1877, Hussey to Sarsfield.

353. M.D.R. 1876/10/331.

354. *The Works of John Ruskin*, ed. Cook and Wedderburn, 1909, vol. XXXVII, p. 618.

355. John Ruskin, *Fors Clavigera*, vol. VII, 1877, pp. 115-20.

356. P.R.O., RG 11/46, ff. 91-4.

357. K.P.L., MSS. 65/34, 43: Post Office, Conveyancing Dept., box 537(1), mortgage, 19 June 1885, Hussey to Taylor.

358. K.P.L., MSS. 65/43, 52.

359. Kensington Vestry Minutes, 30 March, 6 July 1892, pp. 8, 260; 22 May 1895, p. 175.

360. *Ibid.*, 11 Oct. 1899, p. 491.

361. Charles Booth, *Life and Labour of the People in London, First Series, Poverty, 2, Streets and Population Classified*, 1902, App., p. 6.

362. Kensington Borough Council Minutes, 4 Aug. 1903, p. 420.

363. *Ibid.*, 10 April 1906, p. 268; 5 May 1908, p. 356.

364. Post Office, Conveyancing Dept., box 537(1), conveyance, 28 Sept. 1927, Hussey to Brew.

365. *The New Survey of London Life and Labour*, 1930, vol. VII, map-sheet No. 9.

366. Kensington Borough Council Minutes, 24 March, 5 May, 2 June, 28 July 1931, pp. 220-1, 260, 300, 366; 6 March, 1 May, 24 July 1934, pp. 150, 160, 232, 337: T. F. Gibbs, *St. Mary Boltons 1850-1964*, [n.d.], p. 12.

367. Post Office, Conveyancing Dept., box 537(1), correspondence, 12 and 17 Nov. 1937, 24 Nov. 1939.

368. G.L.R.O., MR/TH/12, 45: P.R.O., E179/252/32, book 40; E179/253/30; E179/143/370.

369. *The South Carolina Historical and Genealogical Magazine*, vol. 1, no. 3, July 1900, p. 228 and note: P.R.O., PROB 11/309/142; PROB 11/362/2.

370. P.R.O., PROB 11/430/7.

371. Guildhall Library, MS. 8674/10, p. 257.

372. R.B.: M.D.R. 1765/6/173.

373. P.R.O., PROB 31/638/716.

374. K.P.L., MSS. 58/5630, 63/1379: *Survey of London*, vol. XX, 1940, p. 106; vol. XXXIII, 1966, p. 108: M.D.R. 1713/3/96.

375. Archives of St. Mary's Priory, Fulham Road, indentures, 1-2 Aug. 1769, Davison to Collett; 9-10 Aug. 1769 and 22-23 April 1772, Collett to Landumiey: R.B.

376. Archives of St. Mary's Priory, Fulham Road, leases and releases, 26-27 Jan. 1780, Landumiey to Payne; 29-30 May 1780, Payne to Lochée.

377. *Ibid.*, lease and release, 23-24 Feb. 1803, Lochée to Dagley.

378. R.B.: *D.N.B.*

379. *P.O.D.*: M.B.W. Minutes, 30 July 1869, p. 907.

380. B.A. 52685: B.R. 126248: archives of St. Mary's Priory, Fulham Road, envelope 'Re Parochial Hall'.

381. Archives of St. Mary's Priory, Fulham Road, assignment to attend inheritance, 22 Aug. 1783, Mead to Townsend.

382. M.D.R. 1713/3/96.

383. P.R.O., E179/252/32, book 40.

384. G.L.R.O., MR/TH/9.

385. P.R.O., E179/143/370: G.L.R.O., MR/TH/45.

386. K.P.L., MSS. 58/5630, 63/1379: *D.N.B.*: P.R.O., PROB 11/456/106.

387. Archives of St. Mary's Priory, Fulham Road, assignment to attend the inheritance, 22 Aug. 1783, Mead to Townsend: *Musgrave*.

388. Archives of St. Mary's Priory, Fulham Road, lease and release, 13-14 Aug. 1783, Lewis to Townsend.
389. R.B.: Holden's directories: G.L.R.O., MR/PLT.
390. R.B.: Holden's directories, 1799, 1802-5.
391. R.B.: archives of St. Mary's Priory, Fulham Road, lease and release, 21-22 June 1839, Barnard to Milton; release, 20 July 1866, Milton to Milton: Boase.
392. The account of the church and priory is based largely on Fr. Gerard M. Corr, O.S.M., *Servites in London*, 1952, supplemented by archives in the possession of the Servite Fathers, to which guidance was kindly given by Fr. Philip Allen, O.S.M. It has not, however, been possible to consult some of the sources used by Fr. Corr.
393. Corr, *op. cit.*, pp. 1-37 *passim*.
394. Corr, *op. cit.*, p. 36.
395. Archives of St. Mary's Priory, Fulham Road, envelope C2.
396. Corr, *op. cit.*, p. 53.
397. M.D.R. 1873/18/168.
398. Post Office, Conveyancing Dept., box 537(2), abstract of title.
399. R.I.B.A., Fellowship nomination papers, Joseph Stanislaus Hansom.
400. Corr, *op. cit.*, pp. 56-7.
401. K.P.L., applications to Vestry from M.B.W., no. 108: D.S.R. 1875/25: *P.O.D.*
402. Archives of St. Mary's Priory, Fulham Road, agreement, 16 July 1874, in envelope B2: D.S.R. 1874/126: *The Tablet*, 25 Sept. 1875, p. 402.
403. Corr, *op. cit.*, pp. 57-8.
404. *The Tablet*, 25 Sept. 1875, p. 402.
405. Archives of St. Mary's Priory, Fulham Road, printed notice in envelope B2.
406. *The Tablet*, 25 Sept. 1875, p. 402: *P.O.D.*, 1876.
407. Archives of St. Mary's Priory, Fulham Road, memoranda of agreements in envelope B2: *B.* 25 Sept. 1875, p. 872: *P.O.D.*
408. *P.O.D.*: *The Tablet*, 25 Sept. 1875, p. 402.
409. *B.* 25 Sept. 1875, p. 872: *P.O.D.*
410. *The Tablet*, 16 June 1877, p. 758.
411. Archives of St. Mary's Priory, Fulham Road, drawings by J. A. Hansom and G. M. Hammer: *P.O.D.*
412. *B.* 25 Sept. 1875, p. 872.
413. *B.N.* 22 Oct. 1880, p. 470 and illus.: archives of St. Mary's Priory, Fulham Road, envelopes B2, B3; contract drawings: Corr, *op. cit.*, p. 57.
414. Archives of St. Mary's Priory, Fulham Road, particulars of organ by Henry Jones and Sons, 19 Sept. 1894: *The Tablet*, 25 Sept. 1875, p. 402.
415. *B.N.* 22 Oct. 1880, p. 470.
416. Archives of St. Mary's Priory, Fulham Road, contract drawings: *B.* 21 April 1883, p. 547 and illus.: *B.N.* 6 July 1883, p. 32: *P.O.D.*
417. Archives of St. Mary's Priory, Fulham Road, contract drawings: D.S.R. 1890/5: *Souvenir of the Consecration*, 4 Nov. 1953, p. 13.
418. Archives of St. Mary's Priory, Fulham Road, contract and other drawings; envelope B2; particulars of organ by Henry Jones and Sons, 19 Sept. 1894: D.S.R. 1893/94-5: Corr, *op. cit.*, p. 80.
419. *B.* 4 Jan. 1902, p. 13: archives of St. Mary's Priory, Fulham Road, statement of outgoings and income, 1893-5.
420. Archives of St. Mary's Priory, Fulham Road, in envelope C4.
421. D.S.R. 1896/58.
422. Archives of St. Mary's Priory, Fulham Road, design, n.d. (watermark 1899).
423. *Souvenir of the Consecration*, 1953, p. [15]: *P.O.D.*
424. *Souvenir, ut supra*, pp. 13-14.
425. *The Catholic Building Review, Southern Edition, for the year 1962*, p. 68.
426. Directories.
427. K.P.L., MSS. 58/5630, 63/1379: G.L.R.O., AM/PW/ 1722/50: M.D.R. 1710/1/33; 1725/6/94.
428. M.D.R. 1762/1/25.
429. *Ibid.*, 1762/1/26.
430. *Ibid.*, 1802/5/593.
431. *Survey of London*, vol. XXXVII, 1973, pp. 42, 45, 77, 83.
432. R.B.: M.D.R. 1803/7/7: Holden's triennial directories.
433. M.D.R. 1868/12/909-10; 1868/30/1232-7.
434. B.A. 100115: B.R. 120288.

CHAPTER XII (pp. 195-240)

The Boltons and Redcliffe Square Area

1. J. E. B. Gover, Allen Mawer and F. M. Stenton, *The Place-Names of Middlesex*, 1942, p. 128.
2. E.C.R., 20 April 1554.
3. M.D.R. 1809/4/375: P.R.O., MAF 9/167.
4. K.P.L., MSS. 9019, 9035: M.D.R. 1715/4/80.
5. K.P.L., MSS. 9021, 9035: P.R.O., PROB 11/209/117.
6. K.P.L., MS. 9022.
7. E.C.R., 20 April 1554; 16 May 1558.
8. K.P.L., MS. 9029: P.R.O., PROB 11/558/100.
9. K.P.L., MSS. 9026, 9028-9, 9033: M.D.R. 1719/2/284-5.
10. E.C.R., 27 July 1752: M.D.R. 1754/1/132-3: R. Brooke-Caws, *Notes on the Origin and History of Coutts and Company*, 1950, p. 2.
11. M.D.R. 1762/1/348.
12. *Musgrave*: P.R.O., PROB 11/1207/371: *The Merchant and Tradesman's London Directory for the Year 1787*: Howard Robinson, *The British Post Office, A History*, 1948, p. 110: Kenneth Ellis, *The Post Office in the Eighteenth Century*, 1958, pp. 47, 48, 51, 53: *Memoirs of William Hickey*, ed. Alfred Spencer, vol. I, [n.d.], pp. 114, 131.
13. K.P.L., MS. 9032.
14. M.D.R. 1797/2/295.
15. *Ibid.*, 1797/3/551.
16. *Ibid.*, 1805/7/7.
17. *Ibid.*, 1807/6/261.
18. *Ibid.*, 1805/1/778.
19. *Ibid.*, 1808/8/323-4: K.P.L., particulars of sale, Coleherne Estate, 21 June 1808.
20. M.D.R. 1806/5/392.
21. *Ibid.*, 1801/3/324.
22. *Ibid.*, 1755/2/82-4: J. and J. A. Venn, *Alumni Cantabrigienses*.
23. M.D.R. 1737/2/233.
24. *Ibid.*, 1748/1/58.
25. *Ibid.*, 1754/1/132; 1812/1/731; 1812/6/537.
26. *Ibid.*, 1812/9/33.
27. *Ibid.*, 1786/2/38; 1806/5/392.
28. *Ibid.*, 1807/8/57.
29. P.R.O., E179/252/32, book 40: G.L.R.O., MR/TH/3.

30. B.L., Verney Papers, microfilm, M636/56, Ralph Palmer to Hon. Ralph Verney, 4 Oct. 1716.
31. Randall Davies, *Chelsea Old Church*, 1904, pp. 198-200.
32. G.L.R.O., MR/TH/12, 93: K.P.L., MSS. 58/5630, 63/1379.
33. Faulkner, p. 261.
34. M.D.R. 1784/4/255-6; 1834/4/288; 1836/7/201.
35. E.C.R., 7 Dec. 1753.
36. P.R.O., MAF9/167.
37. G.L.R.O., MR/PLT/4902: E.C.R., 30 April 1641.
38. G.L.R.O., TA9.
39. M.D.R. 1754/1/132.
40. *Ibid.*, 1808/8/323.
41. *Ibid.*, 1808/5/530.
42. *B.* 16 Aug. 1873, p. 647.
43. M.D.R. 1719/2/282; 1721/4/48.
44. K.P.L., MS. 9024.
45. *Ibid.*, particulars of sale, Coleherne Estate, 21 June 1808.
46. M.D.R. 1746/2/467.
47. P.R.O., C54/3191, no. 28.
48. E.C.R., 4 Dec. 1753.
49. O.S. sheet X/19, 1868.
50. John Harvey, *Early Nurserymen*, 1974, pp. 201-2.
51. Faulkner, p. 606: J. C. Loudon, *An Encyclopaedia of Gardening*, 1822, pp. 372, 1213.
52. R.B.: M.D.R. 1835/7/142.
53. B.L., Add. MS. 31326.
54. R.B.
55. R.B.: *P.O.D.*
56. *Ibid.*, 1808/8/323: K.P.L., sale particulars, *ut supra.*
57. K.P.L., MS. 58/5630.
58. Samuel Johnson, *Lives of the English Poets*, with an introduction by L. Archer-Hind, 2 vols. (Everyman Library), [n.d.], vol. 2, p. 22.
59. *The Parish Registers of Kensington from A.D. 1539 to A.D. 1675*, ed. F. N. Macnamara and A. Story-Maskelyne, 1890, p. 36.
60. *Ibid.*, p. 40.
61. G.L.R.O., MR/TH/3.
62. P.R.O., E179/252/32, book 40.
63. G.L.R.O., MR/TH/40, 93: K.P.L., MS. 58/5630.
64. K.P.L., MS. 63/1379, p. 172.
65. M.D.R. 1723/6/102-3.
66. *Ibid.*, 1730/6/231.
67. National Monuments Record, BB67/737.
68. M.D.R. 1723/6/101-3: K.P.L., MS. 58/5630.
69. K.P.L., MSS. 58/5630, 63/1379.
70. M.D.R. 1735/4/61-2: G.L.R.O., Mddx. MS. 131(3).
71. M.D.R. 1739/2/50-1; 1739/3/328.
72. *Ibid.*, 1749/2/439-40.
73. *Ibid.*, 1751/1/644-5.
74. *Ibid.*, 1762/1/347.
75. *Ibid.*, 1810/7/183.
76. G.L.R.O., Print Collection, no. 14720.
77. *The Journal of Beatrix Potter from 1881 to 1897*, transcribed by Leslie Linder, 1966, p. 56.
78. D.S.R. 1871/36.
79. R.B.: Boase.
80. M.D.R. 1864/8/682.
81. R.B.: *P.O.D.*: Boase.
82. O.S. sheets X/8 and X/9, 1867.
83. R.B.: Richard Fawkes, *Dion Boucicault*, 1979, pp. 144-5.
84. *B.* 18 July 1863, p. 523.
85. M.B.W. 928, no. 14, 8 Aug. 1866, plan of Redcliffe Estate.
86. O.S. sheets X/8 and X/9, 1894-6.
87. Corbett Letters, XVII, 375; XXI, 75, 116, 194, 695, 972.
88. K.P.L., cutting from *The Cycling World Illustrated*, 24 June 1896, pp. 337-8.
89. R.B.: Boase: Vincent Orchard, *Tattersalls*, 1953, pp. 256-9.
90. R.B.: M.D.R. 1805/1/778.
91. R.B.: *P.O.D.*: *Plan of . . . Kensington*, published by Thomas Starling, 1822.
92. M.D.R. 1810/3/568.
93. Thomas Faulkner, *An Historical and Topographical Description of Chelsea and its Environs*, 1810.
94. M.D.R. 1810/3/569.
95. *Ibid.*, 1810/3/570; 1812/2/781; 1813/6/250.
96. *Ibid.*, 1813/3/54.
97. *Burke's Landed Gentry*, 18th ed., vol. I, 1965.
98. *The Morning Herald*, 14 Aug. 1820: K.P.L., GC2420.
99. G.L.C., Legal and Parliamentary Dept., Conveyancing (Records) Division, Bousfield School site, Docket 26551, lease 15 Nov. 1836, Gunter to Nixon: K.P.L., MS. 63/13337, p. 208 (insertion).
100. M.D.R. 1838/3/501.
101. J. and J. A. Venn, *Alumni Cantabrigienses.*
102. K.P.L., K70/171.
103. M.D.R. 1857/10/162 (schedule): R.B.: *P.O.D.*
104. R.B.: K.P.L., MS. 63/13349, p. 232 (insertion).
105. R.B.: *P.O.D.*: K.P.L., K60/18: G.L.R.O., H4/PB/E2/1.
106. 1 Geo. IV, c. 34, private: M.D.R. 1820/5/652.
107. M.D.R. 1836/7/201.
108. *Ibid.*, *sub* Robert Gunter.
109. *Ibid.*, 1846/6/181, 552; 1852/1/960.
110. British Telecom, Conveyancing Dept., deeds re Earl's Court Telephone Exchange, photocopy of will of Robert Gunter.
111. C.C., file 20641.
112. D.S.R. 1850/191-4, 275-8.
113. *Ibid.*, 1853/14-17, 42.
114. M.C.S. 292/114.
115. D.S.R. 1854/172-3.
116. *B.* 13 Jan. 1855, p. 24.
117. M.D.R. 1855/2/281.
118. *Ibid.*, 1851/12/995; 1851/13/495: P.R.O., HO 107/1473, f. 475.
119. M.D.R. 1852/9/556-7; 1854/10/846; 1854/12/1033-4; 1854/17/404.
120. *Ibid.*, 1852/1/287-8; 1852/10/761; 1852/12/214, 971; 1853/2/313.
121. *Ibid.*, 1852/1/285-6; 1852/7/823-4.
122. *Ibid.*, 1851/13/45; 1852/3/422.
123. *Ibid.*, 1852/13/330-1.
124. *Ibid.*, 1851/12/843-5; 1851/14/25; 1852/5/61-4.
125. M.C.S. 291/586: D.S.R. 1850/208-9, 230-1, 261-2, 283-4.
126. M.D.R. 1852/1/289-91, 959; 1857/10/162 (schedule).
127. *Ibid.*, 1851/12/995; 1851/13/495.
128. *Ibid.*, 1853/11/908-10.
129. See M.D.R. 1846-51, index, Gunter to Harding (Chelsea).
130. M.D.R. 1851/12/835-42; 1852/1/961-2; 1852/4/815-16; 1852/8/713-14; 1852/16/705.
131. D.S.R. 1851/74-81, 351-7.
132. P.R.O., HO 107/1472-3.
133. M.D.R. 1851/12/995; 1851/13/495.
134. F. M. L. Thompson, *Hampstead: Building a Borough 1650-1964*, 1974, pp. 276-88: Donald J. Olsen, *The Growth of Victorian London*, 1976, pp. 257, 260-2.

135. *P.O.D.*
136. M.C.S. 292/353.
137. *Ibid.*, 290/226; 292/289, 353: D.S.R. 1850/291-2, 298-301, 349-50; 1851/74-81, 83-4, 190-1, 324-5, 351-7.
138. *B.* 4 Sept. 1875, p. 791.
139. M.D.R. 1851/12/835-42; 1852/4/815-16, 961-2; 1852/8/713-14; 1852/16/705.
140. *Ibid.*, 1856/14/433.
141. *Ibid.*, 1857/9/659; 1857/11/821; 1857/15/384, 386; 1859/16/58, 60; 1860/1/782; 1861/1/878-83.
142. *P.O.D.*: Boase.
143. M.D.R. 1860/1/782.
144. *The Estates Gazette*, 1 May 1861, p. 199.
145. *Ibid.*, 16 Aug. 1858, p. 13.
146. G.L.R.O., Mddx. Acc. 208/2.
147. Arundel Castle Muniments, 14th Duke's Correspondence (Undated Letters), 12 Jan [1853?], J. Hughes to Earl of Arundel.
148. Royal Borough of Kensington and Chelsea, Town Planning case 16410, Frere Cholmeley to Postmaster-General, 21 Oct. 1937.
149. Ealing Town Hall, ratebooks 1847-54: M.D.R. 1847/10/314; 1849/8/423.
150. John Summerson, 'The London Suburban Villa', in *The Architectural Review*, vol. 104, Aug. 1948, p. 67 (Plate 3).
151. Cf. M.D.R. 1853/6/467-8 and M.D.R. 1851/7/256; 1853/13/513; 1854/10/846; 1857/14/804; 1859/16/58; 1862/10/11.
152. Cf. M.D.R. 1853/6/467-8 and M.D.R. 1851/7/256; 1853/2/313.
153. *B.* 11 June 1859, p. 400.
154. K.P.L., applications to Vestry from M.B.W., no. 439.
155. M.D.R. 1862/1/349-50; 1862/2/932-3; 1862/15/511-12; 1862/19/138; 1863/4/555; 1863/9/579-80; 1863/12/39-40.
156. *Ibid.*, see index, R. Gunter to Bradley, 1863 onward (Chelsea).
157. Corbett Letters, xiv, 209, 214.
158. M.D.R. 1854/12/1036; 1857/1/186, 801-2; 1858/6/461; 1862/15/650.
159. British Telecom, Conveyancing Dept., deeds re Earl's Court Telephone Exchange, abstract of title to Sidmouth Lodge.
160. *The Times*, 19 Sept. 1905, p. 4c.
161. M.D.R. 1853/9/321-2; 1854/2/1021-2.
162. *Ibid.*, 1854/10/846; 1854/12/1033-4; 1854/17/404.
163. *Ibid.*, 1852/7/823.
164. *Ibid.*, 1855/8/146-7: R.B.
165. M.D.R. 1857/10/162 (schedule): R.B.
166. M.C.S. 297.
167. M.D.R. 1857/3/783; 1867/17/65-6; 1867/19/564-5.
168. *Ibid.*, 1857/14/884; 1858/5/102; 1858/6/593-4; 1858/9/14-15; 1859/2/954-6; 1859/4/579.
169. *Ibid.*, 1862/10/11-12; 1862/13/460-3; 1862/18/806-7; 1864/13/243-8; 1865/3/103-4.
170. *Ibid.*, 1869/19/685.
171. *P.O.D.*: P.R.O., RG 10/53, ff. 73-7.
172. M.D.R. 1859/4/933-4; 1860/9/15-19; 1863/16/913-14; 1865/3/105-7; 1866/17/333.
173. *B.* 20 Jan. 1883, p. 93.
174. M.D.R. 1863/10/281-2, 609-10; 1864/7/239-42: G.L.R.O., C/84/1, 81.
175. *The Journal of Beatrix Potter from 1881 to 1897*, transcribed by Leslie Linder, 1966, p. 196.
176. G.L.R.O., C/84/3, 83.
177. *The Journal of Beatrix Potter, ut supra*, pp. xv, xvi: *The Linder Collection of the Works and Drawings of Beatrix Potter*, 1971, p. 30.
178. M.B.W. 22502.
179. P.R.O., RG 10/53, ff. 52-3, 55-7, 64-6, 73-83.
180. *P.O.D.*: *The South London Press*, 17 Aug. 1872.
181. M.D.R. 1864/21/560-1, 563-6, 746-7, 777-8.
182. *The Times*, 2 Sept. 1908, p. 11e: *P.O.D.*
183. M.D.R. 1865/10/66; 1868/21/383.
184. K.P.L., MSS. 3804-5.
185. M.D.R. 1864/3/69.
186. *Ibid.*, 1864/7/451-2.
187. See *Survey of London*, vol. xxxviii, 1975.
188. Corbett Letters, xiv, 554.
189. G.L.R.O., BRA 641/31-2.
190. Corbett Letters, viii, 79.
191. M.B.W. 6500.
192. *Ibid.*, 928, item 14, 8 Aug. 1866.
193. M.D.R. 1867/16/599.
194. *Ibid.*, 1867/19/926; 1868/6/360.
195. *Ibid.*, 1869/19/692-3.
196. *Ibid.*, 1869/22/907.
197. These figures are derived from the M.D.R.
198. D.S.R.
199. P.R.O., RG 10/53, f. 76; RG 10/54, f. 13.
200. E.g. M.D.R. 1863/21/453; 1864/21/560.
201. M.D.R. 1862/4/914.
202. P.R.O., RG 10/53, f. 76; RG 10/54, ff. 13, 42-6, 66, 82-3.
203. Corbett Letters. xiv, 703, 882, 894.
204. P.R.O., RG 10/53, f. 76.
205. Corbett Letters, iv, 556, and vols. xiv, xvii (Feb. 1878, May 1879).
206. M.B.W. 928, item 14, 8 Aug. 1866: M.D.R. 1865/10/66; 1868/21/383-4.
207. *B.* 21 March 1868, pp. 201-2.
208. Corbett Letters, iii, 270: C. J. Féret, *Fulham Old and New*, 1900, vol. iii, p. 22.
209. Corbett Letters, xxi, 789-90.
210. *B.* 2, 9 Dec. 1871, pp. 952, 961-2: information kindly supplied by Mr. Salmons, Paddington District Surveyor's office.
211. *I.L.N.* 28 Sept. 1872, pp. 302, 339: *B.N.* 4 Oct. 1872, p. 272.
212. Corbett Letters, iv, 558.
213. *B.N.* 20 Sept. 1872, p. 234: *B.* 21 Sept. 1872, p. 752: *The Times*, 6 May 1878, p. 11f: *The Kensington News*, 11 May 1878.
214. Corbett Letters, viii, 282.
215. *B.* 21 March 1868, pp. 201-2: Corbett Letters, xxi, 591.
216. Corbett Letters, viii, 79; xxi, 267.
217. *Ibid.*, vi, 251; xxi, 102.
218. M.D.R. 1864/21/562, 567; 1865/5/644-5; 1865/23/250-2; 1865/26/128-30; 1866/9/781-5; 1866/10/250; 1866/12/721-2; 1866/21/596-7; 1867/3/512-15; 1867/11/875-8; 1867/16/323-9; 1867/20/787-9; 1867/29/426-9; 1868/2/760-3; 1868/17/828-33.
219. *Ibid.*, 1863/10/607-8; 1863/16/114-15; 1865/18/492-3.
220. R.B. (Wharfedale St., 1869).
221. M.D.R. 1869/17/375.
222. *Ibid.*, 1864/21/560-1.
223. *Ibid.*, 1866/21/635-7; 1866/27/265-6.

224. *Ibid.*, 1865/9/145-6; 1865/21/853-4; 1866/10/518-19; 1866/14/594-5.
225. *Ibid.*, 1865/25/753-4; 1866/4/388-92.
226. *Ibid.*, 1865/21/855-8; 1865/25/747-50.
227. *Ibid.*, 1865/5/641-3; 1865/11/105-7.
228. *Ibid.*, 1865/25/193; 1866/3/277-8; 1866/7/594-7; 1866/22/337-41.
229. *Ibid.*, 1869/19/988-97; 1873/4/950-5.
230. *Ibid.*, 1866/8/892-4; 1866/17/316-20; 1866/21/69-72; 1867/16/542-6; 1867/27/453-8; 1868/2/892-6; 1868/13/553-7.
231. *Ibid.* 1867/7/27-9.
232. *Ibid.*, 1868/18/700-1.
233. *Ibid.*, 1868/3/348-51; 1868/15/536-8.
234. Corbett Letters, XVII, 138.
235. *Ibid.*, VIII, 45.
236. *B.* 4 Sept. 1880, p. 301: *B.N.* 10 Sept. 1880, p. 311.
237. Corbett Letters, II, 606v.; XIV, 214.
238. M.D.R. 1867/9/955.
239. *Ibid.*, 1868/9/842.
240. Corbett Letters, XVII, 271.
241. *B.* 26 May 1939, p. 985.
242. P.R.O., RG 10/54, ff. 42-6, 66, 82-6.
243. K.P.L., applications to Vestry from M.B.W., no. 64.
244. Corbett Letters, XXI, 456, 562, 630, 632, 656.
245. M.B.W. Minutes, 5 Aug., 14 Oct. 1881, pp. 263, 498.
246. Corbett Letters, I, 25.
247. *Ibid.*, XIV, 769.
248. M.D.R. 1865/4/575-6: *P.O.D.*
249. What follows is based on the lease-plans on deeds memorialized in the M.D.R.
250. M.D.R. 1853/13/513-14; 1857/15/384, 386.
251. *Ibid.*, 1871/11/364: *P.O.D.*: R.I.B.A. Library, Fellowship nomination papers, 9 April 1883.
252. M.D.R. 1865/25/193.
253. *Ibid.*, 1866/6/929.
254. *Ibid.*, 1872/16/536.
255. *Ibid.*, 1851/7/256-7; 1853/13/513-14; 1862/15/511-12; 1863/4/555; 1863/9/579-80; 1863/12/39-40; 1866/18/98-103; 1866/21/592-3; 1866/26/589-92, 594-6; 1867/4/775-6; 1869/19/992-3.
256. *Ibid.*, 1865/11/104; 1865/20/939-42; 1865/23/250-2; 1865/26/131-4; 1866/23/629-30; 1866/25/728; 1867/3/507-11; 1867/5/282-4; 1867/10/1005-10; 1867/25/813-15; 1868/11/556; 1868/12/909-10; 1868/25/885-6; 1869/1/703-5; 1869/18/674-6; 1869/29/156.
257. Corbett Letters, XXI, 53, 247-8.
258. K.P.L., MSS. 5899, 5904, 5922.
259. Corbett Letters, XXI, 192-3, 789-90, 805, 843.
260. M.D.R. 1865/10/66; 1868/21/383-4.
261. *Ibid.*, 1865/11/325; 1866/25/728.
262. *Ibid.*, 1868/19/437; 1870/18/466.
263. Corbett Letters, XXI, 267.
264. *B.* 11 Feb. 1871, p. 104.
265. Pepperell, advertisement at front.
266. *B.* 16 Aug. 1873, p. 646.
267. *B.N.* 16 May 1873, p. 555.
268. Corbett Letters, VIII, 365.
269. *Ibid.*, XIV, 388.
270. *Ibid.*, IV, 512.
271. *Ibid.*, XXI, 794.
272. *Ibid.*, VIII, 696.
273. These prices are mostly derived from Corbett Letters.

274. *The Kensington News*, 11 May 1878.
275. *The Estates Gazette*, 15 May 1878, p. 217.
276. Chelsea Public Library, deed 3316: *P.O.D.*
277. Corbett Letters, XXI, 33.
278. *Ibid.*, VIII, 822.
279. *Ibid.*, XVII, 115, 118; XXI, 88.
280. *Ibid.*, VIII, 363.
281. *Ibid.*, IV, 596.
282. *Ibid.*, II, 193v.
283. *Ibid.*, XIV, Aug.-Sept. 1878.
284. See Corbett Letters, VIII.
285. Corbett Letters, XXI, 921.
286. *Ibid.*, II, 40v.
287. *Ibid.*, IV, 643.
288. [Rev. Douglas H. G. Sargent], *A Short Historical Sketch of the Parish and Church of Saint Luke, Redcliffe Square, South Kensington, 1871-1934*, [n.d.], p. 30.
289. P.R.O., RG 10/54, ff. 75-82; RG 10/55, ff. 21-33.
290. Charles Booth, *Life and Labour of the People in London*, 1902, *First Series: Poverty, 2, Streets and Population Classified*, App., p. 6, and *Third Series: Religious Influences, 3, The City of London and the West End*, map following p. 135.
291. *Ibid., Third Series, Religious Influences, 3, The City of London and the West End*, p. 114.
292. *B.N.* 10 May 1878, p. 481.
293. *The Times*, 6 May 1878, p. 11f.
294. *The Kensington News*, 15 Feb. 1879: Corbett Letters, XVII, 440-1.
295. *P.O.D.*: Corbett Letters, XIV, 759; XVII, 64: P.R.O., RG 11/81, f. 16.
296. Corbett Letters, XIV, 895; XVII, 73.
297. *Ibid.*, XXI, 881.
298. *Ibid.*, XVII, 381, 410, 485.
299. *Ibid.*, II, 721.
300. E.g. *ibid.*, I, 111.
301. *Ibid.*, I, 60, 77: *Kelly's Directory of Kent*, 1878.
302. Corbett Letters, XXI, 847.
303. *Ibid.*, XXI, 562.
304. *Ibid.*, IV, 556, 558, 572.
305. E.g., *ibid.*, XVII, 271.
306. *Ibid.*, VIII, 696.
307. *Ibid.*, IV, 260v.
308. *Ibid.*, IV, 910, 949; VIII, 738.
309. *Ibid.*, IV, 19v., 421, 910; VI, 901.
310. *Ibid.*, IV, 599.
311. *Ibid.*, VIII, 689.
312. *Ibid.*, IV, 872.
313. M.D.R. 1862/18/808-9; 1869/19/688-90.
314. E.g., *ibid.*, 1863/15/578-9: Corbett Letters, VIII, 316; XIV, 306; XVII, 226.
315. E.g., M.D.R. 1868/23/920.
316. Corbett Letters, XIV, 503.
317. *Ibid.*, XVII, 379.
318. *Ibid.*, VIII, 10, 13, 51, 77, 306, 318.
319. *Ibid.*, I, summer 1871; IV, 154; VIII, early 1877: *Kelly's Directory of Kent*, 1874.
320. Corbett Letters, VIII, 31.
321. *Ibid.*, XIV, 489.
322. *Ibid.*, XIV, 547, 613.
323. *Ibid.*, XIV, 611, 615.
324. *Ibid.*, XIV, 688.
325. *Ibid.*, XIV, 310, 311, 444, 520.
326. *Ibid.*, II, 249: IV, 4, 512; VIII, 225, 652.

327. *Ibid.*, xiv, 214, 306.
328. *Ibid.*, xiv, 311.
329. *Ibid.*, viii, 659.
330. *Ibid.*, vi, July 1875.
331. *Ibid.*, xxi, 879.
332. *Ibid.*, viii, 49.
333. *Ibid.*, xxi, 765, 777.
334. *Ibid.*, xxi, 794.
335. *Ibid.*, xvii, 280, 306.
336. *Ibid.*, xvii, 108.
337. *Ibid.*, xvii, 388.
338. *Ibid.*, iv, 643; viii, 813, 922v., 1002; xiv, 7.
339. *B.* 8 Oct. 1870, p. 800.
340. Corbett Letters, vol. xiv.
341. *Ibid.*, vol. xvii.
342. *Ibid.*, xxi, 192-3, 247-8.
343. *Ibid.*, viii, 659.
344. *Ibid.*, viii, 96.
345. *Ibid.*, xvii, 115; xxi, 88, 262, 336, 382, 419, 504.
346. *Ibid.*, xvii, 8.
347. Margate Public Library, photocopy of typescript, 'Westgate-on-Sea, Isle of Thanet, Kent, 1909-1969, memorized by H. W. (Bill) Hambidge'.
348. Corbett Letters, xvii, 147, 171.
349. M.D.R. 1867/28/945.
350. *Ibid.*, 1875/4/704-6.
351. Joan Bulman, *Jenny Lind*, 1956, pp. 311-17.
352. *P.O.D.*: Boase: *Survey of London*, vol. xxxviii, 1975, pp. 321, 357: A. Charles Sewter, *The Stained Glass of William Morris and his Circle - A Catalogue*, 1975, p. 101.
353. K.P.L., applications to Council from L.C.C., no. 1004.
354. M.D.R.   1884/17/624-6;   1884/20/171-4,   426-9; 1884/22/138-9; 1884/33/405-10; 1884/34/117; 1885/ 2/315-17;   1885/5/542;   1885/8/670;   1885/11/787; 1885/25/431.
355. K.P.L., applications to Vestry from M.B.W., no. 340.
356. D.S.R. 1901/77, 96, 165; 1902/3, 40, 59, 99, 158; 1903/53 (South Kensington district), 36, 384, 553 (Kensington district): K.P.L., applications to Council from L.C.C., no. 837: *The Architectural Review*, vol. xiv, 1903, pp. 162, 165-9: *P.O.D.*
357. W. Shaw Sparrow, *Flats, Urban Houses and Country Homes*, [1907], p. 65: K.P.L., sale particulars, Nos. 136-153 Coleherne Court, [1906].
358. G.L.C., Legal and Parliamentary Dept., Conveyancing (Records) Division, Bousfield School site, Docket 26551, assignments, 2 Aug. 1859 (Godrick and Graham to Graham), 14 June 1880 (Grahams to Webb): *B.* 24 Nov. 1911, pp. 598-61.
359. M.D.R. 1883/39/396: K.P.L., applications to Vestry from M.B.W., no. 325: *B.* 14 Oct. 1882, p. 512.
360. *B.* 6 Feb. 1904, p. 140 and illus.: G.L.C., Legal and Parliamentary Dept., Conveyancing (Records) Division, Bousfield School site, Docket 26561, leases, 28 July 1906 (Gunter to Minter); Docket 54822, application, 16 May 1906 (Cooper and Blake to L.C.C.), covenant, 18 May 1908 (Gunter and Minter): K.P.L., applications to Council from L.C.C., no. 988: *P.O.D.*
361. H.B., photo, Bolton Gardens, 1933.
362. P. G. Konody and Sidney Dark, *Sir William Orpen, Artist and Man*, 1932, p. 210: Bruce Arnold, *Orpen. Mirror to an Age*, 1981, pp. 228, 247-8: Lady Gregory, *Hugh Lane's Life and Achievement*, 1921, p. 159: H.B., Blue Plaque file 766.

363. G.L.C., Legal and Parliamentary Dept., Conveyancing (Records) Division, Bousfield School site, Docket 26551, conveyance, 8 March 1918 (Gunter *et al.* to Jacob); contract, 1 Sept. 1927 (Bergen and Dalziel); surrender, 11 Nov. 1927 (Lund to Dalziel).
364. B.A. 61160: *Architecture Illustrated*, Dec. 1930, pp. 227-8: *Country Life*, 17 March 1934, pp. 287-8.
365. B.A. 61160.
366. *Country Life*, 20 Sept. 1930, pp. 342-7: *B.* 9 Oct. 1931, p. 574: D.S.R. 1929/525, 1117: B.A. 64409: Bruce Arnold, *op. cit.*, pp. 420-2, 425, 427.
367. B.A. 63066: D.S.R. 1929/519: *B.* 11 Dec, 1931, p. 956: *Architecture Illustrated*, Dec. 1931, pp. 182-3.
368. British Telecom, Conveyancing Dept., Earl's Court Telephone Exchange, abstract of title and deeds: B.R. 154358: Royal Borough of Kensington and Chelsea, Town Planning case 16410: *P.O.D.*: date on building.
369. B.A. 102494: B.R. 2932.
370. G.L.C., Legal and Parliamentary Dept., Conveyancing (Records) Division, Bousfield School site, Dockets 26551, 26561, 26564-5, 26571-2.
371. *The Architectural Review*, vol. 117, Jan. 1955, pp. 49-50; vol. 120, Sept. 1956, pp. 150-7.
372. *The Times*, 19 Sept. 1905, p. 4c; 2 Sept. 1908, p. 11e: British Telecom, Conveyancing Dept., Earl's Court Telephone Exchange, photostat of will of Sir Robert Gunter and abstract of title.
373. *The Times*, 12 June 1917, p. 3b: K.P.L., sale particulars, The Gunter Estate, 11 June 1917.
374. Chelsea Public Library, scrapbook, p. 1254 (cutting from *The Star*, 7 Dec. 1916).
375. *The Times*, 22 Aug. 1917, p. 9d.
376. *Report of the Royal Commission on London Squares*, 1928, App. iii.
377. B.R. 110614.
378. B.A. 66099: Sir Charles Wheeler, *High Relief*, 1968, pp. 93-4: inscription on building: information kindly supplied by Miss C. Wheeler and Mr. S. C. Hutchison.
379. G.L.R.O., H4/PB/Y3/1.
380. *Ibid.*: B.R. 102465: *The Architects' Journal*, 22 June 1932, pp. 830-4.
381. B.R. 102465.
382. *Ibid.*, 111621.
383. Kensington Borough Council Minutes, 11 Dec. 1951, pp. 461-2; 11 May, 14 Oct., 11 Nov., 9 Dec. 1952, pp. 201, 356, 407, 453; 13 Oct., 8 Dec. 1953, pp. 354, 434; 7 Dec. 1954, p. 398; 11 Oct. 1955, p. 309; 12 March 1957, p. 89: B.R. 12034, 13546, 13607.
384. Kensington Borough Council Minutes, 19 May, 28 July, 8 Dec. 1953, pp. 197, 301, 435; 11 Oct. 1955, p. 309; 12 Nov. 1957, p. 337: B.R. 15199.
385. Kensington Borough Council Minutes, 18 April 1961, p. 130; 3 July 1962, p. 225; 14 May 1963, p. 187; 28 Oct. 1965, pp. 509, 602.
386. *Ibid.*, 21 March, 2 May, 20 June 1967, pp. 203, 271, 362; 25 June 1968, p. 290; 29 April 1969, p. 190: B.A. 107267: B.R. 150564.
387. Kensington Borough Council Minutes, Oct. 1973.
388. B.R. 16767.
389. B.A. 81464.
390. G.L.C., Architect's Dept., Street Naming Section.
391. B.A. 103139.
392. *Ibid.*, 78766.

393. B.R. 3998.
394. *Ibid.*, 126735, 151285.
395. B.A. 87490: B.R. 14832: information kindly supplied by Sir Hugh Casson.
396. B.A. 91051: *B.* 21 March 1958, pp. 531-3.
397. B.A. 102568: B.R. 154338.
398. B.R. 150803: *The Architectural Review*, vol. 160, Sept. 1976, pp. 170-3: Richard Einzig, *Classic Modern Houses in Europe*, 1981, pp. 150-7.
399. B.R. 16278: *The Architect and Building News*, 25 Jan. 1961, p. 113; 20 June 1962, pp. 889-92; 1 Aug. 1962, p. 147: *Architectural Design*, 1962, p. 134: Alice Hope, *Town Houses*, 1963, pp. 116-18: *The Architectural Review*, vol. 136, Nov. 1964, pp. 357-9: information kindly supplied by Sir Hugh Casson.
400. *House and Garden*, July 1964.
401. *The Daily Telegraph*, 24 March 1982, p. 25.
402. K.P.L., K2581/B.
403. C.C., files 20641, 20643: George Godwin, *Buildings and Monuments, Modern and Mediaeval . . .*, 1850, p. 86.
404. *B.* 16 June 1849, pp. 282-3.
405. Godwin, *op. et loc. cit.*
406. M.D.R. 1849/9/251.
407. *B.* 19 Oct. 1850, p. 499: *The Times*, 2 Feb. 1850, p. 8a.
408. C.C., file 20643.
409. *B.* 19 Oct. 1850, p. 499; 18 Sep. 1858, p. 632: *I.L.N.* 26 Oct. 1850, p. 336.
410. *The Ecclesiologist*, n. s., vol. VIII, 1850, p. 195.
411. Archives of St. Mary, The Boltons, subscription book: *The Land and Building News*, 29 Nov. 1856, p. 875.
412. T. F. Gibbs, *St. Mary Boltons, 1850-1964*, [n.d.], p. 6.
413. Pepperell, pp. 11-13.
414. D.S.R. 1871/440: Gibbs, *op. et loc. cit.*: Basil F. L. Clarke, *Parish Churches of London*, 1966, p. 103.
415. Gibbs, *op. cit.*, p. 7.
416. *B.* 1 July 1882, p. 35; 16 May 1885, p. 710.
417. Archives of St. Mary, The Boltons, records in church vestry, envelope no. 3.
418. *Ibid.*, file, Council for the Care of Churches.
419. Gibbs, *op. cit.*, p. 8.
420. Archives of St. Mary, The Boltons, records in church vestry, envelope no. 5: Gibbs, *op. cit.*, pp. 9-10.
421. C.C., file 41936.
422. *B.* 3 Dec. 1870, p. 958.
423. C.C., file 48151.
424. [Rev. Douglas H. G. Sargent], *A Short Historical Sketch of the Parish and Church of Saint Luke, Redcliffe Square*: Pepperell, p. 20: M.B.W. Minutes, 26 May 1871, p. 753.
425. Sargent, *op. cit.*: *B.* 16 Aug. 1873, p. 646.
426. *B.N.* 16 May 1873, p. 555: *B.* 17 Feb. 1872, p. 134.
427. *B.* 10 Aug. 1872, p. 634: *B.N.* 16 May 1873, p. 555.
428. *B.* 16 Aug. 1873, p. 646: C.C., files 41936, 48151.
429. Sargent, *op. cit.*: *B.* 16 Aug. 1873, p. 646: *B.N.* 22 Dec. 1876, p. 651.
430. G.L.R.O., P84/LUK/43 and 68.
431. Corbett Letters, IV, 233 (also 72, 194, 198, 260, 283).
432. *Ibid.*, IV, 362.
433. *Ibid.*, XIV, 211.
434. *Ibid.*, XIV, 448.
435. *Ibid.*, XIV, 550.
436. *Ibid.*, XIV, 686-7, 691; XVII, 467, 489; XXI, 114, 117, 127, 272.
437. St. Luke's Church Hall papers and deeds (with Messrs.

Payne, Hicks Beach and Co., Dec. 1981).
438. C.C., files 41936, 48151.
439. Sargent, *op. cit.*
440. G.L.R.O., P84/LUK/48.
441. *Ibid.*, P84/LUK/73.
442. R.I.B.A., Fellowship nomination papers, C. S. Peach, 1891.
443. H.B., file 622.
444. K.P.L., applications to Vestry from M.B.W., no. 231.
445. B.A. 102415.
446. Royal Borough of Kensington and Chelsea, Town Planning case 52087.
447. H.B., Blue Plaque file 62.
448. M.B.W. 1786, no. 978.
449. *Kensington and Chelsea Street-Names*, 1968.
450. B.R. 154264.
451. *Ibid.*, 14161.
452. K.P.L., applications to Council from L.C.C., no. 1004.
453. Royal Borough of Kensington and Chelsea, Town Planning case 67836.

CHAPTER XIII (pp. 241-245)
Stamford Bridge and the Billings Area

1. See E. Daw, *Map of . . . Kensington*, 1848 and 1863 eds.
2. J. E. B. Gover, Allen Mawer and F. M. Stenton, *The Place-Names of Middlesex*, 1942, p. 2.
3. Faulkner, p. 26.
4. Gover, *op. cit.*, pp. 102, 128.
5. *Ibid.*, p. 103: Charles James Féret, *Fulham Old and New*, vol. II, 1900, pp. 225-6.
6. K.P.L., MS. 58/5630, 9 June 1703, f. 62v.
7. *Ibid.*, MS. 58/5601, 18 May 1707, p. 22.
8. R.B.: E.C.R., 17 April 1696, 4 May 1710, 1 May 1724, 25 April 1726, 7 May 1728, 12 March 1743.
9. R.B.: E.C.R., 12 March 1743, 11 Oct. 1764, 27 June 1776, 20 Feb., 6 May 1856.
10. B.L., Add. MS. 31326.
11. *P.O.D.*: B.A. 10557.
12. G.L.R.O., MR/LV/9/179.
13. E.C.R., 5 June 1846.
14. D.S.R. 1874/422.
15. G.L.R.O., B/NTG/210: *The Parish Register of Putney, Surrey 1620-1734*, ed. W. Bruce Bannerman, vol. I, 1913, pp. 38, 122: P.R.O., PROB 11/278/334.
16. G.L.R.O., B/NTG/135, 209-10: M.D.R. 1809/8/419; 1812/1/627.
17. M.D.R. 1809/9/65.
18. G.L.R.O., B/NTG/138, 372: M.D.R. 1830/7/192.
19. 5 and 6 Vict. c. 36, local and personal.
20. G.L.R.O., B/NTG/136.
21. *Ibid.*, B/EGLC/1, 5, 19 Jan. 1831: Hermione Hobhouse, *Thomas Cubitt Master Builder*, 1971, pp. 191, 221.
22. G.L.R.O., B/EGLC/1, 19 Jan. 1831.
23. *Ibid.*, B/NTG/372.
24. M.D.R. 1836/2/128.
25. G.L.R.O., B/EGLC/3, 26 June 1838.
26. *Ibid.*, B/EGLC/4, 20 Aug., 10 Sept. 1841, 19 July 1842.
27. *Ibid.*, B/EGLC/4, 10 Dec. 1841; B/EGLC/5, 22 Nov., 23 Dec. 1842.
28. *Ibid.*, B/EGLC/5, 3 Feb. 1843; B/NTG/220.

29. *Ibid.*, B/EGLC/5, 9 May 1843.
30. P.R.O., WORK 6/66, 9 Feb. 1844, p. 378: M.D.R. 1843/4/216, 1844/3/775-6.
31. G.L.R.O., B/EGLC/5, 9 May 1843; B/NTG/220: M.D.R. 1843/4/530.
32. G.L.R.O., B/EGLC/5, 6 June 1843; B/NTG/220: M.D.R. 1843/4/849.
33. G.L.R.O., B/EGLC/5, 28 May, 11 June 1844; B/NTG/204: M.D.R. 1844/7/661.
34. G.L.R.O., B/EGLC/5, 28 May, 11, 18 June, 6, 13 Aug. 1844; B/NTG/153, 204: M.D.R. 1844/10/702.
35. M.D.R. 1844/10/275-7.
36. *Ibid.*, 1844/8/51-2, 57.
37. *Ibid.*, 1844/9/507.
38. *Ibid.*, 1844/10/120.
39. *Ibid.*, 1844/8/869-70; 1845/11/399.
40. *Ibid.*, 1846/5/116.
41. *Ibid.*, 1846/7/614.
42. *Ibid.*, 1844/10/661.
43. *Ibid.*, 1846/7/604.
44. D.S.R. 1845/159: M.D.R. 1846/5/116.
45. M.D.R. 1844/9/251; 1845/8/31.
46. G.L.R.O., B/EGLC/5, 2, 9 July 1844.
47. M.D.R. 1844/8/712-13.
48. *Ibid.*, 1846/4/862.
49. *Ibid.*, 1845/6/522.
50. *Ibid.*, 1845/9/885.
51. *Ibid.*, 1852/16/634.
52. *Ibid.*, 1855/2/99.
53. B.R. 121093: B.A. 101563: Kensington Borough Council Minutes, 2 March 1937, pp. 175-6, 8 March 1938, p. 182, 27 June, 31 Oct. 1939, pp. 373, 452, 19 Dec. 1944, p. 32, 20 Feb. 1945, p. 82, 15 Jan. 1946, p. 46.
54. B.R. 156026.
55. M.D.R. 1855/2/99.
56. *Ibid.*, 1846/1/611; 1852/16/634; 1855/2/99.
57. R.B.
58. *Diagrams of the Parish of St. Mary Abbotts Kensington*, 1847, p. 172.
59. *P.O.D.: Kensington Directories*: P.R.O., RG 9/22, f. 21.
60. G.L.R.O., B/EGLC/5, 2, 9 July 1844.
61. *Ibid.*, B/NTG/314.
62. *Report of Kensington Medical Officer of Health for 1872*, Table H: O.S. sheet X/19, 1865-7, 1894-6.
63. W.C.S. 84, 17 Jan., 7 Feb. 1845, pp. 173, 184.
64. M.D.R. 1851/4/742.
65. *Ibid.*, 1847/1/219, 620.
66. *Ibid.*, 1847/9/46-7.
67. W.C.S. P47/1563.
68. M.D.R. 1847/1/412: Colvin.
69. M.D.R. 1853/1/348.
70. *Ibid.*, 1847/9/261; 1849/9/575; 1853/2/913: R.B.
71. M.D.R. 1850/1/276: R.B.
72. M.D.R. 1847/3/5; 1850/8/44; 1851/8/201; 1852/3/243: R.B.
73. M.D.R. 1849/4/92; 1857/5/519.
74. *Ibid.*, 1846/7/24-5; 1849/4/92; 1849/5/444; 1851/2/956-7.
75. *Ibid.*, 1850/8/443; 1850/9/213; 1851/12/941-3.
76. P.R.O., RG 9/22, ff. 21-34: R.B.
77. P.R.O., RG 11/47, ff. 80-91.
78. Charles Booth, *Life and Labour of the People in London, Third Series: Religious Influences*, vol. 3, 1902, map.
79. *New Survey of London Life and Labour*, vol. VII, [n.d.], maps, sheet 9.
80. *The Sunday Times*, 11 Nov 1962.

CHAPTER XIV (pp. 246-252)
Brompton Cemetery

1. *P.P.*, 1843, XII, *Report on the Practice of Interment in Towns*, pp. 27, 133.
2. P.R.O., WORK 6/65, 14 Aug. 1838, p. 41; 20 Feb. 1839, p. 72; 2 April 1839, p. 77.
3. Boase: *Survey of London*, vol. XXIV, 1952, p. 115: Colvin.
4. P.R.O., WORK 6/65, 20 July 1837, p. 2; 10 Jan. 1839, p. 66.
5. *The Times*, 27 Aug. 1836, p. 2.
6. *Journals of the House of Commons*, vol. XCII, 14, 24 Feb. 1837, pp. 43, 82.
7. 1 Vict., c. 130, local: *Journals of the House of Lords*, vol. LXIX, 24 April 1837, p. 230.
8. P.R.O., WORK 6/65, 20 July 1837, p. 1.
9. H.L.R.O., Minutes of Evidence before Committees, 1837, West of London and Westminster Cemetery Bill, p. 6.
10. P.R.O., WORK 6/65, *passim*.
11. 1 Vict., c. 130, local.
12. P.R.O., C13/2722.
13. *Ibid.*, WORK 6/65, 11 Jan. 1840, p. 122: C13/2722: M.D.R. 1833/7/65; 1839/6/718-19.
14. P.R.O., WORK 6/65, 10 July, 6 Nov. 1838, pp. 36, 49; 23 April 1839, p. 78; 11 Jan. 1840, p. 122.
15. G.L.R.O., B/EGLC/5, 28 Feb., 9 May 1843, pp. 112, 180; B/NTG/220, sale particulars: P.R.O., WORK 6/66, 9 Feb. 1844, p. 378; WORK 6/67, 26 Jan. 1852, p. 619: M.D.R. 1844/3/775-6.
16. P.R.O., WORK 6/65, 1 Nov. 1837, p. 7.
17. *Ibid.*, WORK 6/65, 6, 20 March 1838, pp. 22, 24; 10 Jan. 1839, p. 64.
18. *Ibid.*, WORK 6/65, 19 June 1838, p. 34: *Catalogue of Royal Academy Exhibition*, 1838, no. 1205.
19. P.R.O., WORK 6/65, 5, 7, 20 Sept., 2 Oct. 1838, pp. 44, 46, 47.
20. *B.N.* 30 April 1875, p. 508: Colvin, *sub* Wyatville.
21. P.R.O., WORK 6/65, 25 Sept., 2 Oct. 1838, pp. 46-7.
22. *Ibid.*, WORK 6/65, 7 Jan. 1839, p. 60.
23. *Ibid.*, WORK 6/65, 10 Jan., 2, 16 April, 16 July 1839, 25 Aug., 1 Sept., 1 Dec. 1841, pp. 66, 77, 78, 85, 250, 251, 263.
24. *Ibid.*, WORK 6/65, 19, 20 Feb. 1839, pp. 70, 71.
25. *Ibid.*, Work 6/65, 6 July, 8, 13 Aug. 1839, pp. 85, 89, 90.
26. *Ibid.*, WORK 6/65, 13, 20, 27 Aug., 3 Sept., 15 Oct., 17 Dec. 1839, pp. 90-5, 100, 113: Hermione Hobhouse, *Thomas Cubitt Master Builder*, 1971, p. 151.
27. P.R.O., WORK 6/65, 10, 17 Dec. 1839, pp. 112, 113.
28. *Ibid.*, WORK 6/65, 8 April 1840, p. 147.
29. *Ibid.*, WORK 6/65, 20 May, 2, 9 Sept. 1840, pp. 154, 183, 185.
30. *Ibid.*, WORK 6/65, 4, 11 Feb., 18 March, 2 June, 8 July 1840, 8 Feb. 1841, pp. 132-3, 141-2, 158, 168, 211: B.L. Map Collection, plan of Brompton Cemetery, 1884, pressmark 3542(1).
31. P.R.O., WORK 6/65, 22 April, 10, 17 June, 1, 29

July, 2 Sept. 1840, 17 Feb., 17 May 1841, pp. 149, 161, 163, 166, 174, 183-4, 216, 231.

32. *Ibid.*, WORK 6/65, 17, 26 May, 2, 9, 16, 30 June 1841, pp. 231-4, 237-41.

33. *Ibid.*, WORK 6/65, 21 July 1841, p. 243.

34. *Ibid.*, WORK 6/65, 9 Feb. 1842, p. 277.

35. *The British Almanac for 1841. Companion*, pp. 236-7.

36. K.P.L., 614.61 BRO, K69/96, Brompton Cemetery newspaper cuttings.

37. P.R.O., WORK 6/65, 13 Feb. 1843, p. 328.

38. *Ibid.*, WORK 6/65, 1 March 1843, p. 335.

39. *Ibid.*, WORK 6/66, 29 Jan. 1845, p. 417.

40. *Ibid.*, WORK 6/66, 28 Feb. 1844, p. 383.

41. *Ibid.*, WORK 6/66, 13, 20, 27 March, 3, 17 April 1844, pp. 384, 386, 387, 389.

42. *Ibid.*, WORK 6/66, 29 Jan. 1845, p. 417; 1 July 1846, p. 465; 8 Feb. 1847, p. 477.

43. *B.N.* 30 April 1875, p. 508.

44. P.R.O., WORK 6/66, 20 March, 3 April 1844, pp. 385, 388-9.

45. 8 and 9 Vict., c. 77, local.

46. P.R.O., WORK 6/66, 21 Jan. 1846, p. 453; 3 Feb. 1847, pp. 476-7; 6/67, 28 Jan. 1850, p. 563; 20 Jan. 1851, p. 590.

47. *P.P.*, 1852, I.III, *Minutes of the Board of Health relating to the Metropolitan Interments Act since August 1850*, p. 24.

48. *Ibid.*, 1843, XII, *Report on the Practice of Interment in Towns*.

49. *Ibid.*, 1850, XXI, *Report on a general scheme for extra-mural sepulture*, pp. 72, 75, 78, 81.

50. 13 and 14 Vict., c. 52, public general.

51. *P.P.*, 1852, I.III, *Minutes of the Board of Health, ut supra*, pp. 50, 53, 55: P.R.O., WORK 6/67, 19 March, 23 April 1851, pp. 595, 599.

52. George E. Chadwick, *The Works of Sir Joseph Paxton*, 1961, pp. 205-6: Wolfgang Hermann, *Gottfried Semper im Exil*, 1978, p. 55.

53. P.R.O., WORK 6/67, 19 March 1851, p. 596.

54. *P.P.*, 1852, I.III, *Minutes of the Board of Health, ut supra*, p. 25.

55. P.R.O., WORK 6/67, 19 March 1851, p. 595.

56. *Ibid.*, WORK 6/67, 23, 30 April 1851, pp. 599, 600.

57. *P.P.*, 1852, I.III, *Minutes of the Board of Health, ut supra*, pp. 24, 127.

58. P.R.O., WORK 6/67, 18 June, 30 Oct. 1851, pp. 604, 610.

59. *P.P.*, 1852, I.III, *Minutes of the Board of Health, ut supra*, p. 98.

60. *Ibid.*, pp. 85, 104-5: R.A. Lewis, *Edwin Chadwick and the Public Health Movement 1832-1854*, 1952, pp. 250-5.

61. P.R.O., WORK 6/67, 30 Oct., 1 Nov., 27 Dec. 1851, 26 Jan. 1852, pp. 610-12, 619-20.

62. M.D.R. 1853/1/253.

63. P.R.O., WORK 6/67, 5 Nov. 1852, 24 Aug. 1853, 15 Nov., 20 Dec. 1854, pp. 637, 646, 653, 654.

64. *Annual Report on the Health . . . of the Parish of St. Mary Abbott's Kensington for 1889*, 1890, pp. 172-3.

65. P.R.O., WORK 38/146.

66. *Catalogue of the Burne-Jones Exhibition at the Hayward Gallery*, 1975-6, p. 68.

Index

NOTE

The symbols in the left-hand margin distinguish those persons who have worked, or, it is thought, may have worked, on the fabric of the area, and the authors of unexecuted designs:

*a*Architects, designers, engineers, and surveyors
*b*Builders and allied craftsmen
*c*Artists, craftsmen, and decorators

PLATES

Southern Kensington, aerial view from the south-west in June 1973. The east end of Redcliffe Square appears in the left foreground, The Boltons in the centre, and the museums area and Hyde Park in the distance

2

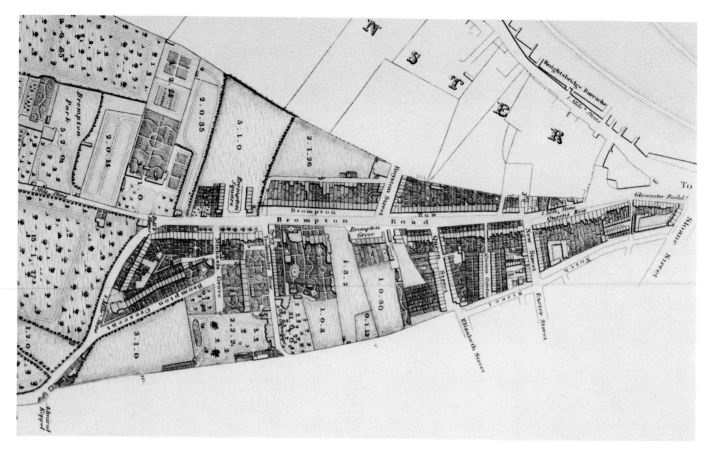

a. Extract from map of Kensington published by T. Starling, 1822

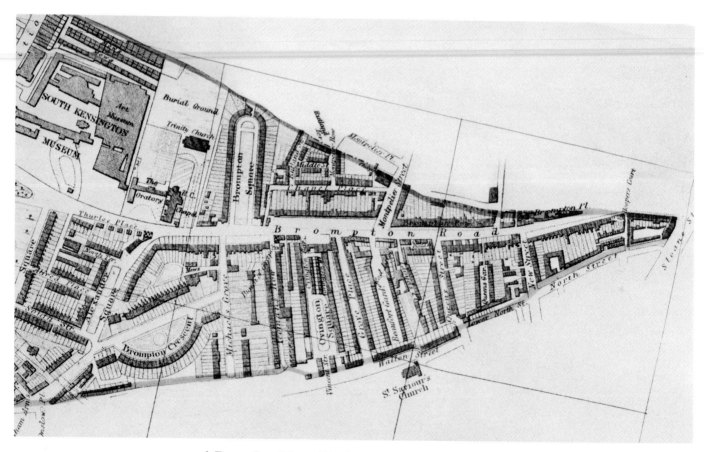

b. Extract from Edmund Daw's map of Kensington, 1879

BROMPTON ROAD, MAPS

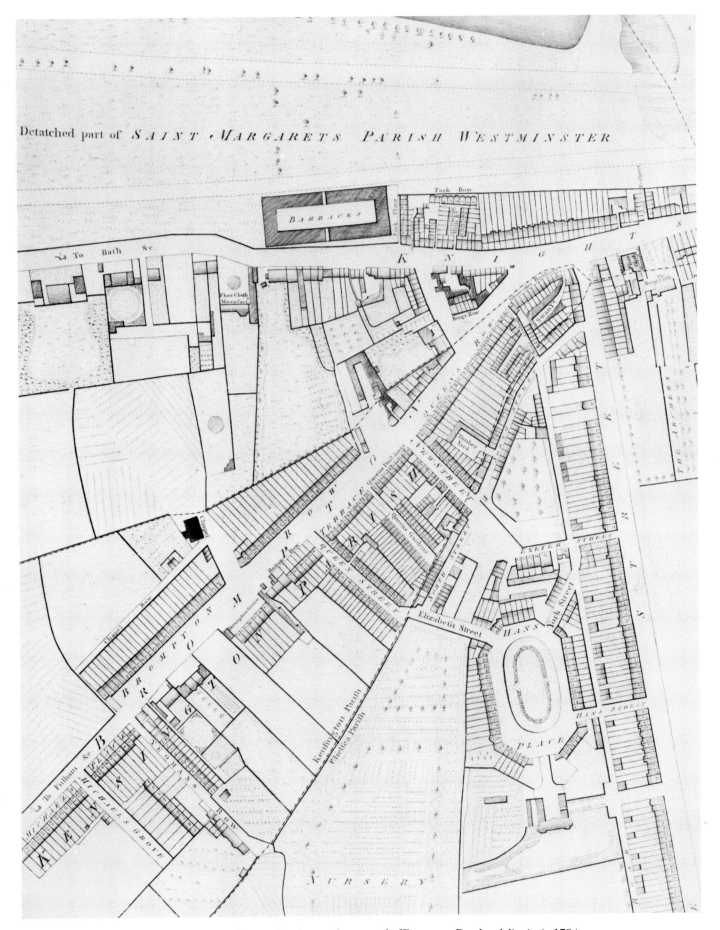

Extract from Horwood's map showing north-east end of Brompton Road and district in 1794

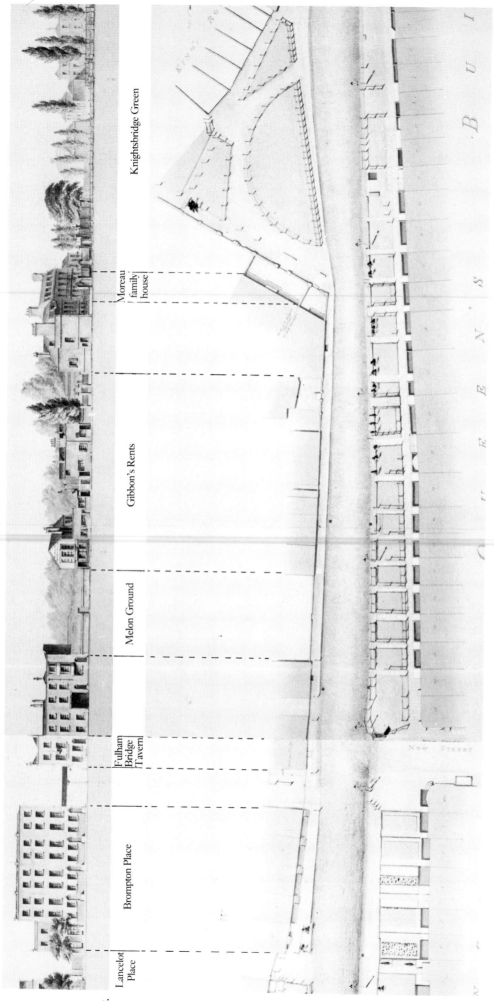

4

BROMPTON ROAD. Extracts from Joseph Salway's survey of 1811. *The house numbers are those assigned in 1863*

Knightsbridge Green

Moreau family house

Gibbon's Rents

Melon Ground

Fulham Bridge Tavern

Brompton Place

Lancelot Place

a.

KING'S ROW

QUEEN'S BUILDINGS

New Street

b.

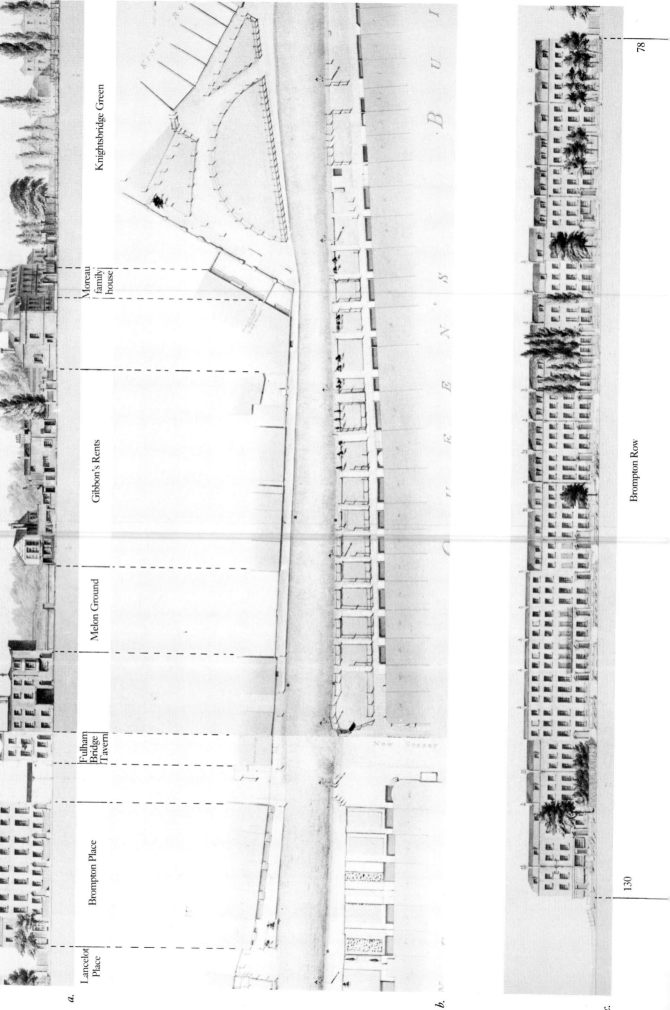

78

Brompton Row

130

c.

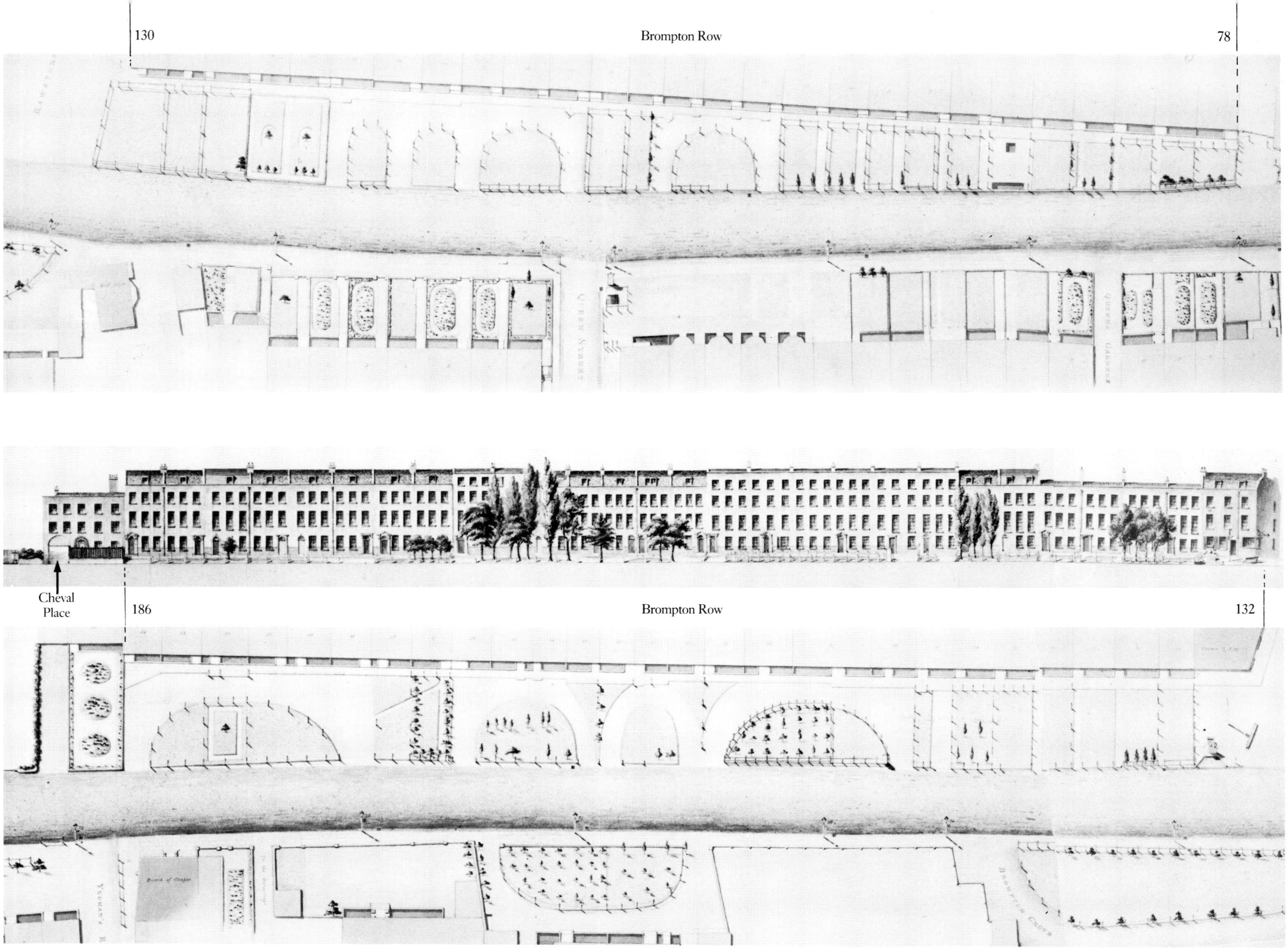

5

a.

78

Brompton Row

130

QUEEN'S GARDENS

QUEEN STREET

b.

132

Brompton Row

186

Cheval
Place

c.

BROMPTON GROVE

YEOMAN'S R

a. Nos. 96-102 in 1952. John and Richard Stokes, bricklayers, building lessees, 1766. *All demolished*

b. No. 188 from rear in *c.*1965. Joseph Clark, carpenter, building lessee, 1768

c. No. 156 in 1975. George Gibbons, carpenter, building lessee, 1766

d. No. 152 in 1975. George Gibbons, carpenter, building lessee, 1766

'BROMPTON ROW', NOS. 78-188 (even) BROMPTON ROAD (pp. 36-8)

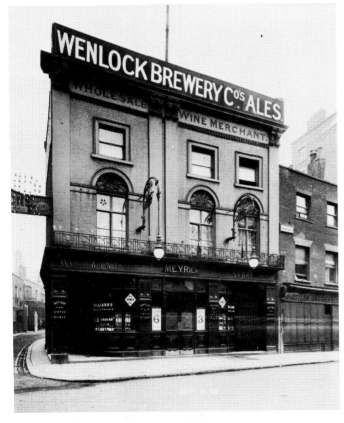

c. Nos. 64 (right) and 66 (The Fulham Bridge). Buildings of 1777-80, variously altered (pp. 34-5)
d. *(right)*. Nos. 48-52 (even). Developed under William Whitehead, builder, 1820-4 (p. 34)

BROMPTON ROAD IN 1902. *All demolished*

b. Brompton Road looking north-east towards Knightsbridge Green in *c.*1905. Nos. 60–86 (even) on left, Harrods on right

a. Nos. 84–120 (even) Brompton Road (right to left) in *c.*1905 (pp. 36–8). *Mostly demolished*

d. Brompton Road in 1980. No. 130 at corner, Nos. 2–14 (even) Montpelier Street on left (pp. 36–8, 39–40)

c. (left). Nos. 1–10 Brompton Place (left to right) in 1975. William Paul, plumber, building lessee, 1825–32 (p. 23)

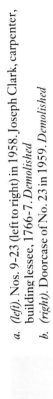

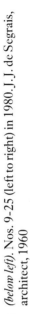

a. *(left).* Nos. 9–23 (left to right) in 1958. Joseph Clark, carpenter, building lessee, 1766–7. *Demolished*

b. *(right).* Doorcase of No. 23 in 1959. *Demolished*

c. *(below left).* Nos. 9–25 (left to right) in 1980. J. J. de Segrais, architect, 1960

d. *(below right).* Nos. 9–33 (left to right) in 1980. Nos. 27–33 (on right) built by John Stuttard, carpenter, *c.*1771

YEOMAN'S ROW, EAST SIDE (pp. 28, 30–1)

10

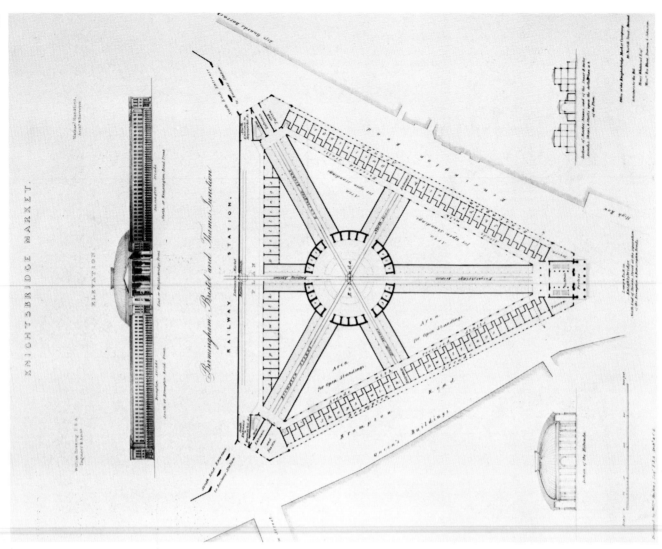

a. Brompton Chapel, Montpelier Street. Thomas Rawstorne, Richard Harrison and Seth Thompson, lessees, 1768 (p. 38)

b. Brompton National School, Brompton Road. George Godwin junior, architect, 1841–2 (p. 34). *Demolished*

c. Knightsbridge Market. Scheme proposed by William Hosking, architect, *c*.1836 (p. 5). *Not executed*

a. (above). The Hermitage in *c*.1840 (p. 27). *Demolished*
b. (above right). The Bell and Horns Inn in 1811 (p. 60). *Demolished*

c. (below). Blemell House School in *c*.1850 (p. 50). *Demolished*
d. (right). Brompton Square in 1843 (pp. 40-6)

12

a. *(above left)*. Nos. 5–9 (consec.) in 1975. Built under William Farlar and James Bonnin, 1823

b. *(left)*. Nos. 43–48 (consec.) in 1975. Built under William Farlar, *c.*1825–30

c. *(above right)*. Nos. 32 and 33 in 1976. Built by William Aslat, *c.*1835, probably to designs by John Blore, architect

BROMPTON SQUARE (pp. 40–6)

13

a. Nos. 11–29 (odd) **Rutland Street** (left to right) in 1982. ?William Aslat, builder, *c.*1830 (p. 44)

b. **Cottage Place**, east side in *c.*1910. Built under William Farlar, 1823 (p. 40). *Demolished*

c. **Cheval Place**, looking west from Montpelier Walk in 1982 (p. 39). Brompton Square and the dome of the Oratory are in the distance

d. Nos. 3–5 (right to left) **Fairholt Street** in 1982. Baillie Scott and Beresford, architects, 1925–8 (p. 39)

a. *(above left)*. Nos. 70-74 (even) in 1903. F. E. Williams, architect, 1896 (p. 35)

b. *(centre left)*. No. 200 Brompton Road (former London and Westminster Bank) in 1969. F. W. Porter, architect, 1881 (p. 45)

c. *(above)*. No. 58A in 1909. Architect unknown, 1890 (p. 35). On left, part of Nos. 60-64 (even), R. A. Briggs, architect, 1905-6

d. *(left)*. Knightsbridge Station at Nos. 29-31 (odd) in *c*.1906. Leslie W. Green, architect, 1903-5 (p. 13)

LATE VICTORIAN AND EDWARDIAN BROMPTON ROAD. *All demolished*

a. Beauchamp Place looking north in *c.*1903

b. Nos. 179-183 (odd) Brompton Road in 1903. Built by William Farlar, 1825. *No. 183 demolished*

c. Nos. 14 and 15 Beauchamp Place, 1844-5, in 1980

BEAUCHAMP PLACE DEVELOPMENT (pp. 24-6)

a. Nos. 197–201 (odd) Brompton Road in 1903.
W. W. Pocock, architect, 1844–5. *Demolished*

b. No. 11 Ovington Gardens in 1903. W. W. Pocock, architect,
1845. *Demolished*

c. Nos. 203 (left) and 205 Brompton Road, 1845, in 1903.
Demolished

d. The Bunch of Grapes, No. 207 Brompton Road, 1845, in
1982. Yeoman's Row is on the right

OVINGTON SQUARE DEVELOPMENT (pp. 28–30)

a. Nos. 30 and 32 Ovington Square in 1975. W. W. Pocock, architect, 1850-1

b. Ovington Square, east side in 1980. Nos. 22-26 (even) in centre designed by Walter and Eva Segal, architects, 1957

c. Nos. 17-19 (right to left) Ovington Gardens in 1980. W. W. Pocock, architect, 1845

d. Nos. 1-7 (right to left) Ovington Gardens in 1980. Charles Aldin, builder, 1867

OVINGTON SQUARE AND GARDENS (pp. 28-30)

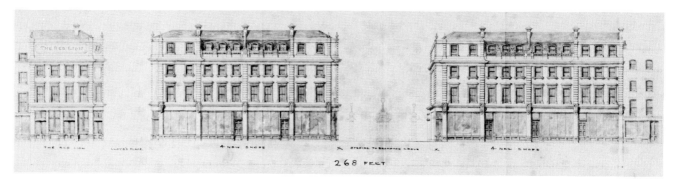

a. Nos. 161-177 (odd) Brompton Road. Drawing of development scheme by G. A. Burn, architect, 1860. Openings are shown to Brompton (formerly Lloyd's) Place on left, and to Beaufort Gardens (formerly Brompton Grove)

b. (above). The Red Lion, No. 161 Brompton Road in 1903. G. A. Burn, architect, 1861
c. (above right). Nos. 163-169 (odd) Brompton Road in 1960. G. A. Burn, architect, 1861. *Demolished*

d. (right). Beaufort Gardens, east side in 1975. Jeremiah and Henry Little, builders, 1861-70

BEAUFORT GARDENS DEVELOPMENT (p. 24)

a. Intersection of Sloane Street (left), Brompton Road (centre right) and Knightsbridge (right)

b. Nos. 1-31 (odd) Brompton Road. Nos. 1-9 (left), W. Duvall Goodwin, architect, 1903-4; Nos. 13-27 (centre right), G. D. Martin and W. F. Harber, architects, 1903-10; Nos. 29-31 (far right), Delissa Joseph, architect, 1910-11 (pp. 13-14)

BROMPTON ROAD IN 1959

a. Nos. 33 and 35 in 1902. James D'Oyley, architect, 1893. *No. 33 demolished*

b. Nos. 57-61 (odd), 1899-1900, in 1902

c. Nos. 33-61 (left to right), 1893-1900, in 1959

THE GODDARD ESTATE, BROMPTON ROAD (pp. 13-14)

a. Nos. 14-34 (even) Hans Road (right to left) in 1980. C. A. Daw and Son builders of Nos. 18-34, 1892-5 (p. 15). Hans Road front of Harrods on extreme right

b. Hans Crescent looking north in 1963. Nos. 32-44 (in centre), C. W. Stephens, architect, 1908 onwards (p. 22); Harrods to left; Basil Street to right. *Demolished*

c. Nos. 79-85 (odd) Brompton Road in 1980. C. W. Stephens, architect, 1903-4 (p. 14)

THE GODDARD ESTATE

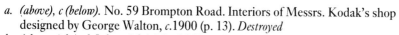

a. *(above)*, c *(below)*. No. 59 Brompton Road. Interiors of Messrs. Kodak's shop
   designed by George Walton, *c*.1900 (p. 13). *Destroyed*
b. *(above right)*, d *(below right)*. No. 12 Hans Road. A. H. Mackmurdo, architect,
   1893-4 (pp. 15-17)

L'Art Nouveau in Brompton

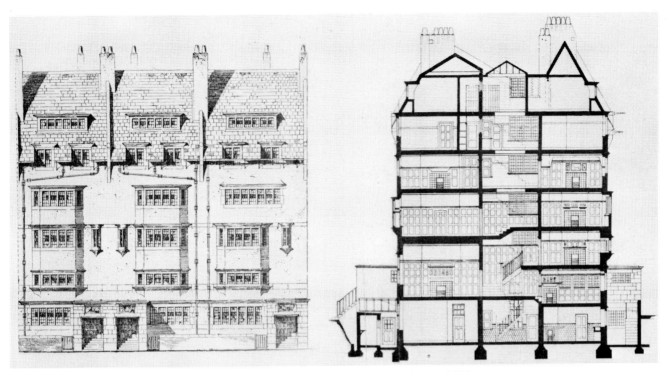

a. *(above).* Preliminary elevation and section of Nos. 12-16. C. F. A. Voysey, architect, 1891
b. *(below).* Nos. 12-16 (left to right), rear view in 1971. A. H. Mackmurdo, architect of No. 12; C. F. A. Voysey, architect of Nos. 14 and 16
c. *(centre right).* Panel in porch of No. 14 in 1971. Conrad Dressler, sculptor
d. *(below right).* Staircase of No. 14 in 1971. C. F. A. Voysey, architect

NOS. 12-16 (even) HANS ROAD (pp. 15-17)

a. Looking east from Ovington Gardens. Centre right, Nos. 187A-191 (odd), Clifford Derwent and Partners, architects, 1964; far right, Nos. 193-195, Denis Clarke Hall and Partners, architects, 1963-4

b. Nos. 78-94 (Princes Court). G. Val. Myer and F. J. Watson-Hart, architects, 1934-5 (pp. 37-8)

c. Knightsbridge Green and Nos. 44-76 (even). Caltex House (in foreground) by Stone, Toms and Partners, architects, 1955-7 (p. 35)

BROMPTON ROAD IN 1980

25

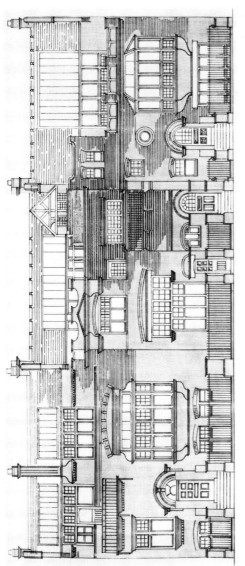

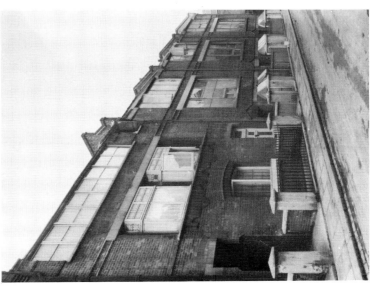

a. (above). Nos. 233–237 (odd) Brompton Road, 1886–8, in 1981
(p. 122)

b. (above right). Nos. 24–28 (right to left) Yeoman's Row. Elevation by
W. Barber, architect, 1897 (p. 126)

c. (right). Nos. 14–20 (right to left) Yeoman's Row in 1937.
W. H. Collbran, architect, lessee, 1898–9 (pp. 125–6)

d. (far right). Nos. 22–28 (even) Yeoman's Row in 1974. No. 22,
Alfred J. Beesley, architect; Nos. 24–28, W. Barber, architect
(pp. 125–6)

b. *(right).* In *c.*1903. Opening into Queen's Gardens in centre

d. *(below).* In *c.*1906. On right, part of Nos. 137–159 (odd), C. W. Stephens, architect, 1903–6

a. *(above).* In *c.*1900. Opening into Queen's Gardens, centre right

c. *(below).* In *c.*1904

HARRODS, BROMPTON ROAD FRONTAGE (pp. 18–20). Rebuilt in 1901–5 by C. W. Stephens, architect

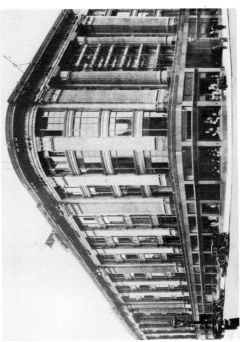

b. *(above)*. Aerial view from the south-west in *c*.1948

a. *(above)*. 'Coronation Tower', Hans Road, in 1980. C. W. Stephens, architect, 1910–12 (p. 20)

c. *(right)*. Basil Street frontage in *c*.1930. Louis D. Blanc, architect, 1929–30 (p. 23)

HARRODS, EXTERIORS

28 *a.* Fancy Leather Goods
Department (ground
floor)

b. Silver Department
(ground floor)

HARRODS, INTERIORS IN
1919 (p. 22). *Destroyed*

a. Blouse Department
(first floor)

b. Ladies' Boots
Department (first floor)

Harrods, Interiors in
1919 (p. 22). *Destroyed*

29

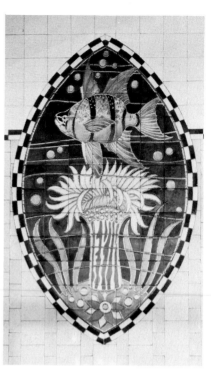

a. Banking Hall in *c.*1935. Louis D. Blanc, architect, 1934 (p. 23). *Destroyed*

b. Detail of Meat Hall in 1979. Ceramic panel by W. J. Neatby, 1903 (p. 22)

c. Meat Hall in 1929. Ceramics by W. J. Neatby, 1903 (p. 22)

HARRODS, INTERIORS

a. From the south-east in 1830

b. From the south in 1843

c. From the north-west in 1965

d. From the south-east in 1979

HOLY TRINITY CHURCH, BROMPTON. T. L. Donaldson, architect, 1826-9 (pp. 46-9)

32

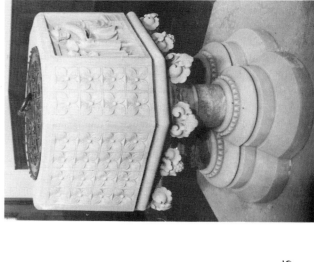

a. *(above left)*. Nave and chancel looking east

b. *(above right)*. Nave looking west

c. *(left)*. Sanctuary. Reredos by Clayton and Bell, 1885

d. *(right)*. Font. E. C. Hakewill, architect, 1863

HOLY TRINITY CHURCH, BROMPTON, IN 1979. Interior recast by Arthur Blomfield, architect, 1879-82 (pp. 46–9)

a. *(left)*. The Church and Oratory House in *c*.1853–8. *Church demolished*

b. *(right)*. The Oratory House in 1857. The building being erected in the foreground is the former Refreshment Room of the South Kensington Museum

c. *(below left)*. Looking east in *c*.1865. *Demolished*

d. *(below right)*. East end in *c*.1878. *Demolished*

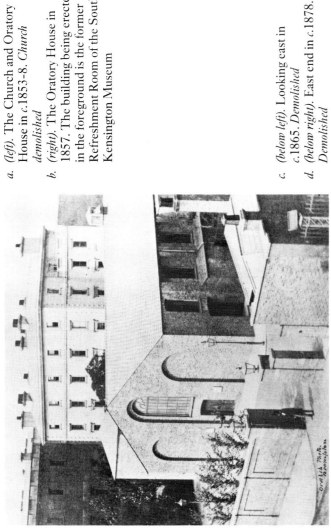

THE ORATORY, 1853–8, J. J. Scoles, architect (pp. 50–1)

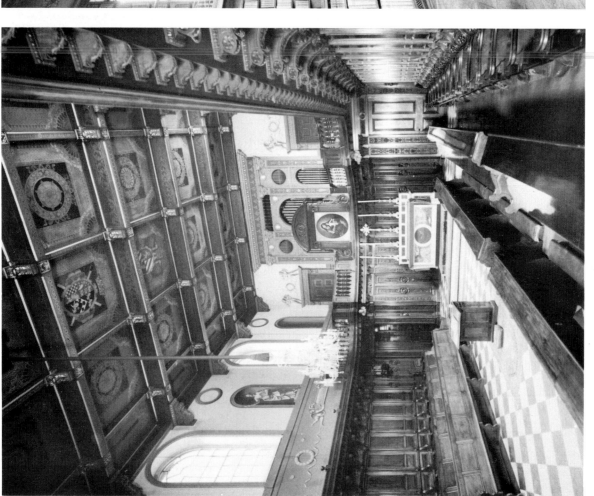

a. The Little Oratory in 1971. J. J. Scoles, architect, 1853: J. Hungerford Pollen, interior designer, 1871-2: A. Brookholding-Jones, designer of the painted decoration, 1954 (pp. 51, 55)

b. The Library in 1971. J. J. Scoles, architect, 1853, with later alterations (pp. 51, 55)

THE ORATORY

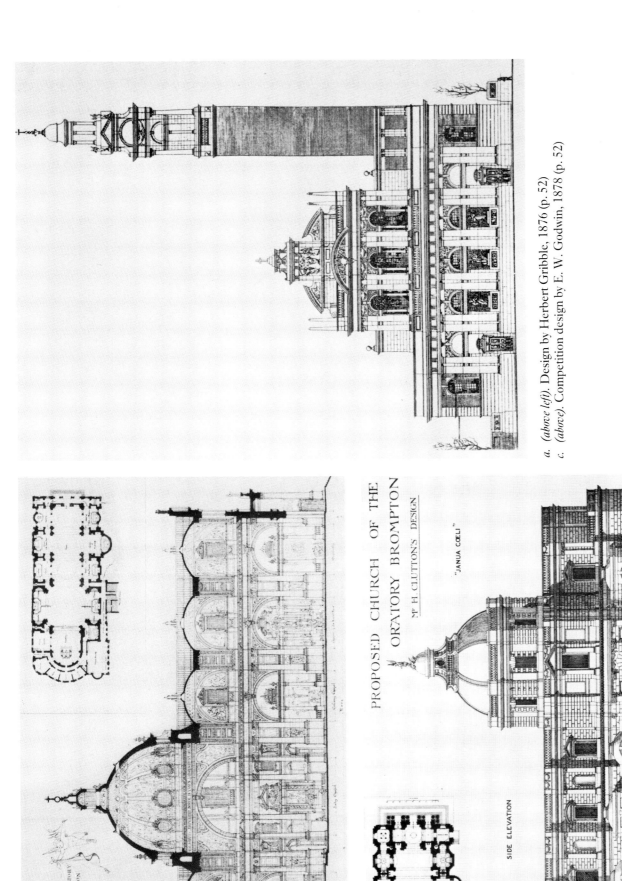

a. (above left). Design by Herbert Gribble, 1876 (p. 52)

c. (above). Competition design by E. W. Godwin, 1878 (p. 52)

b. (left). Competition design by Henry Clutton, 1878 (p. 54)

THE ORATORY CHURCH: unexecuted designs

36

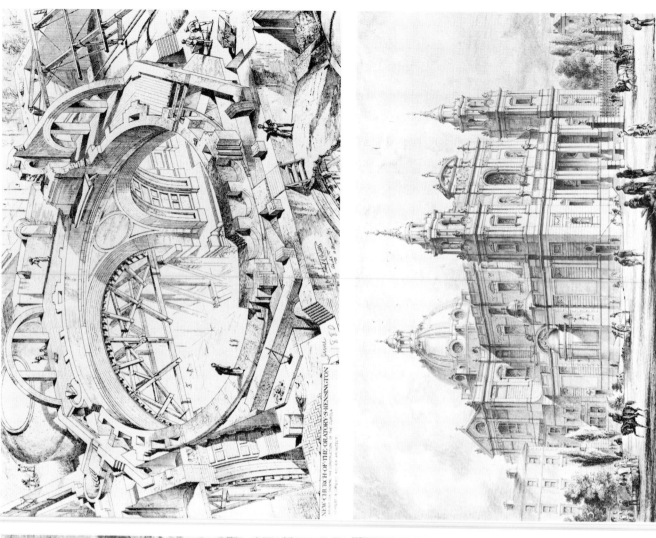

a. *(above).* Design, seen from north, 1879
b. *(above right).* The construction of the drum, 1880

c. *(right).* Design, seen from south-west, 1879

THE ORATORY CHURCH, 1880-4. Drawings by the architect, Herbert Gribble (pp. 54-5)

a. The dome, 1895-6, in 1896. George Sherrin, architect: E. A. Rickards, designer of lantern (p. 55)

b. The exterior in 1948. Body of church, 1880-4; façade, 1892-5; dome, 1895-6 (pp. 54-5)

THE ORATORY CHURCH

THE ORATORY CHURCH, 1880-4, as decorated in 1927-32 by C. T. G. Formilli. The nave looking south in 1948 (pp. 54-6)

a. (above left). Nave, looking towards sanctuary

b. (above). Looking across nave to Lady Altar

c. (left). Nave ceiling
d. (right). The crossing

THE ORATORY CHURCH, 1880-4, as decorated in 1927-32 by C. T. G. Formilli, in 1948 (p. 56)

a. Pulpit, 1932 (C. T. G. Formilli, designer), in 1979 (p. 56)

b. Altar of St. Wilfrid in 1971 (p. 57)

c. Chapel of St. Wilfrid in *c*.1905 (p. 57)

THE ORATORY CHURCH

a. (left). Lady Altar, 1693 (F. Corbarelli and sons, designers), in 1971 (p. 57)

b. (above). Altar of St. Philip, *c.*1882, in 1971 (p. 56)

c, d. (below left). Statues of St. Jude (left) and St. Matthew (right) in 1948. G. Mazzuoli, sculptor, *c.*1679-95 (p. 56)

e. (below). Memorial to Cardinal Newman, 1895-6, in 1982. L. Chavalliaud, sculptor of statue: Bodley and Garner, architects (p. 55)

THE ORATORY

42

a. (above). Brompton Road looking north from Alexander Square towards the Oratory and the Bell and Horns in c.1900. Alexander Place (p. 63) on left

b. (above right). The Bell and Horns at the junction of Thurloe Place and Brompton Road in c.1912. Behind, left and right, are parts of Empire House (pp. 60, 82–3)

c. (right). Empire House at the junction of Thurloe Place and Brompton Road in 1982. Paul Hoffmann, architect, 1910-16. Dalmeny House is on the right (pp. 82–3)

a. No. 7 North Terrace, Alexander House (formerly the Western Grammar School) in 1958. W. F. Pocock, architect, 1835–6 (pp. 67–8)

b. North Terrace and Nos. 1–4 Alexander Square (right), 1827–8, looking to the Western Grammar School in October 1902 (p. 63)

c. Nos 4–10 (even) Alexander Place (right to left), 1829–30, in 1957 (pp. 64–5)

d. Nos. 12–18 (even) Thurloe Street (left to right), 1845–6, in 1957 (p. 76)

THE ALEXANDER ESTATE

44

a. Nos. 13-20 (right to left), 1827-8, in 1958 (p. 64)

b. Entrance to No. 11 in 1957

c. Nos. 5-12 (right to left) in 1974. James Bonnin,
builder, 1830-2 (p. 65)

THE ALEXANDER ESTATE: ALEXANDER SQUARE

45

a. Design for south-east range, *c*.1842 (p. 72)

b. North end looking west from Thurloe Place in *c*.1856. No. 33 on left, Nos. 34-38 in middle distance

c. North-east range, Nos. 20-33 (right to left) in 1938. James Bonnin, junior, builder, 1843-4 (p. 72)

THE ALEXANDER ESTATE: THURLOE SQUARE. George Basevi, architect, 1840-6 (pp. 70-4)

a. No. 19 Thurloe Square, sitting-room in 1911 when in the occupation of Mrs. Salis Schwabe

b. Nos. 18-21 Thurloe Place (left to right) in 1975. Thomas Holmes, builder, 1843-4 (pp. 75-6)

THE ALEXANDER ESTATE

a. Harrington Road looking east to the junction of Thurloe and Pelham Streets (site of South Kensington Station) in *c.*1867, during the construction of the underground railway

b. Thurloe Close in 1980. F. G. Selby, architect, 1927-30 (p. 84)

c. Nos. 25-29 (odd) Thurloe Street in 1974. John Blore, architect, 1846-50 (p. 78)

ELEVATION IN PELHAM STREET

a. Design for the original station, Pelham Street elevation. (Sir) John Fowler, engineer, 1867-8 (p. 80). *Demolished*

b. Piccadilly Line station in Pelham Street shortly after completion in 1907. Leslie W. Green, architect (p. 117)

SOUTH KENSINGTON STATION

a. Nos. 23 and 25 Pelham Place, 1843-4, in 1902 (p. 96)

b. Thurloe Houses, Pelham Place North, 1844-5, in 1902 (p. 94). *Demolished*

c. No. 14 Pelham Crescent (right) and Nos. 2-14 (even) Pelham Place in 1957. George Basevi, architect, James Bonnin, developer, 1837-8 (p. 96)

THE SMITH'S CHARITY ESTATE

50   *a.* Elevational drawings by Basevi for eastern range, 1833

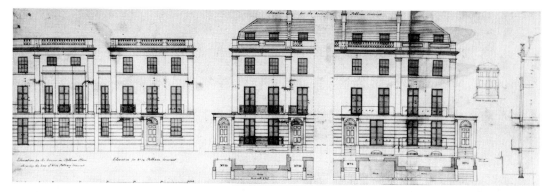

b. Eastern range in *c.*1905

c. Eastern range in 1957

THE SMITH'S CHARITY ESTATE: PELHAM CRESCENT. George Basevi, architect, James Bonnin, developer, 1833–41 (pp. 92-6)

a, b. Egerton Crescent in 1959. George Basevi, architect, James Bonnin, developer, 1844-5 (p. 98)

c. Nos. 33-41 (odd) Egerton Terrace, 1845-50, in 1959 (p. 100)

THE SMITH'S CHARITY ESTATE

52

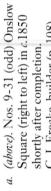

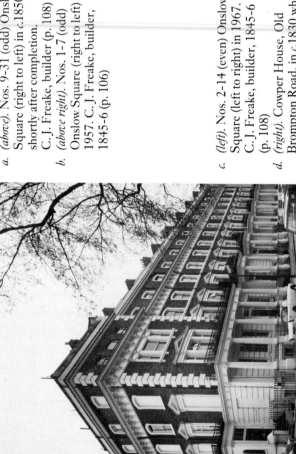

a. *(above)*. Nos. 9-31 (odd) Onslow Square (right to left) in *c.*1850 shortly after completion. C. J. Freake, builder (p. 108)

b. *(above right)*. Nos. 1-7 (odd) Onslow Square (right to left) in 1957. C. J. Freake, builder, 1845-6 (p. 106)

c. *(left)*. Nos. 2-14 (even) Onslow Square (left to right) in 1967. C. J. Freake, builder, 1845-6 (p. 108)

d. *(right)*. Cowper House, Old Brompton Road, in *c.*1830 when in use as a lunatic asylum. View from south with avenue of elms to left (p. 91). *Demolished*

THE SMITH'S CHARITY ESTATE

53

a. *(left).* Nos. 35–48 (consec., right to left), 1867–8, in *c.*1905
b. *(above).* Nos. 49–77 (odd, right to left), 1874–5, in 1980

c. *(below).* Nos. 50–78 (even, left to right), 1873–4, in 1980

THE SMITH'S CHARITY ESTATE: ONSLOW GARDENS. C. J. Freake, builder, 1863–78 (p. 108)

54

c. *(left)*. Library of No. 68 Onslow Gardens in 1891 when in the occupation of Sir Lyon Playfair

a. *(left)*. A drawing-room in Onslow Crescent in 1929. *Demolished*

b. *(right)*. Hall of No. 4 Onslow Square in 1926, as remodelled by Walter Sarel, architect, for his own occupation

THE SMITH'S CHARITY ESTATE

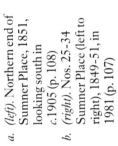

a. *(left)*. Northern end of Sumner Place, 1851, looking south in c.1905 (p. 108)

b. *(right)*. Nos. 25–34 Sumner Place (left to right), 1849–51, in 1981 (p. 107)

d. *(above)*. The Cranley Arms, Fulham Road, 1853–4 with later ground floor, in 1981 (p. 103)

c. *(left)*. Avenue Studios, Sydney Mews, 1870–1, from north-east in 1979 (p. 103)

THE SMITH'S CHARITY ESTATE: BUILDINGS BY C. J. FREAKE

a. *(above).* St. Paul's Church, Onslow Square, in
c.1872. James Edmeston, architect, 1859-60
(pp. 112-14)

b. *(above).* St. Peter's Church,
Cranley Gardens, 1866-7, in
1966 (pp. 114-17). Vicarage to
left: Alfred Williams, architect,
1870 (p. 117)

c. *(left).* St. Peter's Church, east
end from Selwood Place in
1972

THE SMITH'S CHARITY ESTATE: CHURCHES

a. Interior looking west towards chancel

b. Interior looking east

St. Paul's Church, Onslow Square, in 1974 (pp. 112-14)

58

a. Interior looking east in *c.*1905

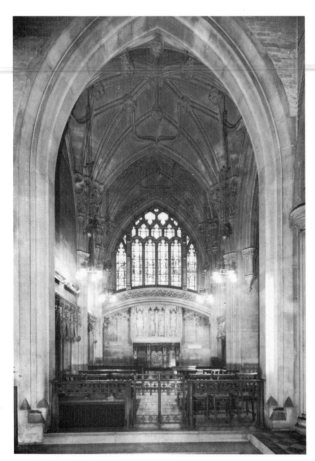

b. Morning chapel in 1972. W. D. Caröe, architect, 1907-9

c. Interior looking east in 1982

ST. PETER'S CHURCH, CRANLEY GARDENS (pp. 114-17)

a. Nos. 50-70 (consec.) Evelyn Gardens (right to left) in 1981. C. A. Daw and Son, builders, 1890-3 (p. 120)

b. Nos. 15-37 (odd) Cranley Gardens (left to right) in 1980. C. H. Thomas, architect, C. J. Freake, builder, 1883-4 (p. 108)

c. Nos. 2-10 (even) Evelyn Gardens (right to left) in 1981. C. A. Daw and Son, builders, 1886 (pp. 119-20)

THE SMITH'S CHARITY ESTATE

60

a. *(above)*. Nos. 20–48 (even) Egerton Gardens (left to right), rear elevations, and communal garden in 1973. M. C. Hulbert, architect, for Matthews Brothers, builders, 1888–90 (p. 123)

b. *(above right)*. Egerton Place in 1973. Left half, Mervyn Macartney, architect, 1892–4; right half, Amos Faulkner, architect, for W. Willett, builder, 1894–7 (pp. 123–5)

c. *(right)*. Nos. 27–49 (odd) Egerton Gardens (left to right) in 1982. M. C. Hulbert, architect, for Matthews Brothers, builders, except for No. 31 (T. H. Smith, architect), 1888–90 (pp. 122–3)

THE SMITH'S CHARITY ESTATE

b. Swimming pool *cum* conservatory

d. Hall and staircase

a. West front

c. Ground-floor drawing-room

THE SMITH'S CHARITY ESTATE: MORTIMER HOUSE, EGERTON GARDENS, 1886-8, IN 1976 (p. 126)

62

a. View of main front from south by F. J. Francis, the architect, 1844

b. Chapel and hospital from north-west before 1876. E. B. Lamb, architect of chapel, 1849-50

c. East front of chapel in 1971, as altered by William White, architect, 1891-2

BROMPTON HOSPITAL, 1844-54 (pp. 130-9)

a. View by Lamb from south-east, *c*.1849

b. Interior looking east in 1971

c. Interior looking west in 1971

BROMPTON HOSPITAL CHAPEL. E. B. Lamb, architect, 1849-50; altered by William White, architect, 1891-2 (pp. 135-9)

a. *(above).* Onslow Chapel, Neville Terrace, from north-west in *c.*1905. W. Mumford, architect, 1856 (p. 143). *Demolished*

b. *(right).* Nos. 9-16 Onslow Gardens (left to right), 1862-3, in 1981 (p. 142)

c. Nos. 1-11 (consec.) Neville Terrace (right to left), 1860-2, in 1982 (p. 142)

THE BROMPTON HOSPITAL ESTATE

a. North side of Selwood Place in 1937. James Ardin, builder, 1825-30 (p. 145)

b. East side of Elm Place in 1957. Christopher Surrey, builder, 1830-6 (p. 146)

c. Nos. 9-14 Selwood Terrace (left to right) in 1976. No. 9, Samuel Archbutt and Christopher Surrey, builders, Nos. 10-14, James Ardin, builder, 1825-6 (p. 145)

THE WARE ESTATE

a. The Anglesea public house and No. 16 Selwood Terrace in 1964. James Ardin, builder, 1825-7 (p. 145)

b. Nos. 4-9 Thistle Grove (left to right) in 1981. Nos. 4-7, *c*.1816-20; Nos. 8 and 9, *c*.1828 (p. 167)

a. Nos. 28-34 (even) Drayton Gardens (right to left), 1859-62, in 1982

b. Nos. 141 and 143 Old Brompton Road (formerly 4-5 Drayton Terrace), 1845-6, in 1971

c. Nos. 1-29 (odd) Drayton Gardens (left to right), 1846-63, in 1982

DRAYTON GARDENS AREA: THE DAY ESTATE. John Blore, architect (pp. 157-60)

a. No. 153 Old Brompton Road, Drayton Arms, in 1975. Gordon, Lowther and Gunton, architects, 1891-2 (p. 161)

b. Drayton Gardens in 1982. Priory Mansions (1894-7, centre) and Drayton Court (1901-2, left), C. J. C. Pawley, architect (p. 169)

c. Drayton Gardens in 1899. Nos. 49 and 51 (1897, left) and 53 (1894, right), J. Norton, architect (p. 169)

d. No. 59 Drayton Gardens in 1904. J. Norton, architect, 1897-8 (p. 169)

DRAYTON GARDENS AREA

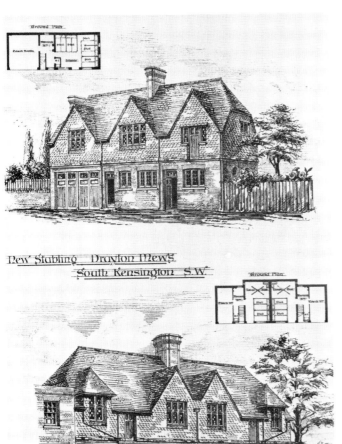

a. *(left)*. Nos. 18 (above) and 21-22 (below) Cresswell Place (here called Drayton Mews) in 1887. H. Phelps Drew, architect, 1885-6 (p. 169)

b. *(above)*. Nos. 80-84 (even) Drayton Gardens (right to left) in 1982. Nos. 80-82, 1888-9; No. 84, 1885-6 (p. 169)

c. *(below left)*. Nos. 13 and 15 Roland Gardens in 1982. C. Aldin and Sons, builders, 1871-3 (p. 152)

d. *(below)*. No. 46 Roland Gardens, 1883-5, in 1980 (p. 153)

a. Showing approximately the same area as Plate 71a opposite

b. Showing approximately the same area as Plate 71b opposite

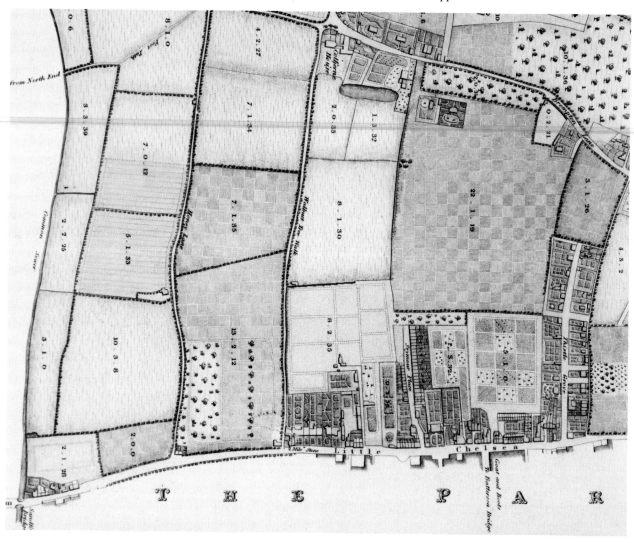

LITTLE CHELSEA AND WEST BROMPTON. Extracts from the map of Kensington published by T. Starling, 1822

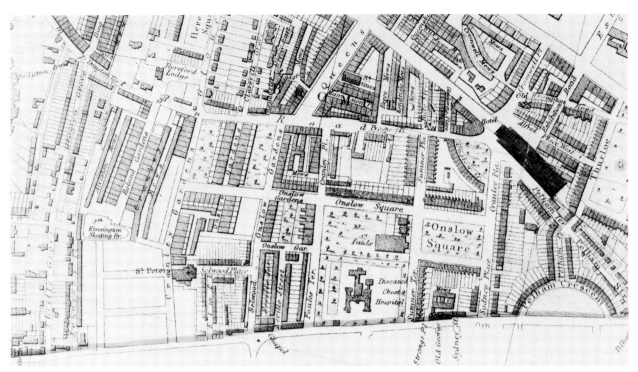

a. From Thurloe Square to Drayton Gardens (then Thistle Grove)

b. From Roland Gardens to Brompton Cemetery

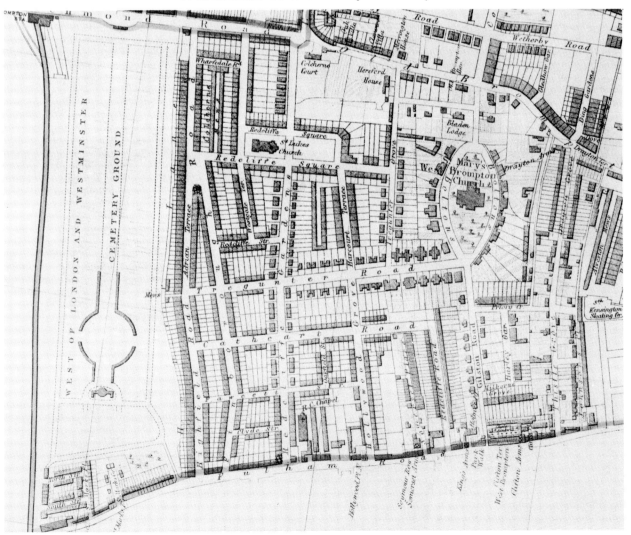

LITTLE CHELSEA AND WEST BROMPTON. Extracts from Edmund Daw's map of Kensington, 1879

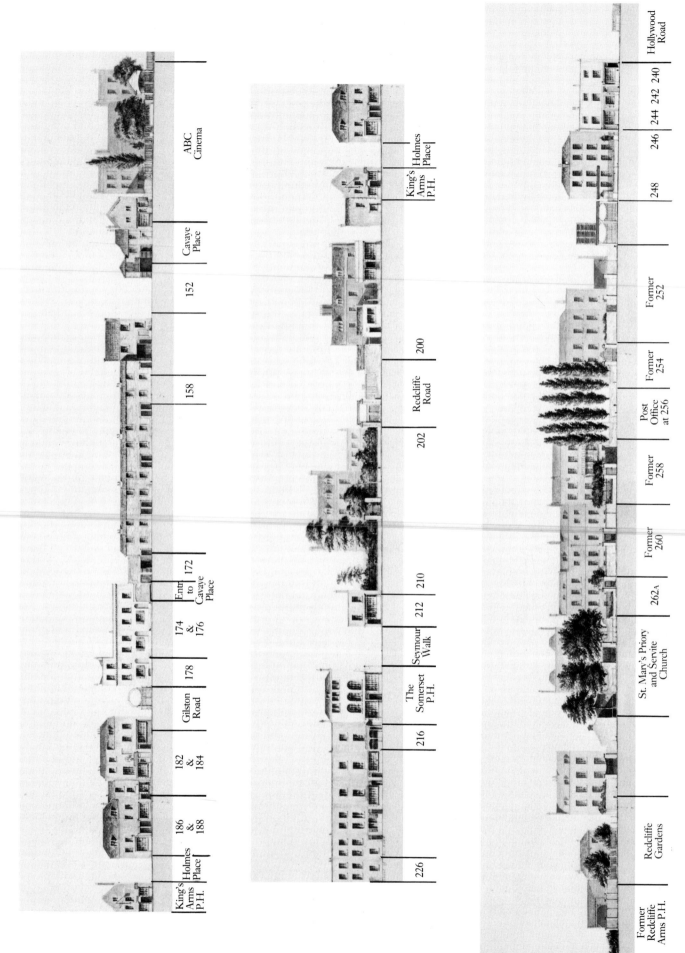

LITTLE CHELSEA IN THE FULHAM ROAD. Extracts from Joseph Salway's survey of 1811. *Modern street openings and some sites are indicated*

a. *(above left).* ABC Cinema in 1973. J. Stanley Beard and Clare, architects, 1930 (pp. 169, 171)

b. *(above right).* No. 152 Fulham Road (left, 1849–50) and No. 1 Cavaye Place (centre right, 1853), John Blore, architect, and Nos. 27 and 28 Cavaye Place (extreme right, 1863) in 1981 (p. 172)

c. *(left).* Nos. 170–176 (even) Fulham Road, 1846–7, in 1981: Nos. 170 (right) and 172, John Blore, architect (p. 172)

d. *(right).* Nos. 186–192 (even) Fulham Road (right to left) in 1981: Nos. 190 and 192, Edward Curtis, senior, builder, 1861 (pp. 174, 175)

FULHAM ROAD

74

a. *(left)*. Nos. 38–46 (even, right to left), *c.*1807–11, in 1974 (p. 178)

b. *(above)*. Looking north in 1973. Nos. 33–47 (odd) on left, T. W. Haylock, builder, 1889–90: Nos. 38–58 (even) on right, *c.*1807–11 (pp. 178, 179)

c. *(right)*. No. 13, *c.* 1807–11, in 1976 (p. 178)

SEYMOUR WALK

75

a. Lochée's Military Academy, Fulham Road, in 1784 (pp. 181–2). *Demolished*

d. Lochée's Military Academy, Fulham Road, nineteenth-century view perhaps based on one of 1782 (pp. 181–2). *Demolished*

b. Hollywood House, Hollywood Road, c.1810, in occupation of Captain E. P. Nisbet (p. 184). *Demolished*

c. Barker Street, looking north in c.1930. T. Hussey, builder, 1877–8 (pp. 188–9). *Demolished*

e. West corner of Hollywood Road and Fulham Road in 1981. Nos. 240–244 Fulham Road (centre to mid-left), c.1790–1; Nos. 246 and 248 (left), c.1801–2 (pp. 182–3)

a. *(above).* Entrance elevation of church, *c.*1873-4, drawn by J. A. Hansom, architect. *Partly concealed by later building*

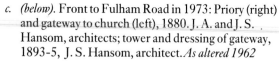

c. *(below).* Front to Fulham Road in 1973: Priory (right) and gateway to church (left), 1880. J. A. and J. S. Hansom, architects; tower and dressing of gateway, 1893-5, J. S. Hansom, architect. *As altered 1962*

b. *(above).* The interior (1874-5, J. A. and J. S. Hansom, architects) with High Altar (1882-3, J. S. Hansom, architect) in 1883. *High Altar, except altar table, demolished*

d. *(below).* Front to Fulham Road of Priory and gateway, 1880, J. A. and J. S. Hansom, architects

CHURCH OF OUR LADY OF SEVEN DOLOURS AND ST. MARY'S PRIORY, NO. 264 FULHAM ROAD (pp. 190-3)

a. Approach to church, 1893-5, J. S. Hansom, architect

b. Nave, looking toward sanctuary, 1874-5, J. A. and J. S. Hansom, architects

c. Chapel of the Blessed Sacrament (formerly Lady Chapel), 1890, J. S. Hansom, architect

d. Baptistery, 1925

CHURCH OF OUR LADY OF SEVEN DOLOURS IN 1979 (pp. 190-3)

a. Hereford House when a cycling club in 1896 (pp. 200-1). Now site of Coleherne Court. *Demolished*

b. Coleherne House: staircase compartment (p. 200). *Demolished*

c. Cresswell Lodge in *c.*1840's. James Faulkner, bricklayer, building lessee, 1809 (p. 201). Now site of Cresswell Gardens. *Demolished*

d. Sidmouth Lodge, 1838, in 1912 (pp. 201-2). Now site of Telephone Exchange. *Demolished*

a. *(above).* South Bolton Gardens looking west in January 1933 across present site of Bousfield School. *Demolished*

b. *(above right).* Gilston Road looking north in *c.*1905

c. *(below).* Nos. 3–6 Bolton Gardens, Old Brompton Road (left to right) in January 1933. J. Spicer, builder, 1863–4 (p. 210). Now site of Bousfield School. *Demolished*

d. *(right).* No. 185 Old Brompton Road in 1974. J. Spicer, builder, 1875 (p. 229)

80

a. Nos. 24-28 (right to left) in 1965

b. Nos. 18-23 (right to left) in 1965

c. Nos. 16-21 (right to left) in 1938

THE BOLTONS, WESTERN CRESCENT. J. Spicer, builder, 1857-60 (p. 206)

a. Nos. 1 and 2 in 1980

b. Nos. 9 and 10 in 1975

THE BOLTONS, EASTERN CRESCENT. H. W. Atkinson and D. Tidey, builders, 1851-2 (p. 205)

82

a. *(right).* Hall and staircase of
   No. 12 in 1979
b. *(far right).* Drawing-room of
   No. 12 in 1979

c. *(right).* Drawing-room
   fireplace of No. 12 in 1979
d. *(far right).* Music room at No.
   16 in occupation of Madame
   Albani in 1893

THE BOLTONS, INTERIORS (p. 207)

a. No. 2 Harley Gardens in 1977. W. Harding, builder, 1851 (p. 208)

b. Nos. 3 and 4 Harley Gardens in 1970. J. Bonnin, junior, builder, 1851 (p. 207)

c. No. 24 Gilston Road from north-west in 1970 (No. 22 on right). W. Harding, builder, 1852 (p. 208)

d. Nos. 25-41 (odd) Gilston Road (left to right) in 1970. S. Peirson probable builder of Nos. 25-39, 1851 (p. 204)

e. Nos. 10-16 (even) Tregunter Road (right to left) in 1970. J. Spicer, builder, 1859 (p. 210)

THE GUNTER ESTATE: HOUSES OF THE 1850's

84

a. *(left)*. Nos. 6-12 (consec.) Priory Walk and No. 26 Gilston Road (left) in 1977. R. Trower, builder, 1850-3 (p. 203)

b. *(right)*. No. 3 Cathcart Road in 1980. Corbett and McClymont, builders, 1864 (p. 212)

c. *(below left)*. Nos. 12-14 (consec.) Harley Gardens (left to right) in 1970: Nos. 10-12 (consec.) Milborne Grove in background. B. and T. Bradley, builders, 1861-3 (p. 208)

d. *(below)*. No. 16 Hollywood Road (formerly studio at rear of No. 27 Cathcart Road) in 1974. A. McClymont, building lessee, 1866 (p. 219)

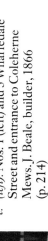

a. *(above left).* Nos. 25–29 (odd) The Little Boltons (left to right). W. Corbett or A. McClymont, building lessees, 1867–8 (p. 217)

b. *(above).* Nos. 26 and 28 The Little Boltons. J. Spicer, builder, 1864 (p. 217)

c. *(left).* Nos. 1 (left) and 3 Wharfedale Street and entrance to Coleherne Mews. J. Beale, builder, 1866 (p. 214)

d. *(right).* Nos. 2 (right) and 4 Redcliffe Square. Corbett and McClymont, building lessees, 1868

THE GUNTER ESTATE: HOUSES OF THE 1860's IN 1980

a. Nos. 7 (left) and 8 Harley Gardens in 1977. T. Hussey and T. Huggett, builders, 1867 (p. 210)

b. Nos. 36 (right) and 38 Tregunter Road, 1866, in 1980 (p. 240)

c. Nos. 29 (left) and 31 Tregunter Road in 1975. Corbett and McClymont, building lessees, 1865

d. Nos. 20 (right) and 22 Tregunter Road, 1865, in 1975 (p. 219)

THE GUNTER ESTATE: HOUSES OF THE 1860's

a. Nos. 5 (right) and 6 Redcliffe Road. Corbett and McClymont, builders, 1861 (p. 175)

b. Nos. 15 (left) and 17 Coleherne Road. J. Beale, builder, 1867-8

c. Nos. 53-59 (odd) Cathcart Road (left to right). Corbett and McClymont, building lessees, 1867

d. Nos. 106-110 (even) Ifield Road (left to right) and entrance to Adrian Mews. B. J. Hudson or W. Spires, building lessees, 1869 (p. 223)

THE REDCLIFFE ESTATE: HOUSES OF THE 1860's IN 1980

a. Coleherne Road looking north

b. Redcliffe Gardens looking north

WEST BROMPTON IN *c.* 1905

a. *(left).* Hollywood Arms, Hollywood Road, in 1974. Corbett and McClymont, building lessees, 1865 (pp. 217, 221)

b. *(above).* Former Redcliffe Arms at No. 268 Fulham Road in 1981. No. 2A Redcliffe Gardens on right; Nos. 270 and 272 Fulham Road on left. Corbett and McClymont, building lessees, 1865 (pp. 217, 221)

c. *(below left).* The Coleherne (formerly Coleherne Arms), Old Brompton Road, in 1980. J. Beale, builder, 1866 (pp. 217, 221)

d. *(below).* Nos. 263-269 (odd) Old Brompton Road in 1980. Corbett and McClymont, building lessees, 1866-7 (p. 217)

THE REDCLIFFE ESTATE: BUILDINGS OF THE 1860's

a. Prospective view of Redcliffe Mansions at Nos. 29-45 (odd) Redcliffe Square (left to right) published in 1871

b. Nos. 29-45 (odd) Redcliffe Square (left to right) in 1975

REDCLIFFE SQUARE, SOUTH-WEST RANGE. G. and H. Godwin, architects, W. Corbett and A. McClymont, building lessees, 1874-6 (p. 217)

a. Nos. 6-20 (even, right to left) in *c.* 1905

b. Nos. 18-22 (even, right to left) in 1975

REDCLIFFE SQUARE, NORTH-EAST RANGES. G. and H. Godwin, architects, W. Corbett and A. McClymont, building lessees, 1870-4 (p. 217)

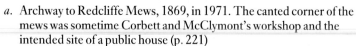

a. Archway to Redcliffe Mews, 1869, in 1971. The canted corner of the mews was sometime Corbett and McClymont's workshop and the intended site of a public house (p. 221)

b. No. 38 Redcliffe Gardens in 1980. A. McClymont, building lessee, 1868

c. Nos. 1–7 (odd) Finborough Road and No. 17 Redcliffe Place (right to left) in 1980. A. M. Greig, builder, sub-lessee, 1867 (pp. 217, 222)

d. Nos. 2 (left) and 4 Finborough Road in 1980. W. Corbett, building lessee, 1867 (pp. 217, 222)

THE REDCLIFFE ESTATE: BUILDINGS OF THE 1860's

93

b. View from the west in 1975

a. View from the south-west as originally proposed

ST. MARY'S CHURCH, THE BOLTONS. George Godwin, the younger, architect, 1849-50; spire added, 1856 (pp. 232-4)

a. Crossing and nave looking west in 1850

b. Interior looking east in 1979

c. Sedilia in 1850

d. Crossing looking north-east in 1979

St. Mary's Church, The Boltons. George Godwin, the younger, architect, 1849-50 (pp. 232-4)

a. Front to Gilston Road

b. Rear to Cavaye Place

FORMER ST. MARY'S SCHOOL at No. 4 Gilston Road in 1974. Joseph Peacock, architect, 1878 (p. 172)

a. (above). View from south-west in *c.* 1905

b. (left). View from east in 1873

c. (below). View from north-east in 1979

St. Luke's Church, Redcliffe Square. G. and H. Godwin, architects, 1872-3 (pp. 235-6)

a. Nave and chancel in *c.* 1905

b. Nave in 1979

c. Chancel in 1979

ST. LUKE'S CHURCH, REDCLIFFE SQUARE. G. and H. Godwin, architects, 1872-3 (pp. 235-6)

a. (above). Altar and reredos, Richard Boulton, carver, 1874
b. (right). Font, copied from Thorvaldsen's Angel of Baptism

c. (below). Pulpit, Richard Boulton, carver, 1876
d. (below right). Lectern and reading desk, Richard Boulton, carver, 1873

St. Luke's Church, Redcliffe Square, in 1979. G. and H. Godwin, architects, 1872-3 (p. 236)

a. South front

b. Entrance courtyard looking west

c. Loggia looking north

BLADON LODGE, SOUTH BOLTON GARDENS, IN 1934. Built 1836, extended and remodelled, 1928,
Clough Williams-Ellis, architect (pp. 201, 230). *Demolished*

a. North front

b. Studio

Nos. 8 and 9 South Bolton Gardens in 1930. J. E. Forbes and J. Duncan Tate, architects for remodelling, 1929 (p. 230)

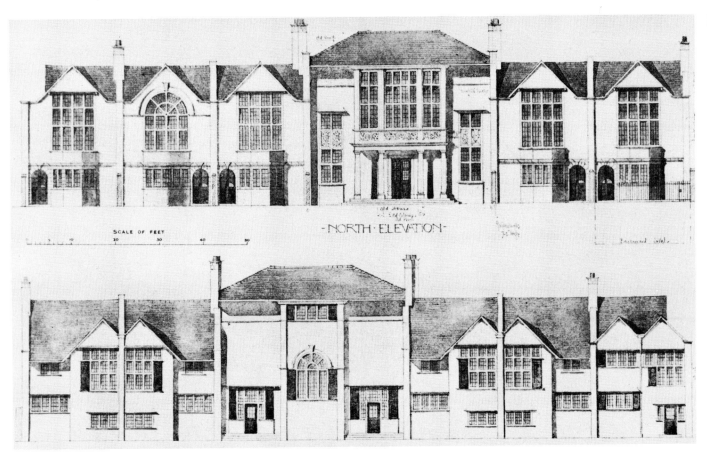

a. South Bolton Gardens. Design for Nos. 4-6 and 8-9, and for remodelling of No. 7 (consec., left to right in North Elevation). W. Cave, architect, 1903 (p. 230). *Nos. 4-6 demolished*·

c. Cathcart Road in 1977. No. 18 (right), W. Paton Orr and Partner, architects, 1961, second floor, Nerios Consultants Group, architects, 1972-3; No. 20 (left), C. J. G. Guest, architect, 1972-5 (p. 232)

b. *(left).* Coleherne Court, front to Redcliffe Gardens, in 1903. W. Cave, architect, 1901-4 (p. 229)

a. (above). From the Black
Bull (extreme right) to
Stamford Bridge in 1811
(p. 241). *All demolished*

b. Nos. 340-356 (even, right
to left), 1844-6, in 1981
(pp. 243-4)

c. The Black Bull, 1874
(p. 241), and Nos. 360-366
(even) in 1981

FULHAM ROAD near Stamford Bridge

a. Nos. 12-19 Billing Street (left to right) in 1982. C. Crew and E. Foster, builders, *c.* 1854 (p. 244)

b. Nos. 1-8 Billing Place (right to left) in 1974. James Wormsley, builder, *c.* 1850 (p. 244)

THE BILLINGS

104

BROMPTON CEMETERY, 1839-42. Bird's-eye view looking north-east in 1973. Benjamin Baud, architect (pp. 247-50)

a. *(above)*. Proposed layout, 1840
b. *(right)*. Chapel in 1970

c. *(below)*. Main avenue looking south to chapel in 1970
d. *(below right)*. North entrance lodge in 1970

BROMPTON CEMETERY, 1839–42. Benjamin Baud, architect (pp. 247–50)

a. (above). Val Prinsep, artist, d.1904
b. (above right). John Jackson, pugilist, d.1845. E. H. Baily, sculptor

c, d. Frederick Leyland, ship-owner, d.1892. Designed by Sir Edward Burne-Jones

BROMPTON CEMETERY: monuments (p. 251)

a. *(left).* Emmeline Pankhurst, suffragette, d.1928
b. *(above).* Robert Coombes, sculler, d.1860

c. *(below left).* Reginald Warneford, V.C., d.1915
d. *(below centre).* Blanche Roosevelt Macchetta, d.1898
e. *(below right).* George Godwin, editor of *The Builder*,
   d.1888

Brompton Cemetery: monuments (pp. 251-2)

Hansom cab and perambulators in Redcliffe Square